NAME	FORM	YEAR
Alice Lucas-Tooth	M IZ D.	1977

Philips'
Modern School
Atlas

Seventy-fourth Edition

Edited by Harold Fullard M.Sc.

George Philip & Son Limited, London

© **1976**

ISBN 0 540 05311 2

Printed in Great Britain by George Philip Printers Ltd., London

Preface

To justify its title and to continue to merit the reput-
ation it has gained over many years among teachers
of geography, each new edition of PHILIPS' MODERN
SCHOOL ATLAS receives most careful editing to en-
sure that every map is up to date and that its contents
meet the changing needs of the geography syllabus.

Philips' Modern School Atlas was first published in
1906 and now, more than seventy years later, the atlas bene-
fits from the improvements made over so many years
and for this edition the wider use of the
metric system has been reflected in conversion to,
or inclusion of metric equivalents where they had not
already been given in previous editions and particularly
on thematic maps and in climate graphs. All maps and
graphs have recently been reproduced afresh after
extensive revision and a new colour scheme has been
developed aimed at clear layer colouring on which the
legibility of names is yet further improved and hill
shading is added on the physical maps of the
continents, to give a graphic impression of principal
relief features.

The Modern School Atlas is designed to meet the
requirements of those intending to take the examina-
tion in Geography for the General Certificate; and
as the list of contents shows in detail the geology,
structure, relief, climate, vegetation and human con-
ditions of the whole world are illustrated, whilst for
detailed regional study there are larger scale maps of
more important political and highly developed regions.

Modern spellings have been adopted in accordance
with the latest official lists, the rules of the Royal
Geographical Society Permanent Committee on Geographical Names, the decision lists of the United
States Board on Geographical Names and other
sources. A selective index of names appearing on the
maps have been included.

Where there are rival claims to territory the *de facto*
boundaries have been shown. This does not denote
international recognition of these boundaries but
shows the states which are administering the areas
on either side of the line.

HAROLD FULLARD

Contents

Scale

The scales given in the contents list and on the maps are those used in the calculation of the map projection and the scale bar is a linear representation of that scale. Great care must be taken in measuring distances on the maps for the linear scale is true only along certain lines, these varying from one projection to another. On the World map centred on London all scales measured outwards from London are true, but all other distances are distorted, e.g. Johannesburg to Rio is 7 100km but measured on this projection appears to be 9 650km. Also such factors as paper shrinkage and expansion can introduce smaller inaccuracies: e.g., although the scale of the series of maps covering the British Isles is given as 1:1 000 000, the true scale measured along a meridian is approximately 1:1 000 780.

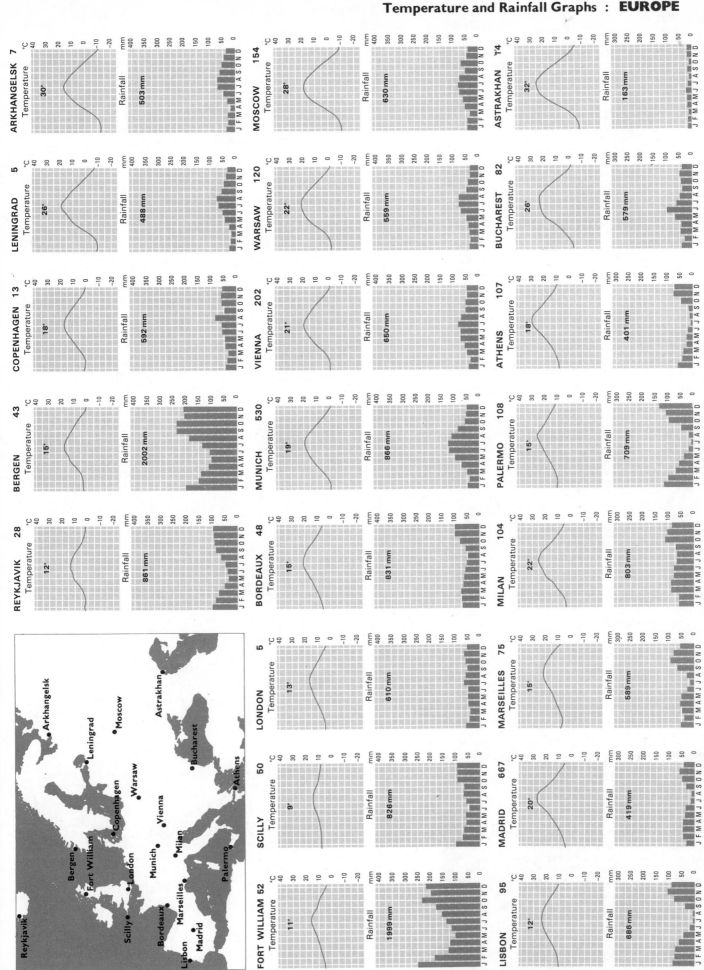

The climate graphs should be used in conjunction with the maps illustrating the climate of the World, and also the more detailed maps of the Continents. The stations have been selected to show the various types of climate to be found throughout the World. On each graph the name of the station is followed by its height in metres above sea-level, so that comparisons between stations can be made after allowing for elevation. The line on the temperature graphs shows the mean monthly temperatures. The mean annual range of temperature (in degrees Celsius) is given above the temperature graphs. The rainfall graphs show the average monthly rainfall and above them is given the average total annual rainfall (in millimetres).

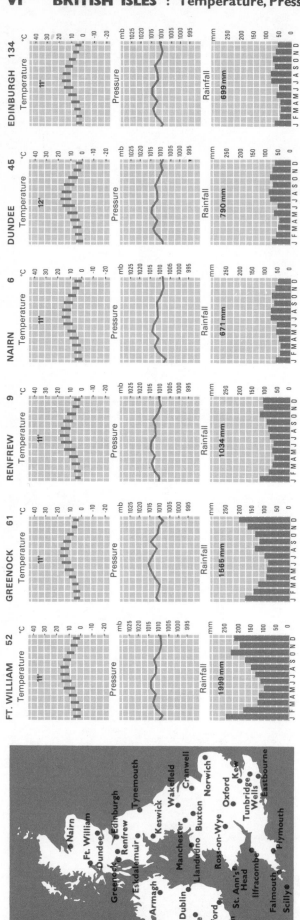

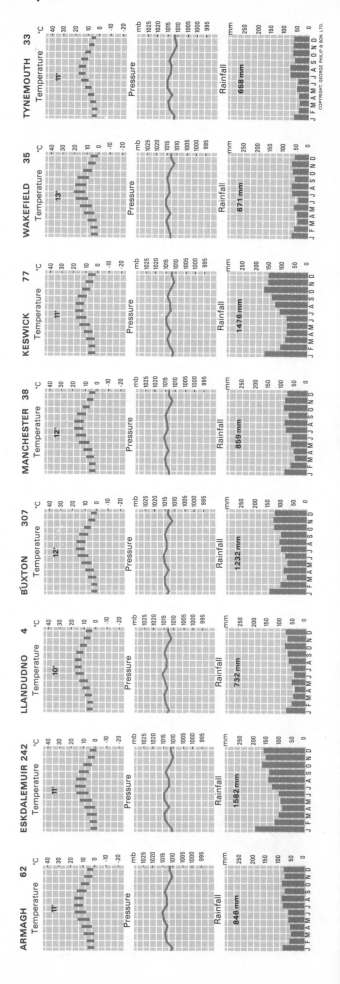

On these climate graphs of the British Isles, in addition to rainfall and temperature, mean monthly pressure is shown (in millibars and reduced to sea-level). Temperature is shown by a bar, the top of the bar representing the mean monthly maximum and the bottom of the bar the mean monthly minimum temperature. A mid point between these is the mean monthly temperature.

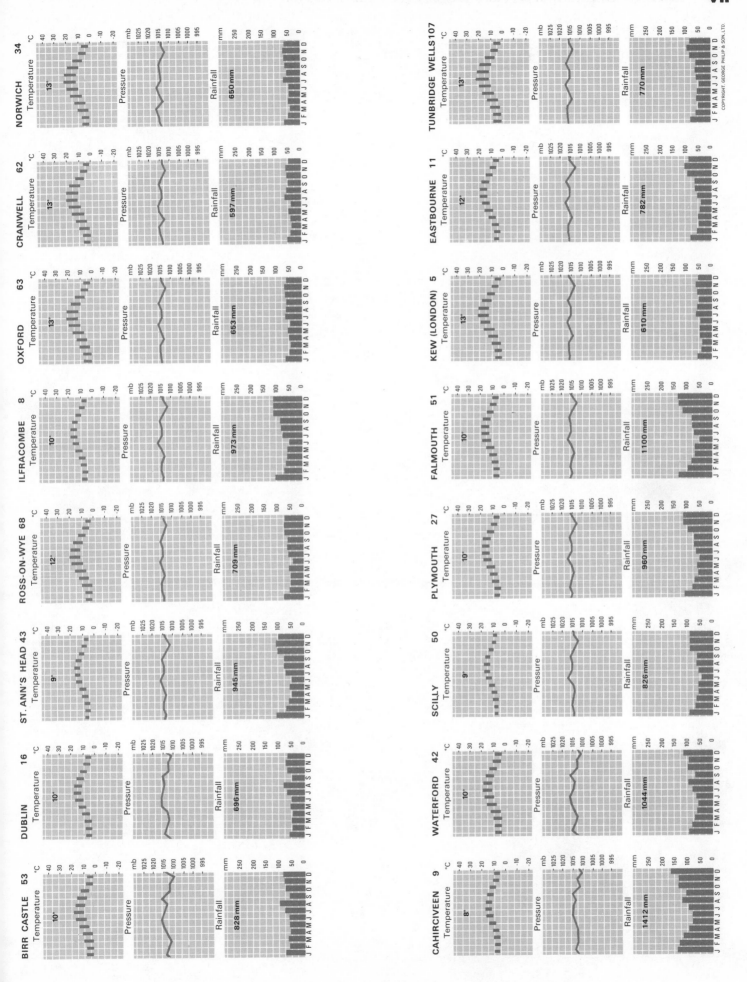

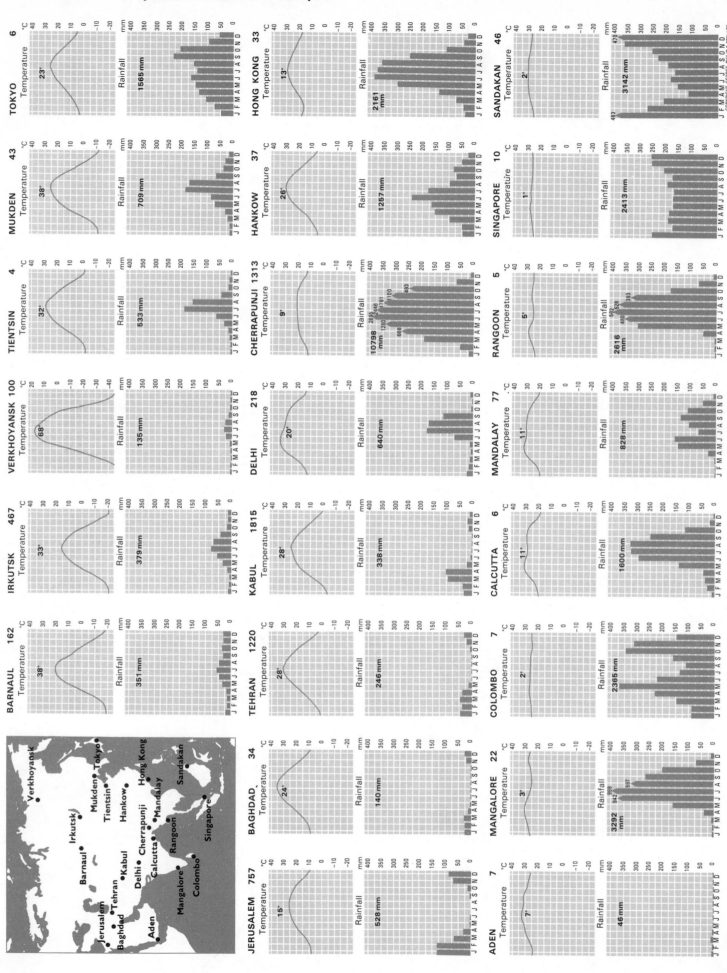

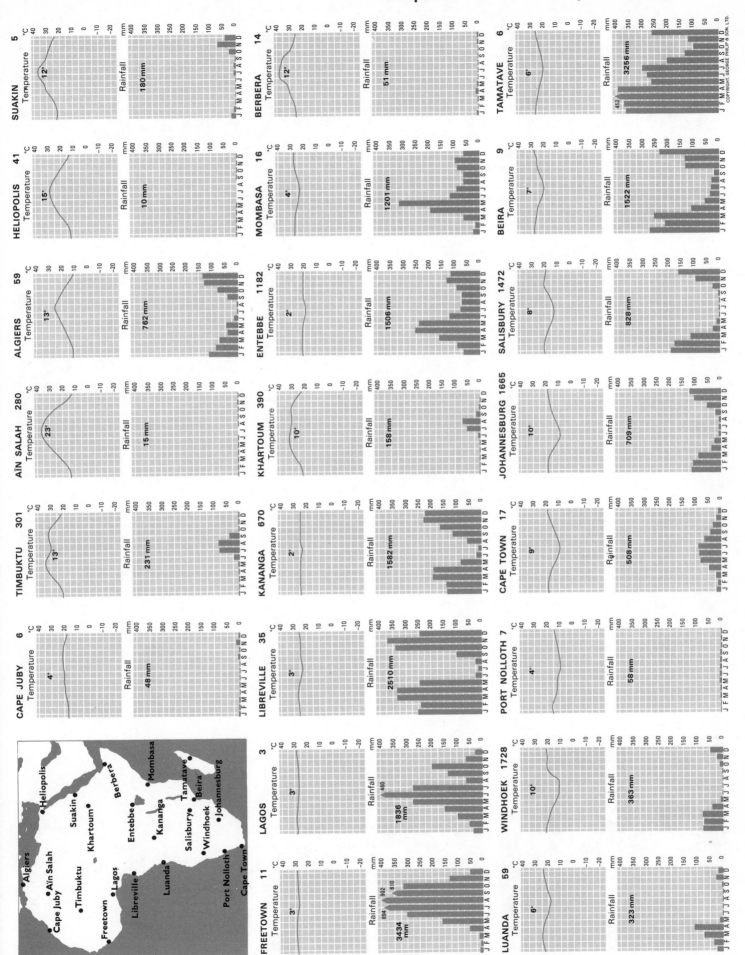

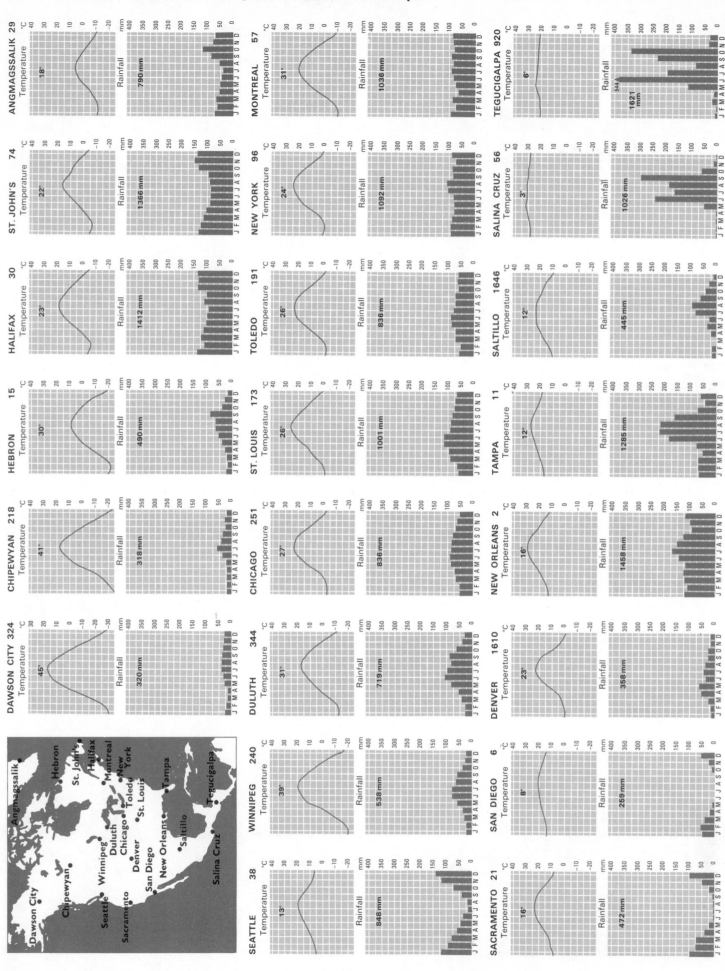

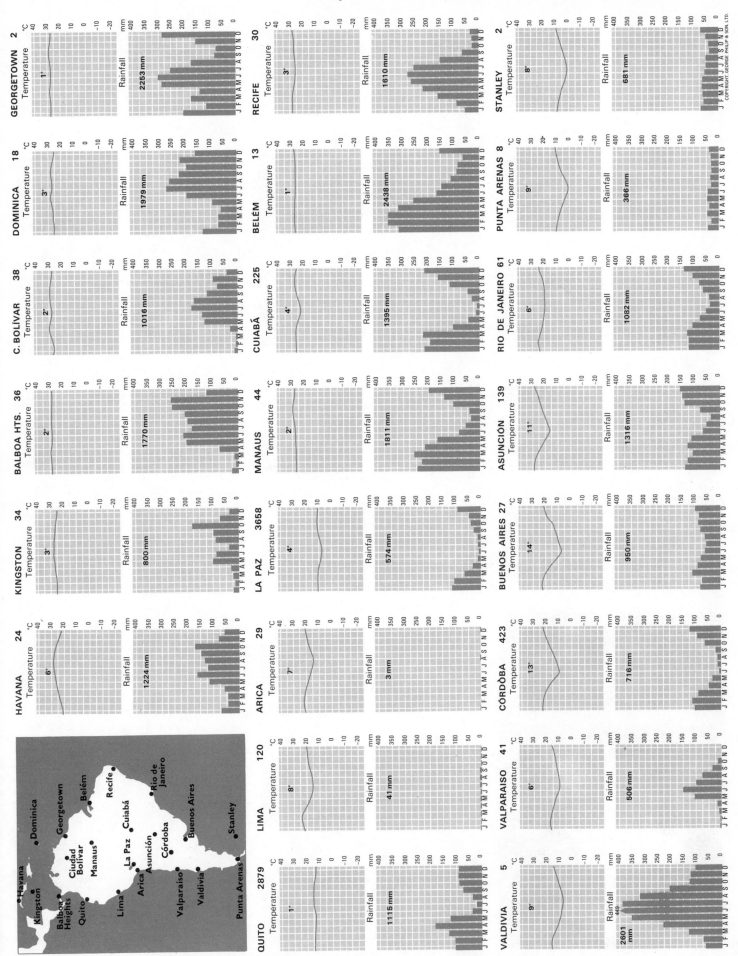

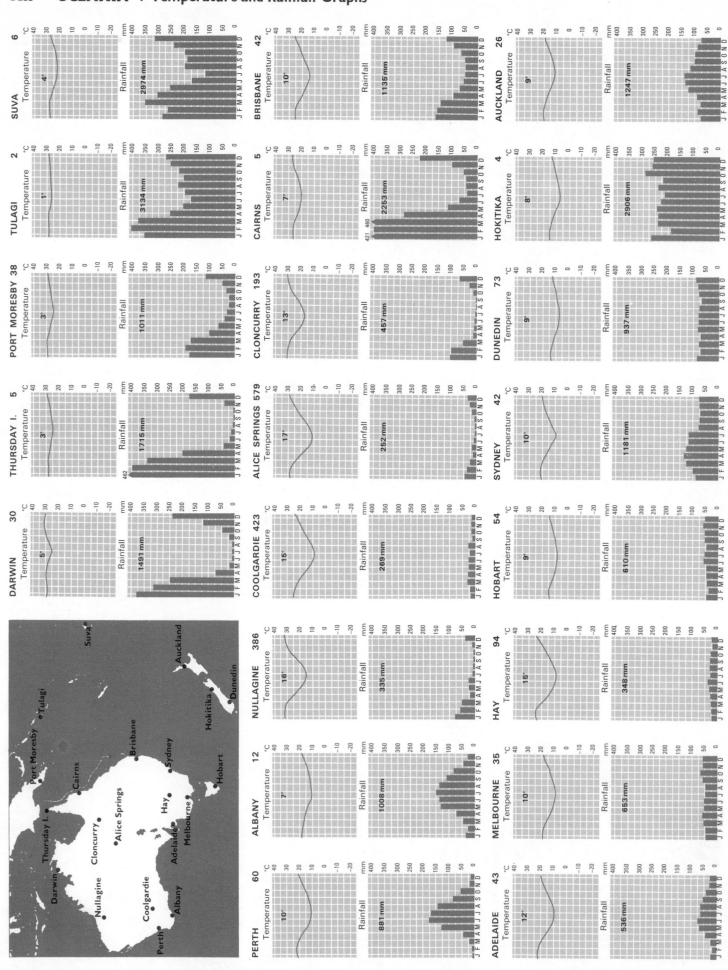

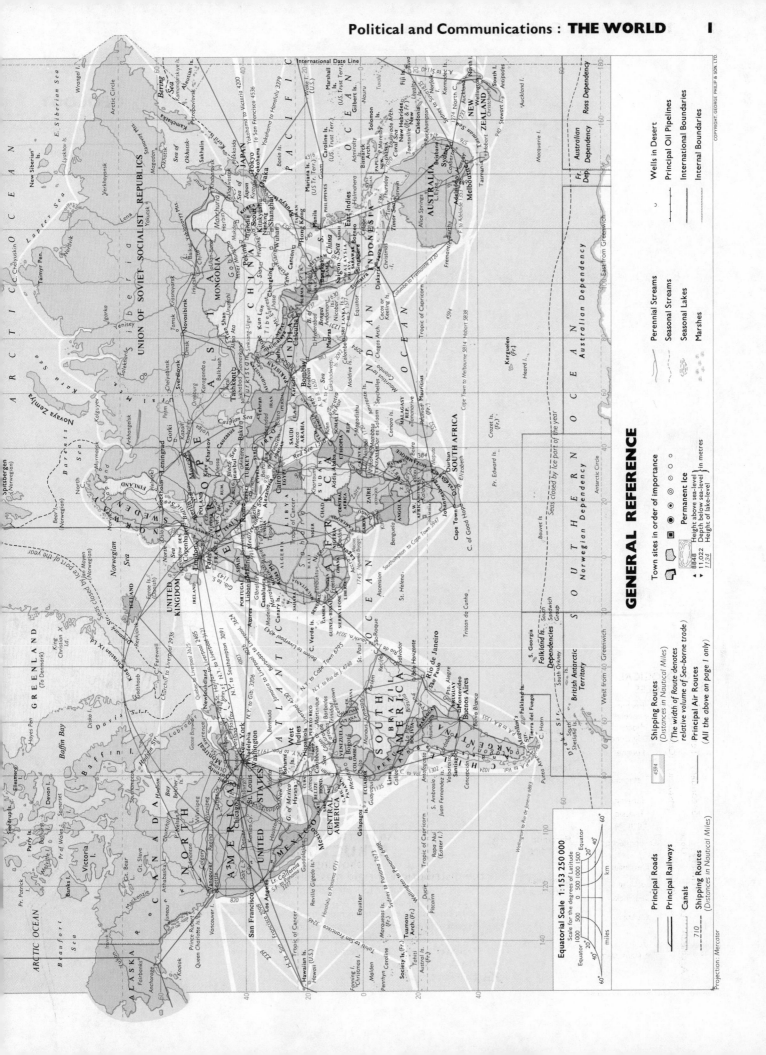

GENERAL REFERENCE

——	Principal Roads
——	Principal Railways
——	Canals
710	Shipping Routes *(Distances in Nautical Miles)*

	Shipping Routes *(Distances in Nautical Miles)* (The width of Route denotes relative volume of Sea-borne trade)
4594	
	Principal Air Routes *(All the above on page I only)*

Town sites in order of importance

Permanent Ice

Height above sea-level 8848 } in metres
Depth below sea-level 11.022 }
Height of lake-level 1134 }

	Wells in Desert
——	Principal Oil Pipelines
——	International Boundaries
——	Internal Boundaries
	Perennial Streams
	Seasonal Streams
	Seasonal Lakes
	Marshes

Equatorial Scale 1:153 250 000

Scale for the degrees of Latitude

Projection: Mercator

GEOLOGY
after
Beyschlag, Nalivkin and others

1:90 000 000

Ⓐ

Arctic Circle

60

40

Tropic of Cancer

20

Equator

160   140   120   100   80   60   40   20   0

20

Tropic of Capricorn

40

60

Antarctic Circle

L A U R E N T I A

Ⓒ **GEOLOGICAL CYCLES**

Quaternary		Recent	
Tertiary	(Cainozoic)	Pliocene	Alpine Folding
		Miocene	
		Oligocene	
		Eocene	
Secondary	(Mesozoic)	Cretaceous	Laramide Folding
		Jurassic	
		Triassic	
Primary Upper	(Palæozoic)	Permian	
		Carboniferous	Hercynian Folding
		Devonian	
Primary Lower		Silurian	Caledonian Folding
		Ordovician	
		Cambrian	
Archæan		Pre-Cambrian	

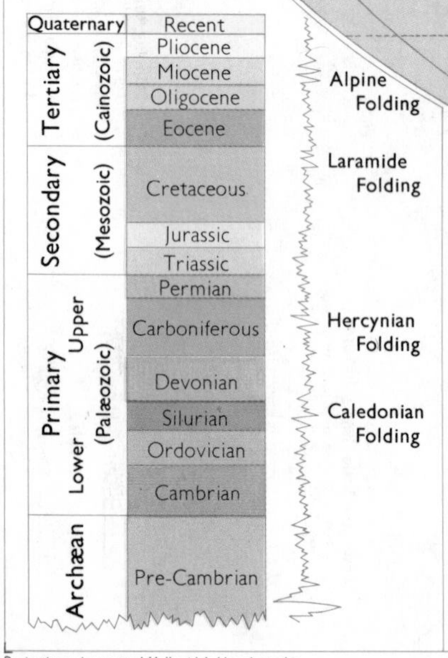

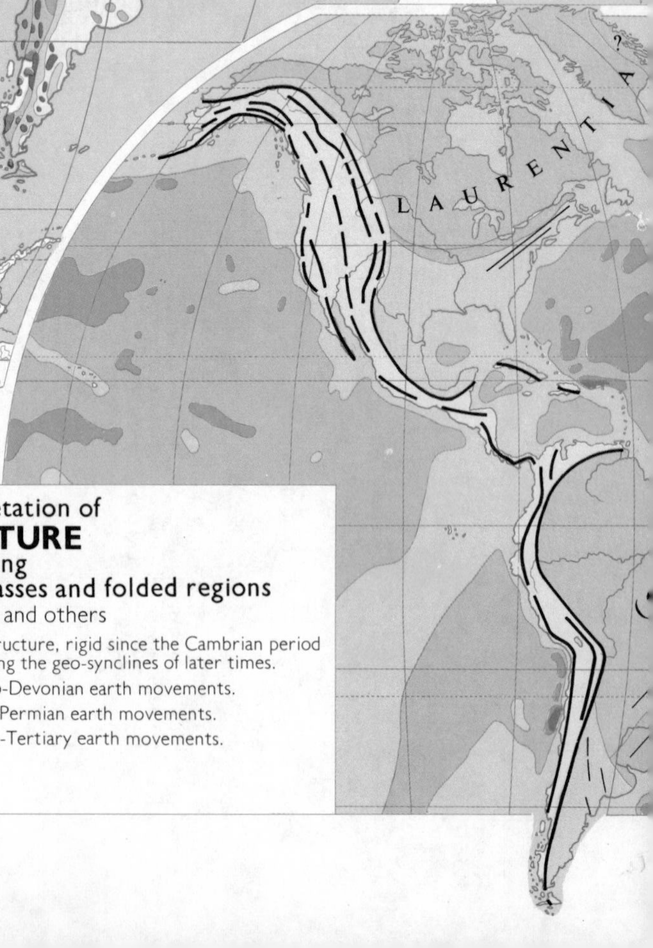

Ⓑ An Interpretation of
STRUCTURE
showing
the distribution of rigid masses and folded regions
after L. Kober and others

Pre-Cambrian tables composite in structure, rigid since the Cambrian period and forming stable elements separating the geo-synclines of later times.

Regions of Caledonian folding; Siluro-Devonian earth movements.

Regions of Hercynian folding; Carbo-Permian earth movements.

Regions of Tertiary folding; Cretaceo-Tertiary earth movements.

The Great Rift Valley

Main Trend lines

Projections: Interrupted Mollweide's Homolographic

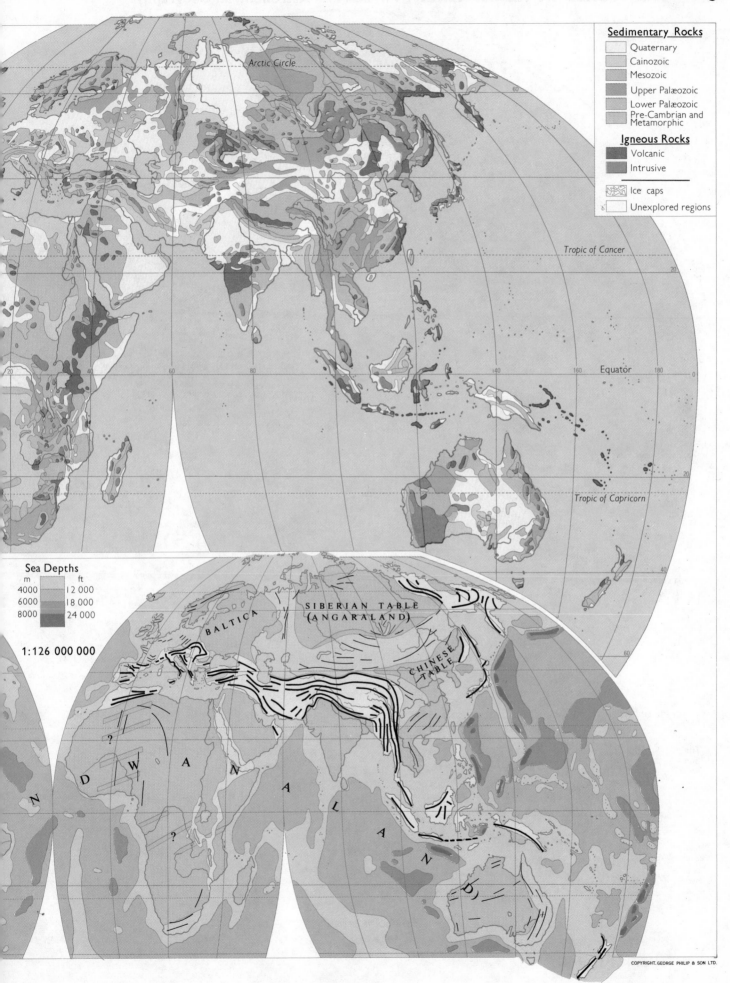

THE WO

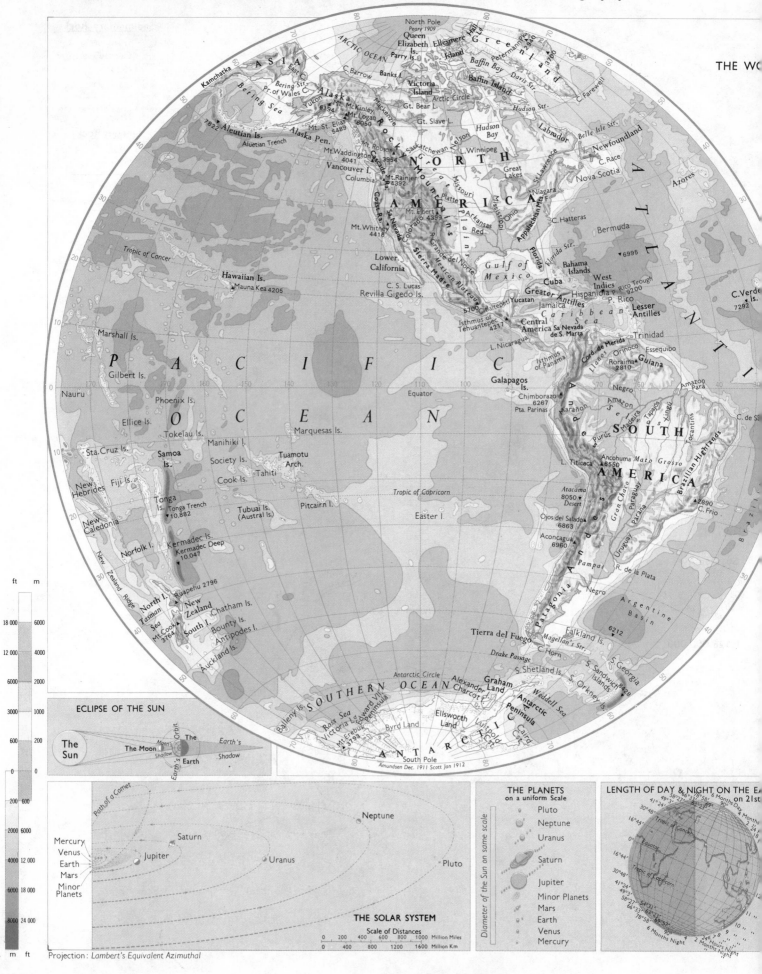

ECLIPSE OF THE SUN

The Sun   The Moon   The Earth

THE SOLAR SYSTEM

Mercury
Venus
Earth
Mars
Minor
Planets

Jupiter

Saturn

Uranus

Neptune

Pluto

Path of a Comet

Scale of Distances

| 0 | 200 | 400 | 600 | 800 | 1000 | Million Miles |
| 0 | 400 | 800 | 1200 | 1600 | | Million Km |

THE PLANETS
on a uniform Scale

Pluto
Neptune
Uranus
Saturn
Jupiter
Minor Planets
Mars
Earth
Venus
Mercury

Diameter of the Sun on same scale

LENGTH OF DAY & NIGHT ON THE EA
on 21st

Tropic of Cancer

Equator

Tropic of Capricorn

6 Months Day

6 Months Night

ft	m
18 000	6000
12 000	4000
6000	2000
3000	1000
600	200
0	0
600	200
6000	2000
12 000	4000
18 000	6000
24 000	8000
ft	m

Projection: *Lambert's Equivalent Azimuthal*

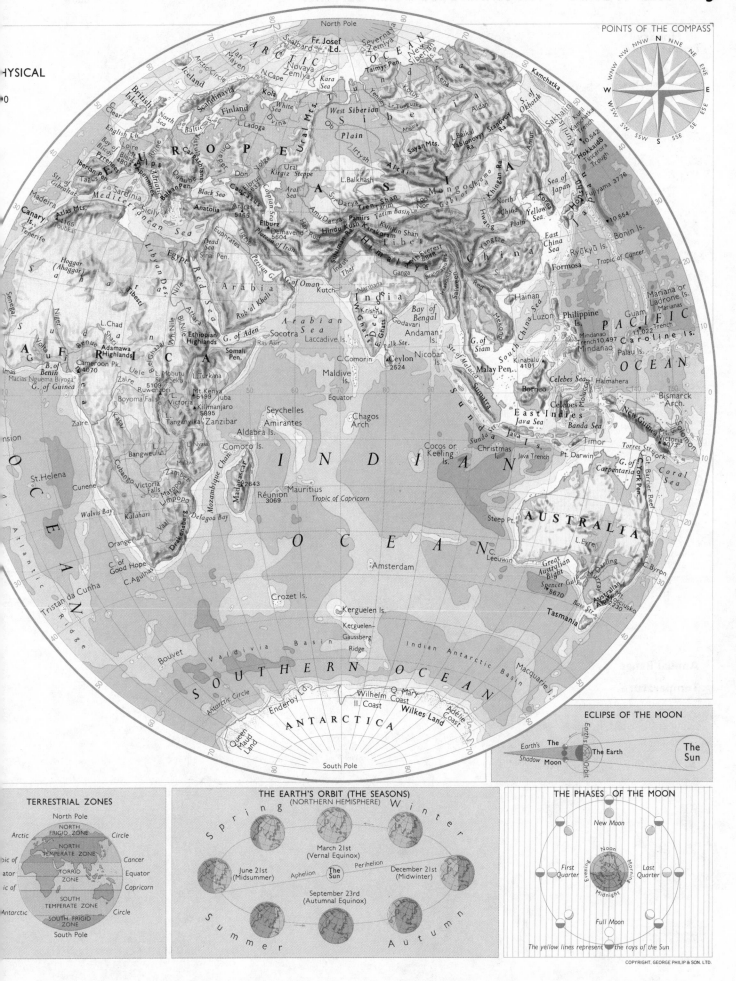

1:190 000 000

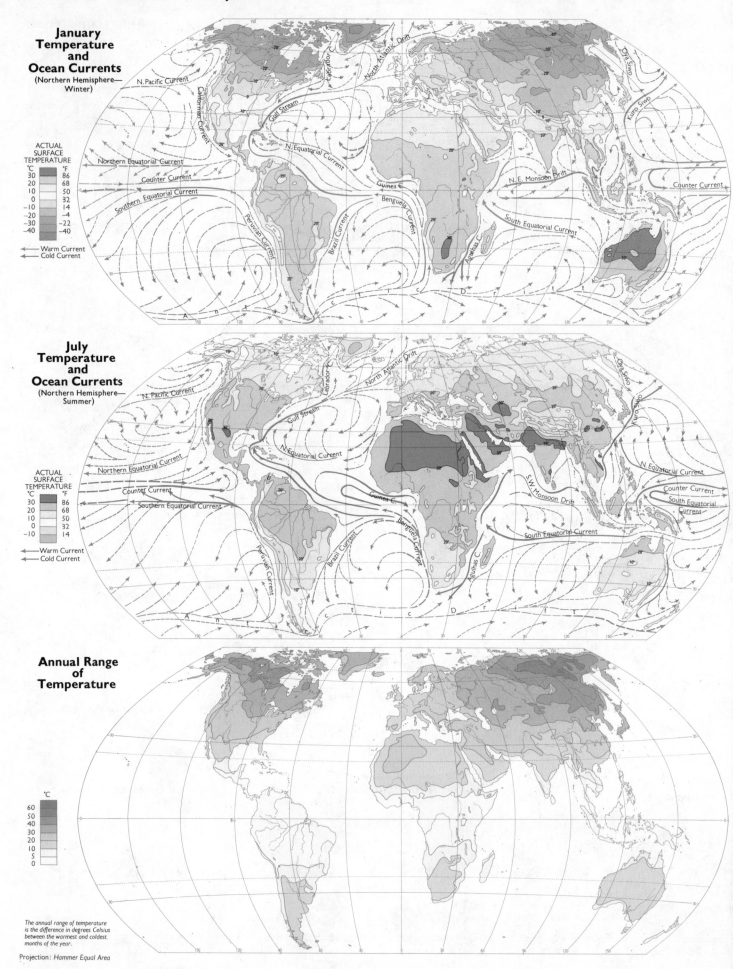

January Temperature and Ocean Currents

(Northern Hemisphere— Winter)

ACTUAL SURFACE TEMPERATURE

°C	°F
30	86
20	68
10	50
0	32
-10	14
-20	-4
-30	-22
-40	-40

← Warm Current
← Cold Current

July Temperature and Ocean Currents

(Northern Hemisphere— Summer)

ACTUAL SURFACE TEMPERATURE

°C	°F
30	86
20	68
10	50
0	32
-10	14

← Warm Current
← Cold Current

Annual Range of Temperature

°C
60
50
40
30
20
10
5
0

The annual range of temperature is the difference in degrees Celsius between the warmest and coldest months of the year.

Projection: *Hammer Equal Area*

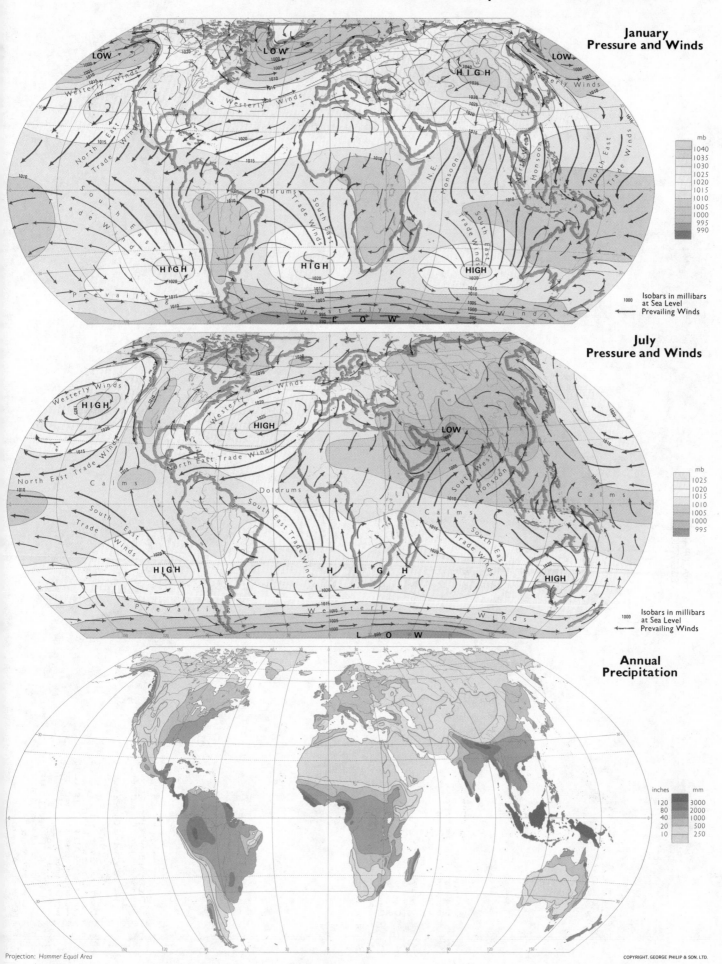

January
Pressure and Winds

July
Pressure and Winds

Annual
Precipitation

Projection: *Hammer Equal Area*

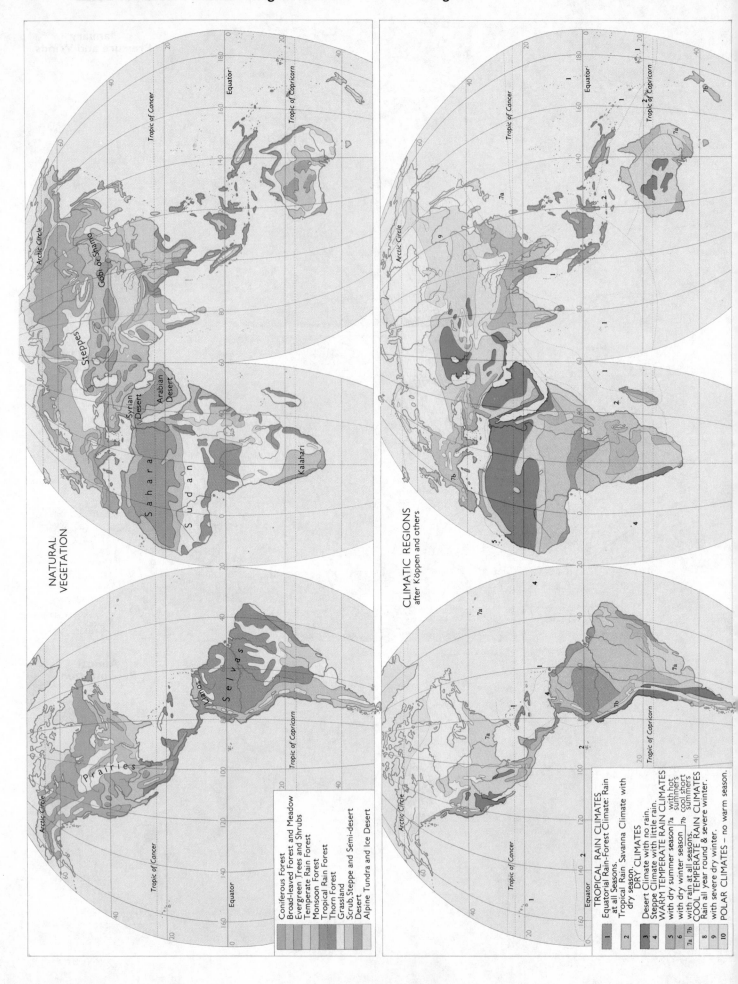

NATURAL VEGETATION

CLIMATIC REGIONS
after Köppen and others

Coniferous Forest
Broad-leaved Forest and Meadow
Evergreen Trees and Shrubs
Temperate Rain Forest
Monsoon Forest
Tropical Rain Forest
Thorn Forest
Grassland
Scrub, Steppe and Semi-desert
Desert
Alpine Tundra and Ice Desert

TROPICAL RAIN CLIMATES
1 Equatorial Rain-Forest Climate: Rain at all Seasons.
2 Tropical Rain Savanna Climate with dry season.
DRY CLIMATES
3 Desert Climate with no rain.
4 Steppe Climate with little rain.
WARM TEMPERATE RAIN CLIMATES
5 with dry summer season
6 with dry winter season
7a with hot summers
7b with cool short summers
7a, 7b with rain at all seasons
COOL TEMPERATE RAIN CLIMATES
8 Rain all year round & severe winter.
9 with severe dry winter.
POLAR CLIMATES – no warm season.
10

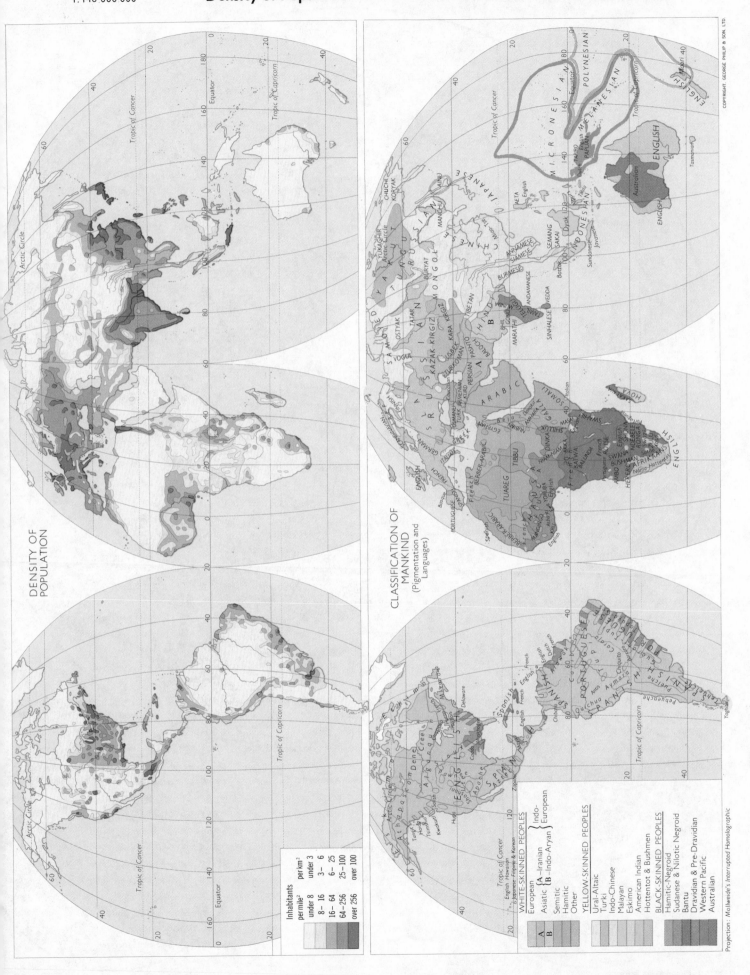

DENSITY OF
POPULATION

CLASSIFICATION OF
MANKIND
(Pigmentation and
Languages)

Inhabitants

per mile²	per km²
under 8	under 3
8 – 16	3 – 6
16 – 64	6 – 25
64 – 256	25 – 100
over 256	over 100

WHITE-SKINNED PEOPLES
European
Asiatic {A – Iranian
{B – Indo-Aryan } Indo-European
Semitic
Hamitic
Other

YELLOW-SKINNED PEOPLES
Ural-Altaic
Turki
Indo-Chinese
Malayan
Eskimo
American Indian
Hottentot & Bushmen

BLACK-SKINNED PEOPLES
Hamitic-Negroid
Sudanese & Nilotic Negroid
Bantu
Dravidian & Pre-Dravidian
Western Pacific
Australian

Projection: Mollweide's Interrupted Homolographic

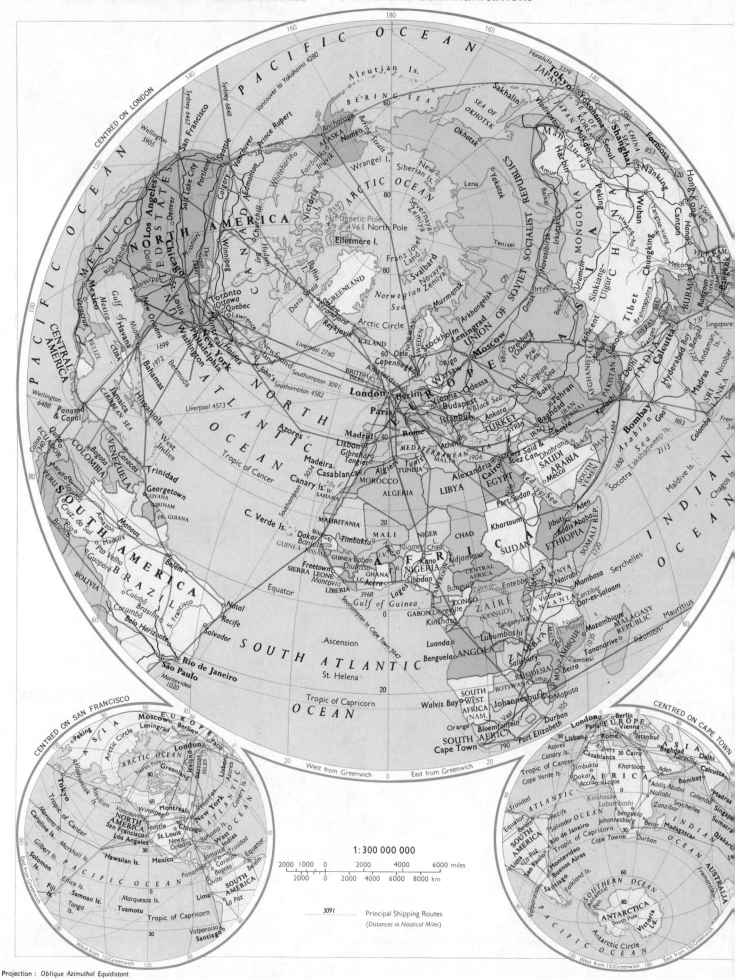

1:300 000 000

2000 1000 0 2000 4000 6000 miles
2000 0 2000 4000 6000 8000 km

3091 Principal Shipping Routes
(Distances in Nautical Miles)

Projection : *Oblique Azimuthal Equidistant*

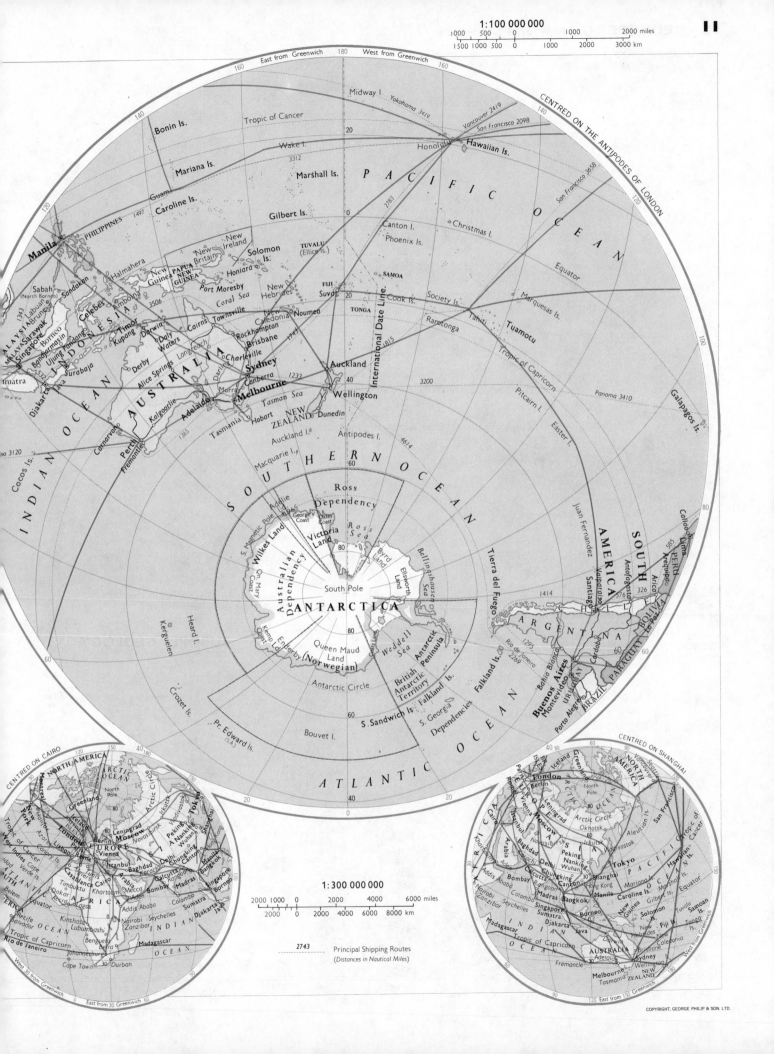

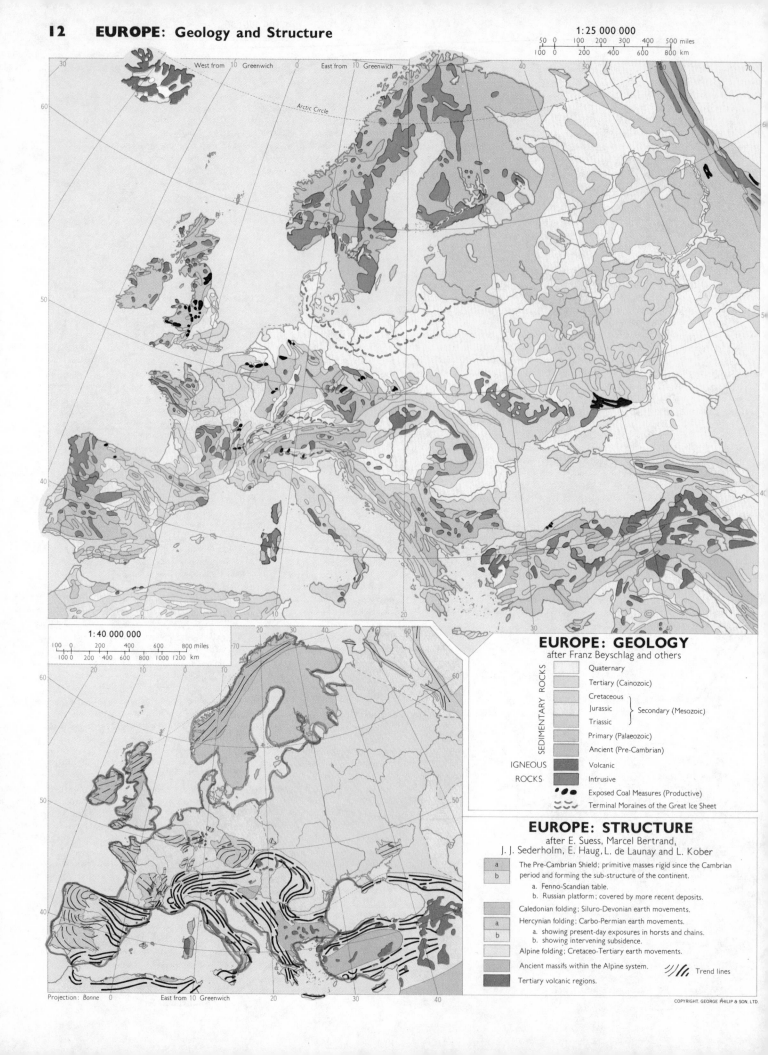

1:25 000 000

50 0 100 200 300 400 500 miles
100 0 200 400 600 800 km

West from 10 Greenwich 0 East from 10 Greenwich

Arctic Circle

1:40 000 000

100 0 200 400 600 800 miles
100 0 200 400 600 800 1000 1200 km

EUROPE: GEOLOGY
after Franz Beyschlag and others

SEDIMENTARY ROCKS

Quaternary

Tertiary (Cainozoic)

Cretaceous ⎫
Jurassic ⎬ Secondary (Mesozoic)
Triassic ⎭

Primary (Palaeozoic)

Ancient (Pre-Cambrian)

IGNEOUS Volcanic

ROCKS Intrusive

Exposed Coal Measures (Productive)

Terminal Moraines of the Great Ice Sheet

EUROPE: STRUCTURE
after E. Suess, Marcel Bertrand,
J. J. Sederholm, E. Haug, L. de Launay and L. Kober

a
b
The Pre-Cambrian Shield; primitive masses rigid since the Cambrian
period and forming the sub-structure of the continent.
a. Fenno-Scandian table.
b. Russian platform; covered by more recent deposits.

Caledonian folding; Siluro-Devonian earth movements.

a
b
Hercynian folding; Carbo-Permian earth movements.
a. showing present-day exposures in horsts and chains.
b. showing intervening subsidence.

Alpine folding; Cretaceo-Tertiary earth movements.

Ancient massifs within the Alpine system.

Tertiary volcanic regions.

Trend lines

Projection: Bonne 0 East from 10 Greenwich 20 30 40

COPYRIGHT. GEORGE PHILIP & SON, LTD.

1:20 000 000

100 ... 100 200 300 400 500 miles
100 0 200 400 600 800 km

COPYRIGHT. GEORGE PHILIP & SON. LTD.

CASPIAN SEA -28

U r a l   M o u n t a i n s

Ob
Ural
1617
884
Pechora
Kanin Peninsula
Kola Peninsula
White Sea
Mezen
N. Dvina
Onega
Onega

O b s h c h i y   S y r t

V o l g a   U p l a n d s

Volga
Volga
Kama
Rybinsk Res.
Tsimlyansk Res.
Don
Don
Manych
Terek
Kuban
Sea of Azov
Crimea
Kerch Str.
Bosporus

C e n t r a l   R u s s i a n   U p l a n d s

C a u c a s u s
5633
5166
Araks
Elbrus
Rion
2211

K u r d i s t a n
A r m e n i a
3710
Euphrates
Taurus
Anatolia
Cyprus 1951

BLACK SEA

L a p l a n d
S c a n d i n a v i a
Vesterålen
Lofoten
2123
2469
3734

NORWEGIAN SEA

F i n l a n d
Gulf of Finland
Gulf of Bothnia
Torne
Ume
Indals
Dal
Klar
Göta
Vänern
Vättern
Mälaren
Gotland
Öland

BALTIC SEA

Chari
Ladoga
Chudskoye
Neva
Dvina
Niemen
Riga
G. of Riga

P r i p y a t   M a r s h e s
Pripyat (Pripet)
Dnestr (Dniester)
Prut
Bug
U k r a i n e
Dnepr (Dnieper)
Danube

C a r p a t h i a n s
2655
Tatra
Transylvanian Alps
Wallachia
Morava
Tisza
Mures
Plain of Hungary
Danube
Drava
Sava
Balkans
Rhodope
Peninsula
Pindus
Morea
C. Matapan 5121
Aegean Sea
Crete
Ida 1766
Marmara
Sea of Marmara

NORTH SEA
FISHER
VIKING
FORTIES
Dogger Bank
HUMBER
THAMES
GERMAN BIGHT
Heligoland
Netherlands
Rhine
Meuse
Ardennes
Eifel
Moselle
Elbe
Weser
Harz 1142
Erz Geb.
Ez Geb.
Bohemian For.
Sudetes
Moravian Heights
Odra (Oder)
Wisła (Vistula)
Black For.
Vosges
1343
Taunus
Hunsrück

Skagerrak
Kattegat
Jutland
Lindesnes
2469

N o r t h   E u r o p e a n   P l a i n

A l p s
4807
Dinaric Alps
Gran Sasso 2914
A p e n n i n e s
Corno
Tiber
Po
Ligurian Sea
Sr. of Bonifacio
Corsica
Sardinia
Tyrrhenian Sea
Sicily 3263
Etna
Str. of Messina
C. Bon
Malta

ADRIATIC SEA
Str. of Otranto
Ionian Is.
Ionian Sea

MEDITERRANEAN SEA

Central Massif
Mt. Dore 1886
Cévennes
Rhône
G. of Lions
Pyrenees
3404
Garonne
Dordogne
Loire
Seine
Brittany
Bay of Biscay
4651
FINISTERRE
C. Finisterre
C. Ortegal
Gironde

English Channel
DOVER
WIGHT
PORTLAND
PLYMOUTH
Land's End
Lundy
FASTNET
SOLE
SHANNON
Valentia
C. Clear

Great Britain
1344
British Isles
Ireland
Irish Sea
1085
HEBRIDES
Hebrides
FAIR ISLE
Orkney Is.
Shetland Is.
CROMARTY
TYNE
FORTH
NORTH
MALIN
IRISH SEA
BAILEY
ROCKALL
Rockall
Fisher Bank
FAEROES
Faroes

ATLANTIC OCEAN

Iceland
2119
Hekla
1491
Myrdal.
NORTH EAST ICELAND
SOUTH EAST ICELAND
Arctic Circle

Cantabrian Mts.
Old Castile
New Castile
Duero
Douro
Mondego
Sa. da Estrela
Tagus
Iberian Peninsula
Sierra Morena
Guadiana
Guadalquivir
Andalusia
Sa. Nevada
3478
Str. of Gibraltar
C. St. Vincent
C. Trafalgar
C. Spartel
Balearic Is.
Maritime Atlas
Plateau of the Shotts

Projection: Bonne   West from Greenwich 0 East from Greenwich
ROCKALL   Sea areas named in
weather forecasts

ft m
12 000 4000
6000 2000
3000 1000
1200 400
600 200
0 0
200-600
2000 6000
4000 12 000
ft m

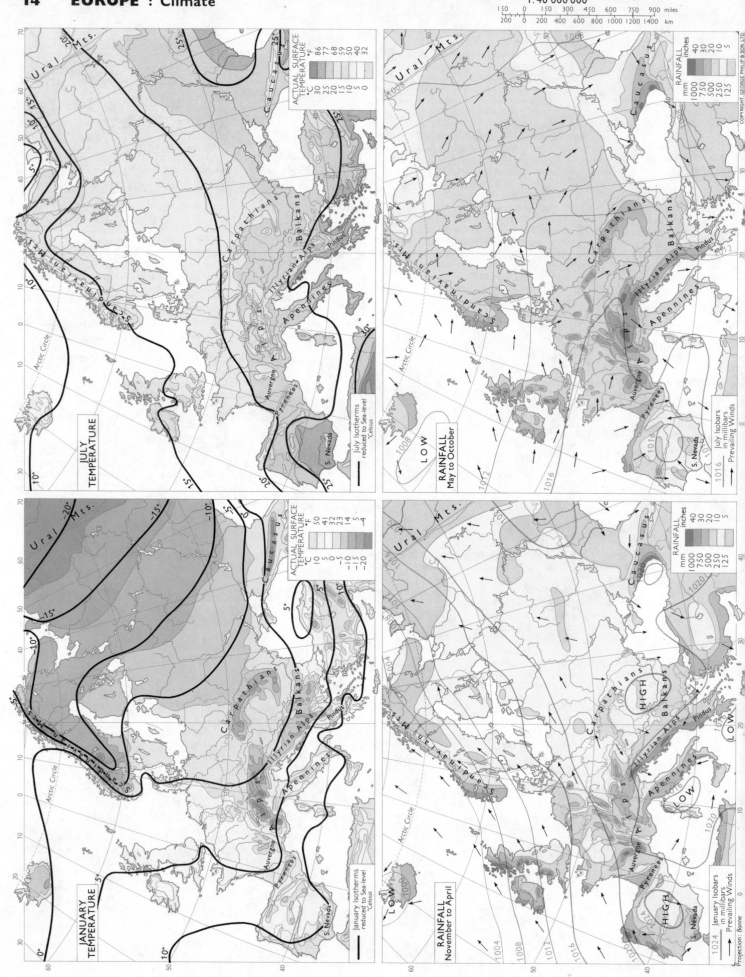

1 : 40 000 000

JULY TEMPERATURE

ACTUAL SURFACE TEMPERATURE

°C   °F
30   86
25   77
20   68
15   59
5   40
0   32

July Isotherms reduced to Sea-level °Celsius

JANUARY TEMPERATURE

ACTUAL SURFACE TEMPERATURE

°C   °F
10   50
5   41
0   32
-5   23
-10 14
-15 5
-20 -4

January Isotherms reduced to Sea-level °Celsius

RAINFALL May to October

RAINFALL
mm   inches
1000 40
750   30
500   20
250   15
125

July Isobars in millibars
Prevailing Winds

RAINFALL November to April

RAINFALL
mm   inches
1000 40
750   30
500   20
250   10
125   5

January Isobars in millibars
Prevailing Winds

COPYRIGHT GEORGE PHILIP & SON LTD

Projection Bonne

1:20 000 000

100   0   100   200   300   400   500 miles

100   0   200   400   600   800 km

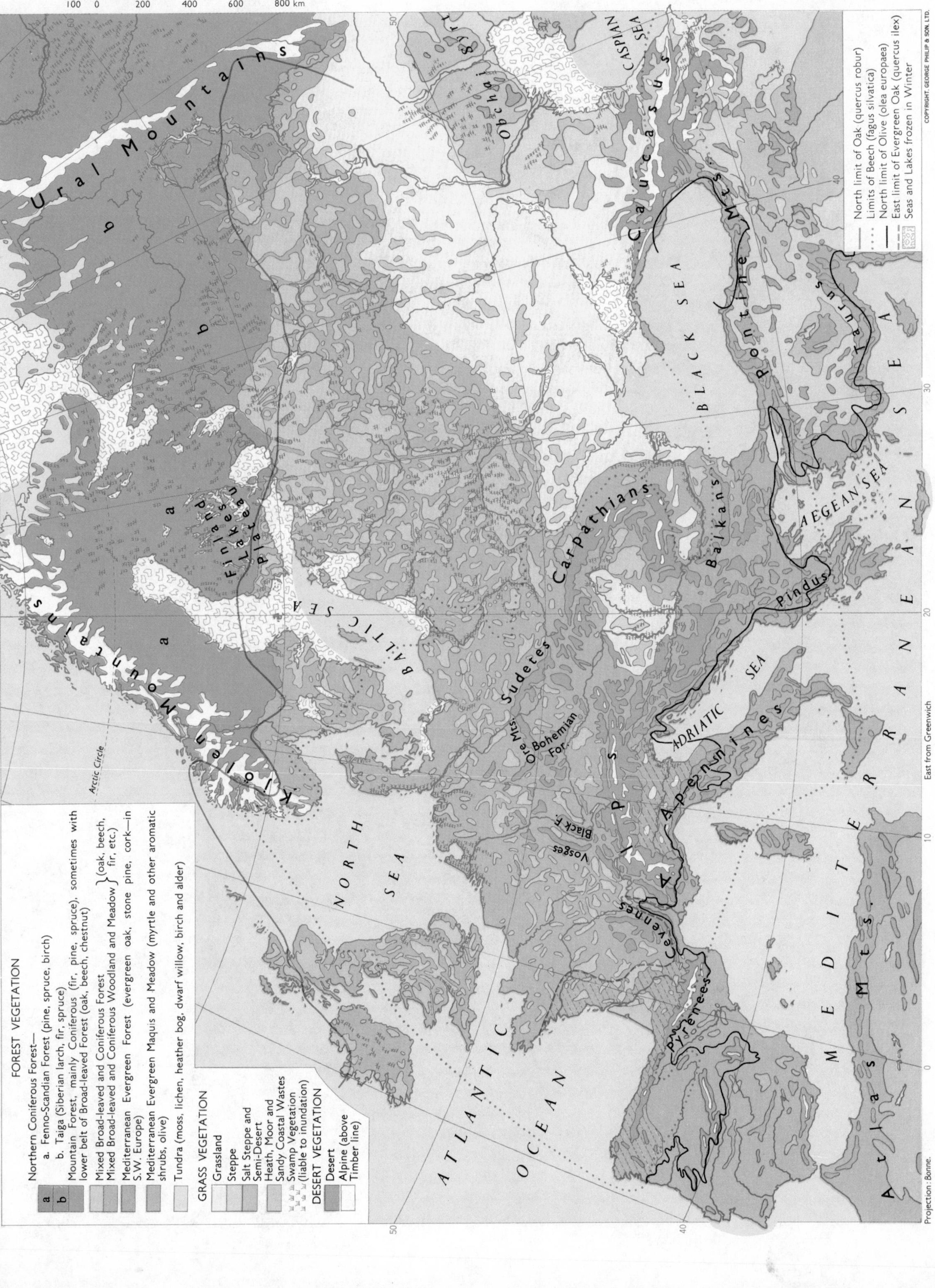

COPYRIGHT. GEORGE PHILIP & SON LTD.

North limit of Oak (quercus robur)
Limits of Beech (fagus silvatica)
North limit of Olive (olea europaea)
East limit of Evergreen Oak (quercus ilex)
Seas and Lakes frozen in Winter

FOREST VEGETATION

Northern Coniferous Forest—
  a. Fenno-Scandian Forest (pine, spruce, birch)
  b. Taiga (Siberian larch, fir, spruce)

Mountain Forest, mainly Coniferous (fir, pine, spruce), sometimes with lower belt of Broad-leaved Forest (oak, beech, chestnut)

Mixed Broad-leaved and Coniferous Forest
Mixed Broad-leaved and Coniferous Woodland and Meadow } (oak, beech, stone pine, cork—in S.W. Europe) (oak, beech, pine, fir, etc.)

Mediterranean Evergreen Forest (evergreen oak, stone pine, cork—in S.W. Europe)

Mediterranean Evergreen Maquis and Meadow (myrtle and other aromatic shrubs, olive)

Tundra (moss, lichen, heather bog, dwarf willow, birch and alder)

GRASS VEGETATION

Grassland
Steppe
Salt Steppe and Semi-Desert
Heath, Moor and Sandy Coastal Wastes
Swamp Vegetation (liable to inundation)

DESERT VEGETATION

Desert
Alpine (above Timber line)

a   b

Projection: Bonne.

East from Greenwich

Map labels: Ural Mountains, Obchai Syrt, CASPIAN SEA, Caucasus, Pontine Mts., Black Sea, Taurus, AEGEAN SEA, Carpathians, Balkans, Pindus, Kjolen Mountains, Finland Lake Plateau, BALTIC SEA, Sudetes, Ore Mts., Bohemian For., Alps, Apennines, ADRIATIC SEA, Black F., Vosges, Cevennes, Pyrenees, Atlas Mts., MEDITERRANEAN SEA, NORTH SEA, ATLANTIC OCEAN, Arctic Circle

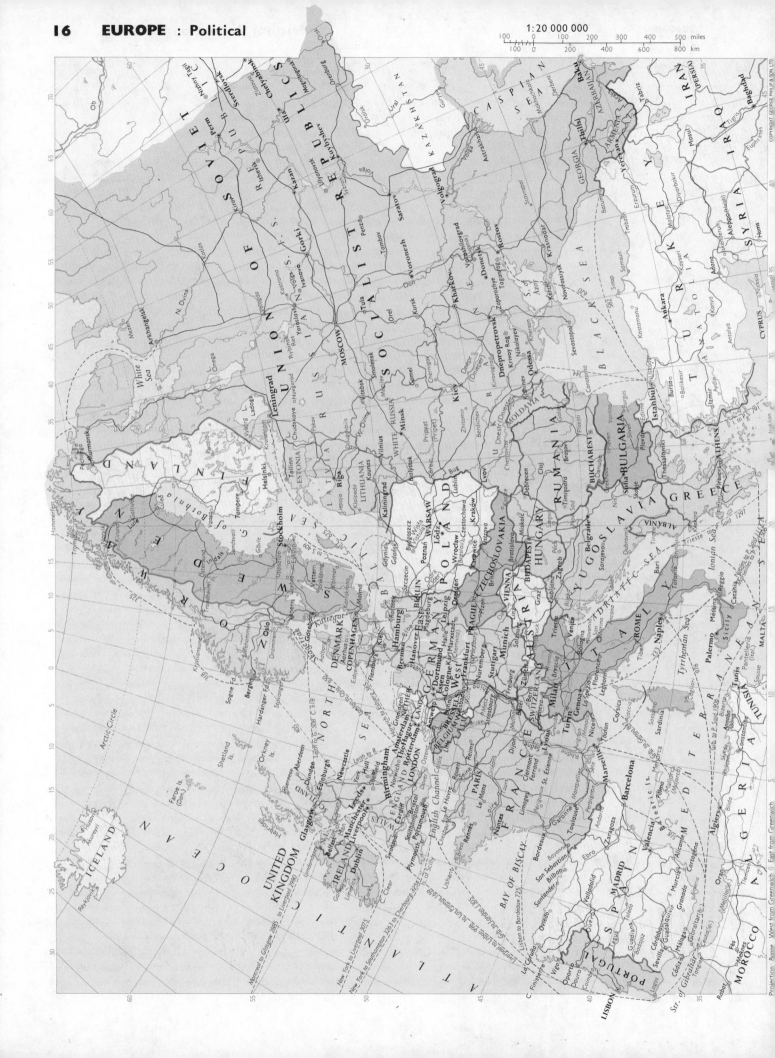

1:40 000 000

150   0   150   300   450   600   750   900 miles
200   0   200   400   600   800   1000 1200 1400 km

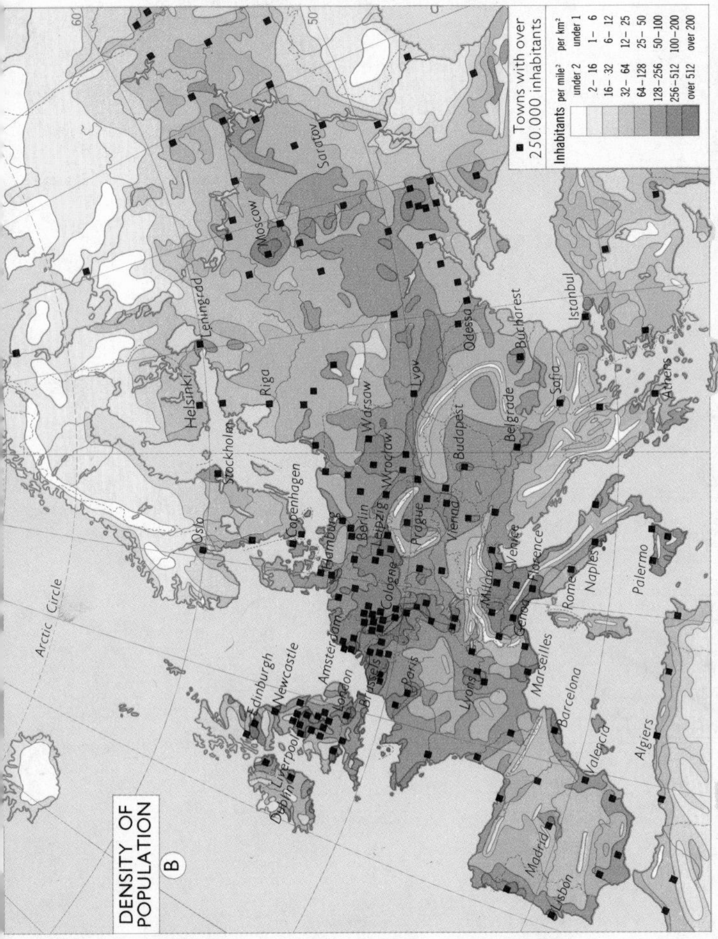

B — DENSITY OF POPULATION

Towns with over 250 000 inhabitants

Inhabitants per mile²	per km²
under 2	under 1
2 – 16	1 – 6
16 – 32	6 – 12
32 – 64	12 – 25
64 – 128	25 – 50
128 – 256	50 – 100
256 – 512	100 – 200
over 512	over 200

Urals · Saratov · Moscow · Leningrad · Helsinki · Riga · Warsaw · Stockholm · Oslo · Copenhagen · Hamburg · Berlin · Łódź · Wrocław · Prague · Vienna · Budapest · Odessa · Bucharest · Istanbul · Sofia · Belgrade · Athens · Naples · Rome · Palermo · Florence · Milan · Venice · Genoa · Turin · Marseilles · Lyons · Paris · Barcelona · Algiers · Valencia · Madrid · Lisbon · London · Amsterdam · Newcastle · Edinburgh · Glasgow · Dublin · Belfast · Arctic Circle

A — ANNUAL RAINFALL

inches	mm
60	1 500
40	1 000
30	750
20	500
10	250

Urals · Caucasus · Carpathians · Balkans · Pindus · Dinaric Alps · Apennines · Alps · Auvergne · Pyrenees · S. Nevada · Atlas Mts. · Scandinavian Mts. · Arctic Circle

D — RELIGIONS

Christianity
Protestant
Roman Catholic
Greek and Russian Orthodox
Mohammedanism
Others

Urals · Caucasus · Carpathians · Balkans · Pindus · Dinaric Alps · Apennines · Auvergne · Pyrenees · S. Nevada · Atlas Mts. · Scandinavian Mts. · Arctic Circle

COPYRIGHT GEORGE PHILIP & SON LTD

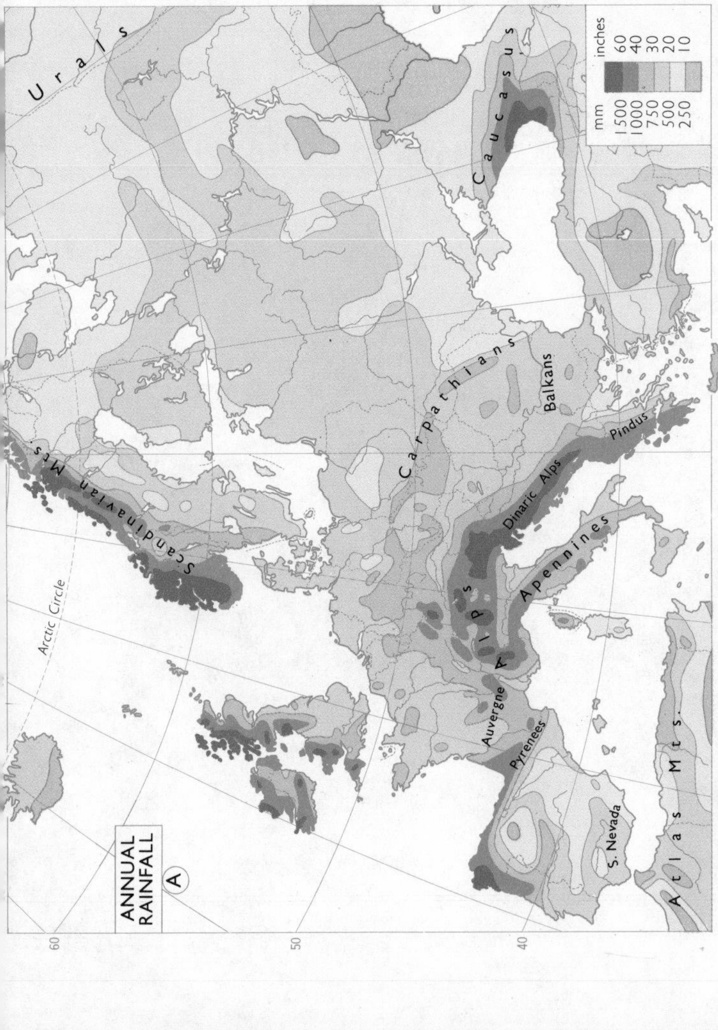

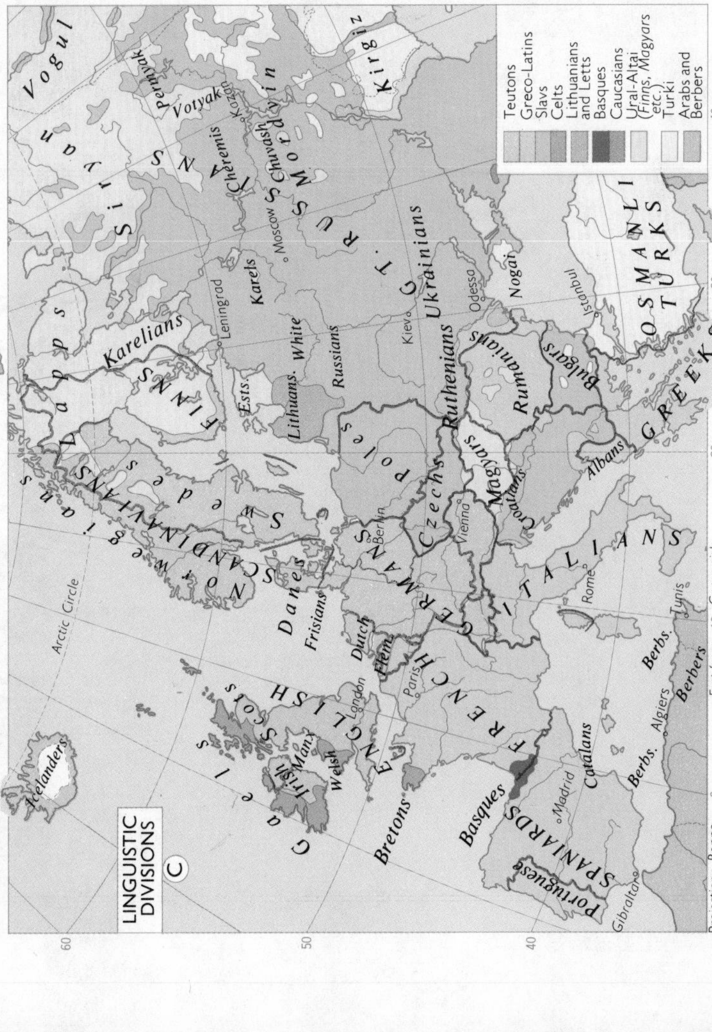

C — LINGUISTIC DIVISIONS

Teutons
Greco-Latins
Slavs
Celts
Lithuanians and Letts
Basques
Caucasians
Ural-Altai (Finns, Magyars etc.)
Turki
Arabs and Berbers

Vogul · Syryan · Kirgiz · Permyak · Votyak · Cheremis · Chuvash · Mordvin · GREAT RUSSIANS · Kazan · Moscow · Karels · Leningrad · Ests · Lithuans · White Russians · Ukrainians · Kiev · Odessa · Nogai · Istanbul · Karelians · LAPPS · FINNS · Swedes · Norwegians · Danes · Frisians · Dutch · GERMANS · Berlin · Czechs · Magyars · Vienna · Ruthenians · Rumanians · Rumni · Bulgars · Serbs · Albans · OSMANLI TURKS · GREEKS · ITALIANS · Rome · FRENCH · Catalans · SPANIARDS · Madrid · Portuguese · BASQUES · Gibraltar · Tunis · Algiers · Berbs · ENGLISH · Scots · Irish · Manx · Welsh · Lundy · Bretons · Gaels · Icelanders

Projection: Bonne

East from 10 Greenwich

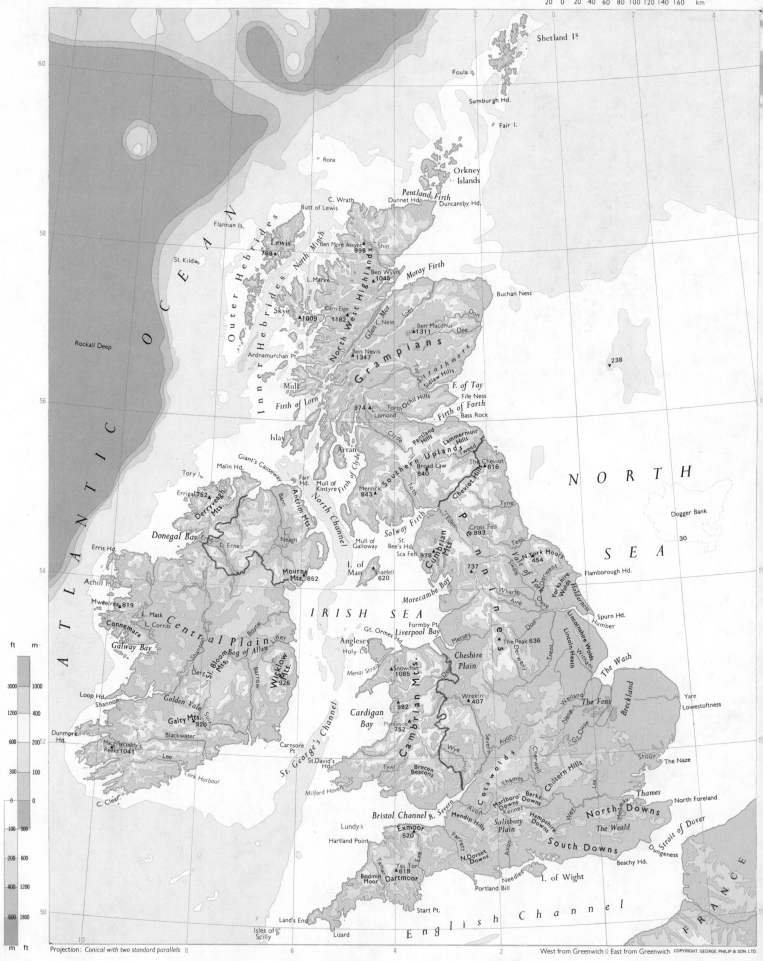

1:5 000 000

20   0   20   40   60   80   100 miles
20 0 20 40 60 80 100 120 140 160 km

Shetland I.ˢ

Foula

Sumburgh Hd.

Fair I.

Rona

Orkney Islands

Pentland Firth

C. Wrath   Dunnet Hd.   Duncansby Hd.

Butt of Lewis

Flannan Is.

Lewis
789 ▲

St. Kilda

Ben More Assynt 998 ▲   L. Shin

North Minch

L. Maree   Ben Wyvis 1045 ▲   Moray Firth

Outer Hebrides

Skye   Carn Eige   Buchan Ness
1009 ▲   1182 ▲

Inner Hebrides

Glen Mor   L. Ness   Ben Macdhui 1311 ▲   Dee

Ardnamurchan Pt.   Ben Nevis 1347 ▲   Grampians   Strathmore

Rockall Deep

Mull   Sidlaw Hills   F. of Tay   Fife Ness

Firth of Lorn   Forth   Ochil Hills   Firth of Forth   Bass Rock

974 ▲   L. Lomond

Islay   Clyde   Pentland Hills   Lammermuir Hills   238 ▲

Arran   Southern Uplands   Tweed

Giant's Causeway   Fair Hd.   Broad Law   The Cheviot
                    840   816 ▲

Tory I.   Malin Hd.   Mull of Kintyre   Firth of Clyde   Merrick   Cheviot Hills
                                                            843 ▲   Nith

Errigal 752 ▲   Antrim Mts.   North Channel   Tyne   NORTH

Derryveagh Mts.   Bann   Solway Firth   Cross Fell 893 ▲   Dogger Bank

Donegal Bay   Erne   L. Neagh   Mull of Galloway   St. Bee's Hd.   Teme   Tees   30   SEA
                                            Sca Fell

Erris Hd.   L. Erne   I. of Man   Sca Fell 978 ▲   Cumbrian Mts.   Swale   N. York Moors 454   Flamborough Hd.

Achill I.   Mourne Mts. 852   Snaefell 620   737 ▲   Ure   Vale of York   Yorkshire Wolds   Holderness

Mweelrea 819   Morecambe Bay   Wharfe   Spurn Hd.
                                                        Humber

L. Mask   IRISH SEA   Aire   Lincolnshire Wolds

Connemara   L. Corrib   Formby Pt.   Mersey   The Peak 636 ▲   Trent   Lincoln Heath   The Wash

Galway Bay   Central Plain   Liffey   Gt. Ormes Hd.   Liverpool Bay   Dee   Cheshire Plain   Witham   Breckland

St. Bloom Mts.   Bog of Allen   Anglesey   Wrekin 407 ▲   The Fens   Yare   Lowestoftness

Derg   Barrow   Holy I.   Snowdon 1085 ▲   Cambrian Mts.   Dove   Welland   Nene

Wicklow Mts. 926   Menai Strait   892 ▲   Derwent   Gt. Ouse   The Naze

Loop Hd.   Golden Vale   Suir   Cardigan Bay   Plynlimon 752   Avon   Cherwell   Chiltern Hills   Stour

Shannon   Galty Mts. 920   Wye   Severn   Cotswolds   Thames

Dunmore Hd.   Blackwater   Carnsore Pt.   Tywi   Brecon Beacons   Berks.   Marlboro' Downs   North Downs   North Foreland

Macgillycuddy's Reeks 1041   Lee   St. George's Channel   St. David's Hd.   Severn   Avon   Kennet   Hampshire Downs   The Weald   Strait of Dover

C. Clear   Cork Harbour   Milford Haven   Bristol Channel   R. Severn   Mendip Hills   Salisbury Plain   South Downs   Dungeness

Lundy   Exmoor 520   Parrett   Avon   Beachy Hd.

Hartland Point   N. Dorset Downs   Portland Bill

Yes Tor 618 ▲   Exe   I. of Wight   Needles

Bodmin Moor   Dartmoor   Portland Bill

Land's End   Start Pt.

Isles of Scilly   Lizard   ENGLISH CHANNEL   FRANCE

ATLANTIC OCEAN

NORTH SEA

ft   m
        m   ft
3000 1000
        100   300
1200   400   200   600
600   200   400   1200
300   100   600   1800
0   0   m   ft

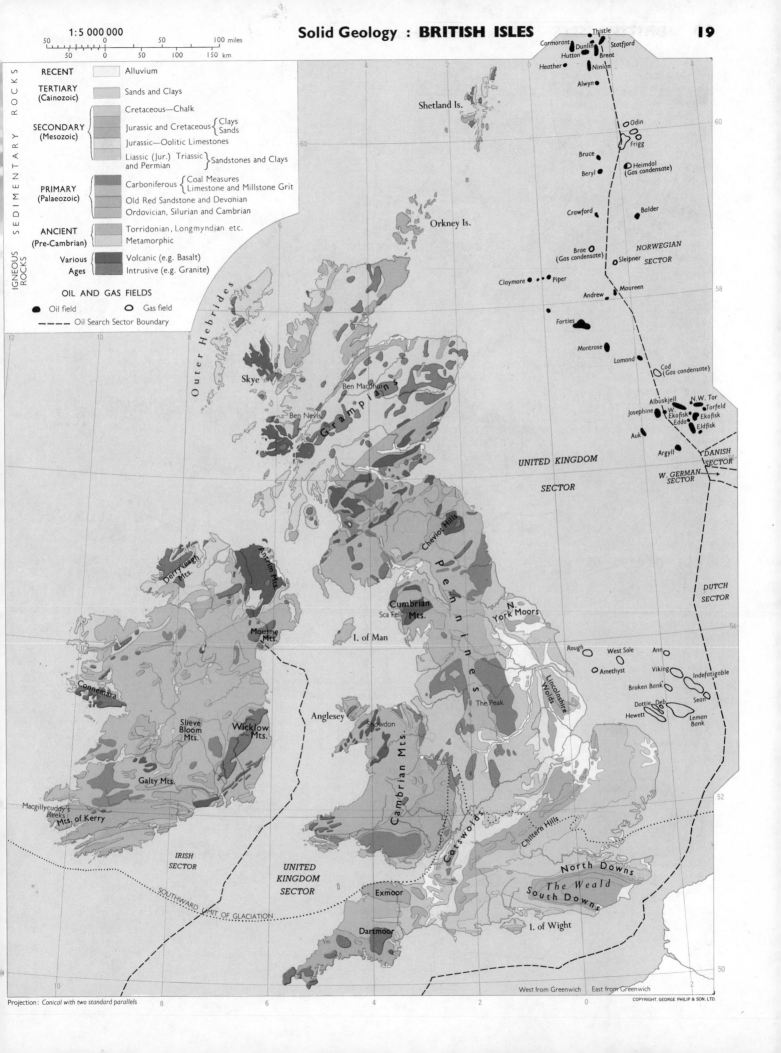

1 : 5 000 000

50   0   50   100 miles
50   0   50   100   150 km

SEDIMENTARY ROCKS

RECENT — Alluvium

TERTIARY (Cainozoic) — Sands and Clays

SECONDARY (Mesozoic)
- Cretaceous—Chalk
- Jurassic and Cretaceous { Clays / Sands
- Jurassic—Oolitic Limestones
- Liassic (Jur.) Triassic and Permian } Sandstones and Clays

PRIMARY (Palaeozoic)
- Carboniferous { Coal Measures / Limestone and Millstone Grit
- Old Red Sandstone and Devonian
- Ordovician, Silurian and Cambrian

ANCIENT (Pre-Cambrian)
- Torridonian, Longmyndian etc.
- Metamorphic

IGNEOUS ROCKS

Various Ages
- Volcanic (e.g. Basalt)
- Intrusive (e.g. Granite)

OIL AND GAS FIELDS

● Oil field   ○ Gas field

- - - Oil Search Sector Boundary

Projection: Conical with two standard parallels

COPYRIGHT. GEORGE PHILIP & SON LTD.

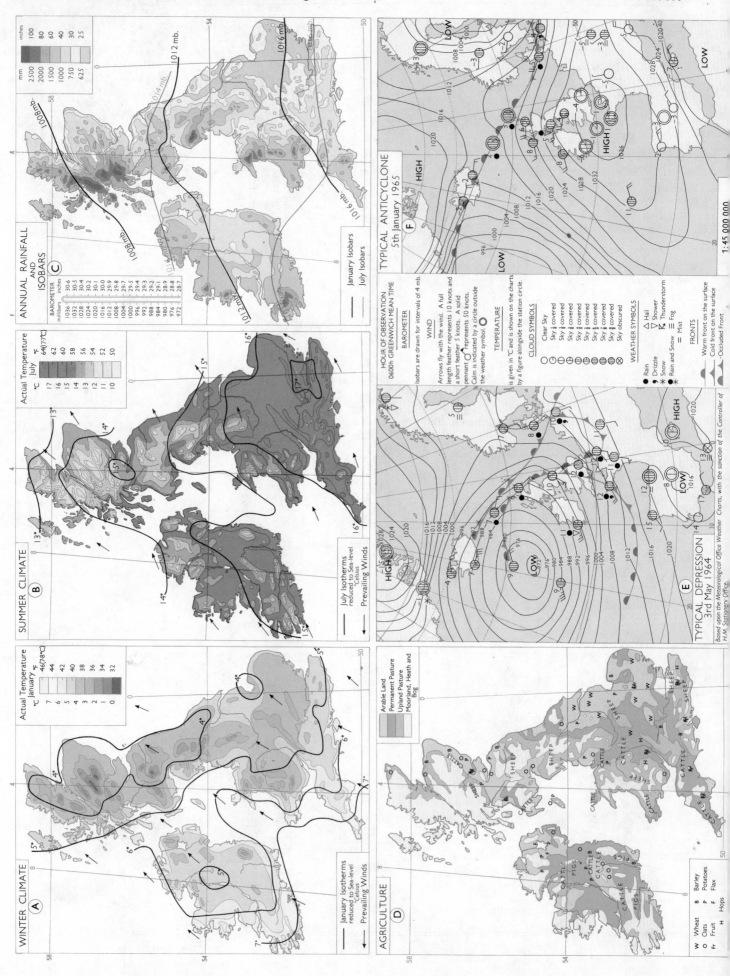

1:10 000 000

WINTER CLIMATE Ⓐ

Actual Temperature January

°C	°F
7	46(78°C)
6	44
5	42
4	40
3	38
2	36
1	34
0	32

—— January Isotherms reduced to Sea-level °Celsius

→ Prevailing Winds

SUMMER CLIMATE Ⓑ

Actual Temperature July

°C	°F
17	64(77°C)
16	62
15	60
14	58
13	56
12	54
11	52
10	50

—— July Isotherms reduced to Sea-level °Celsius

→ Prevailing Winds

ANNUAL RAINFALL AND ISOBARS Ⓒ

inches	mm
100	2500
80	2000
60	1500
40	1000
30	750
25	625

BAROMETER

millibars	inches
1036	30.6
1032	30.5
1028	30.4
1024	30.2
1020	30.1
1016	30.0
1012	29.9
1008	29.8
1004	29.7
1000	29.5
996	29.4
992	29.3
988	29.2
984	29.1
980	28.9
976	28.8
972	28.7

—— January Isobars

—— July Isobars

AGRICULTURE Ⓓ

Arable Land
Permanent Pasture
Upland Pasture
Moorland, Heath and Bog

W Wheat   B Barley
O Oats   P Potatoes
Fr Fruit   F Flax
H Hops

TYPICAL DEPRESSION Ⓔ
3rd May 1964

Based upon the Meteorological Office Weather Charts, with the sanction of the Controller of H.M. Stationery Office.

TYPICAL ANTICYCLONE Ⓕ
5th January 1965

HOUR OF OBSERVATION
0600h GREENWICH MEAN TIME

BAROMETER
Isobars are drawn for intervals of 4 mb.

WIND
Arrows fly with the wind. A full length feather represents 10 knots and a short feather 5 knots. A solid pennant ⊾ represents 50 knots. Calm is indicated by a circle outside the weather symbol. ◯

TEMPERATURE
is given in °C and is shown on the charts by a figure alongside the station circle.

CLOUD SYMBOLS
◯ Clear Sky
◉ Sky ¼ covered
⊕ Sky ¼ covered
⊕ Sky ½ covered
⊕ Sky ¾ covered
⊕ Sky ¾ covered
⊕ Sky ⅞ covered
⊕ Sky ⅞ covered
● Sky covered
⊗ Sky obscured

WEATHER SYMBOLS
● Rain   △ Hail
, Drizzle   ▽ Shower
* Snow   ☒ Thunderstorm
● Rain and Snow   ≡ Fog
*   ≡ Mist

FRONTS
▲ Warm front on the surface
▼ Cold front on the surface
▲▼ Occluded Front

1:45 000 000

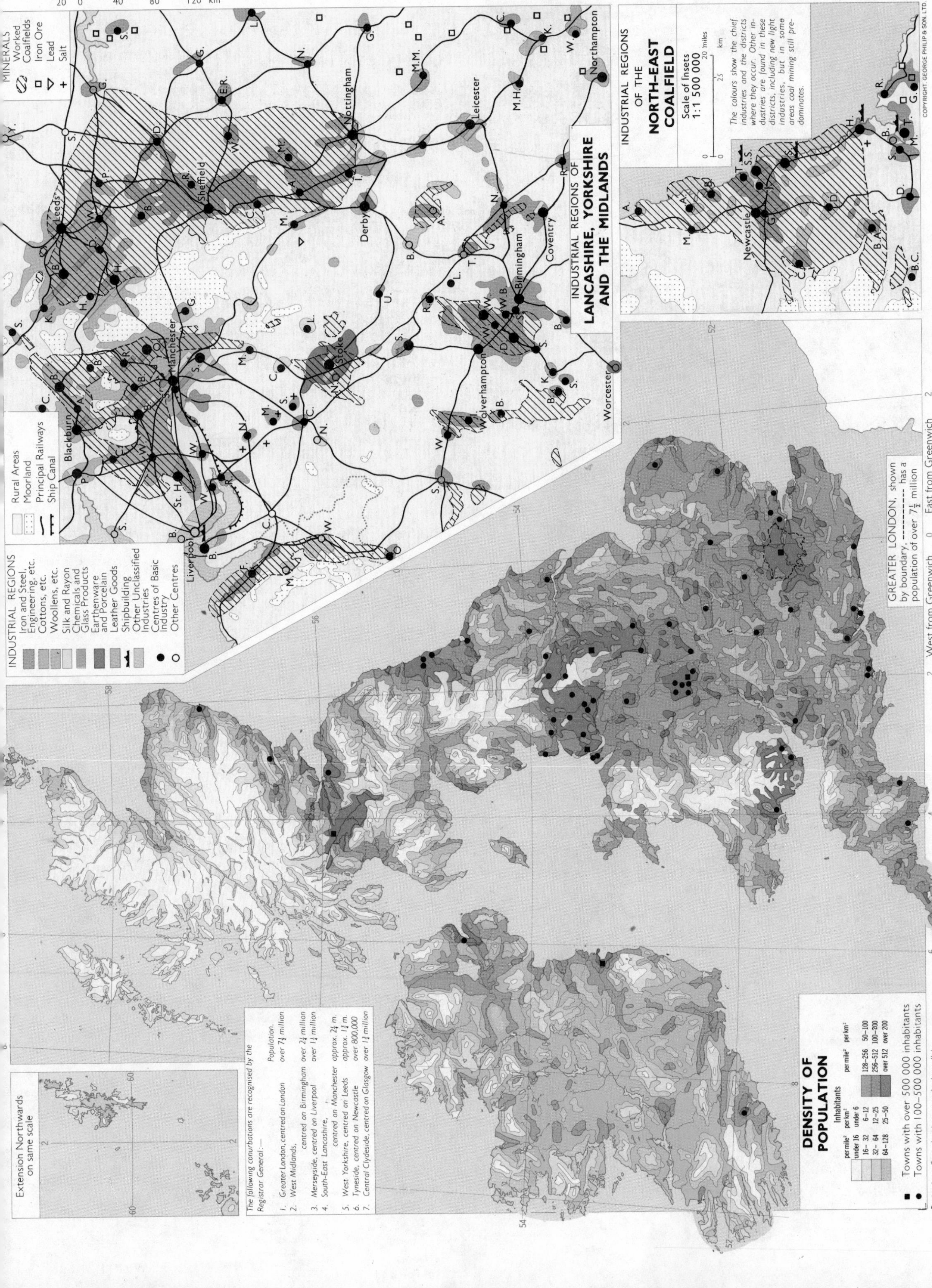

1:5 000 000

20 0 20 40 60 80 miles
20 0 40 80 120 km

MINERALS
≋ Worked
Coalfields
□ Iron Ore
▷ Lead
+ Salt

**INDUSTRIAL REGIONS OF
LANCASHIRE, YORKSHIRE
AND THE MIDLANDS**

INDUSTRIAL REGIONS
Iron and Steel,
Engineering, etc.
Cottons, etc.
Woollens, etc.
Silk and Rayon
Chemicals and
Glass Products
Earthenware
and Porcelain
Leather Goods
Shipbuilding
Other Unclassified
Industries
Centres of Basic ●
Industry
Other Centres ○

Rural Areas
Moorland
Principal Railways
Ship Canal

Leeds
Sheffield
Manchester
Liverpool
Blackburn
St. H.
Stoke
Derby
Nottingham
Leicester
Northampton
Birmingham
Coventry
Wolverhampton
Worcester

**INDUSTRIAL REGIONS OF THE
NORTH-EAST
COALFIELD**

Scale of Insets
1:1 500 000

0 25 20 miles
0 25 km

The colours show the chief
industries and the districts
where they occur. Other industries are found in these
districts, including new light
industries, but in some
areas coal mining still pre-
dominates.

Newcastle

COPYRIGHT GEORGE PHILIP & SON, LTD.

GREATER LONDON, shown
by boundary, ---- has a
population of over 7¼ million

West from Greenwich 0 East from Greenwich

Extension Northwards
on same scale

The following conurbations are recognised by the
Registrar General:—

	Population.
1. Greater London, centred on London	over 7¼ million
2. West Midlands, centred on Birmingham	over 2¼ million
3. Merseyside, centred on Liverpool	over 1¼ million
4. South-East Lancashire, centred on Manchester	approx. 2¼ m.
5. West Yorkshire, centred on Leeds	approx. 1¼ m.
6. Tyneside, centred on Newcastle	over 800,000
7. Central Clydeside, centred on Glasgow	over 1¾ million

**DENSITY OF
POPULATION**

per mile²	per km²		per mile²	per km²
under 16	under 6		128-256	50-100
16 - 32	6-12		256-512	100-200
32 - 64	12-25		over 512	over 200
64-128	25-50			

■ Towns with over 500 000 inhabitants
● Towns with 100–500 000 inhabitants

Projection. Conical with two standard parallels.

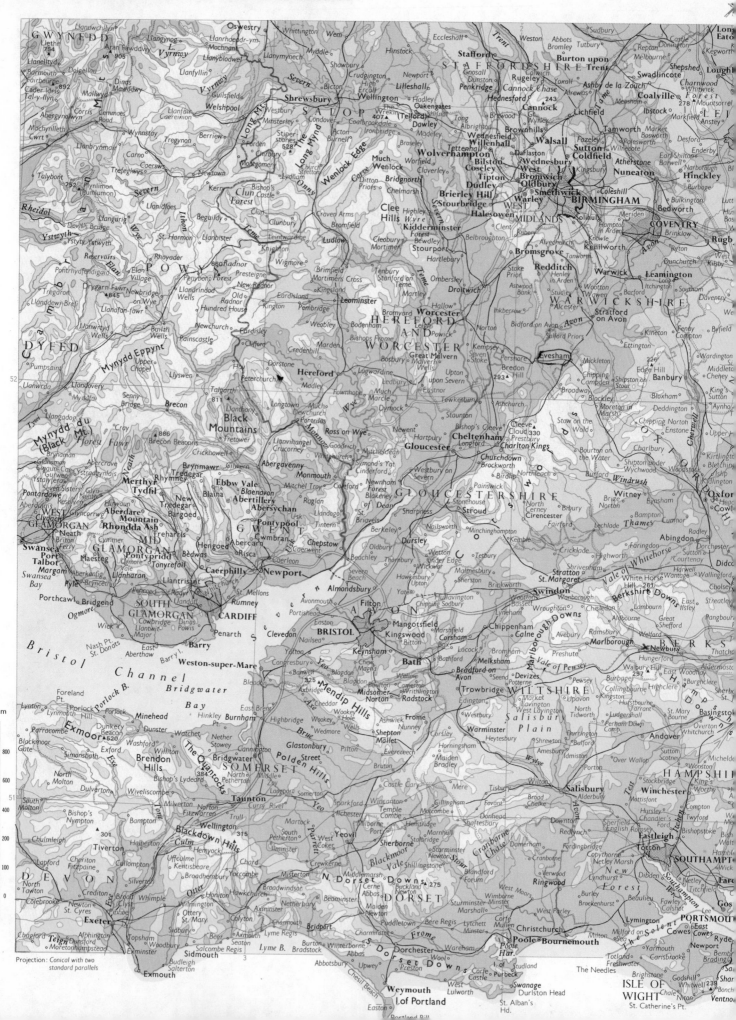

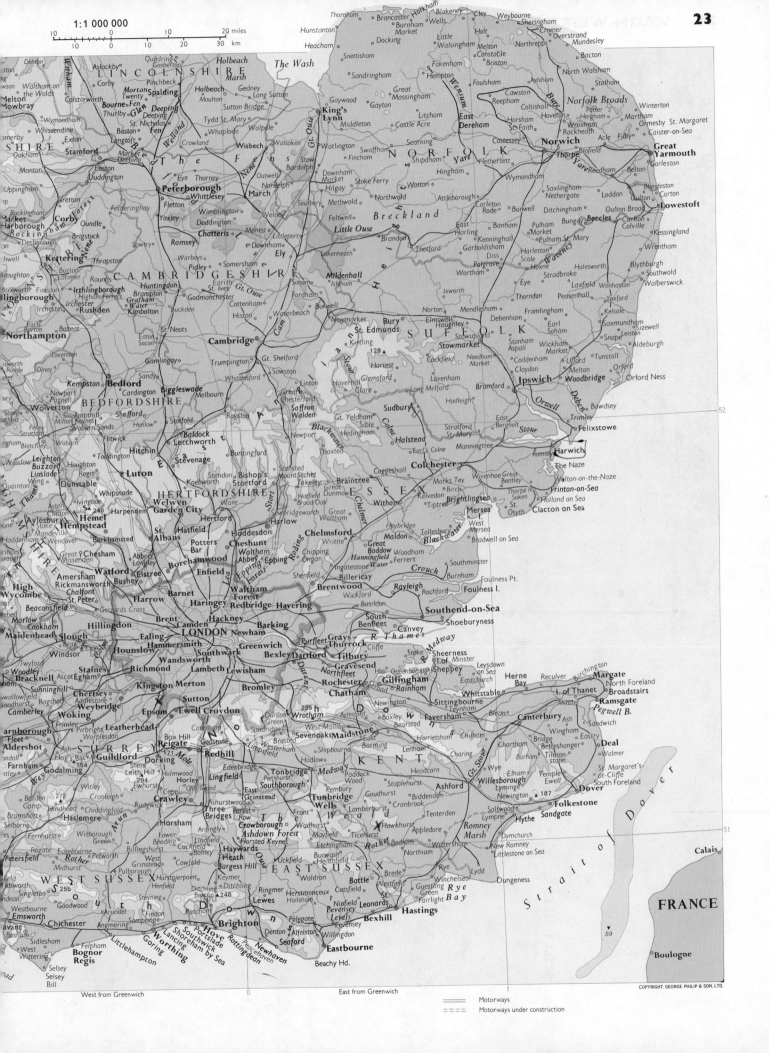

1:1 000 000

West from Greenwich   East from Greenwich

Motorways
Motorways under construction

1:1 000 000

10   0   10   20 miles
10   0   10   20   30 km

BRISTOL CHANNEL

ENGLISH CHANNEL

GWENT

GLAMORGAN

WEST GLAMORGAN

MID GLAMORGAN

SOUTH GLAMORGAN

BRISTOL

CARDIFF

Newport

Swansea

Weston-super-Mare

SOMERSET

DORSET

DEVON

CORNWALL

Bristol Channel

Bridgwater Bay

Barnstaple or Bideford Bay

Lyme Bay

Torbay

PLYMOUTH

Exeter

Taunton

Weymouth

I. of Portland

Portland Bill

Mendip Hills

Quantocks

Brendon Hills

Exmoor

Blackdown Hills

Dartmoor

Bodmin Moor

Start Bay

Falmouth Bay

Lizard Pt.

Land's End

SCILLY ISLES
on same scale

Isles of Scilly

Tresco

St. Martin's

St. Mary's

St. Agnes

Broad Sound

Crow Sound

St. Mary's Sound

Gurnard's Hd. 252

Pendeen

C. Cornwall

St. Just

Sennen

St. Levan

Penzance

Ludgvan

St. Buryan

Land's End

Wolf Rk.

Lundy

West from Greenwich

ft   m   600   400   200   100   0
1800   1200   600   300   150   50   ft
m

1:1 000 000

10 0 10 20 miles
10 0 10 20 30 km

Projection : Conical with two standard parallels

━━━━ Motorways
╌╌╌╌ Motorways under construction

West from Greenwich

COPYRIGHT. GEORGE PHILIP & SON. LTD.

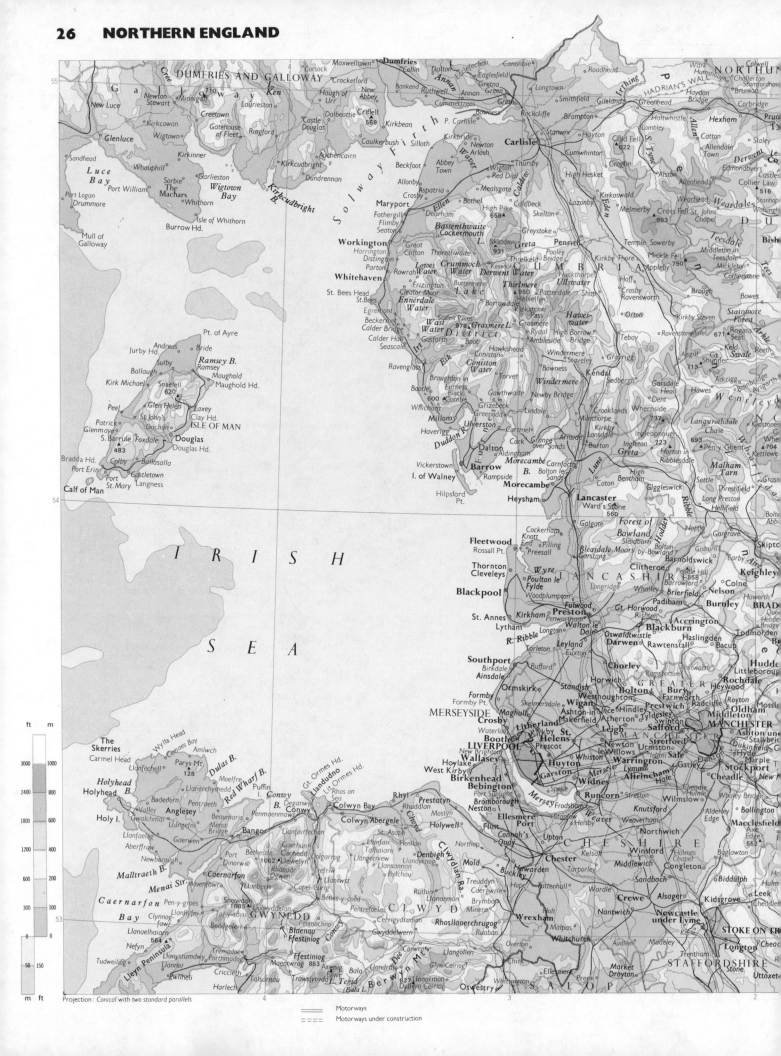

DUMFRIES AND GALLOWAY

Corsock   Maxwelltown   **Dumfries**   Collin   Dalton   Ecclefechan   Canonbie   Roadhead   Wark   NORTHUM
Crocketford   New   Bankend   Ruthwell   Annan   Green   Gretna   Longtown   Smithfield   Gilsland   Greenhead   Haydon Bridge   Chollerton   Humshaugh   Haltwhistle   Corbridge   Allen   Cattan   Prud

Newton Stewart   Minnigaff   710   Haugh of Urr   New Abbey   Crifell   569   Kirkbean   Cummertrees   Bowness   Rockcliffe   Brampton   Gilsland   Greenhead   Haydon Bridge   Hexham

DUMFRIES AND GALLOWAY   Ken   **Carlisle**

New Luce   Kirkcowan   Wigtown   Kirkinner   Garlieston   Isle of Whithorn   Whithorn

Galloway

New Luce   Newton Stewart   Creetown   Gatehouse of Fleet   Ringford   Kirkcudbright   Dundrennan   Auchencairn   Castle Douglas   Dalbeattie   Kirkbride   Silloth   Abbey Town   Newton Arlosh   Wigton   Red Dial   Thursby   Cumwhinton   Croglin   Alston

Glenluce   Wigtown   Sorbie   Port William   The Machars   *Wigtown Bay*   Kirkcudbright   Beckfoot   Allonby   Crosby   Aspatria   Mealsgate   Caldbeck   High Pike 658   Skelton   Penrith

Sandhead   Whauphill   Garlieston   Whithorn   Burrow Hd.   Maryport   Fothergill   Flimby   Seaton   Dearham   Bothel   Greystoke   Pooley Bridge   Mickle Fell 790   Middleton in Teesdale   Mickleton   Cotherstone

Port Logan   Drummore   Isle of Whithorn   **Workington**   Harrington   Distington   Clifton   Great Clifton   Thornthwaite   Bassenthwaite   Cockermouth   L.   Skiddaw 931   Greta   Keswick   CUMBRIA   Hackthorpe   Hoff   Appleby   Temple Sowerby   Brough   Stainmore   Bowes

Mull of Galloway   **Whitehaven**   Frizington   Parton   Rowrah   Lowes Water   Crummock Water   Derwent Water   Thirlmere   950   Patterdale   Ullswater   Shap   Crosby Ravensworth   Orton   Ravenstonedale   671   Rogans Seat

St. Bees Head   St. Bees   Cleator Moor   Ennerdale Water   Borrowdale   Helvellyn   Kirkstone Pass   High Borrow Bridge   Tebay   Newbiggin   Keld   Swale   Reeth

Egremont   Beckermet   Calder Bridge   Scafell Pikes 978   Grasmere L.   Grasmere   Rydal   Ambleside   Hawes water   High Borrow Bridge   Ravenstonedale   Gt. Shunner Fell 713   Askrigg   Aysgarth

Calder Hall   Seascale   Gosforth   Boot   Esk   Coniston   Hawkshead   Windermere   Staveley   Grayrigg   Sedbergh   Garsdale Head   Dent   W e n s l e y

Ravenglass   Broughton in Furness   Black Catnbe 600   Torver   Coniston Water   Bowness   Kendal   Crooklands   Whernside 737   Ingleborough   Langstrothdale Chase   Kettlewell

Bootle   Wficham   Duddon R.   Grizebeck   Greenodd   Lindale   Milnthorpe   Kirkby Lonsdale   Ingleton 723   Horton in Ribblesdale   Pen-y-Ghent 693   Buckden

Millom   Haverigg   Ulverston   Cartmel   Grange over Sands   Arnside   Burton   Settle   Malham Tarn   Threshfield   Kirkby Malham

Vickerstown   Dalton   Aldingham   Morecambe   Carnforth   Lune   High Bentham   Ingleton   Giggleswick   Settle   Long Preston   Hellifield   Bolt Abb

I. of Walney   **Barrow**   Rampside   Bolton le Sands   Caton   Ward's Stone 560   Gargrave   Skipto

Hilpsford Pt.   Heysham   Morecambe   **Lancaster**   Galgate   Cockerham   Knott End   Forest of Bowland   Slaidburn   Hodder   Nappa   Gisburn   Earby   Barnoldswick

Fleetwood   Rossall Pt.   Preesall   Pilling   Garstang   Bleasdale Moors   Dunsop by-Bowland   Clitheroe   Pendle Hill 558   Barrowford   Nelson   Colne   Keighley

Thornton   Cleveleys   Wyre   Poulton le Fylde   Woodplumpton   Longridge   Whalley   Padiham   Brierfield   Burnley   Haworth   Hebden Bridge   BRAD

Blackpool   Fulwood   Gt. Harwood   Rishton   Accrington   Todmorden

St. Annes   Kirkham   **Preston**   Penwortham   Walton le Dale   Oswaldtwistle   **Blackburn**   Haslingden   Rawtenstall   Bacup   Littleboro

Lytham   Longton   Leyland   Euxton   Darwen   Whitworth   Rochdale   Hudd

R. Ribble   Tarleton   Standish   Ramsbottom   Bury   Heywood   Royton   Oldham   Mossl

Southport   Rufford   Chorley   Horwich   **Bolton**   Farnworth   Radcliffe   Prestwich   Middleton   Oldham

Birkdale   Ainsdale   Ormskirk   Skelmersdale   Westhoughton   **Wigan**   Hindley   Atherton   Tyldesley   Swinton   **Salford**   Ashton under   Stalybridge

Formby   Maghull   Ashton-in-Makerfield   Ince   Leigh   **MANCHESTER**   Stretford   Denton   Hyde

Formby Pt.   **MERSEYSIDE**   Crosby   Kirkby   St. Helens   Newton le Willows   Urmston   Sale   Gatley   Stockport   Marple   New

Liverpool   Waterloo   Bootle   Prescot   Whiston   Huyton   Warrington   Lymm   Altrincham   Hale   Cheadle   Hulme   Cheadle   Whaley Bridge

New Brighton   **Wallasey**   Hoylake   West Kirby   **Birkenhead**   Bebington   Garston   Widnes   Runcorn   Stretton   Wilmslow   Alderley Edge   Bollington

Holyhead   Port Sunlight   Bromborough   Neston   Frodsham   Weaver   Weaverham   Northwich   Knutsford   Macclesfield 552

The Skerries   Carmel Head   Cemaes Bay   Amlwch   Ellesmere Port   Stanlow   Helsby   Upton   **CHESHIRE**   Middlewich   Holmes Chapel   Gawsworth

Holyhead   Holyhead B.   Wylfa Head   Llanfechell   Parys Mt. 128   Moelfre   Connah's Quay   Flint   Kelsall   **Chester**   Tarporley   Winsford   Congleton   Biddulph

Holy I.   Valley   Gwalchmai   Bodedern   Pentraeth   Red Wharf B.   Llandudno   Gt. Ormes Hd.   Lit. Ormes Hd.   Rhos on Sea   Colwyn Bay   Mostyn   Holywell   Northop   Mold   Buckley   Hawarden   Tattenhall   Sandbach   Alsager   Kidsgrove

Aberffraw   Llanfaelog   Llangefni   Llanerchymedd   Beaumaris   Menai Bridge   Bangor   Penmaenmawr   Conwy   Deganwy   Conwy B.   Abergele   Rhyl   Prestatyn   Rhuddlan   St. Asaph   Henllan   Denbigh   Llandyrnog   Ruthin   Treuddyn   Coedpoeth   Wrexham   Crewe   Nantwich

Malltraeth B.   Newborough   Gaerwen   Port Dinorwic   Bethesda   Carnedd Llewelyn 1062   Rhaeadr Ogwen   Trefriw   Llanrwst   Llansannan   Bylchau   Cerrigydrudion   Bwlchgwyn   Brymbo   Minera   Holt   Malpas   Wardle   Crewe   Newcastle under Lyme

Menai Str.   Caernarfon   Waenfawr   Llanberis   Snowdon 1085   Dolwyddelan   Betws-y-coed   Pentrefoelas   **CLWYD**   Rhosllanerchrugog   Ruabon   Whitchurch   **STOKE ON TR**

Caernarfon Bay   Pen-y-groes   Clynnog-fawr   Dolbenmaen   Tal-y-sarn   Capel Curig   Penmachno   Conwy   Cerrigydrudion   Llangollen   Chirk   Overton   Prees   Market Drayton   Longton   Chea

Pwllheli   Nefyn   Llanaelhaiarn   584   Llanllyfni   Tremadog   Maentwrog 853   Arenig Fawr   Bala   Corwen   Dee   Llandrillo   Glyn Ceiriog   Whittington   Ellesmere   Leek   Cheadl

Lleyn Peninsula   Tudweiliog   Llanystumdwy   Porthmadog   Blaenau Ffestiniog   Ffestiniog   Trawsfynydd   L. Tegid (Bala L.)   Bala   **Berwyn Mts.**   827   Llanarmon Dyffryn Ceiriog   Oswestry   **SALOP**   Stone   **STAFFORDSHIRE**   Uttoxeter

Criccieth   Talsarnau   Harlech   **GWYNEDD**   Trefor   Madeley   Trentham

Beddgelert   Llanfrothen

I R I S H

S E A

Projection: Conical with two standard parallels

Motorways
Motorways under construction

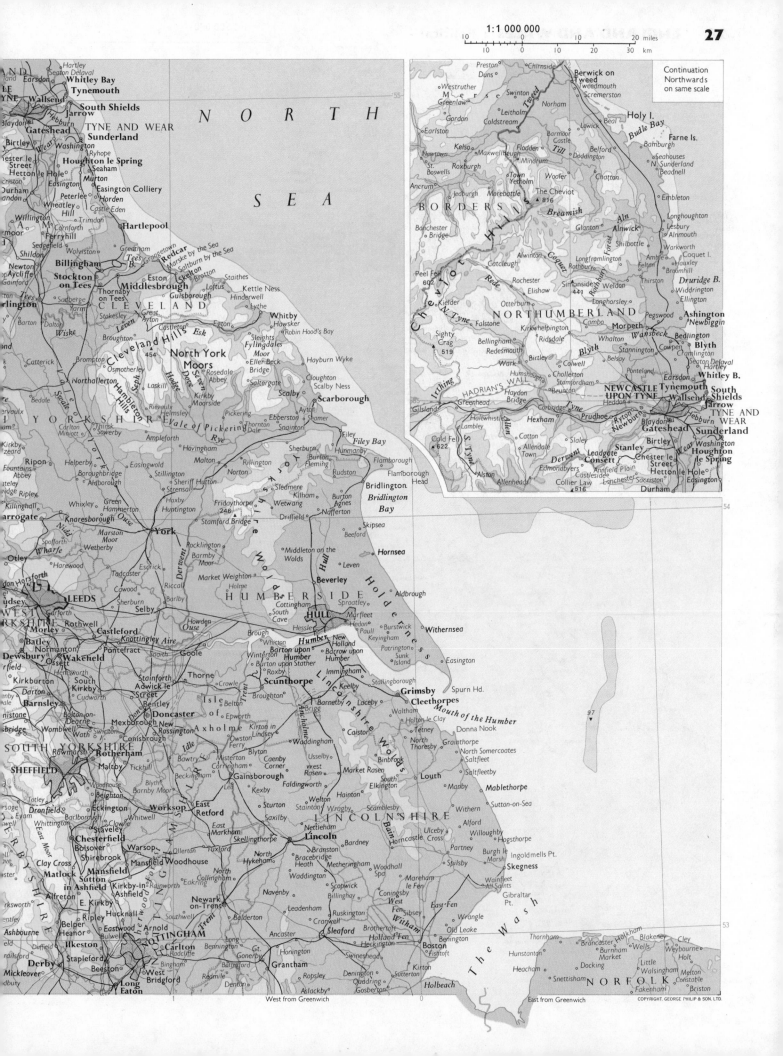

1 : 2 500 000

10 5 0 10 20 30 40 50 60 miles
20 10 0 20 40 60 80 100 km

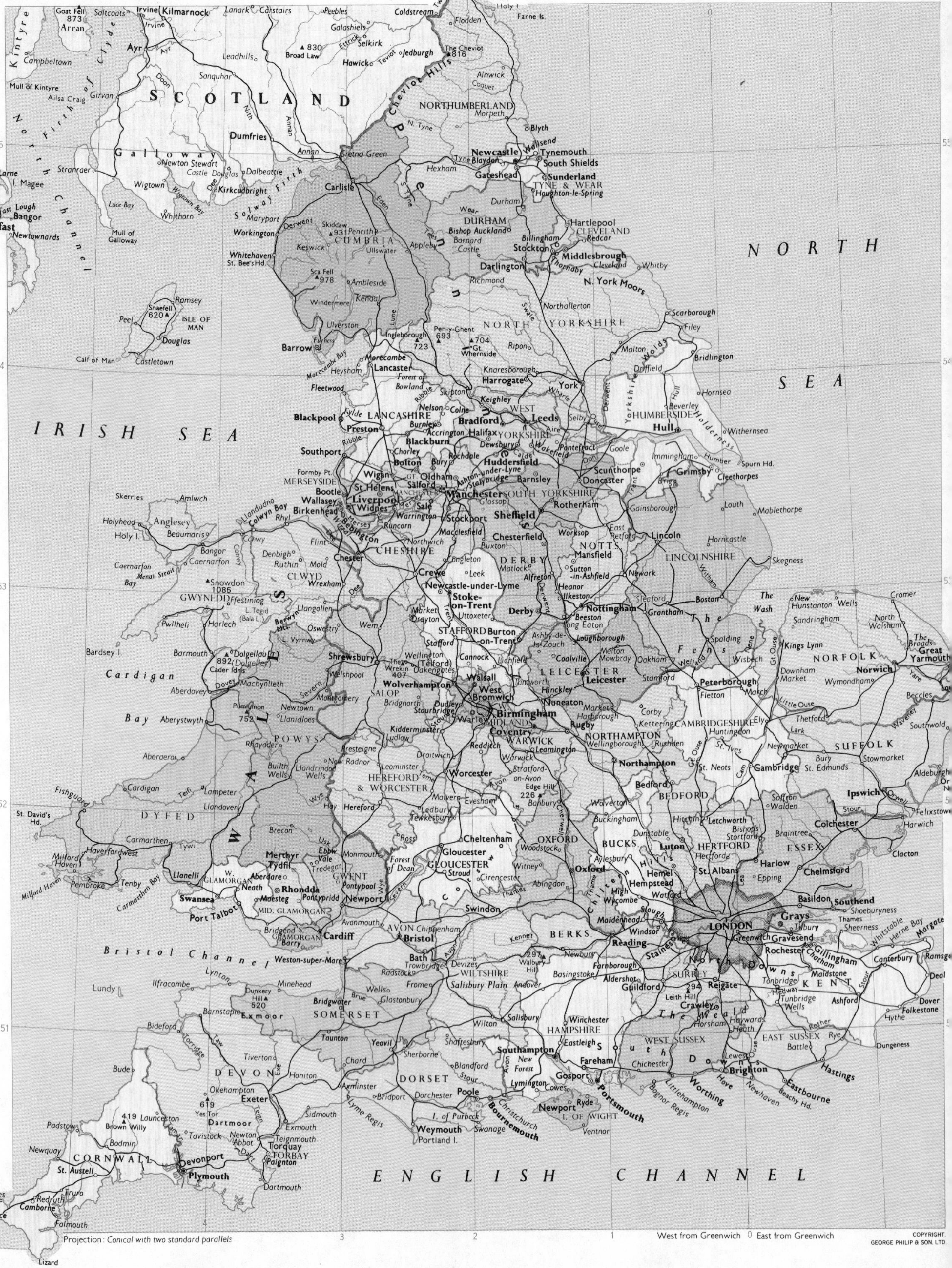

SCOTLAND

NORTH SEA

IRISH SEA

ISLE OF MAN

NORTHUMBERLAND
TYNE & WEAR
DURHAM
CLEVELAND
CUMBRIA
NORTH YORKSHIRE
WEST YORKSHIRE
SOUTH YORKSHIRE
HUMBERSIDE
LANCASHIRE
MERSEYSIDE
GREATER MANCHESTER
CHESHIRE
DERBY
NOTTS
LINCOLNSHIRE
NORFOLK
SUFFOLK
CLWYD
GWYNEDD
POWYS
DYFED
WALES
SALOP
STAFFORD
LEICESTER
CAMBRIDGESHIRE
WEST MIDLANDS
WARWICK
NORTHAMPTON
BEDFORD
HERTFORD
ESSEX
HEREFORD & WORCESTER
GLOUCESTER
OXFORD
BUCKS
BERKS
AVON
WILTSHIRE
SOMERSET
HAMPSHIRE
SURREY
KENT
WEST SUSSEX
EAST SUSSEX
DORSET
DEVON
CORNWALL
I. OF WIGHT
GWENT
GLAMORGAN
MID GLAMORGAN
W. GLAMORGAN

Belfast
Bangor
Newcastle
Sunderland
Gateshead
Middlesbrough
Carlisle
Barrow
Lancaster
Blackpool
Preston
Southport
Liverpool
Birkenhead
Manchester
Sheffield
Leeds
Bradford
Hull
Grimsby
Lincoln
York
Harrogate
Chester
Stoke-on-Trent
Derby
Nottingham
Leicester
Norwich
Great Yarmouth
Ipswich
Cambridge
Peterborough
Northampton
Bedford
Shrewsbury
Wolverhampton
Birmingham
Coventry
Worcester
Gloucester
Oxford
LONDON
Southend
Colchester
Chelmsford
Reading
Bristol
Cardiff
Swansea
Newport
Bath
Southampton
Portsmouth
Bournemouth
Weymouth
Exeter
Plymouth
Penzance
Truro

BRISTOL CHANNEL

ENGLISH CHANNEL

Projection: Conical with two standard parallels

West from Greenwich 0 East from Greenwich

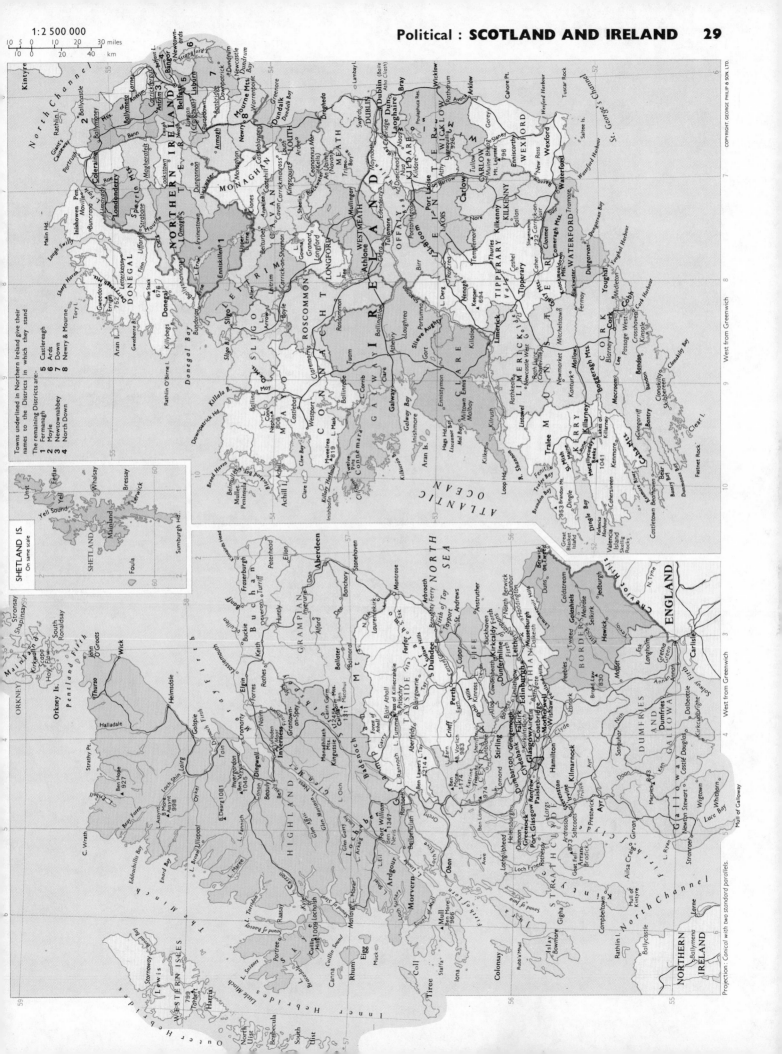

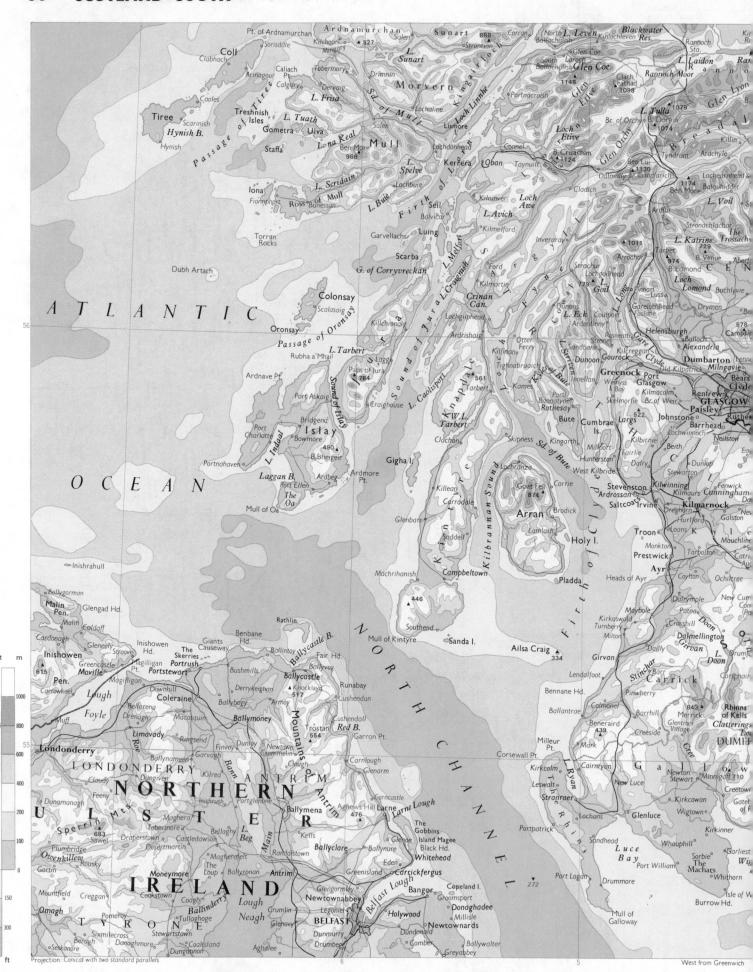

ft m

3000 1000

2400 800

1800 600

1200 400

600 200

300 100

0 0

50 150

100 300

m ft

Projection: Conical with two standard parallels

West from Greenwich

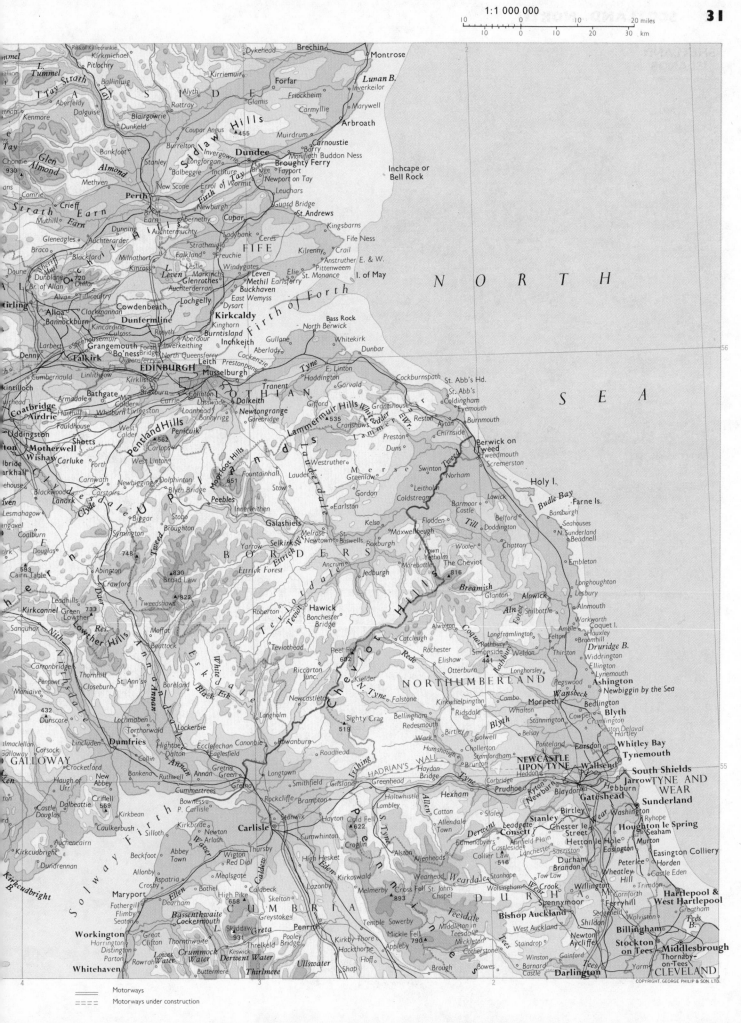

1:1 000 000

10   10   20 miles
10   0   10   20   30 km

NORTH

SEA

COPYRIGHT. GEORGE PHILIP & SON. LTD.

━━━ Motorways
═══ Motorways under construction

SHETLAND ISLANDS
on same scale

SHETLAND

Projection: Conical with two standard parallels

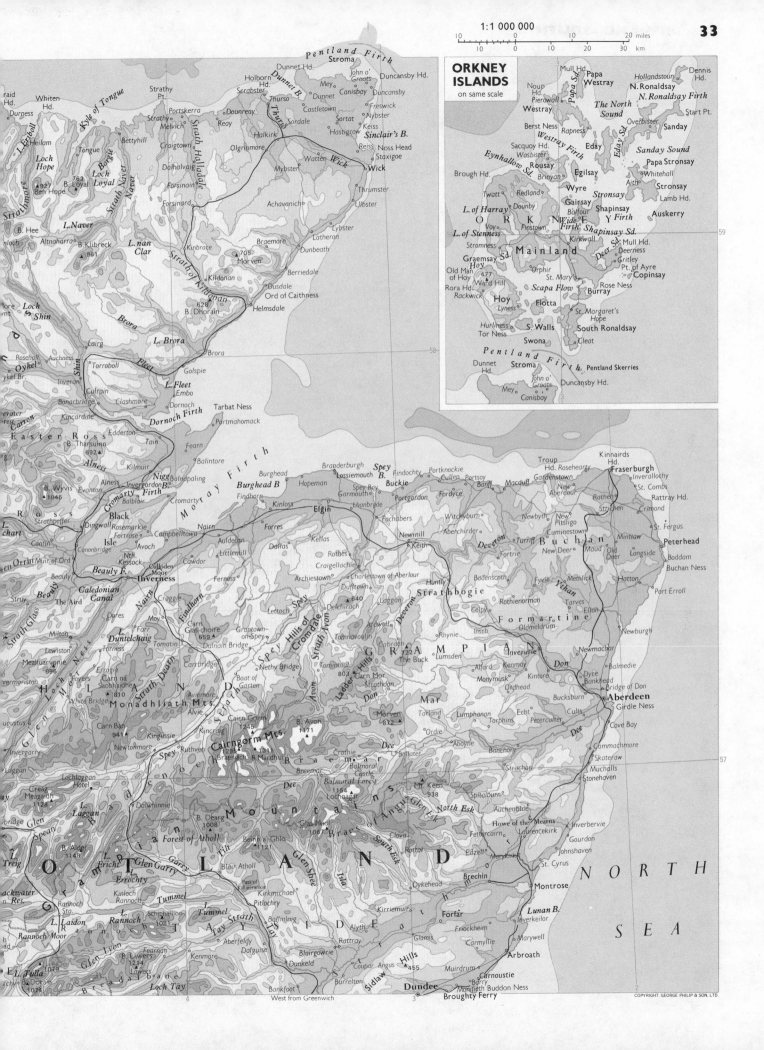

1:1 000 000

10   0   10   20 miles
10   0   10   20   30 km

ORKNEY ISLANDS
on same scale

Mull Hd. Papa
Westray   N. Ronaldsay
Noup   Hollandstoun   Dennis Hd.
Hd. Pierowall   N. Ronaldsay Firth
Westray   Rapness   Overbister   Start Pt.
Berst Ness   The North   Sanday
Sound
Sacquoy Hd.   Eday   Sanday Sound
Wasbister   Papa Stronsay
Eynhallow Sd.   Rousay   Whitehall
Brough Hd.   Brinyan   Egilsay   Stronsay
Twatt   Wyre   Lamb Hd.
Redland   Gairsay   Shapinsay   Auskerry
Dounby   Balfour
L. of Harray   Voy   Finstown   WIDE   Y Firth
Shapinsay Sd.
L. of Stenness   Kirkwall
Stromness   Mainland   Deer Sd.   Deerness
Graemsay Sd.   Orphir   Gritley
Old Man   Hoy   St. Mary's   Pt. of Ayre
of Hoy   477   Copinsay
Rora Hd.   Ward Hill   Rose Ness
Rackwick   Scapa Flow   Burray
Hoy   Lyness   St. Margaret's
Flotta   Hope
Hurliness   Burray   South Ronaldsay
Tor Ness   S. Walls   Cleat
Swona

Pentland Firth   Pentland Skerries
Dunnet   Stroma
Hd.   John o'
Mey   Groats   Duncansby Hd.
Canisby

COPYRIGHT. GEORGE PHILIP & SON. LTD.

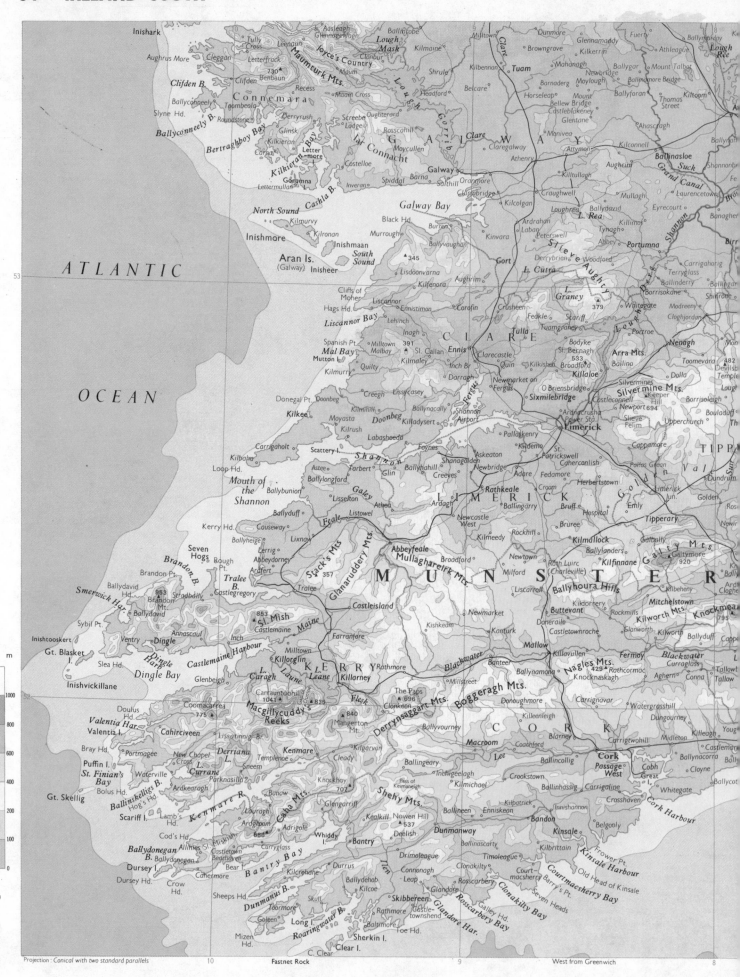

ATLANTIC

OCEAN

Projection: Conical with two standard parallels

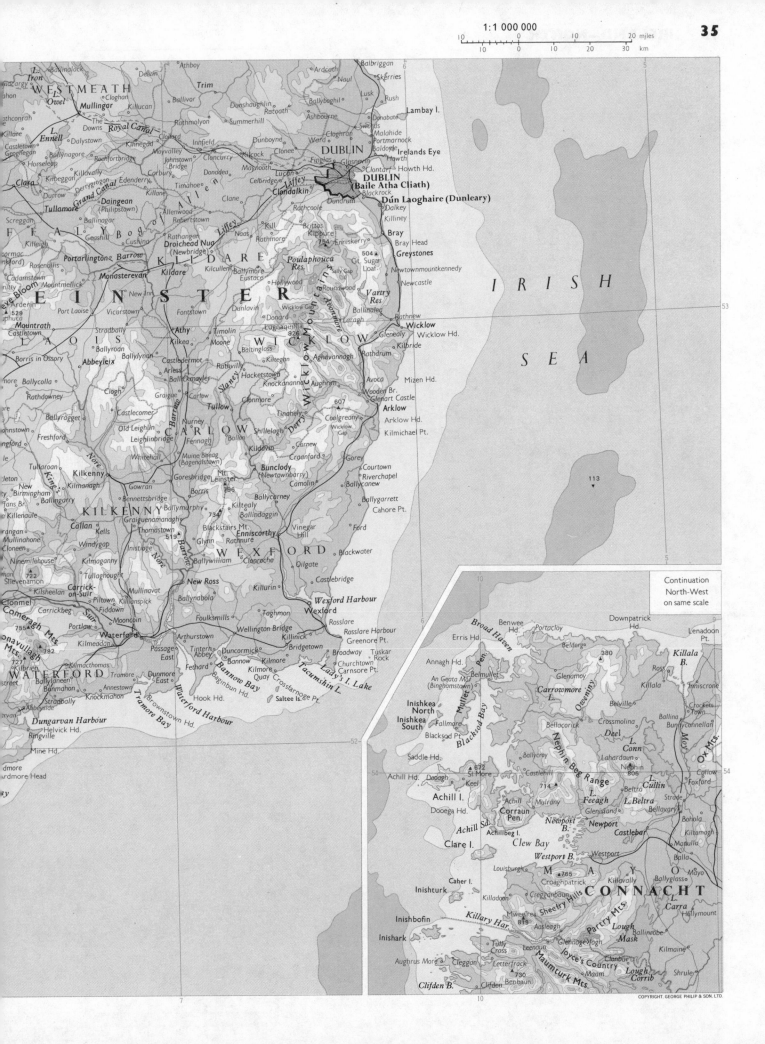

1:1 000 000

10   0   10   20 miles

10   0   10   20   30 km

WESTMEATH
L. Iron
Ballinlack
Delvin
Athboy
Ardcath
Naul
Balbriggan
Skerries
Mullingar
Killucan
Trim
Dunshaughlin
Ratoath
Ashbourne
Lusk
Rush
Lambay I.
Ballyboghil
Donabate
Swords
Malahide
Portmarnock
Baldoyle
Irelands Eye
Howth
Howth Hd.
DUBLIN
DUBLIN
(Baile Atha Cliath)
Blackrock
Dún Laoghaire (Dunleary)
Dalkey
Killiney
Bray
Bray Head
Greystones
Newtownmountkennedy
Newcastle

IRISH
SEA

WICKLOW
Wicklow Mountain
Aghavannagh
Wicklow
Wicklow Hd.
Kilbride
Rathdrum
Avoca
Mizen Hd.
Aughrim
Wooden Br.
Glenart Castle
Arklow
Arklow Hd.
Kilmichael Pt.

CARLOW
LAOIS
KILKENNY
WEXFORD
WATERFORD

113

Continuation
North-West
on same scale

Broad Haven
Benwee Hd.
Portacloy
Downpatrick Hd.
Lenadoon Pt.
Erris Hd.
Belderg
Killala B.
Annagh Hd.
Glenamoy
Ross
Killala
Inniscrone
Carrowmore L.
Belmullet
Owenmore
Belville
Ballina
Crockets Town
Bunnyconnellan
Inishkea North
Inishkea South
Fallmore
Bellacorick
Crossmolina
Blacksod Pt.
Deel
Ox Mts.
Saddle Hd.
Ballycroy
L. Conn
Lahardaun
Nephin
Foxford
Achill Hd.
Dooagh
Keel
Sl. More
Castlehill
Nephin Beg Range
L. Cullin
Strade
Achill I.
714
L. Feeagh
Beltra
L. Beltra
Bellavary
Bohola
Dooega Hd.
Corraun Pen.
Mulrany
Glenisland
Kiltamagh
Balla
Achill Sd.
Newport B.
Newport
Castlebar
Achillbeg I.
Clare I.
Clew Bay
Westport B.
Westport
Mayo
Ballyglass
Caher I.
Louisburgh
765
Croaghpatrick
MAYO
Killavally
L. Carra
Hollymount
Inishturk
Killadoon
Cregganbaun
CONNACHT
Mweelrea
Sheefry Hills
Partry Mts.
Inishbofin
819
Aasleagh
Lough Mask
Ballinrobe
Kilmaine
Killary Har.
Joyce's Country
Glennagevlagh
Maumturk Mts.
Lough Corrib
Shrule
Inishshark
Tully Cross
Leenoun
Maam
Aughrus More
Cleggan
Letterfrack
730
Benbaun
Clifden B.
Clifden

COPYRIGHT, GEORGE PHILIP & SON, LTD.

1:1 000 000

DISTRICTS IN
NORTHERN IRELAND
1 Londonderry
2 Limavady
3 Coleraine
4 Ballymoney
5 Moyle
6 Larne
7 Ballymena
8 Magherafelt
9 Cookstown
10 Strabane
11 Omagh
12 Fermanagh
13 Dungannon
14 Craigavon
15 Armagh
16 Newry and Mourne
17 Banbridge
18 Down
19 Lisburn
20 Antrim
21 Newtownabbey
22 Carrickfergus
23 North Down
24 Ards
25 Castlereagh
26 Belfast

Projection: Conical with two standard parallels

West from Greenwich

1:5 000 000

100 miles

km

East from Greenwich

West from Greenwich

Projection: Conical with two standard parallels

ALGERIA

Algiers · Félix Faure · Boufarik · Koléa · Blida · El Asnam (Orléansville) · Mostaganem · Mohammadia (Perrégaux) · Sig (St. Denis) · Oran · Tighil Izane (Relizane) · Mascara · C. Caxine · C. Falcon · Tres Forcas · C. Tres Forcas · Alboran

MOROCCO · Targa · Tetuán · Tangier (Tanger) · Ceuta · Melilla

FRANCE · Montpellier · Béziers · Agde · Narbonne · Gulf of Lions · Perpignan · Port Vendres · Toulouse · Bayonne · Biarritz · Pau

Pyrenees · Andorra · 3404 · 3351 · Pico de Aneto · Huesca

SPAIN · Barcelona · Sabadell · Hospitalet · Badalona · Tarragona · Lérida · Zaragoza 2316 · Pamplona · Navarra · Logroño · Vitoria · Bilbao · San Sebastián · Santander · Gijón · Oviedo · Mieres · León · Astorga · Lugo · La Coruña · Ferrol · Santiago de Compostela · Pontevedra · Vigo · Orense · Zamora · Valladolid · Salamanca · Ávila · Segovia · Burgos · Palencia · Soria · Sierra de la Demanda 2262 · Guadalajara · MADRID · Sierra de Gredos 2592 · Toledo · Cuenca · Serrania de Cuenca · Teruel 2019 · Castellón · Valencia · Alicante · Elche · Murcia · Lorca · Cartagena · Almería · Guadix · Granada · Sa. Nevada 3478 · Jaén · Linares · Ciudad Real · Córdoba · Seville · Jerez · Cádiz · Huelva · Badajoz · Cáceres · Málaga · Gibraltar (Br.) · La Línea · Algeciras

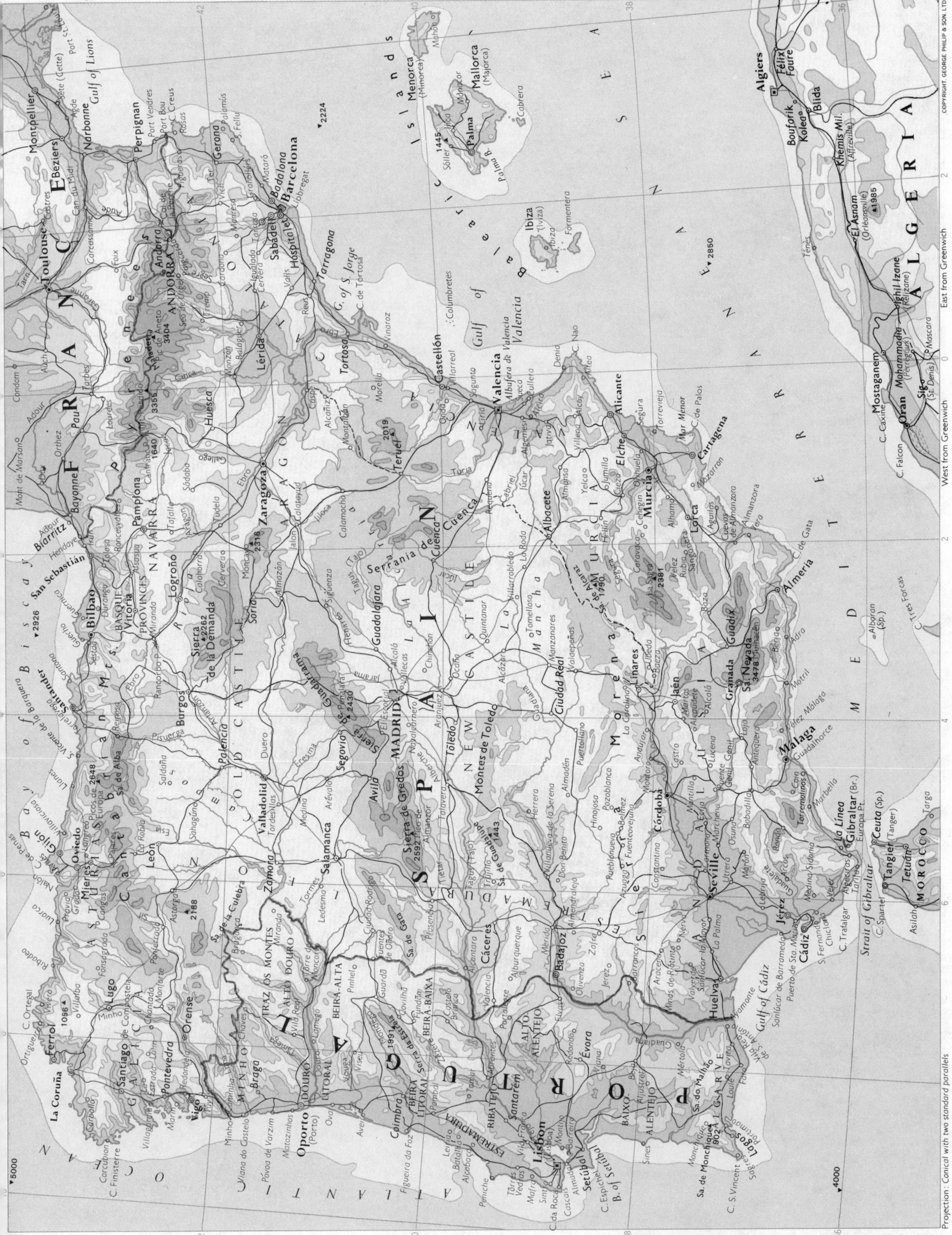

PORTUGAL · Oporto (Porto) · Coimbra · Lisbon · Setúbal · Évora · Santarém

Balearic Islands · Menorca (Minorca) · Mallorca (Majorca) · Palma · Ibiza (Iviza) · Formentera · Cabrera · 1445

BAY of Biscay

ATLANTIC OCEAN

MEDITERRANEAN SEA

Strait of Gibraltar · C. Trafalgar · C. S. Vincent · Gulf of Cádiz

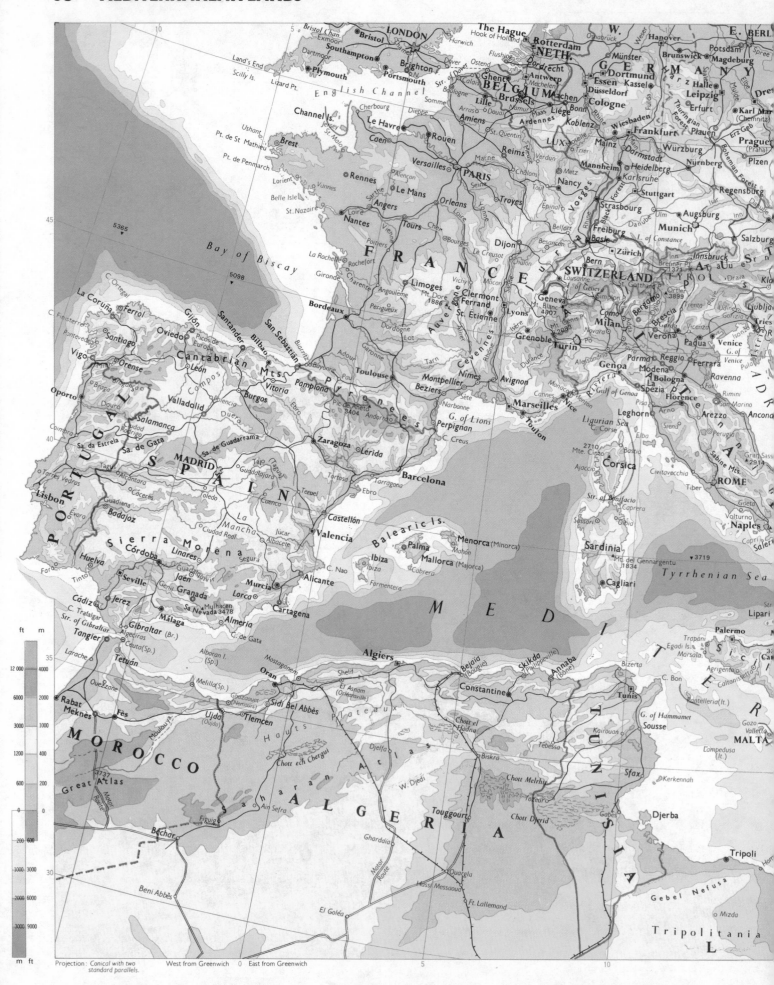

Projection: Conical with two standard parallels.

West from Greenwich 0 East from Greenwich

1:10 000 000

50   0   50   100   150   200 miles
50   0   100   200   300 km

POLAND
Poznań
Łódź
Warsaw (Warszawa)
Wisła (Vistula)
Plock
Brest
Pinsk
Pripyat Marshes
Chernigov
Desna
Sumy
Belgorod
Volgograd

Wrocław
Radom
Lublin
Bug
Pripyat
Goryń
Pyat
Nezhin
Konotop
Kremenchug
Kharkov
Kazanskaya

Ostrava
Kielce
Lutsko
Rovno
Zhitomir
Kiev
Belaya Tserkov
Dnieper
Pereyaslav-Khmelnitski
S. S. R.
Poltava
Slavyansk
Artemovsk
Voroshilovgrad (Lugansk)
Shakhty

Chorzów
Kraków
Tarnów
Przemysl
Lvov
U.
Vinnitsa
U. K. R. A. I. N. E.
Kremenchug
Pavlograd
Gorlovka
Makeyevka
Novocherkassk

CHOS
LOVAKIA
Tatra 2655
Ruthenia
Carpathian
Chernovtsy
Moldavia
Kirovograd
Dnepropetrovsk
Krivoy Rog
Zaporozhye
Donetsk
Rostov
Don
Manych

Bratislava
Banská Bystrica
Košice
Miskolc
Iaşi
Kishinev
Odessa
Nikolayev
Melitopol
Zhdanov (Mariupol)
Taganrog
Azov
L. Manych Gudilo

Budapest
HUNGARY
Debrecen
Oradea
Cluj
RUMANIA
Kherson
Perekop
Sea of Azov
Kerch
Str.
Krasnodar
Stavropol
Armavir

Kecskemét
Szeged
Arad
Braşov
Galaţi
Izmail
G. of Karkinisk
Crimea
Simferopol
Feodosiya
Novorossiysk
Tuapse
Kuban
Maykop

BLACK SEA

Belgrade
SERBIA
BULGARIA
Sofia
Plovdiv
Edirne
Istanbul
Ankara
TURKEY
Kayseri

GREECE
Thessaloniki
Athens
İzmir
Konya
Adana
SYRIA

CYPRUS
Beirut
LEBANON
Damascus

ISRAEL
Tel Aviv-Jaffa
Jerusalem
JORDAN
Amman

MEDITERRANEAN SEA

Alexandria
CAIRO
Suez
EGYPT
Port Said

LIBYA
Benghazi
Cyrenaica
Tobruk

40

SWITZERLAND

Lyons
Villeurbanne
Geneva

DAUPHINÉ

Grenoble

Turin
Torino

PIEDMONT

Avignon

PROVENCE

Marseilles

Nice
Cannes
Monte Carlo

LIGURIAN SEA

Milan
Milano

LOMBARDY

Como
Bergamo
Brescia
Novara
Pavia
Cremona

Piacenza
Parma
Modena
Reggio

EMILIA-ROMAGNA

Bologna

Genoa
(Genova)
Savona
G. of
Genoa
La Spezia
Carrara

Mte. Cimone
2165

Ferrara

TRENTINO-ALTO ADIGE

Bolzano
Trento

VENETO

Verona
Vicenza
Padua
(Padova)

FRIULI VENEZIA GIULIA

Udine
Venice
(Venezia)
Treviso

Trieste

Gulf of Venice

Ravenna
Forlì
Cesena
Rimini

San Marino

Pesaro
Fano
Senigallia
Ancona

Klagenfurt
Maribor

Ljubljana
SLOVENIA
Zagreb
CRO

Rijeka

ADRIATIC

Pula
(Pola)

BOSN
HER

Split

CORSICA

Mte. Cinto
2710

Ajaccio
Calvi
Bastia
Aleria

Elba

Leghorn
(Livorno)

TUSCANY

Florence
(Firenze)

Pisa
Lucca
Prato

Siena
Arezzo

Perugia

UMBRIA

Terni

MARCHES

Macerata
Ascoli Piceno

L'Aquila
ABRU

Gran Sasso
2914

Pescara

Rome
(Roma)

LAZIO

Civitavecchia

Tivoli

MOLISE
Campobasso

Mt. Gargano
1056

Foggia
G. of Manfredónia

Cerignola
Barletta
Andria

SARDINIA

Sassari
Alghero
Bosa
Nuoro
Oristano
G. of Oristano
Mt. Gennargentu
1834
M. Santo

Cagliari
G. of Cagliari
C. Carbonara

Iglesias
Carbonia

Asinara
C. Falcone
Porto Torres
Olbia
(Terranova)

TYRRHENIAN SEA

3719

Naples
(Napoli)
Vesuvius
1277
Salerno
CAMPANIA

BASILICATA

Potenza
Matera
Tarant

Cosenza
1929

CALABRIA

Reggio
Messina
Str. of Messina

Palermo
Trapani
Marsala

SICILY

Mt. Etna
3340
Catánia
Enna
Caltanissetta
Siracusa
(Syracuse)
Ragusa

Lipari Is.
Stromboli
Vulcano

Ustica
(It.)

MEDIT

Pantelleria
(Ital.)

Lampedusa
(Ital.)

Gozo
Comino
Valletta
MALTA

---

ft **m**

12 000 — 4000
9000 — 3000
6000 — 2000
4500 — 1500
3000 — 1000
1200 — 400
600 — 200
0 — 0
200 — 600

m **ft**

MALTA
1:1 000 000

C. S. Dimitri
Gozo
(Ghawdex)
Victoria
(Rabat)
Comino (Kemmuna)

St. Pauls Bay
Mosta
Mdina
Rabat
Valletta
Zurrieq
Marsaxlokk
Birzebbuga

0   10

S.E. EUROPE
POLITICAL
1:25 000 000

FRANCE
SWITZ.
Bern
Liechtenstein
AUSTRIA
Vienna
HUNGARY
Budapest
U.S.S.R.

Venice
Trieste
San Marino
ITALY
Rome

YUGOSLAVIA
Belgrade
RUMANIA
Bucharest

ADRIATIC SEA

Tirane
ALBANIA

Sofia
BULGARIA
Istanbul

TURKEY

Corsica
(Fr.)
Sardinia
Naples

GREECE
Thessaloniki
Athens

Sicily

AEGEAN SEA

MALTA
Crete

MEDITERRANEAN SEA

Projection : Conical with two standard parallels

CHANNEL ISLANDS
1:1 000 000

0   5   10   15   20 miles
0   10   20   30 km

The Casquets · Burhou
St. Anne
Alderney

Cap de la Hague
Auderville · St. Germain
Urville
Jobourg · Beaumont
Anse de Vauville
Cherbourg
Virandeville · 178
Diélette · Breuville
les Pieux

GUERNSEY
St. Sampson
Vale · St. Martin
Herm
St. Peter Port
St. Martin · Sark
Forest · Jerbourg Pt.
Torteval

Bricquebec
St. Jacques
Carteret
Barneville
Portbail
Baudreville

Ecréhou Rocks
Bretteville
St. Germain

JERSEY
Grosnez Pt.
Trinity
St. Peter · St. Martin
Corbière Pt.
Gorey · la Rocque Pt.
St. Brelade's
St. Helier

Pirou
Gouville
Blainville

The Minquiers

Coutainville

2° 30' West from Greenwich   2

Over 300 ft. Over 100 m
0–300 ft 0–100 m

ENGLAND
Lundy I. · Ilfracombe
Hartland Pt. · Minehead · Weston-s-Mare
Bideford · Barnstaple · Bridgwater · Frome · Andover
Bude · Tiverton · Yeovil · Dorchester
Newquay · Okehampton · Yes · Exmouth
St. Ives · Bodmin · Dartmoor · 618 · Newton Abbot
Penzance · Truro · **Exeter**
Land's End · **Torquay**
Falmouth · Dartmouth · Start Pt.
Lizard · Scilly Is.

English Channel

C. de la Hague · Cherbourg
Alderney · Pte. de Barfleur
Guernsey · St. Peter Port · Valognes
Channel Is. (Br.) · Sark · Jersey
St. Helier · Coutances

SWITZERLAND

FRANCE
DEPARTMENTS
1:8 000 000

50   0   50   100 miles
50   0   50   100   150 km

1. VAL d'OISE
2. YVELINES
3. ESSONNE
4. HAUTS-DE-SEINE
5. SEINE-ST. DENIS
6. VAL-DE-MARNE
7. VILLE DE PARIS

ft   m
12 000   4000
9000   3000
6000   2000
4500   1500
3000   1000
1200   400
600   200
0   0
200   600
m   ft

Projection: Conical with two standard parallels

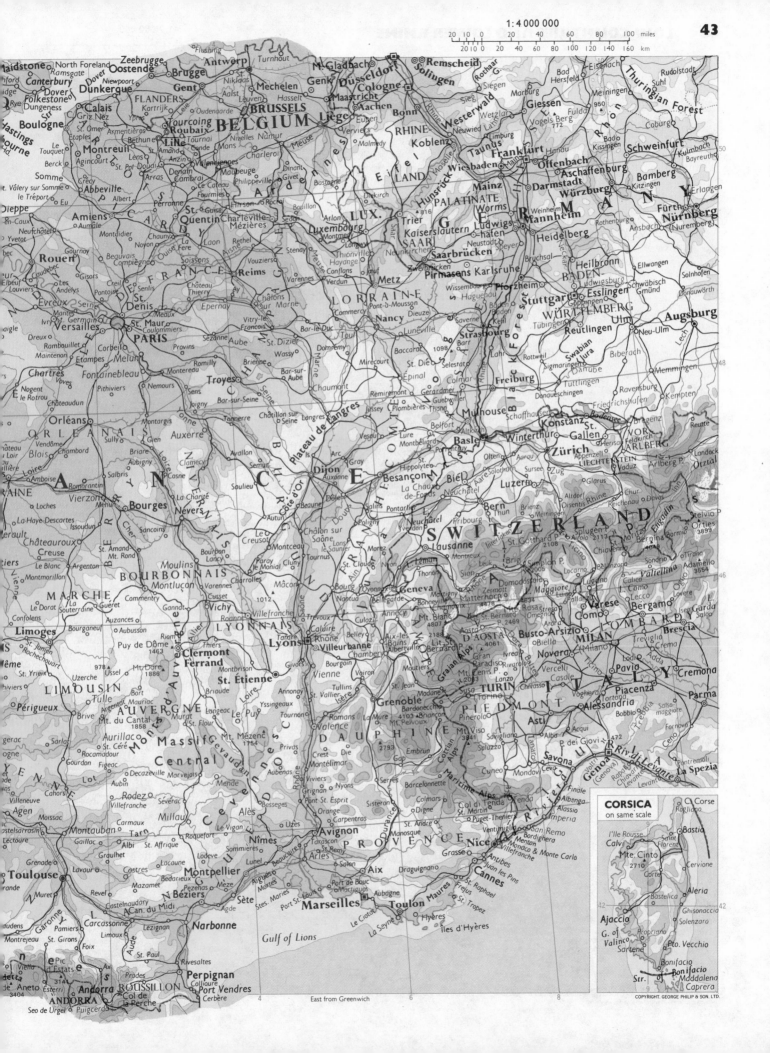

1:2 000 000

10   5   0   10   20   30   40 miles
10   0   10   20   30   40   50   60 km

NORTH SEA

WESTFRIESCHE EILANDEN

Texel · Vlieland · Terschelling · Ameland · Schiermonnikoog · Uithuizen · Jadebusen · Aurich · Gödens · Zetel · Varel

Wadden Zee · Dokkum · Zoutkamp · Delfzijl · Emden · Ostfriesland · Hesel · Westerstede · Apen · Rastede · Bockhorn · Jade

Den Helder · Den Oever · Franeker · Harlingen · Leeuwarden · Bergum · Zuidhorn · Groningen · Winschoten · Weener · Leer · Papenburg · Bad Zwischenahn · Oldenburg · Hunte

Bergen-Binnen · Bolsward · Sneek · Drachten · Roden · Hoogezand · Slochteren · Rhede · Aschendorf · Friesoythe

FRIESLAND · Heerenveen · Smilde · Assen · Borger · Stadskanaal · Meppen · Cloppenburg · NIEDER · SACHSEN

Alkmaar · Heiloo · Workum · Staveren · Lemmer · Wolvega · Beilen · Emmen · Haren · Löningen · Lastrup · Quackenbrück · Lohne

Noordoost Polder · Steenwijk · Hoogeveen · DRENTHE · Coevorden · Emlichheim · Nordhorn · Vechta · Damme · Bramsche

Costricum · Wormerveer · Urk · Emmeloord · Vollenhove · Hardenberg · Ommen · Lingen · Fürstenau · Bersenbrück · Steinfeld

Beverwijk · IJmuiden · Velsen · Zaandam · Marken · Lelystad · Kampen · Zwolle · OVERIJSSEL · Almelo · Ibbenbüren · Westerkappeln · Osnabrück

Haarlem · Zandvoort · Heemstede · AMSTERDAM · Harderwijk · Nunspeet · Epe · Rijssen · Hengelo · Enschede · Gronau · Ochtrup · Emsdetten · Lengerich · 331

Hillegom · Aalsmeer · Bussum · Hilversum · Huizen · Laren · Baarn · Nijkerk · Apeldoorn · 107 · Deventer · Lochem · Ahaus · Burgsteinfurt · Borghorst · Greven

Noordwijk-aan-Zee · Leiden · Alphen · Oude Rijn · Amersfoort · Barneveld · Ede · Zutphen · Doesburg · Winterswijk · Aalten · Coesfeld · Münster · Warendorf · Telgte

Wassenaar · Voorburg · Utrecht · Zeist · Renkum · Arnhem · GELDERLAND · Doetinchem · Stadtlohn · NORD · Dülmen · Lüdinghausen · Ahlen · Beckum

THE HAGUE ('s Gravenhage) · Delft · Gouda · IJsselstein · Wageningen · Elst · Emmerich · Bocholt · Borken · RHEIN · Haltern · Lippe · Werne

Hoek van Holland · Europoort · Rijswijk · Naaldwijk · Lek · Tiel · Waal · Nijmegen · Kleve · Rees · Wesel · Dorsten · Marl · Datteln · Werne

ROTTERDAM · Schiedam · Vlaardingen · Maassluis · Sliedrecht · Leerdam · Gorinchem · Geldermalsen · Oss · Goch · Kevelaer · Recklinghausen · Gelsenkirchen · Lünen · Kamen · Hamm · Werl

Goeree · Overflakkee · Dordrecht · Waalwijk · Hertogenbosch · Uden · Venraij · Geldern · Kamp-Lintfort · Bottrop · Herne · DORTMUND

Schouwen · Brouwershaven · Zierikzee · Made · Oosterhout · Boxtel · Veghel · Gemert · Helmond · Deurne · Venlo · Kempen · Oberhausen · Mülheim · Bochum · Witten · Mengede · Neheim

Noord Beveland · Roosendaal · Breda · Tilburg · Goirle · Eindhoven · Geldrop · Weert · Süchteln · Dülken · Moers · Duisburg · ESSEN · Hattingen · Iserlohn · Hohenlimburg

Walcheren · Middelburg · Goes · Bergen-op-Zoom · Essen · Baarle-Nassau · Turnhout · Valkenswaard · Roermond · Viersen · Krefeld · Velbert · Gevelsberg · Hagen · Lüdenscheid

Vlissingen (Flushing) · West Schelde · Terneuzen · Hulst · Kapellen · Brasschaat · Mol · Leopoldsburg · Maaseik · Mönchen-Gladbach · Neuss · Wuppertal · Werdohl · Plettenberg

Knokke · Zeebrugge · Brugge (Bruges) · Moldegem · Eeklo · Zelzate · ANTWERPEN · Schoten · Lammel · Lanklaar · 95 · Erkelenz · Grevenbroich · Rheydt · DÜSSELDORF · Remscheid · Solingen · Ostend (Oostende)

Blankenberge · Nieuwport · Torhout · Eernegem · St. Niklaas · Antwerp · Deurne · Hoboken · Lier · Herentals · Geel · Tessenderlo · Sittard · Geilenkirchen · Jülich · Leverkusen · Opladen · Bergisch Gladbach · Gummersbach

FLANDRE · Lokeren · St. Amandsberg · Gent · Boom · Willebroek · Duffel · Nethe · Genk · Geleen · Brunssum · Bedburg · Bergheim · COLOGNE (Köln) · Overath · Waldbröl

Diksmuide · Ruiselede · Ledeberg · Wetteren · Mechelen · Demer · Hasselt · Diepenbeek · Heerlen · Kerkrade · Eschweiler · Düren · Brühl · Siegburg · Eitorf · Siegen

Ypres · Roeselare · Tielt · Deinze · Aalst · Lebbeke · Asse · Leuven · Tienen · Maastricht · Tongeren · Aachen · Stolberg · Bonn · Bad Godesberg · Königswinter

Menin · Kortrijk · Oudenaarde · Zottegem · Ninove · BRUSSELS · Brussel Bruxelles · BRABANT · St. Trond · Visé · Herzogenrath · Kornelimünster · Euskirchen · Bad Honnef · Hachenburg · Westerwald · 657

Mouscron · Ronse · Geeraardsbergen · Lessines · Enghien · Halle · Waterloo · Wavre · Herstal · Liège · Eupen · Verviers · Mechernich · Remagen · Andernach · Neuwied

Roubaix · Lille · Tournai · Ath · Leuze · Soignies · Nivelles · Gembloux · St. Georges · Seraing · Theux · Spa · 694 · Schleiden · Nettersheim · Münstereifel · Sinzig · Mayen · Koblenz · Bad Ems · Oberlahnstein

Armentières · Haubourdin · Seclin · Leers · HAINAUT · Mons · La Louvière · Jumet · Charleroi · Namur · Huy · Combiain · Verviers · Hohe Venn · Malmédy · Nürburg · Ahrweiler · Boppard

Bully les Mines · Lens · Liévin · Douai · Orchies · Condé · St. Amand · Valenciennes · Hornu · Jemappes · Binche · Anderlues · Thuin · Fosse · Marchin · Havelange · St. Vith · 697 · 700 · Geroldstein · Prüm · Cochem · Treis · St. Goar · Wiesbaden

Arras · Cambrai · PAS-DE-CALAIS · Denain · Bavay · Maubeuge · Hautmont · Florennes · Dinant · Ciney · Marche · La Roche · Houffalize · Bogny · 652 · Daun · Wittlich · Bernkastel · Bingen · Rüdesheim

Bapaume · Solesmes · Le Quesnoy · Avesnes · Landrecies · Philippeville · Rochefort · Wellin · Bastogne · Wiltz · Bitburg · Kyllburg · Zell · Simmern · Bacharach · Bad Kreuznach

SOMME · Roisel · Oise · Capelle · Hirson · Rocroi · Revin · Fumay · Givet · Beauraing · LUXEMBOURG · St. Hubert · 569 · Libramont · Clervaux · Waxweiler · Prüm · Daun · Mosel · Trarbach · Traben-Trarbach · Kreuznach

St. Quentin · Guise · Vervins · Aubenton · Rumigny · Nouzonville · Mézières · Recogne · Neufchâteau · Sûre · 549 · Diekirch · Echternach · Trier · Saarburg · Idar-Oberstein · 816 · Kirchheim-bolanden · 687

PICARDIE · Noyon · Ham · Marle · La Fère · Sissonne · Château Porcien · Rethel · ARDENNES · Charleville-Mézières · Sedan · Bouillon · Florenville · Virton · Arlon · LUXEMBOURG · Mersch · Grevenmacher · Saarburg · Merzig · Hermeskeil · Kaiserslautern

Compiègne · Chauny · Laon · Craonne · Aisne · Vouziers · Buzancy · Carignan · Montmédy · Longwy · Differdange · Esch · MEURTHE · Mettlach · Dillingen · Merzig · Sulzbach · Neunkirchen · Homburg

OISE · Ribécourt · Soissons · Fismes · Vesle · Attigny · Vouziers · Stenay · Dun · Longuyon · Villerupt · Hayange · Sierck · Saarlouis · St. Wendel · Landstuhl

Crépy-en-Valois · Villers-Cotterêts · Ourcq · Reims · Suippes · Ste. Menehould · Verdun · Étain · Briey · Thionville · Völklingen · Saarbrücken · Stiring Wendel · Zweibrücken · Landau

Château-Thierry · Épernay · Marne · Châtillon · le Grand · Valmy · Montfaucon · Metz · St. Avold · Forbach · Sarreguemines · Pirmasens · Bergzabern · MOSELLE

LUXEMBOURG · MOSEL · RHEINLAND PFALZ · GERMANY · WESTFALEN · HUNSRÜCK · EIFEL

Projection: Conical with two standard parallels

East from Greenwich

ft   m
1200 400
600   200
0   0

1:2 000 000

10   20   30   40   50 miles
10   20   30   40   50   60   70   80 km

LUXEMBOURG

RHEINLAND

PFALZ

FRANKFURT
Wiesbaden
Mainz
Offenbach
Neu-Isenburg
Höchst

Bad Homburg
Hanau
Aschaffenburg
Würzburg
Bamberg
Schweinfurt

HESSEN

Worms
Darmstadt
Bensheim
Weinheim

GERMANY

Trier
Luxembourg
Saarbrücken
Kaiserslautern
Ludwigshafen
Mannheim
Heidelberg

Metz
Nancy

Karlsruhe
Pforzheim

STUTTGART
Esslingen
Tübingen
Reutlingen

BADEN-WÜRTTEMBERG

Ulm
Neu Ulm
Augsburg

Strasbourg
Offenburg
Freiburg

VOSGES

Colmar
Mulhouse

Belfort
Besançon

Basle (Basel)
BASEL-LAND
SOLOTHURN
ZÜRICH
Zürich
Winterthur
Schaffhausen
Konstanz
Bodensee
THURGAU
St. Gallen
Bregenz
VORARLBERG
Dornbirn

AUSTRIA
Innsbruck

LIECHTENSTEIN
Vaduz

Neuchâtel
Bern
LUZERN
ZUG
SCHWYZ
GLARUS
URI
Chur
GRAUBÜNDEN (GRISONS)
Davos-Platz

SWITZERLAND

Lausanne
Fribourg
VAUD
Thun
Interlaken

Geneva (Genève)
VALAIS
Sion
Brig

Montreux

Matterhorn 4478
Zermatt

ITALY

TICINO
Locarno
Bellinzona
Lugano
L. di Como
Maggiore

LOMBARDIA
TRENTINO
ALTO ADIGE

East from Greenwich

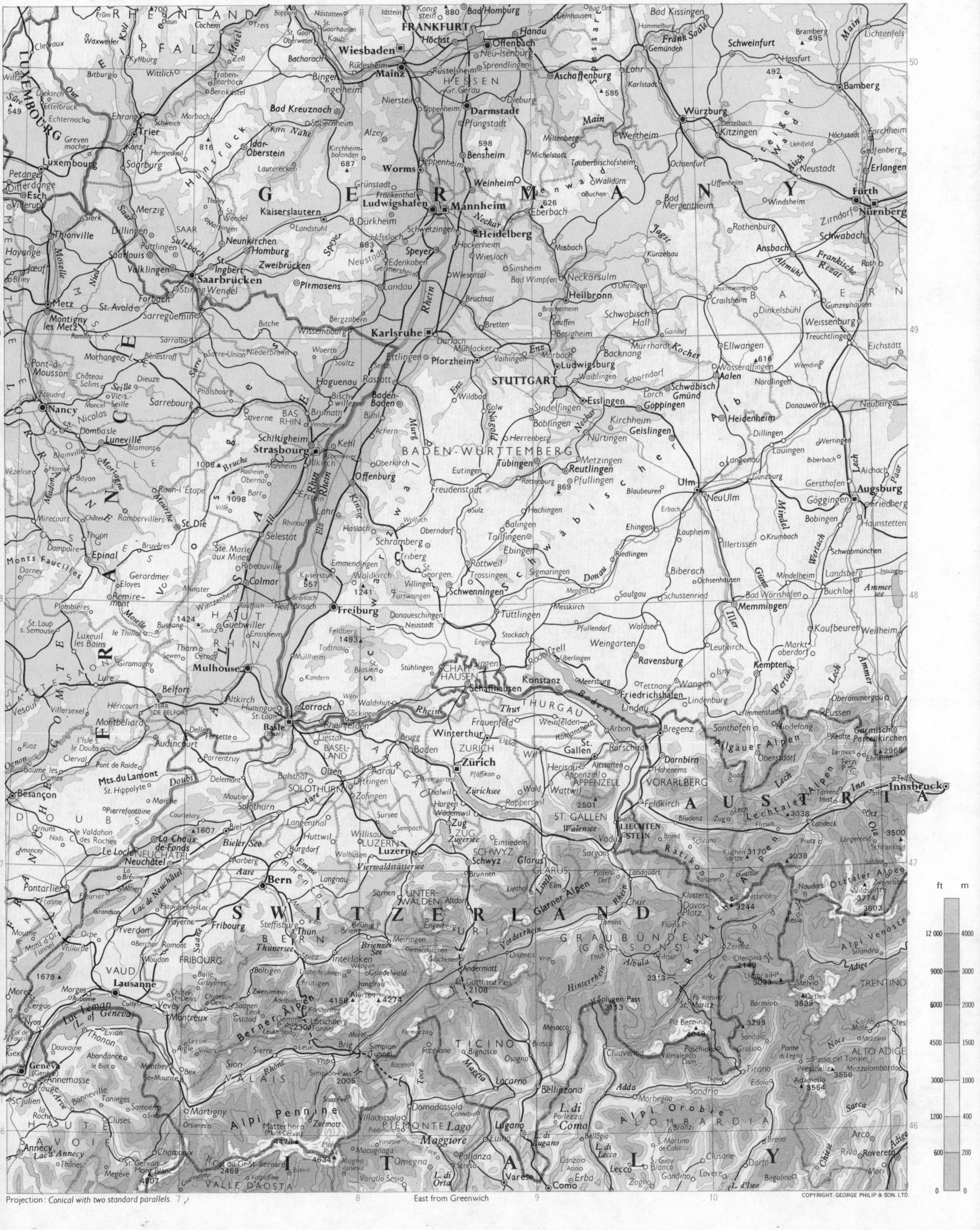

Projection: Conical with two standard parallels.

COPYRIGHT. GEORGE PHILIP & SON. LTD.

NORTH SEA

BALTIC

NETHERLANDS
BELGIUM
LUX.
FRANCE
GERMANY
WEST GERMANY
EAST GERMANY
CZECHOSLOVAKIA
SWITZERLAND
AUSTRIA
ITALY

SCHLESWIG
HOLSTEIN
LOWER SAXONY
NORTH RHINE WESTPHALIA
FLANDERS
RHINE LAND
PALATINATE
SAAR
LORRAINE
WÜRTTEMBERG
BADEN
BAVARIA
HARZ Mts.
THURINGIAN FOREST
BOHEMIAN FOREST
BOHEMIA
MORAVIA
UPPER AUSTRIA
LOWER AUSTRIA
TYROL
SALZBURG
CARINTHIA
STYRIA
BURGENLAND
VORARLBERG
LIECHTENSTEIN
LOMBARDY
PIEDMONT
VENETO
EMILIA ROMAGNA
TRENTINO
ALTO-ADIGE
FRIULI-VENEZIA-GIULIA
DAUPHINÉ
PROVENCE
PPROVENCE

Flensburg
Kiel
Kiel Bay
Fehmarn
Lübeck
Rostock
Stralsund
Rügen
Sassnitz
Swinoujscie
Szczecin (Stettin)
Hamburg
Bremerhaven
Bremen
Schwerin
Wismar
Neu Brandenburg
Oldenburg
Groningen
Leeuwarden
Den Helder
Alkmaar
Haarlem
Amsterdam
The Hague
Leiden
Utrecht
Hilversum
Rotterdam
Dordrecht
Breda
Antwerp
Ghent
Bruges
Ostend
Brussels
Lille
Hanover
Hannover
Hildesheim
Brunswick
Magdeburg
Potsdam
BERLIN
Charlottenburg
Spandau
Brandenburg
Frankfurt
Cottbus
Halle
Leipzig
Dresden
Görlitz
Liberec
Karl Marx Stadt (Chemnitz)
Zwickau
Plauen
Erfurt
Jena
Gera
Kassel
Dortmund
Essen
Duisburg
Düsseldorf
Cologne (Köln)
Bonn
Aachen
Wuppertal
Bochum
Gelsenkirchen
M.Gladbach
Krefeld
Münster
Osnabrück
Bielefeld
Herford
Hamm
Paderborn
Koblenz
Wiesbaden
Frankfurt
Offenbach
Mainz
Worms
Darmstadt
Mannheim
Heidelberg
Karlsruhe
Würzburg
Bamberg
Nuremberg (Nürnberg)
Fürth
Regensburg
Ingolstadt
Augsburg
Munich (München)
Stuttgart
Pforzheim
Heilbronn
Esslingen
Ludwigsburg
Tübingen
Reutlingen
Ulm
Freiburg
Strasbourg
Colmar
Mulhouse
Basle
Besançon
Dijon
Nancy
Metz
Luxembourg
Trier
Kaiserslautern
Saarbrücken
Ludwigshafen
Passau
Linz
Vienna (Wien)
Wiener Neustadt
Graz
Klagenfurt
Innsbruck
Salzburg
Brenner P.
Gr. Glockner
Bolzano
Bressanone
Trento
Merano
Udine
Gorizia
Trieste
Ljubljana
Zagreb
Maribor
Celje
Rijeka
Milan
Turin
Novara
Vercelli
Como
Bergamo
Brescia
Verona
Vicenza
Padua (Padova)
Venice (Venezia)
Treviso
Mantua (Mantova)
Cremona
Pavia
Piacenza
Parma
Reggio
Modena
Bologna
Ferrara
Ravenna
Rimini
Genoa (Genova)
Spezia
Pistoia
Prato
Florence (Firenze)
Lucca
Pisa
San Marino
Nice
Cannes
Monaco
Monte Carlo
Marseilles
Aix
Avignon
Nîmes
Arles
St. Étienne
Lyons
Villeurbanne
Grenoble
Geneva
Lausanne
Bern
Zürich
Luzern
St. Gallen
Neuchâtel
Fribourg
Matterhorn
Mt. Blanc
4807
Mt. Rosa
4634
Gr. Paradiso
4061
Mt. Viso
3841
Aosta
D'AOSTA

ADRIATIC SEA
Gulf of Venice
Gulf of Genoa

Projection: Conical with two standard parallels
East from Greenwich

ft m
12 000   4000
9000   3000
6000   2000
4500   1500
3000   1000
1200   400
600   200
0   0
200   600
m ft

1 : 5 000 000

50   0   50   100 miles
50   0   50   100   150 km

Inset map (Central Europe Political):

DENMARK
Copenhagen
Amsterdam NETH. Hamburg Berlin POLAND Warsaw U.S.S.R.
Brussels BELGIUM WEST GERMANY EAST GERMANY Kiev
LUX. Bonn Prague Lvov
CZECHOSLOVAKIA
FRANCE SWITZ. Bern Liechtenstein Vienna AUSTRIA Budapest HUNGARY RUMANIA
Monaco Trieste Bucharest
ITALY San Marino Belgrade YUGOSLAVIA
Rome BULGARIA Sofia

Main map:

Gdansk Bay Zelenogradsk Kaliningrad Chernyakhovsk LITHUANIA Vilnius
Sopot Gdynia Pregel Gusev Varena S.S.R.
Gdansk Elblag Braniewo Lyna Suwałki 309 WHITE
Starogard Malbork Olsztyn Ketrzyn Gizycko Augustów Grodno RUSSIA
Kwidzyn Ostroda Masurian Lakes Plateau Sokółka 238 Bialystok S.S.R.
Grudziadz Chelmno Mława Ostrołęka Bransk Hajnówka Volkovysk Slonim
Toruń Rypin Ciechanów Ostrów Mazowiecka Czeremcha Bereza
Włocławek Płock Puttusk Zhabinka Brest
Warsaw (Warszawa) Mińsk Mazowiecki Siedlce Biała Podlaska Pripyat
Pruszków Żyrardów Otwock Łuków Międzyrzec Dubrovitsa Marshes 316 Uzh
Łódź Skierniewice Grójec Włodawa Sarny Korosten
Radom Pilica Kozienice Pulawy Chełm Vladimir Volynski Lutsk Korets Novograd Kiev
Kielce Ostrowiec Krasnik Lublin Zamość Sokal Rovno Dubno Ostrog Shepetovka Zhitomir Berdichev Belaya Tserkov
Częstochowa Sandomierz Tarnobrzeg 390 Kamenka Bugskaya Radekhov Brody Kremenets Starokonstantinov Kazatin
Zabrze Bytom Przeworsk Jaroslaw Gorodok Lvov 471 Zolochev Ternopol Khmelnitski 384 Vinnitsa UKRAINE
Gliwice Sosnowiec Kraków Wieliczka Tarnow Przemyśl Sambor Dnestr Buchach Chortkov Zhmerinka Uman S.S.R.
Chorzów Katowice Wisła 1725 Jaslo Krosno Dukla P. 502 Drogobych Stry Zaleshchiki Kamenets Podolski Pervomaisk
Ostrava Bielsko Nowy West Beskids East Beskids Borislav Turka Ivano-Frankovsk Kolomyia Snyatyn Khotin Mogilev-Podolski
Frydek 550 High Tatra 2665 4340 Ruthenia Nadvornaya 1881 2061 Chernovtsy Yedintsy Sorok Kotovsk
Mistek Zilina Ružomberok Prešov Košice Uzhgorod 931 of the Tartars Storozhinets Beltsy MOLDAVIAN
SLOVAKIA Low Tatra Ore Mts. Mukachevo Khust Sighet 2061 Dorohoi 429 Kishinev
Kremnica Banská Bystrica Beregovo Satoraljaujhely Tokaj Botoşani Bendery
Nitra Zvolen Slovakian Miskolc Eger Nyíregyháza Satu Mare Carei Baia Mare 2305 Radauti Suceava Iaşi Tiraspol
Banská Stiavnica Lučenec Mezőkövesd Hajdúböszörmény Pietrosul Vatra-Dornei Roman Vaslui Odessa
Komárno Hron Hatvan Jászberény Debrecen Dej 2102 Bistrita Pietrosul Piatra Neamt Bârlad Belgorod Dnestrovski
Budapest Vác Gyöngyös Szolnok Karcag Oradea Cluj Turda Tirgu Mures Praid Bacau Galati
Győr Tatabánya Székesfehérvár Cegléd Nagykőrös Salonta 1848 Mt. Bihor Aiud Abrud Odorhei Miercurea Ciuc Focşani Braila 467
HUNGARY Kecskemét Kiskunfélegyháza Békéscsaba Gyula Crişu Transylvania Sfântu Gheorghe Tecuci Izmail
Dunaújváros Kiskőrös Szentes Brad Deva Medias Sighişoara Br
Kalocsa Kiskunhalas Hódmezővásárhely Makó Arad Simeria Alba-Iulia Sibiu Fagaras Braşov Ramnicu Sarat Galati
Szekszárd Baja Szeged Mures Lugoj Hunedoara Red Tower Mt. Negoiu 2535 2507 Cimpina Buzau Braila
Pécs Subotica Kikinda Timişoara Caransebes 2518 350 Mt. Omu Cimpulung Ploeşti Constanta
Mohács Senta Banat Resita Peleaga 2509 Parîngul-Mare Tîrgu-Jiu Rimnicu Valcea Trajan's Wall
Osijek Sombor Novi Sad Porta Orientalis Tirgovişte Bucharest (Bucureşti) BLACK SEA
Vinkovci Petrovaradin Vršac Mehadia Iron Gate Orsova Turnu-Severin Wallachia Slatina Dobrogea Cernavoda Constanta
Brčko Sremska Mitrovica Bela Crkva Pančevo Pitaşti Caracal Ruse (Ruschuk) Mangalia
Belgrade (Beograd) Smederevo Pozarevac Craiova Turnu Magurele Giurgiu BULGARIA
YUGOSLAVIA 1346 Danube Zimnicea Sofia
Sarajevo Titovo Užice

COPYRIGHT. GEORGE PHILIP & SON. LTD

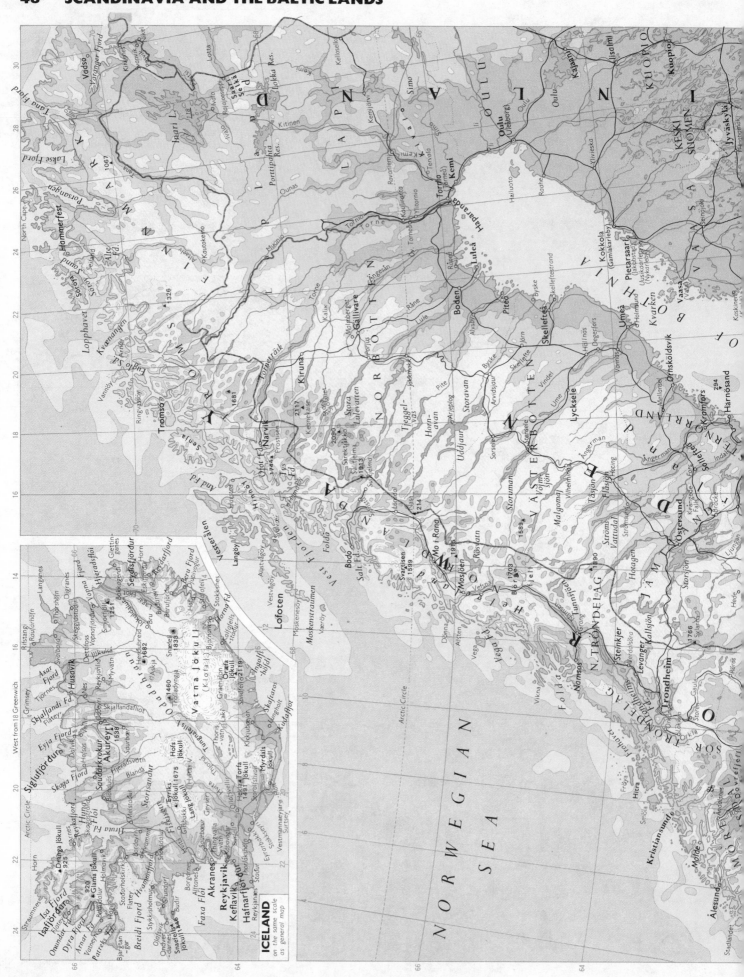

ICELAND
on the same scale
as general map

NORWEGIAN
SEA

1:5 000 000

20 10   0   60   80   100 miles
40 20 0   40   80   120   160 km

Projection: Conical with two standard parallels

East from Greenwich

FINLAND

Heinola, Hämeenlinna, Kotka, Kouvola, Lovisa (Lovisa), Porvoo (Borgå), HELSINKI (Helsingfors), Hanko (Hangö), Rakvere, Rauma, Pori, Turku (Åbo), Uusikaupunki, Ahvenanmaa (Åland), Maarianhamina (Mariehamn), Kokemäen, Tampere, Tavastehus

ESTONIA, **S.S.R.**

Tallinn, Pärnu, Haapsalu, Paldiski, Viljandi, Valga, Tartu, Khiuma (Hiiuma), Kärdla, Sarema (Saaremaa), Kingisepp (Kuressaare), Ruhnu

LATVIA, **S.S.R.**

Riga, G. of Riga, Valmiera, Cēsis, Jelgava (Mitau), Tukums, Kuldīga, Ventspils, Liepaja, Bauska

LITHUANIA

Kaunas, Vilnius, Šiauliai, Panevėžys, Ukmerge, Telšiai, Klaipeda, R. Neman, Tourage

B A L T I C   S E A

Gotland, Visby, Fårö, Gotska Sandön, Hoburg, Burgsvik, Hemse

R.S.F.S.R.

Kaliningrad, Chernyakhovsk, Sovetsk, Elbing, Malbork, Gdynia, Gdansk, G. of Gdansk, Bornholm, Rønne

POLAND

Szczecin, Stargard, Bydgoszcz, Grudziadz, Toruń, Białystok, Grodno, Łomża, Ostroleka, Suwałki, Augustów, Olsztyn

SWEDEN

STOCKHOLM, Uppsala, Västerås, Eskilstuna, Södertälje, Nacka, Nyköping, Norrköping, Oxelösund, Katrineholm, Örebro, Köping, Kumla, Linköping, Motala, Mjölby, Västervik, Oskarshamn, Kalmar, Öland, Nybro, Karlskrona, Karlshamn, Blekinge, Kristianstad, Ystad, Trelleborg, Malmö, Landskrona, Helsingborg, Halmstad, Falkenberg, Varberg, Göteborg, Mölndal, Borås, Alingsås, Uddevalla, Vänersborg, Trollhättan, Lidköping, Skövde, Mariestad, Skara, Falköping, Jönköping, Huskvarna, Värnamo, Ljungby, Växjö, Vetlanda, Nässjö, Tranås, Vetlanda, Ulricehamn

Söderhamn, Gävle, Sandviken, Bollnäs, Ljusne, Hudiksvall, Mora, Siljan, Falun, Borlänge, Hedemora, Avesta, Ludvika, Fagersta, Köping, Hagfors, Karlstad, Kristinehamn, Filipstad, Arvika, Åmål, Säffle, Kongsvinger

DALARNA, **VÄRMLAND**, **VÄSTMANLAND**, **UPPLAND**, **SÖDERMANLAND**, **ÖSTERGÖTLAND**, **SMÅLAND**, **HALLAND**, **GOTLAND**, **ÖLAND**, **KRONOBERG**, **JÖNKÖPING**, **KALMAR**, **BLEKINGE**, **ÄLVSBORG**, **GÖTEBORG AND BOHUS**, **ÖREBRO**, **KOPPARBERG**, **GÄVLEBORG**

NORWAY

OSLO, Bergen, Sogne Fjord, Hardanger Fjord, Stavanger, Sandnes, Haugesund, Kopervik, Egersund (Eigersund), Flekkefjord, Farsund, Lista, Kristiansand, Mandal, Lillesand, Grimstad, Arendal, Risør, Kragerø, Skien, Larvik, Tønsberg, Sandefjord, Horten, Moss, Drammen, Drøbak, Halden, Sarpsborg, Fredrikstad, Kongsberg, Notodden, Rjukan, Hamar, Lillehammer, Gjøvik, Hønefoss, Kongsvinger

VEST-AGDER, **AUST-AGDER**, **TELEMARK**, **BUSKERUD**, **AKERSHUS**, **ØSTFOLD**, **VESTFOLD**, **ROGALAND**, **HORDALAND**, **HEDMARK**, **OPPLAND**

DENMARK

COPENHAGEN, Roskilde, Køge, Korsør, Slagelse, Sjælland, Næstved, Nakskov, Nykøbing, Falster, Maribo, Møn, Odense, Fyn, Svendborg, Nyborg, Kiel B., Store Bælt, Lille Bælt, Aarhus, Randers, Silkeborg, Horsens, Vejle, Fredericia, Kolding, Aabenraa, Sønderborg, Haderslev, Esbjerg, Ribe, Varde, Viborg, Herning, Holstebro, Skive, Struer, Lemvig, Thisted, Hjørring, Frederikshavn, Skagen (The Skaw), Ålborg, Lim Fjord, Nørresundby, Hobro, Ebeltoft, Grenaa, Kalundborg, Sønderborg, Tønder

Skagerrak, **Kattegat**, **The Sound**, **Læsø**, **Anholt**, **Samsø**, **Langeland**, **Lolland**

GERMANY

Hamburg, Lübeck, Kiel, Flensburg, Schleswig, Rendsburg, Neumünster, Rostock, Wismar, Schwerin, Güstrow, Stralsund, Greifswald, Rügen, Sassnitz, Anklam, Neubrandenburg, Neustrelitz, Pasewalk, Usedom, Wolin, Świnoujście, Bremen, Bremerhaven, Cuxhaven, Wilhelmshaven, Oldenburg, Emden, Verden, Lüneburg, Elbe, Weser

NETHERLANDS

Groningen, North Frisian Is., Sylt, E. Frisian Is., Blaavands Huk

Gulf of Finland

m ft

6000 2000
4500 1500
3000 1000
1200 400
600   200
0   0
200   600
ft   m

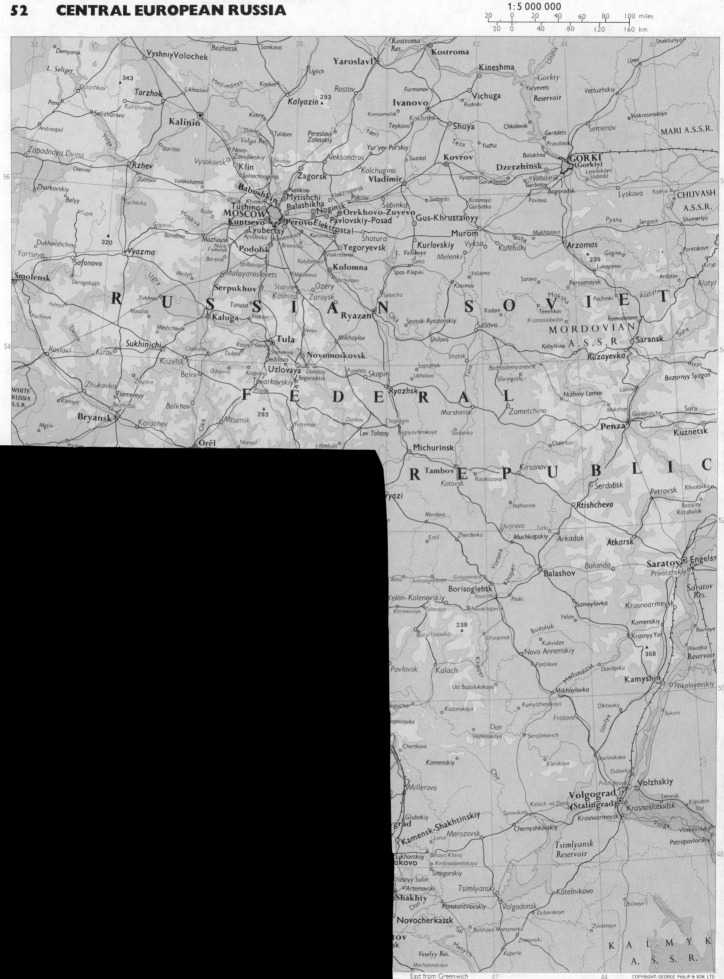

1:5 000 000

COPYRIGHT. GEORGE PHILIP & SON. LTD.

1 Kabardino-Balkar A.S.S.R.
2 North Ossetian A.S.S.R. (Azer.)
3 Nakhichevan A.S.S.R.
4 Checheno-Ingush A.S.S.R.

Karagiye Depression

1:50 000 000

250   0   250   500   750   1000 miles
200 0 200 400 600 800 1000 1200 1400 1600 km

FOREST VEGETATION

Tropical Rain Forest (dipterocarpus, palms, arborescent and climbing ferns, lianas, bamboos, orchids, epiphytes, mangrove swamp forest on coast).

Monsoon Tropophilous Woodland and Open Jungle (eng forest, pyinkado (ironwood), teak, sal, banyan, sandalwood, lianas, bamboos, orchids, jungle, epiphytes; in eastern parts of East Indies, casuarina and eucalyptus).

Sub-tropical and Temperate Rain Forest (evergreen oaks, lauraceae, camellia, tea, magnolia, rhododendrons, crystomeria, arborescent ferns, palms, wistaria, lianas, bamboos, orchids, epiphytes).

Broad-leaved Deciduous Forest and Meadow (oaks, beech, maple, walnut, chestnut, paper mulberry, syringa, ferns, dwarf bamboos).

Temperate Mountain Forest (mainly coniferous, fir, pine, spruce, larch; sometimes at lower altitudes mixed with oak, chestnut, maple, birch; in North-West India, deodar).

Taiga or Northern Coniferous Forest—
  (A) West. Siberian Forest (Siberian fir, stone pine, spruce, silver fir, Siberian larch).
  (B) East Siberian Forest (Siberian fir, eastern larch, stone pine).
  (C) South-East Siberian Transitional Forest (eastern larch, Siberian fir, ayan pitch-pine, Manchu pine, with oak, elm, maple, walnut, wild apple).

Mediterranean Evergreen Forest (evergreen oak, plane, walnut, hornbeam).

Mediterranean Evergreen Maquis and Meadow (myrtle, box, olive).

Open Jungle and Xerophilous Scrub (teak, babul, acacia, tamarisk, tamarind, euphorbia).

Oases and Euphrates and Tigris Valleys.

GRASS VEGETATION

Transitional Zone of Wooded Steppe.

Temperate Grasslands and Steppe (stipa grass)

Savanna.

High Steppe (South-West Asia)

Steppe

Marsh Vegetation

DRY STEPPE & DESERT

Salt Steppe and Semi-desert (artemisia, saxaul, acacia, tamarisk).

Gobi and Central Asiatic Deserts (artemisia).

High Plateau Steppe and Desert (palaeoarctic vegetation).

Desert

Tundra (moss, lichen, heather bog, dwarf willow, birch and alder).

Alpine (ice desert).

Northern Limits of Siberian Larch (larix sibirica).

Limits of Date Palm (phœnix dactylifera).

Limits of Teak (tectona grandis).

Northern Limits of Palms.

Seas and Lakes frozen in Winter.

Projection: Bonne

COPYRIGHT. GEORGE PHILIP & SON. LTD.

East from Greenwich

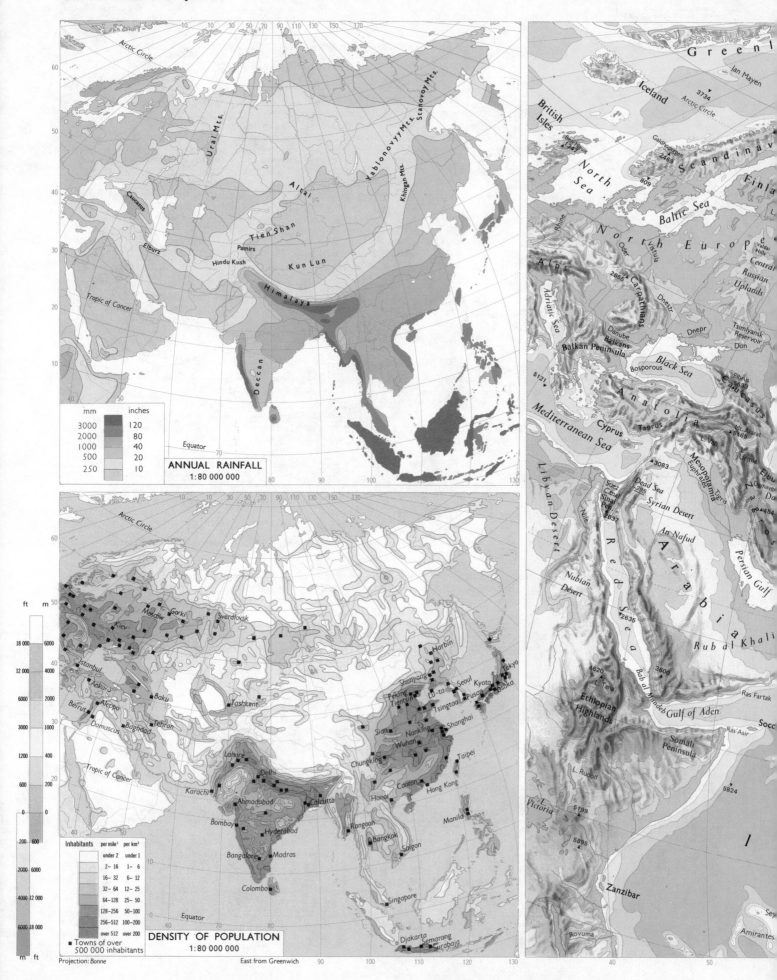

ANNUAL RAINFALL
1:80 000 000

mm	inches
3000	120
2000	80
1000	40
500	20
250	10

DENSITY OF POPULATION
1:80 000 000

Inhabitants	per mile²	per km²
	under 2	under 1
	2– 16	1– 6
	16– 32	6– 12
	32– 64	12– 25
	64–128	25– 50
	128–256	50–100
	256–512	100–200
	over 512	over 200

■ Towns of over
500 000 inhabitants

Projection: *Bonne*   East from Greenwich

1 : 40 000 000

200 0 200 400 600 800 1000 miles
200 0 400 800 1200 1600 km

ARCTIC OCEAN

Ibard
Bear I.
Fr. Josef Land
Severnaya Zemlya
New Siberian Is.
C. Dezhneva (East C.)
Bering Str.

Novaya Zemlya
Kara Sea
C. Chelyuskin
Laptev Sea
Foddeyev
Kotelny
Lyakhov Is.
Bear Is.
Wrangel I.
Chukot Ra.
G. of Anadyr
Koryak Ra.

Barents Sea
Kolguyev
Yamal Pen.
Taimyr Peninsula
Byrrang Mts.
Verkhoyansk Ra.
Indigirka
Kolyma Plain
Kolyma
3147
Bering Sea

N. Dvina
Gydan Pen.
Ob
Yenisey
Kotuy
Lower Tunguska
Olenek
Lena
Aldan
Stanovoy Ra.
Dzhugdzhur Ra.
Shantar Is.
Sea of Okhotsk
Kamchatka Peninsula
Sredinny Ra.
Komandorskiye Is.
7999

Ural Mountains
Narodnaya 1894
West Siberian Plain
Central Siberian Plateau
Stony Tunguska
Angara
2999
Yablonovyy Ra.
Amur
Ta Khingan Shan
Hsiao Khingan Shan
Manchurian Plain
Khanka
Sikhote Alin
Tartary Str.
Sakhalin
La Pérouse Str.
Kuril Is.
10542
Tsugaru Str.
Hokkaido
2290

Kama
Tobol
Irtysh
Ob
Eastern Sayan
Western Sayan
Baikal 1496
Selenga
Ta Khingan Shan
Hsi-liao
2744 Sungari Reservoir
Sea of Japan
4750
Kiyoshevsk Vol.
50
40

Yaman Tau 1640
Kirgiz Steppe
Muyun Kum
53 Syr-Darya
Belukha 4506
3957
Plateau of Mongolia
G. of Chihli
Korea Str.
Honshu
Fuji-yama 3776
30

Aral Sea
Turanian Plain
Kyzyl Kum
L. Balkhash 342
Chu
L. Issyk-Kul
Tien Shan 7439
Turfan Basin -154
Tarim
Lop Nor
Gobi
3015 Ordos Plateau
Ala Shan
2894
Shantung Pen.
Yellow Sea
Kagu Str.
Kyushu
Shikoku
10554

Kum
Amu Darya
Communism Pk. 7495
Pamirs
Takla Makan
Tarim Basin
Altyn Tagh 6346
Nan Shan
Tsaidam
Koko Nor
Chinling Shan 4107
China
Hwang-Ho
Great Plain of China
Yangtze-kiang
East China Sea
Ryukyu Islands
7507
Tropic of Cancer
20

Hindu Kush 7788
Karakoram Ra. 8611
Kunlun Shan 7723
Bayan Kara Shan
Plateau of Tibet
Red Basin
Yangtze-kiang
Ta Liang Shan
Tung-Ting L.
Poyang
Nan Shan Wu Shan
3897
Formosa
7559

Helmand 5143
Sulaiman Ra. 8128
Himalaya
Nam Tso
Tsangpo 4756
2690
2710
Si-kiang
Formosa Str.
Bushi Chan.

Saihan Ra.
Indus
Thar
Indo-Gangetic Plain
82214
Mt. Everest 8848
Kanchenjunga 8598
Brahmaputra
3143
G. of Tonkin
Hainan
Babuyan Is.
Luzon 2928
Philippine Islands
Cape Johnson Deep 10497
8054

Aravalli Ra.
Chenab
Sutlej
Ganga
Khasi Hills
Mt. Victoria 3053
Salween
Irrawaddy
Mekong
3280
South China Sea
5245
Mindoro
Samar
Leyte
10

Chambal
Yamuna
India
Vindhya Mts.
Narmada
Satpura Ra.
Godavari
Ganges Delta
Arakan Yoma
Irrawaddy
Phnom Dong Rak Tonle Sap
Palawan
Sulu Sea 5576
Panay
Negros
Mt. Apo 2954
Mindanao
5842
Morotai

Arabian Sea
Krishna
Deccan
Western Ghats
Eastern Ghats
Malabar Coast
Coromandel Coast
Bay of Bengal
Andaman Is.
Andaman Sea
G. of Martaban
Salween
Mekong
G. of Siam
Ca Mau Pt.
Kinabalu 4101
Celebes Sea
Halmahera
New Guinea
0

Laccadive Is.
Anai Mudi 2698
Palk Str.
Ceylon
Pidurutalagala 2524
Dondra Head
Nicobar Is.
Isthmus of Kra
Malay Peninsula
Natuna Is.
Celebes
7440
Ceram
Banda Sea

5875
Maldive Is.
C. Comorin
G. of Mannar
Str. of Malacca
3466
Borneo
Makassar Str.
2456
Buru
Arafura Sea

INDIAN OCEAN
Equator
Sumatra
Sunda Islands
Java Sea
Java
6073
Bali
Lombok
Semeru 3676
3726
Sumbawa
5123
Flores
Timor
Sumba
Australia

Chagos Arch.

PACIFIC OCEAN

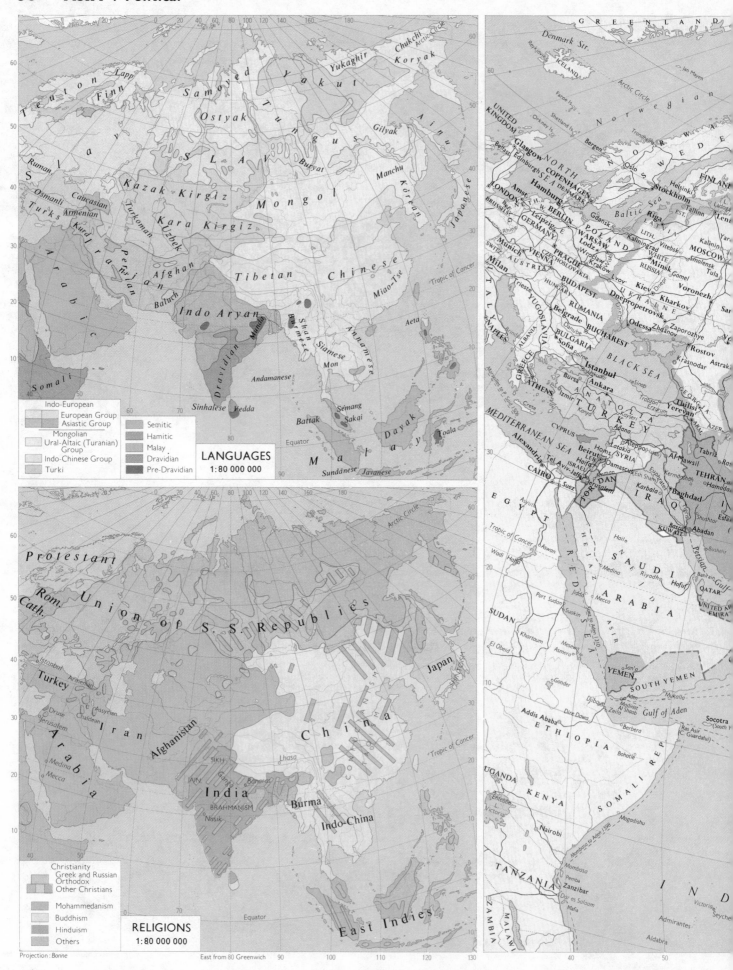

LANGUAGES
1:80 000 000

Indo-European
- European Group
- Asiatic Group

Mongolian
- Ural-Altaic (Turanian) Group
- Indo-Chinese Group
- Turki

- Semitic
- Hamitic
- Malay
- Dravidian
- Pre-Dravidian

Teuton — *Lapp* — *Finn* — *Samoyed* — *Yakut* — *Yukaghir* — *Koryak* — *Chukchi* — Arctic Circle — *Ostyak* — *Tungus* — *Gilyak* — *Ainu* — *Slav* — *Buryat* — *Manchu* — *Korean* — *Japanese* — *Ruman* — *Kazak-Kirgiz* — *Mongol* — *Miao-Tse* — *Osmanli* — *Caucasian* — *Armenian* — *Turkoman* — *Kara Kirgiz* — *Uzbek* — *Turks* — *Kurd* — *Persian* — *Afghan* — *Tibetan* — *Chinese* — Tropic of Cancer — *Arabic* — *Baluch* — *Indo Aryan* — *Shan Burmese* — *Annamese* — *Aeta* — *Dravidian* — *Munda* — *Siamese* — *Mon* — *Somali* — *Andamanese* — *Sinhalese* — *Vedda* — *Battak* — *Semang Sakai* — *Dayak* — *Toala* — Equator — *Malay* — *Sundanese* — *Javanese*

RELIGIONS
1:80 000 000

Christianity
- Greek and Russian Orthodox
- Other Christians

- Mohammedanism
- Buddhism
- Hinduism
- Others

Protestant — *Rom. Cath.* — *Union of S.S.Republics* — *Japan* — *Istanbul* — *Armenian* — *Turkey* — *Druse* — *Chaldean* — *Assyrian* — *Jerusalem* — *Iran* — *Afghanistan* — *China* — *Arabia* — *SIKH* — *Lhasa* — *Medina* — *JAIN* — *Ganges* — *Benares* — *India* — *BRAHMANISM* — *Burma* — *Nasik* — *Indo-China* — *Mecca* — Equator — *East Indies*

Projection: *Bonne*   East from 80 Greenwich   90   100   110   120   130

GREENLAND — Denmark Str. — Reykjavik — ICELAND — Jan Mayen — Arctic Circle — Faroe Is. — Norwegian — UNITED KINGDOM — Orkney Is. — Shetland Is. — Trondheim — Bergen — Oslo — SWEDE — FINLAND — Glasgow — NORTH — Belfast — Edinburgh — SEA — DENMARK — Stockholm — Helsinki — LONDON — Amst. — Hamburg — Copenhagen — Baltic — Riga — EST. — Tallinn — BRUSSELS — GERMANY — Leipzig — Gdansk — LATVIA — Rhine — Munich — BERLIN — POLAND — WARSAW — Kaliningrad — LITH. — Vitebsk — MOSCOW — SWITZ. — AUSTRIA — PRAGUE — Wroclaw — Lodz — Krakow — WHITE — Minsk — Gomel — Kalinin — Milan — VIENNA — CZECHOSLOVAKIA — U K R A I N E — Kiev — RUSSIA — Smolensk — Tula — ITALY — Trieste — HUNGARY — BUDAPEST — Lvov — Dnepr — Kharkov — Voronezh — NAPLES — YUGOSLAVIA — Belgrade — RUMANIA — BUCHAREST — Dnepropetrovsk — Danube — ALBANIA — BULGARIA — Sofia — BLACK SEA — Odessa — Zhdanov — Rostov — Zaporozhye — Krasnodar — Astrak — GREECE — ATHENS — Istanbul — Edirne — Bursa — Ankara — Sinop — Trabzon — Erzurum — GEORGIA — Tbilisi — Yerevan — ARM. — AZER. — MEDITERRANEAN SEA — CYPRUS — TURKEY — Izmir — Konya — Kayseri — ANATOLIA — Crete — Adana — Tabriz — Ras — Aleppo — SYRIA — Mosul — TEHRAN — Hamadan — Alexandria — Beirut — Homs — Damascus — Esh Sham — Euphrates — Baghdad — Esfa — Tel Aviv-Jaffa — ISRAEL — LEB. — CAIRO — Suez — JORDAN — Jerusalem — Amman — Karbala — IRAQ — EGYPT — Asyut — Basra — Abadan — Shushtar — KUWAIT — Hofuf — Hail — Bahrain Gulf — Bushehr — Tropic of Cancer — Aswan — HEJAZ — Medina — SAUDI — Persian Gulf — UNITED A. EMIRA — Wadi Halfa — Port Sudan — Suakin — Jidda — Mecca — Riyadh — ARABIA — QATAR — SUDAN — Khartoum — ASIR — RED SEA — Mesewa — Asmera — YEMEN — San'a — SOUTH YEMEN — El Obeid — Aden — Mukalla — Gonder — Gulf of Aden — Socotra (South) — Addis Ababa — Djibouti — Medinet — Dire Dawa — ETHIOPIA — Zeila — Shaab — Berbera — Ras Asir (C. Guardafui) — Bohotle — UGANDA — KENYA — Bombasa to Aden 1598 — SOMALI REP. — I N D — Entebbe — L.Victoria — Nairobi — TANZANIA — Pemba — Zanzibar — Mogadishu — ZAMBIA — MALAWI — Dar es Salaam — Mafia — Admirantes — Seyche — Aldabra

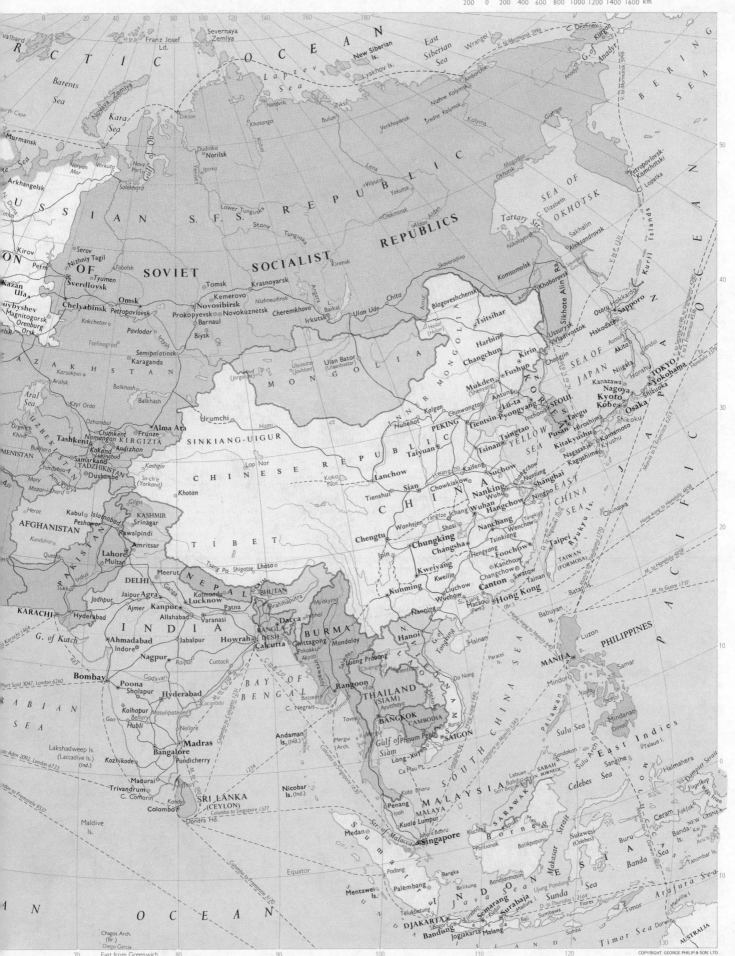

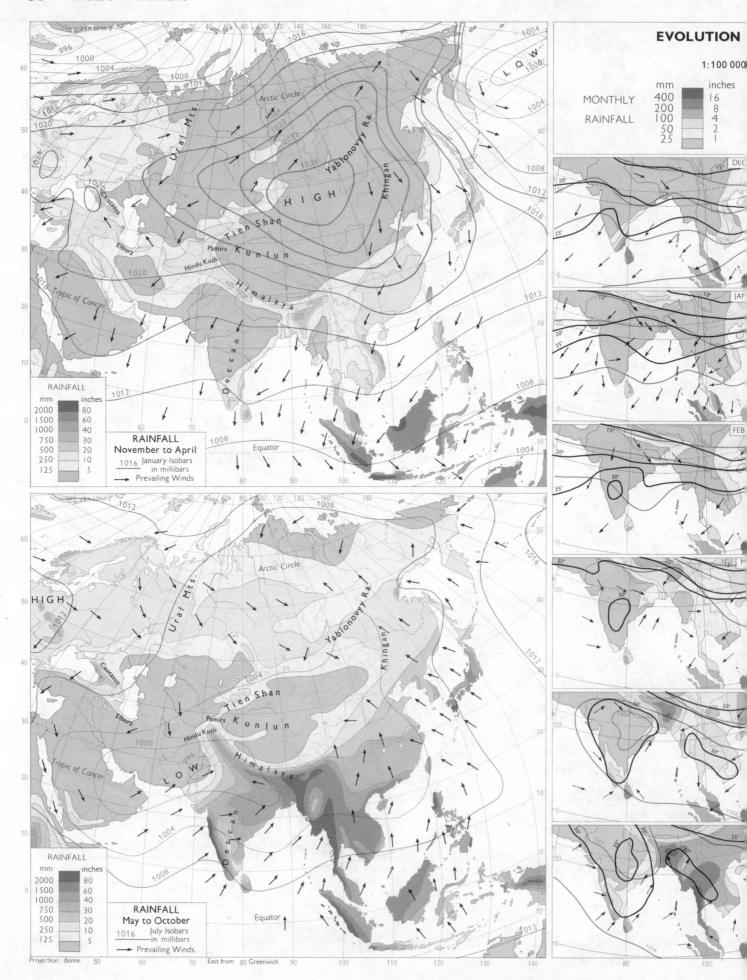

EVOLUTION

1:100 000

	mm	inches
MONTHLY	400	16
RAINFALL	200	8
	100	4
	50	2
	25	1

DEC

JAN

FEB

RAINFALL

mm	inches
2000	80
1500	60
1000	40
750	30
500	20
250	10
125	5

RAINFALL
November to April

1016 January Isobars
in millibars
→ Prevailing Winds

RAINFALL

mm	inches
2000	80
1500	60
1000	40
750	30
500	20
250	10
125	5

RAINFALL
May to October

1016 July Isobars
in millibars
→ Prevailing Winds

Projection: Bonne

East from Greenwich

1:80 000 000

400 0 400 800 1200 1600 miles
400 0 400 800 1200 1600 2000 2400 km

HE MONSOON

0 500 1000 1500 2000 miles
0 500 1000 1500 2000 2500 3000 km

—— Isotherms
reduced to Sea-level °Celsius

1016 Isobars in millibars

→ Winds

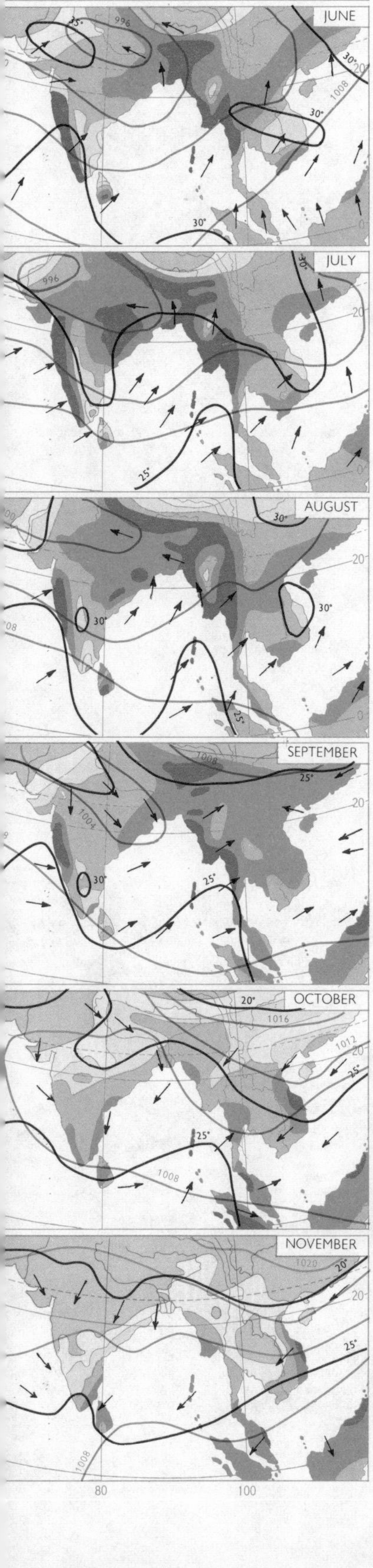

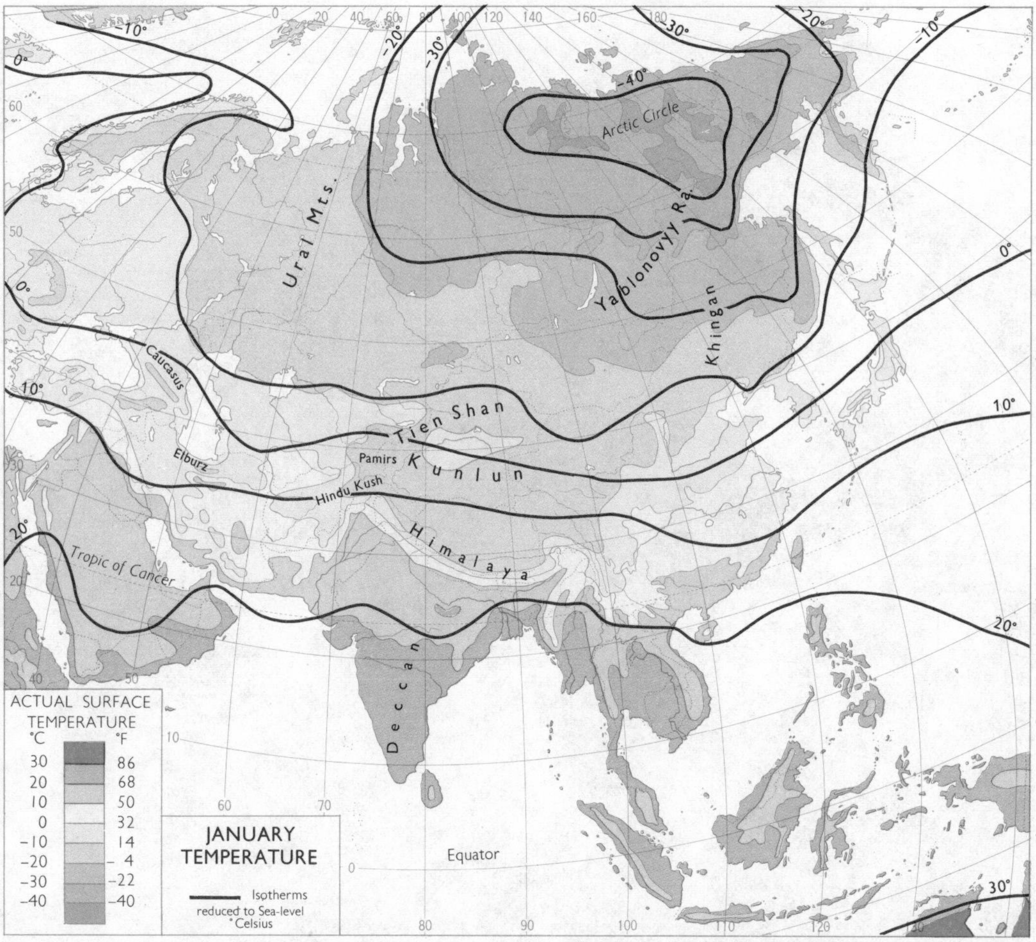

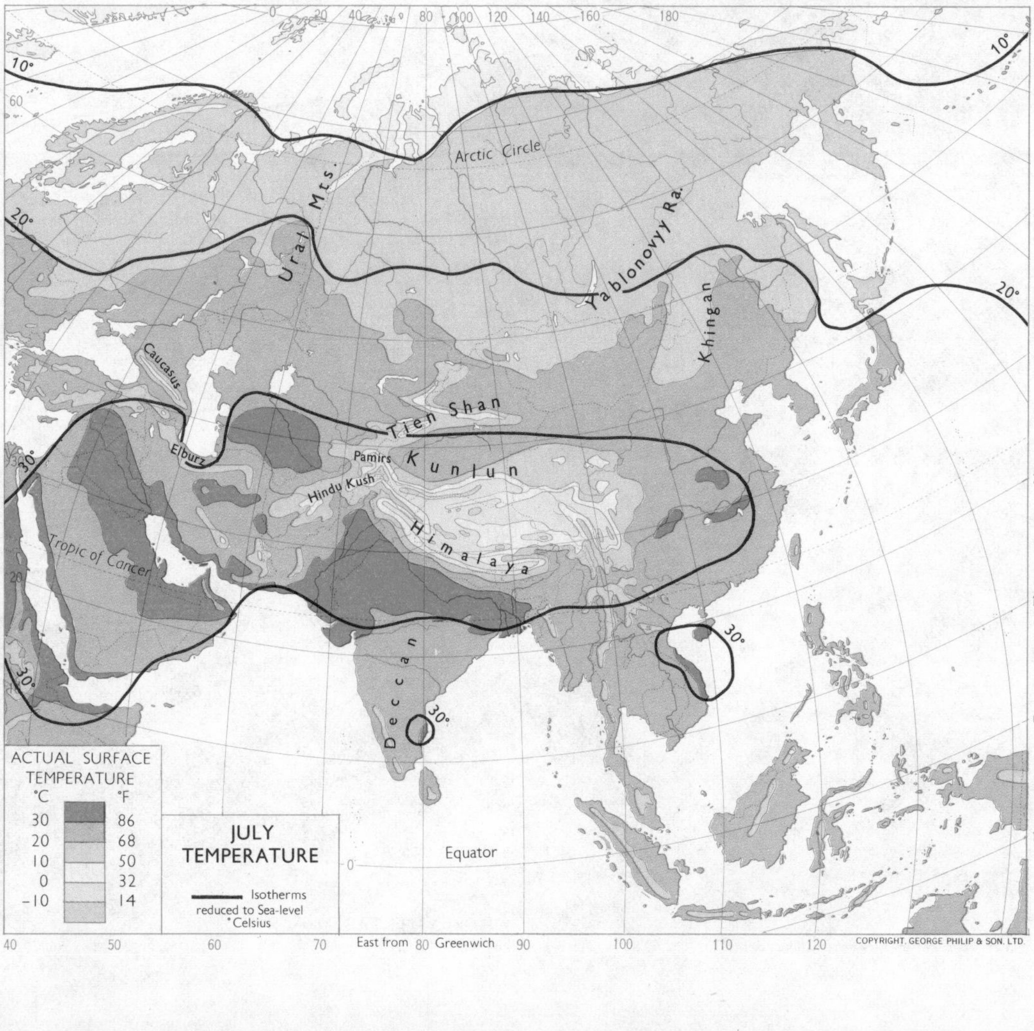

JUNE

JULY

AUGUST

SEPTEMBER

OCTOBER

NOVEMBER

ACTUAL SURFACE
TEMPERATURE

°C	°F
30	86
20	68
10	50
0	32
−10	14
−20	−4
−30	−22
−40	−40

JANUARY
TEMPERATURE

—— Isotherms
reduced to Sea-level
°Celsius

Ural Mts.
Arctic Circle
Yablonovyy Ra.
Khingan
Caucasus
Tien Shan
Elburz
Pamirs Kunlun
Hindu Kush
Himalaya
Tropic of Cancer
Deccan
Equator

ACTUAL SURFACE
TEMPERATURE

°C	°F
30	86
20	68
10	50
0	32
−10	14

JULY
TEMPERATURE

—— Isotherms
reduced to Sea-level
°Celsius

Ural Mts.
Arctic Circle
Yablonovyy Ra.
Khingan
Caucasus
Tien Shan
Elburz
Pamirs Kunlun
Hindu Kush
Himalaya
Tropic of Cancer
Deccan
Equator

East from Greenwich

COPYRIGHT. GEORGE PHILIP & SON. LTD.

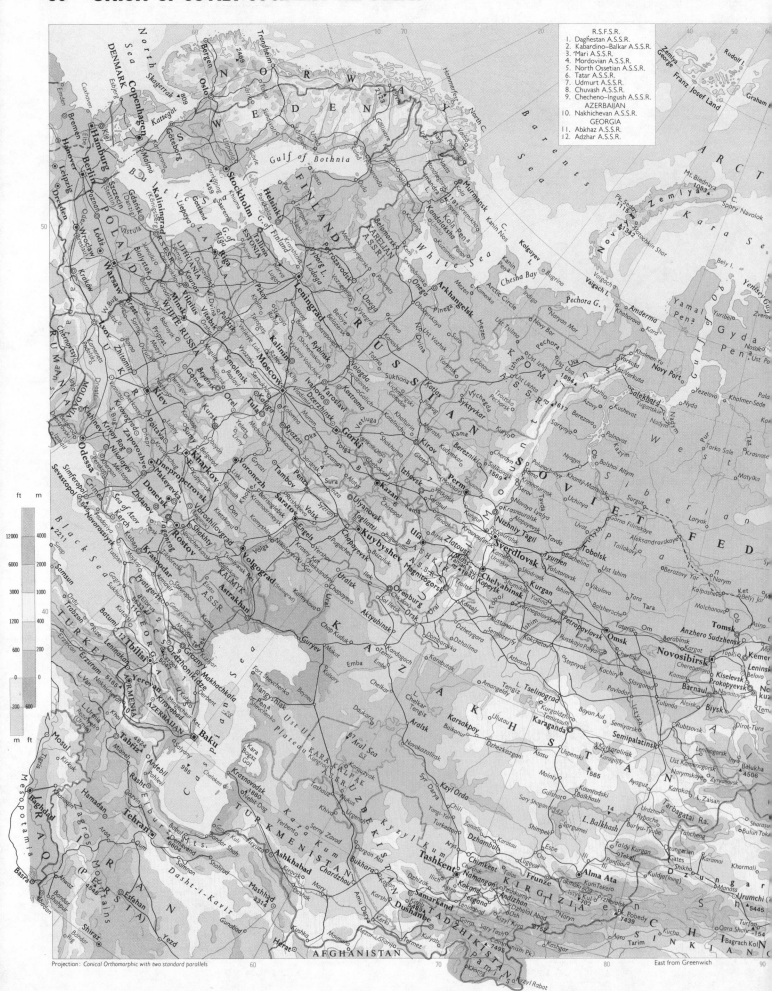

R.S.F.S.R.
1. Daghestan A.S.S.R.
2. Kabardino–Balkar A.S.S.R.
3. Mari A.S.S.R.
4. Mordovian A.S.S.R.
5. North Ossetian A.S.S.R.
6. Tatar A.S.S.R.
7. Udmurt A.S.S.R.
8. Chuvash A.S.S.R.
9. Checheno-Ingush A.S.S.R.
AZERBAIJAN
10. Nakhichevan A.S.S.R.
GEORGIA
11. Abkhaz A.S.S.R.
12. Adzhar A.S.S.R.

Projection: Conical Orthomorphic with two standard parallels

East from Greenwich

1:20 000 000

100   50   0   100   200   300   400   500 miles
100   50   0   200   400   600   800 km

OCEAN

Chukchi Sea

C. Dezhneva
(East C.)

St. Lawrence I.
(U.S.A.)

Gulf of Anadyr

Koryak Range

Bering Sea

Kamchatka Pen.

Petropavlovsk-Kamchatskiy

Komandorskiye Is.

Sea of Okhotsk

Sakhalin

Tartary Str.

Kurile Is.

Yuzhno-Sakhalinsk

Sovetskoye Gavan
(Soviet Harbour)

Sikhote Alin Range

Hokkaidō

Sapporo

Hakodate

Khabarovsk

Komsomolsk

Birobidzhan

Vladivostok

Nakhodka

Ussuriysk

Sea of JAPAN

Honshū

Niigata

Toyama

Kanazawa

JAPAN

Blagoveshchensk

Amur

Manchuria

Harbin

Tsitsihar

Kiamusze

Chita

Ulan Ude

Irkutsk

Lake Baikal

MONGOLIA

Ulan Bator
(Ulaanbaatar)

Gobi

Changchun

Kirin

Mukden
(Shenyang)

Fushan

Anshan

Antung

Yingkow

Lü-ta
(Port Arthur-
Dairen)

Peking

Kalgan

Paotow

NORTH KOREA

Pyongyang

Wonsan

Chongjin

Seoul

Inchon

SOUTH KOREA

Taejon

Pusan

Sea of Japan

East Siberian Sea

Wrangel I.

New Siberian Is.

New Siberia

Laptev Sea

Severnaya Zemlya

Arctic Circle

Verkhoyansk

Yakutsk

A.S.S.R.

Vilyuisk

Olekminsk

Central Siberian Plateau

SOCIALIST REPUBLIC

Stanovoy Ra.

Krasnoyarsk

Nizhneudinsk

Cheremkhovo

Angarsk

Kirensk

Okhotsk

Magadan

Kolyma

Srednekolymsk

Tiksi

Nordvik

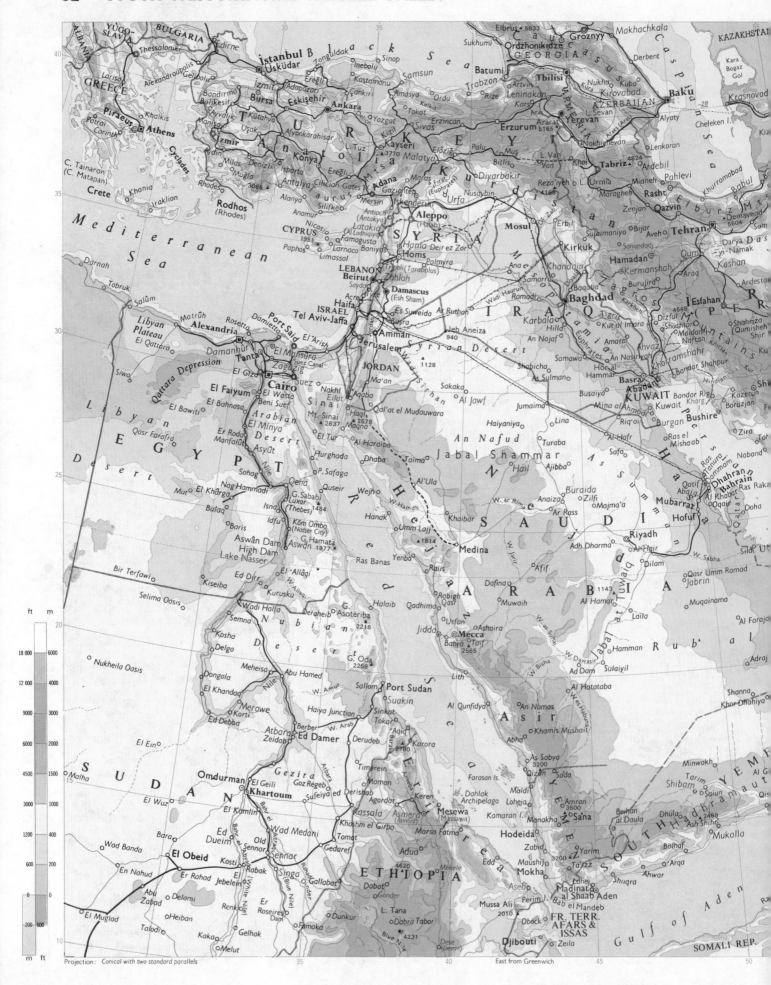

YUGO-SLAVIA
ALBANIA
BULGARIA
Edirne
Thessaloniki
Alexandroupolis
GREECE
Larisa
Istanbul
Usküdar
Black Sea
Zonguldak
Inebolu
Sinop
Samsun
Elbrus 5633
Sukhumi
Makhachkala
Groznyy
Ordzhonikidze
GEORGIA
Batumi
Derbent
Kara Bogaz Gol
KAZAKHSTAN
Krasnovod
Izmit
Izmir
Bandirma
Balikesir
Bursa
Eskişehir
Ankara
Adapazari
Ereğli
Kastamonu
Çankiri
Amasya
Ordu
Trabzon
Rize
Artvin
Tbilisi
Nukha
Kirovabad
Leninakan
Kars
ARMENIA
AZERBAIJAN
Baku
-28
Cheleken I.
Khurramabad
Babul
Piraeus
Athens
Corinth
Patrai
Khalkis
Aydin
Milas
Muğla
Manisa
Uşak
Afyonkarahisar
Kütahya
L. Tuz
Yozgat
Kayseri
3770
Sivas
Erzincan
Kelkit
Malatya
Palu
Muş
Erzurum
Ararat 5165
Nakhichevan
L. Sevan
Yerevan
Aras
Khoi
Tabriz 4824
Ardebil
Pahlevi
Rasht
Qazvin
Elburz Mts
Demavend 5604
Cyclades
C. Tainaron (C. Matapan)
Khania
Iraklion
Crete
Rhodes
Rodhos (Rhodes)
Denizli
Isparta
3086
Antalya
Alanya
Anamur
Cilician Gates
Taurus Mts
Mersin
Silifke
Adana
Gaziantep
Maraş
İskenderun
Urfa
Diyarbakir
Bitlis
L. Van
Van
Reza'iyeh 4166
L. Urmia
Maragheh
Mianeh
KURDISTAN
Zenjan
Qazvin
Mediterranean Sea
Darnah
Tobruk
Salûm
Matrûh
Libyan Plateau
El Qattara
Alexandria
Rosetta
Damietta
Port Said
El Arish
Nicosia
Famagusta
CYPRUS 1951
Paphos
Limassol
Larnaca
Baniyas
Latakia (Al Ladhiqiya)
Antioch (Antakya)
Tripoli (Tarabulus)
Aleppo (Halab)
Hama
Homs
Deir ez Zor
SYRIA
Palmyra
Mosul
Ana
Kirkuk
Khanaqin
Samarra
Sulaimaniya
Bijar
Aveh
Erbil
Zab
Tehran
Darya-yi-Namak
Qum
Hamadan
Kermanshah
Burujird
Kashan
PERSIA
Beirut
Zahlah
Sayda
Tyre
Damascus (Esh Sham)
Haifa
Acre
ISRAEL
Tel Aviv-Jaffa
Busra
At Suweida
Jeb Aneiza 940
Ramadi
Wadi Hauran
Ar Rutbah
Baghdad
Karbala
Hilla
Kut el Imara
Amara
Tigris
Dizful
Shushtar
Naftan
Khuzistan
Maidan Shir
Esfahan
Shahriza (Qumisheh)
Port Said
Suez Canal
Damanhûr
Tanta
El Mansura
Zagazig
Cairo
El Giza
Suez
Nakhl
Amman
JORDAN
Jerusalem
Wadi Sirhan
1128
Syrian Desert
Sakaka
An Najaf
Samawa
An Nasiriyah
Hor al Hammar
Ahvaz
Khorramshahr
Bandar Shahpur
Hindian
Kazerun
Shir
Rosetta
El Faiyum
El Wasta
Beni Suef
El Bahnasa
Er Roda
Arabian
El Minya
Manfalût
Mt. Sinai 2637
Sinai
El Tur
Hagl
Magna
Aqaba
Eilat
Qal'at el Mudawwara
Al Jawf
As Sulmano
Shabicha
Busaiya
As Samawa
Basra
Abadan
KUWAIT
Kuwait
Bandar Rigo
Kharg
Borazjan
Bushire
Zira
Libyan
Qattara Depression
Siwa
EGYPT
Qasr Farafra
Desert
Asyût
El Horaiba
Hurghada
P. Safaga
An Nafud
Haiyaniya
Turaba
Lina
Riq'ai
Burgan
Al-Hafr
Mina al Ahmadi
Ras el Mishaab
Ras Tanura
Naband
Qatif
Dhahran
Bahrain
Al Khobar
Oqair
Doha
Desert
El Kharga
Bulaq
Nag Hammadi
Qena
Quseir
Wejh
Hanak
W. Hamdh
Al'Ula
Khaibar
Jabal Shammar
Hail
Ajibba
Anaiza
Ar Rass
W. ar Rima
Buraida
Zilfi
Majma'a
Hofuf
Mubarraz
Al Hasa
Abqaiq
Al Hofuf
Ras Rakan
Isna
Idfu
Kôm Ombo (Nasser City)
G. Sabahi
Luxor (Thebes) 1484
G. Hamata
Aswân 1977
Umm Lajj
1814
SAUDI
Medina
W. Jarir
Adh Dharma
Riyadh
Al-Hair
Dilam
Qasr Umm Ramad
Jabrin
Al Faraja
Aswân Dam High Dam Lake Nasser
El 'Allâqi
Ras Banas
Yenbo
Rais
ARABIA
Afif
Jabal Tuwaiq
Al Hamar 1143
Laila
Muqainama
Bir Terfawi
Ed Dirr
Kuruşku
Dafina
Dhaba
Taima
Rabigh
Qasr
Qadhima
Muwaih
Ad Dam
Sulaiyil
Adraj
Kiseiba
Selima Oasis
Wadi Halfa
Derahieb
Asoteriba 2216
Halaib
Jidda
Mecca
Usfan
Ashaira
Bahra
Taif 2565
W. as Suba
W. Dawasir
Hamman
Rub' al
Nukheila Oasis
Nubia
Desert
G. Oda 2259
Lith
Al Hatataba
Shanna
Khor Dhahiya
Kosha
Delgo
Meheisa
Abu Hamed
W. Amur
Sallom
Port Sudan
Al Qunfidya
An Namas
Mehaisa
Dongola
El Khandaq
Merowe
Korti
Ed Debba
Haiya Junction
W. Arab
Berber
Suakin
Sinkat
Tokar
Suakin
Aqiq 2780
Karora
Asir
Khamis Mushait
Abha
As Sabya 3200
Minwakh
YEMEN
SUDAN
El Ein
Gezira
Omdurman
El Geili
Atbara
Ed Damer
Zeidab
Derudeb
Goz Regeb
Maman
Timerein
Agordat
Keren
Qizan
Sa'da
Shibam
Saiun
Tarim
Hadhramaut
Malha
El Wuz
Khartoum
El Kamlin
Kassala
Khashm el Girba
Sufeiya ed Derishab
Adua
Asmera (Massawa)
Mesewa (Massawa)
Dahlak Archipelago
Maidi
Loheia
Kamaran I.
Amran 3600
Manakha
Sa'na
Beihan al Daula
Ash Shihr
Mukalla
Bara
Ed Dueim
Wad Medani
Tomat
Gedaref
Kamaran I.
Hodeida
Zabid
Dhula 2469
Bolhaf
Arqa
El Obeid
Kosti
Rabak
Sennar
Singa
Rahad
Dinder
4620
Mekele
Edd
Ta'zz
Maushij 3200
Yarim
Mokha
Madinat al Shaab Aden
El Muglad
Abu Zabad
Delami
Heiban
Er Roseires Dam
Famaka
ETHIOPIA
Dabat
Gönder
Dabra Tabor
L. Tana
Asebo
Mussa Ali 2010
Obock
FR. TERR. AFARS & ISSAS
Djibouti
Zeila
Gulf of Aden
SOMALI REP.
Talodi
Gelhak
Melut
Blue Nile 4231
Dese (Desye)
Bab el Mandeb

ft   m
18 000   6000
12 000   4000
9000   3000
6000   2000
4500   1500
3000   1000
1200   400
600   200
0
200   600
m   ft

1:15 000 000

100   0   100   200   300 miles
100   0   100 200 300 400 500 km

CHINA

Left map (Afghanistan / Pakistan region)

S. S. R.
Dzhizak
Samarkand
Pendzhikent
UZBEKISTAN
Khiva
Bukhara
Chardzhou
Kagan
Karshi
Dushanbe
TADZHIKISTAN
Termez
Surkhob
Pamir
Faizabad
Kashmir
Gilgit
Chitral
Islamabad
Srinagar
Kara Kum
Ashkhabad
Mary
Sarakhs
Kerkio
Kushka
Maimana
Mazar-i-Sharif
Balkh
Tashkurghan
Kundun
Kabul
Jalalabad
Khyber Pass
Peshawar
Kohat
Rawalpindi
Jammu
ENISTAN
Nishapur
Mashhad
2849
Herat
Ghurian
Koh-i-Sangan
3923
AFGHANISTAN
Ghazni
Kuh-i-Mazar
3787
Kalat-i-Ghilzai
Kandahar
Bannu
Tank
Dera Ismail Khan
Ft. Sandeman
Sialkot
Lahore
Multan
Sutlej
Sabzawar
Sabzawar
Birjand
Gunabad
Farah
Lash
Daulatabad
Girishk
Registan
Pishin
Botan Pass
Quetta
Sibi
Khanpur
Dera Ghazi Khan
KRASAN
Neh
Hamun-i-Helmand
Helmand
Khash Rud
Nushki
Kalat
Jacobabad
Sukkur
AD
Dasht-i-Lut
Ravar
Kerman
Saguch
3994
Saidabad
Kunj-i-Lalehzar
4419
Zahidan
Ladis
Shahr-i-Zabul
Kuh-i-Taftan
4042
Dizak
Kharan
Ras Koh
3003
Gandava
Dolbandin
Larkana
Nawabshah
Shikarpur
INDIA
PAKISTAN
Kotri
Hyderabad
Bampur
Magas
Mashkel
Panjgur
Jhao
Bela
Karachi
Daulatabad
Khanu
Haliri
Shomil
Minab
Bandar Abbas
Qishm I.
2057
Ramishk
Kuhran
2163
Fanuch
Dardan Dasht
Pasni
Ormara
Sonmiani
Jask
MAKRAN
Gwadar
Chahbar
Sharja
Kishar Ra
Las Bela
A Sohar
Burqaimi
Al Khabura
Matrah
Muscat
Gulf of Oman
Tropic of Cancer
ARAB
haih
Dhank
J. ash Sham
3019
Sarur
2151
Sur
Batha
Ras al Hadd
O M A N
As Suwaih
Sharkh
Arabian Sea
W. Muaiini
W. Kalbuh
W. Andam
Al Masira
Al Khalaf
Gulf of Masira
Ras al Madraka
Al Ain
Al Juwara
Al Jazir
Saugra Bay
Dhofar
1678
Kuria Muria Is.
Salala
Marbat
Bay
rtak
Socotra (South Yemen)
The Brothers
East from Greenwich
55

Right map (Palestine)

34
36
BEIRUT (Bayrut)
Djounie (Juniyah)
Ghazir
Raisoun
J. Sannini
2628
Ba'labakk (Baalbek)
Bikfaya
Dhour
Rayt
Meri
Zahlah
Rayak
Choueifat
Baabda
Aley
Hammoha
Ser 'aaya
Anti Lebanon
2462
Zabdani
N. el Damour
Beit Eddine
Moukhtara
Joub Jennine
LEBANON
N. Bisri
Jezzine
Sayda (Sidon)
Rachaya
Damascus (Esh Sham)
Dareiya
Ras Sarafand
Hasbaiya
Hermon
2814
Qatana
Kiswe
Tyre (Sur)
Nabatiye el Tahta
Merjayoun
N.F. Litani
Joudiya
Metulla
Banias
Massade
Jebel el Leja
Zakiye
Tibnin
Benni
Ibail
Hula (Reclumed)
Al Quanytirah
Sanamein
Ras en Naqura
Ladder of Tyre
Aolma ech Choab
Me'ona
Rosh Pinna
PIPELINE
Khushniyed
Uassem
Nawa
Nahariya
Beit Janna
1208
Tsefat (Safad)
Butmiya
Izr'a
Acre
Carmiel
Roma
Capernaum
GALILEE
B. of Haifa
Migdal
Kinneret (Sea of Galilee)
Al Aal
Sheikh Miskin
Haifa
Dir Yam
Kfar Ata
Shefar'am
Tiberias
Kafr Kanna
209
Figa
Tsil
N. el Harir
Tirat Karmel
Mt. Carmel
546
Ramat Yohanan
Nazareth
588
Kinneret
Umm Qays
Samar
Dar'a
Daal
Beit Oren
Atlit
Ramat David
Tabor Tor
515
Naharayim
Esh Shuna
W. el Arab
Kerem Mahral
Dor
Ramat Hashofet
Afula
Balfouriya
Beit Yosef
Beit Hashitta
Irbid
Ramtha
Zikhron Ya'aqov
Shelomo
Megiddo
Esdraelon
Taiyiba
Deir
Al Husn
Caesarea
Umm el Fahm
Janin
Beit Shean
Abu Said
PIPE LINE (DISUSED)
Pardes Hanna
Hadera
Karkur
Ya'bad
Qobatiya
1198
Ajlun
Hadera
W. Yabis
Jebel 'Ajlun
1247
El Madwar
Beit Yannai
SAMARIA
Anabta
Tubas
Kutrinja
Ajlun
Jarash
Netanya
Tul Karm
Sabastiya
940
W. el Fara
Zarqa
Arsuf
Taiyiba
Jacob's Well
Ra'anana
Qalqilyah Shariqya
881
Nablus
Huwwarah
Al Jiftalik
Herzliya
Kefar Sava
Al Lubban
Ramat Hashavim
Shilo
As Salt
Jebel Yusha'
1113
Az Zarqa
Benei Berad
Petah Tiqva
Salfit
1016
Suweilh
TEL AVIV-JAFFA
Ramat Gan
Or Yehuda
Giv'atn
Holon
Bat Yam
Bir Zeit
JORDAN
Amman
Rishon Le-Zion
Lod (Lydda)
Ram Allah
Rammun
Na'ar
Sahab
Nes Tsiyona
Ramla
El Bira
Jericho
Shunat Nimrin
Rehovot
Gezer
Mishmar Atarot
Hussein Br.
Hisban
Yavne
Soreq
Nevlat
Kallia
802
Ma'daba
Ashdod
Hattat
Gedera
Jerusalem
Eizariya
Qumran
Ashdod Yam
Beit
Bethlehem
Dead Sea
Ashqelon
Agur
JUDAEA
Helkish
Beit Guvrin
Halhul
1020
Hebron (El Khalil)
Qasr Daba
Beit Hanun
Qiryat Gat
Dura
W. el Heidan
Gaza (Ghazzah)
Beyor Hayil
Az Zahiriyah
Yatta
595
W. el Mujib
Dhiban
Khan Yunis
Gerar
Arad
Al Mazra
Ar Rabbah
Rafah
W. Habesor
Masada
Qatrana Sta.
Sedomo
Beersheba
Al Karak
EGYPT
Hatira
716
El Auja
N E G E V
30
35
36

ISRAEL

PALESTINE

Armistice boundary between Arab States and Israel, 1949

1:1 500 000
10   0   10   20   30 miles
10   0   10   20   30   40 km

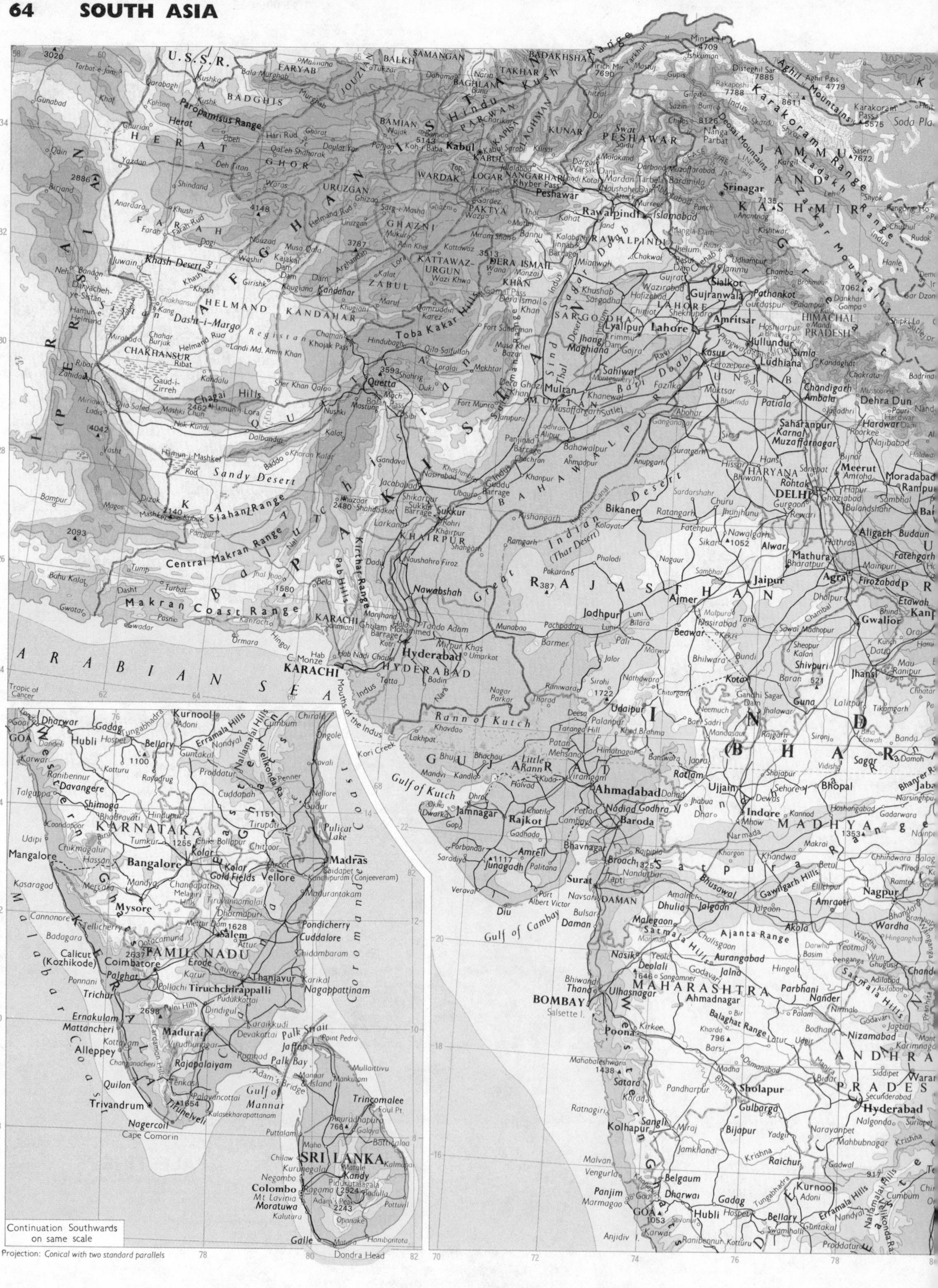

U.S.S.R.

ARABIAN SEA

AFGHANISTAN

PAKISTAN

INDIA (BHARAT)

KARACHI

DELHI

BOMBAY

Madras

Bangalore

Hyderabad

KASHMIR

JAMMU

HIMACHAL PRADESH

PUNJAB

HARYANA

RAJASTHAN

GUJARAT

MADHYA PRADESH

MAHARASHTRA

ANDHRA PRADESH

KARNATAKA

TAMIL NADU

GOA

SRI LANKA

Colombo

Tropic of Cancer

Great Indian (Thar Desert)

Rann of Kutch

Gulf of Kutch

Gulf of Cambay

Mouths of the Indus

Hindu Kush

Karakoram Mountains

Continuation Southwards on same scale

Projection: Conical with two standard parallels

ft	m
18 000	6000
12 000	4000
9000	3000
6000	2000
4500	1500
3000	1000
1200	400
600	200
0	0
600	200
m	ft

1:10 000 000

50　　0　　50　100　150　200 miles
50　0　50　100　150　200　250　300 km

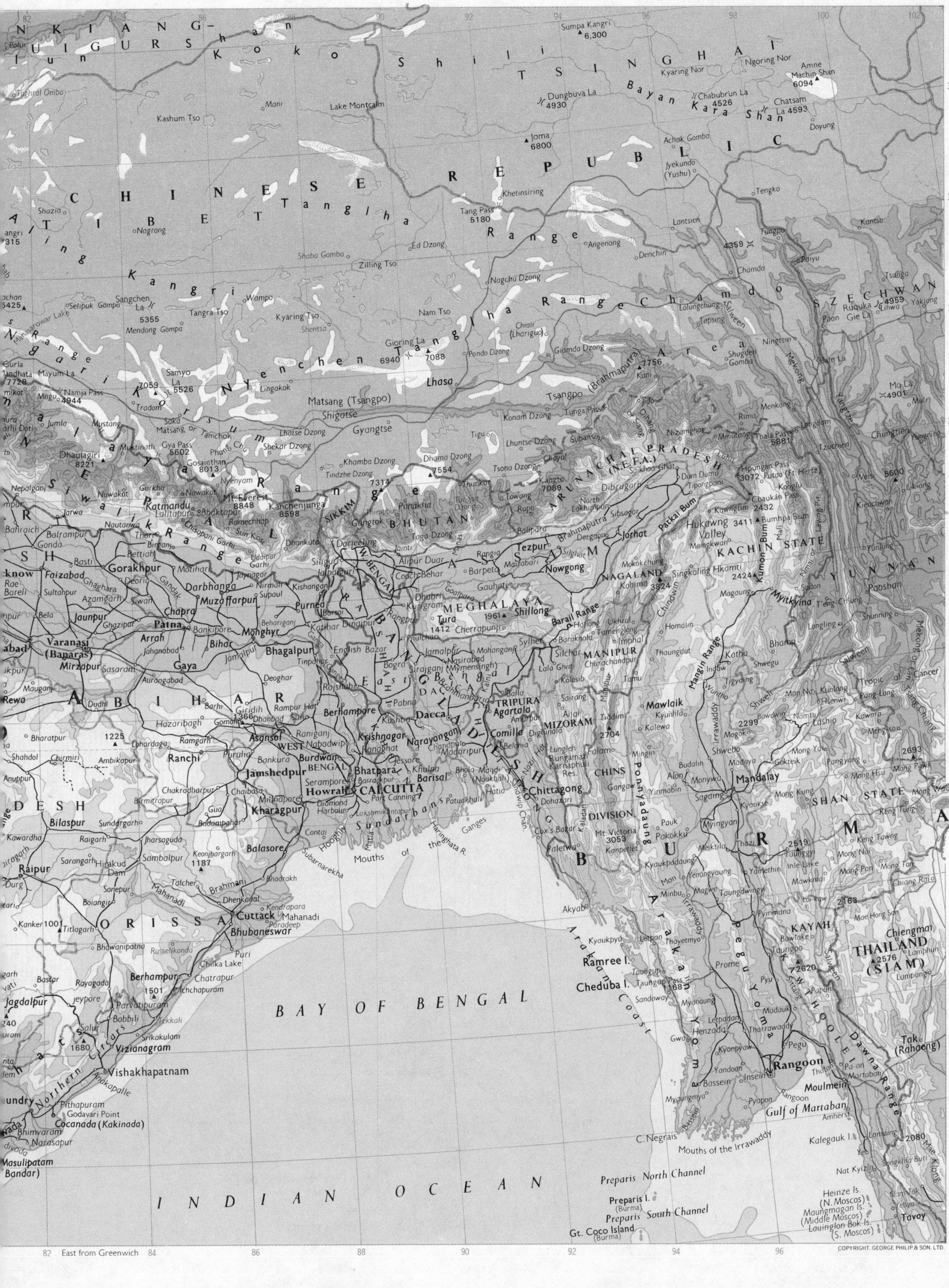

NKIANG-
uiGUR Shan
Koko　Shili
SUMPA Kangri
6,300
Kyaring Nor
Ngoring Nor
Amne Machin Shan
6094
TSINGHAI
Bayan Kara Shan
Dungbuva La 4930
Chabrun La 4526
Chatsam La 4593
Doyung

Kashum Tso
Lake Montcalm
Mani

CHINESE　REPUBLIC

Khetinsiring
Jyekundo (Yushu)
Tengko
Kantse

TIBET
Tang Pass 5180
Range
Angenong
Denchin
4359
Chamdo
Lantsien
Tungpo
SZECHWAN
Ruquka 4959
Pan Gie La Lhwa
Yakiang

Joma 6800

CHINESE
Ting Tanglha
Nagrong
Ed Dzong
Shaba Gomba
Zilling Tso
Nagchu Dzong
Tang Pass

Tang La Range
Chiali (Lhariguo)
Gioring La 6940
Tsangpo
Chamdo Area
Shugden Gomba
Ningtsin
Mo La 4901
Muli

Nam Tso

Nyenchen Tanglha Range
Pondo Dzong
Giamda Dzong
Tsangpo (Brahmaputra)
Jido
Rima
Tzuchen
Chungtien 5600

Lhasa
Matsang (Tsangpo)
Shigatse
Gyangtse
Konam Dzong
Tsela Dzong
Tsangpo
Tunga Pass
Kani
Lum
Menkong
Kiedchrad

Khamba Dzong
Dhama Dzong
Tsona Dzong
ARUNACHAL PRADESH (N.E.F.A.)
Hpungan Pass
Putao (Ft. Hertz)
Weisi

Gya Pass
Tindze Dzong
7554
Thinkor
Kapto 7089
North Lokhimpur
Dam Duma
Tipongdan
Chaukan Pass
Konglu

Mt. Everest 8848
Kanchenjunga 8598
SIKKIM
Gangtok
Punakha
Towang
Rupa
Dibrugarh
Hukawng Valley
Bumhpa Bum
Katha

Katmandu
Darjeeling
BHUTAN
Rangia
ASSAM
Tezpur
Sibsogar
Jorhat
Patkai Bum
Mokokchung
KACHIN STATE
Myitkyina

NEPAL
Siliguri
Jalpaiguri
Cooch Behar
Barpeta
Brahmaputra
Nowgong
NAGALAND
Kohima 3824
Singkaling Hkamti
Mogaung

Gorakhpur
Darbhanga
WEST BENGAL
Dhubri
Goalpara
Gauhati
MEGHALAYA
Tura 1961
Shillong
Barail Range
Haflong
Homalin

BIHAR
Patna
Bhagalpur
Purnea
Dinajpur
Rangpur
Cherrapunji 1412
Sylhet
Silchar
MANIPUR
Imphal
Thaungdut

Varanasi (Banaras)
Arrah
Gaya
Bogra
EAST BENGAL
Mymensingh
Lala
Kolasib
Tamu
Mawlaik

Mirzapur
Deoghar
BANGLADESH
Pabna
Dacca
Comilla
TRIPURA
Agartala
MIZORAM
Aijal
Tiddim 2704
Mingin
Mandalay

Ranchi
Asansol
Burdwan
WEST BENGAL
Krishnagar
Narayanganj
Barisal
CHINS
Falam
Shwebo
Monywa
SHAN STATE

Jamshedpur
Howrah
CALCUTTA
Kharagpur
Khulna
Sundarbans
Chittagong
CHINS DIVISION
Mt. Victoria 3053
BURMA

ORISSA
Cuttack
Bhubaneswar
Puri
Balasore
Mouths of the Ganges
Cox's Bazar
Akyab
Taungup
Prome
KAYAH

Berhampur
Chilka Lake
Mahanadi
Ramree I.
Cheduba I.
Sandoway
THAILAND (SIAM)
Chiengmai

Vishakhapatnam
Godavari Point

BAY OF BENGAL

Arakan Coast
Henzada
Pegu
Rangoon
Moulmein
Gulf of Martaban

Cocanada (Kakinada)
Masulipatam (Bandar)

C. Negrais
Mouths of the Irrawaddy

Preparis North Channel
Preparis I. (Burma)
Preparis South Channel
Gt. Coco Island (Burma)
Heinze Is. (N. Moscos)
Maungmagan Is. (Middle Moscos)
Launglon Bok Is. (S. Moscos)
Tavoy

INDIAN　OCEAN

East from Greenwich
COPYRIGHT. GEORGE PHILIP & SON. LTD.

Projection: Bonne

East from Greenwich

1:15 000 000

| 100 | 0 | 100 | 200 | 300 | 400 | miles |

| 100 | 0 | 100 | 200 | 300 | 400 | 500 | 600 | km |

HONSHU, SHIKOKU AND KYUSHU

1:7 500 000

| 50 | 0 | 50 | 100 | 150 | miles |

| 50 | 0 | 50 | 100 | 150 | 200 | km |

REFERENCE TO PREFECTURES

1 Aomori	16 Tokyo	32 Shimane
2 Akita	17 Saitama	33 Hiroshima
3 Iwate	18 Yamanashi	34 Yamaguchi
4 Yamagata	19 Shizuoka	35 Kagawa
5 Miyagi	20 Aichi	36 Tokushima
6 Fukushima	21 Gifu	37 Kochi
7 Niigata	22 Fukui	38 Ehime
8 Ishikawa	23 Shiga	39 Oita
9 Toyama	24 Mie	40 Fukuoka
10 Nagano	25 Nara	41 Saga
11 Gunma	26 Wakayama	42 Nagasaki
12 Tochigi	27 Osaka	43 Kumamoto
13 Ibaraki	28 Kyoto	44 Miyazaki
14 Chiba	29 Hyogo	45 Kagoshima
15 Kanagawa	30 Tottori	46 Hokkaido
	31 Okayama	

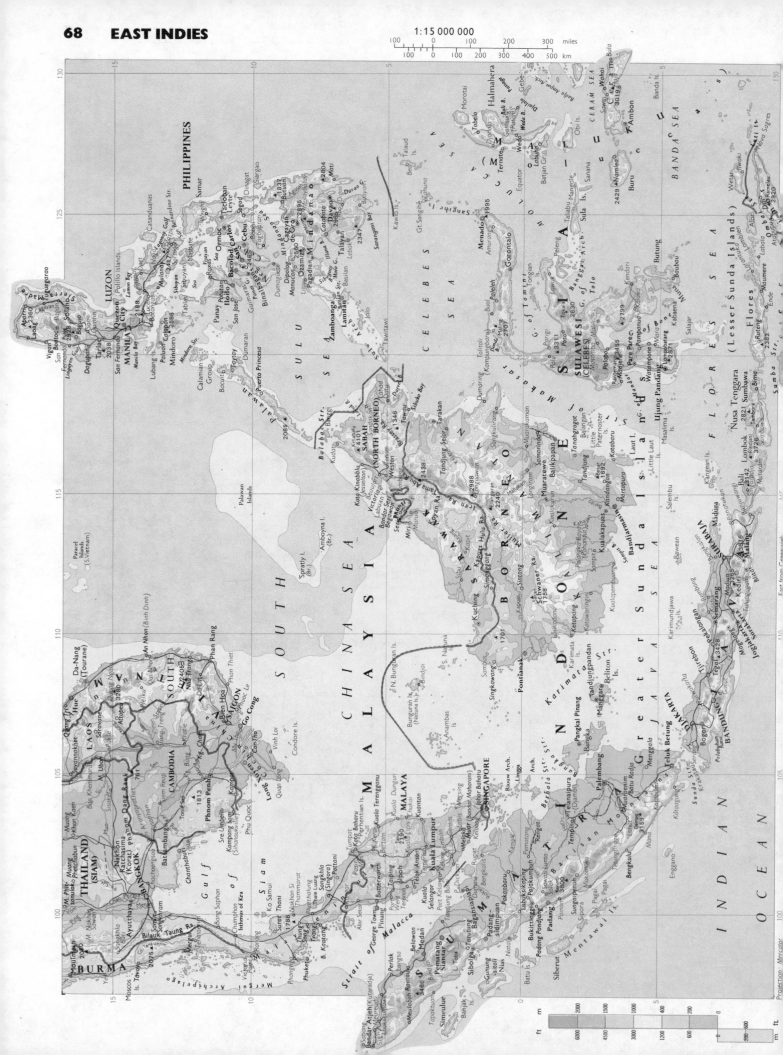

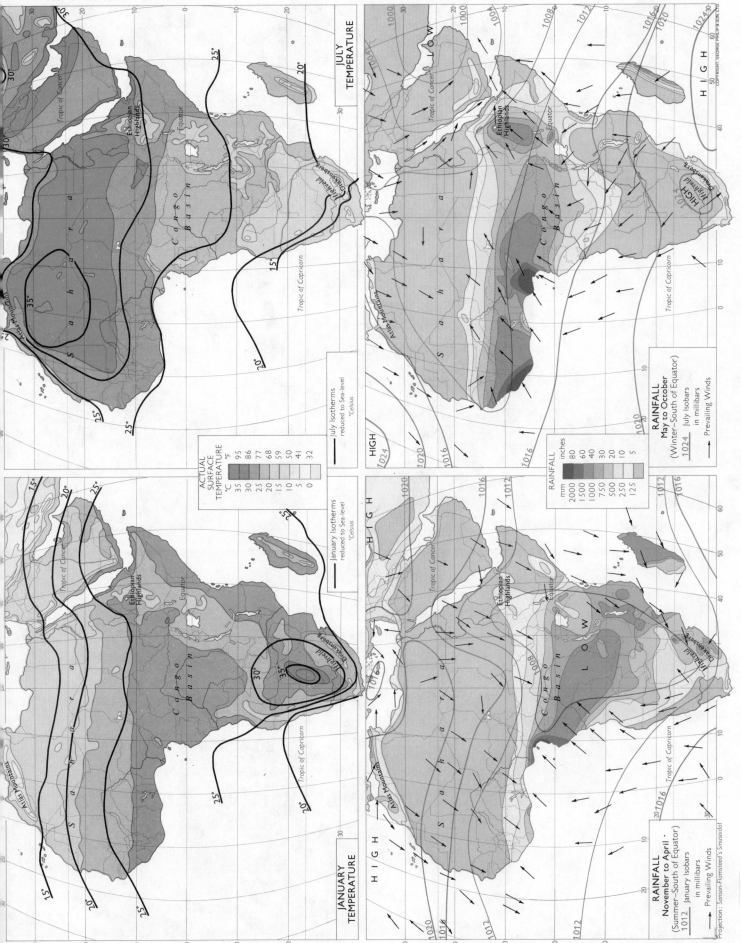

1:80 000 000

400   0   400   800   1200   1600 miles

400   0   400   800 1200 1600 2000 2400 km

JULY
TEMPERATURE

25°

20°

15°

20°

25°

Tropic of Cancer

Ethiopian Highlands

Equator

Congo Basin

Tropic of Capricorn

Atlas Mountains

S a h a r a

Drakensberg

ACTUAL
SURFACE
TEMPERATURE

°C	°F
35	95
30	86
25	77
20	68
15	59
10	50
5	41
0	32

July Isotherms
reduced to Sea-level
°Celsius

January Isotherms
reduced to Sea-level
°Celsius

JANUARY
TEMPERATURE

15°

20°

25°

25°

30°

35°

30°

35°

25°

20°

15°

Tropic of Cancer

Ethiopian Highlands

Equator

Congo Basin

Tropic of Capricorn

Atlas Mountains

S a h a r a

Drakensberg

RAINFALL
May to October
(Winter–South of Equator)
1024 July Isobars
in millibars
→ Prevailing Winds

RAINFALL

mm	inches
2000	80
1500	60
1000	40
750	30
500	20
250	10
125	5

LOW

HIGH

HIGH

HIGH

1000   1000   1004   1008   1012   1016   1020   1024

1024   1020   1016

1020

1016

Tropic of Cancer

Ethiopian Highlands

Equator

Congo Basin

Tropic of Capricorn

Atlas Mountains

S a h a r a

Drakensberg

HIGH

RAINFALL
November to April
(Summer–South of Equator)
1012 January Isobars
in millibars
→ Prevailing Winds

HIGH

LOW

1020   1016   1012   1016

1012

1016

1020

1016   1012

1008

1020   1016

Tropic of Cancer

Ethiopian Highlands

Equator

Congo Basin

Tropic of Capricorn

Atlas Mountains

S a h a r a

Drakensberg

Projection: Sanson-Flamsteed's Sinusoidal

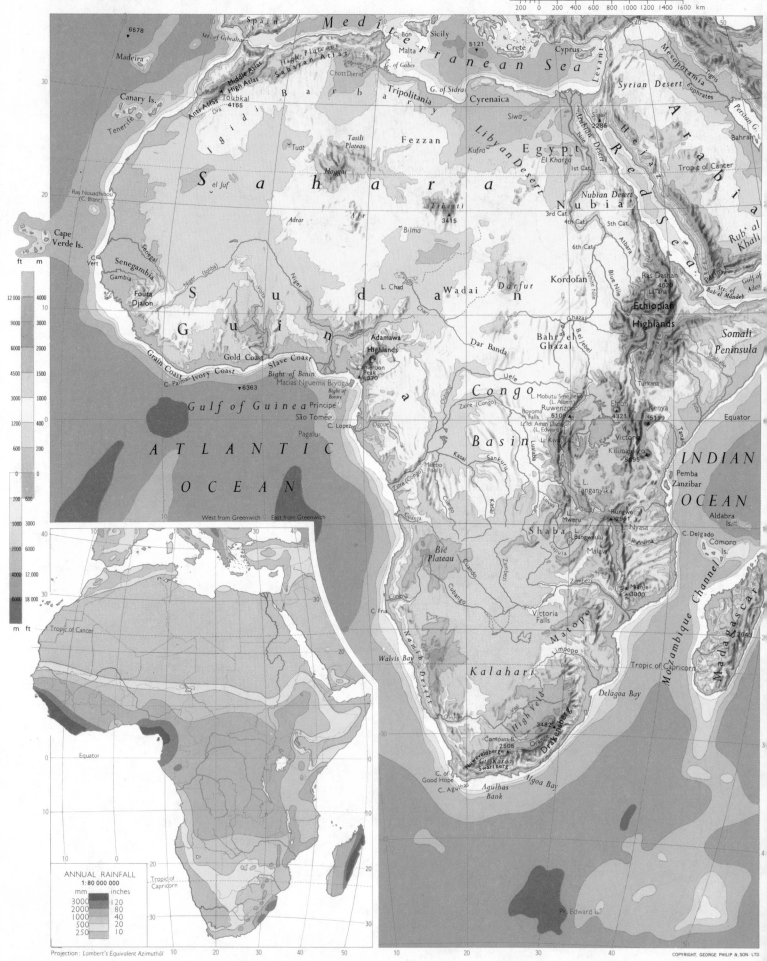

1:40 000 000

| 200 | 0 | 200 | 400 | 600 | 800 | 1000 miles |
| 200 | 0 | 200 | 400 | 600 | 800 | 1000 1200 1400 1600 km |

ANNUAL RAINFALL
1:80 000 000

mm	inches
3000	120
2000	80
1000	40
500	20
250	10

ft   m

12 000	4000
9000	3000
6000	2000
4500	1500
3000	1000
1200	400
600	200
0	0
200	600
1000	3000
2000	6000
4000	12 000
6000	18 000

m   ft

Projection: Lambert's Equivalent Azimuthal

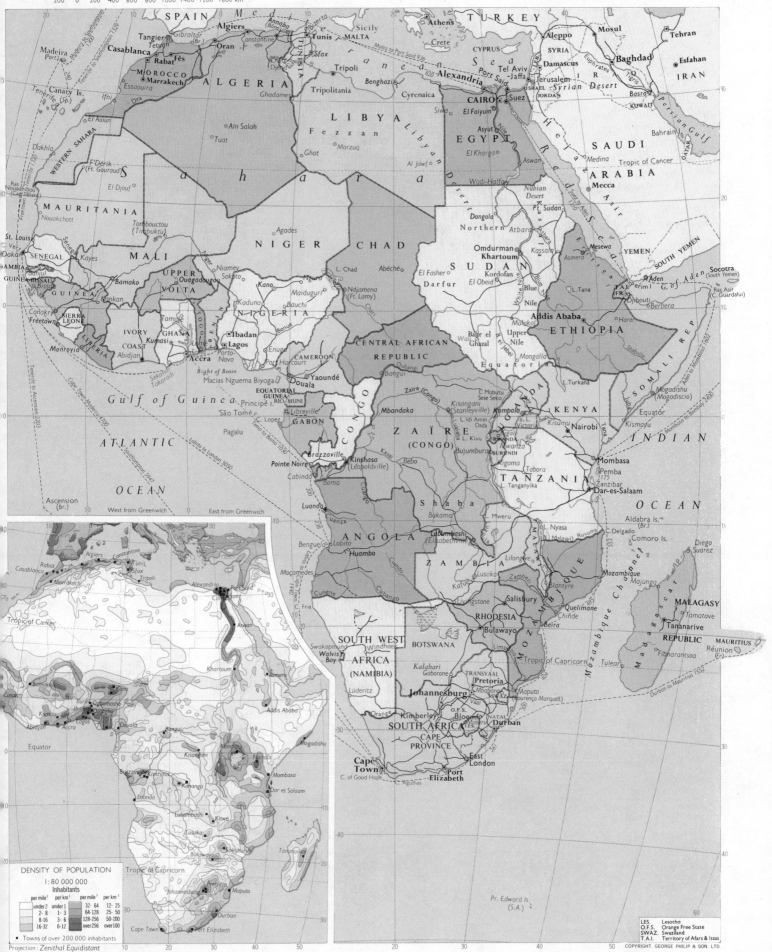

1 : 40 000 000

200   0   200   400   600   800   1000 miles
200   0   200   400   600   800   1000 1200 1400 1600 km

SPAIN   *Medi*   TURKEY
Tangier   Gibraltar   Algiers   Annaba   Bizerta   Sicily   Athens
Madeira   Tetuan   (Br.)   Constantine   TUNISIA   Tunis   MALTA   Crete   CYPRUS   Aleppo   Mosul   Tehran
(Port.)   Casablanca   Rabat   Fès   Oran   Sfax   Malta to Port Said 936   SYRIA   Damascus   IRAN   Esfahan
Canary Is.   Marrakech   Tripoli   Tropolitania   Benghazi   Cyrenaica   Alexandria   Port Said   Tel Aviv   Jerusalem   Baghdad
Tenerife (Sp.)   Essaouira   Ghadames   CAIRO   Suez   ISRAEL   JORDAN   Basra   KUWAIT
Ifni   MOROCCO   Aïn Salah   El Faiyum   Syrian Desert   Bahrain   Persian Gulf
El Aaiun   Tuat   Marzuq   Al Jawf   El Kharga   SAUDI   QATAR
WESTERN SAHARA   Ghat   LIBYA   Siwa   Wadi Halfa   Medina   Tropic of Cancer
Dakhla   S   a   h   a   r   a   Fezzan   Asyut   Aswan   Nubian   Mecca   ARABIA
Ras el   El Djouf   Dongola   Desert   Pt. Sudan
Nouadhibou (Cap Blanc)   MAURITANIA   Northern   Atbara   Mesewa   YEMEN
St. Louis   Nouakchott   Tombouctou   Agades   Omdurman   Khartoum   Kassala   Asmera   SOUTH YEMEN
GAMBIA   Senegal   (Timbuktu)   NIGER   CHAD   L. Chad   Abéché   SUDAN   T.A.I.   Aden   Socotra
Banjul   SENEGAL   MALI   Niamey   Darfur   El Fasher   Kordofan   L. Tana   Djibouti   (South Yemen)
GUINEA BISSAU   Bamako   Sokoto   Kano   Ndjamena   El Obeid   Blue   Addis Ababa   Berbera
Conakry   GUINEA   UPPER   Kaduna   Maiduguri   (Ft. Lamy)   White   Nile   Harer   Ras Asir
Freetown   SIERRA   VOLTA   Bauchi   Bahr el   Nile   ETHIOPIA   (C. Guardafui)
LEONE   Ouagadougou   NIGERIA   Benue   CENTRAL AFRICAN   Ghazal   Upper   SOMALI REP
Monrovia   IVORY   Kumasi   GHANA   Ibadan   Enugu   REPUBLIC   Nile   Mongalla   Equator
LIBERIA   COAST   Tamale   Lagos   Porto   Port Harcourt   Bangui   Equatoria   L. Turkana
Sekondi   Abidjan   Accra   BENIN   Novo   CAMEROON   Yaoundé   Zaïre (Congo)   L. Mobutu   KENYA   INDIAN
Takoradi   TOGO   Bight of Benin   Douala   Sese Seko   Kisangani   Kampala   Kisumu   Nairobi   Kismayu
Macias Nguema Biyogo   EQUATORIAL   (Stanleyville)   L.   Victoria   Mombasa to Bombay 2400
Gulf of Guinea   GUINEA   RIO MUNI   CONGO   Mbandaka   L. Idi Amin   L.   Nairobi
Príncipe I.   Dada   RWANDA   Kivu   ZAÏRE   Bujumbura   BURUNDI   Mombasa
São Tomé   C. Lopez   GABON   Libreville   Kigoma   Tabora   Pemba
Pagalu   Brazzaville   Kinshasa   (CONGO)   Kasai   TANZANIA   Zanzibar
ATLANTIC   Pointe Noire   (Léopoldville)   Ilebo   Dar-es-Salaam
Cabinda   Boma   Shaba   L. Tanganyika
OCEAN   Luanda   Bukama   L. Mweru   Aldabra Is.   OCEAN
Ascension (Br.)   West from Greenwich   East from Greenwich   ANGOLA   Lubumbashi   L. Nyasa   C. Delgado   (Br.)
Benguela   Lobito   (Elisabethville)   (L. Malawi)   Comoro Is.   Diego
Moçâmedes   Huambo   ZAMBIA   Lilongwe   Suarez
SOUTH WEST   Lusaka   Blantyre   Mozambique   MALAGASY
Cunene   RHODESIA   Salisbury   Quelimane   Majunga   REPUBLIC   MAURITIUS
AFRICA   Swakopmund   Windhoek   Bulawayo   Beira   Tananarive   Réunion (Fr.)
(NAMIBIA)   Walvis Bay   BOTSWANA   Chinde   Fianarantsoa   Tuléar
Lüderitz   Kalahari   Limpopo   Tropic of Capricorn
SOUTH AFRICA   TRANSVAAL   Pretoria   Maputo
Johannesburg   SWAZ.   Lourenço Marques
Kimberley   O.F.S.   NATAL   Durban
CAPE   Bloemfontein   LES.
PROVINCE   East London
Cape Town   C. of Good Hope   Port Elizabeth   Pr. Edward Is. (S.A.)
C. Agulhas

DENSITY OF POPULATION
1 : 80 000 000
Inhabitants

per mile²	per km²	per mile²	per km²
under 2	under 1	32–64	12–25
2–8	1–3	64–128	25–50
8–16	3–6	128–256	50–100
16–32	6–12	over 256	over 100

■ Towns of over 200 000 inhabitants

Projection : *Zenithal Equidistant*

LES.   Lesotho
O.F.S. Orange Free State
SWAZ.   Swaziland
T.A.I. Territory of Afars & Issas

COPYRIGHT. GEORGE PHILIP & SON. LTD.

NORTH ATLANTIC

OCEAN

SPAIN

Algiers (Alger)

Constantine

Oran

TUNISIA

Cádiz
C. St. Vincent
Str. of Gibraltar
Gibraltar (Br.)
Tangier
Ceuta (Sp.)
Tétouan
Melilla
Al Hoceima
Oujda
Tlemcen

Kenitra
Salé
Rabat
Fès
Taza

Casablanca
El Jadida
Meknès
Khouribga
Settat
Safi

Madeira (Port.)
Funchal
Pto. Santo

MOROCCO

Middle Atlas
High Atlas
Anti Atlas

Marrakech
Essaouira
Agadir
Ifni
Taroudant
Ouarzazate

Béchar

ALGERIA

El Goléa
Hassi Messaoud
Ghardaïa
Ouargla
El Oued

Plateau du Tademaït
Adrar
In Salah
Aoulef Arab
Reggane

Canary Is. (Span.)
Palma
Lanzarote
Fuerteventura
Arrecife
Tenerife
Gomera
Sta. Cruz
Gran Canaria
Las Palmas
Hierro

EL AAIUN
Smara
C. Bojador

WESTERN SAHARA

Dakhla

MAURITANIA

Tindouf
Ain Ben Tili
Bir Mogrein (Ft. Trinquet)

Chegga

Tanezrouft

Hoggar
Tahat 2918
Tamanrasset (Ft. Laperrine)

Djanet (Ft. Charlet)
Idelès

Nouadhibou (Port Etienne)
C. Blanc

F'Dérik (Ft. Gouraud)
Zouérate
Atar
Chinguetti
Ouadane

Tamsagout
Terhazza
Taoudenni

Adrar
Tessalit

Air (Azbine)
Tamgak Mts.
Agadès
In Gall

Nouakchott
Rachid
Tidjikja
Akreijit
Moudjeria

Araouane
Bou Djebeha
Kidal

Tichit
Tamchakett
Néma
Oualata

MALI
Bamba
Gao
Bourem
Menaka

Tombouctou (Timbuktu)
Goundam
Diré
Kabara
Gourma-Rarous
Ansongo

NIGER

St. Louis
Louga
Thiès
Dakar
Kaolack

SENEGAL
Linguère
Matam

Nioro
Nara
Sokolo

GAMBIA
Banjul

Tambacounda

GUINEA
BISSAU
Bissau

Kayes
Bafoulabé
Bamako
Ségou
Mopti

Ké-Macina
Djenné
San

UPPER
VOLTA

Niamey
Dosso

Tahoua
Madaoua
Maradi
Zinder
Kano

Fouta
Djalon
Tougué

Kita
Koutiala
Sikasso

Ouagadougou
Koudougou
Fada N'Gourma

Birni-n'Koni
Sokoto
Katsina

GUINEA
Conakry
Kankan

Bobo-Dioulasso
Banfora

Kaduna

SIERRA
LEONE
Freetown

IVORY
COAST

Korhogo
Bouna

Tamale
Yendi

TOGO
BENIN

Ogbomosho
Oyo
Ife
Oshogbo
Ibadan

NIGERIA

LIBERIA
Monrovia

Man

Bouaké

GHANA
Kumasi

Lomé
Porto Novo
Cotonou

Lagos
Abeokuta

Benin
City
Onitsha
Enugu
Aba

Abidjan
Accra
Cape Coast

Bight of Benin

Port
Harcourt

CAMEROON

EQUATORIAL GUINEA
Macias Nguema Biyoga

Projection: Sanson Flamsteed's Sinusoidal

West from Greenwich   East from Greenwich

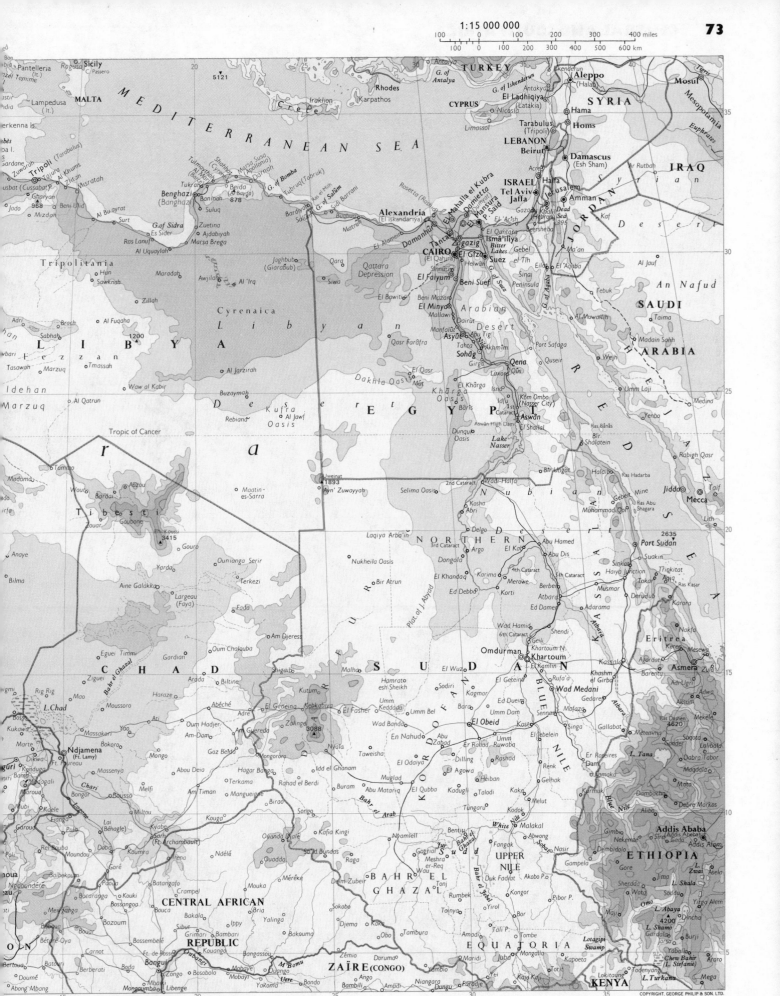

1:15 000 000

100   0   100   200   300   400 miles
100   0   100   200   300   400   500   600 km

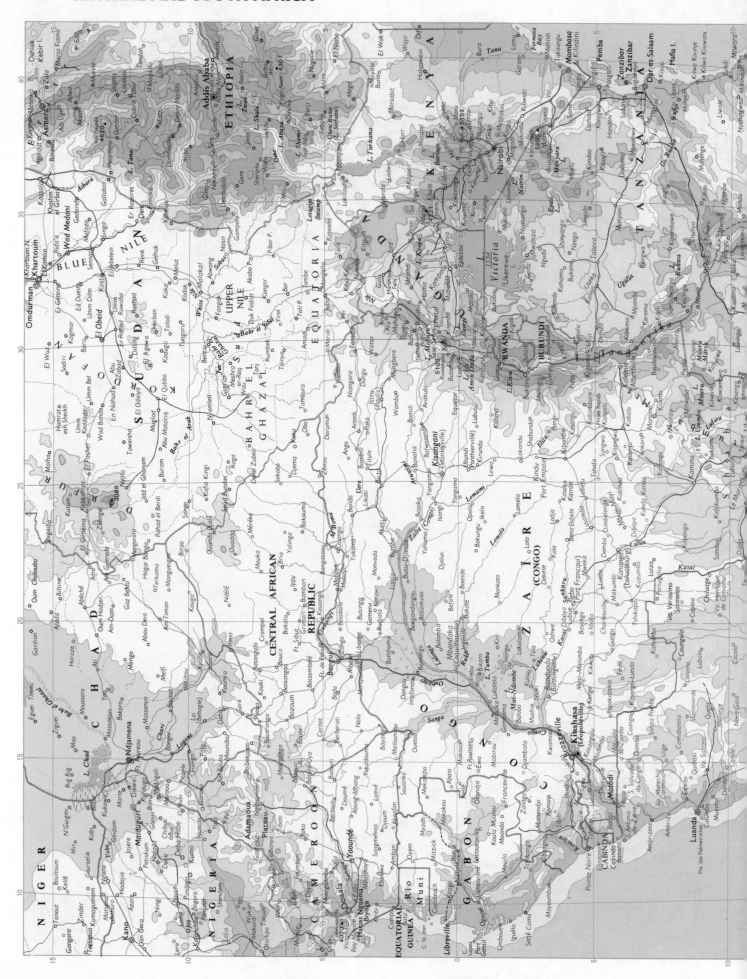

SOUTH AFRICA

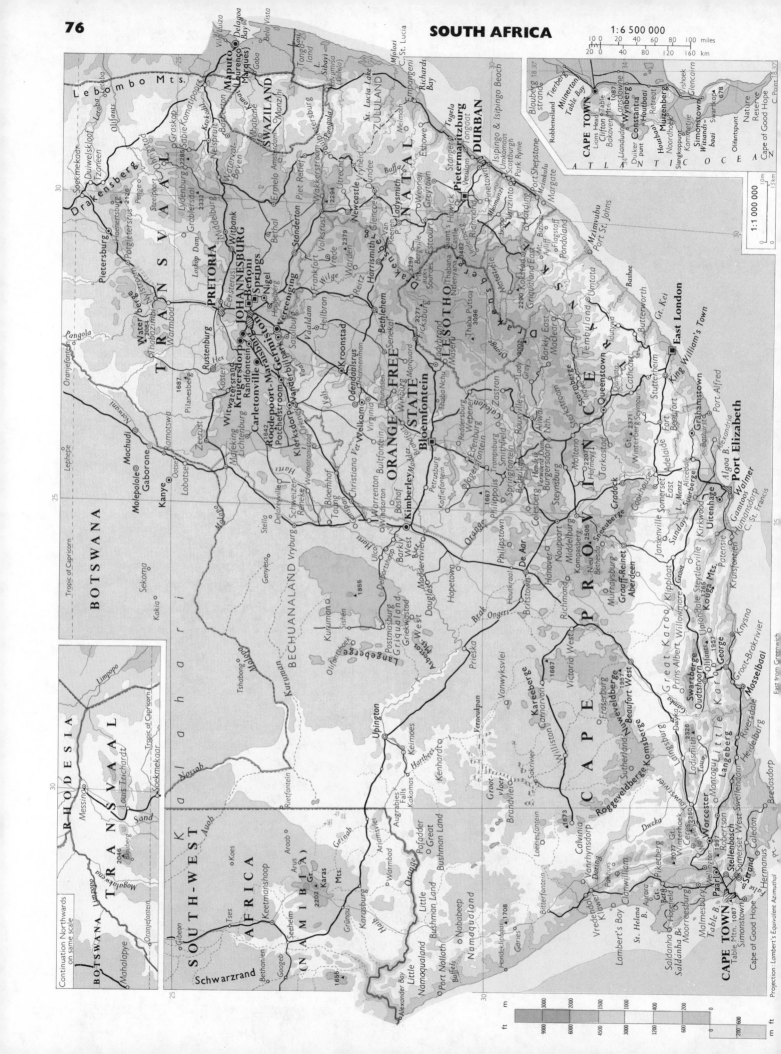

1:40 000 000

200 0 200 400 600 800 miles
200 0 200 400 600 800 1000 1200 km

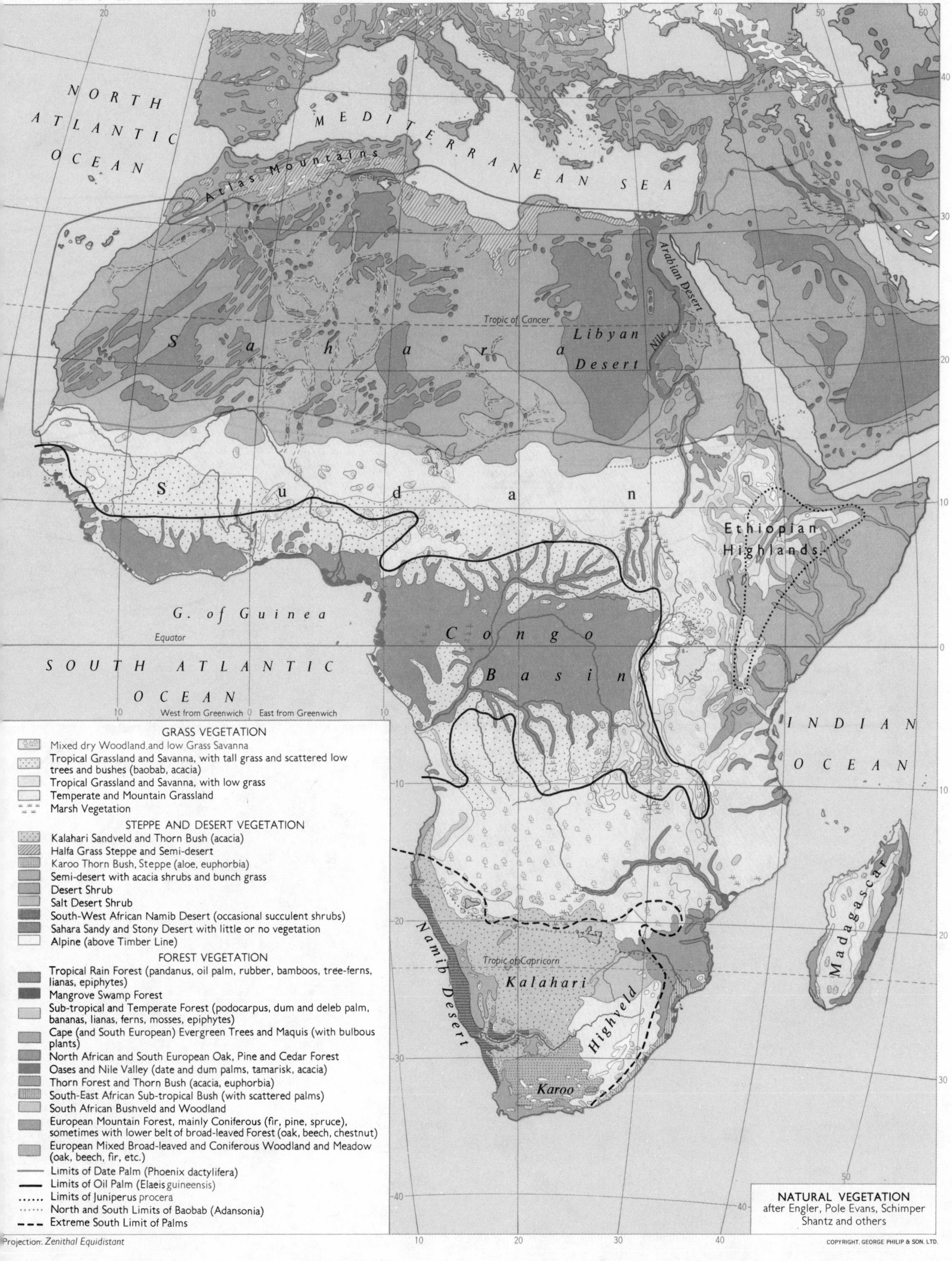

GRASS VEGETATION
Mixed dry Woodland and low Grass Savanna
Tropical Grassland and Savanna, with tall grass and scattered low trees and bushes (baobab, acacia)
Tropical Grassland and Savanna, with low grass
Temperate and Mountain Grassland
Marsh Vegetation

STEPPE AND DESERT VEGETATION
Kalahari Sandveld and Thorn Bush (acacia)
Halfa Grass Steppe and Semi-desert
Karoo Thorn Bush, Steppe (aloe, euphorbia)
Semi-desert with acacia shrubs and bunch grass
Desert Shrub
Salt Desert Shrub
South-West African Namib Desert (occasional succulent shrubs)
Sahara Sandy and Stony Desert with little or no vegetation
Alpine (above Timber Line)

FOREST VEGETATION
Tropical Rain Forest (pandanus, oil palm, rubber, bamboos, tree-ferns, lianas, epiphytes)
Mangrove Swamp Forest
Sub-tropical and Temperate Forest (podocarpus, dum and deleb palm, bananas, lianas, ferns, mosses, epiphytes)
Cape (and South European) Evergreen Trees and Maquis (with bulbous plants)
North African and South European Oak, Pine and Cedar Forest
Oases and Nile Valley (date and dum palms, tamarisk, acacia)
Thorn Forest and Thorn Bush (acacia, euphorbia)
South-East African Sub-tropical Bush (with scattered palms)
South African Bushveld and Woodland
European Mountain Forest, mainly Coniferous (fir, pine, spruce), sometimes with lower belt of broad-leaved Forest (oak, beech, chestnut)
European Mixed Broad-leaved and Coniferous Woodland and Meadow (oak, beech, fir, etc.)

Limits of Date Palm (Phoenix dactylifera)
Limits of Oil Palm (Elaeis guineensis)
Limits of Juniperus procera
North and South Limits of Baobab (Adansonia)
Extreme South Limit of Palms

NATURAL VEGETATION
after Engler, Pole Evans, Schimper Shantz and others

NORTH ATLANTIC OCEAN
MEDITERRANEAN SEA
Atlas Mountains
SOUTH ATLANTIC OCEAN
Equator
G. of Guinea
Sahara
Tropic of Cancer
Libyan Desert
Arabian Desert
Nile
Sudan
Ethiopian Highlands
Congo Basin
INDIAN OCEAN
Madagascar
Namib Desert
Kalahari
Tropic of Capricorn
Highveld
Karoo

West from Greenwich   East from Greenwich

Projection: Zenithal Equidistant

1:60,000,000

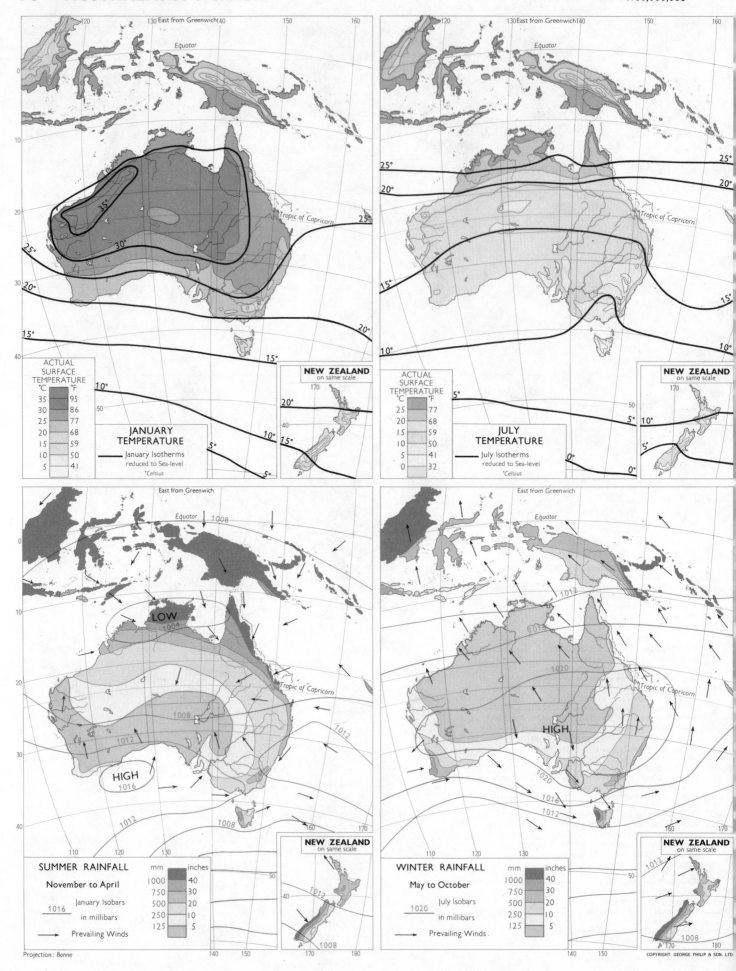

ACTUAL
SURFACE
TEMPERATURE
°C	°F
35	95
30	86
25	77
20	68
15	59
10	50
5	41

JANUARY TEMPERATURE

— January Isotherms
reduced to Sea-level
°Celsius

NEW ZEALAND
on same scale

ACTUAL
SURFACE
TEMPERATURE
°C	°F
25	77
20	68
15	59
10	50
5	41
0	32

JULY TEMPERATURE

— July Isotherms
reduced to Sea-level
°Celsius

NEW ZEALAND
on same scale

SUMMER RAINFALL

November to April

1016 — January Isobars
in millibars

→ Prevailing Winds

mm	inches
1000	40
750	30
500	20
250	10
125	5

NEW ZEALAND
on same scale

WINTER RAINFALL

May to October

1020 — July Isobars
in millibars

→ Prevailing Winds

mm	inches
1000	40
750	30
500	20
250	10
125	5

NEW ZEALAND
on same scale

Projection: Bonne

COPYRIGHT. GEORGE PHILIP & SON. LTD.

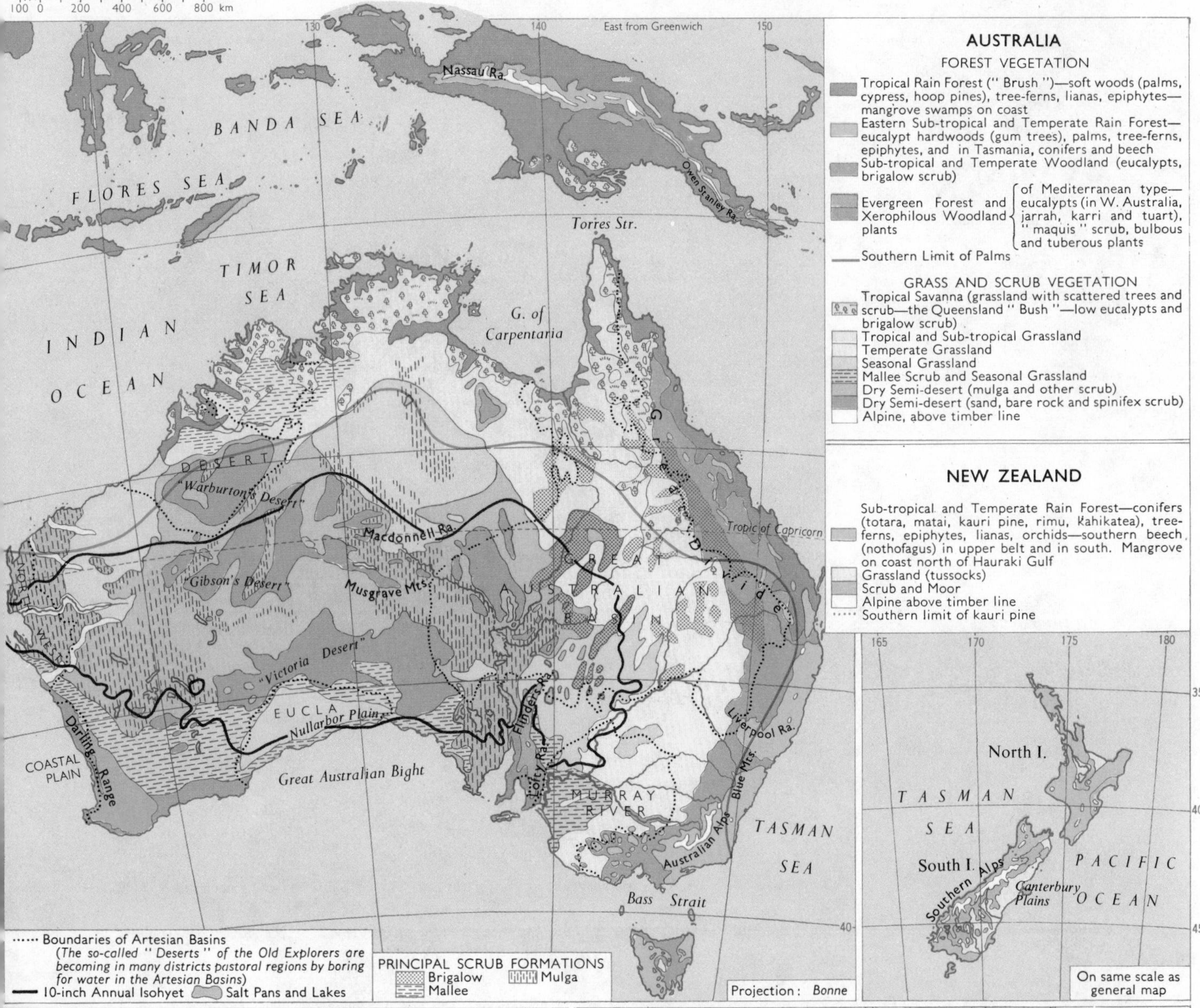

1:30 000 000

100 0 100 200 300 400 500 miles
100 0 200 400 600 800 km

AUSTRALIA
FOREST VEGETATION

Tropical Rain Forest (" Brush ")—soft woods (palms, cypress, hoop pines), tree-ferns, lianas, epiphytes—mangrove swamps on coast

Eastern Sub-tropical and Temperate Rain Forest—eucalypt hardwoods (gum trees), palms, tree-ferns, epiphytes, and in Tasmania, conifers and beech

Sub-tropical and Temperate Woodland (eucalypts, brigalow scrub)

Evergreen Forest and Xerophilous Woodland plants { of Mediterranean type—eucalypts (in W. Australia, jarrah, karri and tuart), " maquis " scrub, bulbous and tuberous plants }

Southern Limit of Palms

GRASS AND SCRUB VEGETATION

Tropical Savanna (grassland with scattered trees and scrub—the Queensland " Bush "—low eucalypts and brigalow scrub)
Tropical and Sub-tropical Grassland
Temperate Grassland
Seasonal Grassland
Mallee Scrub and Seasonal Grassland
Dry Semi-desert (mulga and other scrub)
Dry Semi-desert (sand, bare rock and spinifex scrub)
Alpine, above timber line

NEW ZEALAND

Sub-tropical and Temperate Rain Forest—conifers (totara, matai, kauri pine, rimu, Kahikatea), tree-ferns, epiphytes, lianas, orchids—southern beech (nothofagus) in upper belt and in south. Mangrove on coast north of Hauraki Gulf
Grassland (tussocks)
Scrub and Moor
Alpine above timber line
Southern limit of kauri pine

····· Boundaries of Artesian Basins
(The so-called " Deserts " of the Old Explorers are becoming in many districts pastoral regions by boring for water in the Artesian Basins)
— 10-inch Annual Isohyet ⌗ Salt Pans and Lakes

PRINCIPAL SCRUB FORMATIONS
Brigalow Mulga
Mallee

Projection : *Bonne*

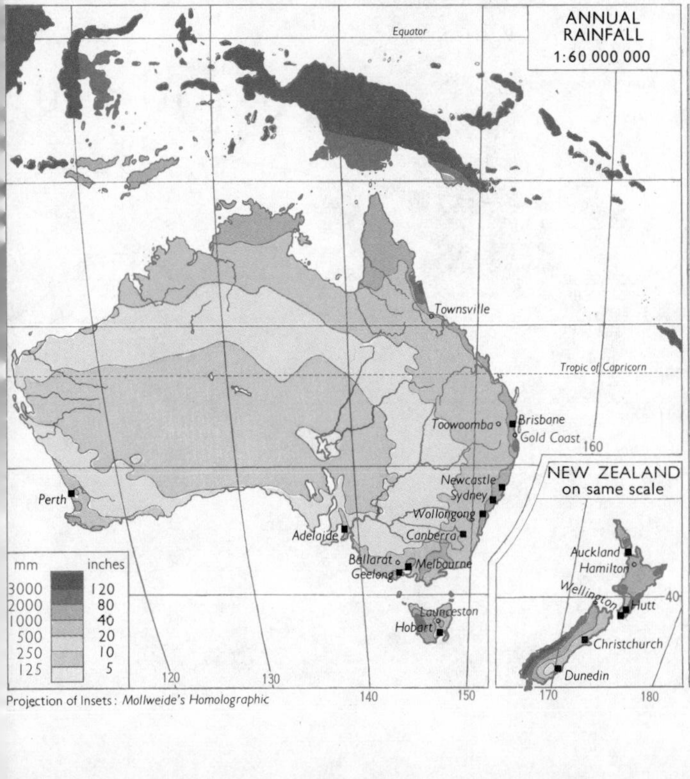

On same scale as general map

BANDA SEA
FLORES SEA
TIMOR SEA
INDIAN OCEAN
Nassau Ra.
Owen Stanley Ra.
Torres Str.
G. of Carpentaria
DESERT
Warburton's Desert
Gibson's Desert
Musgrave Mts.
Macdonnell Ra.
"Victoria Desert"
EUCLA
Nullarbor Plain
Great Australian Bight
COASTAL PLAIN
Darling Range
Tropic of Capricorn
GREAT AUSTRALIAN BASIN
Liverpool Ra.
Blue Mts.
Flinders Ra.
MURRAY RIVER
Australian Alps
TASMAN SEA
Bass Strait
North I.
South I.
TASMAN SEA
Southern Alps
Canterbury Plains
PACIFIC OCEAN

East from Greenwich

ANNUAL RAINFALL
1:60 000 000

Equator
Townsville
Tropic of Capricorn
Toowoomba
Brisbane
Gold Coast
Perth
Newcastle
Sydney
Wollongong
Adelaide
Canberra
Ballarat
Geelong
Melbourne
Launceston
Hobart

NEW ZEALAND on same scale
Auckland
Hamilton
Wellington
Hutt
Christchurch
Dunedin

mm / inches
3000 / 120
2000 / 80
1000 / 40
500 / 20
250 / 10
125 / 5

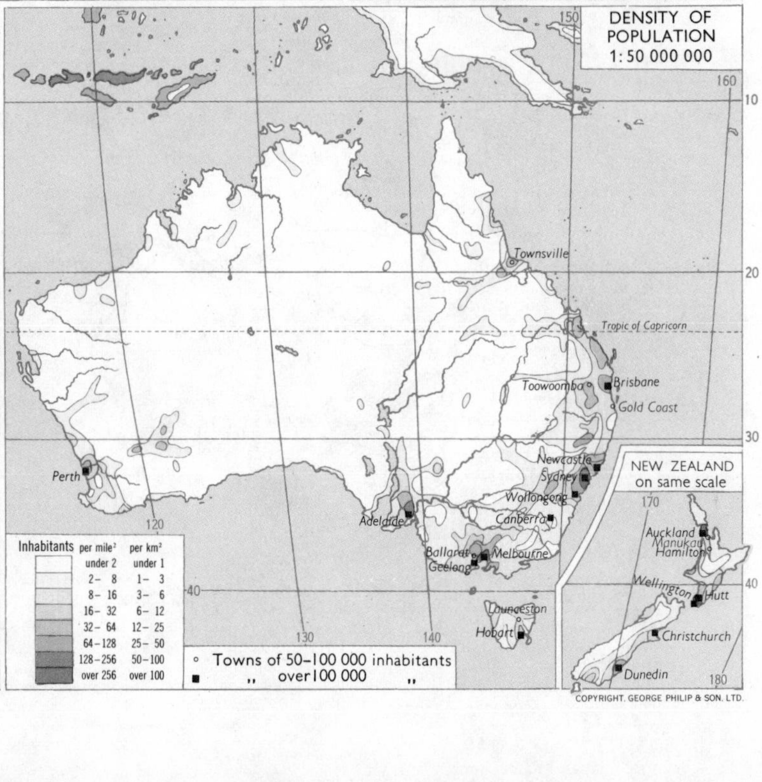

DENSITY OF POPULATION
1:50 000 000

Townsville
Tropic of Capricorn
Toowoomba
Brisbane
Gold Coast
Perth
Newcastle
Sydney
Wollongong
Canberra
Adelaide
Ballarat
Geelong
Melbourne
Launceston
Hobart

NEW ZEALAND on same scale
Auckland
Manukau
Hamilton
Wellington
Hutt
Christchurch
Dunedin

Inhabitants per mile² / per km²
under 2 / under 1
2 – 8 / 1 – 3
8 – 16 / 3 – 6
16 – 32 / 6 – 12
32 – 64 / 12 – 25
64 – 128 / 25 – 50
128 – 256 / 50 – 100
over 256 / over 100

○ Towns of 50–100 000 inhabitants
■ " over 100 000 "

Projection of Insets : *Mollweide's Homolographic*

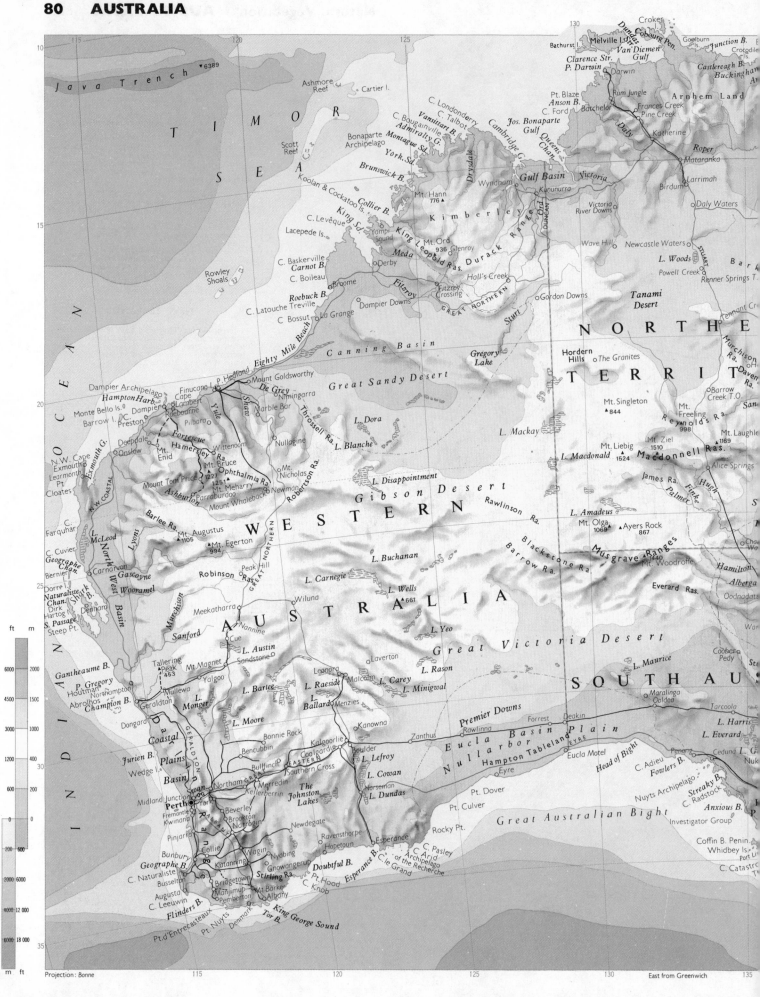

TIMOR SEA

INDIAN OCEAN

Java Trench ▼6389

Ashmore Reef
Cartier I.
Scott Reef
Rowley Shoals

C. Londonderry
C. Talbot
Vansittart B.
Admiralty G.
Montague Sd.
York Sd.
Brunswick B.
Bonaparte Archipelago
Koolan & Cockatoo Is.
Collier B.
King Sd.
C. Lévêque
Lacepede Is.
C. Baskerville
Carnot B.
C. Boileau
Roebuck B.
C. Latouche Treville
C. Bossut

Jos. Bonaparte Gulf
Cambridge G.
Queens Chan.
Wyndham
Kununurra
Gulf Basin
Drysdale
Ord
Duncan

Croker
Cobourg Pen.
Goulburn Is.
Junction B.
Crocodile Is.
Bathurst I.
Melville I.
Dundas
Van Diemen Gulf
Clarence Str.
P. Darwin
Darwin
Castlereagh B.
Buckingham
Arnhem Land

Pt. Blaze
Anson B.
C. Ford
Batchelor
Rum Jungle
Frances Creek
Pine Creek
Katherine
Roper
Mataranka
Victoria
Larrimah
Birdum
Daly Waters

Bark
L. Woods
Powell Creek
Renner Springs
Tanami Desert

Mt. Hann 776
Kimberley
Mt. Ord 936
Glenroy
King Leopold Ras.
Durack Range
Derby
Meda
Hall's Creek
Fitzroy Crossing
Broome
Dampier Downs
La Grange
Fitzroy
Great Northern
Sturt
Gregory Lake
Gordon Downs
Victoria River Downs
Wave Hill
Newcastle Waters

Canning Basin
Eighty Mile Beach
P. Hedland
Mount Goldsworthy
Finucane I.
Cape Lambert
Nimingarra
Marble Bar
Throssell Ra.
Nullagine
L. Blanche
L. Dora
Great Sandy Desert
Hordern Hills
The Granites
Mt. Singleton 844
Mt. Freeling 998
Reynolds Ra.
Barrow Creek T.O.
San
Daveh Ra.
Murchison Ra.

NORTHE
TERRIT

Dampier Archipelago
Monte Bello Is.
Barrow I.
C. Preston
C. Dampier
HamptonHarb.
Roebourne
Pilbara
De Grey
Shaw
Yule
Fortescue
Deepdale
Onslow
Mt. Enid
Wittenoom
Hamersley Ra.
Mt. Bruce 1227
Ophthalmia Ra.
Mount Tom Price 1251
Mt. Meharry
Parraburdoo
Ashburton
Mount Whaleback
Newman
Robertson Ra.
Mt. Nicholas
L. Disappointment
L. Mackay
Mt. Liebig 1510
Mt. Ziel 1169
L. Macdonald 1524
Macdonnell Ras.
Alice Springs
James Ra.
Finke
Hugh
Palmer

N.W. Cape
Exmouth G.
Exmouth
Learmonth
Pt. Cloates
Farquhar
C. Cuvier
Geographe Chan.
Bernier
Dorre I.
Naturaliste Chan.
Dirk Hartog I.
S. Passage
Steep Pt.
Denham
Shark B.
N.W. Coastal
North West
Barlee Ra.
Mt. Augustus 1105
Mt. Egerton 994
Peak Hill
Robinson
Ras.
L. McLeod
Lyons
Gascoyne
Carnarvon
Wooramel
Murchison

WESTERN
Gibson Desert
Rawlinson Ra.
L. Buchanan
Blackstone Ra.
Barrow Ra.
Musgrave Ranges
L. Amadeus
Mt. Olga 1069
Ayers Rock 867
Mt. Woodroffe 1440
Everard Ras.
Hamilton
Alberga
Oodnadat

AUSTRALIA

L. Carnegie
L. Wells 661
L. Yeo
Great Victoria Desert
L. Rason
L. Maurice
Cooper Pedy
Maralinga
Ooldea
SOUTH AU

Meekatharra
Sanford
Nannine
Cue
L. Austin
Sandstone
Wiluna
Laverton
Leonora
Malcolm
L. Carey
L. Minigwal
Premier Downs
Forrest
Rawlinna
Deakin
Tarcoola
L. Harris
L. Everard

Gantheaume B.
P. Gregory
Houtman Abrolhos
Northampton
Champion B.
Geraldton
Dongara
Tallering Peak 453
Mullewa
Yalgoo
Mt. Magnet
L. Barlee
Leonora
L. Raeside
L. Ballard
Menzies
Kanowna
Kalgoorlie
Boulder
Coolgardie
Zanthus
Eucla Basin
Nullarbor Plain
Hampton Tableland
Eucla Motel
Eyre
C. Adieu
Fowlers B.
Nuyts Archipelago
Cedaina
Streaky B.
C. Radstock
Anxious B.
Investigator Group

Jurien B.
Wedge I.
Coastal
Plains
Basin
L. Monger
L. Moore
Bonnie Rock
Bencubbin
Bullfinch
Southern Cross
L. Lefroy
L. Cowan
Norseman
L. Dundas
Pt. Dover
Pt. Culver
Eucla
Head of Bight
Great Australian Bight
Rocky Pt.
Coffin B. Penin.
Whidbey Is.
Port Li
C. Catastro

Midland Junction
Perth
Fremantle
Kwinana
Northam
Merredin
Kellerberrin
York
Beverley
Brookton
Narrogin
Newdegate
The Johnston Lakes
Ravensthorpe
Hopetoun
Esperance
Esperance B.
C. le Grand
C. Arid
Archipelago of the Recherche
C. Pasley
Pinjarra
Collie
Bunbury
Geographe B.
C. Naturaliste
Busselton
Augusta
C. Leeuwin
Pt. d'Entrecasteaux
Pt. Nuyts
Bridgetown
Manjimup
Pemberton
Denham
Wagin
Nyabing
Gnowangerup
Doubtful B.
Pt. Hood
C. le Grand
Katanning
Stirling Ra.
Mt. Barker
Albany
C. Knob
Tor B.
King George Sound
Flinders B.

GREAT
ALBANY
EASTERN
GERALDTON

Scale bar:
ft / m
6000 / 2000
4500 / 1500
3000 / 1000
1200 / 400
600 / 200
0 / 0
200 / 600
2000 / 6000
4000 / 12 000
6000 / 18 000
m / ft

Projection: Bonne

East from Greenwich

1:12 000 000

100   0   100   200   miles
100   0   100   200   300   400 km

AUSTRALASIA
POLITICAL
1:80 000 000

TASMANIA

on same scale

COPYRIGHT. GEORGE PHILIP & SON. LTD

QUEENSLAND

NEW SOUTH WALES

VICTORIA

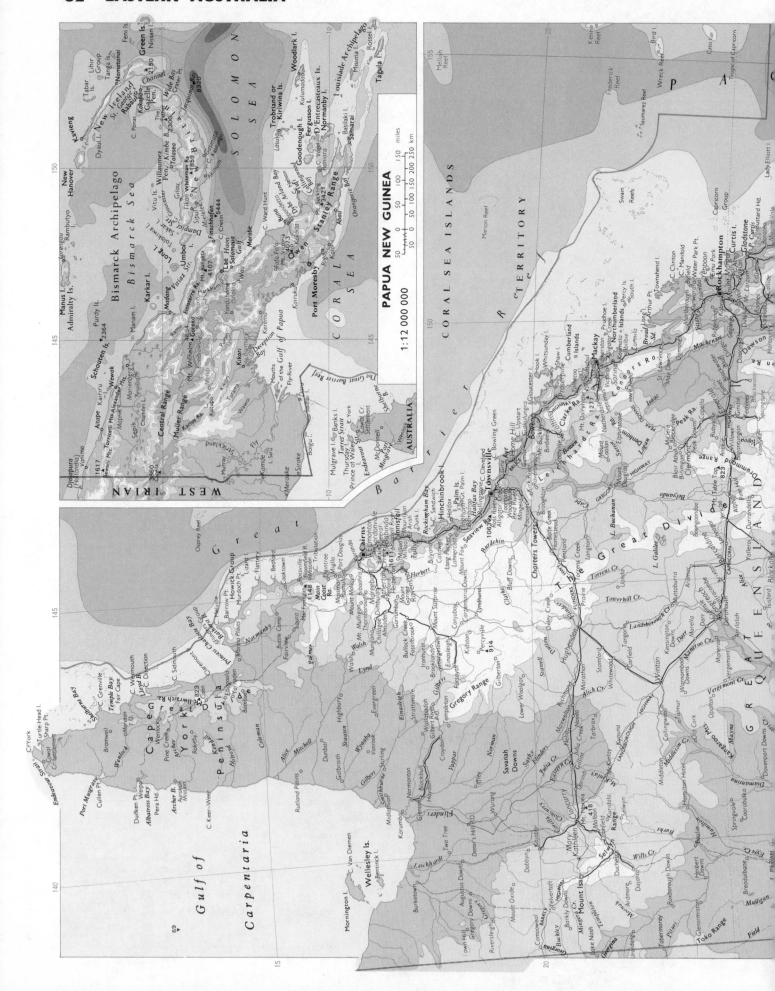

PAPUA NEW GUINEA

1:12 000 000

	miles
0 50 100 150	
0 50 100 150 200 250 km	

1:7 500 000

50   0   50   100   150   200 miles
50   0   50   100   150   200   250   300 km

PA C I F I C   O C E A N

T a s m a n   S e a

BRISBANE

SYDNEY & Port Jackson

Newcastle

NEW SOUTH WALES

Great Dividing Range

CANBERRA
AUSTRALIAN CAPITAL TERR.
COMMONWEALTH

Wollongong

MELBOURNE

VICTORIA

Ballarat   **Bendigo**

SOUTH AUSTRALIA

ADELAIDE

Broken Hill

Lake Eyre North

Lake Eyre South

Lake Torrens

Lake Frome

Lake Gairdner

Darling R.

Murray R.

Murrumbidgee R.

Spencer Gulf

Gulf St Vincent

Kangaroo I.

Bass   Strait

King Island

Flinders Island

Kent Group

TASMANIA

Hobart   **Launceston**

Continuation
Southwards

Projection: Bonne

East from Greenwich

COPYRIGHT: GEORGE PHILIP & SON, LTD.

m   ft
4000   12 000
2000   6000
1000   3000
400   1200
200   600
0   0
200   600
2000   6000
6000   18 000
12 000   24 000
m   ft

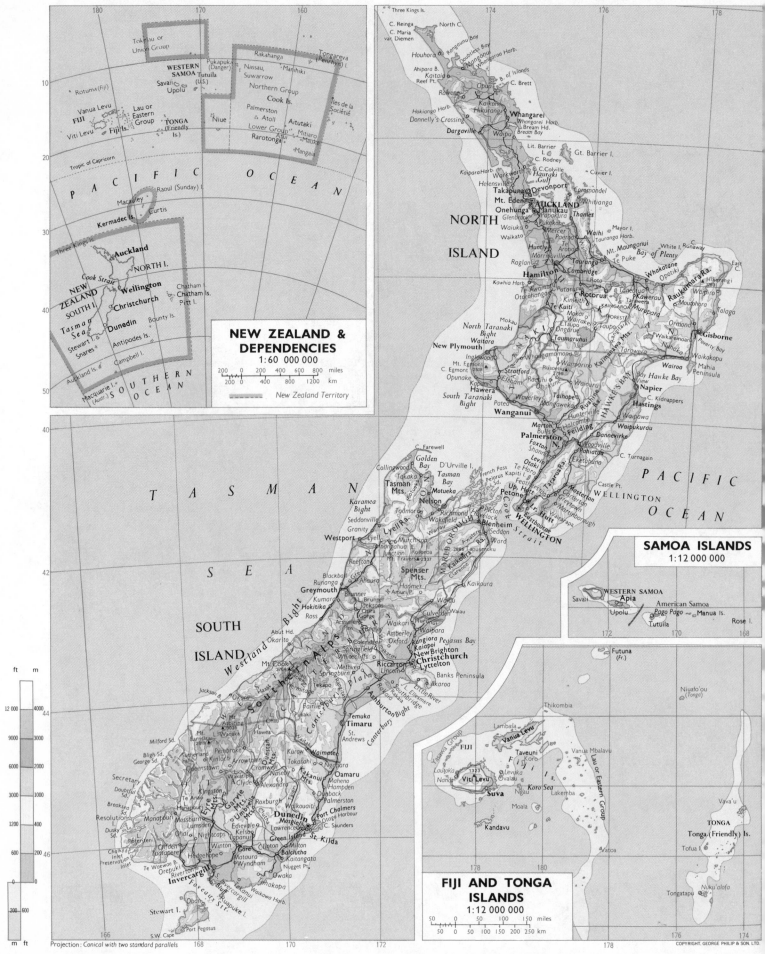

1:6 000 000
20 0 20 40 60 80 100 miles
20 0 20 40 60 80 120 160 km

NEW ZEALAND & DEPENDENCIES
1:60 000 000
200 0 200 400 600 800 miles
200 0 400 800 1200 km
New Zealand Territory

NORTH ISLAND

SOUTH ISLAND

SAMOA ISLANDS
1:12 000 000

WESTERN SAMOA Apia
Savaii Upolu American Samoa Pago Pago Manua Is.
Tutuila Rose I.

FIJI AND TONGA ISLANDS
1:12 000 000
50 0 50 100 150 miles
50 0 50 100 150 200 250 km

FIJI Vanua Levu Taveuni Koro
Viti Levu Suva Koro Sea Lau or Eastern Group

TONGA Tonga (Friendly) Is.

Projection: Conical with two standard parallels

COPYRIGHT. GEORGE PHILIP & SON. LTD.

ft m
12 000 4000
9000 3000
6000 2000
3000 1000
1200 400
600 200
0 0
200 600
m ft

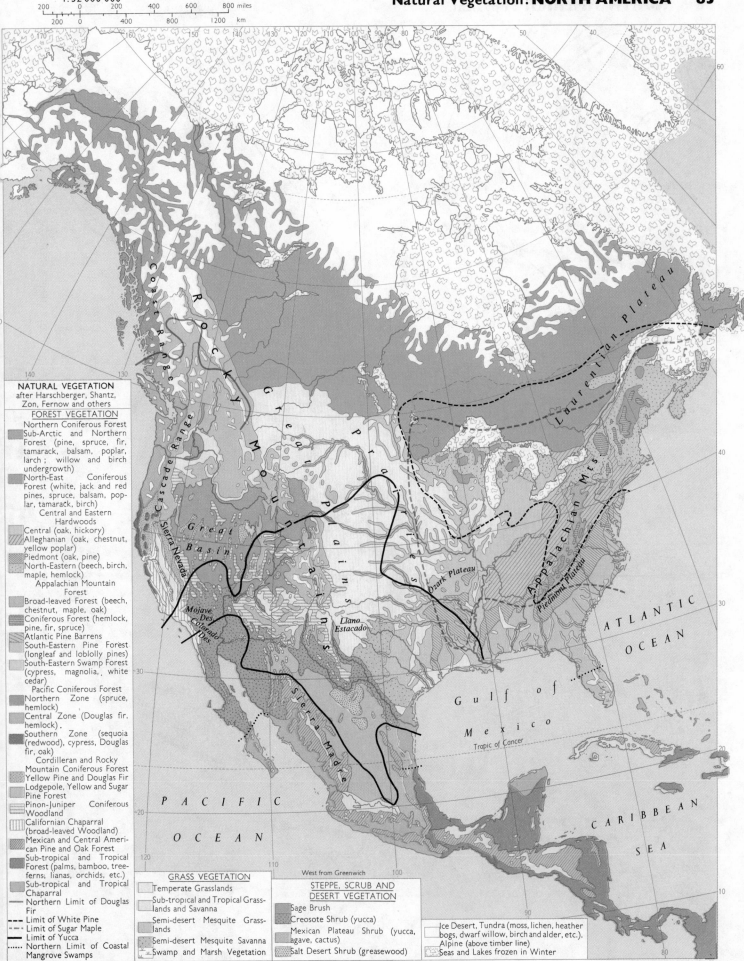

1 : 32 000 000

200   0   200   400   600   800 miles

200   0   200   400   800   1200 km

NATURAL VEGETATION
after Harschberger, Shantz,
Zon, Fernow and others

FOREST VEGETATION
Northern Coniferous Forest
- Sub-Arctic and Northern Forest (pine, spruce, fir, tamarack, balsam, poplar, larch ; willow and birch undergrowth)
- North-East Coniferous Forest (white, jack and red pines, spruce, balsam, poplar, tamarack, birch)

Central and Eastern Hardwoods
- Central (oak, hickory)
- Alleghanian (oak, chestnut, yellow poplar)
- Piedmont (oak, pine)
- North-Eastern (beech, birch, maple, hemlock)

Appalachian Mountain Forest
- Broad-leaved Forest (beech, chestnut, maple, oak)
- Coniferous Forest (hemlock, pine, fir, spruce)
- Atlantic Pine Barrens
- South-Eastern Pine Forest (longleaf and loblolly pines)
- South-Eastern Swamp Forest (cypress, magnolia, white cedar)

Pacific Coniferous Forest
- Northern Zone (spruce, hemlock)
- Central Zone (Douglas fir, hemlock).
- Southern Zone (sequoia (redwood), cypress, Douglas fir, oak)

Cordilleran and Rocky Mountain Coniferous Forest
- Yellow Pine and Douglas Fir
- Lodgepole, Yellow and Sugar Pine Forest
- Pinon-Juniper Coniferous Woodland
- Californian Chaparral (broad-leaved Woodland)
- Mexican and Central American Pine and Oak Forest
- Sub-tropical and Tropical Forest (palms, bamboo, tree-ferns, lianas, orchids, etc.)
- Sub-tropical and Tropical Chaparral
- Northern Limit of Douglas Fir
- - - Limit of White Pine
- - - Limit of Sugar Maple
- —— Limit of Yucca
- · · · · Northern Limit of Coastal Mangrove Swamps

Projection : Polyconic

GRASS VEGETATION
- Temperate Grasslands
- Sub-tropical and Tropical Grasslands and Savanna
- Semi-desert Mesquite Grasslands
- Semi-desert Mesquite Savanna
- Swamp and Marsh Vegetation

West from Greenwich

STEPPE, SCRUB AND DESERT VEGETATION
- Sage Brush
- Creosote Shrub (yucca)
- Mexican Plateau Shrub (yucca, agave, cactus)
- Salt Desert Shrub (greasewood)

- Ice Desert, Tundra (moss, lichen, heather bogs, dwarf willow, birch and alder, etc.). Alpine (above timber line)
- Seas and Lakes frozen in Winter

COPYRIGHT. GEORGE PHILIP & SON. LTD.

1 : 40 000 000

200 0 200 400 600 800 1000 miles
200 0 200 400 600 800 1000 1200 1400 1600 km

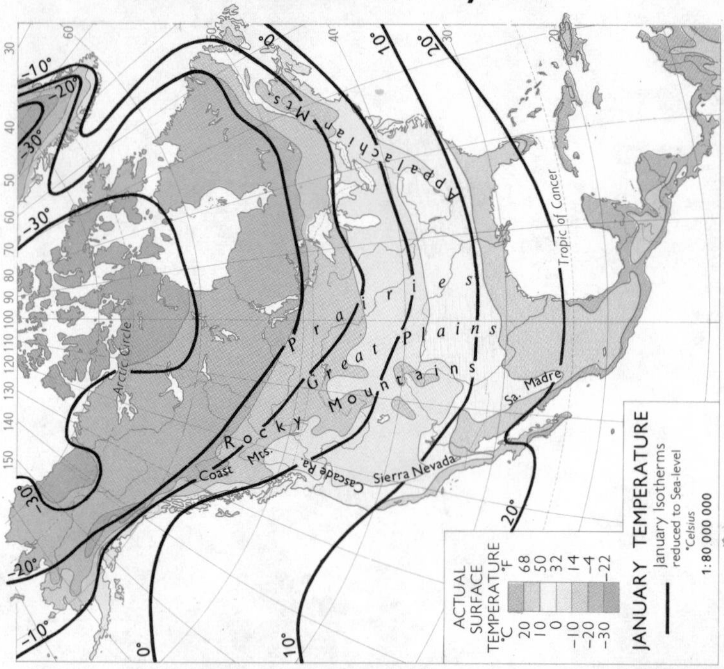

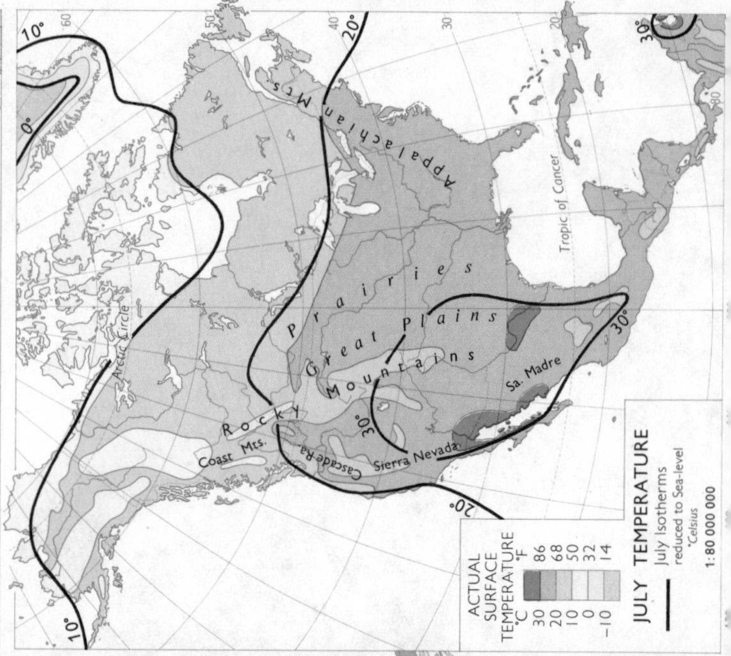

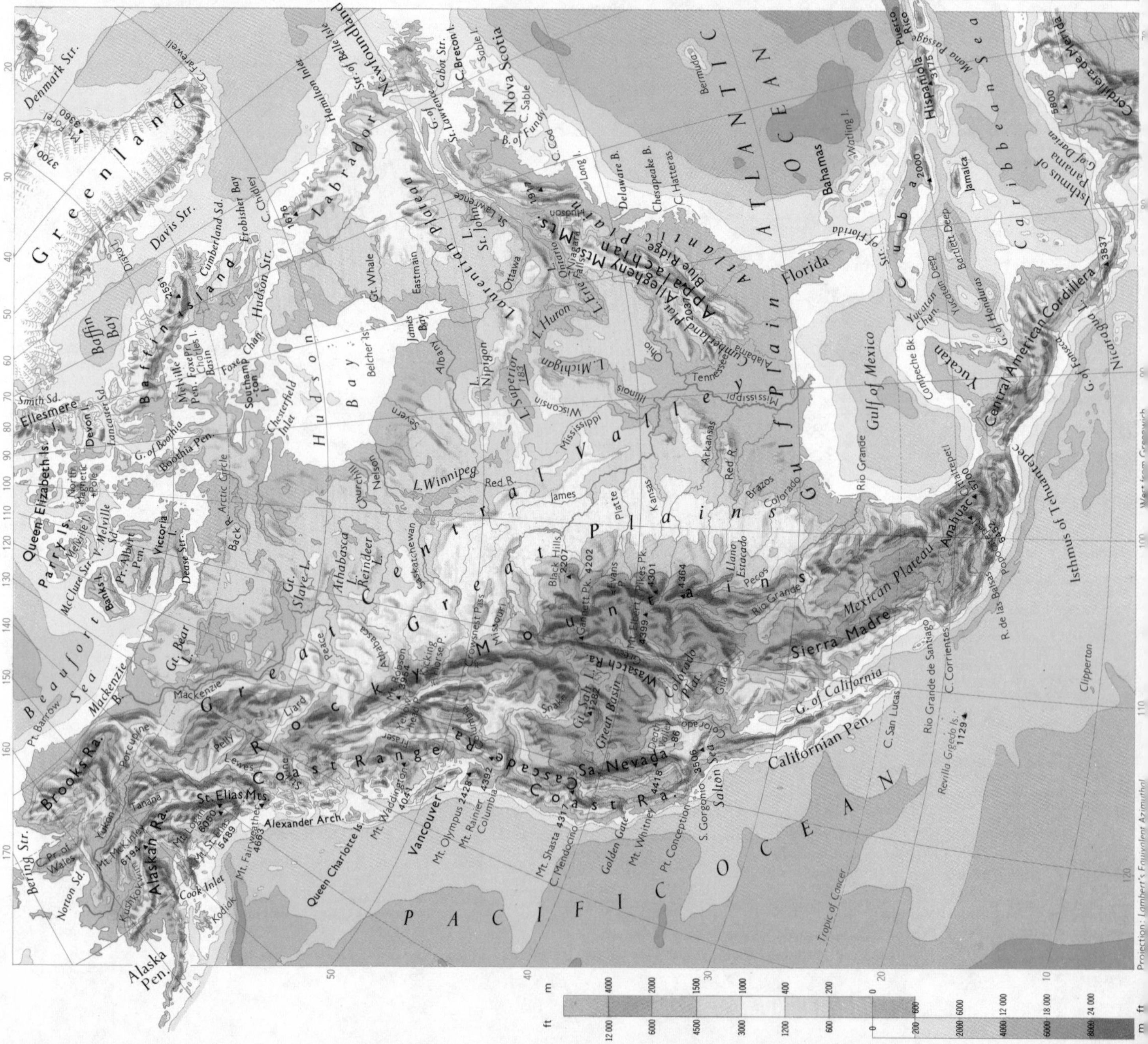

January Temperature map

Appalachian Mts.
Prairies
Great Plains
Rocky Mountains
Coast Mts.
Cascade Ra.
Sierra Nevada
Sa. Madre
Arctic Circle
Tropic of Cancer

ACTUAL SURFACE TEMPERATURE

°C	°F
20	68
10	50
0	32
−10	14
−20	−4
−30	−22

JANUARY TEMPERATURE
January Isotherms reduced to Sea-level
°Celsius
1 : 80 000 000

July Temperature map

Appalachian Mts.
Prairies
Great Plains
Rocky Mountains
Coast Mts.
Cascade Ra.
Sierra Nevada
Sa. Madre
Arctic Circle
Tropic of Cancer

ACTUAL SURFACE TEMPERATURE

°C	°F
30	86
20	68
10	50
0	32
−10	14

JULY TEMPERATURE
July Isotherms reduced to Sea-level
°Celsius
1 : 80 000 000

Physical map

Denmark Str.
Greenland
Mt. Forel 3300
3700
Baffin Bay
Davis Str.
Disko
Frobisher Bay
C. Chidley
1676
Labrador
Newfoundland
Hamilton Inlet
Str. of Belle Isle
Gt. Whale
Eastmain
St. Lawrence
G. of St. Lawrence
Cabot Str.
C. Breton I.
Sable I.
Nova Scotia
C. Sable
B. of Fundy
C. Cod
Long I.
Laurentian Plateau
St. John R.
Ottawa
L. Erie
L. Ontario
Niagara Falls
Allegheny Mts.
Appalachian
Blue Ridge
Cumberland Plateau
Delaware B.
Chesapeake B.
C. Hatteras
Bermuda
ATLANTIC OCEAN
Watling I.
Bahamas
Florida
Str. of Florida
Alabama
Tennessee
Ohio
Illinois
Wisconsin
L. Michigan
L. Huron
L. Superior
L. Nipigon
Albany
James Bay
Belcher Is.
Severn
Nelson
Churchill
L. Winnipeg
Chesterfield Inlet
Hudson Bay
Southampton I.
Foxe Chan.
Foxe Basin
Melville Pen.
Boothia Pen.
G. of Boothia
Baffin Island
Bylot I.
Lancaster Sd.
Devon I.
Ellesmere I.
Smith Sd.
Queen Elizabeth Is.
Parry Is.
Melville I.
Prince Patrick I.
McClure Str.
Banks I.
Victoria I.
King William I.
Prince of Wales I.
Somerset I.
North Magnetic Pole
Gt. Bear L.
Gt. Slave L.
Back
Coppermine
Arctic Circle
Beaufort Sea
Pt. Barrow
Mackenzie B.
Mackenzie
Great Bear L.
Athabasca
Reindeer L.
Saskatchewan
Peace
Slave
Liard
Central Plain
Great Plains
Black Hills 2207
Harney Pk. 4202
Laramie Pk.
Pikes Pk. 4301
Mt. Evans
Long's Pk. 4364
Llano Estacado
Pecos
Rio Grande
Red R.
Arkansas
Kansas
Platte
Missouri
James
Red R.
Colorado
Brazos
Mississippi
Rocky Mountains
Wasatch Ra.
Great Basin
Colorado Plat.
Grand Canyon
Gila
Salton Sea
Sa. Nevada
Mt. Whitney 4418
Mt. Shasta 4317
C. Mendocino
Golden Gate
Pt. Conception
S. Gorgonio
Coast Ra.
Cascade Ra.
Mt. Rainier 4392
Mt. Olympus 2428
Columbia
Snake
Vancouver I.
Queen Charlotte Is.
Mt. Waddington 4042
Alexander Arch.
St. Elias Mts. 5489
Mt. Logan 6050
Mt. Fairweather 4663
Mt. McKinley 6194
Tanana
Yukon
Kuskokwim
Brooks Ra.
Porcupine
Coast Range
Kodiak I.
Cook Inlet
Alaskan Ra.
Alaska Pen.
Bering Str.
Pr. of Wales
Norton Sd.
Nunivak I.
PACIFIC OCEAN
Gulf of Mexico
Campeche Bk.
Yucatan
Yucatan Chan.
Cuba 2000
Isle of Pines
Cayman Is.
Jamaica
Hispaniola 3175
Puerto Rico
Mona Passage
Bartlett Deep 6800
Bartlett Trough
G. of Honduras
Caribbean Sea
Mexican Plateau
Sierra Madre
Orizaba 5700
Anahuac
Popocatepetl 5452
Central American Cordillera 3837
Nicaragua
G. of Tehuantepec
Isthmus of Tehuantepec
Isthmus of Panama
G. of Darien
Cordillera de Mérida
Cabot Deep
Tropic of Cancer
Rio Grande de Santiago
C. Corrientes
G. of California
Californian Pen.
C. San Lucas
Rio Grande de Norte
Revillo Gigedo Is. 1129
Clipperton
West from Greenwich

ELEVATION
m: 4000 2000 1500 1000 400 200 0 200 4000 6000 12000 18000 24000
ft: 12000 6000 4500 3000 1200 600 0 600 12000 18000 24000

Projection : Lambert's Equal-area Azimuthal

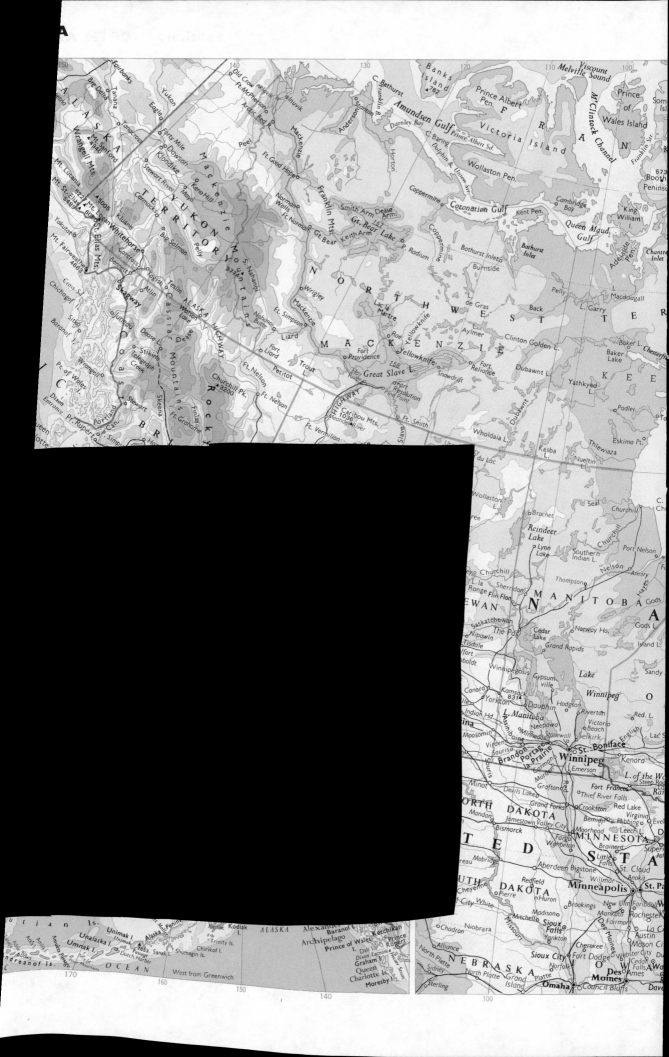

1:40 000 000

RAINFALL
November to April
1:80 000 000

1016 January Isobars
in millibars
→ Prevailing Winds

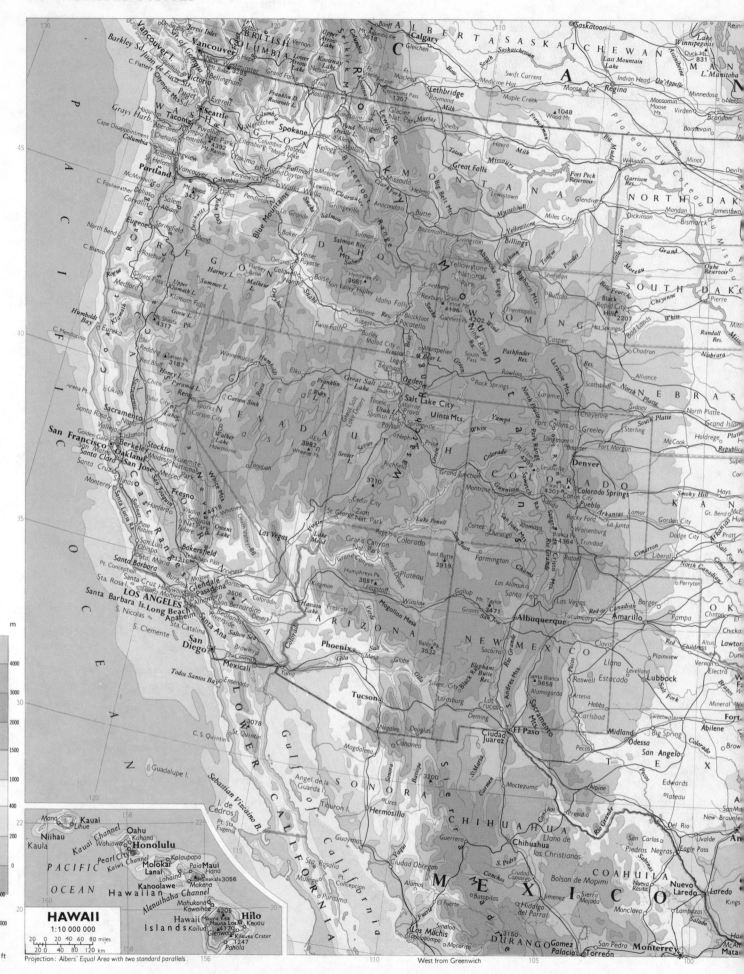

HAWAII
1:10 000 000

Projection: Albers' Equal Area with two standard parallels.

West from Greenwich

1:12 000 000

50 0 50 100 150 200 250 300 miles
50 0 50 100 150 200 250 300 350 400 450 km

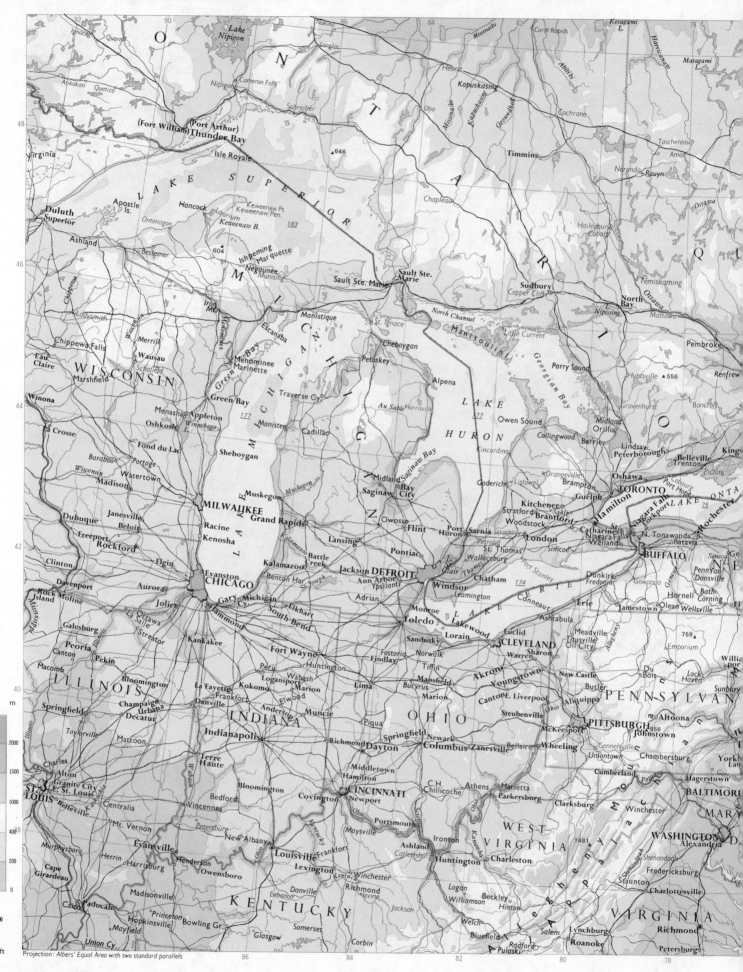

Projection: Albers' Equal Area with two standard parallels

1:6 000 000

50   0   50   100   150 miles
50   0   50   100   150   200 km

Density of Population legend

Inhabitants	
per mile²	per km²
under 2	under 1
2–8	1–3
8–16	3–6
16–32	6–12
32–64	12–25
64–128	25–50
128–256	50–100
256–512	100–200
over 512	over 200

■ Towns of over 200,000 Inhabitants

DENSITY OF POPULATION

1:50 000 000

GULF OF ST. LAWRENCE

NEW BRUNSWICK

NOVA SCOTIA

PRINCE EDWARD ISLAND

MAINE

NEW HAMPSHIRE

VERMONT

MASS.

NEW JERSEY

ATLANTIC OCEAN

MONTREAL · Quebec · BOSTON · NEW YORK · Halifax · Sydney

COPYRIGHT. GEORGE PHILIP & SON. LTD.

West from Greenwich

PANAMA CANAL
1:1 000 000
0   10   20 km
Canal Zone

JAMAICA
1:5 000 000
0   50 km

TRINIDAD
AND TOBAGO
1:5 000 000
0   50 km

LEEWARD
ISLANDS
1:5 000 000
0   50 km

WINDWARD
ISLANDS
1:5 000 000
0   50 km

Projection: Bonne

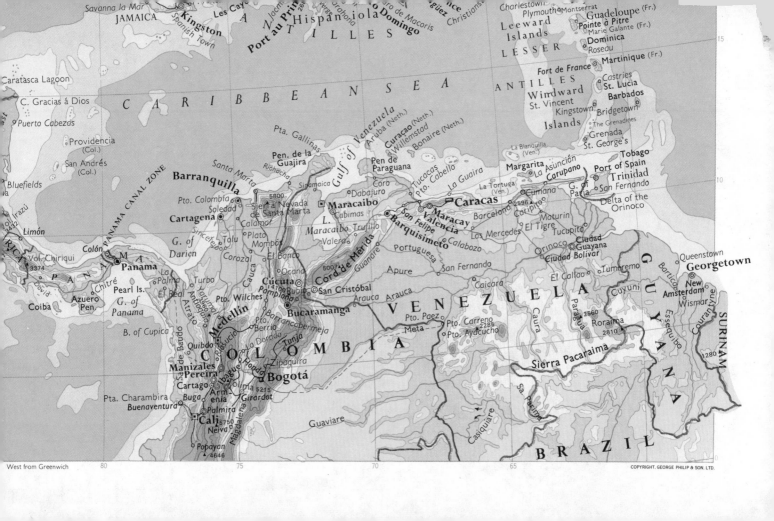

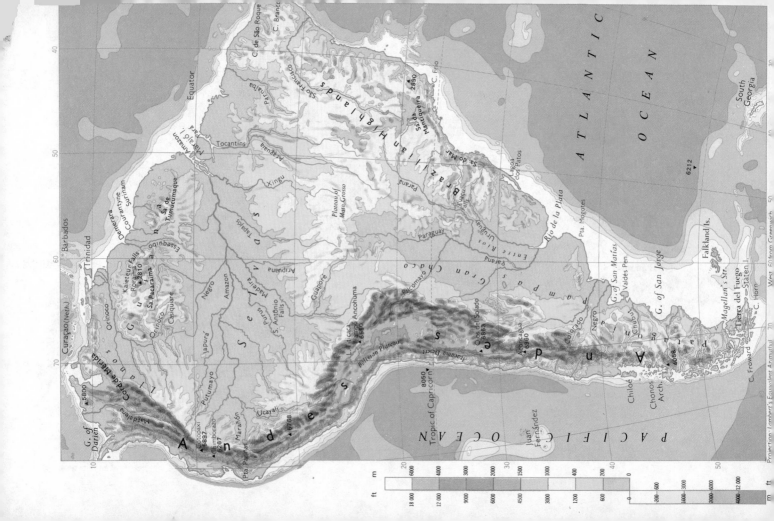

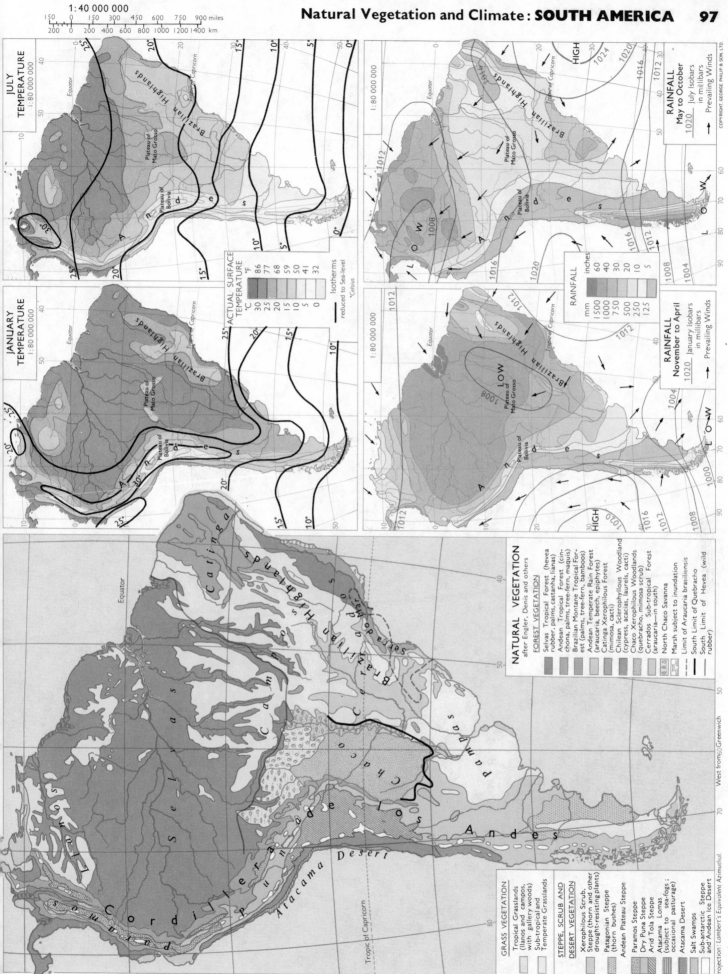

1:40 000 000

150   0   150 300 450 600 750 900 miles
200 0 200 400 600 800 1000 1200 1400 km

JULY TEMPERATURE
1:80 000 000

JANUARY TEMPERATURE
1:80 000 000

ACTUAL SURFACE TEMPERATURE

°F	°C	
86	30	
77	25	
68	20	
59	15	
50	10	
41	5	
32	0	

Isotherms reduced to Sea-level
°Celsius

RAINFALL May to October
1020 July Isobars in millibars
→ Prevailing Winds

RAINFALL November to April
1020 January Isobars in millibars
→ Prevailing Winds

RAINFALL

inches	mm
60	1500
40	1000
30	750
20	500
10	250
5	125

COPYRIGHT. GEORGE PHILIP & SON LTD.

NATURAL VEGETATION
after Engler, Denis and others

FOREST VEGETATION

Selvas Tropical Forest (hevea rubber, palms, castanha, lianas)
Andean Tropical Forest (cinchona, palms, tree-fern, maquis)
Brazilian Montane Tropical Forest (palms, tree-fern, bamboos)
Andean Temperate Rain Forest (araucaria, beech, epiphytes)
Catinga Xerophilous Forest (mimosa, cacti)
Chilean Sclerophyllous Woodland (cypress, acacias, laurels, cacti)
Chaco Xerophilous Woodlands (quebracho, mimosa scrub)
Cerrados Sub-tropical Forest (araucaria—in south)
North Chaco Savanna

— — Marsh subject to inundation
— — Limit of Araucaria brasiliensis
━━ South Limit of Quebracho
— — South Limit of Hevea (wild rubber)

GRASS VEGETATION

Tropical Grasslands (llanos and campos, with gallery woods)
Sub-tropical Temperate Grasslands

STEPPE, SCRUB AND DESERT VEGETATION

Xerophilous Scrub, Steppe (thorn and other drought-resisting plants)
Patagonian Steppe (thorn bushes)
Andean Plateau Steppe
Paramos Steppe
Dry Puna Steppe
Arid Tola Steppe
Atacama Lomas (subject to sea-fogs; occasional pasturage)
Atacama Desert
Salt Swamps
Sub-antarctic Steppe and Andean Ice Desert

Projection: Lambert's Equivalent Azimuthal.

West from Greenwich

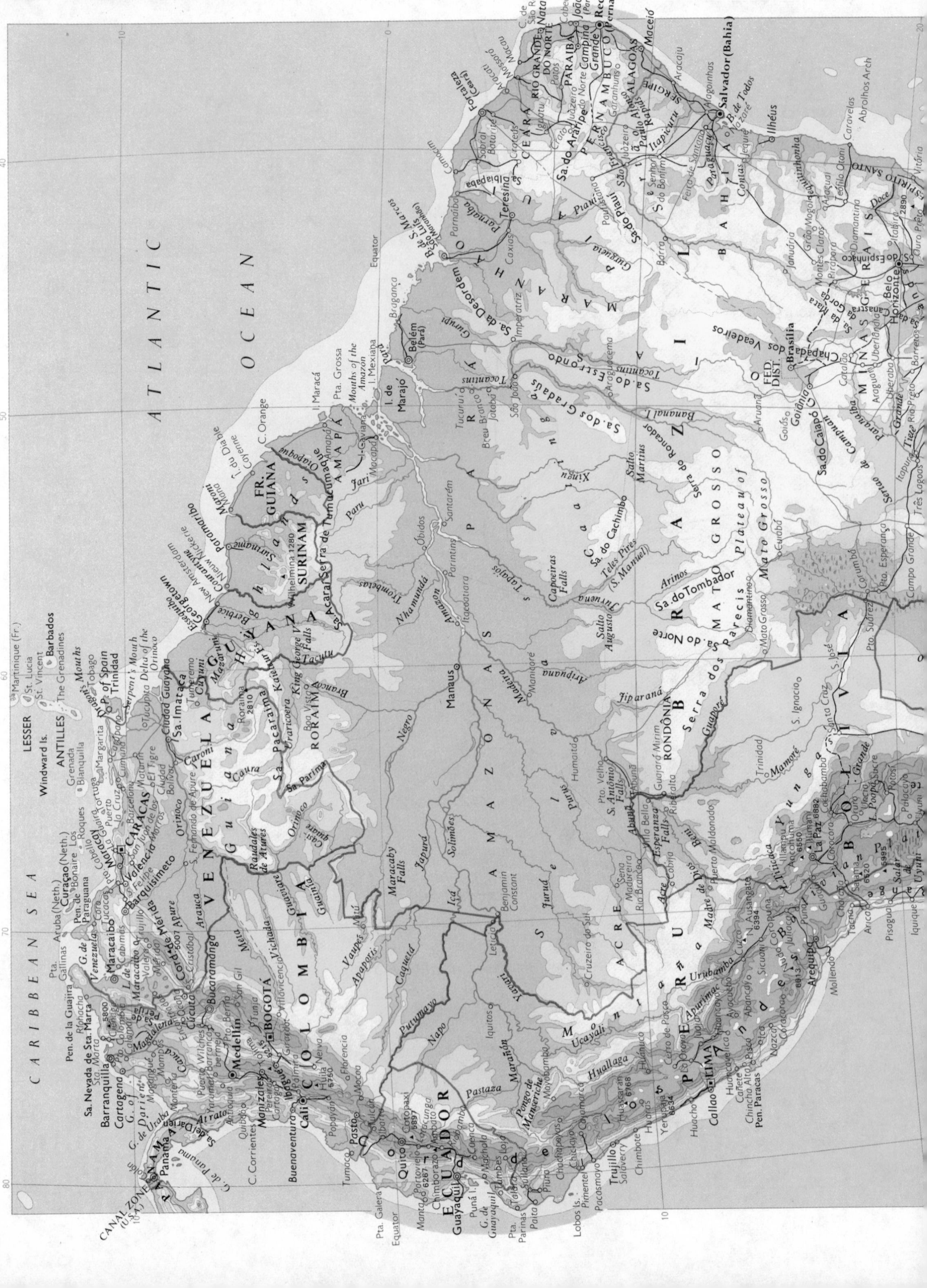

ATLANTIC   OCEAN

CARIBBEAN SEA

LESSER
Windward Is.
ANTILLES
Martinique (Fr.)
St. Lucia
St. Vincent   Barbados
The Grenadines
Grenada
Tobago
P. of Spain
Trinidad

Aruba (Neth.)
Curaçao (Neth.)
Pen. de Bonaire
Los Roques
Margarita
Blanquilla

Sta. Marta
Sa. Nevada de Sta. Marta
Barranquilla
Cartagena
G. of Uraba
Pen. de la Guajira
Gallinas
Pta.

CARACAS
Valencia
Barquisimeto
Maracaibo
L. de Maracaibo

VENEZUELA
Orinoco
Ciudad Bolívar
Ciudad Guayana

GUIANA
Guiana Highlands
Roraima 2810
RORAIMA

FR. GUIANA
Cayenne
SURINAM
Paramaribo
Georgetown
GUYANA

Mouth of the Amazon
Belém (Pará)
I. de Marajó
I. Mexiana

AMAPÁ
PARÁ

MARANHÃO
Teresina
São Luís
Fortaleza
CEARÁ
RIO GRANDE DO NORTE
Natal
PARAÍBA
João Pessoa
PERNAMBUCO
Recife
ALAGOAS
Maceió
SERGIPE
Aracaju
Salvador (Bahia)
B. de Todos
Ilhéus

BAHIA
ESPÍRITO SANTO
Abrolhos Arch.

MINAS GERAIS
Belo Horizonte
Brasília
FED. DIST.
Goiânia

MATO GROSSO
Plateau of Mato Grosso
Cuiabá

RONDÔNIA
ACRE
AMAZONAS
Manaus

COLOMBIA
BOGOTÁ
Medellín
Cali
Bucaramanga
Cúcuta

ECUADOR
Quito
Guayaquil

PERU
LIMA
Callao

BOLIVIA
La Paz
Sucre
Titicaca

Amazon
Negro
Madeira
Purus
Juruá
Tapajós
Xingu
Tocantins
São Francisco
Paraná

Equator

100   0   100   200   300   400   500 miles
100   0   100   200   300   400   500   600   700   800 km

ANNUAL RAINFALL
1:80 000 000

mm	inches
3000	120
2000	80
1000	40
500	20
250	10

Equator

Brazilian Highlands

Plateau of Mato Grosso

Plateau of Bolivia

Tropic of Capricorn

A n d e s

DENSITY OF POPULATION
1:80 000 000

Inhabitants	per mile²	per km²
	under 2	under 1
	2–8	1–3
	8–16	3–6
	16–32	6–12
	32–64	12–25
	64–128	25–50
	over 128	over 50

■ Towns of over 100,000 inhabitants

Equator

Fortaleza
Recife
Belém
Salvador
Belo Horizonte
Rio de Janeiro
Brasília
São Paulo
Curitiba
Asunción
P. Alegre
Santa Fé
Rosário
Córdoba
Tucumán
Buenos Aires
Montevideo
La Plata
Manaus
Caracas
Barranquilla
Medellín
Bogotá
Cali
Quito
Guayaquil
La Paz
Arequipa
Lima
Callao
Valparaíso
Santiago

Tropic of Capricorn

COPYRIGHT GEORGE PHILIP & SON LTD

SÃO PAULO
Santos
Guape
Itanhaém

Main Map

PARANÁ
Iguaçu Falls
Curitiba
SANTA CATARINA
RIO GRANDE DO SUL
Porto Alegre
Lagoa dos Patos
L. Mirim
URUGUAY
MONTEVIDEO
Río de la Plata
Mar del Plata
Asunción
Corrientes
Resistencia
Santiago del Estero
Tucumán
Salta
Córdoba
Rosário
Santa Fé
BUENOS AIRES
Avellaneda
La Plata
Bahía Blanca
Mendoza
SANTIAGO
Valparaíso
Viña del Mar
Concepción
Temuco
Valdivia
Osorno
Chiloé I.
Chonos Arch.
Taitao Pen.
G. de Peñas
Wellington I.
Madre de Dios I.
Hanover I.
Qn. Adelaide Arch.
Magellan's Str.
Santa Inés I.
Tierra del Fuego
C. Horn
Navarino I.
Beagle Chan.
Ushuaia
I. de los Estados (Staten I.)
Le Maire Str.
C. Virgenes
Río Gallegos
B. Grande
L. Argentino
L. Viedma
L. Buenos Aires
Comodoro Rivadavia
C. Tres Puntas
G. S. Jorge
Deseado
Rawson
Trelew
Valdés Pen.
G. S. Matías
G. S. José
Río Negro
Neuquén
L. Nahuel Huapí
San Carlos de Bariloche

ATLANTIC OCEAN

PACIFIC OCEAN

Juan Fernández Is. (Chile)
Más a Tierra
Más Afuera
I. San Félix
I. San Ambrosio

Antofagasta
Taltal
Chañaral
Caldera
Copiapó
Huasco
La Serena
Coquimbo
Ovalle

Tropic of Capricorn

Falkland Is. (Br.)
Stanley
E. Falkland
W. Falkland

West from Greenwich

Projection: Lambert's Equivalent Azimuthal

Elevation scale

m	ft
6000	18 000
4000	12 000
3000	9000
2000	6000
1000	3000
400	1200
200	600
0	0

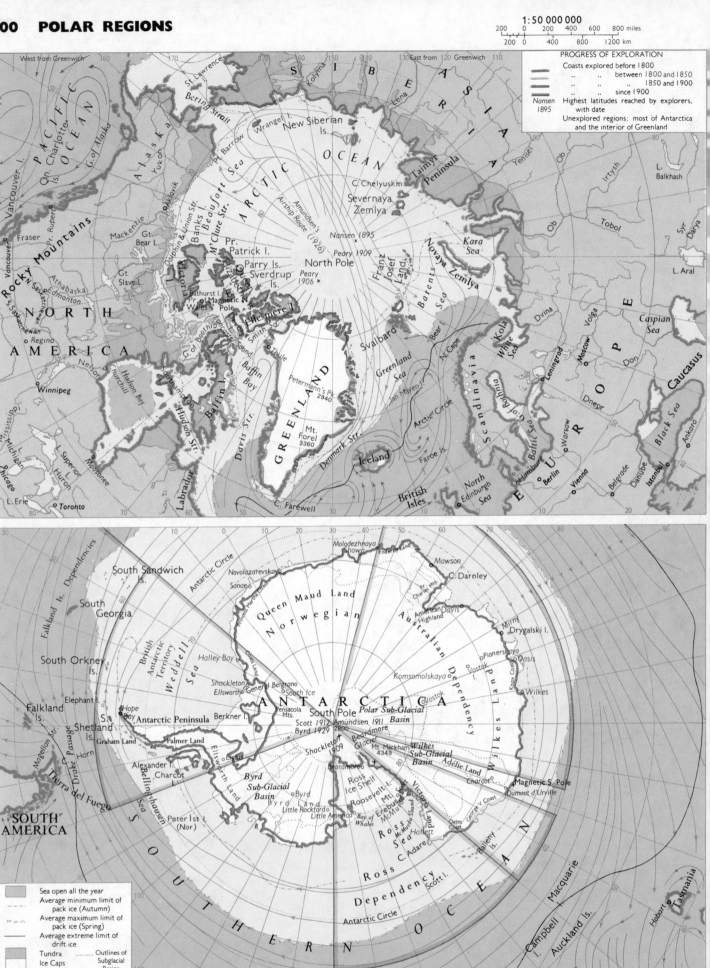

1:50 000 000

200 0 200 400 600 800 miles
200 0 400 800 1200 km

PROGRESS OF EXPLORATION

Coasts explored before 1800
„   „   „   between 1800 and 1850
„   „   „   „   1850 and 1900
„   „   „   since 1900
Nansen 1895 Highest latitudes reached by explorers, with date
Unexplored regions: most of Antarctica and the interior of Greenland

Sea open all the year
Average minimum limit of pack ice (Autumn)
Average maximum limit of pack ice (Spring)
Average extreme limit of drift ice
Tundra
Ice Caps
Cold Currents
Warm Currents
Outlines of Subglacial Basins

Projection: Zenithal Equidistant

COPYRIGHT. GEORGE PHILIP & SON. LTD.

CHF

A.R. – Autonomous Region
A.S.S.R. – Autonomous Soviet Socialist Republic
Afghan. – Afghanistan
Afr. – Africa
Ala. – Alabama
Alg. – Algeria
Amer. – America
Ang. – Angola
Antarc. – Antarctic
Arch. – Archipelago
Arg. – Argentina
Ark. – Arkansas
Atlant. – Atlantic
Austral. – Australia
B. – Bay, Bight, (Baie, Paia, Bahia)
Bangla. – Bangladesh
Belg. – Belgium
Br. – British
Braz. – Brazil
Bur. – Burma
C. – Cape (Cabo)
Cal. – California
Cam. – Cameroon
Can. – Canada, Canal
Cap. – Capital
Cent. – Central
Chan. – Channel
Ches. – Cheshire
Cn. – Canten
Co. – County
Col. – Colony, Colombia
Corn. – Cornwall
Cr. – Creek
Cumbs. – Cumberland
Cy. – City
Cz-slov. – Czechoslovakia
D.C. – District of Columbia
Dan. – Danish

Del. – Delaware
Den. – Denmark
Des. – Desert
Dept. – Department
Dist. – District
Div. – Division
Dom. Rep. – Dominican Republic
E. – East
Eng. – England
Eur. – Europe
F. – Firth
Fd. – Fjord, Fiord
Fed. – Federal
Fin. – Finland
Fla. – Florida
For. – Forest
Fr. – French, France
Fr. T.A. & I. – French Territory of Afars and Issas
Fs. – Falls
G. – Gulf, Gebel
Ga. – Georgia
Ger. – Germany
Gr. – Greater, Greece
Gt. – Great
Guat. – Guatemala
Hants. – Hampshire
Hd. – Head
Herts. – Hertfordshire
Hr. – Harbour, Harbor
Hs. – Hills
Hts. – Heights
Hung. – Hungary
Hunts. – Huntingdonshire
I(s). – Island(s), Isle, Ile(s)
I.O.M. – Isle of Man
I.O.W. – Isle of Wight
Ice. – Iceland
Ill. – Illinois

Ind. – Indian, Indiana
Indon. – Indonesia
Ire. – Ireland
Isth. – Isthmus
It. – Italy
Jap. – Japan
Junc. – Junction
Kan. – Kansas
Ky. – Kentucky
L. – Lake, Loch, Lough, Lago
La. – Louisiana
Lag. – Lagoon, Lagoa, Laguna
Lancs. – Lancashire
Ld. – Land
Leb. – Lebanon
Leics. – Leicestershire
Lincs. – Lincolnshire
Lit. – Little
Lr. – Lower
Lux. – Luxembourg
Madag. – Madagascar
Mad. P. – Madhya Pradesh
Md. – Maryland
Me. – Maine
Medit. – Mediterranean
Mex. – Mexico
Mich. – Michigan
Minn. – Minnesota
Miss. – Mississippi
Mo. – Missouri
Mong. – Mongolia
Mozam. – Mozambique
Mt(s). – Mountain(s), Mount(s)
Mte. – Monte
N. – North, Northern
N.B. – New Brunswick
N.C. – North Carolina
N.H. – New Hampshire
N.J. – New Jersey

N.S.W. – New South Wales
N.Y. – New York
N.Z. – New Zealand
Neb. – Nebraska
Neth. – Netherlands
Newf. – Newfoundland
Nicar. – Nicaragua
Nor. – Norway
Northants. – Northamptonshire
O. – Oasis
O.F.S. – Orange Free State
Oc. – Ocean
Ont. – Ontario
Ore. – Oregon
Okla. – Oklahoma
P. – Pass, Paso, Passo
Pa. – Pennsylvania
Pac. Oc. – Pacific Ocean
Pak. – Pakistan
Pan. – Panama
Para. – Paraguay
Pen. – Peninsula
Phil. – Philippines
Pk. – Peak
Pl. – Plain, Planina
Plat. – Plateau
Pol. – Poland
Port. – Portuguese, Portugal
Pref. – Prefecture
Prov. – Province
Pt. Pte. – Point, Pointe
R. – River, Rio
R.I. – Rhode Island
Ra. – Range
Reg. – Region
Res. – Reservoir
Rhod. – Rhodesia
Rum. – Rumania
S. – South, Sea

S.C. – South Carolina
S.D. – South Dakota
S.S.R. – Soviet Socialist Republic
S., St., Ste., Sta., Sto. – Sao, Saint, Sainte, Santa, Santo
Sa. – Sierra, Serra
Salop. – Shropshire
Scot. – Scotland
Sd. – Sound
Si Arabia – Saudi Arabia
Som. – Somerset
St. – State
Staffs. – Staffordshire
Str. – Strait
Switz. – Switzerland
Span. – Spanish
Tenn. – Tennessee
Terr. – Territory
Tex. – Texas
Tipp. – Tipperary
**Tr. States. – Trucial States
Trans. – Transvaal
Tur. – Turkey
U.S.A. – United States of America
U.S.S.R. – Union of Soviet Socialist Republics
Va. – Virginia
Val. – Valley
Ven. – Venezuela
Vic. – Victoria
Vol. – Volcano
Vt. – Vermont
W. – West, Western, Wadi, Wady
W.I. – West Indies
Wilts. – Wiltshire
Wis. – Wisconsin
Y.-slav. – Yugoslavia
Yorks. – Yorkshire

The latitudes and longitudes are intended primarily as a guide to finding the places on the map and in some cases are only approximate.

Some counties in England and Wales changed in April 1974 and the six counties in N. Ireland were replaced for administrative purposes by 26 districts in October 1973. In April 1975 new regions became effective in Scotland. Where these or other changes affect names in the index a symbol alongside the entry and a corresponding footnote gives the new form.

A

* County incorporated within the region of Grampian

** Now independent and renamed the United Arab Emirates

† Renamed Mobutu Sese Seko, L.

Ale Auc

83 Alexandrina, L., Austral. 35 32s 139 12E
41 Alexandroúpolis, Greece 40 50N 25 55E
63 Aley, Lebanon 33 50N 35 36E
27 Alford, England 53 16N 0 10E
27 Alfreton, England 53 7N 1 24W
48 Alftanes, Iceland 64 29N 22 10W
37 Algarve, Prov., Portugal 37 20N 8 35W
37 Algeciras, Spain 36 11N 5 28W
37 Algemesi, Spain 39 15N 0 29W
72 Algeria, N. Africa 33 40N 3 0E
72 Algiers (Alger), Algeria 36 45N 3 5E
76 Algoa B., S. Africa 33 50s 26 0E
37 Alhama de Murcia, Spain 37 50N 1 30W
64 Alikhel, Afghanistan 33 50N 69 30E
74 Alibo, Ethiopia 9 52N 37 5E
37 Alicante, Spain 38 22N 1 28W
82 Alice, R., Australia 23 50s 145 0E
80 Alice Springs, Australia 23 42s 133 58E
75 Alicedale, S. Africa 33 16s 26 2E
64 Aligarh, India 27 42N 78 25E
65 Aling Kangri, Ra., Tibet, China 32 45N 81 5E
49 Alingsas Sweden 57 57N 12 36E
64 Alipur, Pakistan 29 25N 70 50E
65 Alipur Duar, India 26 35N 89 30E
47 Alitus, U.S.S.R. 54 20N 24 0E
37 Aljustrel, Portugal 37 55N 8 10W
44 Alkmaar, Netherlands 52 38N 4 44E
65 Allahabad, India 25 25N 81 50E
61 Allakn Yun, U.S.S.R. 60 50N 137 5E
31 Allan, Bridge of, Scotland 56 9N 3 56W
92 Allegheny Mts., U.S.A. 39 0N 79 0W
92 Allegheny, R., U.S.A. 42 0N 79 0W
35 Allen, Bog of, Ireland 53 13N 7 20W
36 Allen, L., Ireland 54 8N 8 2W
63 Allenby Bridge, *see* Hussein Bridge
27 Allendale, England 54 55N 2 16W
93 Allentown, U.S.A. 40 40N 75 25W
64 Alleppey, India 9 35N 76 25E
90 Alliance, Neb., U.S.A. 42 8N 102 55W
42 Allier, Dépt., France 46 25N 3 0E
43 Allier, R., France 44 50N 3 42E
31 Alloa, Scotland 56 7N 3 47W
60 Alma Ata, U.S.S.R. 43 20N 76 50E
37 Almada, Portugal 38 45N 9 10W
82 Almaden, Australia 17 22s 144 40E
37 Almadén, Spain 38 48N 4 48W
37 Almansa, Spain 38 50N 1 0W
37 Almazan, Spain 41 30N 2 30W
44 Almelo, Netherlands 52 21N 6 42E
37 Almendralejo, Spain 38 43N 6 28W
37 Almeria, Spain 36 53N 2 33W
24 Almondsbury, England 51 33N 2 34W
27 Aln, R., England 55 24N 1 57W
33 Alness, & R., Scotland 57 45N 4 20W
27 Alnwick, England 55 25N 1 42W
65 Alon, Burma 22 15N 95 10E
68 Alor, & I., Indonesia 8 10s 124 50E
68 Alor Star, Malaya 6 3N 100 25E
92 Alpena, U.S.A. 45 0N 83 35W
42 Alpes Maritimes, Dépt., Fr. 44 5N 7 0E
24 Alphington, England 50 41N 3 32W
45 Alpi Pennine, Mts., Switz. 46 4N 7 35E
90 Alpine, Texas, U.S.A. 30 25N 103 42W
46 Alps, The, Europe 46 to 47 0N 6 to 10 0E
43 Alsace, Dist., France 48 30N 7 30E
26 Alsager, England 53 7N 2 20W
44 Alsdorf, Germany 50 48N 6 10E
32 Alsh, L., Scotland 57 17N 5 40W
26 Alston, England 54 49N 2 28W
66 Altai Mts., Central Asia 48 0N 90 0E
91 Altamaha, R., U.S.A. 31 45N 81 45W
66 Altanbulag, Mongolia 50 15N 106 25E
45 Altdorf, Switzerland 46 53N 8 38E
48 Alte Fjord, Norway 70 0N 23 25E
37 Altea, Spain 38 38N 0 1W
43 Altkirch, France 47 40N 7 15E
75 Alto Molocue, Mozam. 15 50s 37 35E
23 Alton, England 51 8N 0 59W
92 Alton, U.S.A. 38 54N 90 3W
46 Altona, Germany 53 34N 9 51E
92 Altoona, U.S.A. 40 32N 79 27W
26 Altrincham, England 53 24N 2 23W
45 Altstätten, Switzerland 47 23N 9 33E
90 Altus, U.S.A. 34 30N 99 25W
66 Altyn Tagh, Mts., Tibet 39 0N 89 0E
31 Alva, Scotland 56 9N 3 48W
94 Alvarado, Mexico 18 45N 95 50W
22 Alvechurch, England 52 22N 1 58W
49 Alvesta, Sweden 56 57N 14 30E
83 Alvie, Australia 38 15s 143 30E
49 Älvkarleby, Sweden 60 32N 17 40E
49 Alvsborg, Co., Sweden 58 0N 12 30E
48 Älvsby, Sweden 65 42N 21 0E
64 Alwar, India 27 43N 76 40E
51 Alyaty Pristan, U.S.S.R. 39 59N 49 28E
31 Alyth, Scotland 56 38 N 3 14W
47 Alytus, U.S.S.R. 54 25N 24 0E
73 Am-Dam, Chad 12 40N 20 35E
73 Am Djeress, Chad 16 15N 22 50E
73 Am Guereda, Chad 12 53N 21 14E
73 Am Timan, Chad 11 0N 20 10E
80 Amadeus, L., Australia 24 45s 130 45E
73 Amadi, Sudan 5 29N 30 25E
89 Amadjuak & L., Canada 64 0N 72 40W
67 Amagasaki, Japan 34 45N 135 25E
67 Amakusa B. & I., Japan 32 45N 130 5E
49 Amal, Sweden 59 5N 12 35E
64 Amalner, India 21 0N 74 58E
67 Amami O Shima, Is., Japan 27 0N 129 0E
60 Amangeldy, U.S.S.R. 50 10N 65 10E
98 Amapa, st., Brazil 2 0N 52 0W
62 Amara, Iraq 31 58N 47 5E
64 Amaravati, *see* Amraoti
90 Amarillo, U.S.A. 35 6N 101 57W
40 Amaro, Mte., Italy 42 4N 14 5E
51 Amasya, Turkey 40 45N 36 10E
98 Amazon, R., Brazil 1 0s 59 0W
98 Amazonas, st., Brazil 4 30s 64 0W
64 Ambala, India 30 28N 76 50E
74 Amban, Cameroon 2 20N 11 15E
75 Ambanja, Madagascar 13 40s 48 27E
61 Ambarchik, U.S.S.R. 69 40N 162 20E
98 Ambato, Ecuador 1 40s 78 30W
75 Ambatolampy, Madag. 19 0s 47 35E
75 Ambatondrazaka, Madag. 17 55s 48 28E
46 Amberg, Germany 49 27N 11 52E
65 Ambikapur, India 23 10N 83 5E
75 Ambilobé, Madagascar 13 10s 49 3E
27 Amble, England 55 20N 1 36W
26 Ambleside, England 54 26N 2 56W
68 Ambon, Indonesia 3 50s 128 15E
43 Amboise, France 47 24N 1 2E
75 Ambositra, Madagascar 20 30s 47 25E
68 Amboyna, I., S. China Sea 7 0N 113 10E
75 Ambré, C'd', Madagascar 12 0s 49 20E
74 Ambriz, Angola 8 0s 13 20E
74 Ambrizète, Angola 7 18s 12 52E
60 Amderma, U.S.S.R. 69 45N 62 0E
94 Ameca, Mexico 20 26N 104 5W
44 Ameland, I., Netherlands 53 27N 5 45E
61 Amen, U.S.S.R. 68 50N 179 59E
1 America, N. and S., Continents
44 Amersfoort, Netherlands 52 10N 5 24E
23 Amersham, England 51 40N 0 38W
88 Amery, Canada 56 35N 94 5W
91 Ames, U.S.A. 42 3N 93 42W
22 Amesbury, England 51 10N 1 46W
61 Amga, R., U.S.S.R. 61 0N 132 0E
61 Amgu, U.S.S.R. 45 45N 137 15E
61 Amgun, R., U.S.S.R. 52 50N 138 0E
65 Amherst, Burma 16 0N 97 40E
89 Amherst, Canada 45 50N 64 30W
40 Amiata, Mt., Italy 42 49N 11 30E
43 Amiens, France 49 52N 2 15E
5 Amirante Is., Ind. Ocean 6 30s 53 0E
62 Amman, Jordan 31 57N 35 56E
25 Ammanford, Wales 51 48N 4 0W
67 Amoy, China 24 25N 118 15E
75 Ampanihy, Madagascar 24 40s 44 45E
62 Amran, Yemen 15 43N 43 57E
64 Amraoti, India 20 53N 77 15E
64 Amreli, India 21 40N 71 5E
64 Amritsar, India 31 40N 75 20E
64 Amroha, India 29 0N 78 25E
44 Amsterdam, Netherlands 52 23N 4 53E
76 Amsterdam, S. Africa 26 35s 30 40E
93 Amsterdam, U.S.A. 42 58N 74 6W
63 Amu Darya, R., U.S.S.R. 40 30N 62 0E
51 Amul, Iran 36 25N 52 10E
88 Amundsen Gulf, Canada 70 30N 123 0W
61 Amur, R., U.S.S.R. 52 0N 126 30E
68 Amurang, Indonesia 1 15N 124 30E
62 An Nafud, Des., Arabia 28 40N 42 0E
62 An Najaf, Iraq 32 0N 44 20E
62 An Nasiriyah, Iraq 31 0N 46 15E
68 An Nhon, Vietnam 13 40N 109 20E
36 An Uaimh, Ireland 53 40N 6 42W
63 Anabta, Jordan 32 19N 35 7E
90 Anaconda, U.S.A. 46 8N 112 58W
61 Anadyr & G., U.S.S.R. 64 40N 178 0E
61 Anadyr R., U.S.S.R. 65 0N 170 0E
90 Anaheim, U.S.A. 33 50N 118 0W
62 Anaiza, Saudi Arabia 26 4N 44 8E
65 Anakapalle, India 17 25N 82 50E
75 Analalava, Madagascar 14 35s 48 0E
68 Anambas Is., Indonesia 3 0N 106 0E
51 Anamur, Turkey 36 8N 32 58E
64 Anantnag, Kashmir 33 40N 75 3E
62 Anatolia, S.W. Asia 39 0N 32 30E
99 Anatuya, Argentina 28 20s 62 45W
73 Anaye, Niger. 19 28N 13 20E
42 Ancenis, France 47 23N 1 10W
88 Anchorage, Alaska 61 10N 150 0E
98 Anchohuma, Mt., Bolivia 16 0s 68 50W
94 Ancón, Panama Canal Zone (inset)
40 Ancona, Italy 43 38N 13 34E
99 Ancud & G., Chile 42 5s 73 48W
99 Andalgala, Argentina 27 25s 66 30W
48 Åndalsnes, Norway 62 35N 7 43E
37 Andalusia, Prov., Spain 37 20N 5 0W
91 Andalusia, U.S.A. 31 16N 86 30W
63 Andam, Wadi, Oman 21 30N 58 20E
55 Andaman Is., Indian Oc. 12 0N 92 40E
75 Andara, S.W. Africa 18 2s 21 9E
45 Andermatt, Switzerland 46 38N 8 37E
92 Anderson, Ind., U.S.A. 40 1N 85 40W
91 Anderson, S.C., U.S.A. 34 27N 82 36W
96 Andes, Mts., S. America 7 0N to 53 0s 65 0 to 80 0W
64 Andhra Pradesh, st., India 17 0N 81 0E
41 Andikithira I., Greece 35 40N 23 16E
60 Andizhan, U.S.S.R. 41 0N 72 37E
37 Andorra, Europe 42 28N 1 30E
22 Andover, England 51 12N 1 29W
88 Andreanof Is., Alaska 50 30N 178 0W
40 Andria, Italy 41 11N 16 17E
95 Andros I., Bahamas 24 40N 78 15W
41 Andros I., Greece 37 50N 24 53E
37 Andujar, Spain 38 0N 4 5W
72 Anécho, Togo 6 8N 1 32E
61 Angara, R., Siberia 55 0N 103 0E
61 Angarsk, U.S.S.R. 52 30N 104 0E
83 Angaston, Australia 34 28s 139 5E
48 Ånge, Sweden 62 31N 15 35E
49 Angelholm, Sweden 56 15N 12 58E
83 Angellala, Australia 26 20s 146 50E
65 Angenong, China 31 55N 94 10E
42 Angers, France 47 32N 0 33W
*25 Anglesey I. & Co., Wales 53 20N 4 20W
89 Angmagssalik, Greenland 65 40N 37 20W
74 Ango, Zaïre 4 10N 26 5E
99 Angol, Chile 38 0s 72 45W
75 Angola, Port. Terr., Afr. 12 0s 19 0E
43 Angoulême, France 45 40N 0 10E
43 Angoumois, Dist., Fr. 45 43N 0 15E
60 Angren, U.S.S.R. 41 0N 69 10E
95 Anguilla, I., W. Indies 18 0N 63 0W
**33 Angus, Co. & Braes of, Scotland 56 45N 2 55W
49 Anholt, I., Denmark 56 43N 11 25E
66 Anhwei, Prov., China 32 0N 117 0E
64 Anjidiv I., India 14 45N 74 10E
42 Anjou, Prov., France 47 20N 0 50W
75 Anjozorobe, Madagascar 18 22s 47 52E
72 Anka, Nigeria 12 13N 5 58E
51 Ankara, Turkey 39 58N 32 28E
75 Ankazoabo, Madagascar 22 15s 44 45E
75 Ankazobe, Madagascar 18 17s 47 2E
66 Anking, China 30 40N 117 2E
49 Anklam, Germany 53 50N 13 40E
74 Ankoro, Zaïre 6 43s 26 45E
92 Ann Arbor, U.S.A. 42 12N 83 48W
72 Annaba (Bône), Algeria 36 55N 7 45E
68 Annam, reg., Vietnam 16 0N 107 0E
31 Annan, Scotland 55 0N 3 17W
31 Annandale, Dist. & R., Scotland 55 15N 3 25W
92 Annapolis, Md., U.S.A. 39 0N 76 15W
93 Annapolis Royal, Canada 44 45N 65 42W
43 Annecy, France 45 46N 6 5E
26 Annfield Plain, England 54 52N 1 45W
91 Anniston, U.S.A. 33 45N 85 50W
†71 Annobon, I., W. Africa 1 35s 5 35E
43 Annonay, France 45 15N 4 40E
94 Annotto Bay, Jamaica 18 17N 76 43W
83 Annuello, Australia 34 55s 142 55E
91 Anoka, U.S.A. 45 14N 93 29W
45 Ansbach, Germany 49 21N 10 37E
67 Anshan, China 41 2N 122 10E
66 Ansi, China 40 37N 95 50E
72 Ansongo, Mali 15 50N 0 25E
22 Anstey, England 52 41N 1 14W
31 Anstruther, Scotland 56 13N 2 41W
51 Antakya, Turkey 36 10N 36 15E
75 Antalaha, Madagascar 14 57s 50 20E
51 Antalya & G., Turkey 37 0N 30 43E
37 Antequera, Spain 37 4N 4 31W
72 Anti Atlas, Mts., Morocco 30 30N 7 0W
43 Antibes, France 43 40N 7 10E
93 Anticosti, I., Canada 49 30N 63 0W
91 Antigo, U.S.A. 45 10N 89 11W
95 Antigua, I., W. Indies 17 12N 61 45W
95 Antilla, Cuba 20 50N 75 50W
62 Antioch, *see* Antakya
98 Antioquia, Columbia 6 40N 76 0W
4 Antipodes I., S. Pac. Oc. 50 0s 178 0E
99 Antofagasta, Chile 23 45s 70 18W
75 Antonio Enes, Mozam. 16 8s 40 0E
††36 Antrim, & Co., N. Ireland 54 42N 6 12W
36 Antrim, Mts. of N. Ire. 54 55N 6 4W
75 Antsalova, Madagascar 18 40s 44 37E
75 Antsirabe, Madagascar 19 55s 47 2E
75 Antsohihy, Madagascar 14 50s 47 50E
67 Antung, China 40 9N 124 22E
44 Antwerp, & Prov., Belg. 51 13N 4 25E
64 Anupgarh, India 29 10N 73 5E
64 Anuradhapura, Sri Lanka 8 25N 80 23E
80 Anxious, B., Australia 33 20s 134 40E
66 Anyang, China 36 15N 114 35E
60 Anzhero-Sudzhensk, U.S.S.R. 56 10N 85 40E
43 Anzin, France 50 20N 3 30E
40 Anzio, Italy 41 28N 12 37E
67 Aomori, & Pref., Japan 40 40N 140 40E
43 Aosta, Italy 45 46N 7 20E
72 Aoulef Arab, Algeria 27 0N 1 0E
91 Apalachee B., U.S.A. 30 0N 84 10W
91 Apalachicola, U.S.A. 29 47N 85 5W
68 Aparri, Philippines 18 15N 121 50E
44 Apeldoorn, Netherlands 52 13N 5 58E
40 Apennines, Mts., Italy 43 0N 13 0E
84 Apia, Upolu I., Samoa (Inset)
73 Apollonia (Marsa Susa), Libya 32 52N 21 59E
92 Apostle Is., U.S.A. 47 0N 90 45W
92 Appalachians, Mts., U.S.A. 37 0N 80 20W
44 Appenzell, & Cn., Switz. 47 20N 9 24E
44 Appingedam, Netherlands 53 17N 6 45E
26 Appleby, England 54 35N 2 30W
24 Appledore, Devon, England 51 3N 4 12W
23 Appledore, Kent, England 51 2N 0 47E
92 Appleton, U.S.A. 44 17N 88 27W
40 Apulia, Reg., Italy 41 40N 17 20E
95 Apure, R., Venezuela 7 30N 69 15W
98 Apurimac, R., Peru 13 0s 73 0W
73 Aqaba, & Gulf, Jordan 29 0N 35 0E
62 Aqiq, Sudan 18 10N 38 20E
62 Ar Rutbah, Iraq 33 0N 40 10E
62-63 Arab Emirates, Union of 23 50N 52 30E
72 Araba, Nigeria 13 7N 5 0E
62 Arabia, Asia 15 0 to 30 0N; 35 0 to 59 0E
73 Arabian Des., Egypt 28 0N 32 20E
57 Arabian Sea, Indian Oc. 17 0N 65 0E
98 Aracaju, Brazil 11 0s 37 0W
98 Aracati, Brazil 4 20s 37 45W
37 Aracena, Spain 37 53N 6 36W
98 Araçuai, Brazil 16 50s 42 0W
63 Arad, Israel 31 16N 35 13E
47 Arad, Rumania 46 10N 21 13E
37 Aragon, Prov., Spain 41 40N 0 40W
65 Arakan Coast Dist., Bur. 20 43N 93 20E
65 Arakan Yoma, Mts., Burma 20 0N 94 0E
51 Araks, R., Asia 39 0N 47 30E
60 Aral Sea, Cent. Asia 45 0N 59 0E
60 Aralsk, U.S.S.R. 46 50N 61 20E
82 Aramac, Australia 22 58s 145 14E
36 Aran I., Ireland 55 0N 8 32W
34 Aran Is, Ireland 53 5N 9 35W
37 Aranjuez, Spain 40 1N 3 38W
75 Aranos, S.W. Afr. 24 9s 19 7E
91 Aransas Pass, U.S.A. 27 55N 97 0W
72 Araouane, Mali 19 0N 3 30W
51 Araq, Iran 34 0N 49 50E
83 Ararat, Australia 37 30s 142 37E
51 Ararat, Mt., Turkey 39 40N 44 25E
98 Araripe, Sa. do, plat., Brazil 7 0s 40 0W
31 Arbroath, Scotland 56 33N 2 36W
42 Arcachon, France 44 39N 1 13W
37 Arcos, Spain 36 44N 5 47W
64 Arcot, India 12 50N 79 26E
100 Arctic Ocean
88 Arctic Red R., Canada 67 15N 134 0W
32 Ardcharnich, Scotland 57 52N 5 5W
51 Ardebil, Iran 38 24N 48 10E
42 Ardèche, Dépt., France 45 0N 4 40E
36 Ardee, Ireland 53 51N 6 32W
42 Ardennes, Dépt., France 49 33N 4 50E
44 Ardennes, Mts., Belg.-Fr. 50 0N 5 30E
51 Ardestan, Iran 33 22N 52 24E
34 Ardfinnan, Ireland 52 20N 7 53W
36 Ardglass, N. Ireland 54 15N 5 56W
32 Ardhasig, Scotland 57 55N 6 51W
36 Ardkeen, N. Ireland 54 27N 5 53W
35 Ardmore & Hd., Ire. 51 58N 7 44W
91 Ardmore, U.S.A. 34 11N 97 9W
34 Ardnacrusha, Ireland 52 42N 8 38W
32 Ardnamurchan Pt., Scot. 56 46N 6 14W
30 Ardrossan, Scotland 55 39N 4 49W
95 Areciba, Puerto Rico 18 28N 66 30W
49 Arendal, Norway 58 28N 8 43E
25 Arenig Fach, Mt., Wales 52 57N 3 46W
98 Arequipa, Peru 16 30s 71 25W
42 Arès, France 44 46N 1 10W
37 Arévalo, Spain 41 0N 4 45W
40 Arezzo, Italy 43 29N 11 54E
42 Argentan, France 48 43N 0 2W
43 Argentat, France 45 8N 2 0E
96 Argentina, S. Amer. 30 30s 65 0W
99 Argentino, L., Argentina 50 30s 72 54W
43 Argenton, France 46 35N 1 30E
47 Arges, R., Rumania 44 25N 25 40E
72 Argo, L., Sudan 19 30N 30 28E
41 Argolis, G. of, Greece 37 44N 22 54E
41 Argos, Greece 37 39N 22 42E
72 Argungu, Nigeria 12 55N 4 30E
‡30 Argyll, Co. & Dist., Scot. 56 20N 5 25W
98 Arica, Chile 18 37s 70 18W
80 Arid, C., Australia 34 0s 123 20E
42 Ariège, Dépt., France 43 20N 1 30E
94 Arima, Trinidad 10 40N 61 15W
98 Arinos, R., Brazil 12 0s 57 0W
98 Aripuana, R., Brazil 7 30s 60 0W
32 Arisaig, & Sd. of, Scot. 56 54N 5 48W
90 Arizona, st., U.S.A. 34 30N 111 30W
48 Arjeplog, Sweden 66 0N 18 0E
32 Arkaig, L., Scotland 56 58N 5 10W
90 Arkansas, R., U.S.A. 38 5N 103 0W
91 Arkansas, st., U.S.A. 35 0N 92 0W
91 Arkansas City, U.S.A. 37 9N 97 3W
50 Arkhangelsk, U.S.S.R. 64 35N 40 50E
35 Arklow, & Hd., Ireland 52 47N 6 9W
43 Arles, France 43 10N 4 42E
44 Arlon, Belgium 49 41N 5 49E
31 Armadale, Scotland 55 54N 3 42W
††36 Armagh & Co., N. Ire. 54 20N 6 38W
51 Armavir, U.S.S.R. 45 0N 41 7E
51 Armenia, S.S.R., U.S.S.R. 40 0N 45 0E
43 Armentières, France 50 40N 2 55E
83 Armidale, Australia 30 30s 151 40E
48 Arnar Fjord, Iceland 65 45N 23 50W
48 Arnes, Iceland 66 2N 22 32W
44 Arnhem, Netherlands 51 59N 5 55E
80 Arnhem B., Austral. 12 15s 136 4E
80 Arnhem Ld., Australia 13 15s 133 30E
40 Arno, R., Italy 43 41N 10 40W
27 Arnold, England 53 0N 1 8W
48 Arnöy I., Norway 70 5N 20 30E
92 Arnprior, Canada 45 28N 76 26W
76 Aroab, S.W. Afr. 26 41s 19 39E
37 Aroche, Spain 37 58N 7 0W
43 Arona, Italy 45 48N 8 32E
62 Arqa, S. Yemen 13 35N 47 22E
34 Arra Mts., Ireland 52 50N 8 22W
65 Arrah, India 25 40N 84 38E
94 Arraijan, Panama 8 57N 79 38W
30 Arran I., Scotland 55 35N 5 15W
43 Arras, France 50 17N 2 40E
72 Arrecife, Canary Is. 28 58N 13 35W
42 Arrée, Mts. d', France 48 25N 3 35W
36 Arrow L., Ireland 54 3N 8 19W
67 Arshan, China 47 20N 119 55E
41 Arta, Greece 39 10N 20 59E
61 Artem, U.S.S.R. 43 50N 131 55E
52 Artemovsk, U.S.S.R. 48 25N 38 5E
61 Artemovski, U.S.S.R. 54 45N 93 35E
43 Artois, Prov., France 50 30N 2 20E
51 Artvin, Turkey 41 10N 41 3E
74 Arua, Uganda 3 1N 30 58E
95 Aruba I., Neth. W. Indies 12 30N 70 0W
23 Arun, R., England 51 5N 0 27W
31 Arundel, England 50 52N 0 33W
74 Arusha, Tanzania 3 10s 36 50E
74 Aruwimi, R., Zaïre 1 30N 25 0E
42 Arve, R., France 45 56N 6 40E
48 Arvidsjaur, Sweden 65 30N 19 15E
49 Arvika, Sweden 59 43N 12 34E
60 Arys, U.S.S.R. 42 20N 68 30E
52 Arzamas, U.S.S.R. 55 30N 43 45E
72 Arzew, Algeria 35 50N 0 40W
63 As Rabbah, Jordan 31 10N 35 45E
62 As Sabya, Saudi Arabia 17 10N 42 37E
63 As Salt, Jordan 32 5N 35 44E
63 As Sohar, Oman 24 20N 56 40E
63 As Zahiriyah, Jordan 31 24N 34 56E
67 Asahigawa, Japan 43 50N 142 20E
5 Ascension I., Atlantic Oc. 7 55s 14 0W
45 Aschaffenburg, Germany 49 58N 9 10E
40 Ascoli Piceno, Italy 42 54N 13 37E
23 Ascot, England 51 24N 0 41W
62 Aseb, Ethiopia 13 5N 42 38E
74 Asela, Ethiopia 8 0N 39 0E
44 Asfeld, France 49 27N 4 5E
23 Ash, England 51 16N 0 18W
62 Ash Shihr, S. Yemen 14 50N 49 35E
62 Ashaira, Saudi Arabia 21 40N 40 40E
27 Ashbourne, England 53 1N 1 44W
24 Ashburton, England 50 31N 3 46W
84 Ashburton, N.Z. 53 59s 171 52E
80 Ashburton R., Australia 22 20s 115 12E
22 Ashby-de-la-Zouch, Eng. 52 45N 1 30W
63 Ashdod, Israel 31 49N 34 38E
63 Ashdod Yam, Israel 31 47N 34 39E
23 Ashdown Forest, Eng. 51 4N 0 10E
91 Asheville, U.S.A. 35 40N 82 33W
23 Ashford, England 51 8N 0 52E
67 Ashikaga, Japan 36 25N 139 20E
27 Ashington, England 55 12N 1 35W
60 Ashkhabad, U.S.S.R. 38 5N 58 22E
92 Ashland, Ky., U.S.A. 38 30N 82 42W
92 Ashland, Wis., U.S.A. 46 30N 91 0W
63 Ashquelon, Israel 31 40N 34 35E
92 Ashtabula, U.S.A. 41 55N 80 47W
26 Ashton-in-Makerfield, England 53 29N 2 39W
26 Ashton-under-Lyne, Eng. 53 30N 2 8W
5 Asia, Continent
51 Asia Minor, *see* Anatolia
72 Asilah, Morocco 35 30N 6 0W
60 Asino, U.S.S.R. 57 0N 86 0E
62 Asir, Dist., Saudi Arabia 18 25N 43 0E
49 Askersund, Sweden 58 58N 14 8E
23 Aslackby, England 52 53N 0 23W
74 Asmera, Ethiopia 15 20N 38 49E
26 Aspatria, England 54 45N 3 20W
84 Aspiring, Mt., N.Z. 44 31s 168 41E
65 Assam, st., India 25 20N 93 30E
44 Asse, Belgium 50 55N 4 12E
46 Assen, Netherlands 53 0N 6 35E
88 Assiniboia, Canada 49 36N 106 4W
88 Assiniboine R., Canada 49 45N 99 0W
72 Assinie, Ivory Coast 5 9N 3 15W
40 Assisi, Italy 43 5N 12 38E
32 Assynt, L. & Dist., Scot. 58 10N 5 1W
40 Asti, Italy 44 54N 8 15E
37 Astorga, Spain 42 28N 6 9E
90 Astoria, U.S.A. 46 10N 123 45E
51 Astrakhan, U.S.S.R. 46 25N 48 8W
37 Asturias, Prov., Spain 43 20N 5 50E
99 Asunción, Paraguay 25 25s 57 35E
73 Aswan, Egypt 24 12N 32 59W
73 Asyut, Egypt 27 15N 31 0s
99 Atacama Des., Chile 25 0s 70 0W
72 Atakpame, Togo 7 35N 1 0E
72 Atar, Mauritania 20 30N 13 0W
61 Atara, U.S.S.R. 63 10N 129 10E
60 Atasu, U.S.S.R. 48 30N 71 0E
73 Atbara, Sudan 17 20N 35 0E
73 Atbara, R., Sudan 13 50N 36 0E
60 Atbasar, U.S.S.R. 51 50N 68 25E
91 Atchison, U.S.A. 39 31N 95 10W
44 Ath, Belgium 50 39N 3 48E
88 Athabasca, Canada 54 48N 113 15W
88 Athabasca L. & R., Can. 59 20N 109 30W
35 Athboy, Ireland 53 38N 6 57W
34 Athenry, Ireland 53 19N 8 45W
41 Athens, Greece 37 59N 23 42E
91 Athens, Georgia, U.S.A. 33 57N 83 29W
92 Athens, Ohio, U.S.A. 39 28N 82 12W
91 Athens, Tenn., U.S.A. 35 29N 84 42W
22 Atherstone, England 52 35N 1 32W
82 Atherton, Australia 16 54s 145 3E
26 Atherton, England 53 32N 2 30W
34 Athleague, Ireland 53 34N 8 17W
34 Athlone, Ireland 53 27N 7 55W
33 Athol, Forest of, Scot. 56 51N 4 0W
41 Athos, Mt., Greece 40 9N 24 23E
35 Athy, Ireland 53 0N 7 0W
73 Ati, Chad 13 25N 17 0E
92 Atikokan, Canada 48 45N 91 43W
52 Atkarsk, U.S.S.R. 51 55N 45 3E
91 Atlanta, U.S.A. 33 45N 84 25W
93 Atlantic City, U.S.A. 39 24N 74 28W
10 Atlantic Ocean, N. 35 0N 40 0W
10 Atlantic Ocean, S. 20 0s 10 0W
72 Atlas Mts., Morocco 33 0N 1 0W
44 Attigny, France 49 29N 4 35E
23 Attleborough, England 52 32N 1 1E
64 Attock, Pakistan 33 58N 72 32E
68 Attopeu, Laos 14 50N 107 0E
64 Attur, India 11 35N 78 30E
43 Aubagne, France 43 20N 5 30E
42 Aube, Dépt., France 48 30N 4 0E
43 Aube, R., France 48 35N 4 30E
43 Aubenas, France 44 38N 4 20E
44 Aubenton, France 49 50N 4 11E
43 Aubigny, France 47 30N 2 25E
45 Aubonne, Switzerland 46 31N 6 42E
93 Auburn, Me., U.S.A. 44 0N 70 10W
92 Auburn, N.Y., U.S.A. 42 55N 76 38W
43 Auch, France 43 39N 0 32E

* County incorporated within Gwynedd

** County incorporated within the region of Tayside

† Renamed Pagalu, I.

†† In April 1973 districts replaced counties in N. Ireland

‡ County incorporated within the region of Strathclyde

30 Auchinleck, Scotland 55 28N 4 18W
31 Auchterarder, Scotland 56 18N 3 43W
31 Auchterderran, Scotland 56 9N 3 16W
31 Auchtermuchty, Scotland 56 18N 3 15W
32 Auchtertyre, Scotland 57 17N 5 35W
84 Auckland & Dist., N.Z. 36 50S 174 42E
100 Auckland Is., Southern Ocean 51 0S 168 0E
42 Aude, Dépt., France 43 2N 2 25E
43 Aude, R., France 42 47N 2 9E
42 Audierne, France 48 2N 4 38W
36 Aughnacloy, N. Ireland 54 26N 6 59W
35 Aughrus More, Ireland 53 34N 10 10W
45 Augsburg, Germany 48 26N 10 53E
80 Augusta, Australia 34 18S 115 12E
40 Augusta, Italy 37 14N 15 12E
93 Augusta, Me., U.S.A. 44 20N 69 45W
91 Augusta, Ga., U.S.A. 33 30N 82 0W
47 Augustow, Poland 53 51N 22 58E
80 Augustus, Mt., Australia 24 8S 117 0E
44 Aulnoye, France 50 10N 3 50E
43 Aumale, France 49 50N 1 45E
42 Aunis, Dist., France 46 9N 0 57W
64 Aurangabad, India 19 55N 75 30E
42 Auray, France 47 40N 3 0W
43 Aurillac, France 44 58N 2 27E
92 Aurora, Ill., U.S.A. 41 48N 88 15W
75 Aus, S.W. Africa 26 43S 16 12E
49 Aust-Agder, Co., Norway 59 0N 8 30E
91 Austin, Minn., U.S.A. 43 39N 92 59W
90 Austin, Tex., U.S.A. 30 20N 97 46W
81 Austral Downs, Australia 20 45S 137 40E
4 Austral Is., Pacific Ocean 23 0S 150 0W
80-1 Australia, Commonwealth of, 25 0S 135 0E
83 Australian Alps, Australia 37 0S 148 0E
83 Australian Cap. Terr., Australia 35 15N 149 8E
46 Austria, Europe 47 30N 13 20E
48 Austvågöy, I., Norway 68 25N 14 45E
43 Autun, France 47 1N 4 20E
43 Auvergne, Prov., France 45 30N 3 0E
43 Auvergne Monts d', France 45 30N 3 0E
43 Auxerre, France 47 48N 3 33W
74 Avakubi, Zaïre 1 16N 27 30E
43 Avallon, France 47 34N 3 49E
62 Aveh, Iran 35 40N 49 15E
37 Aveiro, Portugal 40 39N 8 39W
40 Avellino, Italy 41 0N 14 42E
40 Aversa, Italy 41 0N 14 10E
42 Avesnes, France 50 9N 3 55E
49 Avesta, Sweden 60 13N 16 4E
42 Aveyron, Dépt., France 44 10N 2 45E
99 Aviá Terai, Argentina 26 30S 60 45W
43 Avignon, France 43 58N 4 54E
37 Avila, Spain 40 39N 4 41W
37 Aviles, Spain 43 33N 6 0W
*35 Avoca, Ireland 52 51N 6 12W
22 Avon, R., Hants, Eng. 51 8N 1 48W
22 Avon, R., Warwick, Eng. 52 22N 1 25W
33 Avon, R., Scotland 57 15N 3 23W
81 Avon Downs, Australia 19 58S 137 25E
22 Avonmouth, England 51 30N 2 43W
42 Avranches, France 48 42N 1 18W
74 Awash, Ethiopia 9 8N 40 7E
30 Awe, L. & R., Scotland 56 17N 5 15W
73 Awjilah, Libya 29 8N 21 7E
48 Axar, Fd., Iceland 66 20N 16 45W
24 Axbridge, England 51 17N 2 50W
24 Axe, R., England 51 17N 2 50W
26 Axe Edge, England 53 13N 1 58W
27 Axholme, I. of, England 53 33N 0 50W
72 Axim, Ghana 4 58N 2 6W
24 Axminster, England 50 46N 3 0W
98 Ayacucho, Peru 12 58S 74 5W
60 Ayaguz, U.S.S.R. 48 10N 80 0E
37 Ayamonte, Spain 37 15N 7 26W
61 Ayan, U.S.S.R. 56 0N 137 0E
41 Aydin, Turkey 37 55N 27 55E
41 Ayios Evstratios, I., Gr. 39 30N 24 59E
23 Aylesbury, England 51 49N 0 48W
23 Aylesford, England 51 18N 0 29E
23 Aylsham, England 52 48N 1 16E
82 Ayr, Australia 19 36S 147 25E
**30 Ayr, & Co., Scotland 55 27N 4 37W
26 Ayre, Pt. of, Isle of Man 54 25N 42 22W
27 Ayton, England 54 15N 0 29W
94 Ayutla, Mexico 17 0N 99 5W
68 Ayutthaya, Thailand 14 30N 100 40E
41 Ayvalik, Turkey 39 20N 26 50E
65 Azamgarh, India 26 15N 83 16E
72 Azare, Nigeria 11 55N 10 10E
51 Azerbaijan, S.S.R., U.S.S.R. 40 20N 48 0E
10 Azores Is., Atlantic Oc. 39 0N 29 0W
52 Azov, U.S.S.R. 47 3N 39 20E
51 Azov, S. of U.S.S.R. 45 53N 35 35E
42 Azpeitia, Spain 43 13N 2 14W
95 Azua, Dominican Rep. 18 15N 70 40W
37 Azuaga, Spain 38 16N 5 42W
99 Azul, Argentina 36 25S 59 40W

B

63 Ba'àbda, Lebanon 33 50N 35 32E
63 Ba'labakk (Baalbek), Leb. 34 0N 36 12E
44 Baarle-Nassau, Neth. 51 27N 4 57E
44 Baarn, Neth. 52 13N 5 17E
62 Bab el Mandeb Str. 12 37N 43 22E
68 Babar Is., Indonesia 8 2S 128 58E
82 Babinda, Australia 17 27S 146 0E
88 Babine L., Canada 54 40N 126 10W
74 Baboua, Central Africa 5 49N 14 58E
62 Babul, Iran 36 40N 52 40E
62 Babushkin, U.S.S.R. 55 50N 38 0E
67 Babuyan Is., Philippines 19 20N 121 45E
47 Bacau, Rumania 46 30N 26 59E
43 Baccarat, France 48 30N 6 45E
60 Bachelina, U.S.S.R. 57 45N 67 20E
45 Backnang, Germany 48 57N 9 26E
68 Bacolod, Philippines 10 40N 123 2E
68 Bacuit, Philippines 11 0N 119 25E
26 Bacup, England 53 44N 2 13W
45 Bad Hersfeld, Germany 50 50N 9 40E
45 Bad Homburg, Germany 50 15N 8 36E
46 Bad Ischl, Austria 47 40N 13 39E
45 Bad Kissingen, Germany 50 10N 10 10E
45 Bad Kreuznach, Germany 49 51N 7 50E
90 Bad Lands, U.S.A. 43 30N 102 10W
45 Bad Mergentheim, Ger. 49 29N 9 46E
64 Badagara, India 11 35N 75 35E
72 Badagri, Nigeria 6 25N 2 55E
37 Badajoz, Spain 38 51N 7 0W
64 Badakhshan, Dist., Afghanistan 36 40N 70 0E
37 Badalona, Spain 41 28N 2 30E
65 Badampahar, India 22 10N 86 10E
64 Baddo R., Pak. 28 20N 65 10E
46 Baden, Austria 48 0N 16 46E
45 Baden, Switzerland 47 29N 8 18E
45 Baden-Baden, Germany 48 44N 8 18E
33 Badenoch, Dist., Scot. 57 5N 4 0W
45 Baden-Württemburg, Länd, Germany 48 45N 9 0E
46 Badgastein, Austria 47 7N 13 9E
64 Badrinath, India 30 45N 79 25E
64 Badulla, Sri Lanka 6 48N 81 7E
89 Baffin B. & I., Canada 73 0N 70 0W
74 Bafia, Cameroon 4 40N 11 10E
72 Bafoulabe, Mali 13 45N 11 0W
63 Bafq, Iran 31 40N 55 28E
74 Bafwasende, Zaïre 1 20N 27 20E
68 Bagansiapiapi, Indonesia 2 5N 101 0E
99 Bagé, Brazil 31 10S 54 10W
35 Bagenalstown, see Muine Bheag
51 Baghdad, Iraq 33 23N 44 30E
32 Bagh nam Faoileann, B., Scotland 57 22N 7 10W
42 Bagnères de Bigorre, Fr. 43 0N 0 5E
42 Bagnères de Luchon, Fr. 42 45N 0 35E
93 Bagotville, Canada 48 28N 70 58W
64 Bagrach Kol, China 42 0N 87 0E
23 Bagshot, England 51 21N 0 39W
68 Baguio, Philippines 16 17N 120 47E
91 Bahama Is., W. Indies 26 0N 77 30W
64 Bahawalpur, Pak. 29 0N 72 0E
98 Bahia Prov., Brazil 12 0S 42 0W
99 Bahia Blanca, Argentina 38 45S 62 25W
99 Bahias, C. dos, Argentina 45 0S 65 30W
62 Bahr el Abyad (White Nile), Sudan 13 30N 33 0E
62 Bahr el Azraq (Blue Nile), Sudan 14 30N 33 30E
73 Bahr el Ghazal, R., Sudan 9 0N 30 0E
73 Bahr el Jebel, R., Sudan 7 30N 30 35E
62 Bahra, Saudi Arabia 21 15N 39 30E
65 Bahraich, India 27 48N 81 30E
62 Bahrain I., Persian G. 26 0N 50 23E
64 Bahu Kalat, Iran 25 40N 61 15E
47 Baia Mare, Rumania 47 40N 23 32E
89 Baie Comeau, Canada 49 25N 68 20W
51 Baikit, U.S.S.R. 61 40N 96 5E
60 Baikonur, U.S.S.R. 47 48N 66 4E
27 Baildon, England 53 52N 1 46W
36 Baillieborough, Ireland 53 56N 6 59W
43 Bain, France 47 52N 1 40W
91 Bainbridge, U.S.A. 31 0N 84 30W
88 Baird Mts., Alaska 60 45 N 160 0W
83 Bairnsdale, Australia 38 0S 147 32E
65 Baitadi, Nepal, India 29 35N 80 25E
47 Baja, Hungary 46 10N 19 0E
74 Bakala, Central Africa 6 15N 20 20E
90 Baker, Ore., U.S.A. 44 45N 117 50W
88 Baker Lake, Canada 64 20N 96 0W
90 Baker, Mt., U.S.A. 48 45N 121 45W
89 Baker's Dozen, Is., Can. 56 45N 79 20W
90 Bakersfield, Calif., U.S.A. 35 22N 119 0W
27 Bakewell, England 53 12N 1 40W
48 Bakkagerdi, Iceland 65 33N 13 58W
47 Bakony Forest, Hungary 47 30N 18 0E
51 Baku, U.S.S.R. 40 27N 49 48E
51 Bala, U.S.S.R. 66 40N 133 5E
25 Bala, tn. & L., Wales 52 55N 3 37W
63 Ba'labakk, Lebanon 34 0N 36 12E
64 Balaghat Ra., India 18 58N 76 0E
37 Balaguer, Spain 41 52N 0 50E
83 Balaklava, Australia 34 2S 138 20E
51 Balaklava, U.S.S.R. 44 27N 33 44E
65 Balangir, India 20 50N 83 25E
51 Balashikha, U.S.S.R. 55 47N 37 59E
52 Balashov, U.S.S.R. 51 35N 43 5E
65 Balasore, India 21 31N 87 10E
47 Balaton, L., Hungary 46 47N 17 40E
31 Balbeggie, Scotland 56 26N 3 19W
94 Balboa, Panama Canal Zone (Inset)
35 Balbriggan, Ireland 53 36N 6 12W
99 Balcarce, Argentina 38 30S 58 0W
41 Balchik, Bulgaria 43 23N 28 11E
84 Balclutha, N.Z. 46 15S 169 50E
23 Baldock, England 51 59N 0 11W
90 Baldy Pk., U.S.A. 33 50N 109 30W
61 Baldzhikan, U.S.S.R. 49 20N 110 30E
37 Balearic Is., Spain 39 40N 3 0E
32 Baleshare I., Scotland 57 30N 7 21W
63 Balfouriya, Israel 32 38N 35 17E
30 Balfron, Scotland 56 4N 4 20W
62 Balhaf, South Yemen 14 0N 48 10E
74 Bali, Cameroon 5 54N 10 0E
68 Bali, I., Indonesia 8 30S 115 20E
41 Balikesir, Turkey 30 40N 28 2E
68 Balikpapan, Indonesia 1 10S 116 55E
33 Balintore, Scotland 57 45N 3 55W
65 Balipara, India 26 54N 92 51E
41 Balkan Mts., Bulgaria 42 50N 24 50E
60 Balkhash, L., U.S.S.R. 46 30N 76 0E
63 Balkh, Afghanistan 36 44N 66 47E
65 Balla, Bangladesh 24 10N 91 35E
30 Ballachulish, Scot., see N. Ballachulish
36 Ballaghaderreen, Ireland 53 55N 8 34W
30 Ballantrae, Scotland 55 6N 5 0W
83 Ballarat, Australia 37 37S 143 50E
33 Ballater, Scotland 57 3N 3 3W
26 Ballaugh, Isle of Man 54 20N 4 32W
100 Balleny Is., S. Ocean 64 0S 160 0E
83 Ballina, Australia 28 48S 153 40E
36 Ballina, Mayo, Ireland 54 8N 9 10W
34 Ballina, Tipperary, Ire. 52 50N 8 27W
36 Ballinalee, Ireland 53 46N 7 40W
36 Ballinamore, Ireland 54 3N 7 48W
34 Ballinasloe, Ireland 53 20N 8 12W
34 Ballincollig, Ireland 51 52N 8 35W
35 Ballindaggin, Ireland 52 34N 6 41 W
36 Ballindine, Ireland 53 40N 8 57W
34 Ballineen, Ireland 51 44N 8 57W
34 Ballingarry, Limerick, Ire. 52 29N 8 50W
34 Ballingarry, Tipp., Ire. 53 1N 8 3W
36 Ballinlough, Ireland 53 45N 8 39W
31 Ballinluig, Scotland 56 38N 3 39W
36 Ballinrobe, Ireland 53 37N 9 12W
36 Ballintoy, Ireland 55 13N 6 20W
36 Ballintra, Ireland 54 35N 8 9W
35 Ballivor, Ireland 53 32N 6 58W
30 Balloch, Scotland 56 0N 4 35W
35 Ballon, Ireland 52 44N 6 47W
36 Ballybay, Ireland 54 8N 6 52W
36 Ballybofey, Ireland 54 48N 7 47W
34 Ballybunion, Ireland 52 31N 9 40W
35 Ballycanew, Ireland 52 37N 6 18W
36 Ballyconnell, Ireland 54 7N 7 35W
34 Ballycotton, Ireland 51 50N 8 0W
36 Ballycroy, Ireland 54 2N 9 49W
34 Ballydavid, Ireland 52 13N 10 21W
34 Ballydehob, Ireland 51 34N 9 29W
34 Ballyduff, Kerry, Ire. 52 27N 9 40W
34 Ballyduff, Waterford, Ire. 52 9N 8 2W
34 Ballyforan, Ireland 53 29N 8 16W
34 Ballygar, Ireland 53 33N 8 20W
36 Ballygarrett, Ireland 52 34N 6 15W
36 Ballygawley, N. Ireland 54 27N 7 2W
36 Ballyhaise, Ireland 54 3N 7 20W
36 Ballyhalbert, N. Ireland 54 30N 5 33W
36 Ballyhaunis, Ireland 53 47N 8 47W
34 Ballyheige, Ireland 52 24N 9 50W
35 Ballyjamesduff, Ireland 53 52N 7 11W
34 Ballylanders, Ireland 52 22N 8 21W
34 Ballylongford, Ireland 52 34N 9 30W
35 Ballylynan, Ireland 52 56N 7 3W
35 Ballymahon, Ireland 53 33N 7 47W
36 Ballymoe, Ireland 53 41N 8 28W
35 Ballymore, Ireland 53 29N 7 40W
35 Ballymore Eustace, Ire. 53 8N 6 38W
36 Ballymote, Ireland 54 5N 8 30W
35 Ballynacargy, Ireland 53 35N 7 32W
36 Ballynahinch, N. Ireland 54 25N 5 54W
36 Ballynure, N. Ireland 54 47 N 5 59W
35 Ballyragget, Ireland 52 47N 7 20W
36 Ballyroan, Ireland 52 57N 7 20W
36 Ballysadare, Ireland 54 12N 8 30W
36 Ballyshannon, Ireland 54 30N 8 10W
34 Ballyvaughan, Ireland 53 7N 9 9W
36 Ballywalter, N. Ireland 54 33N 5 30W
33 Balmoral Castle, Scotland 57 2N 3 14W
30 Balquhidder, Scotland 56 22N 4 22W
65 Balrampur, India 27 25N 82 20E
83 Balranald, Australia 34 40S 143 35E
94 Balsas, R., Mexico 18 30N 102 0W
45 Balsthal, Switzerland 47 20N 7 42E
49 Baltic Sea, Europe 57 0N 19 30E
49 Baltiisk, U.S.S.R. 54 40N 19 10E
34 Baltimore, Ireland 51 29N 9 20W
92 Baltimore, U.S.A. 39 25N 76 40W
64 Baluchistan, Reg., Pak. 27 30N 65 0E
63 Bam, Iran 29 5N 58 23E
72 Bamako, Mali 12 30N 7 45W
72 Bamba, Mali 17 0N 1 0W
74 Bambari, Central Africa 5 40N 20 35E
82 Bambaroo, Australia 18 57S 146 15E
45 Bamberg, Germany 49 53N 11 14E
27 Bamburgh, England 55 37N 1 42W
64 Bamian, Afghanistan 35 0N 67 53E
22 Bampton, England 51 44N 1 33W
63 Bampur, Iran 27 8N 60 8E
68 Ban Aranyaprathet, Thailand 13 40N 102 35E
68 Ban Khemmarat, Thail. 16 0N 105 20E
34 Banagher, Ireland 53 12N 7 59W
74 Banalia, Zaïre 1 40N 25 20E
74 Banana, Zaïre 6 0S 12 20E
65 Banaras, India see Varanasi
47 Banat, Dist., Rumania 45 27N 21 35E
36 Banbridge, N. Ireland 54 20N 6 16W
22 Banbury, England 52 4N 1 20W
33 Banchory, Scotland 57 3N 2 30W
75 Bancroft, Zambia, see Chililabombwe
67 Banda Sea, East Indies 6 0S 127 30E
67 Bandaisan, Mt., Japan 37 40N 140 30E
72 Bandama, R., Ivory Coast 7 0N 5 0W
63 Bandar Abbas, Iran 27 15N 56 23E
68 Bandar Atjeh, Indonesia 5 35N 95 25E
62 Bandar Rig, Iran 29 27N 50 47E
62 Bandar Shah, Iran 37 4N 54 0E
62 Bandar Shapur, Iran 30 10N 48 40E
72 Bandiagara, Mali 14 12N 3 29W
41 Bandirma, Turkey 40 21N 27 58E
68 Bandjarmasin, Indon. 3 20S 114 25E
34 Bandon, Ireland 51 45N 8 43W
74 Bandundu (Banningville), Zaïre 3 12S 17 12E
68 Bangung, Indonesia 6 48S 107 45E
88 Banff, Canada 51 14N 115 38W
†33 Banff, & Co., Scotland 57 41N 2 32W
72 Banfora, Volta 10 40N 4 40W
64 Bangalore, India 12 58N 77 30E
74 Bangassou, Central Africa 4 50N 22 48E
68 Banggai, Arch., Indonesia 1 15S 123 0E
68 Bangka, I., Indonesia 2 20S 106 0E
68 Bangkalan, Indonesia 7 10S 112 50E
68 Bangkok, Thailand 13 55N 100 30E
65 Bangladesh, South Asia 24 0N 90 0E
36 Bangor, N. Ireland 54 39N 5 39W
93 Bangor, Me., U.S.A. 44 45N 68 40W
25 Bangor, Wales 53 14N 4 7W
74 Bangui, Central Africa 4 23N 19 20E
74 Bangweulu, L., Zambia 11 30S 30 5E
63 Banias, Syria 35 7N 36 2E
40 Banja Luka, Yugoslavia 44 45N 17 0E
31 Bankfoot, Scotland 56 30N 3 31W
73 Baninah, Libya 32 10N 20 15E
65 Bankipore, India 25 35N 85 10E
81 Banks I., Australia 10 5S 142 12E
88 Banks I., Canada 73 30N 122 0W
84 Banks Pen., N.Z. 43 47S 173 0E
83 Banks Str., Australia 40 40S 148 10E
65 Bankura, India 23 15N 85 5E
74 Banningville, see Bandundu
31 Bannockburn, Scotland 56 5N 3 55W
64 Bannu, Pakistan 33 0N 70 18E
47 Banská Bystrica, Cz.-slov. 48 46N 19 54E
47 Banská Stiavnica, Cz.-slov. 48 26N 18 54E
34 Banteer, Ireland 52 8N 8 53W
34 Bantry, & B., Ireland 51 1N 9 27W
74 Banyo, Cameroon 6 58N 11 50E
74 Banzyville (Mobayi), Zaïre 4 15N 21 8E
64 Bapatla, India 15 50N 80 30E
44 Bapaume, France 50 8N 2 49E
51 Baquba, Iraq 33 45N 44 50E
41 Bar, Yugoslavia 42 4N 19 7E
91 Bar Harbor, U.S.A. 44 20N 68 17W
43 Bar-le-Duc, France 48 45N 5 8E
43 Bar-s.-Aube, France 48 18N 4 45E
43 Bar-s.-Seine, France 48 6N 4 28E
60 Barabinsk, U.S.S.R. 55 30N 78 35E
92 Baraboo, U.S.A. 43 30N 89 48W
95 Baracoa, Cuba 20 20N 74 20W
95 Barahona, Dom. Rep. 18 0N 71 2W
65 Barail Ra., India 25 15N 93 0E
65 Barakhola, India 25 0N 92 40E
83 Barakula, Australia 26 30S 150 33E
64 Baramula, Kashmir 34 15N 74 25E
64 Baran, India 25 3N 76 30E
88 Baranof I., Alaska 57 0N 135 0W
50 Baranovichi, U.S.S.R. 53 10N 26 0E
98 Barbacena, Brazil 21 0S 44 0W
95 Barbados I., W. Indies 13 15N 59 30W
76 Barberton, Transvaal 25 42S 31 1E
42 Barbezieux, France 45 30N 0 12W
95 Barbuda I., W. Indies 17 43N 61 42W
82 Barcaldine, Australia 23 30S 145 17E
73 Barce (Al Marj), Libya 32 30N 20 50E
37 Barcelona, Spain 41 24N 2 9E
95 Barcelona, Venezuela 10 12N 64 45W
43 Barcelonnette, France 44 20N 6 35E
73 Bardai, Chad 21 15N 17 40E
73 Bardiyah, Libya 31 45 25 0E
27 Bardney, England 53 13N 0 19W
43 Bardonecchia, Italy 45 5N 6 40E
64 Bareilly, India 28 25N 79 32E
100 Barents Sea, Arctic Oc. 73 0N 42 0E
74 Barentu, Ethiopia 15 2N 37 35E
42 Barfleur, France 49 40N 1 20W
65 Barhi, India 24 20N 85 20E
40 Bari, Italy 41 7N 16 53E
64 Bari Doab, Pakistan 30 30N 73 0E
64 Bari Sadri, India 24 20N 74 27E
88 Baring C., Canada 70 0N 116 30W
74 Baringo, L., Kenya 0 35N 36 0E
65 Barisal, Bangladesh 22 50N 90 32E
68 Barisan Mts., Indonesia 4 0S 103 0E
23 Barking, Greater London, England 51 32N 0 5E
80 Barkly Tableland, Australia 19 40S 138 30E
66 Barkol, China 44 18N 90 48E
27 Barlby, England 53 48N 1 3W
80 Barlee L., Australia 29 10S 119 28E
40 Barletta, Italy 41 18N 16 20E
27 Barmby Moor, England 53 55N 0 47W
83 Barmedman, Australia 34 0S 147 16E
64 Barmer, India 25 49N 71 32E
30 Barmoor Castle, England 55 38N 2 0W
25 Barmouth, Wales 52 43N 4 3W
34 Barna, Ireland 53 14N 9 10W
26 Barnard Castle, England 54 33N 1 56W
83 Barnato, Australia 31 35S 145 0E
60 Barnaul, U.S.S.R. 53 10N 83 30E
83 Barnes, Australia 36 2S 144 40E
23 Barnet, Greater London, England 51 40N 0 11W
44 Barneveld, Neth. 52 7N 5 36E
42 Barneville, France 49 23N 1 45W
26 Barnoldswick, England 53 55N 2 11W
27 Barnsley, England 53 34N 1 29W
24 Barnstaple, England 51 5N 4 2W
24 Barnstaple or Bideford Bay, England 51 5N 4 20W
72 Baro, Nigeria 8 50N 6 25E
64 Baroda, India 22 22N 73 17E
75 Barotse, Prov., Zambia 15 30S 23 30E
65 Barpeta, India 26 20N 91 0E
95 Barquisimeto, Venezuela 9 55N 69 15W
43 Barr, France 48 20N 7 20E
98 Barra, Brazil 10 30S 42 28W
32 Barra I., & Sd., Scotland 57 0N 7 30W
83 Barraba, Australia 30 12S 150 40E
65 Barrackpore, India 22 45N 88 30E
37 Barrancos, Portugal 38 10N 7 0W
95 Barranquilla, Colombia 10 49N 74 45W
93 Barre, U.S.A. 44 28N 72 25W
37 Barreiro, Portugal 38 42N 8 56W
75 Barren Is., Madagascar 18 30S 44 0E
30 Barrhead, Scotland 55 47N 4 24W
92 Barrie, Canada 44 30N 79 45W
26 Barrow, England 54 8N 3 12W
80 Barrow I., Australia 20 47S 115 25E
80 Barrow Ra., Mts., Austral. 26 0S 128 0E
27 Barrow upon Humber, England 53 41N 0 22W
26 Barrowford, England 53 51N 2 14W
25 Barry, Wales 51 24N 3 16W
65 Barsoi, India 25 48N 87 57E
91 Bartlesville, U.S.A. 36 48N 96 15W
86 Bartlett Deep, W. Indies 20 0N 85 0W
27 Barton-upon-Humber, England 53 41N 0 27W
42 Bas-Rhin, Dépt., France 48 45N 7 35E
50 Bashkir, A.S.S.R., U.S.S.R. 54 0N 56 0E
68 Basilan, I., Philippines 6 40N 122 0E
23 Basildon, England 51 34N 0 29E
40 Basilicata, Prov., Italy 40 30N 16 0E
22 Basingstoke, England 51 16N 1 5W
80 Baskerville, C., Australia 17 0S 122 5E
45 Basle, & Cn., Switzerland 47 33N 7 34E
74 Basoka, Zaïre 1 20N 23 38E
37 Basque Provinces, Spain 43 20N 2 20W
62 Basra, Iraq 30 30N 47 50E
83 Bass Str., Australia 39 30S 146 0E
88 Bassano, Canada 50 45N 112 30W
40 Bassano, Italy 45 50N 11 40E
75 Bassas da India, Is., Ind. Oc. 21 45S 37 38E
94 Basse Terre, Guadeloupe 16 0N 61 45W
65 Bassein, Burma 17 0N 94 58E
42 Basses Alpes, Dépt., Fr. 44 40N 6 20E
42 Basses-Pyrénées, Dépt., France 43 17N 0 57W
43 Bassigny, Dist., France 48 3N 5 23E
65 Bastar, India 19 30N 81 30E
65 Basti, India 26 45N 82 58E
43 Bastia, Corsica 42 40N 9 20E
44 Bastogne, Belgium 50 0N 5 40E
23 Baston, England 52 43N 0 19W
75 Basutoland, see Lesotho
63 Bat Shelomo, Israel 32 36N 35 0E
63 Bat Yam, Israel 32 0N 34 44E
74 Bata, Rio Muni 1 57N 9 50E
95 Batabano, G., Cuba 22 20N 82 40W
37 Batalha, Portugal 39 40N 8 52W
67 Batan, Is., Philippines 20 25N 122 5E
66 Batang, China 30 20N 98 25E
68 Batangas, Philippines 13 50N 121 5E
92 Batavia, U.S.A. 43 0N 78 2W
52 Bataysk, U.S.S.R. 47 5N 39 45E
83 Bateman's Bay, Australia 35 40S 150 12E
22 Bath, England 51 24N 2 22W
91 Bath, Me., U.S.A. 43 57N 69 58W
63 Batha, Wadi, Oman 22 30N 59 0E
31 Bathgate, Scotland 55 55N 3 38W
83 Bathurst, Australia 33 28S 149 30E
93 Bathurst, Canada 47 37N 65 49W
††72 Bathurst, Gambia 13 20N 16 38W
88 Bathurst Inlet, Canada 67 30N 109 0W
68 Batjan Gr., Is., Indonesia 0 30S 127 0E
27 Batley, England 53 44N 1 38W
83 Batlow, Australia 35 33S 148 10E
72 Batna, Algeria 35 32N 6 20E
91 Baton Rouge, U.S.A. 30 22N 90 50W
74 Batongafo, Central Africa 7 30N 18 20E
74 Batouri, Cameroon 4 30N 14 25E
68 Battambang, Khmer Rep. 13 5N 103 8E
64 Batticaloa, Sri Lanka 7 50N 81 31E
23 Battle, England 50 55N 0 29E
92 Battle Creek, U.S.A. 42 17N 85 10W
89 Battle Harbour, Canada 52 13N 55 42W
88 Battleford, Canada 52 40N 108 12W
68 Batu Is., Indonesia 0 20S 98 5E
74 Batu, Mt., Ethiopia 6 50N 39 30E
68 Batu Radja, Indonesia 4 10S 104 10E
51 Batumi, U.S.S.R. 41 40N 41 30E
98 Baturite, Brazil 4 0S 38 40W
74 Baudouinville (Moba), Zaïre 7 0S 29 48E
42 Bauge, France 47 35N 0 10W
45 Baume les Dames, France 47 21N 6 21E
98 Baurú, Brazil 22 12S 49 8W
49 Bauska, U.S.S.R. 56 24N 24 15E
46 Bautzen, Germany 51 14N 14 23E
46 Bavaria, land, Germany 49 0N 12 0E
72 Bawku, Ghana 11 3N 0 19W
65 Bawlake, Burma 19 0N 97 30E
92 Bay Cy., Mich., U.S.A. 43 38N 83 48W
95 Bayamo, Cuba 20 25N 76 40W
66 Bayan Khara Shan Mts., China 34 0N 98 0E
66 Bayanhongor, Mts., Mongolia 46 35N 99 45E
74 Bayanga, Central Africa 2 55N 16 15E
32 Bayble, Scotland 58 12N 6 13W
42 Bayeux, France 49 20N 0 44W
65 Bayhan Aul, U.S.S.R. 50 50N 75 50E
61 Baykal, L., U.S.S.R. 53 0N 108 0E
42 Bayonne, France 43 30N 1 30W
46 Bayreuth, Germany 49 57N 11 32E
37 Baza, Spain 37 31N 2 46W
52 Bazarnyy Syzgan, U.S.S.R. 53 45N 46 45E

* *Avon, Co., England 51 25N 2 35W*
** *County incorporated within the region of Strathclyde*
† *County incorporated within the region of Grampian*
†† *Renamed Banjul*

83 Beachport, Australia 37 30N 140 0E
23 Beachy Hd., England 50 44N 0 17E
23 Beaconsfield, England 51 36N 0 39W
99 Beagle Chan, Chile 55 0S 68 30W
22 Beaminster, England 50 48N 2 46W
90 Bear, L. & R., U.S.A. 42 0N 111 20W
100 Beardmore, Antarc. 83 30S 175 0E
100 Beardmore Glacier, Antarctica 84 30S 170 0E
42 Béarn, Prov., France 43 20N 0 40W
30 Bearsden, Scotland 55 55N 4 19W
91 Beatrice, U.S.A. 40 20N 96 46W
31 Beattock, Scotland 55 19N 3 27W
43 Beaucaire, France 43 50N 4 35E
83 Beaudesert, Australia 28 0S 152 50E
68 Beaufort, Malaysia 5 25N 115 50E
100 Beaufort Sea, Arctic Oc. 75 0N 160 0W
43 Beaujolais, Dist., France 46 10N 4 30E
33 Beauly, & Firth, Scot. 57 28N 4 28W
25 Beaumaris, Wales 53 17N 4 6W
91 Beaumont, U.S.A. 30 4N 94 10W
43 Beaune, France 47 2N 4 50E
43 Beauvais, France 49 26N 2 2E
88 Beauval, Canada 55 10N 107 55W
91 Beaverdam, U.S.A. 43 30N 88 50W
26 Bebington, England 53 25N 3 1W
23 Beccles, England 52 28N 1 36E
41 Becejo, Yugoslavia 45 33N 20 2E
72 Béchar (Colomb-Béchar), Algeria 31 40N 2 17W
31 Beckfoot, England 54 50N 3 25W
27 Beckingham, England 53 24N 0 49W
92 Beckley, U.S.A. 37 44N 81 42W
27 Bedale, England 54 18N 1 35W
43 Bédarieux, France 43 40N 3 10E
23 Bedford, & Co., England 52 8N 0 28W
92 Bedford, Ind., U.S.A. 39 6N 86 37W
23 Bedford Level, England 52 50N 0 15W
27 Bedlington, England 55 9N 1 35W
25 Bedwas, England 51 36N 3 10W
22 Bedworth, England 52 28N 1 29W
83 Beenleigh, Australia 27 52S 153 0E
27 Beeston, England 52 55N 1 11W
74 Befale, Zaïre 0 5N 21 0E
36 Beg, L., N. Ireland 54 48N 6 25W
83 Bega, Australia 36 48S 149 55E
25 Begelly, Wales 51 45N 4 44W
61 Begichev I., U.S.S.R. 74 20N 112 30E
65 Behariganj, India 25 40N 87 0E
73 Beida (Al Bayda), Libya 32 35N 21 25E
62 Beihan al Daula, South Yemen 14 45N 45 15E
75 Beira, Mozambique 19 45S 35 0E
37 Beira-Alta, Prov., Port. 40 35N 7 35W
37 Beira-Baixa, Prov., Port. 40 0N 7 30W
37 Beira-Litoral Prov., Port. 40 5N 8 30W
63 Beirut (Bayrut), Lebanon 33 55N 35 30E
63 Beit Alfa, Israel 32 31N 35 25E
63 Beit Eddine, Lebanon 33 42N 35 35E
63 Beit Hanun, Israel 31 32N 34 31E
63 Beit Shean, Israel 32 30N 35 30E
63 Beit Yosef, Israel 32 34N 35 33E
75 Beitbridge, Rhodesia 22 12S 30 0E
30 Beith, Scotland 55 45N 4 38W
37 Beja, Portugal 38 2N 7 51W
72 Beja, Tunisia 36 55N 9 5E
72 Bejaia (Bougie), Algeria 36 49N 5 7E
47 Békéscaba, Hungary 46 40N 21 0E
41 Bela Crkva, Y.-slav. 44 54N 21 22E
68 Belawan, Indonesia 3 45N 98 45E
51 Belaya Tserkov, U.S.S.R. 49 40N 30 10E
89 Belcher Is., Canada 56 0N 80 30W
50 Belebei, Russia 54 10N 54 5E
98 Belem (Pará), Brazil 1 25S 48 20W
37 Belem, Portugal 38 40N 9 10W
52 Belev, U.S.S.R. 53 50N 36 5E
36 Belfast, & L., N. Ireland 54 35N 5 57W
93 Belfast, Me., U.S.A. 44 15N 69 0W
43 Belfort, France 47 41N 6 54E
42 Belfort, Dépt., France 47 38N 6 52E
64 Belgaum, India 15 42N 74 40E
44 Belgium, Europe 51 0N 4 10E
52 Belgorod, U.S.S.R. 50 30N 36 40E
51 Belgorod Dnestrovski, U.S.S.R. 46 11N 30 23E
41 Belgrade (Beograd), Yugoslavia 44 48N 20 33E
68 Beliton, I., Indonesia 3 0S 108 0E
94 Belize, Br. Honduras 17 28N 88 20W
83 Bell Bay, Australia 41 2S 146 48E
31 Bell Rock, Scot., 56 26N 2 24W
98 Bell Ville, Argentina 32 30S 62 50W
88 Bella Coola, Canada 52 25N 126 40W
36 Bellaghy, N. Ireland 54 50N 6 31W
45 Bellágio, Italy 45 55N 9 20E
92 Bellaire, Ohio, U.S.A. 40 1N 80 48W
36 Bellanagare, Ireland 53 49N 8 21W
36 Bellananagh, Ireland 53 53N 7 28W
64 Bellary, India 15 12N 77 5E
83 Bellata, Australia 29 58S 149 55E
36 Bellavary, Ireland 53 54N 9 10W
90 Belle Fourche R., U.S.A. 44 40N 104 0W
89 Belle I., Canada 52 10N 55 18W
42 Belle Ile, France 47 20N 3 12W
36 Belleek, N. Ireland 54 30N 8 6W
43 Bellegarde, France 46 4N 5 46E
89 Belleville, Canada 44 15N 77 37W
92 Belleville, Ill., U.S.A. 38 30N 90 7W
43 Belley, France 45 45N 5 45E
83 Bellingen, Australia 30 25S 152 50E
31 Bellingham, Eng., 55 9N 2 16W
90 Bellingham, U.S.A. 48 45N 122 48W
100 Bellingshausen Sea, Antarctica 65 0S 80 0W
45 Bellinzona, Switzerland 46 12N 9 1E
40 Belluno, Italy 46 8N 12 12E
37 Belmez, Spain 38 15N 5 15W
83 Belmont, Australia 33 0S 151 35E
94 Belmopan, Br. Honduras 17 12N 88 0W
35 Belmullet, Ireland 54 13N 9 58W
98 Belo Horizonte, Brazil 19 55S 44 0W
75 Belo sur Tsiribihina, Madagascar 19 40S 44 30W
50 Belomorsk, U.S.S.R. 64 35N 34 30E
65 Belonia, India 23 15N 91 25E
50 Beloretsk, U.S.S.R. 54 0N 58 0E
60 Belovo, U.S.S.R. 54 35N 86 27E
50 Beloye L., U.S.S.R. 60 10N 37 35E
27 Belper, England 53 2N 1 28W
27 Belton (Lincs.), England 53 33N 0 49W
23 Belton (Suff.), England 52 35N 1 39E
91 Belton, Texas, U.S.A. 31 30N 97 30W
36 Beltra, Sligo, Ireland 54 12N 8 36W
47 Beltsy, U.S.S.R. 47 48N 28 0E
36 Belturbet, Ireland 54 6N 7 25W
22 Bembridge, England 50 41N 1 4W
91 Bemidji, U.S.A. 47 30N 94 58W
33 Ben Alder, Scotland 56 49N 4 30W
33 Ben Avon, Scotland 57 7N 3 18W
31 Ben Chonzie, Scotland 56 27N 4 0W
30 Ben Cruachan, Scotland 56 27N 5 5W
33 Ben Dearg, Perth, Scot. 56 54N 3 50W
33 Ben Dhorain, Scotland 58 7N 3 50W
30 Ben Dorain, Scotland 56 30N 4 42W
33 Ben Hope, Scotland 58 26N 4 33W
30 Ben Lawers, Scotland 56 31N 4 17W
30 Ben Lomond, Scotland 56 10N 4 30W
33 Ben Loyal, Scotland 58 25N 4 25W
30 Ben Lui, Scotland 56 23N 4 45W
33 Ben Macdhui, Scotland 57 3N 3 30W
32 Ben Mhor, Lewis, Scot. 57 58N 6 30W
32 Ben Mhor, S. Uist., Scot. 57 16N 7 18W
30 Ben More, Perth, Scot. 56 20N 4 30W
33 Ben More Assynt, Suth., Dist., Scotland 58 9N 4 53W
32 Ben Nevis, Scotland 56 46N 5 0W
33 Ben Sgeirach, Scotland 58 4N 4 39W
32 Ben Sgritheall, Scotland 57 9N 5 34W
32 Ben Stack, Scotland 58 20N 4 58W
30 Ben Venue, Scotland 56 13N 4 28W
30 Ben Vorlich, Scotland 56 22N 4 15W
33 Ben Wyvis, Scotland 57 41N 4 40W
72 Bena, Nigeria 11 20N 5 50E
83 Benalla, Australia 36 34S 146 0E
83 Benanee, Australia 34 26S 142 56E
65 Benares, see Varanasi
34 Benbaun, Mt., Ireland 53 30N 9 50W
32 Benbecula I., Scotland 57 26N 7 20W
80 Bencubbin, Australia 30 56S 118 5E
90 Bend, U.S.A. 44 3N 121 15W
47 Bendery, U.S.S.R. 46 50N 29 28E
83 Bendigo, Australia 36 48S 144 13E
63 Benei Berag, Israel 32 5N 34 50E
40 Benevento, Italy 41 8N 14 50E
73 Benghazi, Libya 32 10N 20 5E
68 Bengkalis, Indonesia 1 38N 102 9E
75 Benguela, Angola 12 20S 13 10E
72 Beni Abbès, Algeria 30 10N 2 0W
73 Beni Mazâr, Egypt 28 32N 30 44E
72 Beni Mellal, Morocco 32 21N 6 14W
73 Beni Suef, Egypt 29 2N 30 58E
73 Beni Ulid, Libya 31 50N 14 20E
72 Benin City, Nigeria 6 20N 5 31E
68 Bengkulu, Indonesia 3 40S 102 40E
88 Bennett, Canada 59 50N 135 0W
61 Bennett I., U.S.S.R., 76 30N 150 0E
35 Bennettsbridge, Ireland 52 36N 7 12W
93 Bennington, U.S.A. 42 55N 73 16W
63 Bennt Jbail, Lebanon 33 7N 35 26E
76 Benoni, Trans. S. Africa 26 11S 28 18E
45 Bensheim, Germany 49 41N 8 36E
82 Bentinck I., Australia 17 15S 139 30E
73 Bentiu, Sudan 9 10N 29 55E
27 Bentley, Yorks., England 53 33N 1 9W
92 Benton Harbor, U.S.A. 42 8N 86 28W
72 Benue R., Nigeria 8 0N 7 30E
41 Beograd, see Belgrade
67 Beppu, Japan 33 15N 131 35E
94 Bequia, W. Indies 13 0N 61 15W
72 Ber Rechid, Morocco 33 0N 7 35E
36 Beragh, N. Ireland 54 34N 7 10W
41 Berat, Albania 40 40N 20 0E
73 Berber, Sudan 18 2N 34 2E
71 Berbera, Somali Rep. 10 30N 45 25E
45 Bercher, Switzerland 46 43N 6 43E
51 Berdichev, U.S.S.R. 49 50N 28 45E
52 Berdyansk, U.S.S.R. 46 42N 36 47E
47 Beregovo, U.S.S.R. 48 15N 22 45E
72 Berekum, Ghana 7 29N 2 34W
47 Bereza, U.S.S.R. 52 45N 25 0E
50 Berezniki, U.S.S.R. 59 25N 56 5E
50 Berezovo, U.S.S.R. 64 5N 65 0E
41 Bergama, Turkey 39 6N 27 20E
40 Bergamo, Italy 45 42N 9 40E
49 Bergen, Norway 60 21N 5 22E
44 Bergen Binnen, Neth. 52 40N 4 40E
44 Bergen-op-Zoom, Neth. 51 30N 4 17E
43 Bergerac, France 44 53N 0 26E
44 Bergum, Netherlands 53 12N 5 59E
76 Bergville, S. Africa 28 40S 29 20E
65 Berhampore, India 24 10N 88 20E
65 Berhampur, India 19 24N 84 50E
61 Bering Sea, Pacific Ocean 57 0N 173 0E
37 Berja, Spain 36 45N 3 0W
22 Berkeley, England 51 42N 2 27W
90 Berkeley, U.S.A. 38 6N 122 0W
23 Berkhamsted, England 51 45N 0 33W
22 Berks. Downs, England 51 30N 1 20W
22 Berkshire, Co., England 51 25N 1 15W
46 Berlin, Germany 52 31N 13 20E
93 Berlin, N.H., U.S.A. 44 28N 71 11W
100 Bermejo, R., Arg. 25 40S 59 40W
42 Bermeo, Spain 43 26N 2 46W
95 Bermuda Is., Atlantic Oc. 32 20N 65 0W
45 Bern and Cn., Switz. 46 57N 7 27E
43 Bernay, France 49 5N 0 32E
46 Bernburg, Germany 51 40N 11 42E
45 Berner Alpen, Mts., Switzerland 46 25N 7 30E
32 Berneray, I., Scotland 56 47N 7 40W
80 Bernier I., Australia 24 58S 113 0E
45 Bernina, Mt., Switzerland 46 22N 9 50E
63 Beror Hayil, Israel 31 34N 34 39E
75 Beroroha, Madagascar 21 40S 45 10E
46 Beroun, Cz.-slov. 50 0N 14 5E
83 Berri, Australia 34 12S 140 38E
33 Berriedale, Scotland 58 10N 3 31W
83 Berry, Australia 34 48S 150 48E
43 Berry, Prov., France 46 48N 2 5E
74 Bertoua, Cameroon 4 30N 13 45E
48 Beru Fjord, Iceland 64 40N 14 15W
48 Berufjordur, Iceland 64 47N 14 28W
*31 Berwick, Co., Scotland 55 45N 2 30W
31 Berwick-upon-Tweed, England 55 47N 2 2W
25 Berwyn Mts., Wales 52 54N 3 25W
75 Besalampy, Madagascar 16 43S 44 29E
43 Besançon, France 47 18N 6 0E
47 Beskids, E., Mts., Eur. 49 8N 22 10E
47 Beskids, W., Mts., Eur. 49 8N 19 0E
47 Bessarabia, reg., U.S.S.R. 47 20N 28 20E
36 Bessbrook, N. Ireland 54 11N 6 23W
43 Bessèges, France 44 20N 4 2E
92 Bessemer, U.S.A. 46 30N 90 0W
73 Betaré-Oya, Cameroon 5 40N 14 15E
76 Bethanien, S.W. Africa 26 32S 17 11E
63 Bethlehem, Jordan 31 42N 35 12E
76 Bethlehem, S. Africa 28 5S 28 30E
93 Bethlehem, Pa., U.S.A. 40 25N 75 30W
76 Bethulie, S. Africa 30 30S 26 0E
43 Béthune, France 50 30N 2 40E
75 Betioky, Madag. 23 48S 44 20E
89 Betsiamites, Canada 48 53N 68 46W
23 Betteshanger, England 51 13N 1 20E
65 Bettiah, India 26 59N 84 38E
64 Betul, India 21 50N 77 50E
25 Betws-y-Coed. Wales 53 5N 3 50W
44 Beveren, Belgium 51 14N 4 16E
80 Beverley, Australia 32 2S 116 58E
27 Beverley, England 53 51N 0 27W
44 Beverwijk, Netherlands 52 28N 4 38E
45 Bex, Switzerland 46 16N 7 2E
23 Bexhill, England 50 50N 0 27E
23 Bexley, Gt. London, Eng. 51 26N 0 10E
41 Beykoz, Turkey 41 6N 29 8E
72 Beyla, Guinea 8 35N 8 30W
51 Beypazari, Turkey 40 11N 31 50E
51 Beysehir Gölü L., Tur. 37 50N 31 30E
52 Bezhitsa, U.S.S.R. 53 25N 34 18E
43 Beziers, France 43 27N 3 15E
64 Bhachau, India 23 20N 70 16E
64 Bhadrakh, India 21 0N 86 30E
65 Bhagalpur, India 25 12N 86 52E
65 Bhamo, Burma 24 16N 96 50E
65 Bhamragarh, India 19 30N 80 30E
64 Bhandara, India 21 8N 79 40E
64 Bharatpur, India 27 19N 77 50E
65 Bhatpara, India 23 0N 88 30E
64 Bhavnagar, India 21 59N 72 19E
64 Bhima, R., India 17 25N 76 0E
65 Bhimvaram, India 16 30N 81 30E
64 Bhiwandi, India 19 15N 72 55E
65 Bhola, Bangladesh 22 45N 90 35E
64 Bhopal, India 23 15N 77 30E
65 Bhubaneswar, India 20 10N 85 50E
64 Bhuj, India 23 10N 69 45E
64 Bhusawal, India 21 10N 75 56E
65 Bhutan, Asia 27 30N 90 20E
†74 Biafra, B. of, W. Africa 3 40N 9 30E
47 Biala Podlaska, Poland 52 2N 23 0E
47 Bialystok, Poland 53 4N 23 12E
42 Biarritz, France 43 30N 1 32W
45 Biasca, Switzerland 46 22N 8 39E
45 Biberach, Germany 48 5N 9 45E
72 Bibiani, Ghana 6 30N 2 8W
82 Biboohra, Australia 16 35S 145 27E
22 Bibury, England 51 46N 1 50W
22 Bicester, England 51 55N 1 9W
25 Bicton, England 52 43N 2 47W
72 Bida, Nigeria 9 2N 6 12E
64 Bidar, India 17 58N 77 35E
23 Biddenden, England 51 7N 0 40E
26 Biddulph, England 53 8N 2 11W
24 Bideford, England 51 1N 4 13W
22 Bidford on Avon, Eng. 52 9N 1 53W
72 Bidon 5, see Poste Maurice Cortier
75 Bié Plateau, Angola 13 0S 16 40E
45 Biel, Switzerland 47 9N 7 15E
46 Bielefeld, Germany 52 2N 8 17E
45 Bieler See, Switzerland 47 7N 7 18E
47 Bielsko, Poland 49 50N 19 10E
68 Bien Hoa, Vietnam 11 0N 107 0E
91 Big Belt, Mts., U.S.A. 46 40N 111 30W
88 Big Salmon, Canada 61 50N 136 0W
90 Big Spring, U.S.A. 32 14N 101 32W
91 Big Stone L., U.S.A. 45 30N 96 30W
89 Big Trout L., Canada 54 30N 90 0W
24 Bigbury, tn. & B., England 50 17N 3 52W
88 Biggar, Canada 52 6N 108 0W
31 Biggar, Scotland 55 38N 3 31W
83 Biggenden, Australia 25 30S 152 0E
23 Biggleswade, England 52 5N 0 17W
90 Bighorn, Mts., U.S.A. 44 30N 107 30W
45 Bignasco, Switzerland 46 20N 8 36E
40 Bihac, Yugoslavia 44 46N 15 57E
65 Bihar, st., India 23 0N 85 30E
65 Bijapur, Mad. P., India 18 50N 80 50E
64 Bijapur, Mysore, India 16 55N 75 57E
62 Bijar, Iran 32 52N 47 35E
41 Bijeljina, Yugoslavia 44 42N 19 15E
64 Bikaner, India 28 1N 73 40E
63 Bikfaiya, Lebanon 33 55N 35 40E
61 Bikin, U.S.S.R. 46 50N 134 15E
74 Bikoro, Zaïre 0 48S 18 15E
64 Bilara, India 26 20N 73 58E
65 Bilaspur, Mad. P., India 22 2N 82 14E
68 Bilauk Taung Ra., Thail. 13 30N 99 15W
37 Bilbao, Spain 43 16N 2 53W
48 Bildudalur, Iceland 65 20N 23 40W
51 Bilecik, Turkey 40 16N 29 52E
61 Bilir, U.S.S.R. 65 40N 131 20E
23 Billericay, England 51 38N 0 25E
23 Billesdon, England 52 38N 0 56W
27 Billingham, England 54 36N 1 18W
90 Billings, U.S.A. 45 58N 108 30W
73 Bilma, Niger 18 5N 13 20E
82 Biloela, Australia 24 25S 150 35E
91 Biloxi, U.S.A. 30 32N 89 0W
22 Bilston, England 52 34N 2 7W
73 Biltine, Chad 14 40N 20 50E
82 Bilyana, Australia 18 5S 145 50E
72 Bimbéréké, Dahomey 10 11N 2 43E
64 Bina-Etawah, India 24 11N 78 12E
44 Binche, Belgium 50 25N 14 12E
83 Binda, Australia 27 50S 147 20E
75 Bindura, Rhodesia 17 15S 31 20E
68 Bindjai, Indonesia 3 30N 98 30E
83 Bingara, Australia 29 40S 150 40E
27 Bingham, England 52 57N 0 55W
93 Binghampton, U.S.A. 42 5N 75 48W
26 Bingley, England 53 51N 1 50W
68 Binh-dinh, see An Nhon
99 Bio Bio, R., Chile 37 40S 71 30W
64 Bir, India 19 4N 75 58E
63 Bir, Iran 25 26N 59 47E
73 Bir Atrun, Sudan 28 15N 26 40E
62 Bir Terfawi, Egypt 22 7N 28 10E
73 Bir Ungat, Egypt 22 8N 33 48E
63 Bir Zeit, Jordan 31 59N 35 11E
73 Birao, Central Africa 10 20N 22 40E
23 Birch, England 51 50N 0 54E
83 Birdsville, Australia 25 58S 139 20E
80 Birdum, Australia 15 30S 133 0E
63 Birjand, Iran 32 52N 59 7E
26 Birkdale, England 53 38N 3 2W
26 Birkenhead, England 53 23N 3 3W
41 Birlad, Rumania 46 15N 27 38E
22 Birmingham, England 52 29N 1 54W
91 Birmingham, U.S.A. 33 37N 86 45W
65 Birmitrapur, India 22 30N 84 10E
72 Birnin-Kebbi, Nigeria 12 32N 4 12E
61 Birobidzhan, U.S.S.R. 48 50N 132 50E
50 Birsk, U.S.S.R. 55 23N 55 35E
31 Birtley, England 54 55N 1 33W
27 Birtley, England 55 5N 2 12W
64 Birur, India 13 30N 75 55E
40 Birzebbuga, Malta 35 52N 14 31E
13 Biscay, B. of, Atlantic Oc. 46 20N 4 0W
27 Bishop Auckland, Eng. 54 40N 1 41W
22 Bishop's Cleeve, England 51 56N 2 3W
24 Bishop's Nympton, Eng. 50 58N 3 44W
23 Bishop's Stortford, Eng. 51 53N 0 10E
24 Bishopsteignton, Eng. 50 32N 3 32W
72 Biskra, Algeria 34 50N 5 45E
90 Bismarck, U.S.A. 46 52N 100 45W
82 Bismarck Arch., Terr. of New Guinea 2 0S 148 0E
82 Bismarck Sea, Terr. of New Guinea 4 30S 149 0E
72 Bissagos Is., Port Guinea 11 0N 16 0W
72 Bissau, Port Guinea 11 50N 15 37W
47 Bistrita, Rumania 47 7N 24 32E
44 Bitburg, Germany 49 59N 6 32E
51 Bitlis, Turkey 38 30N 42 17E
41 Bitola (Monastir) Y.-slav. 41 1N 21 14E
73 Bitter Lakes, Egypt 30 10N 32 0E
76 Bitterfontein, S. Africa 31 0S 18 28E
90 Bitterroot Ra., U.S.A. 46 30N 115 0W
67 Biwa, L., Japan 35 15N 135 45E
60 Biysk, U.S.S.R., 52 40N 85 0E
76 Bizana, S. Africa 30 55S 29 50E
72 Bizerte, Tunisia 37 20N 9 45E
48 Bjargtangar, Iceland 65 30N 24 30W
48 Bjarnanes, Iceland 64 18N 15 10W
40 Bjelovar, Yugoslavia 46 0N 16 45E
49 Blaavands Huk, Denmark 55 33N 8 2E
22 Blaby, England 52 34N 1 10W
47 Black Crisul, R., Rumania 46 40N 22 0E
26 Black Fell, Mt., England 54 47N 2 34W
45 Black Forest, see Schwarzwald, Ger.
27 Black Hills, England 53 33N 1 45W
90 Black Hills, U.S.A. 44 0N 104 0W
33 Black Isle, Scotland 57 35N 4 15W
25 Black Mt., see Mynydd du
25 Black Mts., Wales 51 52N 3 5W
66 Black (Da) R., Viet Nam 21 30N 104 0E
90 Black Range, Mts., U.S.A. 33 0N 107 45W
51 Black Sea, Europe 43 0N 34 0E
72 Black Volta R., W. Africa 10 0N 3 0W
82 Blackall, Australia 24 20S 145 30E
84 Blackball, New Zealand 42 20S 171 35E
82 Blackbull, Australia 18 0S 141 7E
26 Blackburn, England 53 46N 2 30W
24 Blackdown Hills, Eng. 50 57N 3 15W
90 Blackfoot, U.S.A. 43 14N 112 22W
31 Blackford, Scotland 56 15N 3 48W
24 Blackmoor Vale, England 50 54N 2 18W
26 Blackpool, England 53 50N 3 3W
82 Blackwater, Australia 23 35S 149 0E
35 Blackwater, Ireland 52 27N 6 20W
34 Blackwater, R., Cork, Ire. 52 6N 8 30E
23 Blackwater, R., England 51 47N 0 38E
36 Blackwater, R., N. Ireland 54 26N 7 5W
31 Blackwood, Scotland 55 40N 3 56W
25 Blaenavon, England 51 46N 3 5W
61 Blagodarnoye, U.S.S.R. 45 0N 43 45E
61 Blagoveshchensk, U.S.S.R. 50 30N 127 55E
42 Blain, France 47 30N 1 42W
25 Blaina, England 51 46N 3 10W
42 Blainville, France 49 5N 1 32W
82 Blair Athol, Australia 22 50S 147 0E
33 Blair Atholl, Scotland 56 46N 3 50W
31 Blairgowrie, Scotland 56 36N 3 20W
88 Blairmore, Canada 49 40N 114 25W
23 Blakeney, Norfolk, England 52 57N 1 1E
72 Blanc, C., Mauritania 20 40N 17 0W
83 Blanche, L., Australia 29 15S 139 40E
94 Blanchisseuse, Trinidad 10 45N 61 18W
44 Blankenberge, Belgium 51 18N 3 8E
95 Blanquilla I., Venezuela 12 0N 64 30W
75 Blantyre, Malawi 15 50 35 1E
34 Blarney, Ireland 51 58N 8 35W
27 Blaydon, England 54 56N 1 47W
42 Blaye, France 45 8N 0 40W
83 Blayney, Australia 33 35S 149 10E
60 Blednaya, Mt., U.S.S.R. 75 50N 65 30E
46 Bleiburg, Austria 46 40N 14 55E
49 Blekinge, Co., Sweden 56 27N 15 10E
84 Blenheim, New Zealand 41 38S 174 5E
23 Bletchley, England 52 0N 0 45W
72 Blida, Algeria 36 30N 2 50E
68 Blitar, Indonesia 8 12S 112 25E
93 Block, I., U.S.A. 41 12N 71 32W
76 Bloemfontein, S. Africa 29 12S 26 15E
76 Bloemhof, S. Africa 27 30S 25 36E
23 Blofield, England 52 38N 1 25E
43 Blois, France 47 37N 1 19E
48 Blonduös, Iceland 65 40N 20 12W
36 Bloody Foreland, Ireland 55 9N 8 18W
92 Bloomington, Ill., U.S.A. 40 28N 88 59W
92 Bloomington, Ind., U.S.A. 39 10N 86 32W
83 Blue Mts., see Katoomba
90 Blue Mts., U.S.A. 45 0N 119 5W
80 Blue Mud B., Australia 13 30S 136 10E
73 Blue Nile, Dist., Sudan 12 40N 33 30E
73 Blue Nile, R., N.E. Africa 10 0N 35 0E
91 Blue Ridge Mts., U.S.A. 35 0N 82 0W
92 Bluefield, U.S.A. 37 28N 81 4W
95 Bluefields, Nicaragua 12 0N 83 45W
36 Blue Stack, Mt., Ireland 54 45N 8 9W
84 Bluff, New Zealand 46 32S 168 20E
99 Blumenau, Brazil 27 0S 49 0W
23 Blundeston, England 52 33N 1 42E
27 Blyth, England 55 7N 1 31W
31 Blyth Bridge, Scotland 55 41N 3 22W
27 Blyth R., England 55 6N 1 56W
23 Blythburgh, England 52 19N 1 36E
92 Blytheville, U.S.A. 35 56N 89 58W
72 Bo, Sierra Leone 7 55N 11 50W
98 Boa Vista, Brazil 2 55N 60 15W
65 Bobbili, India 18 35N 83 30E
43 Bobbio, Italy 44 50N 9 25E
72 Bobo-Dioulasso, Volta 11 20N 4 0W
46 Bobr, R., Poland 51 30N 15 28E
50 Bobruysk, U.S.S.R. 53 0N 30 0E
72 Bocanda, Ivory Coast 7 5N 4 31W
74 Bocaranga, Central Africa 7 0N 15 35W
44 Bocholt, Germany 51 51N 6 37E
44 Bochum, Germany 51 30N 7 15E
74 Boda, Central Africa 4 19N 17 26E
61 Bodaibo, U.S.S.R. 57 50N 114 0E
33 Boddam, Scotland 57 28N 1 46W
32 Boddam, Shetland Is., Scotland 59 55N 1 16W
48 Boden, Sweden 65 48N 21 45E
45 Bodensee, L., Germany 47 33N 9 30E
64 Bodhan, India 18 45N 77 50E
24 Bodmin Moor, England 50 33N 4 36W
48 Bodö, Il, Norway 67 21N 14 20E
47 Bodrog, R., Hungary 48 20N 21 45E
74 Boende, Zaïre 0 15S 21 12E
35 Bog of Allen, Ireland 53 13N 7 20W
91 Bogalusa, U.S.A. 30 51N 89 56W
83 Bogan, R., Australia 31 0S 147 2E
83 Bogan Gate, Australia 33 0S 147 52E
75 Bogenfels, S.W. Africa 27 31S 15 33E
83 Boggabilla, Australia 28 40S 150 20E
83 Boggabri, Australia 30 45S 150 0E
34 Boggeragh, Mts., Ireland 52 2N 8 55W
72 Boghé, Mauritania 16 45N 14 10W
23 Bognor Regis, England 50 48N 0 42W
68 Bogor, Indonesia 6 30S 106 58E
72 Bogoro, Nigeria 9 37N 9 29E
98 Bogota, Colombia 4 38N 74 15W
60 Bogotol, U.S.S.R. 56 15N 89 50E
65 Bogra, Bangladesh 24 48N 89 24E
44 Bohain, France 49 59N 3 28E
46 Bohemia dist., Cz. 49 50N 15 0E
46 Bohemian For., Cz. 49 15N 13 20E
68 Bohol, I., Philippines 9 45N 124 20E
90 Boise, U.S.A. 43 54N 116 12W
72 Bojador, C., Span. Sahara 26 20N 14 55E
72 Boké, Guinea 10 56N 14 17W
49 Bokna Fd., Norway 59 12N 5 30E
74 Bokote, Zaïre 0 12S 21 8E
74 Bokungu, Zaïre 0 49S 23 12E
72 Bolama, Port. Guinea 11 30N 15 35W
43 Bolbec, France 49 35N 0 30E
46 Bolesawiec, Poland 51 17N 15 37E
47 Bolgrad, U.S.S.R. 45 40N 28 40E
99 Bolivar, Argentina 36 0S 61 0W
98 Bolivia, South America 16 0S 64 30W
49 Böllnäs, Sweden 61 24N 16 27E

* Incorporated within the region of Borders

† Renamed Bonny, B. of

83 Bollon, Australia 28 0s 147 36e
74 Bolobo, Zaïre 2 65s 16 20e
40 Bologna, Italy 44 29n 11 23e
50 Bologoye, U.S.S.R. 57 55n 34 5e
74 Bolomba, Zaïre 0 35n 19 0e
40 Bolsena, L., Italy 42 40n 12 0e
60 Bolshereche, U.S.S.R. 56 5n 74 40e
61 Bolshevik I., U.S.S.R. 78 30n 102 0e
60 Bolshoi I., U.S.S.R. 73 30n 142 0e
61 Bolshoi Altym, U.S.S.R. 62 25n 66 50e
61 Bolshoi Mamyr, U.S.S.R. 56 20n 102 55e
44 Bolsward, Netherlands 53 4n 5 31e
24 Bolt Hd., England 50 13n 3 48w
45 Boltigen, Switzerland 46 37n 7 24e
26 Bolton, England 53 25n 2 25w
26 Bolton Abbey, England 53 59n 1 53w
26 Bolton-by-Bowland, Eng. 53 56n 2 21w
51 Bolu, Turkey 40 46n 31 38e
34 Bolus Hd., Ireland 51 47n 10 21w
51 Bolvadin, Turkey 38 45n 31 57e
40 Bolzano, Italy 46 30n 11 23e
74 Boma, Zaïre 5 57s 12 40e
83 Bomaderry, Australia 34 55s 150 35e
83 Bombala, Australia 37 0s 149 3e
64 Bombay, India 18 55n 73 0e
66 Bomda, China 30 10n 95 10e
74 Bomongo, Zaïre 1 27n 18 21e
73 Bon, C., Tunisia 37 0n 11 0e
88 Bona Mt., Canada 61 20n 140 0w
98 Bonaire I., Neth. W.I. 12 12n 68 15w
83 Bonang, Australia 37 15s 150 35e
80 Bonaparte Arch., Austral. 13 0s 124 0e
33 Bonarbridge, Scotland 57 53n 4 20w
89 Bonavista, Canada 48 42n 53 5w
72 Bône, Algeria, see Annaba
68 Bone, G. of, Indonesia 4 38s 120 10e
31 Bo'ness, Scotland 56 1n 3 5w
74 Bongandanga, Zaïre 1 30n 21 0e
73 Bongor, Chad 10 35n 15 20e
43 Bonifacio, & Str., of, Medit. 41 18n 9 10e
5 Bonin Is., Pacific Oc. 27 0n 142 0e
44 Bonn, W. Germany 50 43n 7 7e
43 Bonneville, France 46 0n 6 30e
80 Bonnie Rock, Australia 30 10s 118 5e
31 Bonnyrigg, Scotland 55 52n 3 8w
72 Bonthé, Sierra Leone 7 30n 12 33w
68 Bontoc, Philippines 17 10n 121 0e
44 Boom, Belgium 51 5n 4 22e
83 Boonah, Australia 28 0s 152 27e
83 Boorindal, Australia 30 25s 146 10e
83 Boorowa, Australia 34 26s 148 47e
26 Boot, England 54 24n 3 18w
88 Boothia, G. & Pen., Can. 70 0n 90 0w
26 Bootle, Cumberland, Eng. 54 17n 3 24w
26 Bootle, Lancs., England 53 28n 3 0w
74 Booué, Gabon 0 5s 11 55e
44 Bor, Yugoslavia 44 16n 22 3e
49 Boras, Sweden 57 45n 12 55e
62 Borazjan, Iran 29 22n 51 10e
42 Bordeaux, France 44 45n 0 38w
83 Bordertown, Australia 36 21s 140 50e
48 Bordeyri, Iceland 65 12n 21 8e
43 Bordighera, Italy 43 50n 7 40e
72 Bordj-in-Eker, Algeria 24 5n 5 10e
23 Borehamwood, England 51 40n 0 15w
48 Borgarnes, Iceland 64 33n 21 55w
48 Borgefjell Mts., Norway 65 20n 13 30e
44 Borger, Netherlands 52 55n 6 46e
90 Borger, U.S.A. 35 43n 101 25w
49 Borgholm, Sweden 56 55n 16 40e
61 Boris Vilkitski Strait, U.S.S.R. 77 40n 105 0e
47 Borislav, U.S.S.R. 49 5n 23 26e
52 Borisoglebsk, U.S.S.R. 51 21n 42 5e
50 Borisov, U.S.S.R. 54 14n 28 20e
44 Borken, Germany 51 50n 6 50e
46 Borkum I., Germany 53 38n 6 41e
49 Borlänge, Sweden 60 28n 14 33e
45 Bormio, Italy 46 30n 10 20e
68 Borneo, I. Asia 1 0n 114 30e
49 Bornholm I., Denmark 55 9n 14 55e
72 Boromo, Volta 11 56n 2 59w
82 Bororen, Australia 24 13s 151 33e
50 Borovichi, U.S.S.R. 58 25n 33 58e
35 Borris, Ireland 52 36n 6 57w
35 Borris-in-Ossory, Ire. 52 57n 7 40w
34 Borrisokane, Ireland 53 0n 8 8w
34 Borrisoleigh, Ireland 52 48n 7 58w
83 Borroloola, Australia 16 7s 136 28e
26 Borrowdale, England 54 30n 3 9w
43 Bort, France 45 20n 2 30e
25 Borth, Wales 52 29n 4 3w
32 Borve, Scotland 58 25n 6 28w
66 Borzya, U.S.S.R. 50 25n 116 0e
40 Bosa, Sardinia, Italy 40 20n 8 25e
40 Bosanska Gradiska, Yugoslavia 45 20n 17 20e
41 Bosna, R., Yugoslavia 45 0n 18 10e
40 Bosnia, & Hercegovina, Fed. Unit, Yugoslavia 44 20n 17 40e
74 Bosobolo, Zaïre 4 14n 19 50e
41 Bosporus, Turkey 41 10n 29 6e
74 Bossangoa, Central Africa 6 35n 17 30e
74 Bossembelé, Cen. Africa 5 25n 17 40e
27 Boston, England 53 0n 0 3w
93 Boston, U.S.A. 42 18n 71 0w
91 Boston Mts., U.S.A. 36 0n 94 0w
48 Bothnia, G. of, Europe 62 0n 19 30e
83 Bothwell, Australia 42 28s 147 2e
47 Botosani, Rumania 47 42n 26 42e
75 Botswana, Africa 22 30s 24 0e
27 Bottesford, England 52 47n 0 48w
72 Botou, Upper Volta 12 45n 2 5e
44 Bottrop, Germany 51 34n 6 59e
72 Bou Arfa, Morocco 33 0n 2 0w
72 Bouaké, Ivory Coast 7 45n 5 0w
42 Bouches du Rhône, Dépt., France 43 28n 5 22e
72 Bougie, Algeria, see Bejaia
72 Bougouni, Mali 11 22n 7 12w
44 Bouillon, Belgium 49 50n 5 2e
80 Boulder, Australia 30 55s 121 28e
90 Boulder, U.S.A. 40 0n 105 0w
82 Boulia, Australia 23 0s 139 50e
43 Boulogne, France 50 42n 1 33e
90 Bountiful, U.S.A. 41 0n 111 58w
4 Bounty I., S. Ocean 48 0s 179 0e
61 Bour Khaya, C., U.S.S.R. 71 50n 133 10e
43 Bourbon Lancy, France 46 39n 3 45e
42 Bourbonnais, Prov., Fr. 46 20n 2 55e
72 Bourem, Mali 17 1n 0 24w
43 Bourg, France 46 14n 5 17e
43 Bourganeuf, France 45 55n 1 46e
43 Bourges, France 47 9n 2 25e
42 Bourgneuf, France 47 5n 1 58w
43 Bourgoin, France 45 38n 5 15e
83 Bourke, Australia 30 8s 145 59e
23 Bourne, England 52 47n 0 21w
22 Bournemouth, England 50 43n 1 54w
22 Bourton-on-the-Water, England 51 53n 1 45w
44 Boussu, Belgium 50 25n 3 42e
72 Boutilimit, Mauritania 17 30n 14 40w
1 Bouvet, Is., S. Atlantic 55 0s 3 30e
24 Bovey Tracey, England 50 36n 3 40w
44 Bovigny, Belgium 50 12n 5 55e
82 Bowen, Australia 19 59s 148 18e
83 Bowen, Mts., Australia 37 5s 148 0e
31 Bowes, England 54 31n 1 59w
27 Bowland Forest, England 54 0n 2 30w
92 Bowling Green, U.S.A. 36 59n 86 25w
83 Bowmans, Australia 34 15s 138 10e
30 Bowmore, Scotland 55 45n 6 17w
83 Bowral, Australia 34 27s 150 30e
83 Bowraville, Australia 30 40s 152 40e
23 Box Hill, England 51 16n 0 16w
44 Boxtel, Netherlands 51 37n 5 17e
36 Boyle, Ireland 53 59n 8 20w
41 Bozca 'Ada I., Turkey 39 50n 26 10e
90 Bozeman, U.S.A. 45 45n 111 5w
74 Bozoum, Central Africa 6 25n 16 35e
44 Brabant, N., Netherlands 51 37n 5 0e
44 Brabant, Prov., Belgium 50 47n 4 30e
40 Brac., I., Yugoslavia 43 20n 16 40e
32 Bracadale, L., Scotland 57 19n 6 30w
40 Bracciano, L., Italy 42 5n 12 15e
73 Brach, Libya 27 50n 14 50e
48 Bräcke, Sweden 62 50n 15 12e
22 Brackley, England 52 3n 1 10w
23 Bracknell, England 51 24n 0 45w
31 Braco, Scotland 56 16n 3 55w
47 Brad, Rumania 46 10n 22 45e
91 Bradenton, U.S.A. 27 30n 82 33w
26 Bradford, Yorks., Eng. 53 48n 1 46w
22 Bradford-on-Avon, Eng. 51 21n 2 15w
23 Bradwell-on-Sea, Eng. 51 44n 0 55e
32 Brae, Scotland 60 23n 1 20w
83 Braemar, Queens., Australia 25 35s 152 15e
83 Braemar, S. Australia 33 15s 139 35e
33 Braemar, Scotland 57 0n 3 24w
33 Braeriach, Mt., Scotland 57 6n 3 45w
31 Braes of Angus, Scotland 56 52n 3 0w
37 Braga, Portugal 41 34n 8 28w
99 Bragança, Brazil 0 56s 47 0w
37 Bragança, Portugal 41 48n 6 51w
65 Brahmani, R., India 20 52n 85 40e
65 Brahmanbaria, Bangla. 23 55n 91 15e
65 Brahmaputra, R., India 26 45n 93 0e
64 Brahmaur, India 32 28n 76 32e
83 Braidwood, Australia 35 28s 149 57e
47 Braila, Rumania 45 18n 27 57e
27 Brailsford, England 52 58n 1 35w
91 Brainerd, U.S.A. 46 16n 94 10w
23 Braintree, England 51 53n 0 33e
76 Brak, R., S. Africa 29 55s 23 12e
64 Bramhapuri, India 20 40n 79 50e
92 Brampton, Canada 43 40n 79 58w
26 Brampton, England 54 57n 2 46w
96 Branco, C., Brazil 7 20s 36 0w
46 Brandenburg, Germany 52 24n 12 31e
33 Branderburgh, Scotland 57 43n 3 17w
76 Brandfort, S. Africa 28 36s 26 28e
88 Brandon, Canada 49 50n 99 57w
47 Braniewo, Poland 54 25n 19 50e
47 Bransk, Poland 52 45n 22 50e
89 Brantford, Canada 43 17n 80 20w
83 Branxholme, Australia 38 0s 141 52e
98 Brasilia (Fed. Dist.), Braz. 16 0s 48 10w
47 Brasov, Rumania 45 35n 25 35e
45 Brasschaat, Belgium 51 17n 4 30e
47 Bratislava, Cz-slov. 48 7n 17 2e
61 Bratsk, U.S.S.R. 56 10n 101 30e
24 Braunton, England 51 6n 4 9w
90 Brawley, U.S.A. 32 58n 115 35w
34 Bray, Ireland 53 11n 6 6w
96 Brazil, S. America 0 0 to 30 0s; 35 0 to 75 0w
90 Brazos, R., U.S.A. 32 30n 97 30w
74 Brazzaville, Congo (Fr.) 4 7s 15 15e
41 Brcko, Yugoslavia 44 55n 18 40e
30 Breadalbane, Dist., Scot. 56 35n 4 15w
84 Bream, B., & Hd., N.Z. 35 56s 174 35e
31 Brechin, Scotland 56 46n 2 30w
23 Breckland, England 52 30n 1 20w
*25 Brecknock, Co., Wales 51 58n 3 25w
25 Brecon, Wales 51 57n 3 24w
25 Brecon Beacons, Wales 51 55n 3 30w
* *Incorporated within the county of Powys*
44 Breda, Netherlands 51 36n 4 46e
83 Bredbo, Australia 36 0s 148 40e
46 Bregenz, Austria 47 28n 9 45e
48 Breidi Fd., Iceland 65 15n 24 0w
49 Bremen, Germany 53 6n 8 51e
49 Bremerhaven, Germany 53 36n 8 40e
45 Bremgarten, Switzerland 47 21n 8 20e
40 Brenner Pass, Austra-Italy 47 1n 11 30e
45 Breno, Italy 45 57n 10 19e
23 Brent, Gt. London, Eng. 51 33n 0 15w
23 Brentwood, England 51 37n 0 19e
40 Brescia, Italy 45 35n 10 17e
42 Bressanone, Italy 46 43n 11 39e
32 Bressay, I. & Sd., Scot. 60 8n 1 5w
43 Bresse, Dist., France 46 25n 5 10e
42 Bressuire, France 46 50n 0 30w
42 Brest, France 48 26n 4 32w
47 Brest, U.S.S.R. 52 10n 23 40e
47 Bretcu, Rumania 46 2n 26 10e
91 Breton Sd., U.S.A. 29 30n 89 15e
84 Brett, C., N.Z. 35 12s 174 20w
42 Bretteville, France 49 18n 1 35w
42 Breuville, France 49 32n 1 40w
83 Brewarrina, Australia 30 0s 146 53e
22 Brewood, England 52 41n 2 10w
43 Briançon, France 44 53n 6 35e
43 Briare, France 47 40n 2 45e
83 Bribie I., Australia 26 55s 153 17e
75 Brickaville, Madagascar 18 49s 49 4e
31 Bridge of Allan, Scotland 56 9n 3 56w
31 Bridge of Earn, Scotland 56 22n 3 21w
30 Bridge of Orchy, Scot. 56 32n 4 46w
25 Bridgend, Wales 51 31n 3 35w
93 Bridgeport, U.S.A. 41 15n 73 13w
93 Bridgeton, U.S.A. 39 30n 75 15w
80 Bridgetown, Australia 33 59s 116 8e
94 Bridgetown, Barbados 13 5n 59 35w
89 Bridgewater, Canada 44 27n 64 30w
24 Bridgwater, England 51 8n 3 1w
22 Bridgnorth, England 52 32n 2 25w
27 Bridlington, England 54 7n 0 12w
83 Bridport, Australia 41 0s 147 32e
22 Bridport, England 50 44n 2 46w
43 Brienne, France 48 23n 4 30e
45 Brienz, Switzerland 46 47n 8 2e
22 Brierley Hill, England 52 29n 2 7w
44 Briey, France 49 15n 5 56e
45 Brig, Switzerland 46 20n 8 0e
27 Brigg, England 53 34n 0 30w
90 Brigham City, U.S.A. 41 35n 111 58w
27 Brighouse, England 53 42n 1 46w
83 Bright, Australia 36 48s 147 0e
23 Brightlingsea, England 51 48n 1 2e
83 Brighton, Australia 35 0s 138 30e
23 Brighton, England 50 49n 0 9w
25 Brimfield, England 52 18n 2 42w
41 Brindisi, Italy 40 40n 17 55e
83 Brinkworth, Australia 33 40s 138 20e
33 Brinyan, Scotland 59 8n 3 0w
93 Brion, I., Canada 47 50n 61 30w
43 Brioude, France 45 18n 3 25e
44 Briquebec, France 49 28n 1 39w
83 Brisbane, Australia 27 30s 153 1e
83 Brisbane R., Australia 27 0s 152 30e
22 Bristol, England 51 28n 2 36w
93 Bristol, R.I., U.S.A. 41 40n 71 15w
24 Bristol Chan., England 51 20n 4 0w
100 British Antarctic Terr. 65 0s 50 0w
88 British Columbia, Prov. Canada 54 0n 125 0w
95 British Guiana, see Guyana
**94 British Honduras, Central America 17 0n 88 40w
13 British Isles, Europe 55 0n 5 0w
25 Briton Ferry, Wales 51 37n 3 50w
76 Britstown, South Africa 30 33s 23 32e
42 Brittany, Prov., France 48 0n 2 10w
35 Brittas, Ireland 53 14n 6 29w
43 Brive, France 45 10n 1 30e
24 Brixham, England 50 23n 3 30w
82 Brixton, Australia 23 32s 144 52e
23 Brixworth, England 52 20n 0 54w
46 Brno (Brünn), Cz. 49 19n 16 38e
64 Broach, India 21 50n 73 10e
35 Broad Haven, Ireland 54 18n 9 54w
25 Broad Haven, Wales 51 46n 5 6w
31 Broad Law, Mt., Scot. 55 27n 3 20w
82 Broad Sd., Australia 22 10s 149 40e
34 Broadford, Ireland 52 48n 8 38w
23 Broadstairs, England 51 21n 1 27e
22 Broadway, England 52 2n 1 51w
88 Brochet, Manitoba, Can. 57 55n 101 40w
46 Brocken, Mt., Germany 51 48n 10 50e
22 Brockenhurst, England 50 49n 1 34w
93 Brockton, Mass., U.S.A. 42 4n 71 0w
41 Brod, Yugoslavia 45 9n 18 0e
89 Brodeur Pen., Canada 72 0n 88 0w
30 Brodick, Scotland 55 33n 5 8w
47 Brody, U.S.S.R. 50 7n 25 8e
83 Broken Hill, Australia 31 59s 141 25e
75 Broken Hill, see Kabwe
26 Bromborough, England 53 20n 3 0w
23 Bromley, England 51 24n 0 2w
27 Brompton, England 54 22n 1 25w
22 Bromsgrove, England 52 20n 2 1w
22 Bromyard, England 52 12n 2 30w
49 Bronderslev, Denmark 57 17n 9 55e
83 Bronte Park, Australia 42 8s 146 30e
36 Brookeborough, N. Ire. 54 19n 7 23w
91 Brookhaven, U.S.A. 31 48n 90 27w
91 Brookings, S. Dak., U.S.A. 44 25n 96 40w
80 Brookton, Australia 32 15s 117 0e
83 Brooloo, Australia 26 28s 152 30e
80 Broome, Australia 18 8s 122 15e
** *Renamed Belize*
33 Brora, & R., Scotland 58 0n 3 51w
22 Broseley, England 52 35n 2 28w
34 Brosna, R., Ireland 53 20n 7 50w
36 Broughshane, N. Ireland 54 54n 6 12w
27 Broughton, Lincs., Eng. 55 33n 0 33w
23 Broughton, Northants., England 52 22n 0 45w
27 Broughton, Yorks., Eng. 54 26n 1 8w
31 Broughton, Scotland 55 37n 3 25w
31 Broughty Ferry, Scotland 56 27n 2 51w
44 Brouwershaven, Neth. 51 45n 3 53e
24 Brown Willy, Mt., Eng. 50 35n 4 35w
22 Brownhills, England 52 38n 1 57w
91 Brownsville, Tex., U.S.A. 26 0n 97 20w
90 Brownwood, U.S.A. 31 42n 99 2w
31 Broxburn, Scotland 55 56n 3 23w
48 Brú, Iceland 65 5n 15 25w
80 Bruce, Mt., Australia 22 40s 117 30e
45 Bruchsal, Germany 49 10n 8 45e
46 Bruck, Austria 47 27n 15 15e
24 Brue R., England 51 11n 2 50w
34 Bruff, Ireland 52 29n 8 35w
44 Bruges, Belgium, see Brugge
45 Brugg, Switzerland 47 28n 8 12e
44 Brugge, Belgium 51 12n 3 10e
44 Bruhl, Germany 50 49n 6 51e
68 Brunei, Borneo 4 55n 114 52e
45 Brunig Pass, Switzerland 46 48n 8 10e
46 Brünn, see Brno
45 Brunnen, Switzerland 47 0n 8 18e
84 Brunner, & L., N.Z. 42 30s 171 23e
46 Brünsbüttel, Germany 53 55n 9 14e
46 Brunswick, Germany 52 17n 10 36e
91 Brunswick, Ga., U.S.A. 31 10n 81 31w
80 Brunswick B., Australia 15 15s 125 0e
83 Bruny I., Australia 43 20s 147 15e
34 Bruree, Ireland 52 35n 8 40w
44 Brussels, Belgium 50 51n 4 22e
83 Bruthen, Australia 37 55s 147 49e
44 Bruxelles, see Brussels
91 Bryan, Texas, U.S.A. 30 17n 96 5w
52 Bryansk, U.S.S.R. 53 25n 34 22e
25 Bryncethin, Wales 51 32n 3 34w
49 Bryne, Norway 58 46n 5 38e
25 Brynmawr, Wales 51 50n 3 8w
47 Brzeg, Poland 50 52n 17 30e
68 Buayan, Philippines 6 5n 125 20e
95 Bucaramanga, Colombia 6 55n 72 58w
47 Buchach, U.S.S.R. 49 5n 25 25e
72 Buchanan, Liberia 5 57n 10 2w
89 Buchans, Canada 48 50n 57 30w
47 Bucharest (Bucuresti), Rumania 44 25n 26 2e
45 Buchs, Switzerland 47 10n 9 30e
33 Buck, The, Mt., Scot. 57 9n 3 0w
31 Buckhaven, Scotland 56 10n 3 2w
33 Buckie, Scotland 57 40n 2 58w
93 Buckingham, Canada 45 40n 75 36w
23 Buckingham & Co., Engl 52 0n 0 59w
25 Buckley, Wales 53 10n 3 5w
30 Bucklyvie, Scotland 56 7n 4 20w
33 Bucksburn, Scotland 57 10n 2 10w
92 Buctouche, Canada 46 30n 64 47w
92 Bucyrus, U.S.A. 40 52n 83 0w
65 Budalin, Burma 22 25n 95 5e
47 Budapest, Hungary 47 33n 19 3e
48 Budareyri, Iceland 65 3n 14 10w
64 Budaun, India 28 15n 79 6e
31 Buddon Ness, Scotland 56 28n 2 43w
24 Bude, England 50 50n 4 32w
48 Budir, Iceland 64 48n 23 21w
74 Budjala, Zaïre 2 50n 19 40e
24 Budleigh Salterton, Eng. 50 37n 3 19w
95 Buenaventura, Colombia 3 55n 77 5w
99 Buenos Aires, Argentina 34 50s 58 37w
92 Buffalo, N.Y., U.S.A. 42 57n 78 50w
90 Buffalo, Wyoming, U.S.A. 44 20n 106 42w
47 Bug, R., Poland 52 39n 21 35e
51 Bug., R., U.S.S.R. 48 17n 30 0e
50 Bugulma, U.S.S.R. 54 35n 52 45e
30 Buie, L., Scotland 56 20n 5 55w
25 Builth Wells, Wales 52 8n 3 24w
44 Buitenpost, Netherlands 53 15n 6 6e
74 Bujumbura, Burundi 3 30s 29 30e
61 Bukachacha, U.S.S.R. 52 55n 116 50e
74 Bukama, Zaïre 9 10s 25 50e
74 Bukavu, Zaïre 2 20s 28 52e
74 Bukene, Tanzania 4 0s 33 0e
60 Bukhara, U.S.S.R. 39 50n 64 10e
68 Bukittingi, Malaysia 0 25s 100 25e
74 Bukoba, Tanzania 1 15s 31 50e
66 Bulak, Sinkiang, China 45 0n 82 0e
64 Bulandshahr, India 28 30n 77 58e
75 Bulawayo, Rhodesia 20 7s 28 38e
66 Bulgan, Mongolia 48 45n 103 0e
81 Bulgroo, Australia 25 40s 143 57e
41 Bulgaria, Europe 42 35n 25 0e
61 Bulinski, U.S.S.R. 68 10n 123 5e
61 Bulkur, U.S.S.R. 71 50n 126 30e
45 Bulle, Switzerland 46 35n 7 6e
80 Bullfinch, Australia 31 10s 119 0e
83 Bulli, Australia 34 12s 150 59e
82 Bullock Creek, Australia 17 40s 144 30e
84 Bulls, N.Z. 40 10s 175 21e
64 Bulsar, India 21 28n 72 35e
61 Bulun, U.S.S.R. 70 37n 126 0e
27 Bulwell, England 53 1n 1 12w
65 Bumhpa Bum Mt., Burma 26 45n 97 10e
74 Buna, Kenya 2 58n 39 30e
82 Buna, Papua 8 35s 148 30e
80 Bunbury, Australia 33 18s 115 40e
35 Bunclody (Newtownbarry), Ireland 52 40n 6 38e
36 Buncrana, Ireland 55 8n 7 25w
83 Bundaberg, Australia 24 54s 152 22e
36 Bundoran, Ireland 54 29n 8 16w
23 Bungay, England 52 27n 1 27e
67 Bungo Chan., Japan 33 0n 132 15e
68 Bunguran Is., Indonesia 3 45n 108 15e
74 Bunia, Zaïre 2 0n 30 20e
36 Bunnanaddan, Ireland 54 3n 8 35w
23 Buntingford, England 51 57n 0 1w
23 Bunwell, England 52 30n 1 9e
74 Bura, Kenya 1 0s 40 0e
62 Buraida ,Saudi Arabia 26 3n 44 0e
22 Buraimi, U.A.E. 24 15n 55 43e
22 Burbage, Wilts., England 51 21n 1 40w
90 Burbank, U.S.A. 34 14n 118 28w
83 Burcher, Australia 33 30s 147 10e
66 Burchun, Sinkiang, China 47 50n 86 30e
51 Burdur, Turkey 37 40n 30 17e
65 Burdwan, India 23 18n 87 50e
61 Bureya, R., U.S.S.R. 50 35n 132 0e
62 Burgan, Kuwait 29 0n 47 59e
41 Burgas, Bulgaria 42 36n 27 26e
45 Burgdorf, Switzerland 47 4n 7 38e
46 Burgenland, Prov., Austria 47 20n 16 20e
76 Burgersdorp, South Africa 31 0s 26 20e
23 Burgess Hill, England 50 57n 0 7w
22 Burghclere, England 51 19n 1 20w
37 Burgos, Spain 42 21n 3 40w
49 Burgsvik, Sweden 57 2n 18 14e
43 Burgundy Prov., France 47 0n 4 50e
50 Burguruslan, U.S.S.R. 53 22n 52 22e
42 Burhou Rocks, Channel Is. 49 45n 2 12w
74 Burji, Ethiopia 5 29n 37 51e
82 Burketown, Australia 17 45s 139 33e
27 Burley, England 53 55n 1 46w
90 Burley, U.S.A. 42 30n 113 55w
91 Burlington, Iowa, U.S.A. 41 0n 91 10w
93 Burlington, Vt., U.S.A. 44 30n 73 12w
60 Burlyu-Tyube, U.S.S.R. 46 30n 79 10e
65 Burma, Asia 21 30n 97 0e
23 Burnham, Essex, England 51 37n 0 50e
83 Burnie, Australia 41 0s 146 0e
26 Burnley, England 53 49n 2 16w
31 Burnmouth, Scotland 55 50n 2 4w
88 Burnside, R., Canada 66 20n 110 0w
31 Burntisland, Scotland 56 3n 3 12w
32 Burravoe, Scotland 60 31n 1 5w
33 Burray I., Scotland 58 50n 2 54w
83 Burren, Australia 30 10s 148 55e
83 Burrinjuck Res., Australia 35 0s 149 0e
25 Burry Port, Wales 51 41n 4 17w
41 Bursa, Turkey 40 8n 29 1e
24 Burton Bradstock, Eng. 50 41n 2 43w
23 Burton Latimer, Eng. 52 23n 0 41w
22 Burton-upon-Trent, Eng. 52 48n 1 38w
83 Burtundy, Australia 33 40s 142 20e
68 Buru, I., Indonesia 3 30s 126 30e
62 Burujird, Iran 33 55n 48 50e
74 Burundi, Africa 3 30s 30 0e
72 Burutu, Nigeria 5 20n 5 29e
26 Bury, England 53 36n 2 18w
23 Bury St. Edmunds, Eng. 52 14n 0 43e
61 Buryat, A.S.S.R., U.S.S.R. 51 0n 104 0e
62 Busaiya, Iraq 30 1n 46 10e
62 Bushire, Iran 29 0n 50 50e
36 Bushmills, N. Ireland 55 14n 6 32w
74 Businga, Zaïre 3 30n 20 50e
49 Buskerud, Co., Norway 60 20n 9 0e
62 Busra, Syria 32 30n 38 27e
80 Busselton, Australia 33 40s 115 20e
44 Bussum, Netherlands 52 18n 5 10e
43 Busto Arsizio, Italy 45 40n 8 50e
74 Buta, Zaïre 2 50n 24 53e
†30 Bute, I., Co. & Kyles of, Scotland 55 50n 5 5w
30 Bute, Sd. of, Scotland 55 45n 5 10w
74 Butembo, Zaïre 0 9n 29 18e
63 Butmiya, Syria 32 57n 35 53e
32 Butt of Lewis, Scotland 58 30n 6 16w
90 Butte, Montana, U.S.A. 46 0n 112 32w
31 Buttermere, England 54 32n 3 16w
68 Butterworth, Malaya 5 20n 100 35e
76 Butterworth, S. Africa 32 20s 28 5e
34 Buttevant, Ireland 52 14n 8 40w
68 Butuan, Philippines 9 0n 125 35e
68 Butung, I., Indonesia 5 0s 123 0e
52 Buturlinovka, U.S.S.R. 50 50n 40 35e
26 Buxton, England 53 16n 1 54w
61 Buyaga, U.S.S.R. 59 50n 127 0e
66 Buyr Nor, L., Mongolia 47 40n 17 40e
47 Buzau, & R., Rumania 45 10n 26 48e
73 Buzaymah, Libya 24 35n 22 0e
50 Buzuluk, U.S.S.R. 52 48n 52 5e
47 Bydgoszcz, Poland 53 7n 17 59e
89 Bylot I., Canada 73 0n 78 0w
100 Byrd, Antarctica 80 5s 120 0w
100 Byrd Basin, Antarctica 80 0s 110 0w
100 Byrd Land, Antarctica 70 30s 125 0w
83 Byrock, Australia 30 40s 146 28e
83 Byron Bay, Australia 28 30s 153 30e
61 Byrrang Mts., U.S.S.R. 75 0n 100 0e
48 Byske, & R., Sweden 64 57n 21 15e
61 Bysyttakh, U.S.S.R. 69 30n 124 10e
47 Bytom, Poland 50 23n 18 58e

C

98 Cabedelo, Brazil 6 45s 35 0w
74 Cabinda, Angola 5 10s 12 10e
89 Cabonge, Res., Canada 47 10n 77 0w
83 Caboolture, Australia 27 5s 152 47e
89 Cabot Str., Canada 47 20n 60 0w
33 Cabrach, Scotland 57 20n 3 0w
37 Cabrera I., Spain 39 8n 2 58e
† *County incorporated within the region of Strathclyde*

41 Cacak, Yugoslavia 43 51N 20 22E
37 Caceres, Spain 39 29N 6 22W
99 Cachoeira, Brazil 30 3S 52 53W
99 Cachoeiro, Brazil 20 45S 41 0W
75 Caconda, Angola 13 40S 15 9E
35 Cadamstown, Ireland 53 7N 7 39W
25 Cader Idris, Mt., Wales 52 40N 3 50W
91 Cadillac, U.S.A. 44 15N 85 28W
37 Cadiz, Spain 36 33N 6 20W
42 Caen, France 49 15N 0 27W
27 Caenby Corner, England 53 23N 0 32W
25 Caerleon, England 51 37N 2 57W
*25 Caernarfon, & Co., Wales 53 9N 4 15W
25 Caernarfon B., Wales 53 4N 4 28W
25 Caerphilly, Wales 51 34N 3 13W
25 Caerwent, England 51 37N 2 47W
63 Caesarea, Israel 32 30N 34 54E
68 Cagayan, R., Philippines 17 30N 121 40E
68 Cagayan de Oro, Phil. 8 32N 124 35E
40 Cagliari, & G., Italy 39 19N 9 8E
95 Caguas, Puerto Rico 18 15N 66 0W
35 Caha Mts., Ireland 51 47N 9 40W
34 Caherconlish, Ireland 52 36N 8 30W
35 Cahir, Ireland 52 21N 7 56W
35 Cahirciveen, Ireland 51 50N 10 14W
35 Cahors, France 44 28N 1 21E
98 Caiapó, Sa. do, Mts., Brazil
17 0S 52 0W
95 Caicos Is., W. Indies 21 45N 72 0W
33 Cairn Gorm Mt., Scot. 57 9N 3 40W
33 Cairn Table, Mt., Scot. 55 30N 4 0W
33 Cairn Toul, Mt., Scotland 57 1N 3 49W
33 Cairngorm Mts., Scotland 57 6N 3 38W
30 Cairnryan, Scotland 54 59N 5 0W
82 Cairns, Australia 17 0S 145 42E
73 Cairo (El Qâhira), Egypt 30 1N 31 14E
91 Cairo, Ill., U.S.A. 37 0N 89 20W
23 Caister-on-Sea, England 52 38N 1 43E
27 Caistor, England 53 31N 0 18W
**33 Caithness, Co., Scotland 58 23N 3 25W
98 Cajamarca, Peru 7 0S 78 18W
72 Calabar, Nigeria 4 59N 8 23E
40 Calabria, Reg., Italy 39 10N 16 20E
41 Calafat, Rumania 43 59N 22 54E
37 Calahorra, Spain 42 20N 2 0W
42 Calais, France 50 59N 1 55E
93 Calais, U.S.A. 45 6N 67 14W
99 Calama, Chile 22 20S 69 0W
95 Calamar, Colombia 10 0N 75 0W
68 Calamian Group, Phil. 11 30N 120 0E
37 Calamocha, Spain 40 57N 1 8W
68 Calapan, Philippines 13 15N 121 15E
47 Calarasi, Rumania 44 35N 27 25E
37 Calatayud, Spain 41 20N 1 40W
68 Calauag, Philippines 14 0N 122 20E
65 Calcutta, India 22 38N 88 21E
26 Calder Hall, England 54 25N 3 30W
99 Caldera, Chile 27 12S 70 48W
90 Caldwell, Idaho, U.S.A. 43 42N 116 45W
36 Caledon, N. Ireland 54 23N 6 52W
81 Caledon B., Australia 12 57S 136 50E
32 Caledonian Can., Scot. 57 28N 4 22W
26 Calf of Man, Isle of Man 54 4N 4 49W
88 Calgary, Canada 51 2N 114 5W
32 Calgary, Scotland 56 34N 6 17W
95 Cali, Colombia 3 30N 76 45W
65 Calicut, India 11 15N 75 43E
94 California, G. of, Mexico 28 0N 112 0W
90 California, st., U.S.A. 37 0N 120 0W
94 California, Lower, Mex. 28 0N 114 0W
83 Callabonna L., Australia 29 45S 140 0E
35 Callan, Ireland 52 33N 7 23W
31 Callander, Scotland 56 14N 4 12W
98 Callao, Peru 11 48S 77 15W
82 Callide, Australia 24 23S 150 33E
83 Calliope, Australia 24 0S 151 16E
22 Calne, England 51 27N 1 55W
83 Caloundra, Australia 26 45S 153 10E
40 Caltagirone, Italy 37 14N 14 33E
40 Caltanisetta, Italy 37 29N 14 7E
74 Calumbo, Angola 9 0S 13 0E
91 Calumet, U.S.A. 47 18N 88 28W
42 Calvados, Dépt., France 49 5N 0 20W
76 Calvinia, S. Africa 31 29S 19 59E
74 Camabatela, Angola 8 20S 15 26E
95 Camaguey, Cuba 21 17N 78 10W
64 Cambay, & G., India 22 27N 72 42E
23 Camberley, England 51 20N 0 44W
68 Cambodia, Rep. 11 45N 105 0E
24 Camborne, England 50 12N 5 17W
44 Cambrai, France 50 11N 3 13E
25 Cambrian Mts., Wales 52 20N 3 30W
23 Cambridge, Eng. 52 11N 0 8E
23 Cambridge & Isle of Ely, Co.,
England 52 15W 0 5E
94 Cambridge, Jamaica 18 16N 77 53W
84 Cambridge, N.Z. 37 52S 175 28E
93 Cambridge, Mass., U.S.A. 42 40N 71 3W
88 Cambridge Bay, Canada 69 10N 105 0W
83 Cambridge G., Australia 14 30S 128 30E
23 Camden Gr. London, Eng. 51 32N 0 8W
91 Camden, Ark., U.S.A. 33 36N 92 52W
93 Camden, N.J., U.S.A. 39 58N 75 0W
92 Cameron Falls, Canada 49 5N 88 16W
74 Cameroon, Mt., Camer. 4 30N 8 55E
74 Cameroon, Africa 6 0N 12 0E
24 Camerton, England 51 18N 2 27W
37 Caminha, Portugal 41 50N 8 50W
83 Camira Creek, Austral. 29 15S 152 58E
98 Camocim, Brazil 2 55S 40 50W
35 Camolin, Ireland 52 37N 6 26W
82 Camooweal, Australia 19 59S 138 8E
99 Campana, Argentina 34 10S 58 40W
99 Campaña I., Chile 48 30S 75 30W
40 Campania, Prov., Italy 40 50N 14 45E

* *County incorporated within Gwynedd*

** *Incorporated within the region of Highland*

100 Campbell I., Southern Oc. 52 0S 169 0E
83 Campbell Town, Austral. 42 0S 147 50E
93 Campbellton, Canada 48 0N 66 57W
83 Campbelltown, Australia 34 5S 150 48E
30 Campbeltown, Scotland 55 26N 5 37W
94 Campêche, & G., Mexico 19 50N 90 30W
83 Camperdown, Australia 38 11S 143 12E
98 Campina Grande, Brazil 7 15S 36 0W
99 Campinas, Brazil 22 50S 47 0W
74 Campo, Cameroon 2 25N 9 55E
98 Campo Grande, Brazil 20 27S 54 40W
40 Campobasso, Italy 41 37N 14 44E
99 Campos, Brazil 21 45S 41 35W
30 Campsie Fells, Scotland 56 2N 4 25W
88 Camrose, Canada 53 0N 112 57W
83 Camurra, Australia 29 25S 149 58E
68 Can Tho, Vietnam 10 0N 105 40E
88-89 Canada, N. America
42 0 to 70 0N; 60 0 to 140 0W
90 Canadian, R., U.S.A. 35 15N 102 0W
41 Canakkale, Turkey 40 5N 26 30E
94 Cananea, Mexico 31 0N 110 25W
72 Canary Is., Atlantic Oc. 28 0N 16 0W
98 Canastra, Sa. da, Mts., Brazil
9 30S 46 30W
95 Canaveral, C., U.S.A., *see* Kennedy, C.
83 Canaway Ra., Australia 25 50S 142 40E
83 Canbelego, Australia 31 28S 146 27E
83 Canberra, Australia 35 15S 149 10E
42 Cancale, France 48 40N 2 0W
41 Candia, *see* Iraklion, Greece
98 Cañete, Peru 13 10S 76 25W
37 Cangas, Spain 43 13N 6 31W
75 Canicado, Mozam., 24 45S 33 15E
51 Cankiri, Turkey 40 43N 33 35E
83 Cann River, Australia 37 40S 149 10E
32 Canna I., Scotland 57 5N 6 35W
64 Cannanore, India 11 59N 75 32E
43 Cannes, France 43 35N 0 0E
80 Canning Basin, Austral. 19 50S 124 0E
24 Cannington, England 51 8N 3 4W
22 Cannock, England 52 42N 2 2W
22 Cannock Chase, Hs., Eng. 52 40N 2 0W
88 Canora, Canada 51 48N 102 36W
83 Canowindra, Australia 33 31S 148 50E
93 Canso, & C., Canada 45 30N 61 0W
37 Cantabrian Mts., Spain 43 12N 5 20W
42 Cantal, Dépt., France 45 5N 3 0E
23 Canterbury, England 51 15N 1 6E
84 Canterbury, Dist., N.Z. 44 0S 171 0E
84 Canterbury Bight, N.Z. 44 20S 172 0E
84 Canterbury Plains, N.Z. 43 30S 172 0E
66 Canton, China 23 15N 113 30E
91 Canton, Miss., U.S.A. 32 37N 90 7W
92 Canton, Ohio, U.S.A. 40 48N 81 20W
23 Canvey, Eng., 51 32N 0 35E
93 Cap Chat, Canada 49 3N 66 40W
95 Cap Haitien, Haiti 20 50N 72 20W
83 Cape Barren I., Austral. 40 25S 148 15E
89 Cape Breton I., Canada 46 25N 61 0W
72 Cape Coast, Ghana 5 5N 1 0W
92 Cape Fear, R., U.S.A. 34 30N 78 30W
92 Cape Girardeau, U.S.A. 37 19N 89 38W
55 Cape Johnson Deep, Pacific Ocean
10 0N 128 0E
76 Cape Province, S. Afr. 32 0S 24 0E
76 Cape Town, S. Africa 33 59S 18 30E
70 Cape Verde Is., Atlantic Oc. 16 0N 24 0W
82 Cape York Pen., Austral. 13 0S 142 30E
25 Capel-Curig, Wales 53 6N 3 55W
82 Capella, Australia 23 2S 148 1E
63 Capernaum, Israel 32 53N 35 34E
98 Capoeiras Falls, Fs., Brazil 7 0S 57 45W
40 Caporetto, Yugoslavia, *see* Kobarid
34 Cappamore, Ireland 52 38N 8 20W
34 Cappoquin, Ireland 52 9N 7 49W
40 Capri, I., Italy 40 35N 14 18E
75 Caprivi Strip, S.W. Africa 17 50S 23 0E
83 Captain's Flat, Australia 35 35S 149 30E
47 Caracal, Rumania 44 10N 24 20E
95 Caracas, Venezuela 10 25N 66 50W
83 Caradoc, Australia 30 35S 142 58E
47 Caransebes, Rumania 45 30N 22 15E
98 Caravelas, Brazil 17 45S 39 0W
40 Carbonara, C., Italy 39 10N 9 33E
89 Carbonear, Canada 47 42N 53 13W
43 Carcassonne, France 43 13N 2 22E
88 Carcross, Canada 60 20N 134 40W
64 Cardamon Hills, India 9 30N 77 0E
95 Cardenas, Cuba 23 0N 81 30W
25 Cardiff, Wales 51 29N 3 10W
25 Cardigan, & Co., Wales 52 6N 4 38W
25 Cardigan B., Wales 52 30N 4 40W
37 Cardona, Spain 41 56N 1 40E
88 Cardston, Canada 49 15N 113 28W
82 Cardwell, Australia 18 14S 146 2E
47 Carei, Rumania 47 45N 22 33E
42 Carentan, France 49 20N 1 20W
80 Carey, L., Australia 29 0S 122 20E
72 Careysburg, Liberia 6 34N 10 30W
42 Carhaix, France 48 20N 2 40W
95 Caribbean Sea, W. Indies 15 30N 73 0W
91 Caribou, U.S.A. 46 52N 68 2W
44 Carignan, France 49 37N 5 10E
83 Carinda, Australia 30 27S 147 52E
46 Carinthia, Prov., Austria 46 50N 14 0E
22 Carisbrooke, England 50 42N 1 19W
93 Carleton Place, Canada 45 4N 76 7W
76 Carletonville, S. Africa 26 25S 27 15E
36 Carlingford, & L., Ireland 54 2N 6 8W
26 Carlisle, England 54 54N 2 57W
31 Carlops, Scotland 55 47N 3 20W
35 Carlow, & Co., Ireland 52 50N 6 56W
90 Carlsbad, U.S.A. 32 25N 104 13W
27 Carlton, England 52 58N 1 6W
31 Carluke, Scotland 55 44N 3 50W
88 Carmacks, Canada 62 0N 136 0W
88 Carman, Canada 49 30N 98 0W
†25 Carmarthen, & Co., Wales 51 52N 4 18W
24 Carmarthen B., Wales 51 37N 4 30W
43 Carmaux, France 44 1N 2 5E
63 Carmel, Mt., Israel 32 45N 35 0E
82 Carmila, Australia 21 53S 149 5E
37 Carmona, Spain 37 28N 5 43W
31 Carmyllie, Scotland 56 36N 2 41W
32 Carn Eige, Mt., Scotland 57 17N 5 9W
33 Carn Glas-choire, Mt., Scotland
57 18N 3 50W
33 Carn na Caim, Mt., Scotland
56 54N 4 10W
42 Carnac, France 47 39N 3 3W
80 Carnarvon, Austral. 24 49S 113 40E
76 Carnarvon, S. Africa 31 0S 22 10E
64 Carnatic, Dist., India 12 30N 79 30E
80 Carnegie, L., Australia 26 0S 122 30E
35 Carnew, Ireland 52 43N 6 30W
26 Carnforth, England 54 8N 2 46W
40 Carnic Alps, Italy 46 34N 12 50E
36 Carnlough, N. Ireland 54 59N 6 0W
73 Carnot, Central Africa 5 0N 15 57E
31 Carnoustie, Scotland 56 30N 2 43W
31 Carnwath, Scotland 56 42N 3 38W
5 Caroline Is., Pacific Ocean 6 0N 146 0E
98 Caroni, R., Venezuela 7 0N 63 0W
47 Carpathian Mts., E. Eur. 48 0N 24 0E
82 Carpentaria, G. of, Australia
15 0S 138 0E
43 Carpentras, France 44 0N 5 0E
83 Carpolac, Australia 36 45S 141 20E
35 Carra, L., Ireland 53 43N 9 15W
40 Carrara, Italy 44 3N 10 9E
83 Carraweena, Australia 29 10S 139 55E
33 Carrbridge, Scotland 57 16N 3 48W
94 Carriacou I., W. Indies 12 30N 61 28W
30 Carrick, Dist., Scotland 55 10N 4 40W
36 Carrick-on-Shannon, Ire. 53 58N 8 5W
35 Carrick-on-Suir, Ireland 52 21N 7 24W
36 Carrickboy, Ireland 53 36N 7 40W
36 Carrickfergus, N. Ireland 54 43N 5 48W
36 Carrickmacross, Ireland 53 59N 6 45W
83 Carrieton, Australia 32 27S 138 30E
34 Carrigaholt, Ireland 52 37N 9 42W
34 Carrigaline, Ireland 51 49N 8 22W
36 Carrigallen, Ireland 53 59N 7 40W
32 Carron, L. & R., Scotland 57 22N 5 35W
31 Carronbridge, Scotland 55 16N 3 46W
36 Carryduff, N. Ireland 54 32N 5 52W
90 Carson City, U.S.A. 39 6N 119 37W
90 Carson Sink, L., U.S.A. 39 45N 118 40W
31 Carsphairn, Scotland 55 13N 4 15W
31 Carstairs, Scotland 55 42N 3 40W
78 Carstenz, Mt., New Guinea,
see Sukarno Pk.
95 Cartagena, Colombia 10 21N 75 35W
37 Cartagena, Spain 37 38N 0 55W
95 Cartago, Colombia 4 30N 76 10W
95 Cartago, Costa Rica 9 50N 83 50W
42 Carteret, France 49 23N 1 48W
91 Carthage, Mo., U.S.A. 37 4N 94 18W
89 Cartwright, Canada 53 40N 56 40W
95 Carúpano, Venezuela 10 40N 63 25W
44 Carvin, France 50 30N 2 56E
72 Casablanca, Morocco 33 30N 7 35W
43 Casale, Italy 45 6N 8 32E
90 Cascade Ra., U.S.A. 45 0N 122 0W
37 Cascais, Portugal 38 45N 9 35W
40 Caserta, Italy 41 8N 14 23E
34 Cashel, Ireland 52 30N 7 52W
83 Casino, Australia 29 0S 152 49E
95 Casiquiare, R., Venezuela 2 40N 66 15W
37 Caspe, Spain 41 15N 0 0
90 Casper, U.S.A. 42 57N 106 30W
51 Caspian Sea, U.S.S.R. 42 30N 51 0E
42 Casquets, The, Channel Is. 49 45N 2 20W
88 Cassiar, Mts., Canada 58 30N 129 0W
75 Cassinga, Angola 15 5S 16 20E
43 Casteljaloux, France 44 20N 0 0
40 Castellammare, Italy 38 1N 12 52E
43 Castelnaudary, France 43 20N 2 0E
37 Castelo Branco, Portugal 39 50N 7 32W
43 Castelsarrasin, France 44 0N 1 5E
40 Castelvetrano, Italy 37 42N 12 47E
83 Casterton, Australia 37 32S 141 25E
37 Castile, New, Prov., Spain 40 0N 3 20W
37 Castile, Old, Prov., Spain 41 30N 3 40W
31 Castle Douglas, Scotland 54 56N 3 57W
36 Castlebellingham, Ireland 53 53N 6 22W
36 Castleblayney, Ireland 54 6N 6 50W
36 Castlebridge, Ireland 52 23N 6 28W
35 Castlecomer, Ireland 52 45N 7 12W
34 Castleconnell, Ireland 52 44N 8 30W
36 Castledawson, N. Ireland 54 47N 6 30W
36 Castlederg, N. Ireland 54 43N 7 36W
35 Castledermot, Ireland 52 55N 6 50W
34 Castlegregory, Ireland 52 15N 10 1W
34 Castleisland, Ireland 52 14N 9 28W
83 Castlemaine, Australia 37 0S 144 15E
34 Castlemaine, Ireland 52 10N 9 44W
34 Castlemaine Hr., Ireland 52 8N 9 52W
34 Castlemartyr, Ireland 51 54N 8 3W
36 Castlepollard, Ireland 53 40N 7 20W
36 Castlereagh, Ireland 53 47N 8 29W
83 Castlereagh R., Australia 31 20S 148 0E
26 Castleton, England 53 22N 1 40W
26 Castletown, I.o.M. 54 4N 4 41W
36 Castletown, Meath, Ire. 53 47N 6 41W
35 Castletown, Laois, Ire. 52 58N 7 30W
35 Castletown, Westmeath, Ireland
53 26N 7 25W
33 Castletown, Scotland 58 35N 3 22W

† *County incorporated within Dyfed*

34 Castletownroche, Ire. 52 10N 8 28W
34 Castletownshend, Ireland 51 31N 9 11W
36 Castlewellan, N. Ireland 54 16N 5 57W
43 Castres, France 43 40N 2 13E
94 Castries, Windward Islands
14 0N 61 0W
99 Castro, Chile 42 30S 73 40W
37 Castro, Spain 37 46N 4 30W
91 Cat I., Bahamas 24 25N 75 30W
99 Catalão, Brazil 18 8S 47 50W
37 Catalonia, Prov., Spain 41 40N 1 30E
99 Catamarca, Argentina 28 28S 65 47W
68 Catanduanas, Phil. 13 45N 124 20E
40 Catania, Italy 37 33N 15 7E
40 Catanzaro, Italy 38 59N 16 34E
23 Caterham, England 51 16N 0 4W
92 Catlettsburg, U.S.A. 38 28N 82 33W
94 Catoche, C., Mexico 21 45N 87 0W
94 Catorce, Mexico 23 50N 100 55W
93 Catskill, Mts., U.S.A. 42 18N 74 30W
27 Catterick, England 54 23N 1 38W
51 Caucasus, Mts., U.S.S.R. 43 0N 44 0E
43 Caudebec, France 49 20N 1 0E
44 Caudry, France 50 7N 3 22E
74 Caungula, Angola 8 15S 18 50E
42 Cauterets, France 43 0N 0 12W
65 Cauvery, R., India 11 0N 78 0E
36 Cavan, & Co., Ireland 54 0N 7 21W
83 Cavendish, Australia 37 35S 142 5E
98 Caviana I., Brazil 0 15N 50 30W
33 Cawdor, Scotland 57 32N 3 53W
64 Cawnpore, *see* Kanpur
98 Caxias, Brazil 4 50S 43 2W
99 Caxias do Sul, Brazil 29 25S 51 10W
98 Cayenne, French Guiana 4 45N 52 15W
92 Cayuga, L., U.S.A. 42 42N 76 35W
36 Ceanannus Mor, Ireland 53 40N 6 55W
98 Ceará, *see* Fortaleza
98 Ceará, st., Brazil 4 30S 39 30W
68 Cebu & I., Philippines 10 20N 123 50E
83 Cecil Plains, Australia 27 32S 151 4E
90 Cedar City, U.S.A. 37 40N 113 7W
91 Cedar Falls, U.S.A. 42 33N 92 30W
91 Cedar Rapids, U.S.A. 42 0N 91 39W
80 Ceduna, Australia 32 0S 133 54E
40 Cefalu, Italy 38 0N 14 0E
37 Cehegin, Spain 38 6N 1 48W
94 Celaya, Mexico 21 0N 101 0W
35 Celbridge, Ireland 53 20N 6 31W
68 Celebes, I., Indonesia, *see* Sulawesi
68 Celebes Sea, Indonesia 4 0N 122 0E
40 Celje, Yugoslavia 46 20N 15 20E
46 Celle, Germany 52 39N 10 3E
25 Cemaes Road, Wales 52 39N 3 41W
43 Cenis, Mt., France 45 17N 7 0E
40 Ceno, R., Italy 44 42N 9 48E
74 Central Africa Rep., Afr. 7 0N 20 0E
13 Central Massif, mts., Fr. 45 0N 2 30E
64 Central Makran Ra., Pakistan
26 30N 64 0E
13 Central Russian Uplands, U.S.S.R.
53 0N 35 0E
61 Central Siberian Plat, U.S.S.R.
65 0N 105 0E
92 Centralia, Ill., U.S.A. 38 30N 89 10W
90 Centralia, Wash., U.S.A.
46 40N 122 55W
41 Cephalonia, I., *see* Kefallinia
68 Ceram, I., Indonesia 3 10S 129 30E
68 Ceram Sea, Indonesia 2 20S 129 0E
43 Cerbère, France 42 25N 3 10E
76 Ceres, Cape Prov., S. Afr. 33 21S 19 18E
40 Cerignola, Italy 41 18N 15 58E
41 Cerigo, I., Greece, *see* Kithira
40 Cerknica, Yugoslavia 45 47N 14 40E
47 Cernavoda, Rumania 44 20N 28 5E
98 Cerro de Pasco, Peru 10 45S 77 0W
37 Cervera, Spain 41 40N 1 30E
43 Cervione, France 42 17N 9 30E
40 Cesena, Italy 44 10N 12 15E
49 Cesis, U.S.S.R. 57 20N 25 15E
47 Cesky Tesin, Cz-slov. 49 45N 18 39E
41 Cesme, Turkey 38 20N 26 20E
83 Cessnock, Australia 33 0S 151 0E
41 Cetinje, Yugoslavia 42 23N 18 54E
72 Ceuta, Morocco 35 50N 5 20W
43 Ceva, Italy 44 25N 8 0E
43 Cevennes, mts., France 44 30N 4 0E
64 Ceylon, *see* Sri Lanka
98 Chachapoyas, Peru 6 15S 77 35W
68 Chachoengsao, Thailand 13 45N 101 12E
64 Chachran, Pakistan 28 55N 70 30E
99 Chaco Central, Argentina 24 0S 61 0W
73 Chad (Tchad), Afr. 13 0N 14 0E
73 Chad, L., Chad 13 50N 14 30E
90 Chadron, U.S.A. 42 52N 103 4W
64 Chagai Hills, Afghan. 29 40N 64 0E
61 Chagda, U.S.S.R. 58 30N 130 43E
55 Chagos Is., Indian Ocean 6 0S 72 0W
64 Chahar Burjak, Afghan. 30 20N 62 0E
63 Chahbar, Iran 25 20N 60 33E
65 Chaibasa, India 22 42N 85 49E
64 Chakhansur, Prov., Afghan.
30 0N 62 0E
65 Chakradharpur, India 22 50N 85 40E
66 Chalainor, China 49 25N 117 30E
67 Chalatun, China 48 0N 122 40E
93 Chaleur, B. de, Canada 47 50N 65 10W
23 Chalfont St. Peter, Eng. 51 36N 0 33W
64 Chalisgaon, India 20 30N 75 0E
42 Challans France 46 50N 1 58W
43 Châlon-s-Saône, France 46 51N 4 52E
42 Chalonnes, France 47 20N 0 44W
43 Châlons-s-Marne, France 49 0N 4 20E
64 Chaman, Pakistan 30 55N 66 50E
64 Chamba, India 32 35N 76 15E
75 Chamba, Tanzania 11 40S 37 0E
64 Chambal, R., India 26 0N 76 55E
43 Chambéry, France 45 35N 5 54E
93 Chambord, Canada 48 27N 72 3W
42 Chamborn, France 47 38N 1 30E
66 Ch'amdo, China 31 30N 97 35E
66 Chamdo, Prov., China 31 0N 95 0E
74 Chamo, L., *see* Shamo
43 Chamonix, France 45 55N 6 50E
42 Champagne, Dist., France 49 0N 4 30E
92 Champaign, U.S.A. 40 12N 88 17W
80 Champion Bay, Australia 28 30S 114 30E
93 Champlain, L., U.S.A. 44 30N 73 20W
99 Chanaral, Chile 26 16S 70 45W
64 Chanda, India 19 59N 79 15E
64 Chandigarh, India 30 32N 76 55E
65 Chandpur, Bangladesh 23 6N 90 35E
66 Changchih, China 35 15 113 0E
66 Changchow, Fukien, China
24 36N 117 40E
67 Changchow, Kiangsu, China
31 55N 119 50E
67 Changchun, China 43 20N 126 30E
66 Changki, Sinkiang, China 44 10N 87 0E
67 Changpai Shan, Mts., China
42 0N 126 30E
66 Changsha, China 28 10N 112 59E
66 Chang Tang, Tibet 34 0N 88 0E
66 Changteh, China 29 2N 111 45E
66 Changyeh, China 39 15N 100 15E
66 Chankiang, *see* Tsamkong, China
64 Channapatna, India 12 40N 77 5E
42 Channel Is., U.K. 49 20N 2 20W
37 Chantada, Spain 42 40N 7 48W
68 Chanthaburi, Thailand 12 35N 102 5E
66 Chanyi, China 25 50N 103 20E
66 Chaochow, China 23 42N 116 25E
66 Chaotung, China 27 22N 103 34E
60 Chap Kuduk, U.S.S.R. 48 40N 55 5E
98 Chapada dos Veadeiros, plat., Brazil
15 0S 48 0W
94 Chapala, L. de, Mexico 20 20N 103 10W
50 Chapayevsk, U.S.S.R. 53 0N 49 50E
26 Chapel-en-le-Fri[illegible], Eng. 53 19N 1 54W
65 Chapra, India 25 58N 84 39E
63 Charak, Iran 26 40N 54 50E
98 Charaña, Bolivia 17 45S 69 10W
100 Charcot, I., Antarctica 70 0S 78 0W
24 Chard, England 50 52N 2 57W
58 Chardzhou, U.S.S.R. 39 0N 63 15E
42 Charente, Dépt., France 46 0N 0 30E
42 Charente-Maritime, Dépt., France
46 5N 0 48W
64 Charikar, Afghan. 35 5N 69 0E
66 Charkhlik, China 39 30N 88 10E
44 Charleroi, Belgium 50 25N 4 27E
93 Charles, C., U.S.A. 37 12N 75 43W
91 Charles City, U.S.A. 43 2N 92 43W
91 Charleston, S.C., U.S.A. 32 48N 80 0W
92 Charleston, W. Va., U.S.A.
38 24N 81 36W
91 Charleston Hr., U.S.A. 32 45N 79 55W
36 Charlestown, Ireland 53 58N 8 48W
95 Charlestown, Nevis, W.I. 17 10N 62 35W
74 Charlesville, Zaïre 5 27S 20 59E
83 Charleville, Australia 26 27S 146 14E
43 Charleville-Mézières, France
49 46N 4 42E
91 Charlotte, N.C., U.S.A. 35 16N 80 50W
95 Charlotte Amalie, Virgin Is.
18 0N 65 0W
80 Charlotte Waters, Australia
25 55S 134 59E
46 Charlottenburg, Ger. 52 31N 13 15E
92 Charlottesville, U.S.A. 38 0N 78 31W
89 Charlottetown, Canada 46 20N 63 22W
83 Charlton, Australia 36 20S 143 30E
89 Charlton I., Canada 52 0N 79 20W
22 Charlton Kings, Eng. 51 52N 2 3W
22 Charnwood Forest, Eng. 52 45N 1 18W
72 Charouin, Algeria 29 10N 0 15W
43 Charrolles, France 46 27N 4 16E
82 Charters Towers, Austral. 20 0S 146 13E
43 Chartres, France 48 29N 1 30E
61 Chasovnya Uchurskaya, U.S.S.R.
57 5N 133 20E
45 Château-d'Oex, Switz. 46 28N 7 10E
43 Château du Loir, France 47 40N 0 30E
42 Château Gontier, France 47 40N 0 42W
43 Château la Vallière, Fr. 47 30N 0 15E
44 Château Porcien, France 49 32N 4 14E
44 Château Thierry, France 49 0N 3 28E
42 Châteaubriant, France 47 45N 1 23W
42 Châteaudun, France 48 0N 1 20E
43 Châteauroux, France 46 51N 1 39E
43 Châtellerault, France 46 46N 0 30E
45 Chatel-St.-Denis, Switz. 46 32N 6 55E
89 Chatham, N.B., Canada 47 0N 65 31W
92 Chatham, Ont., Canada 42 20N 82 18W
23 Chatham, England 51 21N 0 32E
4 Chatham Is., Pacific Oc. 44 0S 176 40W
43 Châtillon-s.-Seine, France 47 50N 4 35E
65 Chatrapur, India 19 25N 84 55E
91 Chattahoochee R., U.S.A. 32 0N 85 7W
91 Chattanooga, U.S.A. 35 2N 85 10W
23 Chatteris, England 52 27N 0 3E
31 Chatton, England 55 34N 1 55W
44 Chaulnes, France 49 48N 2 47E
43 Chaumont, France 48 7N 5 10E
43 Chauny, France 49 40N 3 15E
37 Chaves, Portugal 41 45N 7 35W
75 Chavuma, Zambia 13 10N 22 55E
64 Chayul, Tibet 28 20N 92 50E
26 Cheadle, Ches. Eng. 53 23N 2 14W

26 Cheadle, Staffs., Eng. 43 0N 1 58w
26 Cheadle Hulme, Eng. 53 22N 2 12w
46 Cheb, Czechoslovakia 50 9N 12 20E
50 Cheboksary, U.S.S.R. 56 8N 47 30E
91 Cheboygan, U.S.A. 45 29N 84 15w
72 Chech, Erg, des., Algeria 25 0N 7 0w
51 Checheno-Ingush, A.S.S.R., U.S.S.R. 43 30N 46 0E
22 Cheddar, England 51 16N 2 47w
26 Cheddleton, England 53 5N 2 2w
65 Cheduba, I., Burma 18 48N 93 43E
83 Cheepie, Australia 26 39s 145 0E
67 Chefoo (Yehtai), China 37 30N 121 25E
72 Chegga, Mauritania 25 15N 5 40w
90 Chehalis, U.S.A. 46 35N 122 55w
67 Cheju, Korea 33 30N 126 20E
67 Cheju Do. I. (Quelpart), Korea 33 20N 126 30E
67 Chekiang, Prov., China 29 10N 120 0E
62 Cheleken, I., U.S.S.R. 39 25N 53 15E
50 Chelkar, U.S.S.R. 47 50N 59 32E
47 Chelm, Poland 51 12N 23 39E
47 Chelmno, Poland 53 20N 18 30E
23 Chelmsford, England 51 43N 0 27E
47 Chelmza, Poland 53 10N 18 45E
22 Cheltenham, England 51 54N 2 4w
60 Chelyabinsk, U.S.S.R. 55 20N 61 15E
50 Chemikovsk, U.S.S.R. 54 55N 56 0E
66 Chengchow, China 34 55N 113 40E
66 Cheng-teh, China 41 3N 118 0E
66 Chengtu, China 30 50N 104 5E
22 Chepstow, England 51 39N 2 41w
43 Cher, R. & Dépt., France 47 0N 2 15E
42 Cherbourg, France 49 39N 1 40w
66 Cherchen, China 38 13N 85 27E
66 Cherchen, R., China 39 20N 86 0E
50 Cherdyn, U.S.S.R. 60 20N 56 20E
61 Cheremkhovo, U.S.S.R. 53 5N 103 0E
50 Cherepovets, U.S.S.R. 59 10N 37 50E
51 Cherkassy, U.S.S.R. 49 20N 32 10E
50 Chernigov, U.S.S.R. 51 35N 31 15E
51 Chernovtsy, U.S.S.R. 48 21N 25 58E
61 Chernoye, U.S.S.R. 70 30N 89 10E
49 Chernyakhovsk, U.S.S.R. 54 29N 21.48E
91 Cherokee, U.S.A. 42 46N 95 39w
65 Cherrapunji, India 25 18N 91 57E
61 Cherskiy Ra., U.S.S.R. 64 0N 145 0E
22 Cherwell, R., England 51 55N 1 18w
91 Chesapeake B., U.S.A. 37 0N 76 0w
23 Chesham, England 51 42N 0 36w
26 Cheshire, Co. & Plain, Eng. 53 15N 2 30w
23 Cheshunt, England 51 42N 0 1w
22 Chesil Beach, England 50 38N 2 35w
26 Chester, England 53 12N 2 53w
27 Chesterfield, England 53 15N 1 26w
88 Chesterfield Inlet, Can. 63 45N 92 0w
81 Chesterfield Is., Pac. Oc. 19 52s 158 0E
27 Chester-le-Street, Eng. 54 52N 1 34w
83 Chesterton Ra., Australia 25 50s 146 55E
31 Cheviot Hills, England 55 20N 2 30w
74 Chew Bahir, L., Ethiopia 4 45N 36 50E
90 Cheyenne, U.S.A. 41 20N 104 57w
90 Cheyenne, R., U.S.A. 44 30N 101 45w
64 Chhatarpur, India 25 0N 78 35E
64 Chhindwara, India 22 6N 78 59E
65 Chiali, China 30 25N 93 0E
65 Chiang Mai, Thailand 19 0N 99 55E
65 Chiang Rai, Thailand 19 30N 99 50E
94 Chiapa, R., Mexico 16 45N 92 58w
40 Chiavari, Italy 44 20N 9 20E
40 Chiavenna, Italy 46 20N 9 26E
67 Chiba, & Pref., Japan 35 40N 140 6E
75 Chibia, Angola 15 10s 13 50E
73 Chibuk, Nigeria 10 52N 12 50E
92 Chicago, U.S.A. 41 50N 87 50w
88 Chichagof I., Alaska 57 50N 136 0w
23 Chichester, England 50 50N 0 47w
90 Chickasha, U.S.A. 35 2N 98 0w
37 Chiclana, Spain 36 23N 6 10w
98 Chiclayo, Peru 7 0s 79 30w
99 Chico, R., Argentina 49 0s 70 0w
75 Chicoa, Mozambique 15 35s 32 20E
89 Chicoutimi, Canada 48 24N 71 2w
64 Chidambaram, India 11 20N 79 40E
74 Chiengi, Zambia 8 38s 29 10E
44 Chiers, R., France 49 30N 5 20E
40 Chieti, Italy 42 21N 14 12E
66 Chihli, G., China 40 0N 116 30E
94 Chihuahua, Mexico 28 47N 106 20w
64 Chik Ballapur, India 13 20N 77 40E
65 Chikmagalur, India 13 20N 75 52E
64 Chilaw, Sri Lanka 7 30N 79 50E
83 Childers, Australia 25 15s 152 17E
90 Childress, U.S.A. 34 25N 100 15w
99 Chile, S. America 17 30s to 55 0s 71 15w
99 Chilecito, Argentina 29 0s 67 40w
60 Chili, U.S.S.R. 44 20N 66 59E
75 Chililabombwe, Zambia 12 10s 28 0E
65 Chilka, L., India 19 40N 85 28E
82 Chillagoe, Australia 17 0s 144 10E
99 Chillán, Chile 36 48s 72 12w
91 Chillicothe, Mo., U.S.A. 39 46N 93 34w
92 Chillicothe, Ohio, U.S.A. 39 28N 83 1w
99 Chiloe, I., Chile 43 0s 73 30w
23 Chiltern Hills, England 51 45N 0 45w
66 Chimai, China 33 30N 100 45E
44 Chimay, Belgium 50 2N 4 20E
98 Chimborazo, Mt. Ecuador 1 10s 79 5w
98 Chimbote, Peru 8 55s 78 33w
60 Chimkent, U.S.S.R. 42 40N 69 25E
66 China, Asia 55 0N to 18 30N; 70 0E to 133 0E
94 Chinandega, Nicaragua 12 34N 87 5w
98 Chincha Alta, Peru 13 20s 76 0w
83 Chinchilla, Australia 26 40s 150 8E
37 Chinchon, Spain 40 10N 3 28w
67 Chinchow, China 41 10N 121 2E
75 Chinde, Mozambique 18 45s 36 25E
65 Chindwin, R., Burma 25 0N 95 0E
67 Chingkiang, China 32 7N 119 32E
75 Chingola, Zambia 12 31s 27 53E
72 Chinguetti, Mauritania 20 35s 12 25w
64 Chiniot, Pakistan 31 45N 72 55E
67 Chinnampo, Korea 39 10N 126 0E
43 Chinon, France 47 12N 0 15E
65 Chins Division, Burma 22 30N 93 30E
74 Chinsali, Zambia 10 35s 32 3E
67 Chinwangtao, China 39 58N 119 30E
40 Chioggia, Italy 45 13N 12 17E
75 Chipata, Zambia 13 29s 32 36E
93 Chipman, Canada 46 10N 65 55w
22 Chippenham, England 51 28N 2 7w
91 Chippewa Falls, U.S.A. 44 55N 92 30w
22 Chipping Campden, Eng. 52 4N 1 48w
22 Chipping Norton, Eng. 51 57N 1 33w
64 Chirala, India 15 45N 80 20E
60 Chirchik, U.S.S.R. 41 40N 69 10E
25 Chirk, Wales 52 57N 3 4w
65 Chirmiri, India 23 15N 82 20E
75 Chiromo, Malawi 16 25s 35 12E
75 Chisamba, Zambia 14 55N 28 20E
65 Chisapani Garhi, Nepal 27 30N 84 2E
50 Chistopol, U.S.S.R. 55 22N 50 37E
61 Chita, U.S.S.R. 52 15N 113 50E
75 Chitembo, Angola 13 30s 16 50E
64 Chitorgarh, India 24 58N 74 36E
64 Chitral, India 35 57N 71 46E
95 Chitré, Panama 7 50N 80 25w
65 Chittagong, E. Pak. 22 25N 91 43E
64 Chittoor, India 13 8N 79 5E
40 Chiusi, Italy 43 2N 11 56E
43 Chivasso, Italy 45 15N 7 55E
99 Chivilcoy, Argentina 35 0s 60 4w
75 Chobe Swamp, Botswana 18 25s 24 25E
99 Choele Choel, Argentina 39 15s 65 30w
49 Chojnice, Poland 53 44N 17 40E
22 Cholsey, England 51 34N 1 10w
75 Choma, Zambia 16 57s 26 58E
46 Chomutov, Cz-slov. 50 28N 13 23E
67 Chongjin, Korea 41 40N 129 40E
99 Chonos Arch., Chile 45 0s 74 0w
26 Chorley, England 53 39N 2 38w
51 Chortkov, U.S.S.R. 49 2N 25 46E
47 Chorzow, Poland 50 20N 19 0E
67 Choshi, Japan 35 50N 140 48E
46 Choszczno, Poland 53 7N 15 25E
64 Chotila, India 22 30N 71 3E
72 Chott Djerid, Tunisia 34 10N 8 0E
72 Chott el Hodna, Algeria 35 30N 4 30E
63 Choueifat, Lebanon 33 48N 35 30E
83 Chowilla, Australia 33 58s 140 45E
66 Chowkow (Shanghsui), China 31 10N 105 45E
66 Choybalsan, Mongolia 48 9N 114 30E
66 Chowkow, China 33 40N 115 0E
22 Christchurch, England 50 44N 1 47w
84 Christchurch, N.Z. 43 30s 172 43E
76 Christiana, S. Africa 27 57s 25 8E
95 Christiansted, St. Croix, W. Indies 17 45N 64 45w
5 Christmas I., Indian Oc. 10 0s 105 0E
11 Christmas I., Pac. Oc. 1 58N 157 27w
67 Chüanchow, China 27 0N 118 33E
66 Chuchow, China 27 45N 113 10E
61 Chuckchi or Chukot Sea, U.S.S.R. 69 0N 177 0E
24 Chudleigh, England 50 35N 3 36w
50 Chudskoye L., U.S.S.R. 58 0N 27 30E
67 Chühsien, China 28 55N 119 0E
68 Chukai, Malaysia 4 10N 103 30E
61 Chulman, U.S.S.R. 57 5N 124 50E
66 Chumatien, China 33 0N 114 10E
61 Chumikan, U.S.S.R. 54 45N 135 20E
68 Chumphon, Thailand 10 35N 99 20E
66 Chunking, China 29 32N 106 45E
66 Chungtien, China 27 50N 99 50E
66 Chungwei, China 38 0N 105 0E
74 Chunya, Tanzania 8 20s 34 0E
99 Chuquicamata, Chile 22 30s 69 0w
45 Chur, Switzerland 46 50N 9 30E
22 Church Stretton, Eng. 52 32N 2 49w
22 Churchdown, England 51 53N 2 9w
88 Churchill, & C., Canada 58 45N 94 0w
88 Churchill L., Canada 56 0N 108 30w
89 Churchill Falls, Canada 53 35N 65 20w
88 Churchill R., Canada 55 30N 104 0w
64 Churu, India 28 25N 75 0E
50 Chusovoy, U.S.S.R. 58 15N 57 30E
64 Chusul, Kashmir 33 40N 78 40E
50 Chuvash, A.S.S.R., U.S.S.R. 55 40N 47 0E
47 Ciechanów, Poland 52 55N 20 35E
98 Cienaga, Colombia 11 0N 74 15w
95 Cienfuegos, Cuba 22 13N 80 30w
47 Cieszyn, Poland 49 45N 18 40E
37 Cieza, Spain 38 15N 1 25w
62 Cilician Gates, Turkey 37 20N 34 52E
91 Cimarron, R., U.S.A. 37 10N 102 0w
47 Cîmpina, Rumania 45 10N 25 45E
47 Cîmpulung, Rumania 45 18N 25 0E
37 Cinca, R., Spain 42 20N 0 10E
92 Cincinnati, U.S.A. 39 17N 84 25w
22 Cinderford, England 51 49N 2 30w
44 Ciney, Belgium 50 19N 5 5E
22 Cirencester, England 51 44N 1 58w
94 Citlaltepetl, Mt., Mexico 19 3N 97 16w
95 Ciudad Bolivar, Venezuela 8 0N 63 30w
94 Ciudad Camargo, Mexico 27 40N 105 10w
94 Ciudad del Carmen, Mex. 18 45N 91 45w
95 Ciudad Guayana, Ven. 8 25N 62 30w
94 Ciudad Juaréz, Mexico 31 40N 106 28w
94 Ciudad Madero, Mexico 22 40N 98 10w
94 Ciudad Mante, Mexico 22 40N 99 2w
94 Ciudad Obregon, Mex. 27 40N 109 50w
37 Ciudad Real, Spain 39 0N 3 55w
37 Ciudad Rodrigo, Spain 40 38N 6 33w
94 Ciudad Victoria, Mex. 23 50N 99 0w
40 Civitanova, Italy 43 20N 13 40E
40 Civitavecchia, Italy 42 6N 11 51E
43 Civray, France 46 10N 0 15E
51 Cizre, Turkey 37 27N 42 3E
30 Clachan, Arg., Scot. 55 45N 5 35w
32 Clachan, Invern., Scot. 57 33N 7 20w
*31 Clackmannan, & Co., Scot. 56 6N 3 45w
23 Clacton-on-Sea, England 51 48N 1 9E
30 Cladich, Scotland 56 21N 5 5w
43 Clamecy, France 47 27N 3 30E
88 Claire L., Canada 58 30N 112 0w
35 Clane, Ireland 53 18N 6 40w
76 Clanwilliam, S. Africa 32 13s 18 59E
35 Clara, Ireland 53 20N 7 38w
83 Clare, Australia 33 47s 138 30E
23 Clare, England 52 5N 0 36E
34 Clare, Co., Ireland 52 52N 8 55w
35 Clare, I., Ireland 53 48N 10 0w
34 Clare, R., Ireland 53 30N 8 53w
36 Claremorris, Ireland 53 42N 8 58w
84 Clarence, R., N.Z. 42 15s 173 30E
34 Clarinbridge, Ireland 53 13N 8 55w
83 Clarke I., Australia 40 32s 148 10E
90 Clark Fork, R., U.S.A. 46 45N 114 0w
92 Clarksburg, U.S.A. 39 30N 80 15w
91 Clarksdale, U.S.A. 34 14N 90 31w
91 Clarksville, U.S.A. 36 35N 87 15w
33 Clashmore, Scotland 57 53N 4 8w
36 Claudy, N. Ireland 54 55N 7 10w
27 Clay Cross, England 53 11N 1 26w
27 Claydon, England 52 6N 1 7E
34 Clear, C. & I., Ireland 51 26N 9 30w
91 Clearwater, U.S.A. 28 0N 82 47w
89 Clearwater, L., Canada 56 20N 75 0w
90 Clearwater, R., U.S.A. 46 15N 115 30w
33 Cleat, Scotland 58 45N 2 56w
26 Cleator Moor, England 54 31N 3 32w
91 Cleburne, U.S.A. 32 21N 97 27w
25 Cleddau, R., Wales 51 55N 4 44w
22 Clee Hills, England 52 26N 2 37w
27 Cleethorpes, England 53 33N 0 2w
22 Cleeve Cloud, mt., Eng. 51 57N 2 0w
82 Clermont, Australia 22 45s 147 30E
43 Clermont Ferrand, Fr. 45 46N 3 10E
44 Clervaux, Luxembourg 50 3N 6 2E
83 Cleveland, Australia 27 35s 153 0E
**27 Cleveland, Dist., Eng. 54 32N 1 10w
91 Cleveland, Miss., U.S.A. 33 45N 90 50w
92 Cleveland, Ohio, U.S.A. 41 25N 81 40w
91 Cleveland, Tenn., U.S.A. 35 10N 84 35w
27 Cleveland Hills, England 54 25N 1 11w
35 Clew B., Ireland 53 50N 9 45w
34 Clifden, & B., Ireland 53 30N 10 1w
84 Clifden, New Zealand 46 5s 167 30E
36 Cliffony, Ireland 54 27N 8 31w
22 Clifford, England 52 6N 3 6w
34 Cliffs of Moher, Ireland 52 59N 9 25w
83 Clifton, Australia 27 58s 151 40E
76 Clifton Bakoven, S. Africa 33 57s 18 20E
91 Clinch, Mts., U.S.A. 36 30N 83 0w
88 Clinton, Canada 51 0N 121 40w
84 Clinton, New Zealand 46 24s 169 23E
92 Clinton, Iowa, U.S.A. 41 50N 90 15w
90 Clinton, Okla., U.S.A. 35 30N 98 58w
88 Clinton Colden L., Can. 64 0N 107 0w
26 Clitheroe, England 53 52N 2 24w
80 Cloates, Pt., Australia 22 30s 113 40E
36 Cloghan, Donegal, Ireland 54 48N 7 57w
34 Clogheen, Ireland 52 17N 8 0w
36 Clogher, N. Ireland 54 23N 7 11w
36 Clogher Hd., Ireland 53 47N 6 13w
34 Cloghjordan, Ireland 52 57N 8 2w
34 Clonakilty, & B., Ireland 51 38N 8 52w
82 Cloncurry, Australia 20 38s 140 30E
35 Clondalkin, Ireland 53 20N 6 25w
35 Clonee, Ireland 53 25N 6 28w
36 Clones, Ireland 54 10N 7 13w
34 Clonkeen, Ireland 51 59N 9 20w
36 Clonmany, Ireland 55 16N 7 24w
35 Clonmel, Ireland 52 22N 7 40w
35 Clonroche, Ireland 52 27N 6 42w
36 Cloonfad, Ireland 53 41N 8 45w
31 Closeburn, Scotland 55 13N 3 45w
36 Clough, N. Ireland 54 18N 5 50w
90 Clovis, U.S.A. 34 25N 103 16w
27 Clowne, England 53 16N 1 16w
34 Cloyne, Ireland 51 52N 8 8w
32 Cluanie, L., Scotland 57 8N 5 6w
47 Cluj, Rumania 46 42N 23 36E
22 Clun, England 52 26N 3 1w
83 Clunes, Australia 37 20s 143 45E
43 Cluny, France 46 32N 4 43E
45 Cluses, France 46 4N 6 35E
45 Clusone, Italy 45 54N 9 58E
84 Clutha R., N.Z. 45 39s 168 55E
25 Clwyd, R., Wales 53 15N 3 25w
84 Clyde, New Zealand 45 12s 169 20E
31 Clyde, R., Scot. 55 38N 3 47w
30 Clyde, Firth of, Scotland 55 35N 5 0w
30 Clydebank, Scotland 55 54N 4 25w
31 Clydesdale, Dist., Scot. 55 30N 3 35w
34 Coachford, Ireland 51 57N 8 56w
36 Coagh, N. Ireland 54 40N 6 37w
22 Coalbrookdale, Eng. 52 40N 2 25w
36 Coalisland, N. Ireland 54 33N 6 42w
22 Coalville, England 52 43N 1 21w

* *County incorporated within the region Central*

** *Cleveland, Co., England 54 35N 1 5W*

88 Coast Mts., Canada 56 0N 130 0w
99 Coast Ra., Chile 24 0s 70 0w
90 Coast Ra., N. America 42 0N 123 0w
80 Coastal Plains Basin, Australia 30 30s 115 30E
31 Coatbridge, Scotland 55 51N 4 2w
93 Coaticook, Canada 45 7N 71 50w
88 Coats I., Canada 62 30N 83 0w
100 Coats Ld., Antarctica 78 0s 25 0w
94 Coatzacoalcos, Mexico 18 7N 94 35w
89 Cobalt, Canada 47 30N 79 42w
83 Cobar, Australia 31 29s 145 45E
34 Cobh, Ireland 51 52N 8 17w
83 Cobham, Australia 30 10s 142 5E
83 Cobram, Australia 35 58s 145 35E
75 Cóbué, Mozambique 12 0s 34 58E
46 Coburg, Germany 50 16N 10 57E
65 Cocanada, India 17 0N 82 10E
98 Cochabamba, Bolivia 17 30s 66 27w
68 Cochin China, Vietnam 10 0N 106 0E
89 Cochrane, Canada 49 12N 81 37w
83 Cockburn, Australia 31 58s 141 8E
99 Cockburn Chan., Chile 54 30s 72 30w
31 Cockburnspath, Scotland 55 56N 2 23w
31 Cockenzie, Scotland 55 58N 2 59w
26 Cockerham, England 53 58N 2 49w
26 Cockermouth, England 54 41N 3 19w
23 Cockfield, England 52 8N 0 47E
95 Coco, R., Cent. Amer., *see* Wanks R.
5 Cocos Is., Indian Ocean 12 10s 96 50E
93 Cod, C., U.S.A. 42 8N 70 10w
23 Coddenham, England 52 8N 1 8E
94 Codrington, Barbuda, W.I. 17 40N 61 11w
82 Coen, Australia 13 55s 143 15E
44 Coesfeld, Germany 51 57N 7 11E
90 Coeur d'Alene, U.S.A. 47 58N 116 57w
44 Coevorden, Netherlands 52 29N 6 45E
83 Coff's Harbour, Austral. 30 17s 152 51E
40 Coghinas, R., Sardinia, It. 40 30N 8 50E
42 Cognac, France 45 42N 0 20w
83 Cohuna, Australia 35 57s 144 8E
95 Coiba, I., Panama 7 30N 81 50w
32 Coigach, Scotland 58 0N 5 10w
64 Coimbatore, India 11 0N 77 0E
37 Coimbra, Portugal 40 17N 8 26w
37 Coin, Spain 36 42N 4 46w
45 Col de Faucille, France 46 21N 6 0E
43 Col de la Perche, Spain 42 30N 2 0E
43 Col di Tenda, France 44 10N 7 30E
83 Colac, Australia 38 18s 143 40E
83 Colbinabbin, Australia 36 40s 144 45E
23 Colchester, England 51 53N 0 55E
26 Cold Fell, mt., England 54 56N 2 36w
31 Coldingham, Scotland 55 53N 2 29w
31 Coldstream, Scotland 55 40N 2 14w
24 Colebrooke, England 50 45N 3 44w
22 Coleford, England 51 46N 2 38w
88 Coleman, Canada 49 36N 114 30w
83 Coleraine, Australia 37 47s 141 42E
36 Coleraine, N. Ireland 55 7N 6 39w
22 Coleshill, England 52 30N 1 42w
43 Colico, Italy 46 9N 9 24E
94 Colima, & Vol., Mex. 19 30N 103 50w
30 Coll I., Scotland 56 40N 6 35w
83 Collarenebri, Austral. 29 33s 148 36E
80 Collie, Australia 33 18s 116 5E
80 Collier B., Australia 16 0s 124 0E
26 Collier Law, mt., Eng. 54 47N 1 59w
84 Collingwood, N.Z. 40 40s 172 40E
82 Collinsville, Australia 20 35s 147 50E
43 Collioure, France 42 30N 3 0E
36 Collon, Ireland 53 46N 6 29w
83 Colly Blue, Australia 31 30s 150 2E
43 Colmar, France 48 0N 6 43E
43 Colmars, France 44 10N 6 40E
26 Colne, England 53 52N 2 12w
23 Colne, R., England 51 55N 0 45E
44 Cologne (Köln), Germany 50 56N 6 58E
98 Colombia, Rep., S. Amer. 7 40N 75 0w
64 Colombo, Sri Lanka 6 56N 79 58E
95 Colon, Cuba 22 55N 80 55w
95 Colón, Panama 9 22N 80 12w
30 Colonsay I., Scotland 56 4N 6 13w
94 Colorado I., Panama Canal Zone (Inset)
99 Colorado, R., Argentina 39 30s 63 0w
90 Colorado, R., U.S.A. 38 0N 109 30w
90 Colorado, st., U.S.A. 39 15N 105 30w
90 Colorado Springs, U.S.A. 38 57N 104 59w
33 Colpy, Scotland 57 23N 2 35w
92 Columbia, Dist. of, 38 50N 77 0w
91 Columbia, S.C., U.S.A. 33 59N 81 0w
91 Columbia, Tenn., U.S.A. 35 38N 86 59w
90 Columbia Plat., U.S.A. 47 0N 118 0w
90 Columbia R., U.S.A. 46 15N 124 0w
37 Columbretes Is., Spain 39 53 0 45E
91 Columbus, Ga., U.S.A. 32 30N 84 58w
91 Columbus, Miss., U.S.A. 33 31N 88 17w
91 Columbus, Neb., U.S.A. 41 27N 97 20w
92 Columbus, Ohio, U.S.A. 39 57N 83 2w
25 Colwyn, Wales 53 17N 3 43w
25 Colwyn Bay, Wales 53 19N 3 44w
40 Comacchio, Italy 44 42N 12 17E
94 Comayagua, Honduras 14 10N 87 40w
44 Comblain, Belgium 50 27N 5 34E
35 Comeragh Mts., Ireland 52 16N 7 34w
65 Comilla, Bangladesh 23 27N 91 15E
40 Comino I., Malta 36 0N 14 21E
43 Commentry, France 46 20N 2 45E
43 Commercy, France 48 46N 5 30E
83 Commonwealth Territory, Austral. 35 10s 151 0E
45 Como, & L., Italy 45 49N 9 8E
99 Comodoro Rivadavia, Argentina 45 45s 67 30w
64 Comorin, C., India 8 5N 77 40E
71 Comoro Is., Mozam. Chan. 11 30s 43 17E
88 Comox, Canada 49 50N 125 5w
43 Compiègne, France 49 25N 2 49E
22 Compton, England 51 2N 1 19w
83 Compton Downs, Australia 30 30s 146 35E
31 Comrie, Scotland 56 22N 4 0w
83 Conara Junction, Australia 41 50s 147 20E
72 Conakry, Guinea 9 25N 13 56w
42 Concarneau, France 47 55N 3 55w
99 Concepción, Chile 36 48s 73 5w
75 Conception B., S.W. Afr. 23 55s 14 22E
90 Conceptión Pt., U.S.A. 34 21N 120 40w
99 Conception del Uruguay, Argentina 33 0s 58 40w
93 Concord, U.S.A. 43 7N 71 30w
99 Concordia, Argentina 31 0s 57 48w
83 Condamine, Australia 26 55s 150 5E
42 Condé, Calvados, Fr. 48 55N 0 35w
44 Condé, Nord, France 50 25N 3 35E
83 Condobolin, Australia 33 1s 147 13E
68 Condore Is., Vietnam 8 35N 106 30E
22 Condover, England 52 39N 2 46w
43 Conflans, France 49 10N 5 45E
43 Confolens, France 46 0N 0 45E
26 Congleton, England 53 10N 2 13w
74 Congo, Dem. Rep. of, *see* Zaïre
74 Congo, Africa 0 0 16 0E
74 Congo, R., Africa 2 0N 22 0E
70 Congo Basin, Africa 1 0s 22 0E
27 Conisbrough, England 53 29N 1 12w
26 Coniston Water, Eng. 54 20N 3 7w
82 Conjuboy, Australia 18 35s 144 45E
36 Conn, L., Ireland 54 0N 9 15w
35 Connacht, Prov., Ireland 53 42N 8 55w
25 Connah's Quay, Wales 53 13N 3 6w
92 Conneaut, U.S.A. 41 57N 80 32w
93 Connecticut, st., U.S.A. 41 35N 72 40w
92 Connelsville, U.S.A. 40 0N 79 33w
34 Connemara, Dist., Ire. 53 27N 9 48w
82 Connors Ra., Australia 21 40s 149 10E
83 Conoble, Australia 33 0s 144 45E
26 Consett, England 54 52N 1 50w
45 Constance, L., Switz.-Ger., *see* Bodensee
72 Constantine, Algeria 36 23N 6 29E
47 Constanta, Rumania 44 12N 28 39E
37 Constantina, Spain 37 55N 5 43w
99 Constitución, Chile 35 18s 72 30w
98 Contas, R., Brazil 13 40s 40 30w
36 Convoy, Ireland 54 52N 7 40w
91 Conway, U.S.A. 35 5N 92 30w
25 Conwy, & B., Wales 53 18N 3 52w
25 Conwy, R., Wales 53 0N 3 50w
65 Cooch Behar, India 26 30N 89 20E
11 Cook Is., Pacific Ocean 18 0s 164 0w
84 Cook, Mt., N.Z. 43 30s 170 12E
84 Cook Str., N.Z. 41 15s 174 30E
23 Cookham, England 51 33N 0 42w
76 Cookhouse, S. Africa 32 43s 25 45E
36 Cookstown, N. Ireland 54 39N 6 44w
82 Cooktown, Australia 15 35s 145 10E
83 Coolabah, Australia 30 52s 146 54E
83 Cooladdi, Australia 26 35s 145 28E
83 Coolah, Australia 31 36s 149 50E
83 Coolamon, Australia 34 46s 147 8E
83 Coolangatta, Australia 28 0s 153 5E
36 Coolaney, Ireland 54 11N 8 35w
80 Coolgardie, Australia 30 55s 121 7E
35 Coolgreany, Ireland 52 46N 6 14w
83 Cooma, Australia 36 13s 149 10E
83 Coonabarabran, Austral. 31 5s 149 50E
83 Coonamble, Australia 31 0s 148 21E
64 Coondapoor, India 13 30N 74 40E
83 Coongie, Australia 27 10s 140 5E
83 Coongoola, Australia 27 48s 146 0E
83 Cooper Cr., Australia 27 30s 139 17E
83 Cooroy, Australia 26 18s 152 50E
83 Cootamundra, Australia 34 40s 148 2E
36 Cootehill, Ireland 54 6N 7 3w
83 Cooyar, Australia 27 0s 151 48E
49 Copenhagen, Denmark 55 40N 12 35E
99 Copiapó, Chile 27 15s 70 20w
83 Copley, Australia 30 35s 138 20E
92 Coppercliff, Canada 46 25N 81 6w
88 Coppermine, Canada 68 0N 116 0w
27 Coquet, R. & I., England 55 18N 1 45w
74 Coquilhatville, *see* Mbandaka
99 Coquimbo, Chile 29 50s 71 27w
47 Corabia, Rumania 43 45N 24 30E
98 Coracora, Peru 15 0s 73 40w
91 Coral Gables, U.S.A. 25 46N 80 16w
82 Coral Sea, Australasia 18 0s 152 30E
40 Corato, Italy 41 10N 16 27E
43 Corbeil, France 48 38N 2 30E
26 Corbridge, England 54 58N 2 6w
23 Corby, Lincs., England 52 49N 0 31w
23 Corby, Northants., Eng. 52 30N 0 41w
37 Corcubion, Spain 42 55N 9 14w
91 Cordele, U.S.A. 31 51N 83 49w
99 Cordoba, Argentina 31 22s 64 12w
37 Cordoba, Spain 37 54N 4 48w
99 Cordoba, Sierra de, Arg. 31 30s 65 0w
88 Cordova, Alaska 60 36N 145 45w
22 Corfe Castle, England 50 38N 2 3w
22 Corfe Mullen, England 50 45N 2 0w
82 Corfield, Australia 21 40s 143 21E
41 Corfu, *see* Kérkira
40 Corigliano, Italy 39 37N 16 32E
41 Corinth, Greece 37 40N 22 58E
91 Corinth, U.S.A. 34 54N 88 30w
34 Cork, & Co., Ireland 51 54N 8 28w

34 Cork Harbour, Ireland 51 48N 8 16W
89 Corner Brook, Canada 49 0N 58 0W
83 Cornwall, Australia 41 35S 148 0E
93 Cornwall, Canada 45 2N 75 10W
24 Cornwall Co., England 50 20N 4 50W
95 Coro, Venezuela 11 23N 69 45W
98 Corocoro, Bolivia 17 25S 68 25W
34 Corofin, Ireland 52 52N 9 11W
84 Coromandel, N.Z. 36 33S 175 28E
64 Coromandel Coast, India 13 0N 80 20E
88 Coronation G., Canada 68 0N 110 0W
99 Coronel Pringles, Arg. 38 0S 61 30W
83 Corowa, Australia 36 7S 146 30E
94 Corozal, Br. Honduras 17 20N 88 30W
91 Corpus Christi, U.S.A. 27 50N 97 28W
99 Corral, Chile 40 0S 73 40W
42 Corrèze Dépt., France 45 28N 2 5E
35 Corrib, Lough, Ireland 53 30N 9 20W
99 Corrientes, Argentina 27 15S 58 45W
98 Corrientes, C., Columbia 5 30N 77 30W
94 Corrientes, C., Mexico 20 20N 105 40W
27 Corringham, England 53 25N 0 41W
30 Corryvreckan, G. of, Scot. 56 10N 5 44W
43 Corse, C., Corsica 43 0N 9 20E
†42 Corse, Dépt., France 42 0N 9 0E
22 Corsham, England 51 25N 2 11W
43 Corsica I., Mediterranean 42 0N 9 0E
91 Corsicana, U.S.A. 32 5N 96 31W
31 Corsock, Scotland 55 4N 3 56W
43 Corte, France 42 17N 9 8E
90 Cortez, U.S.A. 37 25N 108 45W
93 Cortland, U.S.A. 42 31N 76 12W
40 Cortona, Italy 43 19N 12 1E
51 Corum, Turkey 40 35N 35 5E
98 Corumba, Brazil 19 0S 57 20W
37 Corunna, see La Coruña, Spain
22 Corve, R., Eng. 52 27N 2 43W
25 Corwen, Wales 52 58N 3 22W
22 Coseley, England 52 33N 2 6W
40 Cosenza, Italy 39 20N 16 13E
22 Cosham, England 50 51N 1 3W
43 Cosne, France 47 22N 3 0E
95 Costa Rica, Cen. Amer. 10 0N 84 0W
34 Costelloe, Ireland 53 17N 9 33W
23 Costessey, England 52 40N 1 11E
68 Cotabato, Philippines 7 0N 124 10E
43 Côte d'Or, Dépt. & Dist., France 47 40N 4 45E
91 Coteau des Prairies, U.S.A. 45 0N 95 30W
43 Cotentin, Dist., France 49 20N 1 30W
42 Côtes du Nord, Dépt., Fr. 48 25N 2 45W
72 Cotonou, Dahomey 6 25N 2 20E
98 Cotopaxi Vol., Ecuador 0 40S 78 30W
22 Cotswold Hills, England 51 45N 2 10W
46 Cottbus, Germany 51 45N 14 24E
23 Cottenham, England 52 18N 0 8E
42 Cottian Alps, France 44 40N 6 50E
27 Cottingham, England 53 47N 0 25W
43 Coulommiers, France 48 46N 3 5E
91 Council Bluffs, U.S.A. 41 22N 95 50W
31 Coupar Angus, Scotland 56 33N 3 15W
95 Courentyne, R., S. Amer. 6 0N 57 3W
45 Courmayeur, Italy 45 47N 7 0E
45 Courtelary, Switzerland 47 10N 7 5E
34 Courtmacsherry, & B., Ire. 51 38N 8 41W
35 Courtown, Ire. 52 37N 6 14W
42 Coutainville, France 49 2N 1 32W
33 Cove Bay, Scotland 57 5N 2 5W
22 Coventry, England 52 25N 1 31W
37 Covilha, Portugal 40 20N 7 27W
92 Covington, U.S.A. 39 0N 84 38W
31 Cowal, Dist., Scotland 56 5N 5 8W
80 Cowan, L., Australia 31 50S 121 50E
83 Cowangie, Australia 35 20S 141 25E
25 Cowbridge, Wales 51 27N 3 28W
31 Cowdenbeath, Scotland 56 7N 3 20W
83 Cowell, Australia 33 35S 136 50E
22 Cowes, England 50 46N 1 18W
22 Cowley, England 51 43N 1 12W
83 Cowra, Australia 33 50S 148 42E
65 Cox's Bazaar, Bangladesh 21 30N 92 5E
94 Cozumel I. de, Mexico 20 30N 87 0W
83 Craboon, Australia 32 2S 149 30E
76 Cradock, S. Africa 32 5S 25 38E
36 Craigavon, N. Ireland 54 28N 6 20W
31 Crail, Scotland 56 16N 2 38W
47 Craiova, Rumania 44 20N 23 49E
27 Cramlington, England 55 5N 1 37W
83 Cranbrook, Australia 42 0S 147 10E
88 Cranbrook, Canada 49 28N 115 58W
23 Cranbrook, England 51 6N 0 33E
22 Cranleigh, England 51 8N 0 29W
31 Cranshaws, Scotland 55 51N 2 30W
27 Cranwell, England 53 2N 0 28W
44 Craonne, France 49 27N 3 42E
98 Crateus, Brazil 5 5S 40 43W
33 Crathie, Scotland 57 2N 3 13W
98 Crato, Brazil 7 0S 39 12W
34 Craughwell, Ireland 53 14N 8 44W
22 Craven Arms, England 52 26N 2 45W
31 Crawford, Scotland 55 28N 3 39W
23 Crawley, England 51 7N 0 12W
33 Creag Meagaidh, Scot. 56 57N 4 37W
43 Crécy, France 50 17N 1 53E
44 Crécy s. Serre, France 49 45N 3 35E
22 Credenhill, England 52 6N 2 48W
24 Crediton, England 50 48N 3 39W
43 Creil, France 49 18N 2 30E
43 Crema, Italy 45 22N 9 40E
43 Cremona, Italy 45 10N 10 1E
43 Crépy, France 49 37N 3 32E
40 Cres, I., Yugoslavia 44 50N 14 25E
83 Cressy, Australia 38 10S 143 48E
43 Crest, France 44 40N 5 0E

† *Divided into 2 new départements, Haute-Corse and Corse-du-Sud.*

91 Creston, U.S.A. 41 2N 94 21W
41 Crete, I., Greece 35 15N 25 0E
37 Creus, C., Spain 42 18N 3 21E
42 Creuse, Dépt., France 45 57N 1 53E
43 Creuse, France 46 40N 1 20E
26 Crewe, England 53 8N 2 23W
24 Crewkerne, England 50 54N 2 48W
30 Crianlarich, Scotland 56 23N 4 36W
25 Crickhowell, Wales 51 52N 3 8W
22 Cricklade, England 51 39N 1 51W
31 Crieff, Scotland 56 23N 3 51W
31 Criffel, Mt., Scotland 54 57N 3 45W
51 Crimea, Pen., U.S.S.R. 45 30N 34 0E
33 Crimond, Scotland 57 35N 1 53W
30 Crinan Canal, Scotland 56 4N 5 30W
94 Cristobal, Panama Canal Zone (Inset)
47 Crisul, Black, R., Rum. 46 40N 22 0E
47 Crisul, White, R., Rum. 46 20N 22 0E
41 Crna, R., Yugoslavia 41 20N 21 59E
41 Crna Gora Mts., Y.-Slav. 42 20N 21 30E
35 Croaghpatrick, Mt., Ire. 53 45N 9 42W
40 Croatia, Fed. unit, Y.-slav. 45 30N 16 0E
32 Comalt Hill, Scotland 58 0N 5 0W
33 Cromarty, Scotland 57 41N 4 2W
33 Cromarty Firth, Scot. 57 40N 4 10W
23 Cromer, England 52 57N 1 19E
84 Cromwell, New Zealand 45 0S 169 12E
23 Crondall, England 51 14N 0 52W
83 Cronulla, Australia 33 58S 151 4E
27 Crook, England 54 44N 1 45W
83 Crookwell, Australia 34 30S 149 28E
34 Croom, Ireland 52 31N 8 44W
31 Crosby, Cumb., Eng. 54 45N 3 25W
26 Crosby, Lancs., Eng. 53 28N 3 2W
26 Cross Fell, mt., England 54 44N 2 32W
88 Cross Sd., Alaska 58 20N 136 30W
36 Crossakiel, Ireland 53 43N 7 1W
36 Crossgar, N. Ireland 54 24N 5 46W
34 Crosshaven, Ireland 51 48N 8 17W
35 Crossmolina, Ireland 54 6N 9 19W
40 Crotone, Italy 39 5N 17 6E
23 Crouch, R., England 51 39N 0 40E
23 Crowborough, England 51 4N 0 9W
83 Crowes, Australia 38 55S 143 22E
27 Crowle, England 53 36N 0 50W
88 Crows Nest P., Canada 49 35N 115 0W
82 Croydon, Australia 18 30S 142 15E
23 Croydon, England 51 21N 0 6W
5 Crozet Is., Indian Ocean 46 0S 51 0E
42 Crozon, France 48 18N 4 30W
26 Crummock Water L. Eng. 54 34N 3 19W
34 Crusheen, Ireland 52 57N 8 54W
98 Cruzeiro do Sul, Brazil 7 30S 72 30W
83 Crystal Brook, Australia 33 20S 138 7E
47 Csongrad, Hungary 46 43N 20 12E
75 Cuangar, Angola 17 28S 18 30E
74 Cuango, Congo 6 20S 16 50E
95 Cuba, West Indies 21 30N 79 30W
75 Cubango, R., Angola 17 30S 18 0E
75 Cuchi, Angola 14 40S 17 5E
23 Cuckfield, England 51 1N 0 9W
27 Cudworth, England 53 34N 1 26W
95 Cúcuta, Colombia 7 40N 72 40W
64 Cuddalore, India 11 42N 79 50E
64 Cuddapah, India 14 30N 78 50E
83 Cudgewa, Australia 36 10S 147 48E
80 Cue, Australia 27 25S 118 0E
98 Cuenca, Ecuador 2 46S 79 10W
37 Cuenca, Spain 40 8N 2 5W
37 Cuenca, Sa. de, mts., Spain 40 20N 1 50W
91 Cuero, U.S.A. 29 20N 97 30W
98 Cuiaba, Brazil 15 30S 56 6W
36 Cuilcagh, Mt., Ireland 54 16N 8 0W
32 Cuillin Hills & Sd., Scot. 57 13N 6 6W
75 Cuima, Angola 13 0S 15 50E
83 Culcairn, Australia 35 40S 147 0E
36 Culdaff, Ireland 55 16N 7 8W
37 Culebra, Sa. de la, mts., Spain 42 0N 6 30W
94 Culiacan, Mexico 24 49N 107 20W
33 Cullen, Scotland 57 42N 2 48W
37 Cullera, Spain 39 10N 0 15W
35 Cullin, L., Ireland 53 57N 9 11W
32 Cullivoe, Scotland 60 42N 1 1W
33 Culloden Moor, Scotland 57 29N 4 8W
24 Cullompton, England 50 52N 3 23W
45 Cully, Switzerland 46 30N 6 44E
43 Culoz, France 45 50N 5 50E
31 Culross, Scotland 56 3N 3 38W
33 Cults, Scotland 57 7N 2 10W
32 Culvain Mt., Scotland 56 55N 5 19W
95 Cumanà, Venezuela 10 30N 64 10W
88 Cumberland, Canada 49 34N 125 0W
*26 Cumberland, Co., Eng. 54 47N 3 0W
92 Cumberland, U.S.A. 39 45N 78 57W
82 Cumberland Is., Austral. 20 25S 149 0E
89 Cumberland Pen., Can. 67 0N 65 0W
91 Cumberland Plat., U.S.A. 36 0N 84 40W
91 Cumberland, R., U.S.A. 36 15N 85 0W
89 Cumberland Sd., Canada 65 0N 65 0W
31 Cumbernauld, Scotland 55 57N 3 59W
30 Cumbrae, Is., Scot. 55 46N 4 55W
83 Cumnock, Australia 32 55S 148 40E
30 Cumnock, Scotland 55 27N 4 16W
22 Cumnor, England 51 44N 1 21W
31 Cumwhinton, England 54 51N 2 49W
75 Cunene, R., Angola 17 0S 15 0E
43 Cuneo, Italy 44 23N 7 32E
83 Cunnamulla, Australia 28 0S 145 42E
30 Cunninghame, Dist., Scot. 55 40N 4 25W
31 Cupar, Scotland 56 19N 3 2W
95 Curaçao, I., Neth. W. I. 12 12N 69 0W
99 Curicó, Chile 35 0S 71 15W
99 Curitiba, Brazil 25 25S 49 45W
34 Currane, L., Ireland 51 50N 10 8W

* *Incorporated within the county of Cumbria*

83 Curraweena, Australia 30 45S 145 55E
31 Currie, Scotland 55 53N 3 17W
82 Curtis I., Australia 23 45S 151 17E
94 Curundu, Panama Can. Zone (Inset)
36 Cushendall, N. Ireland 55 5N 6 4W
91 Cushing, U.S.A. 35 56N 96 50W
43 Cusset, France 46 10N 3 30E
65 Cuttack, India 20 30N 85 57E
49 Cuxhaven, Germany 53 54N 8 42E
98 Cuzco, Peru 13 30S 72 8W
22 Cwmbran, England 51 39N 3 0W
25 Cwrt, Wales 52 35N 3 55W
41 Cyclades, Is., see Kikladhes
83 Cygnet, Tasmania 43 5S 147 3E
62 Cyprus I., Medit. Sea 35 0N 33 0E
73 Cyrenaica, Prov., Libya 28 0N 22 0E
73 Cyrene (Shahhat), Libya 32 39N 21 18E
46-47 Czechoslovakia, Eur. 49 0N 17 0E
47 Czegléd, Hungary 47 15N 19 45E
47 Czeremcha, Poland 52 32N 23 20E
47 Czestochowa, Poland 50 49N 19 4E

D

68 Da Lat, Vietnam 12 0N 108 30E
68 Da-Nang (Tourane), Vietnam 16 20N 108 0E
63 Daal, Syria 32 45N 36 8E
62 Dabat, Ethiopia 13 0N 37 50E
46 Dabie, Poland 53 27N 14 45E
72 Dabola, Guinea 10 50N 11 5W
74 Dabra Tabor, Ethiopia 11 50N 38 0E
47 Dabrowa, Poland 50 10N 21 0E
65 Dacca, Bangladesh 23 49N 90 25E
64 Dadu, Pakistan 26 45N 67 35E
68 Daet, Philippines 14 3N 122 59E
62 Dafina, Saudi Arabia 23 11N 42 0E
72 Dagana, Sénégal 16 30N 15 20W
51 Dagestan, A.S.S.R., U.S.S.R. 43 0N 47 0E
68 Dagupan, Philippines 16 0N 120 20E
62 Dahlak Arch., Red Sea 16 0N 40 10E
††72 Dahomey, Africa 9 0N 2 0E
35 Daingean (Philipstown), Ireland 53 19N 7 18W
67 Dairen-Port Arthur, China, see Lü-ta
73 Dairut, Egypt 27 34N 30 43E
67 Daishoji, Japan 36 15N 136 16E
82 Dajarra, Australia 21 47S 139 20E
72 Dakar, Sénégal 14 45N 17 8W
73 Dakhla Oasis, Egypt 25 55N 27 30E
51 Dakhovskaya, U.S.S.R. 44 15N 40 15E
90 Dakota N. & S., see N. & S. Dakota
41 Dakovica, Yugoslavia 42 25N 20 26E
72 Dakra, Sénégal 15 30N 15 20W
49 Dal, R., Sweden 60 12N 16 40E
66 Dalai Nor, L., China 48 0N 116 30E
66 Dalandzadagad, Mong. 43 55N 104 10E
49 Dalarö, Sweden 59 10N 18 23E
64 Dalbandin, Pakistan 29 0N 64 23E
31 Dalbeattie, Scotland 54 56N 3 50W
83 Dalby, Australia 27 6S 151 18E
33 Dalhalvaig, Scotland 58 27N 3 52W
93 Dalhousie, Canada 48 0N 66 21W
31 Dalkeith, Scotland 55 53N 3 4W
83 Dallarnil, Australia 25 25S 152 0E
90 Dallas, Oregon, U.S.A. 44 50N 123 20W
91 Dallas, Texas, U.S.A. 32 46N 96 55W
30 Dalmally, Scotland 56 24N 4 58W
40 Dalmatia, Prov., Y.-slav. 43 10N 17 10E
30 Dalmellington, Scotland 55 19N 4 24W
30 Dalry, Scotland 55 43N 4 43W
26 Dalton, Lancs., England 54 12N 3 12W
27 Dalton, Yorks., England 54 28N 1 32W
48 Dalvik, Iceland 66 2N 18 20W
80 Daly, R., Australia 14 0S 130 50E
80 Daly Waters, Australia 16 5S 133 30E
64 Daman, India 20 20N 72 59E
75 Damara Ld., S.W. Africa 22 25S 17 0E
63 Damascus (Esh Sham), Syria 33 30N 36 18E
74 Damba, Angola 6 44S 15 29E
73 Dambacha, Ethiopia 10 40N 37 10E
62 Damghan, Persia 36 5N 54 20E
73 Damietta, Egypt 31 30N 31 32E
62 Damman, Saudi Arabia 26 27N 50 3E
64 Damoh, India 23 58N 79 30E
80 Dampier Arch., Austral. 20 30S 116 40E
80 Dampier Downs, Austral. 18 5S 124 10E
82 Dampier Str., Indonesia 0 30S 131 15E
72 Dan Gora, Nigeria 11 30N 8 7E
64 Dandeli, India 15 5N 74 30E
5 Dandeldhura, Nepal 29 25N 80 30E
83 Dandenong, Australia 38 10S 145 14E
64 Dankhar Gompa, India 32 10N 78 10E
49 Dannemora, Sweden 60 13N 17 50E
84 Dannevirke, N.Z. 40 12S 176 8E
92 Dansville, U.S.A. 42 35N 77 40W
47 Danube, R., Europe 45 0N 28 0E
92 Danville, Ill., U.S.A. 40 10N 87 35W
92 Danville, Ken., U.S.A. 37 40N 84 50W
74 Dar es Salaam, Tanzania 6 48S 39 12E
72 Daraj, Libya 30 5N 10 30E
65 Darbhanga, India 26 15N 85 55E
41 Dardanelles (Hellespont), Str., Turkey 40 10N 26 0E
63 Dareiya, Syria 33 28N 36 14E
73 Darfur, Prov., Sudan 15 0N 25 0E
64 Dargai, India 34 20N 71 50E
60 Dargan Ata, U.S.S.R. 40 40N 62 20E
84 Dargaville, N.Z. 36 0S 173 59E
94 Darien, Panama Canal Zone (Inset)
95 Darien, G. of, Colombia 9 0N 77 0W
65 Darjeeling, India 27N 88 18E
22 Darlaston, England 52 35N 2 1W
83 Darling Downs, Australia 27 45S 150 0E

†† *Renamed Benin*

83 Darling, R., Australia 32 0S 143 0E
80 Darling Ra., Australia 32 0S 116 0E
27 Darlington, England 54 33N 1 34W
46 Darlowo, Poland 54 13N 16 19E
45 Darmstadt, Germany 49 52N 8 40E
73 Darnah, Libya 32 40N 22 25E
100 Darnley, C., Antarctica 68 0S 70 0E
82 Darr, Australia 24 34S 144 52E
24 Dart, R., England 50 28N 3 45W
23 Dartford, England 51 26N 0 15E
24 Dartmoor, England 50 39N 3 55W
93 Dartmouth, Canada 44 50N 63 30W
24 Dartmouth, England 50 21N 3 37W
27 Darton, England 53 36N 1 32W
30 Darvel, Scotland 55 37N 4 20W
26 Darwen, England 53 42N 2 28W
80 Darwin, Australia 12 28S 131 0E
62 Darya yi Namak, L., Iran 34 40N 51 30E
63 Dasht-i-Kavir, Des., Iran 35 0N 55 0E
63 Dasht-i-Lut, Des., Iran 31 0N 58 30E
64 Dasht-i-Margo, Des., Afghan. 30 40N 62 30E
50 Daugavpils, U.S.S.R. 56 0N 26 30E
60 Daukara, U.S.S.R. 45 55N 59 30E
64 Daulat Yar, Afghan. 34 35N 65 40E
63 Daulatabad, Afghanistan 32 46N 62 34E
63 Daulatabad, Iran 28 22N 56 38E
88 Dauphin, Canada 51 13N 100 3W
43 Dauphiné, Prov., France 45 5N 5 30E
64 Davangere, India 14 30N 75 50E
68 Davao, & G., Philippines 7 15N 125 35E
92 Davenport, U.S.A. 41 33N 90 34W
22 Daventry, England 52 15N 1 10W
100 Davis, Antarctica 69 10S 79 0E
89 Davis Str., N. America 67 0N 58 0W
45 Davos-Platz, Switzerland 46 50N 9 50E
62 Dawasir, Wadi, Si. Arabia 20 25N 45 30E
24 Dawlish, England 50 35N 3 29W
65 Dawna Ra., Burma 16 30N 98 30E
88 Dawson, Canada 64 10N 139 30W
88 Dawson Cr., Canada 55 45N 120 15W
82 Dawson Ra., Australia 24 45S 149 55E
42 Dax, France 43 41N 1 0W
92 Dayton, Ohio, U.S.A. 39 47N 84 12W
91 Daytona Beach, U.S.A. 29 7N 81 2W
76 De Aar, S. Africa 30 46S 23 54E
80 De Grey R., Australia 20 32S 120 0E
61 De Long Is., U.S.S.R. 77 0N 155 0E
63 Dead Sea, Jordan-Israel 31 30N 35 25E
80 Deakin, Australia 30 34S 129 0E
23 Deal, England 51 13N 1 24E
22 Dean, Forest of, England 51 47N 2 35W
88 Dease Arm, Canada 66 45N 120 6W
88 Dease, R. & L., Canada 59 10N 129 50W
90 Death Valley, U.S.A. 36 0N 117 0W
43 Deauville, France 49 20N 0 0
72 Deba Habe, Nigeria 10 14N 11 20E
41 Debar, Yugoslavia 41 30N 20 30E
23 Deben, R., England 52 12N 1 13E
74 Debre Markos, Ethiopia 10 20N 37 45E
47 Debrecen, Hungary 47 37N 21 54E
91 Decatur, Alabama, U.S.A. 34 29N 86 43W
91 Decatur, Georgia, U.S.A. 33 42N 84 21W
92 Decatur, Ill., U.S.A. 39 53N 88 56W
43 Decazeville, France 44 37N 2 15E
65 Deccan, Reg., India 17 0N 78 30E
72 Dedougou, Volta 12 35N 3 40W
33 Dee, R., Scotland 57 7N 2 10W
25 Dee, R., Wales 52 50N 3 30W
83 Deepwater, Australia 29 25S 151 50E
64 Deesa, India 24 25N 72 20E
25 Deganwy, Wales 53 18N 3 49W
48 Degerfors, Sweden 64 10N 19 48E
46 Deggendorf, Germany 48 49N 12 59E
64 Deh Titan, Afghan. 33 45N 63 50E
72 Dehibat, Tunisia 32 0N 10 10E
64 Dehra Dun, India 30 24N 78 5E
73 Deim Zubeir, Sudan 7 47N 26 20E
44 Deinze, Belgium 50 59N 3 30E
63 Deir Abu Sa'id, Jordan 32 30N 35 42E
62 Deir ez Zor, Syria 35 19N 40 15E
74 Dekese, Zaïre 3 20S 21 21E
90 Del Rió, U.S.A. 29 22N 100 55W
62 Delami, Sudan 11 50N 30 25E
93 Delaware, R., U.S.A. 42 0N 75 15W
91 Delaware, st. & B., U.S.A. 38 45N 75 20W
83 Delegate, Australia 37 14N 148 58E
45 Delemont, Switzerland 47 20N 7 20E
44 Delft, Netherlands 52 1N 4 21E
44 Delfzijl, Netherlands 53 20N 6 55E
74 Delgado, C., Mozambique 10 40S 40 43E
62 Delgo, Sudan 20 1N 30 20E
64 Delhi, India 28 42N 77 20E
51 Delice, R., Turkey 39 45N 34 15E
94 Delicias, Mexico 27 25N 105 0W
83 Deloraine, Australia 41 30S 146 45E
76 Delportshoop, S. Africa 28 25S 24 20E
35 Delvin, Ireland 53 37N 7 4W
37 Demanda, Sa. de la, mts., Spain 42 8N 3 0W
51 Demavend, Mt., Iran 35 50N 52 12E
74 Dembra, Zaïre 5 25S 22 20E
74 Dembidolo, Ethiopia 8 34N 34 50E
44 Demer, R., Belgium 51 0N 5 10E
90 Deming, U.S.A. 32 17N 107 48W
44 Den Burg, Netherlands 53 5N 4 47E
44 Den Helder, Netherlands 52 58N 4 46E
44 Denain, France 50 20N 3 22E
**25 Denbigh & Co., Wales 53 11N 3 26W
65 Denchin, China 31 35N 95 10E
37 Denia, Spain 38 50N 0 5E
83 Deniliquin, Australia 35 31S 144 59E
51 Denizli, Turkey 37 57N 28 41E

** *County incorporated within Clwyd*

48 Denmark, Europe 55 45N 10 20E
100 Denmark Str., N. Atlantic Ocean 66 0N 30 0W
31 Denny, Scotland 56 1N 3 55W
26 Denton, Lancs., England 53 26N 2 10W
23 Denton, Leics., England 52 55N 0 42W
23 Denton, Sussex, England 50 48N 0 5E
91 Denton, U.S.A. 33 10N 97 10W
82 D'Entrecasteaux Is., Papua 9 30S 151 0E
90 Denver, U.S.A. 39 50N 104 57W
65 Deoghar, India 24 40N 86 40E
64 Deolali, India 19 55N 73 45E
65 Deoria, India 26 35N 83 50E
64 Dera Ghazi Khan, Pak. 30 5N 70 53E
64 Dera Ismail Khan, Pak. 31 46N 70 54E
62 Deraheib, Sudan 21 58N 35 7E
51 Derbent, U.S.S.R. 42 0N 48 23E
80 Derby, Australia 17 18S 123 40E
27 Derby, & Co., England 52 56N 1 28W
35 Derg, L., Ireland 53 0N 8 18W
36 Derg, L. & R., Ireland 54 40N 7 40W
65 Dergaon, India 26 40N 94 0E
36 Derry, N. Ireland, see Londonderry
36 Derrygonnelly, N. Ire. 54 25N 7 50W
34 Derryrush, Ireland 53 23N 9 40W
36 Derryveagh Mts., Ireland 55 0N 8 3W
73 Derudub, Sudan 17 30N 36 30E
27 Derwent, R., Derby, Eng. 53 15N 1 38W
27 Derwent, R., Yorks., Eng. 53 50N 1 0W
26 Derwent Water, L., Eng. 54 35N 3 9W
91 Des Moines, & R., U.S.A. 41 42N 93 34W
74 Dese, Ethiopia 10 58N 39 45E
99 Deseado, & R., Argentina 47 0S 68 0W
94 Désirade, I., Leeward Is. 16 15N 61 0W
50 Desna, R., U.S.S.R. 51 30N 32 30E
99 Desolación I., Chile 53 0S 74 30W
98 Desordem, Sa. da, hs., Brazil 4 0S 46 30W
72 Dessa, Niger 14 44N 1 6E
46 Dessau, Germany 51 41N 12 14E
46 Detmold, Germany 51 55N 8 50E
92 Detroit, U.S.A. 42 22N 83 7W
48 Dettifoss, Iceland 65 50N 16 0W
44 Deurne, Belgium 51 13N 4 27E
44 Deurne, Netherlands 51 27N 5 47E
42 Deux Sèvres, Dépt., Fr. 46 30N 0 30W
47 Deva, Rumania 45 55N 22 50E
64 Devakottai, India 9 55N 78 40E
44 Deventer, Netherlands 52 16N 6 10E
33 Deveron, R., Scotland 57 22N 3 0W
22 Devizes, England 51 21N 1 59W
24 Devon, Co., England 50 47N 3 40W
89 Devon Island, Canada 4 30N 85 0W
83 Devonport, Australia 41 8S 146 30E
24 Devonport, England 50 22N 4 10W
84 Devonport, N.Z. 36 49S 174 49E
64 Dewas, India 23 0N 76 0E
27 Dewsbury, England 53 42N 1 38W
61 Dezhneva, C., U.S.S.R. 66 0N 170 0W
62 Dhaba, Saudi Arabia 27 25N 35 50E
62 Dhahran, Saudi Arabia 26 20N 50 10E
65 Dhamtari, India 20 45N 81 30E
65 Dhanbad, India 23 50N 86 25E
65 Dhangarhi, Nepal 28 55N 80 40E
63 Dhank, Oman 23 30N 56 5E
65 Dhankuta, Nepal 27 0N 87 10E
64 Dhar, India 22 40N 75 5E
64 Dharmapuri, India 12 10N 78 5E
64 Dharwar, India 15 39N 75 59E
65 Dhaulagiri, Mt., Nepal 28 45N 83 25E
65 Dhenkanal, India 20 35N 85 30E
41 Dhidhimotikhon, Greece 41 18N 26 33E
41 Dhikti, Mt., Crete 35 10N 25 34E
63 Dhilban, Jordan 31 30N 35 47E
63 Dhofar, Prov., Oman 17 0N 54 10E
64 Dholpur, India 26 45N 77 58E
63 Dhour Chouer, Lebanon 33 53N 35 42E
64 Dhrol, India 22 40N 70 25E
65 Dhubri, India 26 3N 89 58E
62 Dhula, South Yemen 15 10N 48 0E
64 Dhulia, India 21 0N 74 56E
98 Diable, I. du, Fr. Guiana 5 25N 52 35W
94 Diablo Heights, Panama Canal Zone (Inset)
72 Diafarabe, Mali 14 17N 4 57W
99 Diamante, Argentina 32 0S 60 40W
98 Diamantina, Brazil 18 11S 43 45W
82 Diamantina, R., Australia 24 48S 140 0E
98 Diamantino, Brazil 14 25S 56 40W
74 Dibaya, Zaïre 6 30S 23 0E
74 Dibaya-Lubue, Zaïre 4 12S 19 54E
22 Dibden, England 50 53N 1 24W
65 Dibrugarh, India 27 38N 94 55E
90 Dickinson, U.S.A. 46 55N 102 53W
72 Diebougou, Volta 11 0N 3 15W
75 Diego Suarez, Madagascar 12 25S 49 20E
44 Diekirch, Luxembourg 49 52N 6 10E
42 Dielette, France 49 33N 1 54W
44 Diepenbeek, Belgium 50 55N 5 22E
43 Dieppe, France 49 58N 1 13E
44 Dieren, Netherlands 52 3N 6 6E
44 Diest, Belgium 50 59N 5 2E
44 Differdange, Luxembourg 49 32N 5 53E
89 Digby, Canada 44 42N 65 50W
43 Digne, France 44 6N 6 12E
48 Digranes, C., Iceland 66 5N 14 37W
65 Dihang, R., India 28 30N 95 0E
43 Dijon, France 47 20N 5 1E
61 Dikemda, U.S.S.R. 59 0N 121 35E
44 Diksmuide, Belgium 51 3N 2 52E
72 Dikwa, Nigeria 12 6N 14 0E
62 Dilam, Saudi Arabia 23 55N 47 10E
68 Dili, Portuguese Timor 8 45S 125 30E
74 Dimbelenge, Zaïre 5 28S 23 5E

Dimbokro, Ivory Coast 6 45N 4 30W
Dimboola, Australia 36 29S 142 2E
Dimitri Laptev Str., U.S.S.R. 73 0N 140 0E
Dimitovgrad, Bulgaria 42 5N 25 35E
Dinagat I., Philippines 10 10N 125 35E
Dinajpur, Bangladesh 25 40N 88 32E
Dinant, Belgium 50 17N 4 56E
Dinaric Alps, Y-slav. 44 0N 16 0E
Dinas Powis, Wales 51 25N 3 14W
Dincha, Ethiopia 6 15N 37 32E
Dindigul, India 10 22N 78 0E
Dingle, & B., Ireland 52 9N 10 16W
Dingo, Australia 23 40S 149 27E
Dinguiraye, Guinea 11 30N 10 35W
Dingwall, Scotland 57 36N 4 26W
Diourbel, Sénégal 14 40N 15 30W
Dipolog, Philippines 8 35N 123 25E
Dir, Pakistan 35 25N 71 45E
Dirico, Angola 17 52S 20 40E
Dirk Hartog I., Austral. 25 50S 113 0E
Dirranbandi, Australia 28 29S 148 18E
Disappointment, L., Australia 23 20S 123 10E
Discovery B., Australia 38 10S 140 40E
Disko B., & I., Greenland 69 0N 53 0W
Diss, England 52 22N 1 7E
Ditchling, Village & Beacon, England 50 55N 0 7W
Ditton Priors, England 52 29N 2 35W
Diu, India 20 48N 71 0E
Dixon, U.S.A. 41 51N 89 18W
Diyala, R., Iraq 34 0N 45 0E
Diyarbakir, Turkey 37 58N 40 25E
Dizak, Iran 27 20N 62 3E
Dizful, Iran 32 30N 48 33E
Djado, Niger 21 10N 12 5E
Djailolo Passage, Indon. 0 30N 129 20E
Djajapura (Hollandia), Indon. 2 28S 140 38E
Djakarta, Indonesia 6 9S 106 49E
Djambala, Congo (Fr.) 2 25S 14 45E
Djambi, Indonesia, *see* Telanaipura
Djanet, *see* Fort Charlet
Djang, Cameroon 5 30N 10 5E
Djelfa, Algeria 34 39N 3 14E
Djema, Central Africa 6 3N 25 0E
Djenne, Mali 14 0N 4 30W
Djerada, Morocco 34 16N 2 4W
Djerba I., Tunisia 33 50N 10 50E
Djibo, Volta 14 15N 1 35W
Djibouti, Fr. T.A. & I. 11 30N 43 5E
Djidjelli, Algeria 36 45N 5 50E
Djolu, Zaïre 0 45N 22 5E
Djougou, Dahomey 9 40N 1 45E
Djoum, Cameroon 2 46N 12 33E
Djounie (Juniyah), Leb. 33 58N 35 39E
Djugu, Zaïre 1 50N 30 40E
Djupivogur, Iceland 64 38N 14 14W
Dneprodzerzhinsk, U.S.S.R. 48 32N 34 30E
Dnepropetrovsk, U.S.S.R. 48 25N 34 55E
Dnepr, R., U.S.S.R. 47 0N 33 35E
Dnestr, R., U.S.S.R. 48 30N 25 0E
Doba, Chad 8 40N 16 50E
Dobbyn, Australia 19 40S 139 58E
Dobrógea, Reg., Rum. 44 30N 28 20E
Docking, England 52 55N 0 39E
Dodge City, U.S.A. 37 50N 100 4W
Dodecanese Is., Greece 36 40N 27 0E
Dodoma, Tanzania 6 0S 35 50E
Doetinchem, Neth. 51 58N 6 18E
Dogger Bank, North Sea 54 45N 2 0E
Dogi, Afghanistan 32 20N 62 50E
Dogo I., Japan 36 15N 133 20E
Doha, Qatar 25 15N 51 32E
Dohad, India 22 57N 74 20E
Dohazari, Bangladesh 22 10N 92 7E
Dojran, Yugoslavia 41 10N 22 45E
Dokkum, Netherlands 53 20N 6 1E
Dolbeau, Canada 48 25N 72 18W
Dôle, France 47 6N 5 30E
Dolgellau, Wales 52 44N 3 54W
Dolinsk, U.S.S.R. 47 25N 142 48E
Dolisie, Congo (Fr.) 4 0S 13 10E
Dollar, Scotland 56 9N 3 40W
Dolomites, Italy 46 30N 11 40E
Dolores, Argentina 36 15S 57 50W
Dolphin & Union Str., Can. 70 0N 120 0W
Dolphinton, Scotland 55 42N 3 28W
Dolya, U.S.S.R. 69 45N 132 0E
Dombe Grande, Angola 13 0S 13 0E
Domfront, France 48 35N 0 40W
Dominica, I., W. Indies 15 25N 61 20W
Dominican Rep., W.I. 19 0N 70 30W
Domodossola, Italy 46 6N 8 19E
Domrémy, France 48 40N 5 40E
Don, R., England 53 30N 1 15W
Don, R., Scotland 57 15N 2 15W
Don, R., U.S.S.R. 50 0N 42 0E
Don Benito, Spain 38 55N 5 50W
36 Donaghadee, N. Ireland 54 38N 5 32W
33 Donald, Australia 36 25S 142 57E
45 Donaueschingen, Ger. 47 58N 8 31E
45 Donauworth, Germany 48 42N 10 47E
27 Doncaster, England 53 31N 1 8W
74 Dondo, Angola 9 45S 14 32E
75 Dondo, Mozambique 19 32S 34 45E
54 Dondra Hd., Sri Lanka 6 0N 80 40E
36 Donegal, & B., Ireland 54 39N 8 6W
36 Donegal, Co., Ireland 54 52N 8 0W
34 Doneraile, Ireland 52 13N 8 37W
51 Donets, R., U.S.S.R. 48 48N 39 0E
52 Donetsk, U.S.S.R. 48 0N 37 30E
80 Dongara, Australia 29 15S 114 59E
73 Dongola, Sudan 19 8N 20 23E
74 Dongou, Congo 2 4N 17 57E
48 Donna I., Norway 66 5N 12 40E
84 Donnelly's Crossing, N.Z. 35 38S 173 33E
34 Donoughmore, Ireland 52 0N 8 50W
30 Doon, L. & R., Scotland 55 15N 4 22W
34 Doonbeg, R., Ireland 52 44N 9 31W
63 Dor, Israel 32 36N 34 55E
80 Dora, L., Australia 22 0S 122 50E
43 Dora Baltea, R., Italy 45 42N 8 0E
22 Dorchester, Dorset, Eng. 50 42N 2 26W
42 Dordogne, Dépt., France 45 0N 0 7E
43 Dordogne, R., France 44 50N 0 30E
46 Dordrecht, Netherlands 51 47N 4 40E
33 Dores, Scotland 57 22N 4 20W
72 Dori, Volta 14 0N 0 5W
23 Dorking, England 51 14N 0 20W
33 Dornoch, & F., Scotland 57 53N 4 2W
47 Dorohoi, U.S.S.R. 47 55N 26 30E
83 Dorrigo, Australia 30 22S 152 28E
22 Dorset, Co. & Hs., Eng. 50 45N 2 25W
44 Dorsten, Germany 51 40N 6 55E
44 Dortmund, Germany 51 36N 7 28E
74 Doruma, Zaïre 4 50N 27 33E
72 Dosso, Niger 13 0N 3 13E
91 Dothan, U.S.A. 31 13N 85 26W
43 Douai, France 50 22N 3 3E
74 Douala, Cameroon 4 0N 9 45E
42 Douarnenez, France 48 5N 4 20W
42 Doubs, Dépt., France 47 16N 6 35E
43 Doubs, R., France 47 0N 5 30E
72 Douentza, Mali 14 58N 2 48W
31 Douglas, Scotland 55 33N 3 50W
26 Douglas & Hd., I. of Man 54 9N 4 31W
90 Douglad, U.S.A. 31 25N 109 35W
74 Doumé, Cameroon 4 10N 13 30E
31 Doune, Scotland 56 12N 4 3W
33 Dounreay, Scotland 58 35N 3 45W
37 Douro, R., Portugal 41 8N 8 0W
37 Douro Litoral, Prov., Port. 41 10N 8 20W
27 Dove, R. & Dale, Eng. 53 5N 1 38W
83 Dover, Australia 43 26S 147 0E
23 Dover, & Str., England 51 7N 1 19E
93 Dover, Del., U.S.A. 39 19N 75 23W
93 Dover, N.H., U.S.A. 43 13N 70 55W
25 Dovey, R., Wales 52 31N 4 0W
48 Dovrefjell, mts., Norway 62 25N 9 10E
75 Dowa, Malawi 13 38S 33 58E
*36 Down, Co., N. Ireland 54 22N 5 55W
23 Downham, England 52 26N 0 14E
23 Downham Market, Eng. 52 36N 0 22E
36 Downpatrick, N. Ireland 54 19N 5 41W
35 Downpatrick Hd., Ire. 54 19N 9 21W
36 Dowra, Ireland 54 11N 8 2W
65 Doyung, China 33 40N 99 30E
72 Dra, Wadi, Morocco 29 0N 8 0W
44 Drachten, Netherlands 53 7N 6 6E
41 Dragoman P., Bulgaria 43 0N 22 57E
98 Dragons' Mouths, Venezuela-Trinidad 10 40N 61 40W
43 Draguignan, France 43 38N 6 28E
100 Drake Pass, S. America 57 0S 65 0W
76 Drakensberg, mts., S. Afr. 30 0S 29 0E
41 Dráma, Greece 41 9N 24 10E
49 Drammen, Norway 59 45N 10 14E
48 Dranga Jökul, mt., Ice. 66 12N 22 15W
36 Draperstown, N. Ireland 54 48N 6 50W
47 Drava, R., Yugoslavia 45 50N 18 0E
44 Drenthe, Prov., Neth. 52 53N 6 40E
46 Dresden, Germany 51 5N 13 41E
43 Dreux, France 48 42N 1 25E
27 Driffield, England 54 1N 0 27W
41 Drina, R., Yugoslavia 44 30N 19 5E
49 Drobak, Norway 59 39N 10 48E
36 Drogheda, Ireland 53 43N 6 20W
47 Drogobych, U.S.S.R. 49 28N 23 30E
35 Droichead Nua (Newbridge), Ireland 53 11N 6 48W
22 Droitwich, England 52 15N 2 10W
36 Dromara, N. Ireland 54 27N 6 1W
42 Drôme, Dépt., France 44 50N 5 10E
36 Dromore, N. Ireland 54 25N 6 8W
36 Dromore West, Ireland 54 15N 8 50W
82 Dronfield, Australia 21 12S 140 3E
27 Dronfield, England 53 18N 1 29W
36 Drum, Ireland 54 7N 7 8W
32 Drumbeg, Scotland 58 15N 5 12W
88 Drumheller, Canada 51 27N 112 58W
36 Drumlish, Ireland 53 50N 7 47W
82 Drummond Ra., Austral. 23 0S 147 15E
93 Drummondville, Can. 45 54N 72 30W
36 Drumquin, N. Ireland 54 38N 7 30W
36 Drumshanbo, Ireland 54 2N 8 2W
36 Drumsna, Ireland 53 57N 8 0W
100 Drygalski I., Antarctica 68 0S 91 0E
30 Drymen, Scotland 56 4N 4 28W
80 Drysdale R., Australia 15 0S 126 50E
92 Du Bois, U.S.A. 41 6N 78 48W
82 Duaringa, Australia 23 42S 149 42E
88 Dubawnt, L. & R., Can. 63 0N 101 30W
83 Dubbo, Australia 32 15S 148 37E
35 Dublin (Baile Atha Cliath), Ireland 53 21N 6 15W
35 Dublin, Co., Ireland 53 25N 6 20W
91 Dublin, U.S.A. 32 32N 82 57W
47 Dubno, U.S.S.R. 50 24N 25 47E
52 Dubovka, U.S.S.R. 49 3N 44 40E
72 Dubréka, Guinea 9 46N 13 31W
47 Dubrovitsa, U.S.S.R. 51 31N 26 35E
41 Dubrovnik, Yugoslavia 42 40N 18 6E
61 Dubrovskoye, U.S.S.R. 58 55N 111 0E
92 Dubuque, U.S.A. 42 30N 90 45W
82 Duchess, Australia 21 15S 139 57E
1 Ducie, I., Pacific Ocean 25 0S 125 0W
23 Duddington, England 52 36N 0 32W
65 Dudhi, India 24 15N 83 10E
61 Dudinka, U.S.S.R. 69 30N 86 0E
22 Dudley, England 52 30N 2 4W
37 Duero, R., Spain 41 31N 4 20W
27 Duffield, England 52 59N 1 30W
33 Dufftown, Scotland 57 28N 3 7W
47 Dugi Otok, I., Y.-slav. 44 0N 15 0E
44 Duisburg, Germany 51 26N 6 45E
76 Duiwelskloof, S. Africa 23 38S 30 5E
73 Duk Fadiat, Sudan 7 49N 31 31E
64 Duki, Pakistan 30 14N 68 25E
26 Dukinfield, England 53 28N 2 6W
47 Dukla P., Poland-Cz-slov. 49 25N 21 40E
72 Duku, Nigeria 10 43N 10 43E
99 Dulce, R., Argentina 28 30S 63 30W
36 Duleek, Ireland 53 40N 6 25W
82 Dululu, Australia 23 48S 150 15E
92 Duluth, U.S.A. 46 48N 92 10W
24 Dulverton, England 51 2N 3 33W
65 Dum Duma, India 27 35N 95 40E
30 Dumbarton, Scotland 55 57N 4 33W
**31 Dumfries, & Co., Scot. 55 4N 3 35W
100 Dumont d'Urville, Antarctica 67 0S 140 0E
35 Dun Laoghaire, Ireland 53 15N 6 10E
47 Dunaujvaros, Hungary 47 3N 18 58E
84 Dunback, N.Z. 45 23S 170 36E
31 Dunbar, Scotland 56 0N 2 31W
†30 Dunbarton, Co., Scot. 56 0N 4 40W
31 Dunblane, Scotland 56 11N 3 57W
35 Dunboyne, Ireland 53 26N 6 29W
33 Duncansby Hd., Scotland 58 38N 3 2W
22 Dunchurch, England 52 21N 1 18W
36 Dundalk, & B., Ireland 54 0N 6 23W
80 Dundas Str., Australia 11 0S 131 40E
31 Dundee, Scotland 56 27N 2 58W
36 Dundonald, N. Ireland 54 36N 5 50W
35 Dundrum, & B., Ireland 53 17N 6 15W
84 Dunedin, New Zealand 45 51S 170 31E
36 Dunfanaghy, Ireland 55 11N 7 59W
31 Dunfermline, Scotland 56 4N 3 27W
36 Dungannon, N. Ireland 54 31N 6 47W
35 Dungarvan & Hr., Ire. 52 5N 7 38W
23 Dungeness, England 50 54N 0 58E
36 Dungiven, N. Ireland 54 56N 6 55W
36 Dungloe, Ireland 55 0N 8 25W
83 Dungog, Australia 32 27S 151 34E
74 Dungu, Zaïre 3 48N 28 37E
31 Dunkeld, Scotland 56 34N 3 35W
43 Dunkerque, France 51 2N 2 21E
24 Dunkery Beacon, Eng. 51 11N 3 35W
72 Dunkwa, Ghana 6 0N 1 50W
35 Dunlavin, Ireland 53 3N 6 40W
35 Dunleary, *see* Dunlaoghaire, Ireland
36 Dunleer, Ireland 53 49N 6 22W
34 Dunloe, Gap. of, Ireland 52 0N 9 40W
30 Dunlop, Scotland 55 43N 4 32W
34 Dunmanway, Ireland 51 43N 9 6W
35 Dunmore, Ireland 53 37N 8 45W
35 Dunmore, E., Ireland 52 9N 7 0W
33 Dunnet, Scotland 58 37N 3 20W
33 Dunnet B., & Hd., Scot. 58 37N 3 28W
31 Dunning, Scotland 56 18N 3 37W
83 Dunolly, Australia 36 58S 143 44E
30 Dunoon, Scotland 55 57N 4 55W
73 Dunqul Oasis, Egypt 23 38N 31 3E
31 Duns, Scotland 55 46N 2 19W
31 Dunscore, Scotland 55 8N 3 48W
35 Dunshaughlin, Ireland 53 31N 6 31W
23 Dunstable, England 51 54N 0 31W
84 Dunstan Mts., N.Z. 44 50S 169 30E
24 Dunster, England 51 11N 3 28W
23 Dunton Green, England 51 17N 0 11E
32 Dunvegan, Scotland 57 26N 6 35W
32 Dunvegan Head, Scot. 57 32N 6 45W
63 Dura, Jordan 31 30N 35 2E
80 Durack Ra., Australia 17 0S 127 30E
43 Durance R., France 44 0N 6 0E
94 Durango, Mexico 24 12N 105 15W
37 Durango, Spain 43 15N 2 40W
90 Durango, U.S.A. 37 20N 107 55W
91 Durant, U.S.A. 33 58N 96 27W
99 Durazno, Uruguay 33 30S 56 30W
76 Durban, S. Africa 29 57S 30 59E
44 Düren, Germany 50 49N 6 29E
65 Durg, India 21 12N 81 20E
27 Durham, & Co., England 54 47N 1 36W
91 Durham, U.S.A. 36 0N 78 53W
41 Durmitor, Mt., Y.-slav. 43 20N 19 10E
33 Durness, & Kyle of, Scot. 58 34N 4 45W
41 Durres, Albania 41 20N 19 29E
83 Durrie, Australia 25 35S 140 15E
34 Durrus, Ireland 51 37N 9 32W
34 Dursey Hd., & I., Ire. 51 36N 10 16W
22 Dursley, England 51 42N 2 22W
84 D'Urville, I., N.Z. 40 55S 173 50E
60 Dushak, U.S.S.R. 37 20N 60 10E
60 Dushanbe, U.S.S.R. 38 20N 68 30E
44 Düsseldorf, Germany 51 18N 6 47E
88 Dutch Harbor, Alaska 53 40N 166 30W
66 Dutulun Shan, mts., Mongolia 48 45N 111 30E
95 Duverge, Dom. Rep. 18 15N 71 25W
50 Dvina B., U.S.S.R. 65 0N 39 30E
50 Dvina, R., U.S.S.R. 63 0N 42 45E
49 Dvina W., R., U.S.S.R. 56 35N 25 30E
64 Dwarka, India 22 20N 69 0E
76 Dwyka, S. Africa 33 10S 21 30E
33 Dyce, Scotland 57 12N 2 11W
91 Dyersburg, U.S.A. 35 5N 89 10W
89 Dyer, C., Canada 67 0N 61 0W
31 Dysart, Scotland 56 7N 3 6W
52 Dzerzhinsk, U.S.S.R. 56 15N 43 15E
60 Dzhailma, U.S.S.R. 51 30N 61 50E
60 Dzhalal Abad, U.S.S.R. 41 0N 73 0E
61 Dzhalinda, U.S.S.R. 53 40N 124 0E
60 Dzhambul, U.S.S.R. 43 10N 71 0E
51 Dzankoi, U.S.S.R. 45 40N 34 30E
61 Dzhelinde, U.S.S.R. 70 0N 114 0E
60 Dzhetygara, U.S.S.R. 52 10N 61 0E
60 Dzhezkazgan, U.S.S.R. 47 10N 67 40E
61 Dzhugdzhur Ra., U.S.S.R. 57 30N 138 0E
66 Dzungaria, Dist., China 44 20N 88 0E
66 Dzuunmod, Mongolia 47 55N 107 0E

E

88 Eagle, Alaska 64 44N 141 29W
90 Eagle Pass, U.S.A. 28 45N 100 28W
83 Eaglehawk, Australia 36 43S 144 16E
30 Eaglesham, Scotland 55 44N 4 18W
27 Eakring, England 53 9N 0 59W
23 Ealing, Gr. London, Eng. 51 30N 0 19W
25 Eardisland, England 52 14N 2 50W
22 Earl Shilton, England 52 35N 1 20W
23 Earls Colne, England 51 56N 0 43E
31 Earlsferry, Scotland 56 11N 2 50W
31 Earlston, Scotland 55 39N 2 40W
84 Earnslaw, Mt., N.Z. 44 37S 168 28E
27 Earsdon, England 55 4N 1 30W
31 Easington Colliery, Eng. 54 49N 1 19W
31 Easington, England 54 50N 1 24W
27 Easingwold, England 54 8N 1 11W
36 Easky, Ireland 54 17N 8 55W
84 East C., New Zealand 37 39S 178 58E
91 East Pt., U.S.A. 33 38N 84 29W
23 East Anglian Hts., Eng. 52 20N 0 42E
65 East Bengal, reg., Bangla. 24 30N 90 0E
47 East Beskids, Mts., Eur. 49 8N 22 10E
67 East China Sea, Asia 29 30N 125 0E
22 East Cowes, England 50 45N 1 17W
23 East Dereham, England 52 41N 0 57E
23 East Fen, England 53 5N 0 5E
23 East Grinstead, England 51 7N 0 3W
68 East Indies, reg., Asia 0 0 120 0E
27 East Kirby, England 53 5N 1 15W
31 East Linton, Scotland 56 0N 2 40W
76 East London, S. Africa 33 1S 27 58E
24 East Looe, England 50 22N 4 28W
††31 East Lothian, Co., Scot. 55 28N 2 40W
27 East Retford, England 53 20N 0 58W
‡27 East Riding, dist., Eng. 53 57N 0 35W
92 East St. Louis, U.S.A. 38 36N 90 3W
44 East Schelde R., Neth. 51 39N 3 50E
61 East Siberian Sea, U.S.S.R. 73 0N 160 0E
23 East Suffolk, England 52 9N 1 20E
23 East Sussex, England 50 55N 0 15E
83 East Toorale, Australia 30 30S 145 25E
31 East Wemyss, Scotland 56 8N 3 5W
23 Eastbourne, England 50 46N 0 16E
84 Eastbourne, N.Z. 41 50S 174 47E
23 Eastchurch, England 51 23N 0 53E
4 Easter I., Pacific Ocean 27 0S 108 30W
33 Easter Ross, dist., Scot. 57 37N 4 30W
64 Eastern Ghats, Mts., India 13 30N 79 0E
61 Eastern Sayan, Mts., U.S.S.R. 54 0N 96 0E
22 Eastleigh, England 50 58N 1 21W
89 Eastmain, & R., Canada 52 20N 78 30W
22 Easton, Dorset, England 50 30N 2 28W
24 Easton, Somerset, Eng. 51 28N 2 45W
93 Easton, Pa., U.S.A. 40 42N 75 16W
23 Eastry, England 51 15N 1 19E
27 Eastwood, England 53 1N 1 16W
27 Easton, England 52 52N 0 46W
23 Eaton Socon, England 52 13N 0 18W
92 Eau Claire, U.S.A. 44 49N 91 30W
32 Eaval, Mt., Scotland 57 33N 7 12W
25 Ebbw Vale, England 51 47N 3 13W
45 Eberbach, Germany 49 30N 9 0E
46 Eberswalde, Germany 52 50N 13 50E
66 Ebi Nor, L., China 45 0N 82 30E
40 Eboli, Italy 40 38N 15 0E
74 Ebolowa, Cameroon 3 0N 11 11E
37 Ebro, R., Spain 41 0N 0 30E
31 Ecclefechan, Scotland 55 4N 3 16W
26 Eccles, England 53 29N 2 20W
22 Eccleshall, England 52 52N 2 14W
33 Echt, Scotland 57 8N 2 21W
44 Echternach, Luxembourg 49 50N 6 15E
83 Echuca, Australia 36 3S 144 50E
37 Ecija, Spain 37 30N 5 9W
27 Eckington, England 53 21N 1 22W
98 Ecuador, S. Amer. 2 30S 77 30W
73 Ed Damer, Sudan 17 27N 34 0E
73 Ed Debba, Sudan 17 0N 31 12E
73 Ed Dueim, Sudan 13 55N 32 20E
65 Ed Dzong, Tibet 32 10N 90 20E
44 Edam, Netherlands 52 31N 5 3E
33 Eday I. & Sd., Scotland 59 12N 2 47W
74 Edd, Ethiopia 14 0N 41 30E
33 Edderton, Scotland 57 50N 4 10W
32 Eddrachillis, B., Scot. 58 19N 5 8W
44 Ede, Netherlands 52 3N 5 40E
83 Eden, Australia 37 0S 149 55E
26 Eden, R., England 54 50N 2 45W
23 Edenbridge, England 51 12N 0 4E
76 Edenburg, S. Africa 29 42S 25 58E
35 Edenderry, Ireland 53 21N 7 3W
36 Ederny, N. Ireland 54 32N 7 40W
73 Edeyin, Erg, des., Libya 27 0N 10 0E
22 Edge Hill, England 52 9N 1 35W
41 Edhessa, Greece 40 50N 22 5E
84 Edievale, New Zealand 45 20S 169 19E
31 Edinburgh, Scotland 55 57N 3 12W
41 Edirne, Turkey 41 41N 26 36E
83 Edithburgh, Australia 35 2S 137 35E
82 Edmonton, Australia 16 55S 145 45E
88 Edmonton, Canada 53 40N 113 30W
89 Edmundston, Canada 47 22N 68 22W
45 Edolo, Italy 46 11N 10 20E
41 Edremit & G., Turkey 39 35N 27 2E
88 Edson, Canada 53 35N 115 58W
‡‡74 Edward, L., Zaïre-Uganda 0 20S 29 35E
90 Edwards Plateau, U.S.A. 30 30N 100 40W
33 Edzell, Scotland 56 49N 2 39W
44 Eekloo, Belgium 51 11N 3 34E
76 Eersterus, S. Africa 25 45S 28 15E
47 Eger, Hungary 47 57N 20 23E
80 Egerton, Mt., Australia 24 40S 118 0E
23 Egham, England 51 25N 0 35W
33 Egilsay I., Scotland 59 9N 2 56W
75 Egito, Angola 12 0S 13 50E
84 Egmont, C., N.Z. 39 12S 173 45E
84 Egmont, Mt., N.Z. 39 13S 174 7E
26 Egremont, England 54 28N 3 33W
51 Egridir, Turkey 37 55N 30 50E
73 Eguei Timmi, Chad 15 35N 16 25E
73 Egypt, N.E. Africa 26 0N 30 0E
67 Ehime, Pref., Japan 33 30N 132 30E
83 Eidsvold, Australia 25 19S 151 10E
49 Eidsvoll, Norway 60 19N 11 17E
44 Eifel, Mts., Germany 50 5N 6 35E
49 Eigersund, Norway 58 26N 6 3E
45 Eigg, Switzerland 47 29N 8 52E
32 Eigg, I. & Sd. of, Scot. 56 52N 6 15W
80 Eighty Mile Beach, Australia 19 30S 121 0E
32 Eil, L., Scotland 56 50N 5 10W
83 Eildon, L., Australia 37 6S 146 0E
82 Einasleigh, Australia 18 45S 144 15E
44 Eindhoven, Netherlands 51 27N 5 29E
45 Einsiedein, Switzerland 47 9N 8 45E
46 Eisenach, Germany 50 59N 10 21E
63 Eizariya, Jordan 31 47N 35 15E
84 Eketahuna, N.Z. 40 34S 175 40E
61 Ekimchan, U.S.S.R. 53 0N 133 0E
72 El Aaiun, & Prov., Spanish Sahara 27 0N 13 0W
63 El Aal, Syria 32 48N 35 43E
73 El 'Alamein, Egypt 30 40N 29 0E
62 El 'Allâqi, Egypt 23 10N 32 54E
62 El Arish, Egypt 31 3N 33 40E
72 El Asnam (Orleansville), Algeria 36 2N 1 22E
62 El Bawiti, Egypt 28 27N 29 0E
72 El Bayadh (Géryville), Algeria 33 45N 1 0E
63 El Bira, Jordan 31 55N 35 13E
90 El Centro, U.S.A. 32 40N 115 38W
94 El Cuyo, Mexico 21 35N 87 50W
94 El Diaz, Mexico 21 10N 87 30W
62 El Dirr, Egypt 22 40N 32 0E
72 El Djouf, Desert, Mauritania 21 0N 8 0W
91 El Dorado, Ark., U.S.A. 33 14N 92 43W
91 El Dorado, Kan., U.S.A. 37 48N 96 56W
37 El Escorial, Spain 40 38N 4 11W
62 El Faiyum, Egypt 29 20N 30 59E
73 El Fasher, Sudan 13 37N 25 20E
94 El Fuerte, Mexico 26 36N 108 30W
95 El Gallo, Nicaragua 13 5N 84 30W
73 El Geneina, Sudan 13 27N 22 45E
73 El Geteina, Sudan 14 54N 32 30E
73 El Giza, Egypt 30 0N 31 0E
72 El Golea, Algeria 30 40N 3 0E
73 El Gusbat, Libya 32 30N 14 1E
73 El Iskandariya, *see* Alexandria
72 El Jadida, Morocco 33 11N 8 17W
73 El Jebelein, Sudan 12 40N 32 55E
73 El Kab, Sudan 19 30N 32 46E
63 El Khalil, *see* Hebron
73 El Khandaq, Sudan 18 43N 30 38E
73 El Kharga, Egypt 25 30N 30 33E
73 El Mansura, Egypt 31 0N 31 20E
73 El Minya, Egypt 28 12N 30 30E
74 El Niabo, Ethiopia 4 30N 39 55E
73 El Obeid, Sudan 13 15N 30 45E
73 El Odaiya, Sudan 12 0N 27 5E
72 El Oued, Algeria 33 20N 6 40E
72 El Ouig, Mali 19 25N 0 25E
90 El Paso, U.S.A. 31 56N 106 25W
73 El Qâhira, Egypt, *see* Cairo
73 El Qantara, Egypt 31 0N 32 20E
73 El Qasr, Egypt 25 40N 28 42E
62 El Qattara, Egypt 30 10N 27 15E
95 El Real, Panama 8 0N 77 40W
90 El Reno, U.S.A. 35 30N 98 0W
62 El Tur, Egypt 28 14N 33 39E
74 El Wak, Kenya 3 0N 41 0E
62 El Wasta, Egypt 29 25N 31 10E
25 Elan, R., Wales 52 18N 3 34W
51 Elâzig, Turkey 38 37N 39 18E
40 Elba, I., Italy 42 50N 10 20E
41 Elbasan, Albania 41 8N 20 8F
46 Elbe, R., Germany 53 55N 8 50E
43 Elbeuf, France 49 17N 0 58E
47 Elblag, Poland 54 10N 19 22E
51 Elbrus, Mt., U.S.S.R. 43 45N 43 0E
51 Elburz, Mts., Iran 36 0N 51 30E
37 Elche, Spain 38 15N 0 45W
74 Eldoret, Kenya 0 20N 35 40E
90 Electra, U.S.A. 34 2N 98 55W
52 Elektrostal, U.S.S.R. 55 46N 38 30E
100 Elephant I., Falkland Is., Dependency 61 0S 54 0W
91 Eleuthera I., Bahamas 25 0N 76 30W
33 Elgin, Scotland 57 39N 3 20W
92 Elgin, U.S.A. 42 2N 88 15W

* *In April 1973 districts replaced counties in N. Ireland*

** *County incorporated within the region of Dumfries and Galloway*

† *Incorporated within the region of Strathclyde*

†† *Incorporated within the region of Lothian*

‡ *Incorporated within the counties of Humberside and North Yorkshire*

‡‡ *Renamed Idi Amin Dada, L.*

74 Elgon, Mt., Kenya-Uganda
1 30N 34 50E
23 Elham, England 51 9N 1 7E
31 Elie, Scotland 56 11N 2 50W
74 Elila, R., Zaïre 3 0S 27 0E
75 Elisabethville, *see* Lubumbashi
51 Elista, (Stepnoi), U.S.S.R.
46 28N 44 20E
93 Elizabeth, U.S.A. 40 35N 74 8W
57 Elizabeth C., U.S.S.R. 54 0N 143 0E
91 Elizabeth City, U.S.A. 36 17N 76 12W
49 Elk, Poland 53 50N 22 20E
92 Elkhart, U.S.A. 41 39N 85 48W
90 Elko, U.S.A. 40 58N 115 48W
27 Elland, England 53 41N 1 49W
90 Ellensburg, U.S.A. 47 2N 120 32W
26 Ellesmere Port, England 53 17N 2 55W
100 Ellesmere I., Canada 79 0N 80 0W
*78 Ellice Is., Pacific Ocean 7 40S 178 0E
64 Ellichpur (Achalpur), India
21 12N 77 30E
31 Ellington, England 55 14N 1 34W
33 Ellon, Scotland 57 23N 2 3W
100 Ellsworth, Antarctica 78 02 41 0W
100 Ellsworth Land, Antarctica
74 30S 85 0W
51 Elmali, Turkey 36 20N 30 0E
92 Elmira, U.S.A. 42 15N 76 54W
36 Elphin, Ireland 53 51N 8 11W
32 Elphin, Scotland 58 4N 5 3W
23 Elstree, England 51 38N 0 16W
84 Eltham, N.Z. 39 25S 174 20E
65 Eluru, India 16 50N 81 0E
37 Elvas, Portugal 38 52N 7 13W
49 Elverum, Norway 60 55N 11 34E
23 Ely, & Isle of, England 52 23N 0 16E
60 Emba, U.S.S.R. 47 0N 55 45E
60 Emba, R., U.S.S.R. 48 0N 56 0E
43 Embrun, France 44 37N 6 29E
74 Embu, Kenya 0 30S 37 30E
44 Emden, Germany 53 22N 7 12E
82 Emerald, Australia 23 30S 148 1E
88 Emerson, Canada 49 0N 97 10W
73 Emi Koussi, Mt., Chad 20 0N 19 0E
40 Emilia-Romagna, Reg., It.
44 33N 10 40E
34 Emly, Ireland 52 28N 8 20W
44 Emmeloord, Netherlands 52 43N 5 46E
44 Emmen, Netherlands 52 46N 6 50E
44 Emmerich, Germany 51 52N 6 18E
82 Emmet, Australia 24 45S 144 30E
73 Em Nahud, Sudan 12 33N 28 35E
76 Empageni, South Africa 28 43S 31 52E
91 Emporia, Kansas, U.S.A.
38 25N 96 16W
46 Ems, R., Germany 52 47N 7 18E
23 Emsworth, England 50 51N 0 56W
98 Encontrados, Venezuela 9 10N 72 30W
83 Encounter B., Australia 35 50S 139 0E
82 Endeavour Str., Austral. 11 0S 142 0E
22 Enderby, England 52 35N 1 15W
100 Enderby Ld., Antarctica 67 0S 52 0E
41 Enez, Turkey 40 40N 26 5E
23 Enfield, Gr. London, Eng. 51 39N 0 4W
45 Engadin, Dist., Switz. 46 45N 10 10E
45 Engelberg, Switzerland 46 48N 8 24E
52 Engels, U.S.S.R. 51 28N 46 6E
29 England, United Kingdom, Europe
53 0N 2 0W
65 English Bazar, India 24 58N 88 21E
13 English Channel, Europe 50 0N 2 30W
90 Enid, U.S.A. 36 25N 97 52W
44 Enkhuizen, Netherlands 52 42N 5 17E
26 Ennerdale Water, L., Eng. 54 32N 3 24W
83 Enngonia, Australia 29 24S 146 0E
34 Ennis, Ireland 52 51N 8 59W
91 Ennis, U.S.A. 32 21N 96 45W
35 Enniscorthy, Ireland 52 32N 6 43W
34 Enniskean, Ireland 51 44N 8 54W
35 Enniskerry, Ireland 53 12N 6 10W
36 Enniskillen, N. Ireland 54 19N 7 37W
34 Ennistymon, Ireland 52 57N 9 20W
44 Enschede, Netherlands 52 13N 6 53E
94 Ensenada, Mexico 31 45N 116 40W
22 Enstone, England 51 55N 1 25W
74 Entebbe, Uganda 0 3N 32 32E
99 Entre Rios, Prov., Arg. 31 0S 59 0W
80 Entrecasteaux, Pt. d', Australia
34 48S 116 0E
72 Enugu, Nigeria 6 35N 7 30E
44 Epe, Netherlands 52 22N 5 59E
43 Épernay, France 49 3N 3 55E
43 Épinal, France 48 15N 6 25E
41 Epirus, Prov., Greece 39 50N 20 20E
23 Epping, & Forest, Eng. 51 40N 0 6E
23 Epsom, England 51 19N 0 16W
75 Epukiro, & R., S.W. Africa
21 30S 19 0E
73 Equatoria, Dist., Sudan 6 0N 30 0E
71 Equatorial Guinea, Afr. 23 0N 10 0W
73 Er Rahad, Sudan 12 50N 30 47E
62 Er Roda, Egypt 27 45N 30 58E
73 Er Roseires, Sudan 11 55N 34 30E
62 Erbil, Iraq 36 12N 44 7E
61 Ercha, U.S.S.R. 69 40N 147 5E
39 Erciyas Dagi, Turkey 38 30N 36 10E
100 Erebus, Mt., Antarctica 77 0S 166 0E
51 Eregli, Turkey 41 18N 31 25E
62 Eregli, Turkey 38 30N 34 7E
46 Erfurt, Germany 50 59N 11 0E
66 Erhlien, China 43 55N 111 45E
33 Eriboll, L., Scotland 58 33N 4 38W
33 Ericht, L., Scotland 56 50N 4 20W
92 Erie, U.S.A. 42 6N 80 6W
92 Erie, L., N. America 42 0N 81 0W
32 Eriskay, & Sd. of, Scot. 57 4N 7 18W
62 Eritrea, Prov., Ethiopia 15 0N 40 0E
45 Erlangen, Germany 49 38N 11 3E
76 Ermelo, S. Africa 26 30S 29 59E
41 Ermoupolis, Greece 37 10N 24 50E
64 Ernakulam, India 9 58N 76 15E
36 Erne, L. & R., N. Ireland
54 28N 7 50W
36 Erne, Upper L., N. Ire. 54 13N 7 32W
64 Erode, India 11 24N 77 45E
36 Errigal, Mt., Ireland 55 5N 8 12W
35 Erris Hd., Ireland 54 19N 10 0W
46 Erz Gebirge (Ore Mts.), Germany
50 30N 13 0E
51 Erzincan, Turkey 39 49N 39 40E
51 Erzurum, Turkey 39 58N 41 20E
49 Esbjerg, Denmark 55 30N 8 29E
92 Escanaba, U.S.A. 45 47N 87 5W
44 Esch, Luxembourg 49 30N 6 0E
44 Eschweiler, Germany 50 49N 6 14E
94 Escobal, Panama Canal Zone (Inset)
94 Escuinapa, Mexico 22 45N 105 30W
62 Esfahan, Iran 32 40N 51°30E
63 Esh Shuna, Jordan 32 36N 35 35E
76 Eshowe, S. Africa 28 54S 31 30E
27 Esk, R. (Yorks.), Eng. 54 27N 0 52W
31 Esk, R., Scotland 55 12N 3 15W
48 Eskifjördur, Iceland 65 5N 13 55W
49 Eskilstuna, Sweden 59 20N 16 30E
51 Eskisehir, Turkey 39 20N 30 10E
37 Esla, R., Spain 42 30N 5 20W
60 Espe, U.S.S.R. 44 5N 74 0E
80 Esperance, & B., Australia
33 50S 121 57E
99 Espinhaco, Sa. do, mts., Brazil
19 0S 43 45W
99 Espirito Santo, st., Brazil
19 30S 40 30W
88 Esquimalt, Canada 48 30N 123 50W
72 Essaouira, Morocco 31 40N 9 45W
44 Essen, Belgium 51 27N 4 26E
44 Essen, Germany 51 25N 7 0W
98 Essequibo, R., Guyana 6 50N 58 30W
23 Essex, Co., England 51 45N 0 25E
45 Esslingen, Germany 48 45N 9 15E
42 Essonne, Dépt., France 48 30N 2 15E
45 Estavaver-le-Lac, Switz. 46 51N 6 52E
76 Estcourt, S. Africa 29 0S 29 55E
88 Estevan, Canada 49 12N 103 0W
27 Eston, England 54 34N 1 9W
49 Estonia, S.S.R., U.S.S.R. 58 50N 25 40E
37 Estrela, Sa. da., mts., Port.
40 20N 7 20W
37 Estremadura, Prov., Port. 39 0N 8 35W
37 Estremadura, Old Prov., Spain
39 20N 6 20W
99 Estrondo, Sa. do, hs., Brazil
8 0S 48 45W
47 Esztergom, Hungary 47 49N 18 42E
43 Étampes, France 48 26N 2 6E
43 Étaples, France 50 38N 1 40E
64 Etawah, India 26 54N 79 4E
23 Etchingham, England 51 0N 0 27E
71 Ethiopia, E. Africa 8 0N 40 0E
40 Etna, Mt., Italy 37 42N 15 0E
23 Eton, England 51 29N 0 37E
75 Etosha Pan, S.W. Africa 18 45S 16 20E
44 Ettelbrück, Luxembourg 49 51N 6 6E
45 Ettlingen, Germany 48 55N 8 22E
31 Ettrick Water, R., Scot. 55 31N 2 55W
43 Eu, France 50 0N 1 30E
41 Eubœa, *see* Evvoia, Greece
80 Eucla Basin, Austral. 31 41S 127 0E
92 Euclid, U.S.A. 41 39N 81 32W
83 Eucumbene, L., Australia 36 5S 148 40E
90 Eugene, U.S.A. 44 6N 123 8W
83 Eugowra, Australia 33 5S 148 27E
44 Eupen, Belgium 50 38N 6 3E
62 Euphrates, R., Iraq 34 0N 42 40E
42 Eure, Dépt., France 49 0N 1 20E
42 Eure-et-Loire, Dépt., Fr. 48 15N 1 20E
90 Eureka, U.S.A. 40 48N 124 0W
83 Euroa, Australia 36 49S 145 34E
75 Europa, I., Indian Oc. 23 0S 40 30E
37 Europa Pt., Gibraltar 36 2N 6 32E
44 Europoort, Netherlands 51 57N 4 10E
44 Euskirchen, Germany 50 39N 6 47E
49 Eutin, Germany 54 7N 10 38E
92 Evanston, U.S.A. 42 9N 87 43W
92 Evansville, U.S.A. 38 3N 87 27W
80 Everard, L., Australia 31 30S 135 0E
65 Everest, Mt., Himalaya, Nepal-Tibet
28 3N 87 7E
90 Everett, U.S.A. 48 0N 122 13W
91 Everglades, The, region, U.S.A.
26 0N 80 30W
22 Evesham, England 52 5N 1 57W
37 Évora, Portugal 38 37N 7 55W
43 Évreux, France 49 0N 1 5E
41 Evvoia (Eubœa), I., Greece
38 30N 23 50E
23 Ewell, England 51 20N 0 15W
94 Ewarton, Jamaica 18 10N 77 2W
83 Excelsior, Australia 33 5S 150 0E
24 Exe, R., England 50 50N 3 31W
24 Exeter, England 50 44N 3 32W
24 Exminster, England 50 40N 3 29W
24 Exmoor, England 51 10N 3 43W
24 Exmouth, England 50 37N 3 25W
80 Exmouth G., Australia 22 0S 114 20E
74 Eyasi, L., Tanzania 3 30S 35 0E
31 Eyemouth, Scotland 55 52N 2 5W
48 Eyja Fjord, Iceland 66 5N 18 27W
33 Eynhallow Sd., Scotland 59 8N 3 7W
32 Eynort, L., Scotland 57 13N 7 20W
48 Eyrarbakki, Iceland 63 5N 21 2W
80 Eyre, Australia 32 13S 126 20E
83 Eyre, L., Australia 29 20S 137 25E
80 Eyre Pen., Australia 33 30S 135 40E
34 Eyrecourt, Ireland 53 12N 8 8W
48 Eyriks Jökull, mt., Iceland
64 45N 20 20W
62 Ez Zeidab, Sudan 17 30N 33 45E

F

40 Fabriano, Italy 43 20N 12 50E
72 Fachi, Niger 19 5N 11 0E
73 Fada, Chad 17 18N 21 35E
72 Fada N'Gourma, Volta 12 5N 0 30E
61 Faddeyev I., U.S.S.R. 75 30N 144 0E
40 Faenza, Italy 44 19N 11 54E
47 Fagaras, Rumania 45 50N 24 58E
49 Fagernes, Norway 61 1N 9 5E
49 Fagersta, Sweden 60 1N 15 46E
18 Fair I., British Is. 59 30N 1 40W
88 Fairbanks, Alaska 64 59N 148 10W
22 Fairford, England 51 42N 1 48W
84 Fairlie, New Zealand 44 5S 170 48E
91 Fairmont, Minn., U.S.A.
43 40N 94 30W
91 Fairmont, W. Va., U.S.A. 39 30N 80 6W
88 Fairweather, Mt., Alaska
58 50N 137 40W
63 Faizabad, Afghanistan 37 18N 70 45E
65 Faizabad, India 26 50N 82 10E
27 Fakenham, England 52 50N 0 51E
57 Fakfak, Indonesia 2 50S 132 0E
65 Falam, Burma 22 58N 93 50E
27 Faldingworth, England 53 21N 0 22W
49 Falkenberg, Sweden 56 56N 12 30E
31 Falkirk, Scotland 55 59N 3 47W
31 Falkland, Scotland 56 15N 3 13W
99 Falkland Is., S. Atlantic 52 0S 60 0W
100 Falkland Is. Dependencies
55 0S 35 0W
49 Falköping, Sweden 58 10N 13 30E
93 Fall River, U.S.A. 41 43N 71 9W
94 Falmouth, Antigua 17 0N 61 47W
24 Falmouth, & B., Eng. 50 9N 5 4W
94 Falmouth, Jamaica 18 30N 77 42W
76 False B., S. Africa 34 15S 18 40E
49 Falster, I., Denmark 54 50N 11 55E
49 Falsterbo, Sweden 55 21N 13 3E
49 Falun, Sweden 60 38N 15 32E
62 Famagusta, Cyprus 35 10N 33 58E
99 Famatina, Mt., Arg. 28 30S 67 0W
36 Fanad Hd., Ireland 55 15N 7 37W
73 Fangak, Sudan 9 0N 30 50E
32 Fannich, L., Scotland 57 39N 5 0W
40 Fano, Italy 43 50N 13 4E
63 Fanuch, Iran 26 40N 59 35E
74 Faradje, Zaïre 4 0N 29 52E
64 Farah, Afghanistan 32 22N 62 7E
64 Farah Prov., Afghan. 32 0N 62 0E
64 Farah Rud R., Afghan. 32 30N 62 20E
72 Faranah, Guinea 10 3N 10 45W
62 Farasan Is., Red Sea 17 0N 42 0E
22 Fareham, England 50 53N 1 12W
89 Farewell, C., Greenland
60 0N 44 0W
84 Farewell, C., N.Z. 40 30S 172 40E
91 Fargo, U.S.A. 46 57N 96 47W
63 Faria, Wadi el, Jordan 32 12N 35 25E
91 Faribault, U.S.A. 44 16N 93 20W
72 Farim, Port. Guinea 12 27N 15 17W
22 Faringdon, England 51 39N 1 34W
91 Farmington, U.S.A. 44 40N 70 8W
23 Farnborough, Eng. 51 17N 0 46W
27 Farne Is., England 55 38N 1 37W
23 Farnham, England 51 13N 0 48W
26 Farnworth, England 53 33N 2 33W
37 Faro, Portugal 37 5N 7 54W
49 Farö, Sweden 58 0N 19 10E
13 Faroe Is., Atlantic 62 0N 7 0W
34 Farranfore, Ireland 52 10N 9 32W
82 Farrell Flat, Australia 33 50S 139 40E
41 Farsala, Greece 39 20N 22 28E
49 Farsund, Norway 58 3N 6 42E
62 Fasa, Iran 28 57N 53 35E
30 Faslane, Scotland 56 3N 4 49W
29 Fastnet Rock, Ireland 51 23N 9 37W
64 Fatehgarh, India 27 25N 79 35E
64 Fatehpur, Rajasthan, India
27 57N 74 55E
65 Fatehpur, U.P., India 26 0N 80 50E
66 Fatshan, China 23 7N 113 10E
31 Fauldhouse, Scotland 55 50N 3 44W
40 Favara, Italy 37 20N 13 40E
23 Faversham, England 51 18N 0 53E
40 Favignana, Italy 37 55N 12 20E
22 Fawley, England 50 49N 1 20W
48 Faxa Floi, Iceland 64 27N 23 0W
91 Fayetteville, N.C., U.S.A.
35 1N 78 58W
91 Fayetteville, Ark., U.S.A. 36 0N 94 5W
22 Fazeley, England 52 36N 1 42W
64 Fazilka, India 30 30N 74 2E
72 F'Dérik (Fort Gouraud), Mauritania
22 40N 12 45W
91 Fear, C., U.S.A. 33 59N 78 0W
33 Fearn, Scotland 57 47N 4 0W
84 Featherston, N Z. 41 1S 175 23E
43 Fécamp, France 49 47N 0 21E
49 Fehmarn I., Germany 54 27N 11 10E
46 Fehmarn Belt, Str., Den. 54 35N 11 20E
84 Feilding, New Zealand 40 12S 175 30E
75 Feira, Zambia 15 30S 30 15E
45 Feldkirch, Austria 47 12N 9 35E
23 Felixstowe, England 51 58N 1 23E
23 Felpham, England 50 47N 0 38W
48 Femunden L., Norway 62 30N 11 55E
66 Fenglingtu, China 34 40N 110 20E
27 Fenny Bentley, Eng. 53 4N 1 43W
22 Fenny Compton, Eng. 52 9N 1 20W
23 Fenny Stratford, Eng. 51 59N 0 42W
23 Fens, The, Eng. 52 45N 0 2E
51 Feodosiya, U.S.S.R. 45 2N 35 28E
34 Ferbane, Ireland 53 17N 7 50W
60 Fergana, U.S.S.R. 40 50N 71 55E
34 Fergus, R., Ireland 52 45N 9 0W
91 Fergus Falls, U.S.A. 46 25N 96 0W
40 Ferla, Italy 37 5N 14 55E
*36 Fermanagh, Co., N. Ire. 54 22N 7 40W
34 Fermoy, Ireland 52 9N 8 15W
**74 Fernando Poo., I., W. Afr. 3 25N 8 45E
23 Fernhurst, England 51 3N 0 43W
90 Fernie, Canada 49 30N 115 0W
32 Fernilea, Scotland 57 18N 6 24W
64 Ferozepore, India 30 55N 75 20E
40 Ferrara, Italy 44 52N 11 40E
37 Ferrol, Spain 43 32N 8 13W
27 Ferryhill, England 54 42N 1 32W
73 Fès, Morocco 34 5N 4 55W
35 Fethard, Ireland 52 28N 7 43W
32 Fetlar I., Scotland 60 35N 0 50W
33 Fettercairn, Scotland 56 50N 2 33W
73 Fezzan, Dist., Libya 25 40N 16 0E
25 Ffestiniog, Wales 52 58N 3 56W
75 Fianarantsoa, Madagascar 21 30S 47 0E
46 Fichtel Gebirge. Mts., Germany
50 0N 12 0E
76 Ficksburg, S. Africa 28 48S 27 55E
35 Fiddown, Ireland 52 20N 7 20W
31 Fife, Co., Scotland 56 10N 3 10W
31 Fife Ness, Scotland 56 17N 2 35W
43 Figeac, France 44 40N 2 0E
37 Figueira da Foz, Portugal 40 7N 8 54W
37 Figueras, Spain 42 17N 3 0E
72 Figuig, Morocco 32 18N 1 20W
84 Fiji, Pac. Oc. Inset
23 Filby, England 52 40N 1 39E
27 Filey, & B., England 54 14N 0 18W
41 Filiatra, Greece 37 5N 21 35E
49 Filipstad, Sweden 59 42N 14 5E
45 Filisur, Switzerland 46 40N 9 40E
48 Filskivotn, Dist., Ice. 64 50N 20 45W
24 Filton, England 51 29N 2 34E
33 Findhorn, & R., Scot. 57 40N 3 36W
92 Findlay, U.S.A. 41 0N 83 32W
23 Finedon, England 52 20N 0 40W
35 Finglas, Ireland 53 22N 6 18W
75 Fingoé, Mozambique 14 55S 32 10E
42 Finistère, Dépt., France 48 13N 4 4W
37 Finisterre, C., Spain 42 51N 9 19W
49 Finland, Europe 62 20N 26 30E
50 Finland, G. of, Europe 60 0N 26 0E
88 Finlay R., Canada 55 50N 125 10W
83 Finley, Australia 35 50S 145 40E
30 Finnart, Scotland 56 7N 4 48W
36 Finn, R., Ireland 54 50N 7 55W
49 Finnmark, Norway 70 0N 25 0E
82 Finschhafen, N.E. New Guinea
6 33S 147 48E
33 Finstown, Scotland 59 0N 3 8W
36 Fintona, N. Ireland 54 30N 7 20W
63 Fiq, Syria 32 47N 35 41E
62 Firat (Euphrates), R., Turkey
39 0N 38 30E
64 Firozabad, India 27 5N 78 20E
73 First Cataract of Nile, Egypt
24 0N 32 50E
61 Firyuza, U.S.S.R. 38 10N 57 45E
13 Fisher Bank, Europe 61 0N 10 0W
25 Fishguard & B., Wales 51 59N 4 58W
91 Fitzgerald, U.S.A. 31 40N 83 10W
36 Fivemiletown, N. Ireland 54 23N 7 20W
90 Flagstaff, U.S.A. 35 12N 111 38W
49 Flam, Norway 60 52N 7 14E
27 Flamborough Hd., Eng. 54 9N 0 5W
44 Flandre Occidentale, Belg. 51 0N 3 0E
44 Flandre Orientale, Belg. 51 0N 3 30E
48 Flasjön, L., Sweden 64 0N 15 40E
48 Flatey I., Iceland 65 22N 22 57W
48 Flatey I., Iceland 66 12N 17 50W
48 Flateyri, Iceland 66 5N 23 30W
82 Flattery, C., Australia 15 0S 145 30E
90 Flattery, C., U.S.A. 48 30N 124 56W
95 Flatts, The, Bermuda 32 20N 64 44W
44 Flavy le Martel, France 49 43N 3 13E
23 Fleet, England 51 16N 0 50W
33 Fleet, L. & R., Scotland 57 56N 4 2W
26 Fleetwood, England 53 56N 3 2W
49 Flekkefjord, Norway 58 18N 6 39E
49 Flensburg, Germany 54 45N 9 27E
23 Fletton, England 52 34N 0 13W
45 Fleurier, Switzerland 46 55N 6 35E
44 Fleurus, Belgium 50 30N 4 30E
88 Flin Flon, Canada 54 58N 101 58W
80 Flinders B., Australia 34 25S 115 20E
83 Flinders I., Australia 40 0S 148 0E
82 Flinders R., Australia 20 35S 142 30E
83 Flinders Ras., Australia 31 0S 139 0E
92 Flint, U.S.A. 42 59N 83 45W
91 Flint R., U.S.A. 31 15N 84 15W
†25 Flint, & Co., Wales 53 16N 3 10W
27 Flodden, England 55 37N 2 8W
40 Florence (Firenze), Italy
43 48N 11 18E
91 Florence, Ala., U.S.A. 34 51N 87 35W
91 Florence, S. C., U.S.A. 34 12N 79 47W
98 Florencia, Colombia 1 50N 75 50W
44 Florennes, Belgium 50 15N 4 35E
68 Flores, I., Indonesia 8 35S 121 30E
68 Flores Sea, Indonesia 6 50S 122 0E
44 Florenville, Belgium 49 40N 5 19E
99 Florianopolis, Brazil 27 35S 48 25W
91 Florida, st., U.S.A. 28 30N 81 30W
99 Florida, Uruguay 34 10S 56 25W
91 Florida Keys, Is. & B., U.S.A.
25 0N 80 30W
49 Florö, Norway 61 36N 5 0E
33 Flotta, I., Scotland 58 50N 3 8W
45 Fluela Pass, Switz. 46 48N 9 44E
44 Flushing (Vlissingen), Netherlands
51 27N 3 35E
82 Fly R., Papua 8 0S 142 0E
33 Fochabers, Scotland 57 38N 3 5W
47 Focsani, Rumania 45 39N 27 13E
40 Foggia, Italy 41 27N 15 37E
43 Foix, France 42 58N 1 30E
48 Folda Fd., Norway 67 35N 15 25E
49 Folgefonni, Norway 60 0N 6 15E
40 Foligno, Italy 42 58N 12 48E
23 Folkestone, England 51 5N 1 11E
88 Fond du Lac, Canada 59 28N 107 5W
92 Fond du Lac, Wis., U.S.A.
43 50N 88 30W
94 Fonseca, G. of, Central America
13 15N 87 40W
43 Fontainebleau, France 48 20N 2 40E
42 Fontevrault, France 47 17N 0 0
67 Foochow, China 26 10N 119 20E
45 Forbach, France 49 10N 6 52E
83 Forbes, Australia 33 24S 148 1E
30 Ford, Scotland 56 10N 5 27W
35 Ford, Ireland 52 32N 6 15W
25 Forden, England 52 34N 3 8W
22 Fordingbridge, England 50 56N 1 48W
33 Fordyce, Scotland 57 40N 2 45W
86 Forel, Mt., Greenland 67 0N 34 0W
24 Foreland Pt., England 51 14N 3 45W
42 Forest, Guernsey 49 26N 2 35W
26 Forest of Bowland, Eng. 54 0N 2 30W
22 Forest of Dean, England 51 48N 2 35
23 Forest Row, England 51 6N 0 3E
83 Forestier Pen., Australia 43 0S 148 0E
31 Forfar, Scotland 56 40N 2 53W
40 Forli, Italy 44 14N 12 7E
33 Formartine, Dist., Scot. 57 20N 2 15W
26 Formby, & Pt., England 53 34N 3 4W
37 Formentera I., Spain 38 40N 1 33E
99 Formosa, Argentina 26 10S 58 25W
74 Formosa B., Kenya 2 50S 40 10E
67 Formosa (Taiwan) I., China
24 0N 121 0E
67 Formosa Str., China 24 0N 119 0E
43 Fornovo, Italy 44 42N 10 10E
33 Forres, Scotland 57 37N 3 36W
80 Forrest, Australia 30 50S 128 25E
82 Forsayth, Australia 18 50S 143 45E
48 Fors, Sweden 63 1N 16 38E
33 Forsinard, Scotland 58 22N 3 54W
46 Forst, Germany 51 45N 14 40E
83 Forster, Australia 32 2S 152 10E
89 Fort Albany, Ont., Can. 52 10N 81 50
73 Fort Archambault, Chad 9 0N 18 18E
33 Fort Augustus, Scotland 57 9N 4 40W
76 Fort Beaufort, S. Africa 32 44S 26 42
73 Fort Bretonnet, Chad 10 40N 16 50E
72 Fort Charlet (Djanet), Algeria
24 35N 9 20E
89 Fort Chimo, Canada 58 30N 67 10W
88 Fort Chipewyan, Can. 58 50N 111 0W
90 Fort Collins, U.S.A. 40 36N 105 10W
73 Fort Crampel, Cent. Africa
7 2N 19 18E
75 Fort Dauphin, Madagascar
25 0S 46 57E
94 Fort Davis, Panama Canal Zone (Inse
95 Fort de France, Martinique
14 33N 61 2W
91 Fort Dodge, U.S.A. 42 32N 94 11W
73 Fort Foureau, Cam. 12 0N 14 55E
88 Fort Frances, Canada 48 52N 93 25W
72 Fort Gouraud, *see* F'Dérik
65 Fort Hertz, *see* Putao
75 Fort Jameson, *see* Chipata
75 Fort Johnston, *see* Mangoche
72 Fort Lallemand, Algeria 31 30N 6 35E
††73 Fort Lamy, Chad 12 3N 15 3E
72 Fort Laperrine (Tamanrasset), Algeria
22 45N 5 30E
91 Fort Lauderdale, U.S.A. 26 5N 80 5W
72 Fort Miribel, Algeria 29 30N 3 0E
91 Fort Myers, U.S.A. 26 39N 81 48W
88 Fort Nelson, & R., Can. 58 49N 123 0W
88 Fort Norman, Canada 65 0N 125 30W
90 Fort Peck Res., U.S.A. 47 40N 107 0W
91 Fort Pierce, U.S.A. 27 35N 80 25W
74 Fort Portal, Uganda 0 48N 30 20E
88 Fort Providence, Can., 61 20N 117 30W
74 Fort Rosebery, *see* Mansa
74 Fort Rousset, Congo (Fr.) 0 35S 16 5E
88 Fort St. John, Can. 56 15N 120 50W
91 Fort Scott, U.S.A. 37 50N 94 44W
51 Fort Shevchenko, U.S.S.R.
44 37N 50 30E
73 Fort Sibut, Cent. Africa 5 50N 19 12E
88 Fort Simpson, Can. 61 45N 121 30W
88 Fort Smith, North West Territories,
Canada 60 0N 112 25W
91 Fort Smith, U.S.A. 35 10N 94 30W
88 Fort Vermilion, Can. 58 30N 115 57W
75 Fort Victoria, Rhodesia 20 3S 30 50E
92 Fort Wayne, U.S.A. 41 0N 85 3W
92 Fort William, *see* Thunder Bay
32 Fort William, Scotland 56 49N 5 6W
90 Forth Worth, U.S.A. 32 50N 97 20W
88 Fort Yukon, Alaska 66 35N 145 12W
99 Fortaleza (Ceará), Brazil 3 48S 38 38W

* *Renamed Tuvalu*

* *In April 1973 districts replaced counties in N. Ireland*

** *Renamed Macias Nguema Biyoga*

† *County incorporated within Clwyd*

†† *Renamed Ndjamena*

5 Forte Roçadas, Angola 16 38s 15 22E
0 Fortescue R., Australia 22 5s 117 0E
1 Forth, Scotland 55 45N 3 42W
1 Forth, Firth of, Scotland 56 10N 2 45W
0 Forth, R., Scotland 56 8N 4 15W
3 Fortrose, Scotland 57 36N 4 8W
3 Fostoria, U.S.A. 41 8N 83 10W
1 Fothergill, England 54 43N 3 30W
3 Fotheringhay, England 52 32N 0 25W
8 Foula, I., Scotland 60 8N 2 7W
2 Foumban, Cameroon 5 50N 10 58E
3 Fourmies, France 50 0N 4 0E
1 Fournoi I., Greece 37 38N 26 50E
2 Fouta Djalon, Mt., Guinea
11 30N 12 0W
4 Foveaux Str., N.Z. 46 45s 168 15E
4 Fowey, & R., England 50 20N 4 39W
0 Fowler's B., Australia 32 0s 132 50E
6 Foxdale, I. of Man 54 12N 4 38W
9 Foxe Basin, Canada 66 30N 77 0W
9 Foxe Pen., Canada 65 0N 76 0W
6 Foxford, Ireland 53 59N 9 7W
4 Foxton, New Zealand 40 31s 175 13E
6 Foyle, L. & R., N. Ire. 55 5N 7 10W
4 Foynes, Ireland 52 37N 9 5W
3 Framlingham, England 52 12N 1 21E
1 Francavilla Fontana, It. 40 30N 17 34E
3 France, Europe 47 0N 3 0E
3 Frances, Australia 36 40s 140 55E
4 Franceville, Gabon 1 55s 13 40E
3 Franche Comté, Prov., Fr. 47 15N 6 10E
5 Francistown, Botswana 21 6s 27 32E
3 Franeker, Netherlands 53 12N 5 33E
5 Frankenthal, Germany 49 32N 8 20E
2 Frankfort, Ind., U.S.A. 40 18N 86 31W
2 Frankfort, Ken., U.S.A. 38 10N 84 50W
6 Frankfurt-on-Main, Ger. 50 5N 8 42E
6 Frankfurt-on-Oder, Ger. 52 20N 14 32E
8 Franklin B., Canada 70 0N 126 0W
0 Franklin D. Roosevelt L., U.S.A.
48 30N 119 0W
8 Franklin, Mts., Can. 66 0N 125 0W
8 Franklin Str., Canada 72 0N 96 0W
8 Franklin Terr., Canada 71 0N 100 0W
3 Frankston, Australia 38 15s 145 10E
23 Frant, England 51 5N 0 17E
00 Franz Josef Ld. U.S.S.R.
81 0N 60 0E
83 Fraser or Gt. Sandy I., Australia
25 0s 154 0E
8 Fraser R., Canada 53 30N 120 30W
33 Fraserburgh, Scotland 57 42N 2 0W
45 Frauenfeld, Switzerland 47 34N 8 54E
9 Fray Bentos, Uruguay 33 15s 58 25W
49 Fredericia, Denmark 55 36N 9 43E
89 Fredericton, Canada 45 50N 66 40W
89 Frederikshaab, Greenland
62 0N 49 30W
49 Frederikshavn, Den. 57 26N 10 19E
92 Fredonia, U.S.A. 42 25N 79 20W
49 Fredrikstad, Norway 59 16N 10 57E
95 Freeport, Bahama Is. 25 55N 78 20W
92 Freeport, U.S.A. 42 16N 89 42W
72 Freetown, Sierra Leone 8 20N 13 5W
33 Freevater Forest, Scot. 57 52N 4 43W
46 Freiburg, Germany 47 59N 7 53E
46 Freising, Germany 48 30N 11 40E
46 Freistadt, Austria 48 30N 14 30E
43 Fréjus, France 43 12N 6 45E
80 Fremantle, Australia 32 1s 115 50E
91 Fremont, U.S.A. 41 33N 96 28W
96 French Fuiana, S. Amer. 4 0N 53 0W
52 French Somal., see next entry
52 French Territory of Afars and Issas,
Africa 11 30N 42 30E
36 Frenchpark, Ireland 53 53N 8 25W
90 Fresno, U.S.A. 36 42N 119 48W
33 Freswick, Scotland 58 35N 3 5W
31 Freuchie, Scotland 56 14N 3 8W
83 Freycinet Pen., Australia 42 0s 148 15E
75 Fria, C., S.W. Africa 18 34s 12 0E
45 Fribourg, & Cn., Switz. 46 49N 7 9E
45 Friedrichshafen, Ger. 47 38N 9 30E
84 Friendly Is., see Tonga Is. (Inset)
44 Friesland, Prov., Neth. 53 5N 5 50E
94 Frijoles, Panama (Inset)
23 Frimley, England 51 18N 0 43W
23 Frinton-on-Sea, England 51 50N 1 16E
99 Frio, C., Brazil 22 50s 41 50W
46 Frisian Is., Neth.-Ger. 53 30N 6 0E
40 Friuli-Venezia Giulia, Reg., Italy
46 15N 12 50E
26 Frizington, England 54 33N 3 30W
89 Frobisher & B., N.W. Terr., Canada
63 45N 68 30W
88 Frobisher, L., Canada 56 40N 108 20W
26 Frodsham, England 53 17N 2 45W
24 Frome, England 51 15N 2 19W
83 Frome, L., Australia 30 40s 139 45E
22 Frome, R., England 50 45N 2 33W
90 Front Ra., U.S.A. 40 0N 105 10W
40 Frosinone, Italy 41 40N 13 29E
48 Frostisen Mt., Norway 68 17N 17 0E
99 Froward C., Chile 55 0s 71 0W
60 Frunze, U.S.S.R. 42 55N 75 0E
45 Frutigen, Switzerland 46 34N 7 38E
94 Fuego, Vol., Guatemala
14 20N 91 15W
37 Fuenteovejuna, Spain 38 16N 5 28W
37 Fuentes de Onoro, Spain 40 37N 6 45W
37 Fundao, Portugal 40 10N 7 30W
94 Fuerte, R., Mexico 27 0N 108 30W
72 Fuerteventura, I., Canary Is.
28 25N 14 0W
48 Fuglö Sound, Norway 70 0N 20 0E
67 Fujiyama, Mt. Japan 35 30N 139 0E
66 Fukien, Prov., China 25 50N 118 0E
67 Fukui, & Pref., Japan 36 4N 136 8E
67 Fukue Shima, Japan 32 30N 128 40E
67 Fukuoka, & Pref., Japan 33 36N 130 27E
67 Fukushima, & Pref., Japan
37 30N 140 30E
46 Fulda, Germany 50 37N 9 40E
26 Fulwood, England 53 47N 2 41W
44 Fumay, France 49 59N 4 43E
72 Funchal, Madeira 32 40N 16 50W
89 Fundy, B. of, Canada 45 0N 66 0W
83 Furneaux Group, Austral. 40 0s 148 0E
26 Furness, Dist., England 54 18N 3 8W
45 Furth, Germany 49 29N 10 58E
67 Fusin, China 42 0N 121 40E
67 Fushun, China 42 1N 123 59E
84 Futuna, I., Pacific Ocean 14 3s 178 3E
67 Fuyu, China 45 15N 125 15E
30 Fyne, Loch, Scotland 56 0N 5 20W

G

74 Gabela, Angola 10 50s 14 27E
73 Gabes, Tunisia 33 53N 10 4E
74 Gabon, Africa 1 55s 12 0E
76 Gaborone, Botswana 24 38s 25 50E
41 Gabrovo, Bulgaria 42 50N 25 25E
64 Gadag, India 15 10N 75 45E
64 Gadarwara, India 22 58N 78 50E
64 Gadhada, India 21 58N 71 30E
91 Gadsden, U.S.A. 34 5N 85 59W
64 Gadwal, India 16 8N 77 56E
40 Gaeta, Italy 41 18N 13 35E
75 Gago Coutinho, Angola 14 12s 21 20E
43 Gaillac, France 43 58N 1 56E
27 Gainsborough, Eng. 53 25N 0 47W
80 Gairdner, L., Australia 31 30s 136 0E
32 Gairloch, Scotland 57 43N 5 47W
33 Gairsay I., Scotland 59 4N 25 9W
75 Galangue, Angola 13 38s 16 0E
4 Galapagos Is., Pac. Oc. 0 30s 91 0W
31 Galashiels, Scotland 55 37N 2 50W
47 Galati, Rumania 45 28N 28 2E
41 Galatina, Italy 40 10N 18 10E
34 Galbally, Ireland 52 28N 8 17W
49 Galdhöpiggen, Mt., Nor. 61 40N 8 20E
94 Galeana, Mexico 30 2N 107 30W
91 Galesburg, U.S.A. 40 54N 90 20W
50 Galich, U.S.S.R. 58 22N 42 12E
37 Galicia, Old Prov., Spain 42 45N 8 0W
63 Galilee, Dist., Israel 32 52N 35 20E
63 Galilee, Sea of, see Kinneret, L.
62 Gallabat, Sudan 13 10N 36 30E
65 Galle, Sri Lanka 6 2N 80 13E
37 Gallego, R., Spain 42 20N 0 30W
34 Galley Hd., Ireland 51 31N 8 57W
98 Gallinas, Punta, Colombia
12 28N 71 37W
41 Gallipoli, Italy 40 1N 18 0E
41 Gallipoli, Turkey, see Gelibolu
48 Gällivare, Sweden 67 10N 20 32E
30 Galloway, Mull of, Scot. 54 37N 4 52W
90 Gallup, U.S.A. 35 28N 108 50W
83 Galong, Australia 34 40s 148 30E
64 Galoya, Sri Lanka 8 10N 80 55E
92 Galt, Canada 43 25N 80 20W
34 Galty Mts., Ireland 52 22N 8 13W
34 Galtymore Mt., Ireland 52 15N 8 4W
91 Galveston, U.S.A. 29 15N 95 0W
34 Galway, & Co., Ireland 53 18N 9 3W
72 Gambaga, Ghana 10 35N 0 25W
72 Gambia, & R., West Africa
13 50N 15 0W
94 Gamboa, Panama Canal Zone (Inset)
74 Gamboma, Congo (Fr.) 1 45s 16 0E
48 Gamlakarleby, see Kokkola, Finland
65 Gandak, R., India 26 20N 84 56E
64 Gandava, Pakistan 28 40N 67 20E
89 Gander, Newf., Canada 49 1N 54 53W
72 Gandi, Nigeria 12 55N 5 49E
65 Ganga (Ganges), R., India &
Pakistan 24 30N 88 20E
64 Ganganagar, India 29 55N 73 50E
65 Gangtok, Sikkim 27 20N 88 30E
43 Gannat, France 46 8N 3 15E
90 Gannett Pk., U.S.A. 43 10N 110 0W
76 Ganspan, S. Africa 27 55s 24 45E
72 Ganta, Liberia 7 15N 8 59W
72 Gao, Mali 16 25N 0 10W
72 Gaoua, Volta 10 20N 3 15W
72 Gaoual, Guinea 11 35N 13 25W
43 Gap, France 44 35 6 5E
34 Gap of Dunloe, Ireland 52 0N 9 40W
64 Gar Dzong, India 32 20N 79 55E
36 Gara, L., Ireland 53 54N 8 27W
42 Gard, Dépt., France 44 3N 4 20E
40 Garda, L., Italy 45 40N 10 40E
74 Gardala, Ethiopia 5 40N 36 40E
90 Garden City, U.S.A. 38 0N 100 47W
64 Gardez, Afghanistan 33 40N 69 0E
73 Gardian, Chad 15 45N 19 40E
92 Gardner, U.S.A. 42 35N 72 0W
27 Garforth, England 53 48N 1 22W
40 Gargano, Mt., Italy 41 50N 16 5E
76 Garies, S. Africa 30 31s 18 0E
40 Garigliano, R., Italy 41 18N 13 50E
30 Garliestown, Scotland 54 47N 4 22W
60 Garm, U.S.S.R. 39 25N 70 20E
45 Garmisch Partenkirchen, Germany
47 30N 11 6E
33 Garmouth, Scotland 57 40N 3 8W
43 Garonne, R., France 43 20N 1 20E
74 Garoua Malaba, Cam. 9 16N 13 25E
72 Garraway, Liberia 4 35N 8 0W
36 Garrison, Ireland 54 25N 8 5W
88 Garry, L., Canada 66 0N 100 0W
33 Garry, L., Scotland 57 5N 4 52W
74 Garsen, Kenya 2 25s 40 20E
26 Garstang, England 53 53N 2 45W
64 Gartok, Tibet, China 31 33N 80 30E
68 Garut, Java, Indonesia 7 20s 108 0E
36 Garvagh, N. Ireland 55 0N 6 41W
84 Garvie, Mts., N.Z. 45 30s 169 0E
91 Gary, U.S.A. 41 36N 87 10W
60 Gasan Kuli, U.S.S.R. 37 40N 54 20E
43 Gascony, Prov., France 43 40N 0 10E
80 Gascoyne, R., Australia 25 0s 115 0E
72 Gashaka, Nigeria 7 30N 11 30E
89 Gaspé, C., Canada 48 50N 64 5W
37 Gata, Cabo de, Spain 36 42N 2 6W
37 Gata, Sa. de, mts., Spain 40 30N 6 0W
27 Gateshead, England 54 58N 1 38W
93 Gatineau, R., Canada 47 0N 75 50W
26 Gatley, England 53 25N 2 15W
75 Gatooma, Rhodesia 18 15s 29 57E
94 Gatun, & L., Panama Canal Zone
(Inset)
64 Gaud-i-Zirreh, Afghan. 29 45N 62 0E
65 Gauhati, Assam, India 26 12N 91 50E
48 Gaula, R., Norway 63 15N 10 15E
49 Gausta, Mt., Norway 59 48N 8 40E
49 Gauja, R., U.S.S.R. 57 15N 24 50E
49 Gävle, Sweden 60 40N 17 4E
49 Gävleborg, Co., Sweden 61 0N 16 30E
83 Gawler, Australia 34 39s 138 45E
64 Gawilgarh Hills, India 21 15N 76 30E
65 Gaya, India 24 42N 85 0E
83 Gayndah, Australia 25 38s 151 40E
63 Gaza (Ghazzah), Israel 31 30N 34 28E
51 Gaziantep, Turkey 37 10N 37 30E
47 Gdansk, Poland 54 19N 18 40E
50 Gdov, U.S.S.R. 58 40N 27 55E
47 Gdynia, Poland 54 38N 18 28E
35 Geashill, Ireland 53 14N 7 20W
73 Gebeit Mine, Sudan 21 3N 36 29E
62 Gebel Sabahi, Egypt 26 0N 34 0E
73 Gedaref, Sudan 14 0N 35 42E
63 Gedera, Israel 31 49N 34 47E
23 Gedney, England 52 47N 0 5E
74 Gedo, Ethiopia 9 0N 37 0E
49 Gedser, Denmark 54 35N 11 55E
44 Geel, Belgium 51 9N 4 59E
83 Geelong, Australia 38 8s 144 20E
44 Geeraardsbergen, Belg. 50 46N 3 53E
73 Geidam, Nigeria 12 57N 11 57E
45 Geislingen, Germany 48 37N 9 47E
74 Geita, Tanzania 2 40s 32 18E
40 Gela, Italy 37 6N 14 18E
44 Gelderland, Prov., Neth. 52 6N 6 10E
44 Geldermalsen, Neth. 51 53N 5 17E
44 Geldrop, Netherlands 51 24N 5 32E
72 Gelhak, Sudan 11 14N 32 45E
41 Gelibolu (Gallipoli), Turkey
40 30N 26 55E
44 Gelsenkirchen, Germany 51 32N 7 4E
68 Gemas, Malaya 2 35N 102 50E
44 Gembloux, Belgium 50 34N 4 41E
74 Gemena, Zaïre 3 20N 19 40E
45 Gemmi P., Switzerland 46 25N 7 39E
100 General Belgrano, Antarc. 78 0s 38 0W
99 Gen. Pico, Argentina 35 40s 63 45W
45 Geneva, & Cn., Switz. 46 12N 6 8E
45 Geneva, L. of Europe, see Lac Leman
44 Genk, Belgium 50 58N 5 30E
83 Genoa, Australia 37 30s 149 30E
40 Genoa, & G. (Genova), It.
44 25N 8 58E
44 Gent (Ghent), Belgium 51 5N 3 40E
76 Genyesa, S. Africa 26 30s 24 10F
80 Geographe Chan., Austral.
24 20s 113 15E
76 George, S. Africa 34 0s 22 15E
83 George, L., Australia 35 0s 149 0E
74 George, L., Uganda 0 0 30 15E
91 George, L., U.S.A. 29 20N 81 30W
93 George, L., N.Y., U.S.A. 43 40N 73 33W
83 George Town, Australia 41 5s 148 55E
68 George Town, Malaya 5 28N 100 5E
72 Georgetown, Gambia 13 30N 14 47W
94 Georgetown, Guyana 6 40N 58 15W
91 Georgia, st., U.S.A. 33 0N 83 0W
51 Georgia S.S.R., U.S.S.R. 42 0N 44 30E
89 Georgian B., Canada 45 0N 80 30W
51 Georgievsk, U.S.S.R. 44 10N 43 17E
46 Gera, Germany 50 53N 12 6E
80 Geraldton, Australia 28 48s 114 38E
63 Gerar, R., Israel 31 23N 34 35E
43 Gérardmer, France 48 0N 6 50E
46 Germany, East Europe 52 0N 13 0E
46 Germany, West Europe 51 0N 9 0E
76 Germiston, S. Africa 26 16s 28 12E
44 Gerolstein, Germany 50 12N 6 24E
37 Gerona, Spain 41 58N 2 50E
23 Gerrards Cross, England 51 35N 0 32W
42 Gers, Dépt., France 43 31N 0 10E
72 Géryville, Algeria see El Bayadh
92 Gettysburg, U.S.A. 39 50N 77 18W
43 Gevaudan, Dist., France 44 45N 3 30E
48 Geyser, Springs, Iceland
64 22N 20 15W
63 Gezer, Israel 31 51N 34 55E
62 Gezira, Sudan 16 20N 34 0E
72 Ghadames, Libya 30 18N 9 5E
65 Ghaghara (Gogra), R., India
26 40N 82 40E
72 Ghana, Africa 8 0N 1 30W
63 Ghar, Wadi, Jordan 31 30N 35 20E
73 Gharyan, Libya 32 10N 13 0E
72 Ghat, Libya 25 0N 10 20E
65 Ghats, Eastern, Mts., India
13 30N 79 0E
65 Ghats, Western, Mts., India
17 0N 74 0E
72 Ghazaouet (Nemours), Algeria
35 1N 1 48W
64 Ghaziabad, India 28 35N 77 45E
65 Ghazipur, India 25 39N 83 28E
63 Ghazir, Lebanon 34 1N 35 39E
44 Ghent, Belgium, see Gent
65 Giamda Dzong, China 30 2N 93 0E
36 Giant's Causeway, N. Ire. 55 13N 6 31W
40 Giarre, Italy 37 44N 15 10E
75 Gibeon, S.W. Africa 25 11s 17 48E
37 Gibraltar, & Str., Europe 36 10N 5 20W
27 Gibraltar Pt., England 53 7N 0 19E
80 Gibson Des., Australia 24 0s 126 0E
43 Gien, France 47 40N 2 35E
46 Giessen, Germany 50 35N 8 42E
67 Gifu, & Pref., Japan 35 30N 136 54E
26 Giggleswick, England 54 5N 2 19W
30 Gigha I., Scotland 55 42N 5 43W
37 Gijon, Spain 43 32N 5 43 W
90 Gila, R., U.S.A. 33 0N 113 0W
11 Gilbert Is., Pacific Oc. 1 0s 173 0E
82 Gilbert R., Australia 17 0s 141 30E
36 Gilford, N. Ireland 54 22N 6 21W
83 Gilgandra, Australia 31 32s 148 37E
64 Gilgit, Kashmir 35 58N 74 27E
36 Gill, L., Ireland 54 14N 8 15W
82 Gilliat, Australia 20 40s 141 28E
23 Gillingham, England 51 22N 0 33E
44 Gilly, Belgium 50 25N 4 25E
48 Gilsbakki, Iceland 64 42N 21 2W
26 Gilsland, England 55 0N 2 34W
25 Gilwern, Wales 51 49N 3 5W
74 Gimbi, Ethiopia 9 3N 35 42E
41 Giona, Mt., Greece 38 40N 22 10E
51 Giresun, Turkey 40 53 38 19E
65 Giridih, India 24 10N 86 15E
42 Gironde, Dépt., France 44 50N 0 22E
82 Giru, Australia 19 30s 147 5E
30 Girvan, & R., Scotland 55 15N 4 50W
84 Gisborne, N.Z. 38 39s 178 5E
43 Gisors, France 49 20N 1 45E
47 Giurgiu, Rumania 43 53N 25 56E
63 Giv'atayim, Israel 32 4N 34 49E
44 Givet, France 50 8N 4 49E
61 Gizhiga, U.S.S.R. 62 0N 160 27E
47 Gizycko, Poland 54 5N 21 50E
41 Gjirokaster, Albania 40 5N 20 10E
49 Gjövik, Norway 60 47N 10 43E
93 Glace Bay, Canada 46 25N 60 0W
90 Glacier National Park, U.S.A.
48 45N 114 0W
82 Gladstone, Queensland, Australia
24 0s 151 15E
83 Gladstone, S. Australia 33 5s 138 10E
49 Glama, R., Norway 61 0N 11 30E
48 Glama Jökull, Mt., Ice. 65 47N 23 0W
31 Glamis, Scotland 56 37N 3 0W
*25 Glamorgan, Co., Wales 51 35N 3 35W
35 Glanaruddery, Mts., Ire. 52 20N 9 27W
34 Glandore, Ireland 51 33N 9 7W
34 Glanworth, Ireland 52 11N 8 21W
45 Glarner Alpen, Mts., Switzerland
46 54N 9 10E
45 Glarus, Cn., Switzerland 46 55N 9 0E
33 Glas Maol, Mt., Scotland 56 52N 3 20W
30 Glasgow, Scotland 55 52N 4 14W
92 Glasgow, U.S.A. 37 0N 85 55W
36 Glasslough, Ireland 54 20N 6 53W
24 Glastonbury, England 51 8N 2 42W
46 Glauchau, Germany 50 49 12 31E
50 Glazov, U.S.S.R. 58 9N 52 30E
32 Glen Affric, Scotland 57 16N 5 0W
30 Glen Coe, Scotland 56 40N 5 0W
93 Glen Falls, U.S.A. 43 25N 73 40W
32 Glen Garry, Scotland 57 4N 5 10W
83 Glen Innes, Australia 29 42s 151 45E
33 Glen Mor, Scotland 57 15N 4 30W
30 Glen Orchy, Scotland 56 27N 4 52W
32 Glen Shiel, Scotland 57 8N 5 20W
34 Glenamaddy, Ireland 53 40N 8 35W
35 Glenamoy, Ireland 54 14N 9 40W
35 Glenart Castle, Ireland 52 48N 6 12W
36 Glenarm, N. Ireland 54 58N 5 58W
76 Glencairn, S. Africa 34 10s 18 25E
90 Glendale, U.S.A. 34 15N 118 20W
90 Glendive, U.S.A. 47 10N 104 45W
35 Glenealy, Ireland 52 59N 6 10W
83 Glenelg, Australia 35 1s 138 30E
32 Glenelg, Scotland 57 13N 5 36W
83 Glenelg, R., Australia 37 25N 141 30E
30 Glenken, The, reg., Scot. 55 10N 4 15W
30 Glenluce, Scotland 54 53N 4 49W
83 Glenmorgan, Australia 27 15s 149 30E
83 Glenorchy, Australia 42 49s 147 18E
31 Glenrothes, Scotland 56 12N 3 11W
48 Glettinganes, Iceland 65 30N 13 30W
34 Glin, Ireland 52 34N 9 17W
34 Glinsk, Ireland 53 23N 9 49W
47 Gliwice, Poland 50 20N 18 52E
90 Globe, U.S.E. 33 36N 111 0W
46 Glockner, Gr., mt., Austria
47 0N 12 30E
46 Glogow, Poland 51 35N 16 10E
75 Glorieuses Is., Ind. Oc. 11 30N 47 20W
26 Glossop, England 53 27N 1 56W
83 Gloucester, Australia 31 58s 151 56E
22 Gloucester, & Co., Eng. 51 53N 2 14W
93 Gloversville, U.S.A. 43 4N 74 25W
46 Glückstadt, Germany 53 49N 9 29E
46 Gmund, Austria 48 45N 15 0E
46 Gmunden, Austria 47 56N 13 46E
47 Gniezno, Poland 52 30N 17 35E
22 Gnosall, England 52 48N 2 15W
68 Go Cong, Vietnam 10 25N 106 50E
64 Goa, India 15 30N 74 0E
76 Goageb, S.W. Africa 26 40s 17 15E
65 Goalpara, India 26 10N 90 40E
30 Goat Fell, mt., Scotland 55 37N 5 15W
74 Goba, Ethiopia 7 1N 39 59E
75 Goba, Mozambique 26 1s 32 10E
75 Gobabis, S.W. Africa 22 17s 19 5E
66 Gobi (Shamo) Desert, Mongolia
44 0N 108 0E
44 Goch, Germany 51 42N 6 10E
23 Godalming, England 51 11N 0 36W
65 Godavari, R., India 19 20N 76 0E
47 Godeanu, Mt., Rumania 45 25N 22 15E
64 Godhra, India 22 45N 73 56E
88 Gods Lake, Canada 54 40N 94 10W
89 Godthaab, Greenland 64 14N 51 0W
44 Goeree I., Netherlands 51 50N 3 55E
44 Goes, Netherlands 51 31N 3 55E
82 Gogango, Australia 23 40s 150 2E
44 Goggingen, Germany 48 20N 10 52E
65 Gogra, R., see Ghaghara, R., India
73 Gogrial, Sudan 8 30N 28 0E
99 Goiânia, Brazil 16 17s 48 16W
99 Goias, Brazil 15 55s 50 10W
30 Goil, L., Scotland 56 8N 4 54W
64 Gojra, Pakistan 31 5N 72 35E
83 Gold Coast, reg., Austral. 28 0s 153 25E
49 Goldap, Poland 54 18N 22 22E
35 Golden, Ireland 52 30N 8 0W
84 Golden B., N.Z. 40 40s 172 50E
90 Golden Gate, U.S.A. 37 58N 122 30W
34 Golden Vale, Ireland 52 33N 8 20W
91 Goldsboro, U.S.A. 35 26N 77 59W
46 Goleniów, Poland 53 35N 14 50E
33 Golspie, Scotland 57 58N 3 59W
74 Goma, Zaïre 1 40s 29 42E
50 Gomel, U.S.S.R. 52 28N 31 5E
30 Gometra I., Scotland 56 30N 6 18W
94 Gomez (Palacio), Mex. 25 45N 103 28W
65 Gomoh, India 23 52N 86 10E
95 Gonaives, Haiti 19 20N 72 45W
73 Gonder, Ethiopia 12 40N 37 45E
74 Goniri, Nigeria 11 30N 12 15E
76 Good Hope, C of, S. Afr. 34 20s 18 30E
83 Goodooga, Australia 29 1s 147 28E
27 Goole, England 53 42N 0 53W
83 Goondiwindi, Australia 28 31s 150 25E
90 Goose, L., U.S.A. 42 0N 120 0W
89 Goose Bay, Canada 53 25N 60 30W
64 Gop, India 22 5N 69 50E
45 Goppingen, Germany 48 43N 9 38E
65 Gorakhpur, India 26 49N 83 30E
31 Gordon, Scotland 55 41N 2 32W
80 Gordon Downs, Australia 18 30s 129 35E
82 Gordonvale, Australia 17 5s 145 50E
73 Goré, Chad 8 0N 16 48E
73 Gore, Ethiopia 8 12N 35 32E
84 Gore, New Zealand 46 5N 168 55E
35 Goresbridge, Ireland 52 38N 7 0W
42 Gorey, Jersey, Channel Is. 49 12N 2 2W
44 Gorinchem, Netherlands 51 50N 4 59E
23 Goring, England 50 50N 0 21W
40 Gorizia, Italy 45 58N 13 38E
52 Gorki (Gorkiy), U.S.S.R. 56 17N 44 0E
23 Gorleston, England 52 35N 1 44E
46 Görlitz, Germany 51 11N 15 0E
52 Gorlovka, U.S.S.R. 48 25N 37 58E
60 Gorno, Filinskoye, U.S.S.R.
60 15N 70 3E
50 Gornyatski, U.S.S.R. 67 32N 64 15E
47 Gorodok, U.S.S.R. 49 46N 23 32E
68 Gorontalo, Indonesia 0 25N 123 5E
34 Gort, Ireland 53 4N 8 49W
50 Goryn, R., U.S.S.R. 52 0N 27 0E
46 Gorzów, Poland 52 43N 15 15E
65 Gosainthan, Mt., Tibet 28 20N 85 45E
45 Göschenen, Switzerland 46 41N 8 35E
83 Gosford, Australia 33 24s 151 10E
46 Goslar, Germany 51 57N 10 28E
40 Gospic, Yugoslavia 44 35N 15 20E
22 Gosport, England 50 48N 1 9W
48 Gota Can., Sweden 58 40N 14 10E
49 Göteborg, Sweden 57 20N 11 50E
49 Göteborg & Bohus, Co., Sweden
58 15N 11 30E
46 Gotha, Germany 50 56N 10 42E
48 Gothenburg, see Göteborg
48 Gotland, I., Sweden 57 35N 18 30E
49 Gotska Sandon I., Swed. 58 24N 19 15E
46 Göttingen, Germany 51 33N 9 58E
47 Gottwaldov, Cz-slov. 49 15N 17 42E
73 Goubone, Chad 20 45N 17 5E
44 Gouda, Netherlands 52 1N 4 42E
89 Gouin Res., Canada 48 35N 74 40W
83 Goulburn, Australia 34 45s 149 40E
80 Goulburn Is., Australia 11 30s 133 35E
72 Goundam, Mali 16 25N 3 45W
43 Gourdon, France 44 42N 1 25E
72 Gourma-Rarous, Mali 16 55N 2 5W
43 Gournay, France 49 30N 1 45E
30 Gourock, Scotland 55 58N 4 49W
83 Gourock Ra., Australia 36 0s 149 30E
72 Gourselik, Niger 13 40N 10 40E
42 Gouville, France 49 7N 1 32W
25 Gower, Pen., Wales 51 35N 4 10W
35 Gowran, Ireland 52 38N 7 5W
99 Goya, Argentina 29 0s 59 15W
73 Goz Beida, Chad 12 20N 21 30E
62 Goz Regeb, Sudan 16 0N 35 30E
40 Gozo, I., Malta 36 2N 14 18E
76 Graaf Reinet, S. Africa 32 18s 24 37E
72 Grabo, Ivory Coast 4 55N 7 25W

* *Divided into three new counties West, Mid and South Glamorgan*

2 Hebrides, Outer, Scot. 57 40N 7 0W
9 Hebron, Canada 58 10N 62 50W
3 Hebron, Jordan 31 32N 35 5E
3 Hede, Sweden 62 23N 13 43E
9 Hedemora, Sweden 60 18N 15 58E
4 Hedgehope, N.Z. 46 12S 168 34E
9 Hedmark, Co., Norway 61 45N 11 0E
2 Hednesford, England 52 43N 2 0W
4 Heemstede, Netherlands 52 19N 4 37E
4 Heerenveen, Netherlands 52 58N 5 55E
4 Heerlen, Netherlands 50 53N 5 58E
3 Heiban, Sudan 11 13N 30 27E
5 Heidelberg, Germany 49 26N 8 46E
6 Heidelburg, S. Africa 34 5S 20 50E
5 Heidenheim, Germany 48 41N 10 8E
6 Heilbron, S. Africa 27 8S 28 12E
5 Heilbronn, Germany 49 5N 9 19E
7 Heilungkiang, Prov., China 45 0N 130 0E
9 Heinola, Finland 61 13N 26 10E
5 Heinze Is., Burma 14 20N 97 45E
2 Hejaz, dist., Saudi Arabia 25 30N 38 30E
8 Hekla Torfa Jökull, Ice. 64 0N 19 30W
0 Helena, Mont., U.S.A. 46 40N 111 55W
0 Helensburgh, Scotland 56 1N 4 43W
4 Helensville, New Zealand 36 39S 174 28E
8 Helgeland, Dist., Norway 66 0N 13 15E
6 Heligoland I., & B., Ger. 54 11N 7 52E
1 Hellespont, *see* Dardanelles
6 Hellifield, England 54 1N 2 14W
7 Hellin, Spain 38 30N 1 40W
5 Helville, Madagascar 13 20S 48 12E
4 Helmand Rud R., Afghan. 30 25N 63 0E
4 Helmond, Netherlands 51 30N 5 41E
3 Helmsdale, & R., Scot. 58 7N 3 39W
27 Helmsley, England 54 14N 1 3W
9 Helsingfors, *see* Helsinki
9 Helsingör, Denmark 56 2N 12 35E
9 Helsinki (Helsingfors), Fin. 60 13N 24 55E
24 Helston, England 50 6N 5 17W
26 Helvellyn, mt., England 54 30N 3 0W
3 Helwân, Egypt 29 50N 31 20E
23 Hemel Hempstead, Eng. 51 45N 0 28W
9 Hemse, Sweden 57 14N 18 21E
27 Hemsworth, England 53 37N 1 21W
24 Hemyock, England 50 55N 3 14W
37 Henares, R., Spain 41 0N 2 50W
2 Hendaye, France 43 22N 1 50W
92 Henderson, Ken., U.S.A. 37 50N 87 30W
1 Henderson, N.C., U.S.A. 36 17N 78 25W
32 Henderson, Scotland 57 42N 5 47W
33 Hendon, Australia 28 2S 151 55E
57 Hengchun, Taiwan 22 0N 120 40E
44 Hengelo, Netherlands 52 17N 6 48E
24 Hengoed, Wales 51 39N 3 14W
56 Hengyang, China 26 30N 111 58W
44 Hénin-Lietard, France 50 25N 2 58E
23 Henley, England 51 31N 0 54W
23 Henlow, England 52 2N 0 18W
39 Henrietta Maria, C., Can. 55 0N 82 38W
56 Hentiyn Nuruu, mt., Mongolia 49 0N 108 0E
83 Henty, Australia 35 32S 147 2E
55 Henzada, Burma 17 39N 95 37E
64 Herat, Afghanistan 34 28N 62 3E
64 Herat, Prov., Afghan. 34 0N 63 0E
42 Hérault, Dépt., France 43 37N 2 57E
82 Herberton, Australia 17 28S 145 25E
34 Herbertstown, Ireland 52 32N 8 29W
41 Hercegnovi, Y-slav. 42 25N 18 30E
40 Hercegovina, Province, Yugoslavia 43 30N 17 45E
48 Herdhubreid, Mt., Ice. 65 10N 16 21W
22 Hereford, & Co., Eng. 52 4N 2 42W
44 Herentals, Belgium 51 11N 4 51E
46 Herford, Germany 52 8N 8 40E.
45 Herisau, Switzerland 47 24N 9 18E
76 Hermanus, S. Africa 34 15S 19 10E
83 Hermidale, Australia 31 26S 146 54E
84 Hermitage, New Zealand 43 45S 170 7E
63 Hermon, Mt., Syria-Leb. 33 25N 35 50E
47 Hernad, R., Hungary 48 30N 21 5E
23 Herne Bay, England 51 22N 1 9E
49 Herning, Denmark 56 8N 9 0E
89 Heron Bay, Can. 48 50N 86 10W
37 Herrera, Spain 39 12N 5 2W
44 Herstal, Belgium 50 38N 5 35E
23 Herstmonceaux, Eng. 50 53 0 21E
23 Hertford, & Co., Eng. 51 48N 0 4W
44 s'Hertogenbosch, Neth. 51 42N 5 18E
63 Herzliya, Israel 32 10N 34 50E
46 Hesse, Land, Germany 50 27N 9 10E
27 Hessle, England 53 44N 0 26W
27 Hetton-le-Hole, England 54 49N 1 26W
27 Hexham, England 54 58N 2 0W
23 Heybridge, England 51 44N 0 42E
26 Heysham, England 54 4N 2 54W
83 Heywood, Australia 38 12S 141 36E
26 Heywood, England 53 34N 2 19W
91 Hibbing, U.S.A. 47 30N 92 50W
94 Hidalgo del Parral, Mexico 27 0N 105 40W
72 Hierro I., Canary Is. 27 45N 17 58W
26 High Pike, mt., England 54 42N 3 4W
88 High River, Canada 50 30N 114 0W
47 High Tatra, mts., Cz-slov. 49 0N 20 0E
24 High Willhays, England 50 41N 4 1W
23 High Wycombe, England 51 38N 0 45W
23 Higham Ferrers, England 52 18N 0 35W

* *County incorporated within Hereford and Worcester*

22 Highley, England 52 25N 2 23W
22 Highworth, England 51 38N 1 44W
67 Hikone, Japan 35 7N 136 20E
84 Hikurangi, N.Z. 35 42S 174 17E
46 Hildesheim, Germany 52 10N 9 58E
23 Hilgay, England 52 33N 0 24E
62 Hilla, Iraq 32 39N 44 30E
44 Hillegom, Netherlands 52 18N 4 34E
23 Hillingdon, Greater London, England 51 34N 0 27W
91 Hillsboro, U.S.A. 32 0N 97 0W
36 Hillsborough, N. Ireland 54 28N 6 4E
94 Hillsborough, Carriacou, W.I. 12 14N 61 12W
83 Hillston, Australia 33 29S 145 32E
36 Hilltown, N. Ireland 54 12N 6 9W
90 Hilo, Hawaii 19 45N 155 15W
44 Hilversum, Netherlands 52 15N 5 10E
64 Himachal Pradesh, Prov., India 31 30N 77 0E
65 Himalayas, mts., Asia 29 0N 82 0E
64 Himatnagar, India 23 37N 72 57E
67 Himeji, Japan 34 56N 134 48E
67 Himi, Japan 36 55N 137 0E
82 Hinchinbrook I., Australia 18 21S 146 20E
22 Hinckley, England 52 33N 1 22W
74 Hinde Rapids, Zaïre 5 25S 27 3E
62 Hindian, R., Iran 30 20N 50 20E
26 Hindley, England 53 33N 2 35W
63 Hindu Kush, Afghanistan 36 0N 71 30E
64 Hindubagh, Pakistan 30 55N 67 42E
64 Hindupur, India 13 45N 77 25E
88 Hines Cr., Canada 56 20N 118 40W
66 Hingan, China 25 55N 110 40E
66 Hingi, China 25 10N 105 8E
64 Hingol, R., Pakistan 27 30N 66 0E
64 Hingoli, India 19 50N 77 6E
24 Hinkley Pt., England 51 13N 3 7W
48 Hinnöy, I., Norway 68 40N 16 0E
67 Hino, C., Japan 35 25N 132 45E
37 Hinojosa, Spain 38 30N 5 15W
45 Hinterrhein, R., Switz. 46 35N 9 20E
92 Hinton, U.S.A. 37 40N 80 50W
67 Hirosaki, Japan 40 35N 140 30E
67 Hiroshima, & Pref., Japan 34 30N 132 35E
43 Hirson, France 49 55N 4 3E
25 Hirwaun, Wales 51 43N 3 30W
63 Hisban, Jordan 31 48N 35 49E
95 Hispaniola, I., W.I. 17 30N 71 0W
64 Hissar, India 29 11N 75 41E
23 Hitchin, England 51 57N 0 17W
48 Hitra, I., Norway 63 30N 8 45E
49 Hjälmaren, L., Sweden 59 25N 15 50E
48 Hjeradsflói, Iceland 65 40N 14 0W
48 Hjeradsvötn, R., Iceland 65 40N 19 10W
49 Hjorring, Denmark 57 25N 10 0E
66 Hoa-Binh, Vietnam 21 0N 104 25E
83 Hobart, Australia 42 49S 147 6E
90 Hobbs, U.S.A. 32 43N 103 11W
44 Hoboken, Belgium 51 11N 4 21E
49 Hobro, Denmark 56 39N 9 46E
66 Hochih, China 24 45N 107 25E
45 Hochst, Germany 50 6N 8 32E
66 Hochwan, China 30 15N 105 50E
45 Hockenheim, Germany 49 20N 8 32E
62 Hodeida, Yemen 14 50N 42 55E
88 Hodgson, Canada 51 20N 97 40W
47 Hódmezövásarhely, Hungary 46 28N 20 22E
44 Hoek van Holland, Netherlands 52 0N 4 10E
46 Hof, Germany 50 20N 11 54E
48 Hof, Iceland 64 32N 14 35W
66 Hofei, China 31 50N 117 0E
76 Hofmeyr, S. Africa 31 35S 25 45E
48 Hofs Jökull, mt., Iceland 64 45N 19 0W
48 Hofsos, Iceland 65 52N 19 19W
67 Hofu, Japan 34 0N 131 30E
62 Hofuf, Saudi Arabia 25 20N 49 40E
72 Hoggar, mts., Algeria 23 0N 6 30E
23 Hog's Back, England 51 13N 0 40W
27 Hogsthorpe, England 53 13N 0 19E
66 Hohsien, China 24 35N 111 20E
66 Hoihow (Haikow), China 20 0N 110 10E
74 Hoima, Uganda 1 25N 31 25E
67 Hokang, China 47 25N 130 35E
84 Hokitika, New Zealand 42 44S 171 2E
67 Hokkaido, I., & Pref., Japan 43 30N 143 0E
66 Hokow, China 22 55N 103 10E
23 Holbeach & Marsh, Eng. 52 48N 0 1E
83 Holbrook, Australia 35 42S 147 15E
27 Holderness, Dist., Eng. 53 48N 0 5W
90 Holdrege, U.S.A. 40 30N 99 21W
95 Holguin, Cuba 20 50N 76 20W
75 Hollams Bird I., S.W. Afr. 24 35S 14 30E
23 Holland Dist., England 52 50N 0 3W
44 Holland, N., Prov., Neth. 52 29N 4 47E
44 Holland, S., Prov., Neth. 52 5N 4 30E
82 Hollandia, *see* Djajapura
36 Hollymount, Ireland 53 39N 9 7W
35 Hollywood, Ireland 53 6N 6 36W
90 Hollywood, U.S.A. 34 10N 118 28W
48 Holmavik, Iceland 65 42N 21 43W
27 Holmfirth, England 53 34N 1 47W
48 Holmsund, Sweden 63 42N 20 20E
63 Holon, Israel 32 2N 34 47E
89 Hólsteinsborg, Greenland 67 0N 53 20W
24 Holsworthy, England 50 48N 4 21W
23 Holt, England 52 55N 1 6E
25 Holt, Wales 53 5N 2 54W
27 Holy I., England 55 41N 1 47W
30 Holy I., Scotland 55 31N 5 4W
25 Holy I., Wales 53 18N 4 38W
25 Holyhead, & B., Wales 53 20N 4 39W
92 Holyoke, U.S.A. 42 12N 72 40W
25 Holywell, Wales 53 17N 3 15W
36 Holywood, N. Ireland 54 39N 5 50W
65 Homalin, Burma 25 0N 94 55E
72 Hombori, Mali 15 20N 1 38W
45 Homburg, Germany 49 18N 7 18E
89 Home, B., Canada 68 40N 67 0W
82 Home Hill, Australia 19 40S 147 20E
88 Homer, Alaska 59 40N 151 35W
82 Homestead, Australia 20 20S 145 40E
62 Homs, Syria 34 55N 36 43E
76 Hondeklipbaai, S. Africa 30 22S 17 18E
94 Honduras, & G. of, Central America 15 0N 86 30W
49 Hönefoss, Norway 60 10N 10 10E
43 Honfleur, France 49 24N 0 12E
66 Hong Kong, China 22 20N 114 10E
24 Honiton, England 50 48N 3 12W
67 Honjo, Japan 39 28N 140 0E
90 Honolulu, Pac. Oc. 21 20N 158 0W
67 Honshu, I., Japan 36 0N 139 0E
90 Hood, Mt., U.S.A. 45 20N 121 0W
44 Hoogeveen, Netherlands 52 45N 6 30E
44 Hoogezand, Netherlands 53 11N 6 45E
82 Hook I., Australia 20 4S 149 0E
44 Hoorn, Netherlands 52 40N 5 4E
91 Hope, U.S.A. 33 43N 93 38W
100 Hope Bay, Antarctica 60 0S 57 0W
89 Hopedale, Canada 55 27N 60 22W
76 Hopefield, S. Africa 33 0S 18 22E
83 Hopetoun, Australia 35 48S 142 26E
80 Hopetoun, Australia 33 52S 120 0E
76 Hopetown, S. Africa 29 42S 24 10E
92 Hopkinsville, U.S.A. 36 55N 87 29W
90 Hoquiam, U.S.A. 47 0N 123 58W
62 Hor al Hammar, Iraq 30 50N 46 0E
49 Hordaland, Co., Norway 60 8N 6 20E
31 Horden, England 54 46N 1 18W
45 Horgen, Switzerland 47 16N 8 35E
23 Horley, England 51 11N 0 11W
46 Horn, Austria 48 40N 15 40E
48 Horn (North C.), Ice. 66 29N 22 27W
99 Horn, C., Chile 55 47S 67 0W
36 Horn Hd., Ireland 55 13N 7 57W
48 Horna, Fjord, Iceland 64 17N 15 10E
48 Hornavan, L., Seden 66 30N 18 0E
27 Horncastle, England 53 12N 0 8W
23 Horndean, England 50 55N 1 0W
92 Hornell, U.S.A. 42 20N 77 44W
83 Hornsby, Australia 33 36S 151 2E
27 Hornsea, England 53 54N 0 9W
35 Horseleap, Ireland 53 24N 7 34W
49 Horsens, Denmark 55 53N 9 45E
27 Horsforth, England 53 51N 1 38W
23 Horsham, England 51 3N 0 20W
83 Horsham, Australia 36 42S 142 13E
23 Horsham St. Faith, England 52 41N 1 15E
49 Hörten, Norway 59 25N 10 27E
26 Horton-in-Ribblesdale, England 54 10N 2 19W
88 Horton, R., Canada 69 0N 124 0W
26 Horwich, England 53 36N 2 33W
64 Hoshangabad, India 22 50N 77 58E
64 Hoshiarpur, India 31 45N 75 58E
64 Hospet, India 15 10N 76 15E
34 Hospital, Ireland 52 28N 8 28W
37 Hospitalet, Spain 41 22N 2 4E
99 Hoste, I., Argentina 55 30S 70 0W
91 Hot Springs, U.S.A. 34 25N 93 2W
49 Hoting, Sweden 64 4N 16 20E
44 Houffalize, Belgium 50 8N 5 48E
27 Houghton-le-Spring, Eng. 54 51N 1 28W
84 Houhora, New Zealand 34 49S 173 9E
93 Houlton, U.S.A. 46 15N 68 0W
91 Houma, U.S.A. 29 41N 90 43W
32 Hourn, L., Scotland 57 7N 5 35W
23 Hounslow, England 51 28N 0 23W
91 Houston, U.S.A. 29 45N 95 27W
76 Houtbaai, S. Africa 34 3S 18 27E
76 Houtkraal, S. Africa 30 30S 24 0E
66 Hovd, (Jargalant), Mongolia 48 0N 91 30E
23 Hove, England 50 49N 0 10W
83 Howard, Australia 25 18S 152 35E
27 Howden, England 53 46N 0 52W
83 Howe, C., Australia 37 30S 149 58E
33 Howe of the Mearns, Scotland 56 50N 2 30W
76 Howick, S. Africa 29 30S 30 12E
82 Howick Group, Australia 14 20S 145 30E
65 Howrah, India 22 40N 88 15E
35 Howth, & Hd., Ireland 53 23N 6 3W
33 Hoy, I. & Sd., Scotland 58 50N 3 19W
49 Höyanger, Norway 61 25N 6 5E
26 Hoylake, England 53 23N 3 12W
46 Hradec Králové, Cz-slov. 50 8N 15 52E
48 Hruta Fjord, Iceland 65 30N 21 7W
65 Hsenwi, Burma 23 15N 98 0E
55 Hsiao Khingan Shan, Mts., China 50 0N 128 0E
55 Hsi-liao, R., China 43 0N 122 0E
66 Hsuchang, China 34 0N 115 10E
67 Hualien, Taiwan 23 55N 121 30E
98 Huallaga, R., Peru 8 30S 76 10W
98 Huancavelica, Peru 12 50S 75 0W
98 Huascaran, Mt., Peru 8 45S 77 30W
99 Huasco, Chile 28 20S 71 15W
94 Huatabampo, Mexico 26 50N 109 40W
64 Hubli, India 15 20N 75 2E
67 Huchow, China 30 46N 120 10E
27 Hucknall, England 53 3N 1 12W
27 Huddersfield, England 53 38N 1 47W
49 Hudiksvall, Sweden 61 47N 17 5E
93 Hudson, & R., U.S.A. 42 0N 74 0W
89 Hudson B., Canada 59 0N 86 0W
89 Hudson Str., Canada 62 0N 70 0W
68 Hué, Vietnam 16 33N 107 40E
37 Huelva, Spain 37 16N 6 59W
37 Huesca, Spain 42 9N 0 25W
82 Hughenden, Australia 20 58S 144 5E
66 Huhehot, China 40 50N 111 20E
98 Huila, Mt., Colombia 3 0N 76 5W
94 Huixtla, Mexico 15 15N 92 45W
65 Hukawng, Valley, Burma 26 30N 96 0E
63 Hula, L., Israel 33 4N 35 38E
89 Hull, Canada 45 30N 75 48W
27 Hull, & R., England 53 45N 0 20W
44 Hulst, Netherlands 51 17N 4 4E
67 Hulun, China, *see* Hailar
27 Humber, R., England 53 35N 0 20W
88 Humboldt, Canada 52 25N 105 12W
90 Humboldt, R., U.S.A. 41 0N 117 30W
83 Hume L., Australia 36 5S 147 30E
48 Huna Floi, Iceland 65 45N 20 50W
66 Hunan, Prov., China 27 0N 111 30E
67 Hunchun, China 43 0N 130 12E
47 Hunedoara, Rumania 45 44N 22 53E
47 Hungary, Europe 47 12N 19 10E
22 Hungerford, England 51 25N 1 30W
66 Hungkiang, China 27 5N 109 20E
67 Hungnam, Korea 39 55N 127 45E
66 Hungshui, R., China 23 50N 108 0E
67 Hungtze Hu., L., China 33 20N 118 30E
27 Hunmanby, England 54 11N 0 19W
46 Hunsrück, Mts., Germany 50 0N 7 20E
27 Hunstanton, England 52 57N 0 29E
83 Hunter I., Australia 40 30S 144 46E
30 Hunterston, Scotland 55 45N 4 55W
84 Hunterville, N.Z. 39 56S 175 31E
**23 Huntingdon & Peterborough, Co., England 52 20N 0 11W
23 Huntingdon, England 52 20N 0 12W
92 Huntington, Ind., U.S.A. 40 55N 85 28W
91 Huntington, W. Va., U.S.A. 38 21N 82 32W
84 Huntly, New Zealand 37 30S 175 8E
33 Huntly, Scotland 57 27N 2 47W
92 Huntsville, Canada 45 23N 79 13W
91 Huntsville, Alabama, U.S.A. 34 44N 86 17W
91 Huntsville, Texas, U.S.A. 30 44N 95 35W
83 Huonville, Australia 43 2S 147 0E
66 Hupei, prov., China 31 30N 113 0E
62 Hurghada, Egypt 27 15N 33 50E
30 Hurlford, Scotland 55 35N 4 29W
82 Huron, L., N. America 45 0N 82 30W
90 Huron, U.S.A. 44 25N 98 18W
23 Hurstpierpoint, England 50 56N 0 11W
48 Husavik, Iceland 66 3N 17 15W
49 Huskvarna, Sweden 57 50N 14 19E
63 Hussien Bridge, Jordan 31 43N 35 32E
90 Hutchinson, U.S.A. 38 0N 98 0W
45 Huttwil, Switzerland 47 7N 7 50E
44 Huy, Belgium 50 30N 5 16E
26 Huyton, England 53 25N 2 52W
48 Hvammr, Iceland 65 10N 21 50W
48 Hvammsfjord, Iceland 65 5N 22 30W
40 Hvar, I., Yugoslavia 43 10N 16 42E
48 Hvitá, R., Iceland 64 40N 21 30W
48 Hvitarvatn, L., Iceland 64 35N 19 50W
66 Hwai-ho, R., China 33 0N 116 0E
66 Hwainan, China 32 40N 117 30E
66 Hwaiyang, mts.. China 31 30N 115 0E
66 Hwang-ho, R., China 39 0N 107 0E
66 Hwang (Ma) R., China 34 0N 100 30E
66 Hwangshih, China 30 15N 115 0E
66 Hweitseh, China 26 50N 103 0E
66 Hyargas Nuur, Mongolia 49 0N 93 30E
26 Hyde, England 53 27N 2 5W
64 Hyderabad, India 17 25N 78 35E
64 Hyderabad, Pak. 25 20N 68 30E
43 Hyères, & Is., France 43 8N 6 6E
90 Hyndman, Pk., U.S.A. 44 0N 114 0W
67 Hyogo, Pref., Japan 35 0N 135 0E
23 Hythe, Kent, England 51 4N 1 4E
49 Hyvinkaa, Finland 60 38N 25 0E

I

34 Iar Connaught, Dist., Ire. 53 18N 9 20W
47 Iasi, Rumania 47 10N 27 37E
72 Ibadan, Nigeria 7 40N 3 50E
95 Ibagué, Colombia 4 30N 75 25W
67 Ibaraki, Pref., Japan 36 20N 140 20E
98 Ibarra, Ecuador 0 23N 78 15W
72 Ibi, Nigeria 8 7N 9 56E
98 Ibiapaba, Sa. da, mts., Brazil 4 0S 41 10W
99 Ibicuy, Argentina 33 40S 59 10W
37 Ibiza, I. & Tn., Spain 39 0N 1 30E
22 Ibstock, England 52 42N 1 23W
98 Icá, R., Brazil 3 0S 69 0W
98 Ica, Peru 14 5S 75 30W
16 Iceland, Atlantic Oc. 65 0N 17 30W
61 Icha, U.S.S.R. 55 45N 154 4E
66 Ichang, China 30 59N 111 23E
65 Ichchapuram, India 19 5N 84 40E
67 Ichinohe, Japan 40 8N 141 18E
41 Ida, Mt., Turkey 39 40N 27 15E
90 Idaho, st., U.S.A. 44 0N 115 50W

** *Incorporated within the county of Cambridge*

90 Idaho Falls, U.S.A. 43 30N 112 2W
45 Idar-Oberstein, Germany 49 43N 7 17E
73 Idd el Ghanam, Sudan 11 30N 24 25E
73 Idehan, Erg, Des., Libya 27 30N 12 0E
73 Idehan Marzuq, Dunes, Libya 24 50N 13 51E
72 Idelès, Algeria 23 58N 5 58E
73 Idfu, Egypt 24 57N 32 58E
41 Idhi, Mt., Crete 35 15N 24 50E
41 Idhra, I., Greece 37 20N 23 25E
74 Idiofa, Zaïre 5 0S 19 45E
27 Idle, R., England 53 28N 0 58W
22 Idmiston, England 51 8N 1 43W
23 Idsworth, England 50 56N 0 56W
41 Ierapetra, Crete 35 5N 25 40E
40 Ierzu, Italy 39 42N 9 35E
75 Ifanadiana, Madagascar 21 19S 47 50E
72 Ife, Nigeria 7 30N 4 31E
72 Iferouane, Niger 19 6N 8 30E
72 Ifni, Morocco 29 15N 10 0W
61 Igarka, U.S.S.R. 67 25N 87 20E
72 Igbetti, Nigeria 8 44N 4 8E
49 Iggesund, Sweden 61 43N 17 6E
40 Iglesias, Sardinia, Italy 39 21N 8 33E
92 Ignace, Canada 49 30N 91 40W
94 Iguala, Mexico 18 30N 99 15W
99 Iguape, Brazil 24 50S 47 45W
99 Iguassu, R. & Falls, Brazil 25 30S 54 30W
99 Iguatú, Brazil 6 8S 39 15W
74 Iguéla, Gabon 2 5S 9 16E
48 Ii, & R., Finland 65 15N 25 30E
48 Iisalmi, Finland 63 35N 27 12E
72 Ijebu Ode, Nigeria 7 0N 3 58E
44 Ijmuiden, Netherlands 52 28N 4 35E
44 Ijsselmeer, Netherlands 52 45N 5 15E
41 Ikaria, I., Greece 37 35N 26 10E
67 Ikeda, Japan 34 0N 133 56E
67 Ilagan, Philippines 17 0N 121 58E
99 Ilapel, Chile 31 30S 71 0W
47 Ilawa, Poland 53 40N 19 31W
43 Ile de France, Prov., Fr. 49 0N 2 30E
43 Ile Rousse. France 42 35N 8 50E
74 Ilebo (Port Francqui), Zaïre 4 17S 20 47E
50 Ilek, R., U.S.S.R. 51 0N 55 15E
24 Ilfracombe, England 51 11N 4 7W
82 Ilfracombe, Australia 23 30S 144 28E
99 Ilhéus, Brazil 14 44S 39 18W
66 Ili, R., Sinkiang, China 43 20N 81 0E
60 Ili, & R., U.S.S.R. 44 10N 77 25E
60 Ilich, U.S.S.R. 41 0N 68 20E
41 Iliodhromia I., Greece 39 10N 23 45E
72 Ilizi, Algeria 26 32N 8 33E
27 Ilkeston, England 52 59N 1 18W
26 Ilkley, England 53 55N 1 50W
42 Ille-et-Vilaine, Dépt., Fr. 48 22N 1 55W
45 Iller, R., Germany 47 48N 10 7E
98 Illimani, Mt., Bolivia 16 20S 67 40W
92 Illinois, st., & R., U.S.A. 40 15N 90 0W
50 Ilmen, L., U.S.S.R. 58 20N 31 28E
24 Ilminster, England 50 55N 2 56W
68 Iloilo, Philippines 10 40N 122 38E
72 Ilorin, Nigeria 8 30N 4 23E
51 Iman, U.S.S.R. 45 50N 133 50E
50 Imandra, L., U.S.S.R. 67 40N 33 0E
67 Imabari, Japan 34 0N 133 0E
45 Immenstadt, Germany 47 33N 10 14E
27 Immingham, England 53 39N 0 13W
40 Imola, Italy 44 20N 11 40E
74 Impfondo, Congo (Fr.) 1 35N 18 10E
65 Imphal, India 24 15N 94 0E
41 Imroz, I., Turkey 40 10N 26 0E
72 In Belbel, Algeria 27 55N 1 12E
72 In Gall, Niger 16 58N 6 57E
72 In Salah, *see* Ain Salah
67 Ina, Japan 35 56N 138 0E
84 Inangahua Junction, New Zealand 41 50S 171 52E
48 Inari, L., Finland 69 0N 28 0E
26 Ince, England 53 32N 2 38W
51 Ince, C., Turkey 42 2N 35 0E
31 Inchcape Rock, Scotland 56 26N 2 24W
67 Inchinomiya, Japan 35 20N 136 40E
67 Inchon, Korea 37 30N 126 30E
31 Inchture, Scotland 56 26N 3 8W
75 Incomati, R., Mozam. 25 13S 32 26E
30 Indaal, L., Scotland 55 44N 6 20W
48 Indals, R., Sweden 62 40N 16 50E
65 Indaw, Burma 24 10N 96 10E
88 Indian Head, Canada 50 32N 103 35W
5 Indian Ocean 10 0S 70 0E
91 Indian River, & Inlet, U.S.A. 28 0N 80 30W
64–65 India, Asia 22 0N 78 0E
91 Indiana, st., U.S.A. 40 0N 86 0W
91 Indianapolis, U.S.A. 39 48N 86 15W
61 Indigirka, R., U.S.S.R. 69 10N 147 20E
68 Indonesia, S.E. Asia 0 0 110 0E
64 Indore, India 22 42N 75 52E
65 Indravati, R., India 19 12N 81 30E
42 Indre, Dépt., France 47 2N 1 33E
42 Indre-et-Loire, Dépt., Fr. 47 12N 0 43E
64 Indus, R. & Delta, Pak. 24 30N 65 30E
76 Indwe, S. Africa 31 28S 27 24E
51 Inebolu, Turkey 41 58N 33 58E
74 Ingende, Zaïre 0 12S 18 57E
82 Ingham, Australia 18 22S 146 0E
26 Ingleborough, Mt. Eng. 54 10N 2 35W
83 Inglewood, Australia 28 30S 151 2E
84 Inglewood, New Zealand 39 8S 174 14E
48 Ingolfshodi, Iceland 63 50N 16 45W
46 Ingolstadt, Germany 48 47N 11 20E
93 Ingonish, Canada 46 42N 60 25W
75 Inhambane, Mozambique 24 0S 35 45E.

75 Inhamingo, Mozambique 18 25S 35 0E
75 Inharrime, Mozambique 24 25N 35 1E
36 Inishfree, Bay, Ireland 55 4N 8 20W
35 Inishkea, Is., Ireland 54 7N 10 13W
34 Inishmaan, I., Ireland 53 5N 9 35W
34 Inishmore I., Ireland 53 8N 9 45W
35 Inishturk I., Ireland 53 43N 10 8W
35 Inistioge, Ireland 52 30N 7 5W
83 Injune, Australia 25 48S 148 30E
65 Inle Lake, Burma 20 30N 96 55E
46 Inn, R., Austria-Ger. 47 16N 11 0E
30 Innellan, Scotland 55 54N 4 58W
32 Inner Hebrides, Scotland 56 40N 6 50W
66 Inner Mongolia, Autonomous Reg., China 42 0N 111 0E
32 Inner Sd., Scotland 57 30N 5 55W
31 Innerleithen, Scotland 55 37N 3 6W
45 Innertkirchen, Switzerland 46 43N 8 16E
35 Inniscrone, Ireland 54 13N 9 5W
88 Innisfail, Canada 52 0N 114 0W
82 Innisfail, Australia 17 32S 146 5E
34 Innishannon, Ireland 51 46N 8 40W
45 Innsbruck, Austria 47 12N 11 20E
74 Inongo, Zaïre 1 50S 18 22E
47 Inowroclaw, Poland 52 56N 18 20E
33 Insch, Scotland 57 20N 2 39W
65 Insein, Burma 16 45N 95 30E
45 Interlaken, Switzerland 46 42N 7 53E
88 Inuvik, Canada 68 2N 135 30W
36 Inver, & B., Ireland 54 40N 8 16W
33 Inverallochy, Scotland 57 40N 1 56W
30 Inveraray, Scotland 56 14N 5 4W
33 Inverbervie, Scotland 56 50N 2 17W
84 Invercargill, N.Z. 46 28S 168 28E
83 Inverell, Australia 29 50S 151 0E
33 Invergordon, Scotland 57 42N 4 10W
31 Invergowrie, Scotland 56 29N 3 5W
31 Inverkeilor, Scotland 56 38N 2 33W
31 Inverkeithing, Scotland 56 2N 3 24W
93 Inverness, Canada 46 20N 60 15W
*33 Inverness, & Co., Scot. 57 28N 4 12W
32 Invershiel, Scotland 57 13N 5 25W
33 Inverurie, Scotland 57 17N 2 22W
80 Investigator Group, Australia 33 42S 134 25E
83 Investigator Str., Austral. 35 30S 137 0E
60 Inya, U.S.S.R. 50 40N 86 55E
75 Inyanga, Rhodesia 18 12S 32 40E
41 Ioannina, Greece 39 40N 20 52E
30 Iona I., Scotland 56 20N 6 30W
41 Ionian Is. & S., Greece 38 40N 20 0E
41 Ios I., Greece 36 42N 25 20E
91 Iowa, st., U.S.A. 42 15N 93 30W
91 Iowa City, U.S.A. 41 45N 91 40W
66 Ipin, China 29 15N 104 0E
68 Ipoh, Malaya 4 32N 101 0E
74 Ippy, Central Africa 6 5N 21 7E
23 Ipswich, England 52 4N 1 10E
83 Ipswich, Australia 27 38S 152 45E
98 Iquique, Chile 20 20S 70 5W
98 Iquitos, Peru 3 48S 73 12W
41 Iraklion, (Candia), Crete 35 20N 25 10E
62 Iran (Persia), Asia 33 50N 54 0E
94 Irapuato, Mexico 20 50N 101 28W
62 Iraq, S.W. Asia 33 30N 45 0E
95 Irazu, Vol., Costa Rica 10 0N 83 43W
63 Irbid, Jordan 32 34N 35 50E
95 Ireland I., Bermudas 32 21N 64 52W
29 Ireland, Europe 53 0N 8 0W
29 Ireland, N., British Isles 54 40N 6 50W
61 Iret, U.S.S.R. 60 5N 154 5E
74 Iringa, Tanzania 7 50S 35 30E
94 Iriona, Honduras 16 0N 84 58W
18 Irish Sea, British Isles 53 50N 5 0W
61 Irkineyeva, U.S.S.R. 58 30N 97 0E
61 Irkutsk, U.S.S.R. 52 20N 104 0E
26 Irlam, England 53 26N 2 27W
83 Iron Baron, Australia 33 0S 137 0E
47 Iron Gate, Rum.-Y-slav. 44 43N 22 25E
83 Iron Knob, Australia 32 41S 137 0E
91 Iron Mt., U.S.A. 45 54N 88 0W
22 Ironbridge, England 52 38N 2 27W
65 Irrawaddy, R. & Delta, Burma 16 0N 95 0E
26 Irthing, R., England 55 0N 2 37W
23 Irthlingborough, England 52 20N 0 37W
60 Irtysh, R., U.S.S.R. 59 0N 69 30E
37 Irun, Spain 43 20N 1 50W
30 Irvine, Scotland 55 37N 4 39W
36 Irvinestown, N. Ireland 54 28N 7 40W
83 Irymple, Australia 34 4S 142 1E
48 Isa Fjord, Iceland 66 10N 23 0W
48 Isafjördur, Iceland 66 10N 23 15W
74 Isangi, Zaïre 0 50N 24 10E
46 Isar, R., Germany 48 40N 12 30E
40 Ischia I., Italy 40 46N 13 54E
43 Iseo, Italy 45 39N 10 2E
42 Isère, Dépt., France 45 25N 5 40E
60 Ishim, & R., U.S.S.R. 56 15N 69 30E
67 Ishinomaki, Japan 38 26N 141 18E
64 Ishkuman, Kashmir 36 40N 73 45E
91 Ishpeming, U.S.A. 46 30N 87 40W
74 Isiolo, Kenya 0 19N 37 39E
76 Isipingo Beach, S. Africa 30 0S 30 55E
74 Isiro (Paulis), Zaïre 2 53N 27 58E
61 Isitskoye, U.S.S.R. 60 55N 125 0E
51 Iskenderun, & G., Turkey 36 48N 36 17E
39 Iskur R., Bulgaria 43 0N 24 0E
64 Islamabad, Pakistan 33 40N 73 20E
36 Island Magee, Pen., N. Ire. 54 50N 5 45W
30 Islay, I. & Sd., Scotland 55 45N 6 15W
27 Isle of Axholme, England 53 33N 0 50W
23 Isle of Ely, dist., England 52 30N 0 0
26 Isle of Man, Br. Isles 54 10N 4 35W
95 Isle of Pines, Cuba 21 45N 82 50W
22 Isle of Purbeck, England 50 38N 2 0W
30 Isle of Whithorn, Scot. 54 42N 4 23W
22 Isle of Wight, England 50 40N 1 20W
92 Isle Royale, U.S.A. 48 0N 88 40W
73 Isma'iliya, Egypt 31 0N 32 0E
73 Isna, Egypt 25 12N 32 30E
51 Isnik Gölü, L., Turkey 40 30N 30 0E
74 Isoka, Zambia 10 10S 32 42E
62 Isparta, Turkey 37 30N 31 5E
63 Israel, S.W. Asia 32 0N 35 0E
43 Issoudun, France 47 0N 2 0E
60 Issyk Kul, L., U.S.S.R. 42 50N 77 30E
51 Istanbul, Turkey 41 1N 28 56E
40 Istra, Dist., Y-slav. 45 18N 13 50E
99 Itabira, Brazil 19 30S 43 10W
99 Itacoatiara, Brazil 3 0S 58 20W
40 Italy, Europe 42 0N 13 0E
22 Itchen, R., England 51 0N 1 20W
92 Ithaca, U.S.A. 42 28N 76 28W
41 Ithaki, Greece 38 25N 20 43E
67 Iturup I., U.S.S.R. 45 0N 148 0E
99 Ivai, R., Brazil 23 30S 53 20W
48 Ivalo, & R., Finland 68 38 27 35E
83 Ivanhoe, Australia 32 55S 144 20E
52 Ivanovo, U.S.S.R. 57 5N 41 0E
89 Ivigtut, Greenland 62 0N 47 30W
37 Iviza, & I., *see* Ibiza
72 Ivory Coast, Africa 7 0N 5 0W
43 Ivrea, Italy 45 30N 7 50E
43 Ivry, France 48 55N 1 30E
67 Iwakuni, Japan 34 10N 132 10E
67 Iwanuma, Japan 38 7N 140 58E
67 Iwate, Pref., Japan 39 30N 140 20E
76 Ixopo, S. Africa 30 10S 30 5E
44 Izegem, Belgium 50 55N 3 13E
50 Izhevsk, U.S.S.R. 56 50N 53 0E
47 Izmail, U.S.S.R. 45 21N 28 40E
41 Izmir, & G., Turkey 38 21N 27 8E
51 Izmit, Turkey 40 45N 29 50E
63 Izr'a, Syria 32 52N 36 15E
67 Izumo, Japan 35 25N 133 0E

J

62 Jabal At Tuwaiq, mts., Saudi Arabia 22 30N 46 0E
62 Jabal Shammar, Mts., Saudi Arabia 27 30N 42 30E
64 Jabalpur, India 23 10N 80 0E
41 Jablanica, Mt., Albania 41 20N 20 30E
46 Jablonec, Cz-slov. 50 43N 15 10E
62 Jabrin, Saudi Arabia 23 10N 48 32E
37 Jaca, Spain 42 35N 0 32W
99 Jachal, Argentina 30 5S 69 10W
83 Jackson, Australia 26 40S 149 35E
84 Jackson B., N.Z. 43 58S 168 40E
92 Jackson, Mich., U.S.A. 42 15N 84 29W
91 Jackson, Miss., U.S.A. 32 20N 90 13W
91 Jackson, Tenn., U.S.A. 35 36N 88 45W
84 Jacksons, New Zealand 42 46S 171 33E
91 Jacksonville Fla., U.S.A. 30 28N 81 40W
91 Jacksonville, Ill., U.S.A. 39 44N 90 16W
95 Jacmel, Haiti 18 15N 72 35W
64 Jacobabad, Pakistan 28 20N 68 27E
63 Jacob's Well, Jordan 32 12N 35 17E
99 Jacui, R., Brazil 30 0S 52 0W
73 Jado, Libya 32 0N 12 0E
74 Jadotville, *see* Likasi
37 Jaén, Spain 37 48N 3 43W
63 Jaffa, *see* Tel Aviv-Jaffa
64 Jaffna, Sri Lanka 9 45N 80 0E
64 Jagdalpur, India 19 1N 82 7E
76 Jagersfontein, S. Africa 29 40S 25 28E
73 Jaghbub, Libya 29 42N 24 38E
64 Jagraon, India 30 40N 75 40E
62 Jahrum, Iran 28 27N 53 30E
64 Jaipur, India 27 0N 75 50E
72 Jajere, Nigeria 11 58N 10 25E
94 Jalapa Enriquez, Mexico 19 32N 96 55W
64 Jalgaon, India 20 57N 76 30E
64 Jalna, India 19 45N 75 50E
37 Jalon, R., Spain 41 26N 1 35W
65 Jalpaiguri, India 26 15N 88 0E
95 Jamaica, I., West Indies 18 15N 77 30W
65 Jamalpur, India 25 20N 86 30E
89 James, B., Canada 53 30N 81 0W
90 James, R., S. Dak., U.S.A. 43 40N 97 40W
80 James Ra., Australia 24 10S 132 40E
83 Jamestown, Australia 33 11S 138 30E
90 Jamestown, North Dakota, U.S.A. 46 58N 98 38W
92 Jamestown, N.Y., U.S.A. 42 8N 79 17W
64 Jamkhandi, India 16 30N 75 5E
64 Jammu, India 32 50N 74 58E
64 Jammu and Kashmir, Asia 34 0N 77 0E
64 Jamnagar, India 22 32N 70 5E
65 Jamshedpur, India 22 50N 86 10E
48 Jämtland, Co., Sweden 62 45N 14 30E
100 Jan Mayen I., Arctic Oc. 71 0N 8 0W
64 Jand, Pakistan 33 30N 71 57E
83 Jandowae, Australia 26 40S 151 2E
92 Janesville, U.S.A. 42 48N 88 59W
63 Janin, Jordan 32 28N 35 18E
99 Januaria, Brazil 15 30S 44 30W
64 Jaora, India 23 42N 75 5E
67 Japan, E. Asia 36 0N 138 0E
67 Japan Sea, E. Asia 40 0N 134 30E
37 Jarama, R., Spain 40 50N 3 30W
63 Jarash, Jordan 32 17N 35 54E
62 Jarir, Wadi, Si. Arabia 24 10N 42 0E
47 Jaroslaw, Poland 50 0N 22 40E
27 Jarrow, England 54 59N 1 30W
65 Jarwa, India 27 52N 82 36E
63 Jask, Iran 25 52N 57 50E
47 Jaslo, Poland 49 45N 21 30E
47 Jaszbereny, Hungary 47 37N 19 58E
37 Jativa, Spain 39 1N 0 32W
98 Jauja, Peru 11 45S 75 25W
65 Jaunpur, India 25 42N 82 55E
68 Java I., Indonesia 7 0S 110 0E
68 Java Sea, Indonesia 5 0S 111 30E
65 Jaynagar, India 26 43N 86 9E
62 Jeb Aneiza, Mt., Iraq 32 10N 39 20E
73 Jebel Abyad, Plat. of, Sudan 17 30N 28 40E
63 Jebel 'Ajlun, mts., Jordan 32 20N 35 50E
63 Jebel el Leja, Syria 33 17N 36 5E
62 Jebel Ibrahim, mt., Si. Arabia 20 26N 41 15E
63 Jebel Sanmini, mt., Lebanon 33 56N 35 55E
31 Jedburgh, Scotland 55 29N 2 32W
47 Jedrzejów, Poland 50 35N 20 15E
91 Jefferson City, U.S.A. 38 40N 92 18W
91 Jeffersonville, U.S.A. 38 22N 85 49W
72 Jega, Nigeria 12 15N 4 23E
46 Jelenia Góra, Poland 50 50N 15 45E
49 Jelgava, U.S.S.R. 56 39N 23 45E
44 Jemeppe, Belgium 50 37N 5 29E
46 Jena, Germany 51 0N 11 30E
61 Jennette I., U.S.S.R. 77 25N 157 20E
91 Jennings, U.S.A. 30 15N 92 45W
83 Jeparit, Australia, 36 10S 142 5E
37 Jerez, Spain 36 42N 6 10W
82 Jericho, Australia 23 38S 146 6E
63 Jericho, Jordan 31 51N 35 28E
83 Jerilderie, Australia 35 20S 145 40E
93 Jersey City, U.S.A. 40 50N 74 10W
42 Jersey I., Channel Is. 49 17N 2 10W
63 Jerusalem, Israel 31 47N 35 13E
68 Jesselton, *see* Kota Kinabalu
65 Jessore, Bangladesh 23 12N 89 10E
44 Jette, Belgium 50 52N 4 18E
65 Jeypore, India 18 45N 82 32E
63 Jezziné, Lebanon 33 33N 35 34E
64 Jhal Jhao, Pakistan 26 20N 65 30E
64 Jhalawar, India 24 35N 76 10E
64 Jhang Maghiana, Pak. 31 8N 72 15E
64 Jhansi, India 25 40N 78 49E
65 Jharsuguda, India 21 50N 84 5E
64 Jhelum, & R., Pak. 32 58N 73 45E
65 Jiachan, Tibet, China 31 40N 81 5E
62 Jidda, Saudi Arabia 21 30N 39 0E
46 Jihlava, & R., Cz-slov. 49 21N 15 38E
94 Jimenez, Mexico 27 10N 104 55W
73 Jima, Ethiopia 7 50N 37 0E
83 Jindabyne, Australia 36 30S 148 35E
74 Jinja, Uganda 0 30N 33 15E
47 Jiu, R., Rumania 44 50N 23 50E
99 Joao Pessöa, Brazil 7 12S 35 0W
42 Jobourg, France 49 49N 1 54W
64 Jodhpur, India 26 10N 73 0E
50 Joensuu, Finland 62 40N 29 49E
43 Joeuf, France 49 12N 6 0E
68 Jogjakarta, Indonesia 7 50S 110 24E
76 Johannesburg, S. Africa 26 15S 28 4E
33 John o'Groats, Scotland 58 38N 3 5W
91 Johnston City, U.S.A. 36 29N 82 20W
74 Johnston Falls, Zambia 10 45S 28 45E
30 Johnstone, Scotland 55 50N 4 30W
35 Johnstown, Ireland 52 46N 7 34W
92 Johnstown, U.S.A. 40 20N 78 52W
68 Johor Baharu, Malaya 1 35N 103 40E
43 Joigny, France 48 0N 3 25E
48 Jokkmokk, Sweden 66 32N 19 56E
92 Joilet, U.S.A. 41 36N 88 0W
89 Joliette, Canada 46 1N 73 40W
68 Jolo I., Philippines 6 3N 121 3E
91 Jonesboro, U.S.A. 35 50N 90 45W
49 Jönköping, Sweden 57 48N 14 12E
89 Jonquière, Canada 48 27N 71 10W
91 Joplin, U.S.A. 36 58N 94 30W
63 Jordan, R., Jordan-Israel 32 15N 35 32E
62 Jordan, S.W. Asia 32 0N 37 0E
65 Jorhat, India 26 42N 94 15E
48 Jörn, Sweden 65 8N 20 0E
72 Jos, Nigeria 9 53N 8 51E
80 Joseph Bonaparte G., Australia 13 45S 129 0E
49 Jötunheimen, Mts., Nor. 61 35N 8 20E
63 Jouaïya, Lebanon 33 14N 35 20E
63 Joub Jennine, Lebanon 33 38N 35 48E
88 Juan de Fuca Str., North America 48 30N 124 30W
75 Juan de Nova I., Madagascar 17 10S 43 45E
99 Juan Fernandez, I., Pacific Ocean 33 15S 79 0W
99 Juazeiro, Brazil 9 30S 40 30W
73 Juba, Sudan 5 0N 31 35E
70 Juba, R., East Africa 1 45N 42 42E
72 Juby, C., Morocco 27 50N 13 45W
37 Júcar, R., Spain 40 5N 2 10W
94 Juchitan, Mexico 16 30N 95 15W
63 Judaea, Wilderness of, Jordan 31 25N 35 18E
63 Judaean Hills, Jordan 31 45N 35 15E
66 Juikin, China 26 5N 115 25E
99 Juiz de Fora, Brazil 21 35S 43 40W
99 Jujuy, Argentina 24 5S 65 30W
82 Julia Creek, Australia 20 40S 141 55E
46 Julian Alps, Y-slav. 46 15N 13 40E
89 Julianehaab, Greenland 60 40N 45 40W
44 Jülich, Germany 50 56N 6 20E
64 Jullundur, India 31 20N 75 40E
62 Jumaima, Saudi Arabia 29 40N 43 37E
44 Jumet, Belgium 50 28N 4 27E
64 Jumna, R., *see* Yamuna
64 Junagadh, India 21 34N 70 30E
91 Junction City, U.S.A. 39 5N 96 58W
82 Jundah, Australia 24 56S 143 5E
88 Juneau, Alaska 58 13N 134 0W
83 Junee, Australia 34 53S 147 36E
45 Jungfrau, mt., Switz. 46 30N 7 50E
99 Junin, Argentina 34 25S 61 0W
42 Jura, Dépt., France 46 46N 5 40E
30 Jura, I. & Sd., Scotland 55 57N 5 55W
43 Jura Mts., France-Switz. 46 40N 6 5E
80 Jurien Bay, Australia 30 20S 115 0E
98 Juruá, R., Brazil 6 0S 68 0W
43 Jussey, France 47 50N 5 55E
73 J'Uweinat, mt., Egypt 22 40N 25 0E
49 Jylland (Jutland), Den. 56 10N 9 0E
48 Jyvaskyla, Finland 62 12N 25 47E

K

64 K2 Mt., Kashmir 36 0N 77 0E
68 Kabaena, I., Indonesia 5 15S 122 0E
72 Kabala, Sierra Leone 9 38N 11 37W
74 Kabale, Uganda 1 15S 30 0E
74 Kabalo, Zaïre 6 0S 27 0E
74 Kabambare, Zaïre 4 40S 27 44E
51 Kabardino-Balkar, A.S.S.R., U.S.S.R. 43 30N 43 30E
74 Kabinda, Zaïre 6 3S 24 20E
75 Kabompo, R., Zambia 13 30S 24 30E
74 Kabongo, Zaïre 7 18S 25 40E
82 Kabra, Australia 23 25S 150 25E
64 Kabul, & R., Afghanistan 34 30N 69 13E
75 Kabwe, Zambia 13 39S 28 38E
60 Kachiry, U.S.S.R. 53 20N 75 55E
72 Kaddi, Nigeria 13 40N 5 40E
83 Kadina, Australia 33 58S 137 48E
52 Kadiyevka, U.S.S.R. 48 17N 38 17E
73 Kadugli, Sudan 11 0N 29 45E
72 Kaele, Cameroon 10 15N 14 15E
67 Kaesong, Korea 38 0N 126 40E
74 Kafakumba, Zaïre 9 40S 23 40E
51 Kafan, U.S.S.R. 39 10N 46 15E
72 Kafanchan, Nigeria 9 49N 8 20E
63 Kafr Kanna, Israel 32 45N 35 20E
75 Kafue, & R., Zambia 15 45S 28 25E
74 Kafulwe, Zambia 9 0S 29 10E
60 Kagan, U.S.S.R. 39 50N 64 30E
47 Kagul, U.S.S.R. 45 50N 28 15E
67 Kagoshima, & Pref., Japan 31 48N 130 40E
74 Kahama, Tanzania 3 50S 32 25E
83 Kahmoomulga, Austral. 25 58S 145 51E
72 Kaiama, Nigeria 9 36N 4 1E
84 Kaiapoi, New Zealand 43 24S 172 40E
98 Kaieteur Falls Fs., Guyana 5 5N 59 0W
66 Kaifeng, China 34 45N 114 40E
84 Kaikohe, New Zealand 35 25S 173 49E
84 Kaikoura, & Ra., N.Z. 42 23S 173 43E
65 Kailas Ra., Tibet 31 0N 82 0E
84 Kaimanawa Mts., N.Z. 39 0S 176 15E
84 Kaipara Hr., N.Z. 36 22S 174 10E
72 Kairouan, Tunisia 35 48N 10 8E
47 Kaiserslautern, Germany 49 29N 7 46E
84 Kaitaia, New Zealand 35 7S 173 17E
84 Kaitangata, N.Z. 46 18S 170 0E
48 Kajaani, Finland 64 15N 27 45E
82 Kajabbi, Australia 20 0S 140 0E
73 Kajo Kaji, Sudan 3 58N 31 40E
73 Kaka, Sudan 10 38N 32 10E
84 Kakanui, Mts., N.Z. 45 15S 170 35E
51 Kakhovka Res., U.S.S.R. 46 30N 33 50E
64 Kalabagh, Pakistan 33 0N 71 30E
41 Kalábaka, Greece 39 40N 21 35E
75 Kalabo, Zambia 14 58S 22 33E
52 Kalach, U.S.S.R. 50 38N 41 10E
65 Kaladan, R., Burma 21 15N 93 0E
75 Kalahari, des., Africa 23 0S 22 0E
61 Kalakan, U.S.S.R. 55 20N 116 55E
41 Kalamata, Greece 37 2N 22 7E
92 Kalamazoo, U.S.A. 42 15N 85 35W
92 Kalamazoo, R., U.S.A. 42 35N 86 0W
64 Kalat, Pakistan 29 5N 66 32E
63 Kalbuh, Wadi, Oman 22 0N 57 50E
74 Kalemie (Albertville), Zaïre 5 55S 29 9E
65 Kalewa, Burma 23 5N 94 20E
48 Kalfafellsstadur, Iceland 64 11N 15 45W
66 Kalgan, China 40 50N 114 50E
80 Kalgoorlie, Australia 30 40S 121 28E
39 Kaliakra, C., Bulgaria 43 23N 28 26E
74 Kalima, Zaïre 2 38S 26 37E
68 Kalimantan, prov., Indonesia 0 30S 115 0E
52 Kalinin, U.S.S.R. 56 47N 35 55E
61 Kalinina, U.S.S.R. 60 0N 108 10E
49 Kaliningrad, U.S.S.R. 54 42N 20 30E
90 Kalispell, U.S.A. 48 18N 114 27W
47 Kalisz, Poland 51 48N 18 5E
74 Kaliua, Tanzania 5 0S 31 59E
48 Kalix, R., Sweden 67 30N 21 15E
53 Kallia, Jordan 31 46N 35 29E
48 Kallsjön, L., Sweden 63 35N 13 10E
49 Kalmar, & Co., Sweden 56 42N 16 20E
51 Kalmyk, A.S.S.R., U.S.S.R. 46 30N 45 30E
60 Kalmykovo, U.S.S.R. 49 0N 51 50E
47 Kalocsa, Hungary 46 31N 18 58E
75 Kalomo, Zambia 16 54S 26 30E
46 Kalovy Vary, Cz-slov. 50 15N 12 55E
52 Kaluga, U.S.S.R. 54 35N 36 20E
65 Kalutara, Sri Lanka 6 35N 80 0E
52 Kalyazin, U.S.S.R. 57 18N 37 45E
50 Kama, R., U.S.S.R. 60 0N 56 0E
67 Kamaishi, Japan 39 20N 142 0E
62 Kamaran I., Red Sea 15 28N 42 30E
61 Kamchatka, Pen., U.S.S.R. 56 0N 160 0E
60 Kamen, U.S.S.R. 53 50N 81 30E
51 Kamenets-Podolski, U.S.S.R. 48 45N 26 10E
47 Kamenka Bugskaya, Pol. 50 8N 24 16E
60 Kamensk-Uralskiy, U.S.S.R. 56 30N 62 50E
52 Kamensk Shakhtinskiy, U.S.S.R. 48 23N 40 20E
61 Kamenskoye, U.S.S.R. 62 40N 165 0E
30 Kames, Scotland 55 54N 5 15W
74 Kamina, Zaïre 8 40S 25 3E
88 Kamloops, Canada 50 40N 120 20W
44 Kamp Lintfort, Ger. 51 30N 6 38E
74 Kampala, Uganda 0 20N 32 30E
44 Kampen, Netherlands 52 34N 5 54E
68 Kampot, Khmer Rep. 10 30N 104 0E
88 Kamsack, Canada 51 40N 102 0W
52 Kamyshin, U.S.S.R. 50 10N 45 30E
67 Kanagawa, Pref., Japan 35 25N 139 20E
74 Kananga (Luluabourg), Zaïre 5 55S 22 18E
50 Kanash, U.S.S.R. 55 48N 47 32E
67 Kanazawa, Japan 36 40N 136 48E
65 Kanchenjunga, Mt., Nepal 27 45N 88 15E
66 Kanchow, China 25 50N 114 45E
74 Kanda Kanda, Zaïre 6 55S 23 33E
51 Kandagach, U.S.S.R. 49 20N 57 15E
64 Kandahar, Afghanistan 31 42N 65 40E
64 Kandahar, Prov., Afghan 31 0N 65 0E
50 Kandalaksha, U.S.S.R. 67 3N 32 30E
64 Kandalu, Afghanistan 29 55N 63 20E
84 Kandavu I., Fiji Is. 19 0S 178 15E
45 Kandersteg, Switzerland 46 28N 7 40E
72 Kandi, Dahomey 11 15N 3 0E
64 Kandla, India 23 0N 70 7E
83 Kandos, Australia 32 55S 150 0E
64 Kandy, Sri Lanka 7 20N 80 35E
83 Kangaroo I., Australia 35 45S 137 15E
74 Kango, Gabon 0 11N 10 5E
61 Kangotovo, U.S.S.R. 63 30N 87 40E
89 Kaniapiskau, R., Can. 56 20N 68 40W
92 Kankakee, U.S.A. 41 7N 87 50W
72 Kankan, Guinea 10 27N 9 15W
65 Kanker, India 20 10N 81 40E
66 Kan-kiang, R., China 27 0N 115 0E
64 Kannod, India 22 45N 76 40E
72 Kano, Nigeria 11 58N 8 20E
80 Kanowna, Australia 30 30S 121 37E
64 Kanpur, India 26 30N 80 23E
90 Kansas, st., & R., U.S.A. 38 30N 98 30W
91 Kansas City, U.S.A. 39 4N 94 37W
66 Kansen, China 37 45N 92 35E
61 Kansk, U.S.S.R. 56 20N 95 30E
66 Kansu, Prov., China 39 0N 105 0E
66 Kantse, China 31 30N 100 25E
34 Kanturk, Ireland 52 11N 8 52W
75 Kanye, Botswana 24 58S 25 20E
75 Kaoko Otavi, S.W. Afr. 18 12S 13 45E
72 Kaolack, Sénégal 14 10N 15 47W
74 Kapanga, Zaïre 8 15S 22 32E
46 Kapela, Mts., Y-slav. 44 40N 15 40E
84 Kapiti, I., New Zealand 40 45S 174 55E
47 Kaposvár, Hungary 46 20N 17 40E
68 Kapuas, R., Indon. 0 5S 110 30E
83 Kapunda, Australia 34 20S 138 57E
84 Kapuni, New Zealand 39 30S 174 5E
92 Kapuskasing, Canada 49 25N 82 25W
60 Kara, U.S.S.R. 69 15N 65 26E
60 Kara Bogaz Gol., L., U.S.S.R. 41 30N 53 30E
60 Kara-Kalpak, A.S.S.R., U.S.S.R. 42 0N 60 0E
60 Kara Kum, Des., U.S.S.R. 39 40N 60 0E
60 Kara Sea, U.S.S.R. 75 0N 62 0E
64 Karachi, Pakistan 25 0N 67 0E
60 Karaganda, U.S.S.R. 49 50N 73 10E
64 Karaikal, India 10 55N 79 50E
64 Karaikkudi, India 10 2N 78 45E
60 Karakas, U.S.S.R. 48 26N 83 27E
64 Karakoram Ra. & P., India 35 0N 78 0E
51 Karaköse (Agri), Turkey 39 45N 43 0E
84 Karamea Bight, N.Z. 41 40S 172 0E
76 Karasburg, S.W. Africa 28 0S 18 44E
60 Karasino, U.S.S.R. 66 50N 86 50E
60 Karauzyak, U.S.S.R. 43 35N 59 25E
62 Karbala, Iraq 32 47N 44 2E
47 Karcag, Hungary 47 20N 21 0E
41 Kardhitsa, Greece 39 20N 21 55E
49 Kardla, U.S.S.R. 58 58N 22 46E
73 Kareima, Sudan 18 35N 31 50E
50 Karelian A.S.S.R., U.S.S.R. 64 0N 34 0E
74 Karema, Tanzania 6 45S 30 30E
60 Kargat, U.S.S.R. 55 20N 80 30E
75 Kariba Gorge & Lake, Africa 16 30S 29 15E
75 Karibib, S.W. Africa 22 0S 15 50E
68 Karimata Str., Indonesia 2 0S 109 0E
64 Karimnagar, India 18 28N 79 5E
60 Karkaralinsk, U.S.S.R. 49 27N 75 37E
82 Karkar I., Terr. of New Guinea 4 40S 146 0E
62 Karkheh R., Iran 33 0N 47 30E
51 Karkinitsk, Gulf of, U.S.S.R. 46 0N 33 0E
63 Karkur, Israel 32 28N 35 0E
46 Karl Marx Stadt (Chemnitz), Germany 50 49N 12 50E
40 Karlovac, Yugoslavia 45 26N 15 34E

* *County incorporated within the regions of Highland and Western Isles*

9 Karlsborg, Sweden 58 30N 14 29E
9 Karlskroga, Sweden 59 21N 14 26E
9 Karlskrona, Sweden 56 13N 15 37E
9 Karlshamn, Sweden 56 17N 14 50E
5 Karlsruhe, Germany 49 3N 8 26E
9 Karlstad, Sweden 59 21N 13 20E
4 Karnai, India 29 35N 76 58E
5 Karnaphuli Reservoir, Bangladesh 22 40N 92 20E
1 Karnobat, Bulgaria 42 40N 27 0E
3 Karoonda, Australia 35 0S 140 5E
4 Karonga, Malawi 9 57S 33 55E
6 Karora, Sudan 17 44N 38 15E
1 Karpathos I., Greece 35 47N 27 10E
0 Karpinsk, U.S.S.R. 59 45N 59 45E
4 Karram R., India 32 45N 71 0E
6 Karreeberge, S. Africa 30 50S 22 0E
1 Kars, Turkey 40 50N 43 0E
0 Karsakpay, U.S.S.R. 47 55N 66 50E
0 Karst, Plat., Yugoslavia 45 35N 14 0E
0 Karshi, U.S.S.R. 39 5N 65 50E
0 Karsun, U.S.S.R. 54 10N 47 15E
0 Kartaly, U.S.S.R. 53 15N 60 50E
4 Karungu, Tanzania 0 45S 34 10E
4 Karur, India 10 55N 78 5E
4 Karwar, India 14 55N 74 13E
4 Kasai, R., Zaïre 4 0S 19 30E
4 Kasama, Zambia 10 10S 31 12E
74 Kasanga, Tanzania 8 23S 31 12E
74 Kasangulu, Zaïre 4 15S 15 15E
75 Kasempa, Zambia 13 15S 25 43E
52 Kashan, Iran 34 0N 51 30E
50 Kashgar, China 39 30N 76 10E
57 Kashing, China 30 50N 120 45E
54 Kashmir & Jammu, st., Asia 34 45N 76 0E
52 Kasimov, U.S.S.R. 54 58N 41 28E
48 Kaskinen (Kaskö), Finland 62 22N 21 13E
38 Kaslo, Canada 49 58N 117 0W
74 Kasongo, Zaïre 4 18S 26 40E
74 Kasongo-Lunda, Zaïre 6 32S 16 59E
46 Kassal, Germany 51 22N 9 30E
73 Kassala, Sudan 15 35N 36 27E
51 Kastamonu, Turkey 41 35N 34 2E
41 Kastoria, Greece 40 31N 21 18E
74 Kasulu, Tanzania 4 29S 30 7E
83 Katamatite, Australia 36 5S 145 40E
74 Katanga, reg., Zaïre 9 50S 26 0E
64 Katangi, India 21 56N 79 50E
80 Katanning, Australia 33 40S 117 32E
36 Katesbridge, Ireland 54 18N 6 8W
65 Katha, Burma 24 16N 96 13E
80 Katherine, Australia 14 30S 132 15E
64 Kathgotlam, India, *see* Haldwani
65 Katihar, India 25 40N 87 40E
65 Katmandu, Nepal 27 58N 85 23E
75 Katombora, Zambia 18 0S 25 30E
83 Katoomba (Blue Mountains), Australia 33 42S 150 18E
47 Katowice, Poland 50 18N 19 2E
30 Katrine, L., Scotland 56 15N 4 30W
49 Katrineholm, Sweden 59 3N 16 12E
72 Katsina, Nigeria 13 0N 7 35E
67 Katsuura, Japan 35 10N 140 20E
49 Kattegat, Europe 56 50N 11 15E
44 Katwijk-aan-Zee, Neth. 52 12N 4 25E
61 Katylyktakh, U.S.S.R. 68 55N 134 10E
90 Kauai, I., Hawaiian Is. 22 0N 159 40W
48 Kauliranta, Finland 66 28N 23 46E
49 Kaunas, U.S.S.R. 54 54N 23 54E
72 Kaura Namoda, Nigeria 12 40N 6 30E
48 Kautokeino, Norway 69 0N 23 8E
41 Kaválla, Greece 41 0N 24 4E
82 Kavieng, Terr. of New Guinea 3 0S 151 0E
67 Kawagoe, Japan 36 0N 139 30E
65 Kawardha, India 21 58N 81 15E
67 Kawasaki, Japan 35 40N 139 35E
84 Kawerau, New Zealand 38 5S 176 50E
84 Kawhia Hr., New Zealand 38 5S 174 40E
65 Kawthoolei, state, Burma 18 0N 97 0E
65 Kayah, State, Burma 19 0N 97 30E
72 Kayes, Mali 14 15N 11 27W
51 Kayseri, Turkey 38 52N 35 30E
61 Kazache, U.S.S.R. 70 50N 137 0E
60 Kazakhstan, S.S.R., U.S.S.R. 49 0N 70 0E
50 Kazan, U.S.S.R. 55 48N 49 0E
41 Kazanluk, Bulgaria 42 39N 25 27E
39 Kazanskaya, U.S.S.R. 49 33N 41 25E
47 Kazatin, U.S.S.R. 49 45N 28 35E
62 Kazerun, Iran 29 30N 51 40E
51 Kazbek Mt., U.S.S.R. 42 48N 44 29E
60 Kazym R., U.S.S.R. 63 30N 69 2E
72 Ke-Macina, Mali 14 5N 5 20W
41 Kea, I., Greece 37 36N 24 22E
36 Keady, N. Ireland 54 15N 6 41W
30 Keal, Loch na, Scotland 56 29N 6 5W
48 Kebnekaise, Mt., Sweden 68 0N 18 30E
68 Kediri, Indonesia 7 44S 112 5E
72 Kedougou, Sénégal 12 35N 12 10W
26 Keele, England 53 2N 2 17W
67 Keelung (Chilung), China 25 10N 121 45E
92 Keene, U.S.A. 42 58N 72 16W
75 Keetmanshoop, S.W. Africa 26 30S 18 5E
88 Keewatin, Terr., Canada 63 20N 88 30W
41 Kefallinia (Cephalonia), I., Greece 38 15N 20 33E
63 Kefar Sava, Israel 32 10N 34 55E
72 Keffi, Nigeria 8 58N 7 47E
48 Keflavik, Iceland 64 2N 22 35W
45 Kehl, Germany 48 34N 7 50E
26 Keighley, England 53 52N 1 54W
76 Keimoes, S. Africa 28 45N 20 55E
33 Keith, Scotland 57 33N 2 57W
68 Kelang, Malaya 3 0N 101 35E
51 Kelkit R., Turkey 40 9N 38 0E
33 Kellas, Scotland 57 33N 3 24W
74 Kellé, Congo (Fr.) 0 7S 14 20E
72 Kellé, Niger 14 18N 10 10E
80 Kellerberrin, Australia 31 34N 117 42E
90 Kellogg, U.S.A. 47 37N 116 13W
35 Kells, Ireland 52 33N 7 18W
36 Kells, *see* Ceannus Mor
36 Kells, N. Ireland 54 49N 6 14W
88 Kelowna, Canada 49 56N 119 26W
23 Kelsale, England 52 15N 1 30E
25 Kelsall, England 53 14N 2 44W
84 Kelso, New Zealand 45 53S 169 16E
31 Kelso, Scotland 55 37N 2 27W
68 Keluang, Malaya 1 50N 103 30E
23 Kelvedon, England 51 50N 0 43E
50 Kem, & R., U.S.S.R. 65 0N 34 40E
60 Kemerovo, U.S.S.R. 55 35N 86 7E
48 Kemi & R., Finland 65 48N 24 43E
48 Kemijärvi, Finland 66 42N 27 30E
33 Kemnay, Scotland 57 14N 2 28W
83 Kempsey, Australia 31 5N 152 53E
23 Kempston, England 52 7S 0 30W
45 Kempten, Germany 47 45N 10 20E
31 Ken, L., & R., Scotland 55 0N 4 0W
26 Kendal, England 54 20N 2 45W
83 Kendall, Australia 31 33S 152 36E
68 Kendari, Indonesia 4 0S 122 35E
72 Kenema, Sierra Leone 7 55N 11 13W
65 Keng Tawng, Burma 20 50N 98 25E
74 Kenge, Zaïre 5 0S 16 55E
65 Keng Tung, Burma 21 5N 99 30E
76 Kenhardt, S. Africa 29 28S 21 6E
22 Kenilworth, England 52 21N 1 34W
72 Kenitra, Morocco 34 15N 6 40W
34 Kenmare, & R., Ireland 51 53N 9 35W
93 Kennebec, R., U.S.A. 45 0N 69 50W
95 Kennedy, C., (C. Canaveral), U.S.A. 28 28N 80 31W
90 Kennewick, U.S.A. 46 12N 119 8W
88 Keno Hill, Canada 64 0N 135 40W
91 Kenogami, R., Canada 50 0N 85 0W
89 Kenora, Canada 49 48N 94 20W
92 Kenosha, U.S.A. 42 40N 87 49W
23 Kent, Co., England 51 10N 0 45E
24 Kentisbeare, England 50 51N 3 18W
91 Kentucky, R., U.S.A. 37 30N 83 30W
91 Kentucky, st., U.S.A. 37 20N 85 0W
89 Kentville, Canada 45 6N 64 29W
71 Kenya, Africa 0 30S 38 30E
74 Kenya, Mt., Kenya 0 12S 37 30E
91 Keokuk, U.S.A. 40 27N 91 28W
64 Kerala, st., India 10 0N 77 0E
83 Kerang, Australia 35 47S 143 59E
51 Kerch, & Str., U.S.S.R. 45 12N 36 35E
63 Kerem Maharal, Israel 32 39N 35 0E
5 Kerguelen I., Indian Oc. 49 30S 69 40E
74 Kericho, Kenya 0 22S 35 14E
68 Kerintji, mt., Indonesia 1 35S 100 40E
73 Kerkenna, I., Tunisia 34 48N 11 12E
60 Kerki, U.S.S.R. 37 50N 65 25E
41 Kérkira I. (Corfu), Gr. 39 30N 19 50E
84 Kermadec Is., Pacific Oc. 31 0S 178 0W
62 Kerman, Iran 30 15N 57 0E
62 Kermanshah, Iran 34 18N 47 5E
41 Kerme G., Turkey 36 55N 27 45E
30 Kerrera, I., Scotland 56 24N 5 32W
88 Kerrobert, Canada 52 0N 109 10W
34 Kerry, Co., Ireland 52 5N 9 30W
34 Kerry Hd., Ireland 52 20N 9 55E
25 Kerry, Wales 52 30N 3 15W
36 Kesh, N. Ireland 54 31N 7 43W
48 Keski Suomen, Co., Finland 63 0N 25 15E
27 Kesteven, Dist., England 52 58N 0 30W
26 Keswick, England 54 36N 3 7W
60 Ket, R., U.S.S.R. 58 50N 85 0E
72 Keta, Ghana 5 49N 1 0E
68 Ketapang, Indonesia 1 55S 110 0E
47 Ketrzyn, Poland 54 5N 21 21E
23 Kettering, England 52 25N 0 42W
26 Kettlewell, England 54 8N 2 2W
91 Kewanee, U.S.A. 41 17N 89 56W
92 Keweenaw, B., U.S.A. 47 0N 88 0W
92 Keweenaw Pen., U.S.A. 47 0N 88 0W
36 Key, L., Ireland 54 0N 8 15W
91 Key West, U.S.A. 24 40N 82 45W
24 Keynsham, England 51 25N 2 30W
61 Kezhma, U.S.S.R. 59 15N 100 57E
63 Kfar Ata, Israel 32 48N 35 7E
61 Khabarovsk, U.S.S.R. 48 20N 135 5E
62 Khaibar, Saudi Arabia 26 2N 39 28E
65 Khairagarh, India 21 15N 81 0E
64 Khairpur, & Prov., Pakistan 27 32N 68 45E
41 Khalkis, Greece 38 25N 23 40E
60 Khalmer-Sede, U.S.S.R. 67 25N 78 50E
60 Khalmer Yu, U.S.S.R. 68 0N 65 10E
65 Khamba Dzong, Tibet, China 28 25N 88 30E
62 Khamis Mushait, Si. Arabia 18 15N 42 45E
64 Khanapur, India 15 25N 74 30E
62 Khanaqin, Iraq 34 30N 45 25E
64 Khandwa, India 21 50N 76 22E
64 Khanewal, Pakistan 30 25N 71 55E
66 Khangai, Mts., Mongolia 47 0N 99 0E
41 Khania, Crete 35 20N 24 0E
64 Khanpur, Pakistan 28 35N 70 30E
63 Khanu, Iran 28 0N 57 45E
66 Khara Usu Nur, *see* Har Us Nuur
65 Kharagpur, India 22 20N 87 20E
64 Kharda, India 18 40N 75 40E
64 Khargon, India 21 45N 75 35E
52 Kharkov, U.S.S.R. 49 50N 36 15E
73 Khartoum, Sudan 15 40N 32 52E
64 Khash, Afghanistan 31 28N 62 40E
64 Khash Desert, Afghan. 31 45N 62 30E
73 Khashm el Girba, Sudan 14 52N 35 30E
41 Khaskovo, Bulgaria 41 56N 25 30E
61 Khatanga, U.S.S.R. 72 0N 102 40E
61 Khatyn, U.S.S.R. 62 10N 174 55E
64 Khed Brahma, India 24 7N 73 5E
72 Khemis Miliana (Affreville), Algeria 36 14N 2 20E
72 Khenchela, Algeria 35 25N 7 12E
72 Khenifra, Morocco 32 58N 5 46W
51 Kherson, U.S.S.R. 46 47N 32 43E
61 Kheta R., U.S.S.R. 71 0N 97 0E
66 Khetinsiring, Tibet, China 33 0N 91 40E
61 Khilok, U.S.S.R. 51 30N 110 50E
67 Khingan Mts., China 47 0N 119 30E
41 Khios, Greece 38 20N 26 0E
66 Khirgiz Nur, *see* Hyargas Nuur
62 Khirsan R., Iran 31 15N 51 10E
52 Khiuma I., U.S.S.R. 59 0N 22 30E
60 Khiva, U.S.S.R. 41 27N 60 10E
62 Khoi, Iran 38 39N 45 0E
64 Khojak P., Afghanistan 30 57N 66 40E
**68 Khmer Rep., Indo-China 11 45N 105 0E
51 Khonu, U.S.S.R. 66 36N 143 10E
62 Khor Dhahiya, South Yemen 18 50N 51 35E
41 Khora Sfakion, Crete 35 15N 24 10E
60 Khorog, U.S.S.R. 37 50N 71 50E
57 Khotan, China 37 8N 79 57E
47 Khotin, U.S.S.R. 48 31N 26 27E
72 Khouribga, Morocco 32 58N 6 50W
65 Khulna, Bangladesh 22 45N 89 34E
62 Khurramabad, Iran 36 37N 51 12E
64 Khush, Afghanistan 32 55N 62 10E
64 Khushab, Pakistan 32 25N 72 20E
63 Khushniye, Syria 33 0N 35 49E
47 Khust, U.S.S.R. 48 10N 23 18E
64 Khyber P., Pak. Afghan. 34 0N 71 15E
66 Kialing, R., China 33 0N 103 30E
83 Kiama, Australia 34 38S 150 58E
74 Kiambi, Zaïre 7 18S 27 59E
67 Kiamusze, China 46 20N 130 40E
66 Kian, China 27 0N 114 50E
66 Kiangling, China 30 25N 112 20E
66 Kiang-si, Prov., China 27 45N 115 30E
67 Kiangsu, Prov., China 33 0N 120 0E
67 Kiaohsien, China 36 5N 120 40E
74 Kibombo, Zaïre 3 54S 25 54E
23 Kibworth Beauchamp, England 52 33N 0 59W
88 Kicking Horse P., Can. 51 30N 116 10W
22 Kidderminster, England 52 23N 2 15W
22 Kidlington, England 51 49N 1 18W
26 Kidsgrove, England 53 6N 2 15W
25 Kidwelly, Wales 51 45N 4 17W
49 Kiel, B. & Can., Ger. 54 18N 10 5E
47 Kielce, Poland 50 52N 20 38E
27 Kielder, England 55 14N 2 35W
51 Kiev, U.S.S.R. 50 24N 30 28E
72 Kiffa, Mauritania 16 48N 11 15W
74 Kigali, Rwanda 1 58S 30 0E
74 Kigoma, Tanzania 4 49S 29 45E
66 Kikiang, China 29 0N 106 10E
41 Kikinda, Yugoslavia 45 47N 20 31E
41 Kikladhes (Cyclades) Arch., Greece 37 30N 25 15E
82 Kikori, Papua 7 45S 144 10E
74 Kikwit, Zaïre 4 50S 18 45E
90 Kilauea, Mt., Hawaii, I. 19 40N 155 30W
35 Kilbeggan, Ireland 53 21N 7 30W
30 Kilbirnie, Scotland 55 45N 4 42W
30 Kilbrennan Sd., Scot. 55 40N 5 23W
34 Kilbrittain, Ireland 51 40N 8 42W
35 Kilcock, Ireland 53 24N 6 40W
34 Kilcoe, Ireland 51 33N 9 26W
34 Kilconnell, Ireland 53 20N 8 25W
83 Kilcoy, Australia 27 0S 152 28E
30 Kilcreggan, Scotland 56 0N 4 50W
35 Kilcullen, Ireland 53 8N 6 45W
35 Kildare, & Co., Ireland 53 9N 6 54W
33 Kildonan & Strath, Scot. 58 10N 3 50W
34 Kildorrery, Ireland 52 14N 8 26W
34 Kilfenora, Ireland 53 0N 9 13W
30 Kilfinan, Scotland 55 57N 5 19W
34 Kilfinnane, Ireland 52 21N 8 30W
34 Kilgarvan, Ireland 51 45N 9 28W
74 Kilimanjaro, Mt., Tanzania 3 0S 37 0E
74 Kilindini, Kenya 4 10S 39 30E
47 Kiliya, U.S.S.R. 45 28N 29 16E
35 Kilkea, Ireland 52 57N 6 55W
34 Kilkee, Ireland 52 40N 9 37W
36 Kilkelly, Ireland 53 53N 8 50W
35 Kilkenny, & Co., Ireland 52 39N 7 13W
24 Kilkhampton, England 50 53N 4 30W
34 Kilkieran B., Ireland 53 17N 9 50W
34 Kilkishen, Ireland 52 49N 8 45W
35 Kill, Kildare, Ireland 53 15N 6 36W
34 Killadysert, Ireland 52 42N 9 7W
35 Killala, & B., Ireland 54 11N 9 13W
34 Killaloe, Ireland 52 49N 8 28W
36 Killard Pt., N. Ireland 54 19N 5 32W
83 Killarney, Australia 28 27S 152 1E
34 Killarney, Ireland 52 4N 9 30W
35 Killary Hr., Ireland 53 35N 9 57W
34 Killeagh, Ireland 51 56N 8 0W
35 Killeigh, Ireland 53 13N 7 26W
35 Killenaula, Ireland 52 35N 7 40W
36 Killeshandra, Ireland 54 0N 7 30W
33 Killiecrankie P., Scot. 56 43N 3 44W
34 Killimor, Ireland 53 9N 8 17W
30 Killin, Scotland 56 27N 4 20W
41 Killini, Mt., Greece 37 57N 22 31E
27 Killinghall, England 54 1N 1 33W
34 Killorglin, Ireland 52 6N 9 48W
36 Killough, N. Ireland 54 16N 5 40W
35 Killucan, Ireland 53 30N 7 10W
35 Killurin, Ireland 52 20N 6 34W
36 Killybegs, Ireland 54 36N 8 30W
36 Killyleagh, N. Ireland 54 24N 5 40W
30 Kilmacolm, Scotland 55 54N 4 39W
35 Kilmacthomas, Ireland 52 12N 7 28W
35 Kilmaganny, Ireland 52 26N 7 20W
34 Kilmallock, Ireland 52 27N 8 11W
30 Kilmarnock, Scotland 55 37N 4 29W
30 Kilmaurs, Scotland 55 37N 4 33W
34 Kilmeedy, Ireland 52 25N 8 55W
30 Kilmelford, Scotland 56 16N 5 30W
34 Kilmihill, Ireland 52 44N 9 18W
83 Kilmore, Australia 37 20S 144 55E
35 Kilmore, Ireland 52 12N 6 33W
33 Kilmuir, Scotland 57 44N 4 7W
34 Kilmurry, Ireland 52 47N 9 30W
36 Kilnaleck, Ireland 53 52N 7 20W
30 Kilninver, Scotland 56 20N 5 30W
74 Kilosa, Tanzania 6 40S 37 2E
36 Kilrea, N. Ireland 54 48N 6 34W
31 Kilrenny, Scotland 56 15N 2 40W
34 Kilronan, Ireland 53 8N 9 40W
35 Kilsheelan, Ireland 52 23N 7 37W
31 Kilsyth, Scotland 55 58N 4 3W
35 Kilteely, Ireland 52 34N 6 45W
35 Kiltamagh, Ireland 53 51N 9 0W
74 Kilwa, Zaïre 9 15S 28 15E
74 Kilwa Kisiwani, Tanzania 8 58S 39 12E
74 Kilwa Kivinje, Tanzania 8 45S 39 15E
30 Kilwinning, Scotland 55 40N 4 42W
34 Kilworth, Ireland 52 10N 8 15W
34 Kilworth, Mts., Ireland 52 14N 8 15W
80 Kimba, Australia 33 14S 136 22E
76 Kimberley, S. Africa 28 42S 24 59E
68 Kinabalu, Mt., Malaysia 5 55N 116 45E
33 Kinbrace, Scotland 58 16N 3 56W
92 Kincardine, Canada 44 8N 81 38W
33 Kincardine, Scotland 57 51N 4 21W
***33 Kincardine, Co., Scot. 56 55N 2 25W
72 Kindia, Guinea 10 0N 12 52W
74 Kindu-Port Empain, Zaïre 3 0S 25 25E
52 Kineshma, U.S.S.R. 57 30N 42 0E
22 Kineton, England 52 10N 1 30W
83 King I., Australia 39 55S 144 0E
83 King Sd., Australia 16 30S 123 15E
89 King Frederick VI Coast, Greenland 63 0N 43 0W
89 King George Is., Canada 57 30N 80 0W
98 King George V Falls, Fs., Guyana 3 0N 58 0W
80 King Leopold Ra., Australia 17 0S 125 30E
88 King William I., Canada 69 0N 97 0W
76 King William's Town, S. Africa 32 50S 27 17E
30 Kingairloch, Dist., Scot. 56 37N 5 30W
83 Kingaroy, Australia 26 35S 151 38E
31 Kinghorn, Scotland 56 4N 3 10W
49 Kingisepp, U.S.S.R. 58 15N 22 15E
90 Kingman, U.S.A. 35 15N 114 10W
23 King's Lynn, England 52 45N 0 24E
35 Kings, R., Ireland 52 33N 7 20W
22 Kingsbury, England 52 33N 1 41W
83 Kingscote, Australia 35 40S 137 45E
89 Kingston, Canada 44 23N 76 37W
23 Kingston, England 51 23N 0 17W
95 Kingston, Jamaica 18 0N 76 47W
84 Kingston, New Zealand 45 15S 168 47E
93 Kingston, U.S.A. 41 55N 74 0W
27 Kingston-upon-Hull, *see* Hull
83 Kingston South East, Australia 36 50S 139 52E
95 Kingstown, St. Vincent, W.I. 13 10N 61 15W
90 Kingsville, U.S.A. 27 30N 97 55W
24 Kingswood, England 51 26N 2 21W
67 Kingtehchen, China 28 45N 118 50E
22 Kington, England 52 12N 3 2W
33 Kingussie, Scotland 57 5N 4 4W
35 Kinitty, Ireland 53 6N 7 44W
66 Kinyang, China 36 10N 107 35E
67 Kinhwa, China 28 55N 119 30E
74 Kinkala, Congo (Fr.) 4 18S 14 48E
84 Kinleith, New Zealand 38 25S 176 0E
31 Kinloch, Scotland 57 0N 6 18W
33 Kinloch, Sutherland, Scotland 58 17N 4 50W
30 Kinloch Rannoch, Scot. 56 41N 4 12W
33 Kinloss, Scotland 57 38N 3 37W
36 Kinlough, Ireland 54 27N 8 16W
35 Kinnegad, Ireland 53 28N 7 8W
63 Kinneret, Israel 32 43N 35 33E
63 Kinneret, L., (Sea of Galilee), Israel 32 50N 35 25E
†31 Kinross, & Co., Scot. 56 12N 3 25W
34 Kinsale, & Hr., Ireland 51 43N 8 31W
34 Kinsale, Old Head of, Ireland 51 37N 8 32W
66 Kinsha, R., *see* Yangtze R.
74 Kinshasa (Leopoldville), Zaïre 4 40S 15 30E
91 Kinston, U.S.A. 35 15N 77 34W
32 Kintaravay, Scotland 58 4N 6 42W
33 Kintore, Scotland 57 14N 2 20W
30 Kintyre, Mull of, Scot. 55 17N 5 48W
30 Kintyre, Pen. & Dist., Scotland 55 35N 5 35W
34 Kinvara, Ireland 53 5N 8 48W
74 Kioga, L., *see* Kyoga, L., Uganda
41 Kiparissia & G., Greece 37 15N 21 32E
35 Kippure, Mt., Ireland 53 10N 6 15W
75 Kipushi, Zaïre 11 55S 27 20E
45 Kirchheim, Germany 48 38N 9 29E
36 Kircubbin, N. Ireland 54 30N 5 33W
61 Kirensk, U.S.S.R. 57 55N 108 30E
55 Kirgiz Steppe, U.S.S.R. 50 0N 70 0E
60 Kirgizia, S.S.R., U.S.S.R. 42 0N 75 0E
50 Kirillov, U.S.S.R. 59 58N 38 10E
67 Kirin, China 43 50N 127 2E
67 Kirin, Prov., China 44 20N 128 0E
41 Kirkagaç, Turkey 39 0N 27 45E
27 Kirkburton, England 53 36N 1 42W
26 Kirkby, England 53 29N 2 55W
27 Kirkby-in-Ashfield, Eng. 53 6N 1 15W
26 Kirkby Lonsdale, England 54 13N 2 38W
27 Kirkby Moorside, Eng. 54 17N 0 55W
26 Kirkby Stephen, Eng. 54 27N 2 23W
31 Kirkcaldy, Scotland 56 6N 3 9W
30 Kirkcolm, Scotland 54 59N 5 4W
31 Kirkconnel, Scotland 55 23N 4 0W
30 Kirkcowan, Scotland 54 53N 4 38W
††31 Kirkcudbright, & Co., Scotland 54 49N 4 3W
48 Kirkenes, Norway 69 40N 30 1E
26 Kirkham, Lancs., Eng. 53 48N 2 54W
31 Kirkintilloch, Scotland 55 56N 4 9W
48 Kirkjubaejar, Iceland 63 50N 18 1W
89 Kirkland Lake, Canada 48 15N 80 0W
41 Kirklareli, Turkey 41 45N 27 15E
31 Kirkliston, Scotland 55 55N 3 27W
31 Kirkmichael, Scotland 56 43N 3 31W
91 Kirksville, U.S.A. 40 10N 92 40W
62 Kirkuk, Iraq 35 30N 44 21E
33 Kirkwall, Scotland 58 58N 2 57W
76 Kirkwood, S. Africa 33 20S 25 25E
50 Kirov, U.S.S.R. 58 38N 49 30E
51 Kirovabad, U.S.S.R. 40 48N 46 35E
50 Kirovgrad, U.S.S.R. 57 30N 60 0E
51 Kirovograd, U.S.S.R. 48 35N 32 20E
60 Kirovsk, U.S.S.R. 38 0N 60 25E
31 Kirriemuir, Scotland 56 40N 3 0W
52 Kirsanov, U.S.S.R. 52 40N 42 35E
51 Kirsehir, Turkey 39 20N 34 0E
23 Kirtling, England 52 11N 0 29E
27 Kirton, England 52 56N 0 3W
48 Kiruna, Sweden 67 50N 20 8E
74 Kirundu, Zaïre 0 50S 25 40E
74 Kisangani (Stanleyville), Zaïre 0 40N 25 18E
62 Kiseiba, Egypt 22 30N 30 0E
60 Kiselevsk, U.S.S.R. 54 10N 86 35E
47 Kishinev, U.S.S.R. 47 2N 28 52E
64 Kishtwar, India 33 25N 75 57E
74 Kisii, Kenya 0 42S 34 44E
74 Kisiju, Tanzania 7 15S 39 28E
47 Kiskörös, Hungary 46 40N 19 20E
47 Kiskunhalas, Hungary 46 28N 19 21E
72 Kissidougou, Guinea 9 0N 10 0W
74 Kisumu, Kenya 0 2S 34 57E
63 Kiswe, Syria 33 23N 36 14E
72 Kita, Mali 13 5N 9 25W
60 Kitab, U.S.S.R. 39 25N 66 55E
67 Kitakami, R., Japan 39 30N 141 8E
67 Kitakyushu, Japan 33 52N 130 45E
74 Kitale, Kenya 1 0N 35 5E
89 Kitchener, Canada 43 30N 80 41W
74 Kitega, Burundi 3 28S 29 59E
48 Kitenen, R., Finland 67 45N 26 40E
41 Kithira, Greece 36 10N 22 57E
41 Kithira, I., Greece 36 15N 23 0E
41 Kithnos, I., Greece 37 27N 24 28E
88 Kitimat, Canada 54 5N 128 30W
74 Kitui, Kenya 1 0S 38 0E
75 Kitwe, Zambia 12 55S 28 10E
45 Kitzingen, Germany 49 40N 10 7E
67 Kiuchuan, China 39 50N 98 15E
66 Kiukiang, China 29 45N 116 0E
48 Kivalo, mts., Finland 66 10N 26 3E
74 Kivu, L., Zaïre 2 0S 29 5E
50 Kizel, U.S.S.R. 59 0N 57 0E
51 Kizil, R., Turkey 40 30N 34 15E
60 Kizil Kiva, U.S.S.R. 40 20N 72 25E
63 Kizyl Arvat, U.S.S.R. 38 55N 56 30E
51 Kizlyar, U.S.S.R. 43 52N 46 45E
13 Kjolen, Mts., Europe 66 0N 15 0E
46 Kladno, Czechoslovakia 50 13N 14 2E
46 Klagenfurt, Austria 46 39N 14 19E
49 Klaipeda, U.S.S.R. 55 42N 21 6E
90 Klamath Falls, U.S.A. 42 15N 121 46W
90 Klamath R., U.S.A. 42 30N 123 10W
49 Klar, R., Sweden 60 45N 13 0E
46 Klatovy, Cz-slov. 49 20N 13 20E
76 Klawer, S. Africa 31 45S 18 40E
76 Klerksdorp, Transvaal 26 45S 27 11E
44 Kleve, Germany 51 48N 6 9E
52 Klin, U.S.S.R. 56 30N 36 45E
76 Klipplaat, S. Africa 33 0S 24 15E
46 Klodzko, Poland 50 28N 16 35E
88 Klondike, Canada 64 5N 139 0W
45 Klosters, Switzerland 46 54N 9 50E
72 Klouto, Togo 7 0N 0 59E
61 Klyuchevsk, U.S.S.R. 55 45N 160 27E
27 Knaresborough, England 54 1N 1 27W
34 Knockhoy, Mt., Ireland 51 49N 9 27W
44 Knokke, Belgium 51 20N 3 17E
27 Knottingley, England 53 42N 1 15W
22 Knowle, England 52 24N 1 43W

* Renamed Shaba

** Reverted to its former name Cambodia

*** Incorporated within the region of Grampian

† County incorporated within the region of Tayside

†† County incorporated within the region of Dumfries and Galloway

100 Knox Coast, Antarctica 68 0S 108 0E
91 Knoxville, U.S.A. 35 50N 83 55W
32 Knoydart, Dist., Scot. 57 4N 5 35W
26 Knutsford, England 53 19N 2 23W
40 Kobarid, Yugoslavia 46 15N 13 30E
66 Kobdo, Mongolia, see Hovd
67 Kobe, Japan 34 45N 135 12E
44 Koblenz, Germany 50 24N 7 32E
41 Kocane, Yugoslavia 41 55N 22 20E
40 Kocevje, Yugoslavia 45 40N 14 50E
61 Kocheya, U.S.S.R. 52 30N 120 27E
67 Kochi, & Pref., Japan 33 35N 133 40E
88 Kodiak, I., Alaska 57 0N 153 0W
73 Kodok (Fashoda), Sudan 9 57N 32 3E
76 Koes, S.W. Africa 26 1S 19 8E
76 Koffiefontein, S. Africa 29 23S 25 0E
72 Koforidua, Ghana 6 19N 0 15W
67 Kofu, Japan 35 38N 138 30E
67 Kogota, Japan 38 30N 141 5E
63 Koh-i-Sangan Mt., Afghan 33 30N 64 59E
64 Kohat, Pakistan 33 30N 71 33E
60 Kokand, U.S.S.R. 41 0N 71 0E
60 Kokchetov, U.S.S.R. 53 25N 69 30E
49 Kokemaen Is., Finland 61 16N 21 0E
66 Kokiu, China 23 30N 102 55E
48 Kokkola (Gamlakarleby), Finland 63 56N 23 0E
66 Koko Nor, L., China 37 0N 100 0E
66 Koko Shili, Mts., China 35 40N 90 0E
61 Kokora, U.S.S.R. 71 40N 144 40E
76 Kokstad, S. Africa 30 32S 29 29E
67 Kokura, Japan 33 45N 131 0S
50 Kola, U.S.S.R. 68 50N 32 35E
50 Kola, B. & Pen., U.S.S.R. 69 0N 35 0E
64 Kolar, India 13 10N 78 5E
64 Kolar Goldfields, India 12 55N 78 15E
64 Kolayat, India 27 50N 72 50E
72 Kolda, Sénégal 12 55N 14 50W
49 Kolding, Denmark 55 30N 9 24E
74 Kole, Zaïre 3 16S 22 42E
64 Kolhapur, India 16 40N 74 15E
61 Kolin, Czechoslovakia 50 2N 15 16E
44 Köln, (Cologne), Ger. 50 56N 6 56E
47 Kolo, Poland 52 14N 18 45E
46 Kolobrzeg, Poland 54 10N 15 32E
52 Kolomna, U.S.S.R. 55 10N 38 50E
51 Kolomyya, U.S.S.R. 48 30N 25 5E
60 Kolpashevo, U.S.S.R. 58 30N 83 5E
74 Kolwezi, Zaïre 10 50S 25 20E
55 Kolyma Plain, U.S.S.R. 68 0N 155 0E
61 Kolyma R., U.S.S.R. 65 0N 152 0E
73 Kôm Ombo (Nasser City), Egypt 24 30N 32 57E
61 Komandorskiye Is., U.S.S.R. 55 0N 167 0E
47 Komarno, Cz-slov. 47 49N 18 5E
76 Komati, R., Swaziland 26 0S 31 30E
76 Komatipoort, S. Africa 25 30S 31 50E
67 Komatsu, Japan 36 25N 136 30E
50 Komi, A.S.S.R., U.S.S.R. 62 0N 55 0E
52 Kommunarsk (Voroshilovsk), U.S.S.R. 48 28N 38 40E
41 Komotini, Greece 41 6N 25 32E
76 Kompasberg, mt., S. Africa 31 45S 24 35E
68 Kompong Cham, Khmer Rep. 12 0N 105 30E
68 Kompong Som (Sihanoukville), Khmer Rep. 10 35N 103 35E
61 Komsomolsk, U.S.S.R. 50 9N 136 0E
100 Komsomolskaya, Antarctica 74 30S 97 0E
65 Konam Dzong, China 29 5N 92 55E
74 Kondoa, Tanzania 5 0S 36 0E
61 Kondrasheyo, U.S.S.R. 57 25N 98 30E
73 Konduga, Nigeria 11 35N 13 26E
66 Kongmoon, China 22 41N 113 5E
74 Kongolo, Zaïre 5 15S 26 55E
49 Kongsberg, Norway 59 41N 9 38E
49 Kongsvinger, Norway 60 15N 12 0E
41 Konjic, Yugoslavia 43 42N 18 0E
52 Konotop, U.S.S.R. 51 20N 33 10E
47 Konskie, Poland 51 16N 20 22E
52 Konstantinovka, U.S.S.R. 48 33N 37 45E
45 Konstanz, Germany 47 41N 9 10E
72 Kontagora, Nigeria 10 30N 5 32E
51 Konya, Turkey 38 0N 32 35E
74 Konza, Kenya 1 50S 37 10E
83 Koondrook, Australia 35 32S 144 5E
83 Koorawatha, Australia 34 0S 148 47E
90 Kootenay L. & R., Can. 49 30N 116 43W
41 Kopaonik, Plat., Y-slav. 43 17N 21 0E
40 Koper, Yugoslavia 45 55N 13 50E
49 Kopervik, Norway 59 16N 5 18E
49 Koping, Sweden 59 30N 16 0E
60 Kopeysk, U.S.S.R. 55 0N 61 50E
49 Kopparberg, & Co., Sweden 59 55N 15 0E
41 Kora Sfakion, Crete 35 17N 24 9E
68 Korat, Thailand, see Nakhon Ratchasima
41 Korce, Albania 40 37N 20 50E
40 Korcula, I., Y-slav 42 55N 16 50E
61 Korda, U.S.S.R. 55 20N 104 25E
73 Kordofan, Dist., Sudan 13 0N 30 0E
67 Korea North, Asia 40 0N 127 0E
67 Korea South, Asia 36 0N 128 0E
67 Korea, B., Korea 39 30N 124 0E
47 Korets, U.S.S.R. 50 30N 27 5E
72 Koro, Ivory Coast 8 40N 7 30W
84 Koro Sea, Fiji Islands (Inset)
83 Koroit, Australia 38 27S 142 24E
61 Korsakov, U.S.S.R. 46 50N 142 50E
49 Korsör, Denmark 55 19N 11 8E
47 Korsze, Poland 54 10N 21 3E
73 Korti, Sudan 18 2N 31 40E
44 Kortrijk, Belgium 50 51N 3 20E
61 Koryak, Ra., U.S.S.R. 62 0N 170 0E
41 Kos, I., Greece 36 40N 27 10E
51 Koschagyl, U.S.S.R. 46 45N 58 45E
46 Koscian, Poland 52 2N 16 40E
83 Kosciusko, Mt., Austral. 36 25S 148 12E
76 Kosi, L., S. Africa 26 45S 32 45E
46 Kosice, Czechoslovakia 48 42N 21 15E
41 Kosovska Mitrovica, Yugoslavia 42 50N 20 54E
76 Koster, S. Africa 25 55S 26 40E
62 Kosti, Sudan 13 7N 32 38E
52 Kostroma, U.S.S.R. 57 52N 41 0E
46 Kostrzyn, Poland 52 24N 14 38E
46 Koszalin, Poland 54 12N 16 8E
64 Kota, India 25 20N 75 50E
68 Kota Baharu, Malaya 6 10N 102 22E
68 Kota Kinabalu (Jesselton), Malaysia 5 50 116 13E
68 Kotabaru, Indonesia 3 20S 116 20E
63 Kotcha R., Afghanistan 36 5N 70 0E
60 Kotelnich, U.S.S.R. 58 20N 48 12E
61 Kotelny I., U.S.S.R. 75 10N 140 0E
49 Kotka, Finland 60 27N 27 8E
50 Kotlas, U.S.S.R. 61 13N 46 40E
41 Kotor, Yugoslavia 42 23N 18 47E
47 Kotovsk, U.S.S.R. 47 55N 29 35E
64 Kotri, Pakistan 25 28N 68 15E
65 Kottagudem, India 17 30N 80 40E
64 Kottayam, India 9 30N 76 30E
64 Kotturu, India 14 45N 76 10E
73 Kouga, Chad 9 59N 21 30E
74 Koula Moutou, Gabon 1 10S 12 30E
72 Koulikoro, Mali 13 0N 7 42W
82 Koumala, Australia 21 38S 149 15E
82 Kounradski, U.S.S.R. 47 15N 75 5E
50 Kovel, U.S.S.R. 51 18N 24 39E
52 Kovrov, U.S.S.R. 56 25N 41 19E
66 Kowloon, Hong Kong 22 7N 114 15E
41 Kozani, Greece 40 13N 21 58E
64 Kozhikode, see Calicut
50 Kozhva, U.S.S.R. 65 0N 56 50E
47 Kozienice, Poland 51 32N 21 30E
72 Kpandu, Ghana 6 58N 0 16E
68 Kra, Isthmus of, Thailand 10 25N 99 20E
48 Kragero, Norway 58 55N 9 22E
41 Kragujevac, Yugoslavia 44 2N 20 55E
68 Krakatau, Indonesia 6 10S 105 30E
47 Krakow, Poland 50 7N 19 55E
41 Kraljevo, see Rankovicevo, Yugoslavia
52 Kramatorsk, U.S.S.R. 48 45N 37 35E
48 Kramfors, Sweden 62 55N 17 43E
48 Krangede Falls, Sweden 63 10N 16 8E
47 Krásnik, Poland 51 0N 22 5E
51 Krasnodar, U.S.S.R. 45 1N 39 0E
50 Krasnokamsk, U.S.S.R. 58 0N 56 0E
50 Krasnoturinsk, U.S.S.R. 59 45N 60 5E
51 Krasnovodsk, U.S.S.R. 40 5N 53 5E
61 Krasnoyarsk, U.S.S.R. 56 20N 92 50E
68 Kratie, Khmer Rep. 12 30N 106 4E
44 Krefeld, Germany 51 22N 6 34E
40 Kremen, Mt., Yugoslavia 44 28N 15 55E
52 Kremenchug, U.S.S.R. 49 10N 33 30E
47 Kremenets, U.S.S.R. 50 8N 25 43E
61 Krestovski, U.S.S.R. 71 50N 101 40E
74 Kribi, Cameroon 3 0N 10 0E
64 Krishna, R., India 16 20N 76 30E
65 Krishnagar, India 23 25N 88 30E
49 Kristiansand, Norway 58 7N 7 59E
49 Kristianstad, & Co., Sweden 56 6N 14 7E
48 Kristiansund, Norway 63 9N 7 45E
48 Kristiinankaupunki (Kristinestad), Finland 62 18N 21 25E
48 Kristinehamn, Sweden 59 20N 14 8E
52 Krivoy Rog, U.S.S.R. 47 58N 33 20E
40 Krk, I., Yugoslavia 45 5N 14 35E
76 Krokodil, R., S. Africa 25 30S 31 20E
49 Kronoberg, Co., Sweden 56 45N 14 30E
50 Kronshtadt, I., U.S.S.R. 60 2N 30 39E
76 Kroonstad, O.F.S. 27 32S 27 48E
61 Kropotkin, U.S.S.R. 58 50N 115 10E
47 Krosno, Poland 49 35N 21 55E
47 Krotoszyn, Poland 51 41N 17 19E
76 Krugersdorp, Transvaal 26 10S 27 45E
41 Krusevac, Yugoslavia 43 35N 21 21E
72 Ksar el Kebir, Morocco 35 0N 5 57W
72 Ksar es Souk, Morocco 31 58N 4 28W
68 Kuala Lipis, Malaya 4 5N 102 10E
68 Kuala Lumpur, Malaya 3 10N 101 40E
68 Kuala Selangor, Malaya 3 25N 101 20E
68 Kuala Terengganu, Malaya 5 20N 103 15E
68 Kualakapuas, Indonesia 3 0S 114 30E
68 Kuantan, Malaya 3 57N 103 15E
51 Kuba, U.S.S.R. 41 22N 48 21E
51 Kuban, R., U.S.S.R. 45 12N 40 0E
66 Kucha, China 41 40N 82 22E
67 Kuchihotsu, Japan 32 36N 130 8E
68 Kuching, Sarawak 1 40N 111 2E
64 Kuda, India 23 10N 71 15E
48 Kudafljot, Iceland 63 30N 18 15W
68 Kudus, Java 6 40S 111 0E
73 Kufra Oasis, Libya 25 0N 23 0E
63 Kufrinja, Jordan 32 18N 35 42E
46 Kufstein, Austria 47 30N 12 10E
62 Kuh-i-Bul, Mt., Iran 30 35N 53 20E
63 Kuh-i-Lalehzar, mt., Iran 29 30N 57 20E
63 Kuh-i-Taftan, mt., Iran 28 55N 61 0E
73 Kukawa, Nigeria 12 58N 13 30E
64 Kulasekharapatnam, India 8 20N 78 3E
49 Kuldiga, U.S.S.R. 57 0N 22 0E
43 Kulmbach, Germany 50 5N 11 30E
60 Kulunda, U.S.S.R. 52 45N 79 20E
83 Kulwin, Victoria 35 0S 142 46E
60 Kulyab, U.S.S.R. 38 0N 69 50E
60 Kum Tekei, U.S.S.R. 43 15N 79 18E
51 Kuma, R., U.S.S.R. 44 45N 44 30E
67 Kumamoto, & Pref., Japan 32 40N 130 45E
67 Kumano B., Japan 33 50N 136 30E
41 Kumanovo, Yugoslavia 42 9N 21 42E
84 Kumara, New Zealand 42 37S 171 12E
72 Kumasi, Ghana 6 40N 1 35W
50 Kumertau, U.S.S.R. 53 10N 56 15E
72 Kumo, Nigeria 10 1N 11 12E
64 Kunar, & Prov., Afghan. 34 30N 71 3E
61 Kunashir I., U.S.S.R. 44 0N 146 0E
64 Kunch, India 26 0N 79 8E
49 Kunda, U.S.S.R. 59 31N 26 35E
66 Kungho, China 36 25N 100 25E
49 Kungsbacka, Sweden 57 30N 12 7E
50 Kungur, U.S.S.R. 57 24N 56 45E
82 Kungurri, Australia 21 3S 148 46E
65 Kunlong, Burma 23 30N 98 45E
66 Kunlun Shan, mts., Asia 36 0N 90 0E
66 Kunming, China 25 3N 102 40E
67 Kunsan, Korea 36 0N 126 35E
52 Kuntsevo, U.S.S.R. 55 35N 37 30E
82 Kunwarara, Australia 22 55S 150 7E
66 Kunyang, China 24 50N 102 15E
48 Kuopio, Finland 62 59N 27 37E
40 Kupa, R., Yugoslavia 45 30N 15 10E
52 Kupyansk, U.S.S.R. 49 50N 37 45E
51 Kura, R., U.S.S.R. 41 40N 47 0E
82 Kuranda, Australia 16 48S 145 35E
51 Kurdistan, Dist., Turkey 37 30N 43 30E
67 Kure, Japan 34 15N 132 40E
61 Kurgen, U.S.S.R. 64 5N 172 50W
63 Kuria Muria Islands, Arabian Sea 17 23N 56 0E
61 Kuril Is., U.S.S.R. 45 0N 150 0E
66 Kurla, China 41 58N 86 10E
52 Kurlovskiy, U.S.S.R. 55 26N 40 40E
73 Kurmuk, Sudan 10 30N 34 22E
64 Kurnool, India 15 50N 78 0E
84 Kurow, New Zealand 44 40S 170 30E
83 Kurri Kurri, N.S.W. 32 53S 151 22E
52 Kursk, U.S.S.R. 51 51N 36 5E
41 Kursumlija, Yugoslavia 43 10N 21 18E
76 Kuruman & R., S. Africa 27 8S 23 20E
67 Kurume, Japan 33 20N 130 27E
64 Kurunegala, Sri Lanka 6 52N 80 4E
62 Kurusku, Egypt 22 40N 32 12E
61 Kurya, U.S.S.R. 61 10N 108 10E
60 Kushevat, U.S.S.R. 65 15N 65 55E
67 Kushiro, Japan 43 0N 144 25E
64 Kushk, Afghanistan 35 0N 62 15E
64 Kushka, Afghanistan 35 15N 62 15E
60 Kushka, U.S.S.R. 33 35N 62 20E
88 Kushkokwim R., Alaska 61 0N 158 0W
65 Kushtia, Bangladesh 23 50N 89 5E
60 Kustanai, U.S.S.R. 53 25N 63 45E
62 Kut al Imara, Iraq 32 37N 45 40E
51 Kutahya, Turkey 39 30N 30 2E
51 Kutaisi, U.S.S.R. 42 10N 42 58E
68 Kutaradja, Indonesia, see Banda Atjeh
64 Kutch, Rann of, India 24 0N 70 0E
47 Kutno, Poland 52 18N 19 20E
62 Kuwait, Asia 29 0N 47 30E
67 Kuwana, Japan 35 0N 136 43E
52 Kuybyshev, U.S.S.R. 53 12N 50 0E
61 Kuyumba, U.S.S.R. 61 0N 97 5E
52 Kuznetsk, U.S.S.R. 53 13N 46 29E
48 Kvarken Is., Finland 63 20N 21 10E
40 Kvarnevic B., Yugoslavia 44 50N 14 30E
74 Kwamouth, Zaïre 3 9S 16 20E
66 Kwanan, China 30 45N 106 0E
66 Kwanghua, China 31 45N 112 10E
67 Kwangju, Korea 35 10N 127 0E
66 Kwangsi-Chuang, Autonomous Reg., China 24 0N 107 30E
66 Kwangtung, China 25 30N 101 20E
66 Kweichow, Prov., China 26 30N 107 0E
66 Kweilin, China 25 12N 110 10E
66 Kweiping, China 23 25N 109 15E
66 Kwei-yang, China 26 50N 106 55E
49 Kwidzyn, Poland 53 45N 18 58E
80 Kwinana, Australia 32 20S 115 50E
82 Kyabram, Australia 36 19S 145 4E
61 Kyakhta, U.S.S.R. 50 30N 106 25E
65 Kyaring Tso, L., Tibet 31 0N 88 15E
65 Kyaukpyu, Burma 19 28N 93 40E
30 Kyle, Dist., Scotland 55 27N 4 27W
33 Kyle of Durness, Scot. 58 35N 4 49W
32 Kyle of Lochalsh, Scot. 57 20N 5 50W
33 Kyle of Tongue, Scot. 58 33N 4 24W
30 Kyles of Bute, Scotland 55 55N 5 10W
44 Kyllburg, Germany 50 2N 6 35E
83 Kyneton, Australia 37 20S 144 30E
74 Kyoga, L., Uganda 1 30N 33 20E
67 Kyo, C., Japan 35 40N 135 8E
83 Kyogle, Australia 28 37S 152 44E
65 Kyonpyaw, Burma 17 15N 95 0E
67 Kyoto & Pref., Japan 35 0N 135 30E
61 Kystatym, U.S.S.R. 67 0N 123 20E
61 Kytalyktakh, U.S.S.R. 65 30N 123 30E
61 Kyulyunken, U.S.S.R. 64 10N 137 0E
65 Kyunhla, Burma 23 25N 95 15E
67 Kyushu I., Japan 32 30N 131 0E
41 Kyustendil, Bulgaria 42 2S 22 40E
83 Kywong, N.S.W. 34 59S 146 42E
61 Kyzyl, U.S.S.R. 51 45N 94 35E
60 Kyzyl Kum Des., U.S.S.R. 42 10N 66 0E
60 Kyzyl Orda, U.S.S.R. 44 56N 65 30E
60 Kyzyl Rabat, U.S.S.R. 37 50N 74 50E

L

37 La Alcarria, Dist., Spain 40 30N 2 10W
95 La Blanquilla, I., W.I. 12 0N 64 35W
72 La Calle, Algeria 36 55N 8 33E
44 La Capelle, France 49 59N 3 52E
37 La Carolina, Spain 38 17N 3 38W
94 La Ceiba, Honduras 15 45N 86 50W
43 La Charité, France 47 16N 3 2E
45 La Chaux de Fonds, Switz. 47 7N 6 50E
94 La Chorrera, Panama Canal (Inset)
43 La Ciotat, France 43 10N 5 32E
37 La Coruna, Spain 43 20N 8 28W
92 La Crosse, U.S.A. 43 49N 91 13W
37 La Estrada, Spain 42 43N 8 28W
92 La Fayette, U.S.A. 40 24N 86 45W
42 La Ferté Mace, France 48 38N 0 20W
42 La Flêche, France 47 42N 0 5W
90 La Grande, U.S.A. 45 22N 118 7W
91 La Grange, U.S.A. 33 3N 85 1W
95 La Guaira, Venezuela 10 37N 66 48W
90 La Junta, U.S.A. 38 3N 103 35W
44 La Louvière, Belgium 50 29N 4 12E
37 La Mancha, Dist., Spain 39 10N 2 50W
43 La Mure, France 45 0N 5 30E
98 La Oroya, Peru 11 42S 75 57W
95 La Palma, Panama 8 15N 78 2W
37 La Palma, Spain 37 20N 6 35W
98 La Paz, Bolivia 16 30S 68 0W
94 La Paz, & B., Mexico 24 5N 110 14W
67 La Pérouse Str., Japan 45 30N 142 0E
99 La Plata, Argentina 35 0S 57 50W
99 La Quiâca, Argentina 22 15S 65 45W
42 La Réole, France 44 38N 0 2W
99 La Rioja, Argentina 29 20S 66 50W
42 La Roche-sur-Yon, France 46 41N 1 26W
42 La Rochelle, France 46 10N 1 10W
37 La Roda, Spain 39 15N 2 12W
95 La Romana, Dom. Rep. 18 30N 68 55W
88 La Ronge, L., Canada 55 10N 105 15W
37 La Sagra, Mt., Spain 38 0N 2 35W
92 La Salle, U.S.A. 41 25N 89 5W
99 La Serena, Chile 29 55S 71 25W
43 La Seyne, France 43 0N 5 50E
40 La Spezia, Italy 44 9N 9 47E
42 La Teste, France 44 40N 1 10W
42 La Tremblade, France 45 42N 1 10W
93 La Tuque, Canada 47 30N 72 57W
95 La Vega, Dominican Rep. 19 10N 70 35W
34 Labasheeda, Ireland 52 37N 9 15W
46 Labe (Elbe), R., Czechoslovakia 50 0N 15 30E
72 Labé, Guinea 11 24N 12 16W
89 Labrador, dist., Canada 55 50N 60 30W
68 Labuan, I., Sabah 5 22N 115 19E
88 Lac la Biche, Canada 54 45N 111 50W
*55 Laccadive Is., Indian Oc. 13 0N 72 30E
89 Lachine, U.S.A. 45 30N 73 50W
83 Lachlan, R., N.S.W. 33 46S 145 0E
93 Lachute, Canada 45 42N 74 25W
36 Lackagh Hills, Ireland 54 14N 8 0W
88 Lacombe, Canada 52 30N 113 50W
93 Laconia, U.S.A. 43 32N 71 30W
64 Ladakh, Ra., India 34 0N 77 30E
64 Ladis, Iran 29 0N 61 15E
50 Ladoga, L., U.S.S.R. 61 30N 31 0E
76 Lady Grey, S. Africa 30 45S 27 12E
31 Ladybank, Scotland 56 16N 3 8W
88 Ladysmith, Canada 49 0N 124 0W
76 Ladysmith, Natal 28 36S 29 42E
82 Lae, Terr. of New Guinea 6 50S 146 50E
49 Laeso, I., Denmark 57 17N 11 0E
91 Lafayette, La., U.S.A. 30 16N 92 3W
72 Lafia, Nigeria 8 34N 8 30E
36 Lagan, R., N. Ireland 54 29N 6 10W
48 Lagar Fliot, R., Iceland 65 10N 14 40W
49 Lagen, R., Norway 61 30N 10 20E
33 Laggan, Scotland 57 3N 4 48W
32 Laggan L., Scotland 56 56N 4 30W
72 Laghouat, Algeria 33 50N 2 49E
36 Laghy, Ireland 54 37N 8 7W
99 Lagoa dos Patos, Brazil 31 15S 51 0W
72 Lagos, Nigeria 6 20N 3 20E
37 Lagos, Portugal 37 7N 8 42W
94 Laguna de la Madre, Mexico 24 55N 97 30W
94 Laguna de Terminos, Mexico 18 30N 91 30W
91 Laguna Madre, U.S.A. 26 30N 97 0W
68 Lahat, Sumatra 3 40S 103 35E
62 Lahej, South Yemen 13 5N 44 50E
44 Lahn, R., Germany 50 38N 8 20E
49 Laholm, Sweden 56 30N 13 2E
64 Lahore, Pakistan 31 30N 74 23E
45 Lahr, Germany 48 21N 7 52E
50 Lahti, Finland 60 59N 25 42E
73 Lai (Béhagle), Chad 9 25N 16 30E
83 Laidley, Australia 27 35S 152 6E
43 Laigle, France 48 45N 0 40E
62 Laila, Saudi Arabia 22 25N 46 27E
76 Laingsburg, S. Africa 33 6S 20 59E
66 Laipin, China 23 50N 108 25E
33 Lairg, Scotland 58 1N 4 23W
83 Lake Cargelligo, Austral. 33 15S 146 22E
91 Lake Charles, U.S.A. 30 15N 93 7W
91 Lake City, U.S.A. 30 14N 93 10W
89 Lake of the Woods, L., Can. 49 30N 94 30W
91 Lakeland, U.S.A. 28 4N 81 59W
23 Lakenheath, England 52 25N 0 30E
83 Lakes Entrance, Victoria 38 0S 147 58
92 Lakewood, U.S.A. 41 30N 81 54W
65 Lakhimpur, India 27 55N 80 55E
64 Lakhpat, India 23 48N 68 40E
48 Laki, Mt., Iceland 64 10N 18 10W
63 Lakkish, R., Israel 31 40N 34 42E
41 Lakonia, G. of, Greece 36 30N 22 45E
72 Lakota, Ivory Coast 5 50N 5 30W
48 Lakse Fjord, Norway 70 40N 27 0E
65 Lala Ghat, India 24 30N 92 35E
73 Lalibala, Ethiopia 12 8N 39 10E
37 Lalin, Spain 42 40N 8 12W
64 Lalitpur, India 24 45N 78 20E
65 Lamaing, Burma 15 30N 97 50E
74 Lambarene, Gabon 0 50S 10 2E
35 Lambay I., Ireland 53 30N 6 2W
23 Lambeth, Greater London, England 51 26N 0 5W
22 Lambourn, England 51 33N 1 30W
72 Lame, Nigeria 10 25N 9 20E
37 Lamego, Portugal 41 0N 7 50W
94 Lamentin, Martinique I. 14 37N 61 0W
44 Lammel, Belgium 51 15N 5 20E
31 Lammermuir, Dist., Scot. 55 50N 2 25W
31 Lammermuir Hills, Scotland 55 50N 2 40W
65 Lampang, Thailand 18 15N 99 35E
40 Lampedusa I., Italy 35 32N 12 38E
25 Lampeter, Wales 52 8N 4 4W
65 Lamphun, Thailand 18 40N 99 5E
67 Lan Yu, I., Taiwan 22 0N 121 30E
90 Lanai, I., Hawaii, U.S.A. 20 50N 157 0W
**29 Lanark, & Co., Scotland 55 40N 3 47W
28 Lancashire, Co., England 53 30N 2 45W
26 Lancaster, England 54 3N 2 48W
91 Lancaster, Ohio, U.S.A. 39 44N 82 43W
92 Lancaster, Pa., U.S.A. 40 8N 76 18W
89 Lancaster Sd., Canada 74 0N 84 0W
27 Lanchester, England 54 50N 1 44W
66 Lanchow, China 36 0N 104 0E
40 Lanciano, Italy 42 15N 14 22E
23 Lancing, England 50 49N 0 19W
92 Lancing, U.S.A. 42 40N 84 30W
74 Lândana, Angola 5 11S 12 5E
45 Landau, Germany 49 11N 8 7E
45 Landeck, Austria 47 6N 10 37E
44 Landen, Belgium 50 45N 5 5E
43 Landerneau, France 48 30N 4 20W
42 Landes, Dépt., France 44 5N 0 40W
64 Landi Muhamed Amin Khan, Afghanistan 30 30N 63 50E
45 Landquart, Switzerland 46 57N 9 32E
44 Landrecies, France 50 7N 3 42E
24 Land's End, England 50 4N 5 43W
45 Landsberg, Germany 48 4N 10 53E
45 Landshut, Germany 48 33N 12 10E
49 Landskrona, Sweden 56 0N 12 57E
36 Lanesborough, Ireland 53 40N 8 0W
48 Lang Jökull, Mts., Ice. 64 35N 20 30W
48 Langanes, C., Iceland 66 27N 15 30W
43 Langeac, France 45 5N 3 30E
76 Langeberge, mts., S. Africa 34 0S 21 30E
45 Langenthal, Switz. 47 11N 7 50E
31 Langholm, Scotland 55 9N 3 0W
45 Langnau, Switzerland 46 57N 7 48E
42 Langon, France 44 35N 0 20W
43 Langres, & Plat., France 47 54N 5 20E
68 Langsa, Indonesia 4 30N 97 48E
26 Langstrothdale Chase, England 54 14N 2 13W
23 Langtoft, England 52 42N 0 19W
43 Languedoc, Prov., Fr. 43 50N 3 30E
42 Lannion, France 48 41N 3 22W
92 Lansing, U.S.A. 42 40N 84 31W
65 Lantsien, China 32 2N 96 5E
72 Lanzarote I., Canary Is. 29 0N 13 35W
43 Lanzo, Italy 45 20N 7 40E
68 Laoag, Philippines 18 25N 120 40E
29 Laois, Co., Ireland 52 57N 7 20W
43 Laon, France 49 35N 3 35E
57 Laos, S.E. Asia 18 0N 105 0E
48 Lapi, Co., Finland 67 0N 27 0E
13 Lappland, N. Europe 68 30N 25 0E
61 Laptev Sea, U.S.S.R. 76 0N 125 0E
73 Laqiya Arba'in, Sudan 19 50N 28 18E
40 L'Aquila, Italy 42 20N 13 24E
62 Lar, Iran 27 48N 54 2E
72 Larache, Morocco 35 10N 6 5W
90 Laramie, & Ra., U.S.A. 41 22N 105 38W
31 Larbert, Scotland 56 2N 3 50W
90 Laredo, U.S.A. 27 32N 99 28W
44 Laren, Netherlands 52 16N 5 12E
30 Largs, Scotland 55 50N 4 50W
41 Lárisa, Greece 39 38N 22 26E
64 Larkana, Pakistan 27 30N 68 0E
31 Larkhall, Scotland 55 44N 3 57W
62 Larnaca, Cyprus 34 58N 33 33E
36 Larne & L., N. Ireland 54 50N 5 48W
42 Laruns, France 43 0N 0 30W
49 Larvik, Norway 59 7N 10 3E
60 Laryak, U.S.S.R. 61 20N 80 3E
92 Las Cruces, U.S.A. 32 25N 106 47W
72 Las Palmas, Canary Is. 28 0N 15 45W
94 Las Tres Marias, Is., Mexico 21 25N 106 20W
90 Las Vegas, Nevada, U.S.A. 36 12N 115 12W
90 Las Vegas, N. Mexico, U.S.A. 35 35N 105 20W
65 Lashio, Burma 22 58N 97 58E
31 Lasswade, Scotland 55 53N 3 8W

* Renamed Lakshadweep Is.

** County incorporated within the region of Strathclyde

4 Lastoursville, Gabon 0 48s 12 59E
0 Lastovo I., Yugoslavia 42 47N 16 53E
9 Latacunga, Ecuador 0 45s 78 30w
2 Latakia, Syria 35 27N 35 58E
3 Latheron, Scotland 58 17N 3 22w
0 Latium, Prov., Italy 42 0N 12 20E
3 Latrobe, Tasmania 41 5s 146 40E
4 Latur, India 18 35N 76 42E
9 Latvia, S.S.R., U.S.S.R. 56 50N 24 0E
4 Lau or Eastern Group, Fiji 17 0s 178 0w
1 Lauder, & Dale, Scotland 55 43N 2 44w
5 Lauenberg, Germany 53 22N 10 34E
5 Laugharne, Wales 51 47N 4 28w
3 Launceston, Australia 41 24s 147 5E
4 Launceston, England 50 39N 4 22w
5 Launglon Bok Is. (S. Moscos Is.), Burma 13 50N 97 50E
2 Laura, Australia 15 45s 144 30E
1 Laurel, U.S.A. 31 45N 89 0w
3 Laurencekirk, Scotland 56 50N 2 28w
5 Lausanne, Switzerland 46 31N 6 39E
6 Lausitz (Lusatian), mts., Cz-slov. 50 40N 15 0E
8 Laut I., Indonesia 3 30s 116 15E
5 Lauterbrunnen, Switz. 46 36N 7 54E
2 Laval, France 48 4N 0 46w
3 Lavaur, France 43 40N 1 50E
3 Lavendon, England 52 11N 0 39w
0 Laverton, Australia 28 36s 122 27E
1 Lavrion, Greece 37 41N 24 2E
5 Lawng Pit, Mts., Burma 26 15N 98 15E
2 Lawra, Ghana 10 39N 2 51w
1 Lawrence, Kan., U.S.A. 38 59N 95 16w
3 Lawrence, Mass., U.S.A. 42 46N 71 2w
4 Lawrence, N.Z. 46 0s 169 45E
0 Lawton, U.S.A. 34 35N 98 30w
6 Laxey, I. of Man, Eng. 54 15N 4 23w
6 Laytown, Ireland 53 40N 6 15w
3 Le Blanc, France 46 40N 1 3E
3 Le Cateau, France 50 8N 3 30E
4 Le Chesne, France 49 31N 4 45E
3 Le Creusot, France 46 52N 4 25E
4 Le François, Martinique, Fr. W.I. 14 35N 60 55w
2 Le Havre, France 49 32N 0 5E
2 Le Kef, Tunisia 36 12N 8 47E
5 Le Locle, Switzerland 47 3N 6 44E
4 Le Marinel, Zaïre 10 25s 25 25E
9 Le Maire Str., Arg. 55 0s 65 0w
2 Le Mans, France 48 0N 0 15E
4 Le Moule, Guadeloupe I. 16 17N 61 22w
3 Le Puy, France 45 3N 3 53E
4 Le Quesnoy, France 50 15N 3 37E
3 Le Touquet, France 50 20N 1 45E
2 Le Verdon, France 45 33N 1 5w
3 Le Vigan, France 44 0N 3 32E
3 Lea, R., England 51 38N 0 1w
7 Leadenham, England 53 13N 0 33w
7 Leadgate, England 54 52N 1 48w
1 Leadhills, Scotland 55 27N 3 48w
0 Leadville, U.S.A. 39 20N 106 18w
5 Lealui, Zambia 15 10s 23 20E
2 Leamington, England 52 17N 1 32w
4 Leane, L., Ireland 52 0N 9 30w
0 Learmonth, Australia 22 30s 114 10E
3 Leatherhead, England 51 18N 0 20w
1 Leavenworth, U.S.A. 39 16N 94 59w
1 Lebanon, Mo., U.S.A. 37 43N 93 44w
1 Lebanon, Tenn., U.S.A. 36 13N 86 15w
3 Lebanon Mts., Lebanon 33 45N 35 45E
2 Lebanon, S.W. Asia 33 30N 35 40E
7 Lebrija, Spain 36 50N 6 2w
9 Lebu, Chile 37 47s 73 45w
1 Lecce, Italy 40 11N 18 12E
5 Lecco, Italy 45 51N 9 24E
5 Lech, R., Germany 47 45N 10 45E
3 Lectoure, France 43 55N 0 32E
7 Leczyca, Poland 52 2N 19 30E
4 Ledeberg, Belgium 51 3N 3 40E
9 Ledesma, Argentina 23 45s 64 50w
7 Ledesma, Spain 41 0N 6 0w
8 Leduc, Canada 53 20N 113 30w
2 Lee, England 50 47N 1 11w
4 Lee, R., Ireland 51 54N 8 50w
7 Leeds, Yorkshire, Eng. 53 49N 1 33w
6 Leek, England 53 6N 2 2w
4 Leer, Germany 53 15N 7 22E
3 Leeton, N.S.W. 34 23s 146 28E
4 Leeuwarden, Neth. 53 13N 5 48E
0 Leeuwin, C., Australia 34 21s 115 2E
5 Leeward Is., West Indies 17 0N 64 0w
8 Legaspi, Philippines 13 10N 123 46E
0 Leghorn (Livorno), Italy 43 34N 10 20E
6 Legnica, Poland 51 12N 16 10E
4 Leh, India 34 10N 77 50E
4 Lehinch, Ireland 52 56N 9 20w
28 Leicester, & Co., Eng. 52 37N 1 6w
2 Leichhardt Ra., Austral. 20 46s 147 40E
4 Leiden, Netherlands 52 10N 4 30E
4 Leie, R., Belgium 51 0N 3 30E
26 Leigh, Lancs., England 53 30N 2 31w
22 Leigh, Worcs., England 52 10N 2 21w
3 Leigh Creek, Australia 30 25s 138 20E
23 Leighton Buzzard, Eng. 51 55N 0 38w
6 Leine, R., Germany 52 35N 9 40E
4 Leinster, Prov., Ireland 52 55N 6 55w
6 Leipzig, Germany 51 20N 12 21E
7 Leiria, Portugal 39 46N 8 50w
23 Leiston, England 52 13N 1 35E
31 Leith, Scotland 55 59N 3 10w
23 Leith Hill, England 51 10N 0 23w
31 Leitholm, Scotland 55 42N 2 16w
29 Leitrim, & Co., Ireland 54 0N 8 3w
44 Lek, R., Netherlands 51 56N 4 50E
44 Lelystad, Netherlands 52 32N 5 28E
45 Leman (Geneva), L., Switz. 46 28N 6 30E
44 Lemmer, Netherlands 52 49N 5 42E
49 Lemvig, Denmark 56 33N 8 20E
61 Lena R., U.S.S.R. 64 30N 127 0E
35 Lenadoon Pt., Ireland 54 19N 9 3w
30 Lendalfoot, Scotland 55 12N 4 55w
60 Leninabad, U.S.S.R. 40 10N 69 50E
51 Leninakan, U.S.S.R. 41 0N 43 40E
50 Leningrad, U.S.S.R. 60 0N 30 25E
52 Leninsk, U.S.S.R. 48 40N 45 15E
60 Leninsk Kuznetskiy, U.S.S.R. 55 15N 86 15E
60 Leninogorsk, U.S.S.R. 50 30N 83 45E
45 Lenk, Switzerland 46 28N 7 27E
51 Lenkoran, Azerbaijan 38 46N 48 50E
30 Lennox Hills, Scotland 56 2N 4 15w
30 Lennoxtown, Scotland 55 58N 4 14w
44 Lens, France 50 27N 2 49E
40 Lentini, Italy 37 20N 15 0E
72 Léo, Volta 11 3N 2 2w
46 Leoben, Austria 47 22N 15 4E
22 Leominster, England 52 14N 2 44w
94 León, Mexico 21 5N 101 50w
94 Leon, Nicaragua 12 25N 86 47w
37 Leon, & Prov., Spain 42 35N 5 35w
83 Leongatha, Victoria 39 0s 146 0E
80 Leonora, Australia 28 49s 121 19E
*74 Léopold II L., Zaïre 2 0s 18 30E
74 Léopoldville, *see* Kinshasa
50 Lepel, U.S.S.R. 54 45N 28 30E
61 Lepikha, U.S.S.R. 64 45N 126 55E
94 Lerdo, Mexico 25 35N 103 35w
72 Lere, Nigeria 10 22N 8 31E
37 Lerida, Spain 41 38N 0 38E
32 Lerwick, Scotland 60 9N 1 10w
43 Les Andelys, France 49 18N 1 30E
95 Les Cayes, Haiti 18 0N 74 0w
42 Les Landes, Dist., France 44 20N 1 5w
42 Les Pieux, France 49 30N 1 50w
42 Les Sables d'Olonne, Fr. 46 34N 1 50w
31 Lesbury, England 55 25N 1 37w
41 Leskovac, Yugoslavia 42 55N 21 59E
31 Leslie, Scotland 56 12N 3 12w
31 Lesmahagow, Scotland 55 38N 3 55w
76 Lesotho, Africa 29 30s 28 0E
61 Lesozavodsk, U.S.S.R. 45 25N 133 30E
95 Lesser Antilles, W. Indies 14 0N 61 30w
88 Lesser Slave L., Canada 55 30N 115 30w
68 Lesser Sunda Is., *see* Nusa Tenggara
44 Lessines, Belgium 50 43N 3 50E
41 Lésvos I., Greece 39 10N 26 34E
46 Leszno, Poland 51 53N 16 37E
76 Letaba, S. Africa 23 45s 31 40E
23 Letchworth, England 51 58N 0 13w
88 Lethbridge, Canada 49 45N 112 48w
68 Lèti Is., East Indies 8 0s 128 0E
98 Leticia, Colombia 4 0s 70 0w
65 Letpadan, Burma 17 45N 96 0E
36 Letterkenny, Ireland 54 57N 7 43w
31 Leuchars, Scotland 56 23N 2 53w
45 Leuk, Switzerland 46 20N 7 38E
45 Leukerbad, Switzerland 46 22N 7 38E
44 Leuven, Belgium 50 53N 4 42E
44 Leuze, Belgium 50 37N 3 36E
52 Lev Tolstoy, U.S.S.R. 53 13N 39 27E
48 Levanger, Norway 63 47N 11 35E
43 Levanto, Italy 44 10N 9 35E
30 Leven, L., Argyll, Scot. 56 40N 5 5w
31 Leven, L., Kinross, Scot. 56 10N 3 25w
80 Levêque, C., Australia 16 15s 122 55E
44 Leverkusen, Germany 51 2N 6 59E
84 Levin, New Zealand 40 35s 175 15E
89 Levis, Canada 46 45N 71 15w
41 Lévka Ori, Mt., Crete 35 20N 24 0E
41 Levkás I., Greece 38 40N 20 35E
84 Levuka, Fiji Is. 17 34s 179 0E
23 Lewes, England 50 52N 0 1E
32 Lewis, Butt of, Scotland 58 30N 6 16w
32 Lewis I., Scotland 58 10N 6 40w
90 Lewis Ra., U.S.A. 48 15N 114 0w
23 Lewisham, Greater London, England 51 26N 0 5E
90 Lewiston, Idaho, U.S.A. 46 27N 117 2w
90 Lewistown, Mont., U.S.A. 47 11N 109 30w
92 Lexington, U.S.A. 38 2N 84 37w
26 Leyland, England 53 41N 2 42w
68 Leyte I., Philippines 10 30N 125 0E
43 Lezignan, France 43 10N 2 50E
52 Lgov, U.S.S.R. 51 41N 35 17E
64 Lhasa, Tibet 29 42N 91 10E
67 Liaoning, prov., China 42 0N 125 0E
67 Liaotung, G. of, China 40 30N 121 30E
67 Liaotung, Pen., China 40 0N 122 40E
67 Liaoyüan, China 43 52N 123 28E
88 Liard, R., Canada 61 15N 122 30w
74 Libenge, Zaïre 3 40N 18 55E
46 Liberec, Cz-slov. 50 47N 15 7E
72 Liberia, W. Africa 6 0N 9 30w
74 Libreville, Gabon 0 25N 9 25E
73 Libya, N. Africa 27 0N 16 0E
73 Libyan Des., N. Africa 27 0N 27 0E
62 Libyan Plateau, Egypt 31 0N 26 0E
40 Licata, Italy 37 8N 13 58E
22 Lichfield, England 52 41N 1 49w
76 Lichtenburg, S. Africa 26 10s 26 18E
49 Lida, U.S.S.R. 53 53N 25 15E
49 Lidköping, Sweden 58 31N 13 14E
46 Liechtenstein, Europe 47 2N 10 0E
44 Liège, & Prov., Belgium 50 38N 5 30E
46 Lienz, Austria 46 50N 12 10E
49 Liepája, U.S.S.R. 56 30N 21 0E
44 Lier, Belgium 51 9N 4 34E
45 Liestal, Switzerland 47 29N 7 44E
35 Liffey, R., Ireland 53 20N 6 31w
36 Lifford, Ireland 54 49N 7 29w
40 Liguria, prov., Italy 44 20N 8 30E
40 Ligurian Sea, Medit. S. 43 20N 8 40E
65 Lihwa, China 30 5N 100 20E
74 Likasi (Jadotville), Zaïre 10 52s 26 47E
74 Likati, Zaïre 3 20N 24 0E
66 Likiang, China 26 50N 100 5E
43 Lille, France 50 38N 3 0E
49 Lille Bælt, Denmark 55 8N 10 0E
49 Lillehammer, Norway 61 10N 10 29E
49 Lillesand, Norway 58 12N 8 23E
22 Lilleshall, England 52 45N 2 22w
49 Lilleström, Norway 59 56N 11 7E
88 Lillooet, Canada 50 44N 122 0w
75 Lilongwe, Malawi 14 0s 33 40E
49 Lim Fjord, Denmark 56 38N 8 23E
98 Lima, Peru 12 10s 77 5w
92 Lima, U.S.A. 40 40N 84 5w
62 Limassol, Cyprus 34 20N 33 0E
36 Limavady, N. Ireland 55 3N 6 56w
44 Limbourg, Prov., Belg. 51 0N 5 30E
44 Limburg, Germany 50 25N 8 5E
44 Limburg, Prov., Neth. 51 15N 6 0E
29 Limerick, & Co., Ireland 52 40N 8 37w
34 Limerick Junction, Ire. 52 30N 8 12w
41 Límnos, I., Greece 39 50N 25 10E
43 Limoges, France 45 51N 1 15E
95 Limón, Costa Rica 10 0N 83 2w
43 Limousin, Prov., France 45 35N 1 30E
43 Limoux, France 43 0N 2 15E
75 Limpopo, R., Mozam. 25 10s 33 30E
23 Limpsfield, England 51 15N 0 1E
74 Limuru, Kenya 1 6s 36 38E
99 Linares, Chile 36 0s 71 35w
94 Linares, Mexico 24 50N 99 20w
37 Linares, Spain 38 10N 3 42w
28 Lincoln, & Co., England 53 16N 0 33w
84 Lincoln, New Zealand 43 37s 172 30E
91 Lincoln, Neb., U.S.A. 40 55N 96 46w
27 Lincolnshire Wolds, Eng. 53 30N 0 20w
45 Lindau, Germany 47 33N 9 40E
49 Lindesnes, C., Norway 57 58N 7 3E
92 Lindsay, Canada 44 28N 78 53w
27 Lindsey, Dist., England 53 25N 0 20w
68 Lingayen Gulf, Phil. 16 30N 120 20E
63 Lingeh, Iran 26 35N 54 47E
44 Lingen, Germany 52 36N 7 19E
23 Lingfield, England 51 11N 0 1w
68 Lingga, Arch., E. Indies 0 0 104 37E
72 Linguéré, Senegal 15 25N 15 5w
67 Lini, China 35 10N 118 30E
49 Linköping, Sweden 58 24N 15 35E
31 Linlithgow, Scotland 55 58N 3 38w
25 Linney Head, Wales 51 37N 5 4w
30 Linnhe, L., Scotland 56 35N 5 30w
66 Linsia, China 35 40N 102 30E
23 Linslade, England 51 55N 0 40w
45 Linth, R., Switzerland 47 0N 9 0E
23 Liston, Cambs., England 52 6N 0 19E
66 Lintsing, China 36 55N 116 0E
43 Lions, G. of France 43 0N 4 0E
40 Lipari Is., Italy 38 40N 15 7E
52 Lipetsk, U.S.S.R. 52 45N 39 45E
47 Lipno, Poland 52 50N 19 15E
44 Lippe, R., Germany 51 40N 7 20E
74 Lira, Uganda 2 15N 32 55E
37 Liria, Spain 39 35N 0 35w
74 Lisala, Zaïre 2 15N 21 37E
36 Lisbellaw, N. Ireland 54 20N 7 32w
37 Lisbon, Portugal 38 43N 9 10w
36 Lisburn, N. Ireland 54 31N 6 3w
34 Liscannor, & B., Ireland 52 55N 9 27w
34 Liscarroll, Ireland 52 15N 8 44w
34 Lisdoonvarna, Ireland 53 2N 9 18w
24 Liskeard, England 50 28N 4 26w
52 Liski, U.S.S.R. 51 3N 39 20E
83 Lismore, Australia 28 47s 153 20E
34 Lismore, Ireland 52 8N 7 58w
36 Lisnaskea, N. Ireland 54 15N 7 28w
23 Liss, England 51 3N 0 53w
44 Lisse, Netherlands 52 17N 4 33E
92 Listowel, Canada 43 45N 80 57w
34 Listowel, Ireland 52 28N 9 28w
66 Litang, China 23 25N 108 10E
26 Litherland, England 53 29N 3 0w
83 Lithgow, Australia 33 30s 150 14E
41 Lithinon, C., Crete 35 0N 24 45E
49 Lithuania, S.S.R., U.S.S.R. 55 35N 24 0E
46 Litomerice, Cz-slov. 50 33N 14 10E
91 Little Abaco I., Bahamas 26 51N 77 45w
100 Little America, Antarc. 79 0s 164 0w
76 Little Bushman Ld., S. Africa 29 0s 18 30E
46 Little Carpathians, mts., Czechoslovakia 48 30N 17 20E
92 Little Current, Canada 45 58N 81 59w
76 Little Karroo, S. Africa 33 44s 22 0E
67 Little Khinyan, mts., China 48 0N 128 0E
32 Little Minch, Scotland 57 37N 6 50w
90 Little Missouri R., U.S.A. 46 0N 104 0w
64 Little Rann, India 23 25N 71 25E
91 Little Rock, U.S.A. 34 50N 92 25w
45 Little St. Bernard, Mt., Fr. 45 40N 6 47E
26 Littleborough, England 53 38N 2 8w
23 Littlehampton, England 50 48N 0 32w
23 Littleport, England 52 27N 0 18E
66 Liuchow, China 24 21N 109 5E
75 Liuwa Plain, Zambia 14 30s 22 35E
83 Liverpool, Australia 33 59s 150 52E
89 Liverpool, Canada 44 0N 65 0w
26 Liverpool, England 53 25N 3 0w
83 Liverpool Ra. & Pl., Australia 31 40s 150 30E
31 Livingston, Scotland 55 52N 3 33w
90 Livingston, U.S.A. 45 43N 110 41w
75 Livingstone, Zambia 17 48s 25 58E
74 Livingstonia, Malawi 10 33s 34 5E
40 Livorno, *see* Leghorn
99 Livramento, Brazil 30 50s 55 30w
74 Liwale, Tanzania 9 45s 38 0E
34 Lixnaw, Ireland 52 24N 9 38w
24 Lizard Pt., England 49 58N 5 11w
40 Ljubljana, Yugoslavia 46 4N 14 50E
48 Ljungan, R., Sweden 62 30N 14 30E
49 Ljungby, Sweden 56 50N 13 56E
49 Ljusdal, Sweden 61 50N 16 5E
49 Ljusna, Sweden 61 50N 16 5E
49 Ljusnan, R., Sweden 62 0N 15 20E
25 Llanaelhaiarn, Wales 52 59N 4 24w
25 Llanafan-fawr, Wales 52 12N 3 29w
25 Llanarth, Wales 52 12N 4 19w
25 Llanberis, Wales 53 6N 4 4w
25 Llanddewi-Brefi, Wales 52 11N 3 57w
25 Llandeilo, Wales 51 53N 3 59w
25 Llandogo, England 51 43N 2 42w
25 Llandovery, Wales 51 59N 3 48w
25 Llandrillo, Wales 52 56N 3 27w
25 Llandrindod Wells, Wales 52 15N 3 23w
25 Llandudno, Wales 53 20N 3 51w
25 Llandygwydd, Wales 52 3N 4 33w
25 Llandyrnog, Wales 53 10N 3 19w
25 Llandyssul, Wales 52 3N 4 20w
25 Llanelli, Wales 51 41N 4 8w
37 Llanes, Spain 43 30N 4 50w
25 Llanfaelog, Wales 53 13N 4 29w
25 Llanfair Caereinion, Wales 52 39N 3 20w
25 Llanfairfechan, Wales 53 15N 3 58w
25 Llangefni, Wales 53 15N 4 20w
25 Llangelynin, Wales 52 39N 4 7w
25 Llangennech, Wales 51 41N 4 10w
25 Llangollen, Wales 52 58N 3 11w
25 Llanharan, Wales 51 32N 3 28w
25 Llanidloes, Wales 52 26N 3 32w
25 Llanllyfni, Wales 53 2N 4 18w
25 Llannor, Wales 52 55N 4 25w
90 Llano Estacado (Staked Plains), U.S.A. 33 30N 103 0w
25 Llanon, Wales 52 17N 4 9w
96 Llanos, Reg., Columbia & Ven. 5 0N 67 0w
99 Llanquihue, L., Chile 41 2s 72 55w
25 Llanrhidian, Wales 51 36N 4 11w
25 Llanrwst, Wales 53 9N 3 48w
25 Llanstephan, Wales 51 46N 4 24w
25 Llantrisant, Wales 51 32N 3 25w
25 Llantwit-Major, Wales 51 24N 3 29w
25 Llanwenog, Wales 52 6N 4 11w
25 Llanystymdwy, Wales 52 56N 4 17w
25 Llethr, Mt., Wales 52 47N 3 58w
25 Lleyn Penin, Wales 52 55N 4 35w
88 Lloydminster, Canada 53 20N 110 3w
99 Llullaillaco, Mt., Chile 24 40s 68 30w
31 Loanhead, Scotland 55 53N 3 10w
76 Lobatse, Botswana 25 15s 25 30E
75 Lobito, Angola 12 0s 13 0E
98 Lobos Is., Peru 6 15s 81 0w
45 Locarno, Switzerland 46 11N 8 48E
32 Lochaber, Dist., Scotland 57 0N 5 0w
30 Lochaline, Scotland 56 32N 5 47w
30 Lochans, Scotland 54 52N 5 1w
32 Lochcarron, Scotland 57 25N 5 30w
30 Lochdonhead, Scotland 56 27N 5 40w
44 Lochem, Netherlands 52 10N 6 26w
43 Loches, France 47 10N 1 0E
31 Lochgelly, Scotland 56 7N 3 18w
30 Lochgilphead, Scotland 56 3N 5 25w
30 Lochgoilhead, Scotland 56 10N 4 54w
32 Lochinver, Scotland 58 9N 5 15w
31 Lochmaben, Scotland 55 8N 3 27w
30 Lochnagar, Mt., Scotland 56 56N 3 15w
30 Lochranza, Scotland 55 42N 5 18w
30 Lochwinnoch, Scotland 55 47N 4 39w
30 Lochy, L., & R., Scot. 56 57N 4 55w
92 Loch Haven, U.S.A. 41 7N 77 33w
31 Lockerbie, Scotland 55 6N 3 22w
83 Lockhart, Australia 35 10s 146 48E
91 Lockport, U.S.A. 43 10N 78 45w
63 Lod (Lydda), Israel 31 57N 34 54E
43 Lodi, Italy 45 20N 9 32E
74 Lodja, Zaïre 3 28s 23 35E
74 Lodwar, Kenya 2 58N 35 25E
47 Lódz, Poland 51 48N 19 22E
76 Loeriesfontein, S. Africa 30 56s 19 28E
48 Lofoten Is., Norway 68 30N 15 0E
27 Loftus, England 54 33N 0 52w
90 Logan, U.S.A. 41 42N 111 47w
86 Logan, Mt., Yukon, Canada 60 48N 138 40w
92 Logansport, U.S.A. 40 48N 86 20w
74 Loge, R., Angola 7 35s 14 15E
37 Logrono, Spain 42 25N 2 21w
65 Lohardaga, India 23 30N 84 36E
62 Loheia, Yemen 15 45N 42 40E
66 Loho, China 33 30N 114 0E
45 Lohr, Germany 49 59N 9 33E
65 Loikaw, Burma 19 43N 97 20E
49 Loimaa, Finland 60 51N 22 53E
42 Loir-et-Cher, Dépt., Fr. 47 33N 1 50E
42 Loire, Dépt., France 45 40N 4 5E
43 Loire, R., France 47 40N 2 30E
42 Loire-Atlant., Dépt., Fr. 47 32N 1 48w
42 Loiret, Dépt. France 48 5N 2 20E
98 Loja, Ecuador 4 0s 79 16w
37 Loja, Spain 37 10N 4 15w
44 Lokeren, Belgium 51 6N 3 59E
74 Lokitaung, Kenya 4 18N 35 45E
48 Lokka Res., Finland 68 00N 27 30E
48 Lökken, Norway 63 8N 9 45E
72 Lokoja, Nigeria 7 48N 6 43E
74 Lokolama, Zaïre 2 10s 19 50E
49 Lolland, Denmark 54 50N 11 30E
65 Lolungchung, China 30 45N 96 10E
41 Lom, Bulgaria 43 52N 23 20E
40 Lombardy, Prov., Italy 45 22N 9 50E
68 Lomblen I., Indonesia 8 30s 123 32E
68 Lombok, I., Indonesia 8 35s 116 30E
72 Lome, Togo 6 8N 1 10E
74 Lomela & R., Zaïre 2 5s 23 52E
74 Lomié, Cameroon 3 13N 13 38E
30 Lomond, L., Scotland 56 4N 4 34w
89 London, Canada 43 0N 81 21w
23 London, Greater, Eng. 51 30N 0 5w
**36 Londonderry, & Co., N. Ireland 55 0N 7 18w
99 Londrina, Brazil 23 30s 50 45w
91 Long Bay, U.S.A. 33 30N 78 30w
90 Long Beach, Calif., U.S.A. 33 50N 118 6w
22 Long Eaton, England 52 53N 1 15w
93 Long I., U.S.A. 40 50N 73 0w
30 Long, L., Scotland 56 5N 4 52w
25 Long Mt., Wales 52 38N 3 3w
23 Long Melford, England 52 5N 0 44E
22 Long Mynd, mt., Eng. 52 30N 2 56w
23 Long Sutton, England 52 47N 0 9E
68 Long Xuyen, Vietnam 10 15N 105 25E
32 Longa I., Scotland 57 45N 5 50w
65 Longdam, China 28 15N 98 15E
83 Longford, Australia 41 47s 147 4E
36 Longford, & Co., Ireland 53 44N 7 46w
31 Longforgan, Scotland 56 28N 3 8w
89 Longlac, Canada 49 45N 86 25w
65 Longling, China 24 35N 98 35E
90 Longmont, U.S.A. 40 14N 105 10w
82 Longreach, Australia 23 29s 144 13E
26 Longridge, England 53 50N 2 37w
33 Longside, Scotland 57 30N 1 57w
26 Longton (Lancs.), Eng. 53 43N 2 48w
26 Longton (Staffs.), England 53 0N 2 8w
26 Longtown, Cumb., Eng. 55 0N 2 58w
44 Longuyon, France 49 27N 5 35E
91 Longview, U.S.A. 32 28N 94 29w
43 Longwy, France 49 31N 5 46E
43 Lons le Saunier, France 46 42N 5 31E
48 Lönsdal, Norway 66 45N 15 30E
34 Loop Hd., Ireland 52 34N 9 56w
66 Lop Nor, L., China 40 0N 90 0E
74 Lopez, C., Gabon 0 47s 8 40E
65 Lora, R., Afghanistan 32 0N 67 15E
92 Lorain, U.S.A. 41 29N 82 10w
64 Loralai, Pakistan 30 25N 68 30E
37 Lorca, Spain 37 40N 1 41w
81 Lord Howe I., Pac. Oc. 31 0s 159 0E
82 Lorengau, Terr. of New Guinea 2 0s 147 0E
40 Loreto, Italy 43 26N 13 40E
42 Lorient, France 47 45N 3 22w
30 Lorn, Firth of, Scot. 56 20N 5 40w
83 Lorne, Australia 38 35s 144 0E
45 Lorrach, Germany 47 37N 7 38E
43 Lorraine, reg., France 48 58N 6 0E
99 Los Andes, Chile 32 42s 70 25w
99 Los Angeles, Chile 37 42s 72 20w
90 Los Angeles, U.S.A. 33 50N 118 22w
94 Los Mochis, Mexico 25 50N 109 0w
61 Loshkalakh, U.S.S.R. 62 40N 147 5E
40 Losinj, I., Yugoslavia 44 55N 14 45E
33 Lossiemouth, Scotland 57 44N 3 16w
42 Lot, Dépt., France 44 52N 1 48E
43 Lot, R., France 44 30N 1 45E
99 Lota, Chile 37 15s 73 20w
73 Lotagipi Swamp, Sudan & Kenya 4 28N 35 0E
42 Lot-et-Garonne, Dépt., Fr. 44 33N 0 22E
74 Loto, Zaïre 2 18s 23 0E
45 Lotschberg Tunnel, Switz. 46 25N 7 40E
48 Lotta, R., U.S.S.R. 68 30N 29 0E
42 Loudeac, France 48 15N 2 45w
72 Louga, Senegal 15 38N 16 7w
22 Loughborough, England 52 45N 1 12w
36 Loughbrickland, N. Ire. 54 19N 6 19w
25 Loughor, Wales 51 39N 4 5w
34 Loughrea, Ireland 53 14N 8 35w
36 Loughros More B., Ireland 54 47N 8 34w
37 Louie, Portugal 37 8N 8 0w
76 Louis Trichardt, S. Africa 25 5s 29 50E
82 Louisiade Arch., Papua 10 0s 153 0E
91 Louisiana, st., U.S.A. 31 0N 92 0w
92 Louisville, U.S.A. 38 16N 85 48w
42 Lourdes, France 43 15N 0 3w
†75 Lourenço Marques, Moz. 25 59s 32 42E
27 Louth, England 53 24N 0 2w
36 Louth, & Co., Ireland 53 56N 6 31w
44 Louvain, *see* Leuven
43 Louviers, France 49 15N 1 10E
43 Lovere, Italy 45 50N 10 5E
49 Loviisa, Finland 60 26N 26 20E
93 Lowell, U.S.A. 42 44N 71 15w
46 Lower Austria, prov., Austria 48 0N 16 0E

* *Renamed Mai-Ndombe, L.*

** *In April 1973 districts replaced counties in N. Ireland*

† *Renamed Maputo*

94 Lower California, Mex. 28 0N 113 30W
84 Lower Hutt, N.Z. 41 10S 174 55E
46 Lower Saxony, Länd, Ger. 52 45N 9 0E
61 Lr. Tunguska, R., U.S.S.R. 64 0N 98 0E
23 Lowestoft, England 52 29N 1 47E
47 Lowicz, Poland 52 3N 19 59E
31 Lowther Hills, Scotland 55 20N 3 40W
83 Loxton, Australia 34 28S 140 31E
78 Loyalty Is., Pac. Oc. 20 20S 168 0E
66 Loyang, China 34 55N 112 15E
42 Lozère, Dépt., France 44 28N 3 30E
74 Luacano, Angola 11 15S 21 40E
74 Luanda, Angola 8 58S 13 9E
66 Luang Prabang, Laos 19 52N 101 50E
75 Luangwa, R., Zambia 12 0S 32 28E
75 Luanshya, Zambia 13 8S 28 25E
75 Luashi, Zaïre 11 3S 23 38E
90 Lubbock, U.S.A. 33 37N 101 50W
46 Lübeck, & B., Germany 53 52N 10 41E
47 Lublin, Poland 51 18N 22 32E
75 Lubumbashi (Elisabethville), Zaïre 11 30S 27 31E
35 Lucan, Ireland 53 21N 6 27W
88 Lucania, Mt., Alaska 61 10N 140 20W
40 Lucca, Italy 43 52N 10 35E
30 Luce B., Scotland 54 45N 4 45W
94 Lucea, Jamaica 18 25N 78 10W
68 Lucena, Philippines 14 0N 121 35E
37 Lucena, Spain 37 28N 4 28W
47 Luzenéc, Cz-slov. 48 18N 19 42E
66 Luchow, China 29 5N 105 0E
75 Lucira, Angola 14 0S 12 35E
46 Luckenwalde, Germany 52 15N 13 10E
65 Lucknow, India 26 57N 80 59E
42 Luçon, France 46 30N 1 10W
75 Lüderitz, S.W. Africa 26 40S 15 19E
64 Ludhiana, India 30 53N 76 2E
91 Ludington, U.S.A. 43 55N 86 29W
22 Ludlow, England 52 22N 2 42W
49 Ludvika, Sweden 60 15N 15 5E
45 Ludwigsburg, Germany 48 53N 9 11E
45 Ludwigshafen, Germany 49 30N 8 27E
74 Luebo, Zaïre 5 10S 21 24E
74 Lufira, R., Zaïre 9 20S 27 0E
91 Lufkin, U.S.A. 31 17N 94 46W
45 Lugano, Switzerland 46 1N 8 48E
45 Lugano, L. di., Switz. 46 2N 8 57E
52 Lugansk, *see* Voroshilovgrad
75 Lugenda, R., Mozam. 12 30S 36 20E
35 Lugnaquillia, Mt., Ire. 52 57N 6 25W
37 Lugo, Spain 43 2N 7 34W
47 Lugoj, Rumania 45 38N 21 57E
60 Lugovoi, U.S.S.R. 43 10N 72 50E
22 Lugwardine, England 52 4N 2 38W
33 Luichart, L., Scotland 57 38N 4 44W
66 Luichow Pen., China 20 40N 110 0E
30 Luing, I., Scotland 56 15N 5 40W
45 Luino, Italy 45 59N 8 43E
74 Luisa, Zaïre 7 40S 22 30E
75 Lukanga Swamp, Zambia 14 30S 27 50E
74 Lukenie, R., Zaïre 3 0S 18 30E
74 Lukolela, Zaïre 1 30S 17 8E
47 Lukow, Poland 51 58N 22 22E
48 Lule, R., Sweden 66 20N 21 0E
48 Lulea, Sweden 65 33N 22 8E
66 Luliang Mts., China 37 30N 111 0E
74 Lulonga, R., Zaïre 1 0N 18 40E
74 Lulua, R., Zaïre 6 20S 22 40E
74 Luluabourg, *see* Kananga
75 Lumai, Angola 13 20S 21 25E
33 Lumphanan, Scotland 57 8N 2 41W
84 Lumsden, N.Z. 45 41S 168 29E
49 Lund, Sweden 55 44N 13 6E
75 Lundazi, Zambia 12 30S 33 20E
24 Lundy, I., Bristol Chan. 51 11N 4 40W
26 Lune, R., England 54 10N 2 40W
46 Lüneburg, Germany 53 13N 10 22E
43 Lunel, France 43 40N 4 5E
93 Lunenburg, Canada 44 25N 64 32W
43 Luneville, France 48 39N 6 30E
48 Lungholt, Iceland 63 30N 18 5W
67 Lungkow, China 37 38N 120 25E
65 Lungleh, India 22 55N 92 45E
74 Luofu, Zaïre 0 1N 29 15E
40 Luqa, Malta 35 50N 14 27E
40 Lure, France 47 40N 6 30E
36 Lurgan (Craigavon), N. Ireland 54 28N 6 20W
75 Lusaka, Zambia 15 3S 28 30E
74 Lusambo, Zaïre 4 55S 23 20E
74 Lushoto, Tanzania 4 50S 38 10E
35 Lusk, Ireland 53 32N 6 10W
30 Luss, Scotland 56 6N 4 38W
67 Lü-ta (Dairen-Port Arthur), China 39 0N 121 33E
23 Luton, England 51 52N 0 25W
47 Lutsk, U.S.S.R. 50 50N 25 15E
22 Lutterworth, England 52 27N 1 14W
74 Luwingu, Zambia 10 15S 30 2E
44 Luxembourg, Prov., Belg. 49 58N 5 30E
44 Luxembourg, Lux. 49 37N 6 8E
44 Luxembourg, Europe 49 45N 6 20E
73 Luxor, Egypt 25 40N 32 38E
42 Luz, France 42 50N 0 2W
45 Luzern, & Cn., Switz. 47 3N 8 18E
46 Luzické Hory (Lusatian Mts.), Cz-slov., *see* Lausitz mts.
68 Luzon, I., Philippines 16 30N 121 0E
47 Lvov, U.S.S.R. 49 51N 24 0E
61 Lyakhov Is., U.S.S.R. 73 30N 143 0E
33 Lybster, Scotland 58 18N 3 16W
51 Lycian Taurus, Mts., Tur. 37 0N 30 30E
23 Lydd, England 50 56N 0 54E
63 Lydda, *see* Lod
76 Lydenburg, S. Africa 25 0S 30 27E
24 Lydford, England 50 38N 4 7W
48 Lyeksele, Sweden 64 32N 18 40E
84 Lyell, & Ra., N.Z. 41 46S 172 4E
24 Lyme Bay, England 50 38N 2 55W
24 Lyme Regis, England 50 43N 2 57W
22 Lymington, England 50 47N 1 34W
26 Lymm, England 53 23N 2 30W
47 Lyna, R., Poland 54 17N 21 0E
92 Lynchburg, U.S.A. 37 28N 79 12W
22 Lyndhurst, England 50 51N 1 36W
83 Lynd Ra., Australia 25 35S 149 20E
24 Lyneham, England 51 30N 1 57W
24 Lynmouth, England 51 14N 3 50W
92 Lynn, U.S.A. 42 30N 71 0W
43 Lyonnais, Prov., France 45 50N 4 20E
42 Lyons, France 45 47N 4 50E
26 Lytham, England 53 45N 2 58W
84 Lyttelton, New Zealand 43 38S 172 46E
52 Lyubertsy, U.S.S.R. 55 41N 37 54E

M

66 Ma, R., *see* Hwang
62 Ma'an, Jordan 30 15N 35 37E
49 Maarianhamina, Finland 60 12N 20 0E
44 Maas, R., Netherlands 51 48N 5 30E
44 Maaseik, Belgium 51 7N 5 47E
44 Maastricht, Netherlands 50 52N 5 42E
73 Maatin-es-Sarra, Libya 21 45N 22 0E
74 Mabirou, Congo (Fr.) 1 10S 15 48E
27 Mablethorpe, England 53 21N 0 14E
91 McAlester, U.S.A. 34 58N 95 50W
66 Macao, & Port. Terr., China 22 15N 113 35E
98 Macapá, Brazil 0 5N 52 0W
26 Macclesfield, England 53 16N 2 8W
86 McClure Str., Can. 74 20N 120 0W
91 McComb, U.S.A. 31 30N 90 27W
80 Macdonald, L., Australia 23 30S 128 40E
80 Macdonnell Ranges, Australia 23 30S 133 0E
88 Macdougall L., Canada 66 20N 98 30W
33 Macduff, Scotland 57 41N 2 29W
41 Macedonia, Prov., Greece 40 45N 23 0E
41 Macedonia, Fed. Unit, Yugoslavia 41 30N 21 30E
98 Maceio, Brazil 9 30S 35 40W
72 Macenta, Guinea 8 35N 9 20W
40 Macerata, Italy 43 18N 13 33E
34 Macgillacuddy's Reeks, Mts., Ireland 52 0N 9 48W
98 Machala, Ecuador 3 10S 79 59W
30 Machars, The, dist., Scot. 54 45N 4 30W
61 Machevna, U.S.S.R. 61 5N 172 0E
93 Machias, U.S.A. 44 45N 67 30W
83 Macintyre, R., Australia 28 32S 150 25E
82 Mackay, Australia 21 6S 149 14E
80 Mackay, L., Australia 23 0S 131 0E
92 McKeesport, U.S.A. 40 22N 79 41W
88 Mackenzie, Terr., Can. 64 30N 115 0W
88 Mackenzie Mts., Canada 64 0N 130 0W
82 Mackenzie R., Australia 23 30S 148 45E
88 Mackenzie R., Canada 62 0N 122 0W
83 Macksville, Australia 30 40S 152 56E
83 Maclean, Australia 29 29S 153 15E
83 Macleay R., Australia 30 56S 153 0E
88 McLennan, Canada 55 50N 117 0W
100 McMurdo, & Sd., Antarctica 78 0S 166 0E
88 McMurray, Canada 56 35N 111 30W
90 McPherson, U.S.A. 38 25N 97 45W
83 McPherson Ra., Australia 28 20S 153 0E
43 Mâcon, France 46 21N 4 45E
91 Macon, U.S.A. 32 40N 83 28W
75 Macondo, Angola 12 40S 23 48E
83 Macquarie, Hr., Austral. 42 2S 145 10E
100 Macquarie, I., S. Ocean 54 0S 159 0E
75 Macumba R., Australia 27 0S 136 0E
62 Madaba, Jordan 31 42N 35 48E
73 Madagali, Nigeria 10 56N 13 33E
74 Madagascar I., Africa 19 0S 46 0E
73 Madama, Niger 21 35N 13 50E
82 Madang, N.E. New Guinea 5 15S 145 46E
72 Madaoua, Niger 14 5N 6 27E
65 Madaripur, Bangladesh 23 10N 90 10E
40 Maddalena I., Italy 41 20N 9 22E
94 Madden L., Panama 9 15N 79 35W
32 Maddy, L., Scotland 57 36N 7 6W
72 Madeira, I., Atlant. Oc. 32 40N 17 20W
98 Madeira, R., Brazil 6 0S 61 0W
94 Madera, Mexico 29 15N 107 55W
64 Madhya Pradesh, st., Ind. 23 0N 78 0E
62 Madinat al Shaab, S. Yemen 13 0N 44 45E
74 Madingou, Congo (Fr.) 4 10S 13 33E
92 Madison, Wis., U.S.A. 43 15N 89 30W
68 Madiun, Indonesia 7 27S 111 30E
68 Madjene, Indonesia 3 29S 119 4E
64 Madras, India 13 2N 80 22N
94 Madre, Sa., mts., Mex. 25 0N 106 0W
68 Madre, Sa., mts., Phil. 17 30N 122 0E
99 Madre de Dios, I., Chile 50 30S 75 30W
37 Madrid, Spain 40 27N 3 42W
68 Madura, I., Indonesia 7 0S 114 0E
64 Madurai, India 9 50N 78 5E
65 Mae Hong Son, Thailand 19 25N 98 5E
25 Maesteg, Wales 51 36N 3 40W
75 Maevatanana, Madag. 16 57S 46 50E
76 Mafeking, S. Africa 25 48S 25 30E
83 Maffra, Australia 38 45S 147 0E
62 Mafraq, Jordan 32 21N 36 12E
61 Magadan, U.S.S.R. 59 40N 150 50E
74 Magadi, Kenya 1 40S 36 20E
98 Magangue, Colombia 9 15N 74 50W
72 Magburaka, Sierra Leone 8 41N 11 45W
98 Magdalena, R., Colombia 9 0N 74 40W
46 Magdeburg, Germany 52 8N 11 35E
68 Magelang, Indonesia 7 45S 110 20E
99 Magellan's Str., Chile 52 20S 69 0W
45 Maggia, R., Switzerland 46 17N 8 40E
45 Maggiore, L., Italy 46 0N 8 40E
36 Maghera, N. Ireland 54 51N 6 40W
36 Magherafelt, N. Ireland 54 45N 6 38W
50 Magnitogorsk, U.S.S.R. 53 20N 59 0E
93 Magog, Canada 45 20N 72 6W
36 Maguires' Bridge, N. Ire. 54 18N 7 28W
64 Mahabaleshwar, India 17 58N 73 50E
68 Mahakam, R., Indonesia 0 25N 116 30E
75 Mahalapye, Botswana 23 0S 26 48E
73 Mahalla el Kubra, Egypt 31 10N 31 0E
65 Mahanadi, R., India 20 30N 84 30E
64 Mahbubnagar, India 16 45N 77 55E
73 Mahdia, Tunisia 35 30N 11 2E
84 Maheno, New Zealand 45 8S 170 50E
84 Mahia Pen., N.Z. 39 12S 177 53E
62 Maidan-i-Naftan, Iran 32 0N 49 27E
23 Maidenhead, England 51 31N 0 42W
23 Maidstone, England 51 15N 0 32E
73 Maiduguri, Nigeria 12 0N 13 5E
65 Maijdi, Bangladesh 22 45N 91 25E
65 Maikala, Ra., India 21 50N 81 0E
64 Maimana, Afghanistan 35 55N 64 35E
45 Main, R., Germany 49 50N 9 30E
42 Maine, Prov., France 48 10N 0 0
91 Maine, st., U.S.A. 45 0N 68 30W
42 Maine-et-Loire, Dépt., France 47 17N 0 23W
33 Mainland, I., Orkneys, Scotland 59 0N 3 0W
32 Mainland, I., Shetlands, Scotland 60 15N 1 20W
43 Maintenon, France 48 35N 1 38E
75 Maintirano, Madag. 18 3S 44 5E
45 Mainz, Germany 50 0N 8 13E
99 Maipo Vol., Chile 34 0S 70 0W
83 Maitland, Australia 32 49S 151 38E
67 Maizuru, Japan 35 25N 135 25E
62 Majma'a, Saudi Arabia 25 52N 45 28E
37 Majorca, I., *see* Mallorca
75 Majunga, Madag. 15 40S 46 25E
72 Maka-Koulibentane, Sénégal 13 40N 14 13W
75 Makarikari Salt Pan, Botswana 20 45S 26 20E
*68 Makasar, & Str., Indon. 5 10S 119 20E
51 Makat, U.S.S.R. 47 40N 53 25E
72 Makeni, Sierra Leone 8 56N 12 5W
52 Makeyevka, U.S.S.R. 48 0N 38 0E
52 Makhachkala, U.S.S.R. 42 58N 47 40E
66 Makhai, China 38 30N 93 40E
47 Makó, Hungary 46 16N 20 27E
74 Makokou, Gabon 0 35N 12 55E
61 Makorovo, U.S.S.R. 57 30N 107 40E
64 Makrai, India 22 2N 77 0E
63 Makran, dist., Iran 26 0N 60 30E
64 Makran Coast Ra., Pakistan 25 30N 64 0E
60 Maksimoyarskoye, U.S.S.R. 58 50N 87 5E
64 Malabar Coast, India 12 0N 75 25E
68 Malacca, Str. of, Malaya 4 0N 100 0E
37 Maladetta, Mt., Spain 42 40N 0 30E
37 Malaga, Spain 36 46N 4 47W
75 Malagasy Rep., Africa 19 0S 46 0E
35 Malahide, Ireland 53 27N 6 10W
73 Malakal, Sudan 9 37N 31 45E
64 Malakand, Pakistan 34 30N 72 0E
68 Malaku (Moluccas), Is., Indonesia 2 0S 127 30E
61 Malamyzh, U.S.S.R. 50 0N 136 50E
68 Malang, Indonesia 8 0S 112 34E
74 Malanje, Angola 9 30S 16 17E
49 Mälaren L., Sweden 59 30N 16 50E
51 Malatya, Turkey 38 37N 38 35E
74 Malawi (Nyasaland), E. Africa 12 30S 33 40E
75 Malawi, L., *see* Nyasa L.
55 Malay Pen., S.E. Asia 4 30N 102 0E
68 Malaya, st., S.E. Asia 4 0N 103 0E
68 Malaysia, S.E. Asia 4 0N 110 0E
51 Malazgirt, Turkey 39 13N 42 30E
82 Malbon, Australia 21 5S 140 17E
47 Malbork, Poland 54 3N 19 10E
80 Malcolm, Australia 28 58S 121 30E
44 Maldegem, Belgium 51 12N 3 27E
55 Maldive Is., Indian Ocean 5 0N 73 0E
23 Maldon, England 51 43N 0 41E
64 Malegaon, India 20 35N 74 25E
48 Malgomaj, L., Sweden 64 45N 16 5E
73 Malha, Sudan 15 8N 25 10E
26 Malham Tarn, England 54 6N 2 11W
37 Malhao, Sa. do, mts., Port. 37 25N 8 0W
90 Malheur, L., U.S.A. 43 20N 118 50W
72 Mali, West Africa 18 0N 1 0W
65 Mali, R., Burma 26 30N 97 50E
36 Malin Hd. & Pen., Ire. 55 23N 7 22W
66 Malipo, China 23 25N 104 45E
32 Mallaig, Scotland 57 0N 5 48W
73 Mallawi, Egypt 27 44N 30 44E
37 Mallorca I., Balaeric Is., Spain 39 30N 3 0E
34 Mallow, Ireland 52 9N 8 38W
25 Malltraeth B., Wales 53 7N 4 25W
48 Malmberget, Sweden 67 13N 20 32E
44 Malmédy, Belgium 50 26N 6 2E
22 Malmesbury, England 51 36N 2 6W
49 Malmö, Sweden 55 38N 12 57E
49 Malmöhus, Co., Sweden 55 45N 13 15E
40 Malta, I., Medit. Sea 35 54N 14 28E
27 Maltby, England 53 25N 1 12W
27 Malton, England 54 10N 0 45W
64 Malvan, India 16 0N 73 30E
61 Maly I., U.S.S.R. 74 20N 140 30E
43 Mamers, France 48 20N 0 20E
72 Mamfe, Cameroon 5 59N 9 40E
98 Mamore, R., Bolivia 16 30S 63 20W
72 Mamou, Guinea 10 15N 12 0W
72 Man, Ivory Coast 7 30N 7 40W
26 Man, I. of, British Isles 54 10N 4 35W
65 Man-Na, Burma 23 25N 97 20E
37 Manacor, Mallorca, Spain 39 37N 3 46E
68 Manado, Indonesia 1 35N 124 50E
94 Managua, Nicaragua 12 0N 86 20W
75 Manakara, Madagascar 22 5S 48 5E
62 Manakha, Yemen 15 2N 43 50E
82 Manam I., Terr. of New Guinea 4 10S 145 0E
75 Mananjary, Madagascar 21 10S 48 28E
75 Manantenina, Madagas. 24 6S 47 20E
84 Manapouri, New Zealand 45 30S 167 33E
65 Manasarowar L., Tibet, China 30 40N 81 20E
66 Manass, China 44 20N 86 20E
98 Manaus, Brazil 3 0S 60 10W
42 Manche, Dépt., France 48 57N 1 20W
26 Manchester, England 53 28N 2 15W
93 Manchester, U.S.A. 43 0N 71 22W
66 Manchouli, China 49 40N 117 0E
67 Manchuria, reg., China 44 30N 126 0E
55 Manchurian Plain, China 45 0N 125 0E
74 Manda, Tanzania 10 37S 34 52E
75 Mandabé, Madagascar 21 0S 44 55E
49 Mandal, Norway 58 0N 7 22E
65 Mandalay, Burma 22 0N 96 12E
41 Mandalya, G., Turkey 37 15N 27 15E
68 Mandar G., Indonesia 3 30S 119 30E
64 Mandi, India 31 40N 76 55E
65 Mandla, India 22 45N 80 26E
64 Mandya, India 12 30N 76 50E
62 Manfalut, Egypt 27 20N 31 0E
40 Manfredonia, G. of, Italy 41 39N 15 54E
47 Mangalia, Rumania 43 50N 28 37E
64 Mangalore, India 12 58N 75 0E
84 Mangaweka, N.Z. 39 47S 175 43E
34 Mangerton, Mt. Ireland 51 57N 9 29W
68 Manggar, Indonesia 3 0S 108 15E
65 Mangin Ra., Burma 24 15N 95 45E
75 Mangoche (Fort Johnston), Malawi 14 25S 35 16E
68 Mangole, I., Indonesia 1 45S 126 0E
60 Mangyshlak, Pen., U.S.S.R. 43 40N 52 30E
91 Manhattan, U.S.A. 39 20N 96 40W
65 Mani, Tibet, China 34 45N 87 10E
89 Manicouagan R., Can. 50 25N 68 32W
68 Manila, Philippines 14 30N 121 12E
68 Manila Bay, Phil. 14 20N 120 30E
83 Manilla, Australia 30 45S 150 36E
65 Manipur, st., India 24 44N 94 0E
41 Manisa, Turkey 38 38N 27 24E
92 Manistee, U.S.A. 44 19N 86 15W
88 Manitoba, L. & Prov., Canada 51 0N 98 55W
91 Manitowoc, U.S.A. 44 10N 87 42W
98 Manizales, Columbia 5 30N 75 56W
91 Mankato, U.S.A. 44 10N 94 0W
72 Mankono, Ivory Coast 8 10N 6 10W
75 Mankoya, Zambia 14 58S 24 57E
83 Manly, Australia 33 48S 151 20E
83 Manna Hill, Australia 32 29S 140 0E
64 Mannar, & G., Sri Lanka 9 0N 79 49E
45 Mannheim, Germany 49 32N 8 32E
23 Manningtree, England 51 56N 1 3E
83 Mannum, Australia 34 57S 139 12E
75 Manombo, Madagascar 22 55S 43 30E
74 Manono, Zaïre 7 19S 27 23E
36 Manorhamilton, Ireland 54 19N 8 10W
43 Manosque, France 43 50N 5 45E
37 Manresa, Spain 41 46N 1 51E
74 Mansa, Zambia 11 7S 28 54E
89 Mansel I., Canada 62 10N 80 0W
83 Mansfield, Australia 37 4S 146 5E
27 Mansfield, England 53 9N 1 12W
92 Mansfield, U.S.A. 40 45N 82 38W
27 Mansfield Woodhouse, England 53 12N 1 11W
98 Manta, Ecuador 1 0S 80 40W
43 Mantes, France 49 0N 1 45E
64 Manthani, India 18 40N 79 35E
98 Mantiqueira, Sa. da, mts., Brazil 22 0S 44 30W
48 Mänttä, Finland 61 59N 24 32E
40 Mantua, Italy 45 8N 10 47E
84 Manukau, N.Z. 37 0S 174 40E
82 Manus I., Terr. of New Guinea 2 0S 147 0E
74 Manyara, L., Tanzania 3 40S 35 50E
51 Manych-Gudila L., U.S.S.R. 46 17N 42 55E
74 Manyoni, Tanzania 5 55S 35 0E
64 Manzai, Pakistan 32 25N 70 12E
37 Manzanares, Spain 39 0N 3 22W
95 Manzanillo, Cuba 20 25N 77 10W
94 Manzanillo, Mexico 19 12N 104 12W
76 Manzini, Swaziland 26 30S 31 20E
73 Mao, Chad 14 45N 15 50E
62 Maqna, Saudi Arabia 28 30N 35 0E
74 Maquela do Zombo, Ang. 6 2S 15 22E
99 Maquinchao, Argentina 41 0S 68 30W
33 Mar, Dist., Scotland 57 8N 2 55W
99 Mar, Sa. do, mts., Brazil 23 0S 45 0W
99 Mar Chiquita, L., Arg. 30 30S 62 40W
99 Mar del Plata, Argentina 38 0S 57 39
98 Maraca, I., Brazil 2 10N 50 20W
98 Maracaby Fall, Fs., Brazil 0 10S 66 50W
98 Maracaibo & L., of, Venezuela 10 37N 71 40W
98 Maracay, Venezuela 10 15N 67 35W
51 Maragheh, Iran 37 25N 46 10E
98 Marajo, I., Brazil 1 0S 49 30W
74 Maralal, Kenya 1 0N 36 38E
80 Maralinga, Australia 30 15S 131 30E
75 Marandellas, Rhodesia 18 5S 31 35E
98 Maranhao, st., Brazil 5 0S 44 30W
83 Maranoa, R., Australia 27 40S 148 0E
98 Maranón, R. Peru 4 40S 75 30W
51 Maras, Turkey 37 50N 36 58E
82 Marathon, Australia 20 51S 143 32E
41 Marathon, Greece 38 10N 23 55E
37 Marbella, Spain 36 33N 4 53W
80 Marble Bar, Australia 21 5S 119 43E
43 Marburg, Germany 50 45N 8 50E
23 March, England 52 32N 0 6E
44 Marche, Belgium 50 14N 5 21E
43 Marche, Prov., France 46 10N 1 40E
37 Marchena, Spain 37 23N 5 27W
40 Marches, Prov., Italy 43 20N 13 20E
44 Marchin, Belgium 50 26N 5 12E
64 Mardan, Pakistan 34 20N 72 0E
51 Mardin, Turkey 37 20N 41 0E
82 Mareeba, Australia 17 0S 145 27E
42 Marennes, France 45 50N 1 5W
27 Marfleet, England 53 45N 0 15W
25 Margam, Wales 51 34N 3 44W
94 Margarita, Panama Canal Zone (Inset
98 Margarita, I., Venezuela 11 0N 64 0W
23 Margate, England 51 23N 1 25E
76 Margate, S. Africa 30 50S 30 15E
50 Mari, A.S.S.R., U.S.S.R. 56 30N 48 0E
83 Maria I., Australia 42 39S 147 57E
84 Maria van Diemen, C., N.Z. 34 29S 172 36E
5 Mariana Is., Pac. Oc. 18 0N 146 0E
90 Marias, R., U.S.A. 48 30N 111 30W
40 Maribor, Yugoslavia 46 15N 15 40E
89 Maricourt, Canada 61 30N 72 0W
94 Marie Galante I., W.I. 16 0N 61 15W
44 Mariembourg, Belgium 50 6N 4 31E
92 Marietta, U.S.A. 39 28N 81 28W
60 Mariinsk, U.S.S.R. 56 10N 87 20E
98 Marilia, Brazil 22 0S 50 0W
37 Marin, Spain 42 22N 8 46W
92 Marinette, U.S.A. 45 3N 87 38W
92 Marion, Ind., U.S.A. 40 35N 85 37W
92 Marion, Ohio, U.S.A. 40 33N 83 13W
43 Maritime Alps, France 44 10N 6 52E
41 Maritsa, R., Bulgaria 42 10N 24 20E
44 Marken, Netherlands 52 27N 5 6E
22 Market Bosworth, Eng. 52 37N 1 24W
25 Market Drayton, Eng. 52 55N 2 30W
23 Market Harborough, Eng. 52 29N 0 55W
27 Market Rasen, England 53 23N 0 21W
27 Market Weighton, Eng. 53 52N 0 40W
100 Markham, Mt., Antarc. 82 0S 160 0E
31 Markinch, Scotland 56 12N 3 8W
50 Marks, U.S.S.R. 51 43N 46 45E
44 Marl, Germany 51 40N 7 6E
82 Marlborough, Australia 22 46S 149 52E
22 Marlborough, England 51 25N 1 43W
84 Marlborough, dist., N.Z. 41 46S 173 30E
44 Marle, France 49 43N 3 47E
23 Marlow, England 51 35N 0 46W
64 Marmagao, India 15 25N 73 45E
43 Marmande, France 44 30N 0 10E
41 Marmara, Sea of, Turkey 40 40N 28 0E
40 Marmolada, Mt., Italy 46 20N 11 55E
42 Marne, Dépt., France 49 12N 4 5E
43 Marne, R., France 48 30N 5 0E
75 Maroantsetra, Madagascar 15 28S 49 40E
98 Maroni, R., S. America 5 50N 54 0W
83 Maroochydore, Australia 26 35S 153 10E
83 Maroona, Australia 37 30S 142 57E
73 Maroua, Cameroon 10 50N 14 5E
75 Marovoay, Madagascar 16 10S 46 35E
76 Marquard, S. Africa 28 35S 27 30E
92 Marquette, U.S.A. 46 30N 87 27W
72 Marrakech, Morocco 31 32N 8 0W
83 Marree, Australia 29 35S 137 55E
75 Marromeu, Mozambique 18 8S 35 45E
75 Marrupa, Mozambique 13 5S 37 40E
73 Marsa Brega, Libya 30 30N 19 45E
74 Marsa Fatma, Ethiopia 14 50N 40 15E
73 Marsa Susa, Libya 32 45N 21 48E
74 Marsabit, Kenya 2 10N 38 0E
42 Marseilles, France 43 21N 5 22E
91 Marsh I., U.S.A. 29 40N 91 50W
72 Marshall, Liberia 6 8N 10 22W
91 Marshall, Mo., U.S.A. 39 11N 93 16W
4 Marshall Is., Pac. Oc. 9 30N 167 0E
91 Marshalltown, U.S.A. 42 5N 93 0W
92 Marshfield, U.S.A. 44 47N 90 10W
27 Marske by the Sea, Eng. 54 36N 1 1W
49 Marstrand, Sweden 57 53N 11 35E
65 Martaban, & G., Burma 16 42N 97 45E
73 Marte, Nigeria 12 23N 13 46E
44 Martelange, Belgium 49 50N 5 44E
93 Martha's Vineyard, I., U.S.A. 41 27N 70 43W
45 Martigny, Switzerland 46 7N 7 5E
43 Martigues, France 43 20N 5 2E
95 Martinique, I., Fr. W.I. 14 40N 61 0W
84 Marton, N.Z. 40 5S 175 14E
37 Martos, Spain 37 44N 3 58W
43 Marvejois, France 44 35N 3 15E
64 Marwar, India 25 40N 73 30E

* *Town renamed Ujung Pandang*

60 Mary, U.S.S.R. 37 40N 61 43E
82 Mary Kathleen, Austral. 20 40S 139 55E
83 Maryborough, Queens., Australia 25 32S 152 30E
83 Maryborough, Victoria, Australia 37 0S 143 48E
91 Maryland, st., U.S.A. 39 30N 77 0W
26 Maryport, England 54 43N 3 31W
33 Marywell, Scotland 56 35N 2 31W
73 Marzuq, Libya 25 50N 13 50E
63 Masada, Israel 31 20N 35 19E
74 Masaka, Uganda 0 20S 31 48E
74 Masasi, Tanzania 11 0S 39 0E
68 Masbate, I., Phil. 12 15N 123 30E
72 Mascara, Algeria 35 28N 0 2E
76 Maseru, Lesotho 29 35S 27 20E
63 Mashhad, Iran 36 15N 59 30E
67 Mashike, Japan 43 48N 141 20E
74 Mashkel, R., Iran 27 7N 63 0E
64 Mashki Chah, Pakistan 29 0N 62 25
74 Masi Manimba, Zaïre 4 40S 18 5E
91 Masillon, U.S.A. 40 52N 81 28W
74 Masindi, Uganda 1 40N 31 40E
63 Masira, G., Oman 20 0N 58 0E
34 Mask, L., Ireland 53 36N 9 20W
91 Mason City, U.S.A. 43 11N 93 17W
40 Massa, Italy 44 1N 10 12E
93 Massachusetts, st., U.S.A. 42 20N 72 0
73 Massenya, Chad 11 45N 16 25E
43 Massif Central, mts., Fr. 44 50N 3 0E
75 Massinga, Mozambique 23 15S 35 22E
84 Masterton, N.Z. 40 51S 175 41E
64 Mastuj, Pakistan 36 20N 72 35E
64 Mastung, Pakistan 29 50N 66 42E
67 Masuda, Japan 34 48N 131 58E
65 Masulipatam, India 16 12N 81 12E
47 Masurian Lakes, Poland 53 45N 21 40E
98 Mata da Corda, Sa. da, mts., Brazil 17 30S 45 30W
74 Matadi, Zaïre 5 55S 13 13E
94 Matagalpa, Nicaragua 13 5N 85 36W
92 Matagami, L., Canada 49 50N 77 35W
64 Matale, Sri Lanka 7 37N 80 40E
72 Matam, Sénégal 15 34N 13 17W
94 Matamoros, Mex. 25 50N 97 27W
89 Matane, Canada 48 48N 67 37W
95 Matanzas, Cuba 23 0N 80 40W
64 Matara, Sri Lanka 5 58N 80 30E
68 Mataram, Indonesia 8 35S 116 18E
37 Mataro, Spain 41 37N 2 30E
94 Matehuala, Mexico 23 50N 100 39W
40 Matera, Italy 40 40N 16 38E
64 Mathura, India 27 39N 77 48E
27 Matlock, England 53 9N 1 32W
98 Mato Grosso, plateau & st., Brazil 15 0S 56 0W
70 Matopo, S. Africa 20 0S 30 0E
37 Matozinhos, Portugal 41 15N 8 42W
63 Matrah, Oman 23 31N 58 27E
65 Matsang, R., Tibet, China 29 30N 89 0E
67 Matsue, Japan 35 28N 133 5E
67 Matsumoto, Japan 36 8N 138 0E
67 Matsuyama, Japan 33 56N 132 56E
91 Mattagami, R., Canada 49 40N 81 40W
64 Mattancheri, India 9 50N 76 15E
45 Matterhorn, mt., Switz. 45 58N 7 30E
92 Mattoon, U.S.A. 39 28N 88 27W
64 Matun, Afghanistan 33 15N 69 55E
95 Maturin, Venezuela 9 42N 63 18W
60 Matylka, U.S.S.R. 63 55N 82 0E
43 Maubeuge, France 50 18N 3 58E
65 Mauganj, India 24 50N 81 55E
26 Maughold Hd., I. of Man 54 18N 4 20W
90 Maui I., Hawaiian Is. 21 0N 156 30W
42 Mauleon, France 43 15N 1 0W
34 Maumtuck Mts., Ireland 53 33N 9 35W
75 Maun, Botswana 20 0S 23 30E
65 Maunmagan Is., Burma 14 10N 97 45E
43 Maures, Mts., France 43 20N 6 30E
72 Mauritania, Africa 20 0N 10 0W
72 Mauritius, I., Indian Oc. 20 20S 57 10E
62 Maushij, Yemen 13 44N 43 17E
100 Mawson, Antarctica 67 0S 62 0E
93 May, C., U.S.A. 38 58N 75 0W
31 May, I. of, Scotland 56 13N 2 41W
94 May Pen., Jamaica 17 55N 77 12W
61 Maya R., U.S.S.R. 58 20N 135 0E
95 Mayaguana I., Bahamas 22 12N 73 0W
95 Mayaguez, Puerto Rico 18 10N 67 0W
30 Maybole, Scotland 55 21N 4 41W
42 Mayenne, Dépt., France 48 17N 0 40W
51 Maykop, U.S.S.R. 44 38N 40 11E
35 Maynooth, Ireland 53 23N 6 35W
29 Mayo, Co., Ireland 53 46N 9 0W
92 Maysville, Ky., U.S.A. 38 40N 83 45W
65 Mayum La, pass, Tibet, China 30 20N 82 20E
75 Mazabuka, Zambia 15 50S 27 45E
43 Mazamet, France 43 30N 2 20E
63 Mazar-i-Sharif, Afghan. 36 50N 67 0E
37 Mazarron, Spain 37 39N 1 17W
98 Mazaruni, R., Guyana 6 0N 60 0W
94 Mazatlan, Mexico 23 20N 106 20W
75 Mbabane, Swaziland 26 30S 31 30E
74 Mbaiki, Central Africa 4 0N 18 0E
74 Mbala, Zambia 8 49S 31 20E
74 Mbale, Uganda 1 10N 34 0E
74 Mbalmayo, Cameroon 3 33N 11 33E
74 Mbandaka (Coquilhatville), Zaïre 0 3S 18 20E
74 Mbuji-Mayi, Zaïre 6 10S 23 29E
40 Mdina, Malta 35 54N 14 22E
90 Mead, L., U.S.A. 36 10N 114 20W
92 Meadville, U.S.A. 41 39N 80 7W
33 Mealfuarvonie, Mt., Scot. 57 16N 4 46W
29 Meath, Co., Ireland 53 37N 6 35W
43 Meaux, France 48 59N 2 52E
62 Mecca, Saudi Arabia 21 20N 40 13E
44 Mechelen, Belgium 51 2N 4 29E
72 Mecheria, Algeria 33 35N 0 15W
68 Medan, Indonesia 3 45N 98 45E
72 Medéa, Algeria 36 12N 2 50E
98 Medellin, Colombia 6 10N 75 40W
72 Médenine, Tunisia 33 15N 10 35E
72 Mederdra, Mauritania 17 0N 15 35W
90 Medford, U.S.A. 42 25N 123 0W
47 Medias, Rumania 46 5N 24 21E
90 Medicine Front Ra., U.S.A. 41 0N 105 40W
88 Medicine Hat, Canada 50 0N 110 30W
62 Medina, Saudi Arabia 24 20N 39 55E
37 Medina, Spain 41 18N 4 52W
37 Medina Sidonia, Spain 36 30N 5 58W
5 Mediterranean Sea 36 0N 15 0E
42 Médoc, Dist., France 45 15N 1 0W
52 Medveditsa, R., U.S.S.R. 50 20N 44 0E
61 Medvezhi Is., U.S.S.R. 71 0N 161 0E
23 Medway, R., England 51 13N 0 25E
80 Meekatharra, Australia 26 30S 118 27E
64 Meerut, India 29 0N 77 45E
74 Mega, Ethiopia 3 57N 38 30E
93 Megantic, Canada 45 30N 70 42W
40 Megara, Greece 38 0N 23 20E
65 Meghalaya, st., India 25 30N 91 0E
63 Megiddo, Israel 32 37N 35 9E
39 Megiste (Kastellórizon), Greece 36 8N 29 35E
41 Mehadia, Rumania 44 55N 22 22E
62 Meheisa, Sudan 19 37N 33 0E
64 Mehsana, India 23 39N 72 26E
43 Mehun, France 47 15N 2 12E
65 Meiktila, Burma 20 56N 95 58E
43 Meiningen, Germany 50 35N 10 25E
45 Meiringen, Switzerland 46 45N 8 10E
46 Meissen, Germany 51 11N 13 23E
74 Meiyganga, Cameroon 6 20N 14 10E
99 Mejillones, Chile 23 15S 70 32W
74 Mekambo, Gabon 1 5N 13 50E
73 Mekele, Ethiopia 13 30N 39 20E
64 Mekhtah, Pakistan 30 30N 69 15E
72 Meknes, Morocco 34 0N 5 25W
55 Mekong, R., S.E. Asia 16 30N 104 50E
64 Melagiri Hills, India 12 25N 77 30E
68 Melaka, Malaya 2 20N 102 12E
83 Melbourne, Australia 37 45S 144 50E
50 Melekess, U.S.S.R. 54 20N 49 30E
73 Melfi, Chad 11 0N 17 59E
88 Melfort, Canada 53 0N 104 56W
72 Melilla, Morocco 35 17N 2 55W
52 Melitopol, U.S.S.R. 46 53N 35 20E
46 Melk, Austria 48 15N 15 20E
22 Melksham, England 51 22N 2 9W
48 Mellansel, Sweden 63 26N 18 12E
49 Mellerud, Sweden 58 40N 12 28E
76 Melmoth, S. Africa 28 35S 31 20E
99 Melo, Uruguay 32 15S 54 0W
83 Melrose, Australia 32 40S 146 58E
31 Melrose, Scotland 55 36N 2 45W
48 Melstadur, Iceland 65 20N 20 55W
23 Melton, England 52 6N 1 21E
23 Melton Mowbray, Eng. 52 45N 0 52W
43 Melun, France 48 35N 2 40E
62 Melut, Sudan 10 30N 32 20E
32 Melvaig, Scotland 57 48N 5 49W
33 Melvich, Scotland 58 34N 3 55W
82 Melville B., Australia 12 5S 136 45E
82 Melville, C., Australia 14 20S 144 50E
82 Melville, I., Australia 11 30S 131 0E
89 Melville, L., Canada 53 40N 59 0W
89 Melville Pen., Canada 67 40N 84 0W
36 Melvin, L., Ireland 54 27N 8 10W
45 Memmingen, Germany 47 59N 10 12E
91 Memphis, U.S.A. 35 10N 89 49W
25 Menai Bridge & Str., Wales 53 14N 4 10W
72 Ménaka, Mali 16 0N 2 10E
68 Menam, R., Thailand 15 0N 100 30E
92 Menasha, U.S.A. 44 18N 88 28W
43 Mende, France 44 33N 3 30E
24 Mendip Hills, England 51 17N 2 40W
90 Mendocino, C., U.S.A. 40 25N 124 25W
65 Mendong Gomba, Tibet, China 31 0N 85 15E
99 Mendoza, Argentina 32 45S 68 39W
41 Menemen, Turkey 38 18N 27 10E
40 Menfi, Italy 37 35N 12 55E
68 Menggala, Indonesia 4 25S 105 26E
67 Mengtsz, China 23 22N 103 45E
44 Menin, Belgium 50 48N 3 8E
83 Menindee, Australia 32 22S 142 22E
83 Meningie, Australia 35 38S 139 27E
65 Menkong, China 28 40N 98 15E
92 Menominee, U.S.A. 45 15N 87 37W
92 Menominee, R., U.S.A. 45 50N 88 12W
37 Menorca I., Balearic Is., Spain 40 0N 4 0E
68 Mentawai Is., Indonesia 2 30S 99 30E
43 Menton, France 43 50N 7 30E
73 Menzel Temime, Tunisia 36 50N 11 0E
80 Menzies, Australia 29 42S 121 2E
63 Me'ona, Israel 33 0N 35 15E
44 Meppel, Netherlands 52 42N 6 12E
41 Merabéllou B., Greece 35 15N 25 50E
40 Merano, Italy 46 39N 11 12E
83 Merbein, Australia 34 10S 142 0E
64 Mercara, India 12 40N 75 40E
90 Merced, U.S.A. 37 16N 120 26W
99 Mercedes, Argentina 29 15S 58 10W
99 Mercedes, Arg. 33 5S 65 21W
99 Mercedes, Uruguay 33 58S 58 5W
84 Mercer, New Zealand 37 15S 175 5E
89 Mercy C., Canada 65 0N 62 30W
22 Mere, England 51 6N 2 16W
73 Méréke, Central Africa 7 35N 23 0E
68 Mergui, Burma 12 30N 98 40E
94 Mérida, Mexico 20 55N 89 40W
37 Merida, Spain 38 56N 6 26W
98 Mérida, Venezuela 8 30N 71 2W
22 Meriden, England 52 26N 1 38W
93 Meriden, U.S.A. 41 28N 72 54W
*28 Merioneth, Co., Wales 52 52N 3 50W
44 Merksem, Belgium 51 17N 4 25E
73 Merowe, Sudan 18 57N 32 15E
80 Merredin, Australia 31 29S 118 23E
92 Merrill, U.S.A. 45 16N 89 40W
83 Merriwa, Australia 32 10S 150 28E
83 Merriwagga, Australia 33 47S 145 43E
83 Merrygoen, Australia 31 55S 149 10E
44 Mersch, Luxembourg 49 44N 6 7E
31 Merse, The, Scotland 55 40N 2 25W
46 Merseburg, Germany 51 22N 12 0E
**26 Mersey, R., England 53 20N 2 55W
51 Mersin, Turkey 36 52N 34 29E
68 Mersing, Malaya 2 30N 103 50E
25 Merthyr Tydfil, Wales 51 45N 3 22W
37 Mertola, Portugal 37 39N 7 39W
23 Merton, Greater London, England 51 23N 0 9W
74 Meru, Kenya 0 2N 37 35E
44 Merzig, Germany 49 27N 6 39E
90 Mesa, U.S.A. 33 25N 111 50W
74 Mesewa, Ethiopia 15 35N 39 25E
73 Meshra el Req, Sudan 8 25N 29 18E
45 Mesocco, Switzerland 46 24N 9 14E
41 Mesolongion, Greece 38 25N 21 25E
62 Mesopotamia, Dist., S.W. Asia 32 30N 45 0E
40 Messina, & Str., Italy 38 13N 15 33E
75 Messina, S. Africa 22 18S 29 50E
41 Messini, Greece 37 0N 22 0E
41 Mesta, R., Greece 41 10N 25 0E
98 Meta, R., Colombia 5 50N 70 0W
31 Methil, Scotland 56 11N 3 1W
84 Methven, N.Z. 43 37S 171 40E
31 Methven, Scotland 56 24N 3 36W
75 Metil, Mozambique 16 24S 39 0E
64 Mettur Dam, India 11 45N 77 45E
63 Metulla, Israel 33 17N 35 34E
43 Metz, France 49 10N 6 10E
42 Meurthe-et-Moselle, Dépt., France 48 53N 5 53E
42 Meuse, Dépt., France 49 3N 5 53E
44 Meuse, R., Fr., Belgium 50 29N 5 5E
24 Mevagissey, & B., Eng. 50 15N 4 40W
27 Mexborough, England 53 30N 1 17W
98 Mexiana I., Brazil 0 0 49 30W
94 Mexicali, Mexico 32 40N 115 30W
86 Mexican Plat., Mexico 23 0N 104 0W
94 Mexico, Cent. Amer. 23 0N 102 0W
94 Mexico City, Mexico 19 25N 99 5W
94 Mexico, G. of, Mexico 25 0N 89 0W
43 Mèze, France 43 30N 3 30E
50 Mezen, R., U.S.S.R. 64 34N 46 30E
47 Mezökovesd, Hungary 47 44N 20 35E
47 Mezötúr, Hungary 47 0N 20 45E
64 Mhow, India 22 25N 75 51E
91 Miami, Fla., U.S.A. 25 55N 80 23W
75 Miandrivazo, Madagascar 19 40S 45 40E
51 Mianeh, Iran 37 27N 47 39E
64 Mianwali, Pakistan 32 33N 71 43E
75 Miarinarivo, Madag. 18 50S 46 58E
60 Miass, U.S.S.R. 55 00N 60 00E
92 Michigan City, U.S.A. 41 40N 86 58W
92 Michigan, L., N. America 44 0N 87 0W
92 Michigan, st., U.S.A. 45 0N 85 30W
89 Michikamau, L., Canada 54 0N 64 0W
91 Michipicoten, I., Canada 47 45N 86 0W
52 Michurinsk, U.S.S.R. 53 0N 40 30E
26 Mickle Fell, mt., Eng. 54 36N 2 10W
27 Mickleover, England 52 55N 1 32W
31 Mid Calder, Scotland 55 53N 3 23W
44 Middleburg, Netherlands 51 31N 3 37E
91 Middlesboro, U.S.A. 36 42N 83 40W
27 Middlesbrough, England 54 34N 1 16W
94 Middlesex, Br. Honduras 16 50N 88 40W
23 Middleton, England 52 43N 0 29E
22 Middleton Cheney, Eng. 52 5N 1 10W
27 Middleton-on-the-Wolds, England 53 50N 0 35W
93 Middletown, N.Y., U.S.A. 41 29N 74 28W
92 Middletown, Ohio, U.S.A. 39 30N 84 7W
26 Middlewich, England 53 12N 2 28W
92 Midland, Mich., U.S.A. 43 35N 84 15W
90 Midland, Texas, U.S.A. 32 0N 102 8W
80 Midland Junc., Austral. 31 40S 116 0E
34 Midleton, Ireland 51 54N 8 7W
†31 Midlothian, Co., Scot. 55 50N 3 20W
65 Midnapore, India 22 18N 87 30E
24 Midsomer Norton, Eng. 51 17N 2 29W
11 Midway I., Pac. Oc. 28 0N 178 0W
67 Mie, Pref., Japan 34 20N 136 30E
47 Miedzyrzec, Poland 52 0N 22 45E
37 Mieres, Spain 43 16N 5 48W
63 Migdal, Israel 32 50N 35 30E
41 Mikinai, Greece 37 45N 22 45E
74 Mikindani, Tanzania 10 0S 40 0E
49 Mikkeli, Finland 61 43N 27 25E
48 Mikkeli, Co., Finland 62 0N 28 0E
41 Mikonos I., Greece 37 30N 25 24E
67 Mikura Shima, I., Japan 33 50N 139 30E
40 Milan, Italy 45 28N 9 12E
83 Milang, Australia 35 39S 139 0E
62 Milas, Turkey 37 20N 27 50E
40 Milazzo, Italy 38 14N 15 14E
23 Mildenhall, England 52 21N 0 29E
83 Mildura, Australia 34 13S 142 5E
83 Miles, Australia 26 35S 150 18E
90 Miles City, U.S.A. 46 30N 105 47W
25 Milford Haven, Wales 51 41N 5 9W
22 Milford-on-Sea, Eng. 50 44N 1 34W
84 Milford Sd., N.Z. 44 35S 167 50E
90 Milk R., N. America 49 0N 107 0W
43 Millau, France 44 8N 3 10E
91 Milledgeville, U.S.A. 33 0N 83 20W
83 Millicent, Australia 37 50S 140 25E
91 Millinocket, U.S.A. 45 44N 68 31W
83 Millmerran, Australia 27 52S 151 8E
26 Millom, England 54 12N 3 16W
30 Millport, Scotland 55 45N 4 55W
34 Millstreet, Ireland 52 3N 9 4W
34 Milltown, Ireland 52 10N 9 42W
76 Milnerton, S. Africa (Inset) 33 55S 18 29E
30 Milngavie, Scotland 55 57N 4 19W
41 Milos, I., Greece 36 40N 24 27E
83 Milparinka, Australia 29 46S 141 57E
84 Milton, New Zealand 46 8S 169 59E
23 Milton Keynes, England 52 3N 0 45W
34 Miltown Malbay, Ire. 52 53N 9 22W
24 Milverton, England 51 2N 3 15W
92 Milwaukee, U.S.A. 43 5N 88 5W
67 Mimitsu, Japan 32 55N 131 30E
66 Min Kiang, R., China 26 40N 117 30E
62 Mina al Ahmadi, Kuwait 29 0N 47 0E
63 Minab, Iran 27 7N 57 7E
99 Minas (Lavelleja), Uruguay 34 20S 54 48W
93 Minas Basin, Canada 45 14N 64 20W
37 Minas de Rio Tinto, Spain 37 45N 6 36W
98 Minas Gerais, st., Brazil 19 15S 45 0W
67 Minato, Japan 36 24N 140 38E
32 Minch, The, Scotland 58 10N 5 50W
22 Minchinhampton, Eng. 51 42N 2 10W
68 Mindanao, I., Philippines 8 0N 125 0E
46 Minden, Germany 52 18N 8 57E
91 Minden, U.S.A. 32 44N 93 19W
68 Mindoro, I., Philippines 12 40N 121 0E
35 Mine Hd., Ireland 52 0N 7 33W
24 Minehead, England 51 14N 3 30W
90 Mineral Wells, U.S.A. 32 50N 98 10W
51 Mingechaur Res., U.S.S.R. 40 45N 46 30E
65 Mingin, Burma 22 55N 94 30E
32 Minginish, Dist., Scot. 57 17N 6 15W
32 Mingulay I., Scotland 56 49N 7 35W
37 Minho, & Prov., Port. 41 25N 8 20W
37 Minho, R., Spain 43 10N 7 30W
67 Minhow, *see* Foochow
91 Minneapolis, U.S.A. 45 0N 93 30W
91 Minnesota, st., U.S.A. 46 0N 94 30W
37 Minorca I., *see* Menorca
83 Minore, Australia 32 15S 148 25E
90 Minot, U.S.A. 48 15N 101 10W
50 Minsk, U.S.S.R. 54 0N 27 30E
47 Minsk Mazowiecki, Pol. 52 10N 21 30E
61 Minusinsk, U.S.S.R. 53 50N 92 15E
65 Minutang, India 28 20N 96 30E
62 Minwakh, South Yemen 15 59N 49 28E
66 Minya Konka, mt., China 30 0N 101 15E
89 Miquelon I., St. Pierre & Miquelon, North America 47 0N 56 30W
73 Mir, Niger 14 6N 11 58E
94 Miraflores, Panama Canal Zone (Inset)
64 Miraj, India 16 57N 74 46E
64 Miram Shah, Pakistan 33 0N 70 0E
37 Miranda, Portugal 41 33N 6 20W
37 Miranda, Spain 42 40N 2 53W
43 Mirande, France 43 30N 0 20E
43 Mirecourt, France 48 20N 6 5E
62 Mirfa, U.A.E. 24 0N 53 24E
68 Miri, Sarawak, Malaysia 4 30N 114 5E
82 Miriam Vale, Australia 24 20S 151 39E
99 Mirim, L., S. America 33 0S 53 0W
100 Mirny, Antarctica 66 30S 96 0E
64 Mirpur Khas, Pakistan 25 33N 68 0E
65 Mirzapur, India 25 8N 82 39E
93 Miscou, I., Canada 48 0N 64 32W
67 Mishan, China 45 30N 131 30E
63 Mishmar Aiyalon, Israel 31 57N 34 58E
47 Miskolc, Hungary 48 8N 20 46E
73 Misratah, Libya 32 20N 15 7E
92 Missinaibi, R., Canada 49 30N 83 15W
91 Mississippi R., U.S.A. 35 0N 90 0W
91 Mississippi, st., U.S.A. 33 0N 89 30W
91 Mississippi Delta, U.S.A. 29 15N 90 30W
90 Missoula, U.S.A. 46 57N 113 58W
90 Missouri, R., U.S.A. 42 0N 98 30W
91 Missouri, st., U.S.A. 38 0N 92 30W
89 Mistassini, L., Canada 51 0N 73 35W
23 Misterton, England 50 51N 2 35W
98 Misti, Vol., Peru 16 30S 71 0W
40 Mistretta, Italy 38 0N 14 20E
67 Misumi, Japan 32 34N 130 32E
73 Misurata, Libya, *see* Misratah
25 Mitchel Troy, England 51 46N 2 45W
83 Mitchell, Australia 26 30S 147 58E
90 Mitchell, U.S.A. 43 45N 98 2W
82 Mitchell, R., Australia 16 0S 142 30E
34 Mitchelstown, Ireland 52 17N 8 15W
41 Mitilini, Greece 39 8N 26 36E
67 Mito, Japan 36 28N 140 26E
75 Mitsinjo, Madagascar 15 35S 45 45E
83 Mittagong, Australia 34 25S 150 25E
98 Mitú, Colombia 1 0N 70 0W
74 Mitumba Mts., Zaïre 7 0S 27 0E
74 Mitwaba, Zaïre 8 37S 27 28E
74 Mitzick, Gabon 0 45N 11 40E
67 Miyagi, Pref., Japan 38 15N 141 0E
67 Miyake Jima, Japan 34 0N 139 30E
67 Miyako, Japan 39 40N 141 45E
67 Miyakonojo, Japan 31 30N 131 0E
67 Miyasu, Japan 35 40N 135 8E
67 Miyazaki, & Pref., Japan 31 58N 131 30E
72 Mizdah, Libya 31 40N 13 12E
34 Mizen Hd., Ireland 51 27N 9 49W
65 Mizoram, st., India 23 20N 93 0E
49 Mjölby, Sweden 58 19N 15 4E
49 Mjosa L., & R., Norway 60 40N 11 0E
46 Mlada Boleslav, Cz-slov. 50 28N 15 0E
70 Mlanje, mt., Mozambique 16 0S 35 55E
47 Mlawa, Poland 53 6N 20 20E
74 Moanda, Gabon 1 5S 13 0E
35 Moate, Ireland 53 24N 7 42W
91 Moberley, U.S.A. 39 28N 92 27W
91 Mobile, U.S.A. 30 47N 88 10W
76 Mochudi, Botswana 24 25S 26 5E
98 Mocoa, Colombia 1 15N 76 45W
43 Modane, France 45 20N 6 25E
76 Modder, R., S. Africa 28 48S 26 15E
40 Modena, Italy 44 38N 10 54E
90 Modesto, U.S.A. 37 36N 120 58W
40 Modica, Italy 36 54N 14 50E
83 Moe, Australia 38 12S 146 19E
44 Moers, Germany 51 27N 6 39E
31 Moffat, Scotland 55 18N 3 25W
71 Mogadishu, Somali Republic 2 1N 45 25E
72 Mogador, *see* Essaouira
67 Mogami, R., Japan 38 50N 140 0E
65 Mogaung, Burma 25 26N 96 55E
50 Mogilev, U.S.S.R. 54 17N 30 30E
51 Mogilev-Podolski, U.S.S.R. 48 25N 27 50E
75 Mogincual, Mozambique 15 30S 40 22E
61 Mogocha, U.S.S.R. 53 40N 119 50E
65 Mogok, Burma 23 0N 96 30E
47 Mohacs, Hungary 45 59N 18 40E
75 Mohembo, Botswana 18 15S 21 43E
34 Moher Cliffs, Ireland 52 58N 9 26W
32 Moidart, L. & Dist., Scot. 56 50N 5 52W
60 Mointy, U.S.S.R. 47 40N 73 45E
36 Moira, N. Ireland 54 29N 6 14W
49 Moisäkula, U.S.S.R. 58 2N 25 12E
89 Moisie, Canada 50 17N 66 0W
43 Moissac, France 44 8N 1 0E
61 Moiyero R., U.S.S.R. 67 30N 104 0E
90 Mojave Desert, U.S.A. 35 0N 116 20W
67 Moji, Japan 33 56N 131 0E
65 Mokokchung, India 26 15N 94 25E
67 Mokpo, Korea 34 50N 126 30E
44 Mol, Belgium 51 11N 5 7E
25 Mold, Wales 53 10N 3 9W
51 Moldavia S.S.R., U.S.S.R. 47 40N 28 0E
48 Molde, Norway 62 45N 7 8E
23 Mole, R., England 51 18N 0 20W
75 Molepolole, Botswana 24 28S 25 28E
40 Molfetta, Italy 41 12N 16 40E
92 Moline, U.S.A. 41 30N 90 25W
74 Moliro, Zaïre 8 5S 30 30E
40 Molise, Reg., Italy 41 30N 14 30E
49 Molndal, Sweden 57 35N 12 0E
90 Molokai, I., Hawaiian Is. (Inset)
83 Molong, Australia 33 0S 149 0E
68 Molucca Sea, Indonesia 4 0S 126 0E
68 Moluccas, Indonesia, *see* Maluku
71 Mombasa, Kenya 4 0S 39 40E
41 Momchilgrad, Bulgaria 41 33N 25 23E
98 Mompos, Colombia 9 15N 74 25W
49 Mön, I., Denmark 54 57N 12 23E
65 Mon, R., Burma 20 30N 94 30E
32 Monach Is., Scotland 57 31N 7 40W
43 Monaco, Europe 43 46N 7 23E
33 Monadhliath Mts., Scot. 57 8N 4 20W
36 Monaghan, & Co., Ire. 54 14N 6 58W
32 Monar, L. & Forest, Scot. 57 26N 5 4W
35 Monasterevan, Ireland 53 10N 7 7W
73 Monastir, Tunisia 35 40N 10 50E
35 Monavullagh, Mts., Ire. 52 10N 7 40W
37 Moncayo, Mt., Spain 41 47N 1 50W
44 Mönchen-Gladbach, Ger. 51 13N 6 26E
37 Monchique, Portugal 37 16N 8 40W
37 Monchique, Sa. de, mts., Portugal 37 20S 8 40W
94 Monclova, Mexico 27 0N 101 20W
93 Moncton, Canada 46 10N 65 0W
37 Mondego, R., Portugal 40 30N 7 50W
40 Mondovi, Italy 44 25N 7 50E
34 Moneygall, Ireland 52 53N 7 58W
37 Monforte, Spain 42 30N 7 33W
65 Mong Pawk, Burma 22 0N 99 20E
65 Mong Ton, Burma 20 20N 98 55E
65 Mong Wa, Burma 21 25N 100 25E
65 Mong Kung, Burma 21 50N 97 35E
73 Mongalla, Sudan 5 10N 31 50E
80 Monger, L., Australia 29 10S 117 0E
65 Monghyr, India 25 20N 86 22E
73 Mongo, Chad 12 14N 18 43E
66 Mongolia, Asia 45 20N 105 30E
73 Mongororo, Chad 12 01N 22 28E
75 Mongu, Zambia 15 16S 23 3E
31 Monifieth, Scotland 56 29N 2 49W
34 Monivea, Ireland 53 28N 8 42W
74 Monkoto, Zaïre 1 30S 21 0E
††22 Monmouth, & Co., Great Britain 51 48N 2 43W
40 Monopoli, Italy 40 57N 17 18E
91 Monroe, La., U.S.A. 32 30N 92 1W
92 Monroe, Mich., U.S.A. 41 54N 83 27W

* *Incorporated within the county of Gwynedd*
** *Merseyside, Co., England 53 25N 2 55W*
† *Incorporated within the region of Lothian*
†† *Renamed Gwent*

72 Monrovia, Liberia 6 15N 10 43W
44 Mons, Belgium 50 26N 3 58E
75 Mont Aux Sources, S. Africa
28 54S 28 50E
43 Mont Blanc, Fr. & Italy 45 52N 6 50E
43 Mont Cenis, mt., France 45 20N 7 5E
42 Mont de Marsan, France
43 58N 0 34W
43 Mont Dore, mt., France 45 32N 2 30E
43 Mont du Cantal, mt., Fr. 45 10N 2 20E
93 Mont Joli, Canada 48 35N 68 10N
93 Mont Laurier, Canada 46 35N 75 30W
43 Mont Mézenc, mt., Fr. 44 45N 4 35E
43 Mont St. Michel, France 48 40N 1 32W
37 Montalban, Spain 40 50N 0 48W
90 Montana, St., U.S.A. 47 0N 109 0W
43 Montargis, France 48 0N 2 40E
43 Montauban, France 44 1N 1 20E
43 Montbeliard, France 47 32N 6 48E
43 Montbrison, France 45 35N 4 0E
43 Montceau, France 46 40N 4 25E
44 Montcornet, France 49 42N 4 0E
43 Montdidier, France 49 40N 2 30E
40 Monte Argentario, mt., Italy
42 25N 11 10E
80 Monte Bello Is., Austral. 20 30S 115 30E
43 Monte Carlo, Monaco 43 46N 7 23E
99 Monte Caseros, Arg. 30 10S 57 50W
40 Monte Cimone, mt., Italy 44 10N 10 40
43 Monte Cinto, mt., France 42 20N 9 10E
40 Monte Rosa, Italy & Switz.
46 0N 8 0E
40 Monte S. Angelo, Italy 41 40N 16 0E
95 Montego Bay, Jamaica 18 30N 77 50W
43 Montélimar, France 44 34N 4 48E
94 Montemorelos, Mexico 25 8N 99 30W
40 Montenegro, Fed. Unit, Yugoslavia
42 52N 19 20E
43 Montereau, France 48 20N 3 0E
90 Monterey, U.S.A. 36 39N 121 45W
94 Monterrey, Mexico 25 42N 100 22W
98 Montes Claros, Brazil 16 20S 43 0W
37 Montes de Toledo, Spain 39 30N 4 30W
74 Monteverde, Angola 8 45S 16 45E
99 Montevideo, Uruguay 34 50S 56 15W
42 Montfort, France 48 10N 2 0W
91 Montgomery, U.S.A. 32 17N 86 20W
*25 Montgomery, & Co., Wales
52 33N 3 9W
64 Montgomery, Pakistan, *see* Sahiwal
45 Monthey, Switzerland 46 15N 6 56E
45 Montigny les Metz, Fr. 49 6N 6 9E
36 Montijo, Portugal 38 40N 8 56W
37 Montilla, Spain 37 36N 4 40W
43 Montluçon, France 46 21N 2 37E
43 Montmédy, France 49 35N 5 25E
43 Montmorillon, France 46 23N 0 50E
82 Monto, Australia 24 58S 151 0E
37 Montoro, Spain 38 0N 4 0W
93 Montpelier, Ver., U.S.A. 44 15N 72 30W
43 Montpellier, France 43 40N 3 50E
93 Montreal, Canada 45 42N 73 50W
42 Montreuil, France 50 30N 1 48E
45 Montreux, Switzerland 46 27N 6 54E
31 Montrose, Scotland 56 43N 2 28W
90 Montrose, U.S.A. 38 30N 107 53W
95 Montserrat, I., W.I. 16 30N 62 0W
74 Monveda, Zaïre 3 0N 21 35E
65 Monywa, Burma 22 5N 95 8E
75 Monze, Zambia 16 23S 27 28E
64 Monze C., Pakistan 24 47N 66 37E
37 Monzon, Spain 41 53N 0 12E
35 Mooncoin, Ireland 52 18N 7 16W
35 Moone, Ireland 52 58N 6 49W
83 Moonie, R., Australia 28 0S 149 20E
83 Moonta, Australia 34 6S 137 32E
80 Moore, L., Australia 30 0S 117 30E
31 Moorfoot Hills, Scotland 55 45N 3 5W
91 Moorhead, U.S.A. 47 0N 96 42W
83 Mooroopna, Australia 36 30S 145 25E
93 Moosehead L., U.S.A. 45 45N 69 48W
88 Moosejaw, Canada 50 24N 105 25W
72 Mopti, Mali 14 34N 4 0W
64 Moradabad, India 28 50N 78 54E
75 Morafenobe, Madag. 17 50S 44 53E
75 Moramanga, Madag. 18 58S 48 15E
94 Morant Point, Jamaica 17 55N 76 10W
32 Morar, & L., Scotland 56 57N 5 40W
64 Moratuwa, Sri Lanka 6 45N 80 0E
47 Morava, R., Yugoslavia 44 10N 21 20E
46 Moravia, Dist., Cz-slov. 49 27N 16 55E
46 Moravian Hts., Cz-slov. 49 20N 15 20E
**33 Moray, Co., Scotland 57 30N 3 25W
42 Morbihan, Dépt., France 47 55N 2 45W
42 Morcenx, France 44 0N 1 0W
88 Morden, Canada 49 12N 98 10W
52 Mordovian, A.S.S.R., U.S.S.R.
54 20N 44 30E
33 More L., Scotland 58 18N 4 50W
48 Möre and Romsdal, Co., Norway
62 30N 8 0E
26 Morecambe, & B., Eng. 54 5N 2 52W
83 Moree, Australia 29 25S 149 46E
45 Morel, Switzerland 46 23N 8 2E
94 Morelia, Mexico 19 48N 101 0W
82 Morella, Australia 23 0S 143 47E
37 Morena, Sa. de, mts., Spain
38 20N 4 40W
83 Moreton I., Austral. 27 0S 153 15E
43 Morez, France 46 32N 6 0E
83 Morgan, Australia 34 3S 139 40E
91 Morgantown, U.S.A. 39 43N 79 59W
45 Morges, Switzerland 46 31N 6 30E
67 Morioka, Japan 39 48N 141 8E
83 Morkalla, Australia 34 18S 141 4E

* *County incorporated within Powys*

** *Incorporated within the region of Grampian*

42 Morlaix, France 48 38N 3 51W
27 Morley, England 53 46N 1 36W
83 Mornington, Australia 38 15S 145 5E
36 Mornington, Ireland 53 42N 6 17W
82 Mornington I., Austral. 16 30S 139 20E
68 Moro G., Philippines 7 0N 123 0E
82 Morobe, Terr. of, N. Guinea
7 57S 147 50E
72 Morocco, N. Africa 32 0N 5 0W
74 Morogoro, Tanzania 7 0S 37 50E
75 Morombé, Madagascar 21 38S 43 27E
95 Moron, Cuba 21 0N 78 45W
37 Moron, Spain 37 5N 5 30W
74 Morondava, Madag. 20 25S 44 30E
74 Moroto, Uganda 2 50N 34 0E
27 Morpeth, England 55 10N 1 42W
51 Morphou, Cyprus 35 17N 32 56E
84 Morrinsville, N.Z. 37 38S 175 30E
91 Morristown, U.S.A. 36 23N 83 18W
52 Morshansk, U.S.S.R. 53 28N 41 48E
42 Mortagne, France 47 0N 1 0W
22 Mortimer's Cross, Eng. 52 15N 2 47W
83 Mortlake, Australia 38 4S 142 50E
83 Moruya, Australia 35 55S 150 2E
33 Morven, Mt., Scotland 58 12N 3 40W
83 Morwell, Australia 38 12S 146 8E
24 Morwenstow, England 50 53N 4 32W
90 Moscow, U.S.A. 46 47N 117 2W
52 Moscow, U.S.S.R. 55 50N 37 40E
42 Moselle Dépt., France 49 5N 6 45E
46 Moselle, R., W. Europe 50 10N 7 10E
90 Moses Lake, U.S.A. 41 5N 119 0W
84 Mosgiel, New Zealand 45 53S 177 21E
74 Moshi, Tanzania 3 10S 37 30E
48 Mosjöen, Norway 66 0N 13 15E
48 Moskenstraumen, Norway 67 45N 13 0E
52 Moskva, R., U.S.S.R. 55 45N 36 0E
95 Mosquito Coast, Nicaragua
13 0N 84 0W
49 Moss, Norway 59 26N 10 40E
83 Moss Vale, Australia 34 38S 150 29E
84 Mossburn, New Zealand 45 40S 168 15E
75 Mosselbaai, S. Africa 34 10S 22 9E
74 Mossendjo, Congo (Fr.) 2 55S 12 55E
83 Mosgiel, Australia 33 5S 144 33E
99 Mossoró, Brazil 5 0S 37 15W
75 Mossuril, Mozambique 14 57S 40 42E
46 Most, Czechoslovakia 50 31N 13 38E
41 Mostar, Yugoslavia 43 21N 17 46E
36 Mostrim, Ireland 53 42N 7 38W
47 Mosty, U.S.S.R. 53 30N 24 30E
25 Mostyn, England 53 18N 3 14W
62 Mosul, Iraq 36 5N 43 15E
73 Mota, Ethiopia 11 5N 37 50E
49 Motala, & Can., Sweden 58 30N 15 20E
31 Motherwell, Scotland 55 47N 4 0W
65 Motihari, India 26 45N 85 0E
37 Motril, Spain 36 45N 3 34W
41 Moudhros, Greece 39 53N 25 18E
45 Moudon, Switzerland 46 41N 6 49E
74 Mouila, Gabon 1 50S 11 0E
73 Mouka, Central Africa 7 18N 21 50E
43 Moulins, France 46 36N 3 21E
65 Moulmein, Burma 16 30N 97 52E
73 Moundou, Central Africa 8 40N 16 10E
90 Mount Adams, Mt., U.S.A.
46 12N 121 35W
76 Mount Ayliff, S. Africa 30 50S 29 20E
83 Mount Barker, S. Australia
35 8S 138 52E
80 Mount Barker, W. Australia
34 40S 117 50E
34 Mount Bellow Bridge, Ire. 53 29N 8 27W
75 Mount Darwin, Rhodesia
16 30S 31 35E
82 Mount Douglas, Australia
21 35S 146 50E
83 Mount Gambier, Austral. 37 45S 140 45E
80 Mount Goldsworthy, Australia
20 25S 119 39E
90 Mount Hood, Mt., U.S.A.
45 15N 121 40W
83 Mount Hope, Australia 32 48S 146 0E
80 Mount Isa, Australia 20 40S 139 30E
90 Mount Lassen, Mt., U.S.A.
40 32N 121 15W
64 Mount Lavinia, Sri Lanka 6 50N 79 50E
83 Mount Lofty Ras, Austral. 35 0S 139 30E
84 Mount Maunganui, N.Z.
37 35S 176 30E
82 Mount Morgan, Austral. 23 35S 150 28E
90 Mount Rainier, Mt., U.S.A.
46 48N 121 43W
90 Mount Shasta, Mt., U.S.A.
41 30N 122 1W
82 Mount Surprise, Austral. 18 10S 144 17E
90 Mount Taylor, Mt., U.S.A.
35 20N 107 35W
80 Mount Tom Price, Austral. 22 40S 118 9E
90 Mount Vernon, U.S.A. 38 22N 88 44W
80 Mount Whaleback, Australia
24 38S 113 33E
90 Mount Whitney, Mt., U.S.A.
36 25N 118 13W
24 Mount's B., England 50 4N 5 25W
25 Mountain Ash, Wales 51 42N 3 23W
36 Mountcharles, Ireland 54 38N 8 13W
35 Mountmellick, Ireland 53 8N 7 17W
35 Mountrath, Ireland 53 0N 7 29W
72 Mourdhia, Mali 14 35N 7 25W
36 Mourne Mts., N. Ireland 54 8N 6 2W
36 Mourne, R., N. Ireland 54 45N 7 24W
44 Mouscron, Belgium 50 45N 3 15E
73 Moussoro, Chad 13 48N 16 48E
43 Moutiers, France 45 30N 6 30E
36 Moville, Ireland 55 11N 7 2W
36 Moy, N. Ireland 54 27N 6 41W
72 Moyamba, Sierra Leone 8 15N 12 30W
34 Moylough, Ireland 53 29N 8 35W
98 Moyobamba, Peru 6 5S 77 5W
75 Mozambique, Africa 15 3S 40 43E
75 Mozambique, Port. prov., Africa
19 0S 35 0E
70 Mozambique Channel, Indian Ocean
18 0S 42 0E
74 Mpanda, Tanzania 6 22S 30 40E
75 Mpangwe, Zambia 14 8S 32 10E
75 Mpika, Zambia 11 54S 31 32E
74 Mpwapwa, Tanzania 6 30S 36 30E
73 Msaken, Tunisia 35 49N 10 33E
75 Msoro, Zambia 13 35S 32 0E
74 Mtwara, Tanzania 10 16S 40 10E
68 Muang Khon Kaen, Thailand
16 59N 102 40E
68 Muang Nakhon Sawan, Thailand
15 40N 100 5E
68 Muang Phetchabun, Thailand
16 30N 101 10E
66 Muang Phitsanulak, Thailand
16 45N 100 3E
68 Muang Ubon, Thailand 15 20N 104 55E
68 Muar, Malaya 2 0N 102 40E
68 Muaraenim, Indonesia 3 35S 103 50E
68 Muaratewe, Indonesia 0 55S 114 50E
62 Mubarraz, Saudi Arabia 25 29N 49 40E
74 Mubende, Uganda 0 40N 31 21E
74 Mubi, Nigeria 10 16N 13 17E
22 Much Wenlock, Eng. 52 35N 2 33W
32 Muck I., Scotland 56 49N 6 13W
83 Mudgee, Australia 32 33S 149 32E
36 Muff, Ireland 55 4N 7 16W
75 Mufulira, Zambia 12 40S 28 2E
51 Mugla, Turkey 37 15N 28 30E
73 Muglad, Sudan 11 10N 27 35E
65 Mugu, Nepal 29 50N 82 30E
73 Muhammad Qol, Sudan 20 58N 37 0E
46 Mühlhausen, Germany 51 14N 10 26E
35 Muine Bheag, Ireland 52 41N 6 48W
31 Muirdrum, Scotland 56 31N 2 40W
31 Muirhead, Scotland 55 45N 4 5W
76 Muizenberg, S. Africa 34 7S 18 27E
63 Mujib, Wadiel, Jordan 31 28N 35 45E
47 Mukachevo, U.S.S.R. 48 27N 22 45E
62 Mukalla, South Yemen 14 38N 49 0E
67 Mukden, China 41 50N 124 0E
65 Muktinath, Nepal 28 37N 83 55E
64 Muktsar, India 30 40N 74 30E
46 Mulde, R., Germany 51 30N 12 38E
94 Muleje, Mexico 26 50N 112 15W
93 Mulgrave, Canada 45 40N 61 30W
37 Mulhacen, Mt., Spain 36 45N 2 47W
44 Mulheim, Germany 51 0N 7 4E
43 Mulhouse, France 47 46N 7 19E
65 Muli, China 28 20N 100 40E
30 Mull I., Scotland 56 28N 6 0W
30 Mull of Galloway, Scot. 54 37N 4 52W
36 Mull of Kintyre, Scot. 55 17N 5 48W
30 Mull of Oa, Scotland 55 35N 6 20W
36 Mullagh, Ireland 53 49N 6 58W
35 Mullaghareirk Mts., Ire. 52 18N 9 10W
64 Mullaitivu, Sri Lanka 9 15N 80 50E
32 Mullardoch, L., Scotland 57 20N 5 0W
35 Mullet Pen., Ireland 54 10N 10 4W
80 Mullewa, Australia 28 33S 115 28E
35 Mullinahone, Ireland 52 32N 7 30W
35 Mullinavat, Ireland 52 22N 7 10W
35 Mullingar, Ireland 53 31N 7 19W
83 Mullumbimby, Austral. 28 30S 153 10E
64 Multan, Pakistan 30 3N 71 30E
25 Mumbles, The, Wales 51 35N 3 50W
25 Mumbles Hd., Wales 51 34N 3 59W
75 Mumbwa, Zambia 15 0S 27 2E
68 Muna I., Indonesia 5 0S 122 35E
64 Munabao, India 25 45N 70 15E
92 Muncie, U.S.A. 40 15N 85 22W
46 Münden, Germany 51 25N 9 40E
83 Mungallala, R., Austral. 26 25S 147 34E
82 Mungana, Australia 17 8S 144 27E
74 Mungbere, Zaïre 2 35N 28 35E
83 Mungindi, Australia 28 55S 149 0E
75 Munhango, Angola 12 15S 18 35E
46 Munich, Germany 48 9N 11 30E
92 Munising, U.S.A. 46 25N 87 0W
45 Munsingen, Switzerland 46 54N 7 37E
44 Münster, Germany 51 58N 7 39E
34 Munster, Prov., Ireland 52 25N 8 30W
44 Munstereifel Germany 50 33N 6 47E
48 Muonio, Finland 68 20N 23 0E
75 Mupa, Angola 16 5S 15 50E
62 Muqainama, Si. Arabia 22 9N 48 51E
46 Mur, R., Cent., Europe 46 30N 16 30E
50 Murashi, U.S.S.R. 59 30N 49 0E
43 Murat, France 45 10N 2 55E
84 Murchison, New Zealand 41 45S 172 23E
74 Murchison Falls, Fs., Uganda
2 24N 31 55E
80 Murchison, R., Austral. 27 35S 115 0E
80 Murchison Ra., Austral. 20 0S 135 0E
37 Murcia, Spain 38 0N 1 8W
37 Murcia, Prov., Spain 38 35N 1 50W
47 Mures, R., Rumania 46 0N 22 10E
43 Muret, France 43 26N 1 16E
64 Murghab, R., Afghan. 35 4N 64 5E
83 Murgon, Australia 26 5S 151 55E
46 Muritz, L., Germany 53 30N 12 25E
50 Murmansk, U.S.S.R. 69 0N 33 50E
52 Murom, U.S.S.R. 55 31N 42 4E
67 Muroran, Japan 42 20N 141 5E
83 Murray Bridge, Australia 35 2S 139 8E
93 Murray Hr., Canada 46 0N 62 32W
83 Murray, R., Australia 34 30S 141 40E
64 Murree, Pakistan 33 50N 73 25E
45 Murren, Switzerland 46 33N 7 58E
34 Murrough, Ireland 53 8N 9 17W
83 Murrumbidgee R., Australia
34 37S 144 30E
83 Murrumburrah, Austral. 34 35S 147 30E
83 Murrurundi, Australia 31 42S 150 51E
83 Murtoa, Australia 36 42S 142 28E
31 Murton, England 54 51N 1 22W
84 Murupara, New Zealand 38 25S 176 45E
65 Murwara, India 23 46N 80 28E
83 Murwillumbah, Austral. 28 21S 153 2E
73 Murzuq, Libya 25 53N 13 38E
46 Mürzzuschlag, Austria 47 5N 15 35E
51 Mus, Turkey 38 50N 41 28E
64 Musa Qala, Afghan. 32 23N 64 48E
41 Musala, Mt., Bulgaria 42 15N 23 35E
63 Musallim, Wadi, Oman 22 0N 56 30E
63 Muscat, Oman 23 40N 58 38E
63 Muscat & Oman, *see* Oman
78 Musgrave Ras., Austral. 26 10E 131 30E
91 Muskegon, U.S.A. 43 13N 86 10W
91 Muskegon, R., U.S.A. 43 25N 85 40W
91 Muskogee, U.S.A. 35 46N 95 32W
73 Musmar, Sudan 18 6N 35 40E
74 Musoma, Tanzania 1 31S 33 58E
62 Mussa Ali, Ethiopia 12 25N 42 15E
31 Musselburgh, Scotland 55 54N 3 3W
90 Musselshell, R., U.S.A. 46 35N 108 30W
64 Mussooree, India 30 23N 78 10E
94 Mustique, I., W.I. 12 50N 61 10W
83 Muswellbrook, Australia 32 18S 151 0E
62 Mut, Egypt 25 27N 29 0E
67 Mutankiang, Manchuria 44 34N 129 45E
75 Mutana, Angola 16 40S 15 1E
61 Mutarai, U.S.S.R. 61 20N 100 55E
74 Mutshatsha, Zaïre 10 35S 24 20E
67 Mutsu B., Japan 41 8N 141 0E
82 Muttaburra, Australia 22 30S 144 30E
34 Mutton I., Ireland 52 50N 9 33W
62 Muwaih, Saudi Arabia 22 35N 41 32E
74 Muxima, Angola 9 25S 13 52E
55 Muyun Kum, U.S.S.R. 47 0N 65 0E
64 Muzaffarabad, Kashmir 34 30N 73 25E
64 Muzaffarnagar, India 29 27N 77 40E
65 Muzaffarpur, India 26 15N 85 29E
60 Muzhi, U.S.S.R. 65 25N 64 40E
66 Muztagh, Mt., China 36 30N 87 22E
74 Mwanza, Tanzania 2 30S 33 1E
74 Mwaya, Tanzania 9 30S 33 58E
74 Mweka, Zaïre 4 12S 21 56E
74 Mwenga, Zaïre 3 7S 28 27E
74 Mweru, L., Zaïre 9 0S 28 50E
74 Mweru Marsh, Zambia 8 40S 29 40E
75 Mwinilunga, Zambia 11 43N 24 27E
68 My Tho, Vietnam 10 0N 106 48E
74 Myadhi, Gabon 1 16N 13 10E
65 Myaungmya, Burma 16 27N 94 58E
41 Mycenae, Greece 37 45N 22 45E
66 Myingyan, Burma 21 35N 94 40E
65 Myitkyina, Burma 25 50N 97 15E
65 Mymensingh, Pakistan, *see* Nasirabad
25 Mynydd du, Wales 51 45N 3 45W
25 Mynydd Epynt, Mt., Wales
52 3N 3 30W
25 Mynydd Prescelly, Mt., Wales
51 56N 4 45W
48 Myrdals Jökull, mts., Ice. 63 40N 19 0W
†64 Mysore, & st., India 12 18N 76 37E
52 Mytishchi, U.S.S.R. 55 54N 37 47E
48 Myvatn, L., Iceland 65 35N 16 55W

N

46 Naab, R., Germany 49 40N 12 10E
49 Naantali, Finland 60 32N 21 55E
44 Naaldwijk, Netherlands 52 0N 4 15E
63 Na'ar, Jordan 31 53N 35 50E
35 Naas, Ireland 53 14N 6 39W
76 Nababeep, S. Africa 29 35S 17 35E
65 Nabadwip, India 23 25N 88 20E
62 Naband, Iran 27 12N 52 38E
73 Nabeul, Tunisia 36 30N 10 40E
63 Nabulus, Jordan 32 13N 35 15E
75 Nacala, Mozambique 14 40S 40 40E
94 Nacaome, Honduras 13 40N 87 35W
74 Nachingwea, Tanzania 10 32S 38 48E
49 Nacka, Sweden 59 17N 18 14E
94 Nacozari, Mexico 30 30N 109 50W
64 Nadiad, India 22 41N 72 56E
47 Nadvornaya, U.S.S.R. 48 37N 24 30E
60 Nadym, & R., U.S.S.R. 65 30N 73 0E
72 Nafada, Nigeria 11 0N 11 20E
68 Naga, Philippines 13 37N 123 5E
65 Nagaland, st., India 26 0N 94 30E
74 Nagalle, Ethiopia 5 20N 39 30E
67 Nagano, & Pref., Japan 36 38N 138 6E
67 Nagaoka, Japan 37 30N 138 55E
65 Nagappattinam, India 10 40N 79 50E
64 Nagar Parkar, Pak. 24 30N 70 35E
67 Nagasaki, & Pref., Jap. 32 40N 129 48E
67 Nagashima, Japan 34 10N 136 15E
65 Nagchu Dzong, Tibet, China
31 25N 91 57E
64 Nagercoil, India 8 12N 77 33E
34 Nagles mts., Ireland 52 3N 8 30W
67 Nagoya, Japan 35 17N 137 0E
64 Nagpur, India 21 5N 79 5E
47 Nagykorös, Hungary 46 55N 19 48E
67 Naha, Japan 26 10N 127 45E
63 Naharayim, Jordan 32 38N 35 34E
63 Nahariya, Israel 33 0N 35 6E
63 Nahr Bisri, R., Lebanon 33 34N 35 25E
63 Nahr edDâmour, R., Leb.
33 44N 35 35E

† *State renamed Karnataka*

63 Nahr El-Litani, R., Leb. 33 20N 35 20E
99 Nahuel Huapi L., Arg. 41 0S 71 40W
89 Nain, Canada 56 38N 62 0W
64 Nainpur, India 22 30N 80 10E
††29 Nairn, & Co., Scotland 57 36N 3 51W
33 Nairn R., Scotland 57 25N 4 10W
74 Nairobi, Kenya 1 15S 36 49E
74 Naivasha, Kenya 0 50S 36 30E
67 Najin, Korea 42 10N 130 10E
67 Nakadori Shima, Japan 33 0N 129 5E
67 Nakamura, Japan 33 0N 133 0E
67 Nakatsu, Japan 33 40N 131 15E
51 Nakhichevan, & A.S.S.R., U.S.S.R.
39 20N 45 30E
67 Nakhodka, U.S.S.R. 42 50N 132 50E
68 Nakhon Ratchasima, Thailand
15 0N 105 40E
68 Nakhon Si Thammarat, Thailand
8 30N 100 6E
92 Nakina, Canada 50 8N 86 35W
62 Nakhl, Egypt 29 55N 33 43E
75 Nakop, S.W. Africa 28 1S 20 1E
49 Nakskov, Denmark 54 45N 11 12E
74 Nakuru, Kenya 0 10S 36 0E
51 Nalchik, U.S.S.R. 43 24N 43 32E
64 Nalgonda, India 17 4N 79 8E
64 Nallamalai Hs., India 16 0N 79 0E
73 Nalut, Libya 31 55N 11 2E
66 Nam Dinh, Vietnam 20 20N 106 15E
65 Nam Tso L., Tibet 30 45N 90 30E
60 Namangan, U.S.S.R. 41 30N 71 45E
76 Namaqualand, Dist., S. Africa
29 45S 18 0E
83 Nambour, Australia 26 31S 152 50E
83 Nambucca Heads, Australia
30 40S 152 48E
66 Namcha Barwa, Mt., China
29 50N 95 10E
70 Namib Des., S.W. Africa 24 0S 15 0E
83 Namoi, R., Australia 30 20S 150 30E
90 Nampa, U.S.A. 43 32N 116 35W
48 Namsen, R., Norway 64 40N 12 45E
48 Namsos, Norway 64 25N 11 30E
65 Namtu, Burma 23 0N 97 25E
44 Namur, & Prov., Belgium
50 28N 4 52E
75 Namutoni, S.W. Africa 18 50S 17 0E
75 Namwala, Zambia 15 50S 26 12E
66 Nan Ling, mts., China 25 30N 112 30E
55 Nan Shan, mts., China 38 30N 98 0E
88 Nanaimo, Canada 49 7N 123 58W
83 Nanango, Australia 26 40S 152 1E
67 Nanao, Japan 37 0N 137 0E
66 Nanchang, China 28 22N 115 49E
66 Nanchung, China 31 0N 105 20E
43 Nancy, France 48 44N 6 10E
64 Nanda Devi, mt., India 30 45N 80 0E
65 Nander, India 19 10N 77 16E
84 Nandi, Viti Levu, Fiji 17 40S 177 20E
64 Nandurbar, India 21 20N 74 15E
64 Nanga Parbat, mt., India
35 10N 75 0E
64 Nangrahar Prov., Afghan. 35 0N 71 0E
67 Nanking, China 32 5N 118 55E
80 Nannine, Australia 26 50S 118 16E
66 Nanning, China 22 50N 107 8E
67 Nanping, China 26 45N 118 15E
42 Nantes, France 47 17N 1 34W
92 Nanticoke, U.S.A. 41 10N 76 0W
43 Nantua, France 46 10N 5 35E
93 Nantucket I., U.S.A. 41 5N 70 5W
57 Nantung, China 31 50N 120 55E
26 Nantwich, England 53 5N 2 31W
66 Nanyang, China 33 1N 112 37E
74 Nanyuki, Kenya 0 1N 37 3E
37 Náo, C., Spain 38 25N 0 15E
67 Naoetsu, Japan 37 6N 138 9E
90 Napa, U.S.A. 38 24N 122 17W
84 Napier, New Zealand 39 37S 176 52E
40 Naples, (Napoli), Italy 40 53N 14 18E
67 Nara, & Pref., Japan 34 30N 135 40E
83 Naracoorte, Australia 36 55S 140 50E
83 Naradhan, Australia 33 30S 146 27E
65 Narasapur, India 16 50N 81 48E
65 Narayanganj, Bangla. 23 35N 90 30E
64 Narayanpet, India 16 50N 77 12E
25 Narberth, Wales 51 48N 4 45W
43 Narbonne, France 43 12N 3 1E
22 Narborough, England 52 34N 1 12W
41 Nardo, Italy 40 10N 18 0E
49 Narew, R., Poland 53 12N 21 50E
64 Narmada R., India 22 0N 75 15E
55 Narodnaya Mt., U.S.S.R. 65 10N 60 50E
83 Narooma, Austral. 36 14S 150 4E
83 Narrabri, Australia 30 26S 149 47W
83 Narrandera, Australia 34 46S 146 0E
80 Narrogin, Australia 32 50S 117 12E
83 Narromine, Australia 32 1S 148 8E
64 Narsinghpur, India 23 0N 79 6E
50 Narva, Estonia, U.S.S.R. 59 25N 28 5E
48 Narvik, Norway 68 27N 17 30E
50 Naryan-Mar, U.S.S.R. 68 0N 53 0E
60 Narymskoye, U.S.S.R. 49 15N 84 15E
60 Naryn, U.S.S.R. 41 30N 76 10E
48 Nasa, mt., Norway 66 32N 16 0E
23 Naseby, England 52 23N 1 0W
91 Nashua, U.S.A. 42 46N 71 30W
91 Nashville, U.S.A. 36 0N 86 50W
64 Nasik, India 20 0N 74 0E
65 Nasirabad, Bangladesh 24 50N 90 25E
64 Nasirabad, India 26 14N 74 44E
73 Nassar City, Egypt, *see* Kôm Ombo
91 Nassau, Bahamas 25 2N 77 20W
73 Nasir, Sudan 8 30N 33 2E
73 Nasser, L., Egypt 24 0N 32 40E

†† *Incorporated within the region of Highland*

49 Nässjö, Sweden 57 38N 14 45E
99 Natal, Brazil 5 48s 35 20w
76 Natal Prov., S. Africa 28 40s 30 30E
89 Natashquan, & R., Can. 50 14N 61 46w
91 Natchez, U.S.A. 31 35N 91 20w
91 Natchitoches, U.S.A. 31 40N 93 3w
83 Natimuk, Australia 36 52s 142 0E
74 Natron, L., Tanzania 2 0s 36 0E
80 Naturaliste, C., Australia 33 35s 115 1E
46 Naumburg, Germany 51 10N 11 45E
65 Nauntanwa, India 27 20N 83 25E
64 Naushahra, Pakistan 34 0N 72 0E
66 Naushki, U.S.S.R. 50 30N 106 0E
37 Navalcarnero, Spain 40 15N 4 0w
36 Navan, *see* An Uaimh
99 Navarino I., Chile 55 0s 67 30w
37 Navarra, Prov., Spain 43 0N 1 45w
33 Naver, L. & R., Scot. 58 18N 4 20w
94 Navojoa, Mexico 27 10N 109 25w
50 Navolok, U.S.S.R. 62 50N 40 0E
41 Nápaktos, Greece 38 23N 21 26E
41 Návplion, Greece 37 33N 22 50E
64 Navsari, India 20 58N 72 45E
63 Nawa, Syria 32 54N 36 3E
64 Nawabshah, Pakistan 26 20N 68 25E
65 Nawakot, Nepal 28 2N 83 55E
61 Nayakhon, U.S.S.R. 62 5N 159 0E
41 Naxos, I., Greece 37 5N 25 29E
99 Nazare, Brazil 12 52s 39 15w
63 Nazareth, Israel 32 42N 35 17E
94 Nazas, R., Mexico 25 30N 104 0w
22 Naze, The, England 51 52N 1 19E
65 Nazir Hat, Bangladesh 22 40N 91 50E
73 Ndélé, Central Africa 8 30N 20 37E
74 N'Djolé, Gabon 0 10s 10 45E
75 Ndola, Zambia 12 54s 28 35E
36 Neagh, L., N. Ireland 54 35N 6 25w
25 Neath, & R., Wales 51 40N 3 47w
83 Nebine, Cr., Australia 28 30s 146 50E
60 Nebit Dag., U.S.S.R. 39 50N 54 30E
90 Nebraska, st., U.S.A. 42 15N 100 30w
91 Nebraska City, U.S.A. 40 44N 95 55w
45 Neckar, R., Germany 48 37N 9 15E
99 Necochea, Argentina 38 30s 58 50w
22 Needles, The, England 50 40N 1 35w
64 Neemuch, India 24 25N 74 50E
88 Neepawa, Canada 50 19N 99 30w
92 Negaunee, U.S.A. 46 30N 87 32w
63 Negev, Israel 30 50N 34 50E
51 Negoiu, mt., Rumania 45 20N 25 0E
64 Negombo, Sri Lanka 7 10N 79 54E
41 Negotin, Yugoslavia 44 15N 22 34E
65 Negrais, C., Burma 16 0N 94 18E
99 Negro R., Argentina 40 0s 64 0w
98 Negro R., Brazil 1 0s 63 0w
68 Negros, I., Philippines 10 0N 123 0E
63 Neh, Iran 31 30N 59 58E
66 Neikiang, China 29 45N 104 25E
30 Neilston, Scotland 55 47N 4 26w
46 Neisse, R., Pol.-Ger. 51 27N 14 59E
98 Neiva, Colombia 3 0N 75 25w
62 Nejd, reg., Si. Arabia 25 15N 45 0E
74 Nekemte, Ethiopia 9 4N 36 30E
49 Nekso, Denmark 55 4N 15 8E
61 Nelka, U.S.S.R. 57 50N 136 0E
64 Nellore, India 14 30N 80 1E
61 Nelma, U.S.S.R. 47 30N 139 0E
88 Nelson, Canada 49 25N 117 17w
26 Nelson, England 53 50N 2 14w
84 Nelson, New Zealand 41 18s 173 20E
83 Nelson, C., Australia 38 18s 141 40E
84 Nelson, Dist., N.Z. 41 20s 173 23E
88 Nelson, R., Canada 56 22N 95 0w
76 Nelspruit, S. Africa 25 29s 30 59E
72 Néma, Mauritania 16 30N 7 0w
49 Neman, R., U.S.S.R. 55 5N 23 0E
72 Nemours, Algeria, *see* Ghazaouet
43 Nemours, France 48 16N 2 40E
61 Nemui, U.S.S.R. 55 35N 136 0E
67 Nemuro, Japan 43 20N 145 30E
23 Nene, R., England 52 38N 0 50w
34 Nenagh, Ireland 52 53N 8 12w
65 Nepal, Asia 28 0N 83 40E
65 Nepalganj, Nepal 28 0N 81 30E
90 Nephi, U.S.A. 39 43N 111 50w
35 Nephin, mt., Ireland 54 0N 9 22w
35 Nephin Beg Ra., Ireland 54 0N 9 35w
41 Neretva, R., Y-slav. 43 10N 17 53E
61 Nerchinsk, U.S.S.R. 52 1N 116 25E
61 Nerchinski Zavod, U.S.S.R. 51 10N 119 35E
37 Nerva, Spain 37 43N 6 30w
48 Nes, Iceland 65 50N 17 18w
44 Nesle, France 49 45N 2 53E
33 Ness, L. & R., Scotland 57 15N 4 28w
26 Neston, England 53 17N 3 4w
49 Nesttun, Norway 60 17N 5 31E
63 Netanya, Israel 32 20N 34 51E
82 Netherdale, Australia 21 10s 148 33E
44 Netherlands, Europe 52 20N 6 0E
27 Nettleham, England 53 15N 0 28w
46 Neu Brandenburg, Ger. 53 35N 13 15E
45 Neuchâtel, & Cn., Switz. 47 0N 6 56E
45 Neuchâtel, Lac de, Switz. 46 55N 6 50E
44 Neufchâteau, Belgium 49 50N 5 26E
43 Neufchâtel, France 49 42N 1 30E
44 Neufchâtel sur Aisne, Fr. 49 27N 4 0E
46 Neumünster, Germany 54 5N 10 0E
45 Neunkirchen, Germany 49 20N 7 0E
99 Neuquen & R., Arg. 39 5s 68 5w
46 Neuruppin, Germany 52 52N 12 48E
44 Neuss, Germany 51 13N 6 39E
46 Neusiedler, L., of, Austria 47 58N 16 47E
45 Neustadt, Germany 47 53N 8 14E
46 Neustrelitz, Germany 53 19N 13 0E
44 Neuwied, Germany 50 27N 7 30E
50 Neva, R., U.S.S.R. 59 55N 31 0E
91 Nevada, U.S.A. 37 51N 94 28w
90 Nevada, st., U.S.A. 39 30N 118 0w
37 Nevada, Sa. de, mts., Spain 37 10N 3 20w
95 Nevada de Chita, Colombia 6 30N 72 0w
61 Nevelski mt., U.S.S.R. 50 0N 143 25E
43 Nevers, France 47 3N 3 12E
83 Nevertire, Australia 31 38s 147 50E
94 Nevis I., W. Indies 17 0N 62 30w
32 Nevis, L., Scotland 57 0N 5 45w
31 New Abbey, Scotland 54 58N 3 37w
91 New Albany, U.S.A. 38 20N 85 50w
98 New Amsterdam, Guyana 6 12N 57 30w
91 New Bedford, U.S.A. 41 30N 71 0w
35 New Birmingham, Ire. 52 36N 7 38w
90 New Braunfels, U.S.A. 29 40N 98 13w
26 New Brighton, England 53 27N 3 4w
84 New Brighton, N.Z. 43 29s 172 43E
93 New Britain, U.S.A. 41 35N 72 50w
82 New Britain, I., Terr. of New Guinea 6 0s 150 0E
89 New Brunswick, Prov., Canada 46 30N 66 30w
81 New Caledonia, I., Pacific Ocean 21 15s 165 0E
37 New Castile, prov., Spain 40 5N 3 20w
92 New Castle, U.S.A. 41 2N 80 20w
30 New Cumnock, Scot. 55 24N 4 3w
83 New England Ra., Austral. 30 0s 152 0E
22 New Forest, England 50 52N 1 48w
31 New Galloway, Scotland 55 4N 4 9w
93 New Glasgow, Canada 45 35N 62 57w
78 New Guinea, I., E. Indies 5 0s 140 0E
82 New Guinea, Terr. of, Austral. Trust Terr. 5 0s 145 0E
91 New Hampshire, st., U.S.A. 43 20N 71 30w
82 New Hanover, I., Pacific Ocean 2 18s 150 0E
91 New Haven, U.S.A. 41 15N 72 58w
81 New Hebrides, Is., Pacific Ocean 16 0s 166 30E
91 New Iberia, U.S.A. 30 0N 91 46w
82 New Ireland, I., Terr. of New Guinea 3 0s 152 0E
93 New Jersey, st., U.S.A. 39 50N 74 30w
93 New London, U.S.A. 41 20N 72 5w
31 New Luce, Scotland 54 56N 4 51w
90 New Mexico, st., U.S.A. 34 40N 106 0w
26 New Mills, England 53 22N 2 0w
30 Newmilns, Scotland 55 36N 4 19w
83 New Norfolk, Australia 42 45s 146 59E
91 New Orleans, U.S.A. 30 0N 90 0w
84 New Plymouth, N.Z. 39 2s 174 5E
91 New Providence, Bahamas 25 0N 77 25w
25 New Quay, Wales 52 12N 4 22w
25 New Radnor, Wales 52 14N 3 9w
23 New Romney, England 50 59N 0 56E
35 New Ross, Ireland 52 25N 6 57w
27 New Rossington, England 53 30N 1 4w
61 New Siberian Is., U.S.S.R. 75 30N 140 0E
83 New South Wales, st., Australia 32 20s 147 0E
25 New Tredegar, Wales 51 43N 3 15w
91 New Ulm, U.S.A. 44 19N 94 35w
88 New Westminster, Can. 49 12N 122 50w
93 New York, & st., U.S.A. 40 45N 74 0w
84 New Zealand 40 0s 173 0E
74 Newala, Tanzania 11 0s 39 0E
27 Newark, England 53 5N 0 49w
93 Newark, Del., U.S.A. 39 45N 75 45w
93 Newark, N.J., U.S.A. 40 45N 74 0w
92 Newark, Ohio, U.S.A. 40 8N 82 30w
91 New Bern, U.S.A. 35 7N 77 4w
27 Newbiggin-by-the-Sea, England 55 12N 1 30w
31 Newbigging, Scotland 55 42N 3 33w
36 Newbliss, Ireland 54 9N 7 8w
35 Newbridge, *see* Droichead Nua
25 Newbridge-on-Wye, Wales 52 13N 3 26w
31 Newburgh, Scotland 56 21N 3 14w
93 Newburgh, U.S.A. 41 33N 74 0w
27 Newburn, England 54 58N 1 44w
22 Newbury, England 51 24N 1 19w
83 Newcastle, Australia 32 59s 151 49E
35 Newcastle, Ireland 53 5N 6 4w
36 Newcastle, N. Ireland 54 13N 5 54w
25 Newcastle Emlyn, Wales 52 4N 4 28w
80 Newcastle Waters, Australia 17 13s 133 42E
27 Newcastle-on-Tyne, Eng. 54 58N 1 36w
26 Newcastle-under-Lyme, England 53 1N 2 16w
80 Newdegate, Australia 33 0s 119 30E
22 Newent, England 51 56N 2 24w
89 Newfoundland, prov., Canada 49 0N 56 0w
23 Newham, Greater London, England 51 31N 0 3E
23 Newhaven, England 50 47N 0 3E
23 Newington, England 51 6N 1 8E
91 Newman, U.S.A. 33 32N 84 35w
23 Newmarket, England 52 15N 0 24E
34 Newmarket, Ireland 52 10N 9 0w
94 Newmarket, Jamaica 18 8N 77 53w
34 Newmarket-on-Fergus, Ireland 52 46N 8 54w
22 Newnham, England 51 48N 2 27w
22 Newport, Salop, Eng. 52 46N 2 23w
25 Newport, Monmouth, U.K. 51 35N 3 0w
35 Newport, & B., Mayo, Ireland 53 53N 9 33w
34 Newport, Tipperary, Ire. 52 43N 8 24w
31 Newport, Scotland 56 57N 2 56w
91 Newport, Ark., U.S.A. 35 44N 91 17w
91 Newport, Ken., U.S.A. 39 3N 84 28w
93 Newport, R.I., U.S.A. 41 30N 71 17w
93 Newport, Vt. U.S.A. 44 47N 72 12w
91 Newport News, U.S.A. 37 6N 76 25w
23 Newport Pagnell, Eng. 52 5N 0 43w
24 Newquay, England 50 25N 5 6w
36 Newry, N. Ireland 54 10N 6 18w
91 Newton, Iowa, U.S.A. 41 43N 93 4w
91 Newton, Kansas, U.S.A. 38 6N 97 17w
24 Newton Abbot, England 50 32N 3 37w
27 Newton Aycliffe, England 54 36N 1 33w
30 Newton Stewart, Scot. 54 57N 4 28w
26 Newton-le-Willows, Eng. 53 27N 2 37w
31 Newtown, Scotland 55 34N 2 38w
25 Newtown, Wales 52 30N 3 22w
36 Newtown Forbes, Ireland 53 46N 7 50w
36 Newtown Hamilton, N. Ireland 54 12N 6 34w
36 Newtown Monasterboice, Ireland 53 46N 6 26w
36 Newtownabbey, Ireland 54 40N 5 55w
36 Newtownards, N. Ireland 54 36N 5 42w
36 Newtownbutler, N. Ireland 54 11N 7 21w
36 Newtowncunninghamn, Ireland 54 59N 7 31w
35 Newtownmountkennedy, Ireland 53 6N 6 6w
36 Newtownstewart, N. Ireland 54 43N 7 23w
50 Nezhin, Ukraine, U.S.S.R. 51 3N 32 5E
75 Ngami, Ll (Former), Botswana 20 35s 22 35E
73 Ngaoundere, Cameroon 7 23N 13 20E
84 Ngapara, New Zealand 44 57s 170 46E
66 Ngoring, Nor, L., China 35 0N 97 15E
74 Ngudu, Tanzania 3 25s 32 2E
73 Nguigmi, Niger 14 20N 13 20E
68 Nha Trang, Vietnam 12 15N 109 15E
83 Nhill, Australia 36 18s 141 40E
81 Nhulunbuy, Australia 12 18s 137 0E
92 Niagara Falls, N. America 43 12N 79 0w
72 Niamey, Niger 13 31N 2 20E
68 Nias, Is., East Indies 1 0N 97 20E
94 Nicaragua, & L., Central America 12 30N 85 0w
41 Nicastro, Italy 39 0N 16 18E
43 Nice, France 43 45N 7 17E
55 Nicobar Is., India 8 0N 93 20E
62 Nicosia, Cyprus 35 7N 33 2E
27 Nidd, R., England 54 2N 1 40w
46 Nienburg, Germany 52 38N 9 12E
76 Nieu Bethesda, S. Africa 31 55s 24 30E
44 Nieuwpoort, Belgium 51 9N 2 46E
42 Nièvre, Dépt., France 47 17N 3 40E
51 Nigde, Turkey 38 0N 34 40E
72 Niger, W. Africa 15 0N 9 0E
72 Niger, R., W. Africa 16 0N 0 20E
72 Niger Delta, Nigeria 4 0N 5 0E
72 Nigeria, W. Africa 9 30N 8 0E
33 Nigg, B., Scotland 57 42N 4 0w
84 Nightcaps, New Zealand 45 58s 168 3E
67 Niigata, & Pref., Japan 38 0N 139 5E
90 Niihau, Hawaii 21 45N 160 10w
44 Nijkerk, Netherlands 52 14N 5 29E
44 Nijmegen, Netherlands 51 50N 5 52E
67 Nikko, Japan 36 50N 139 30E
51 Nikolayev, U.S.S.R. 46 58N 32 7E
61 Nikolayevski, Siberia 53 30N 140 10E
52 Nikopol, U.S.S.R. 47 20N 34 20E
41 Niksic, Yugoslavia 42 47N 18 57E
73 Nile, R., N.E. Africa 27 20N 31 0E
43 Nîmes, France 43 51N 4 21E
83 Nimmitabel, Australia 36 42s 149 0E
83 Nindigully, Australia 28 27s 149 0E
67 Ningan, China 44 30N 129 45E
67 Ningpo, China 30 0N 121 40E
66 Ningsia, *see* Yinchwan
66 Ningsia Hui, Autonomous Region, China 37 0N 106 0E
65 Ningtsin, China 29 50N 98 25E
66 Ningtu, China 26 50N 115 30E
44 Ninove, Belgium 50 51N 4 2E
72 Nioro, Mali 15 30N 9 30w
42 Niort, France 46 22N 0 43w
88 Nipawin, Canada 53 20N 104 0w
89 Nipigon, & B., Canada 49 10N 88 20w
89 Nipigon, L., Canada 49 40N 88 30w
62 Niriz, Iran 29 15N 54 5E
65 Nirmali, India 26 25N 86 30E
41 Nis, Yugoslavia 43 17N 21 53E
99 Niteroi, Brazil 22 52s 42 55w
31 Nith, R., Scotland 55 27N 3 58w
31 Nithsdale, Scotland 55 13N 3 45w
47 Nitra, Czechoslovakia 48 20N 18 4E
84 Niuafo'ou, I., Pacific Ocean (Inset)
44 Nivelles, Belgium 50 36N 4 20E
43 Nivernais, Prov., France 47 20N 3 25E
64 Nizamabad, India 18 45N 78 7E
61 Nizhne Kolymsk, U.S.S.R. 68 35N 160 55E
61 Nizhneudinsk, U.S.S.R. 55 0N 99 25E
50 Nizhniy Tagil, U.S.S.R. 57 45N 60 0E
72 Nkambe, Camer. 6 35N 10 40E
74 Nkhata Bay, Malawi 11 35s 34 20E
75 Nkhota Kota, Malawi 13 0s 34 20E
65 Nmai, mts., Burma 25 45N 98 0E
65 Noakhali, *see* Maijdi
36 Nobber, Ireland 53 49N 6 45w
67 Nobeoka, Japan 32 35N 131 40E
94 Nogales, Mexico 31 30N 111 0w
90 Nogales, U.S.A. 31 25N 111 0w
43 Nogent le Rotou, Fr. 48 20N 0 50E
52 Noginsk, U.S.S.R. 55 50N 38 28E
61 Noginsk, U.S.S.R. 64 30N 90 50E
42 Noirmoutier, I. de, Fr. 47 0N 2 17w
61 Nokhtuisk, U.S.S.R. 60 10N 117 15E
88 Nokomis, Canada 51 10N 105 10w
64 Nok Kundi, Pakistan 28 55N 62 55E
83 Noondoo, Australia 28 35s 148 25E
44 Noord Beveland I., Neth. 51 35N 3 45E
44 Noord Brabant, prov., Netherlands 51 40N 5 0E
44 Noord Holland, prov., Netherlands 52 30N 4 45E
76 Noordhoek, S. Africa 34 7s 18 25E
44 Noordoost Polder, Neth. 52 45N 5 45E
92 Noranda, Canada 48 20N 79 0w
42 Nord, Dépt., France 50 27N 3 20E
88 Nordegg, Canada 52 0N 116 47w
23 Nordelph, England 52 34N 0 18E
46 Norderney I., Germany 53 43N 7 12E
46 Nordhausen, Germany 51 30N 10 43E
44 Nordhorn, Germany 52 29N 7 3E
13 Nordkinn, C., Europe 71 3N 28 0E
48 Nordland, Co., Norway 66 30N 14 30E
61 Nordvik, U.S.S.R. 73 45N 110 57E
28 Norfolk, Co., England 52 42N 1 0E
91 Norfolk, Neb., U.S.A. 42 6N 97 28w
91 Norfolk, Va., U.S.A. 36 55N 76 12w
23 Norfolk Broads, Eng. 52 45N 1 30E
78 Norfolk I., Pacific Ocean 29 0s 167 55E
27 Norham, England 55 42N 2 10w
82 Norman R., Australia 19 20s 142 25E
82 Normanby, I., Papua 10 0s 151 0E
82 Normanby, R., Australia 15 0s 145 0E
42 Normandy, Prov., France 49 0N 0 0
82 Normanton, Australia 17 52s 140 58E
27 Normanton, England 53 42N 1 25w
48 Norrbotten, Co., Sweden 66 40N 20 0E
49 Nörresundby, Denmark 57 5N 9 52E
49 Norrköping, Sweden 58 39N 16 6E
80 Norseman, Australia 32 8s 121 45E
61 Norsk, U.S.S.R. 52 30N 130 5E
98 Norte, Sa. do, mts., Brazil 12 0s 59 0w
32 North Ballachulish, Scot. 56 42N 5 9w
88 North Battleford, Can. 52 48N 108 6w
89 North Bay, Canada 46 20N 79 30w
90 North Bend, U.S.A. 43 28N 124 15w
31 North Berwick, Scotland 56 3N 2 43w
68 North Bunguran Is., Indonesia 4 40N 108 0E
93 North C., Canada 47 0N 60 28w
84 North C., New Zealand 34 22s 173 1E
49 North C., Norway 71 0N 26 0E
91 North Carolina, st., U.S.A. 35 30N 79 0w
30 North Channel, U.K. 55 0N 5 30w
92 North Chan., L. Huron 46 5N 83 0w
90 North Dakota, st., U.S.A. 47 30N 100 0w
22 North Dorset Downs, England 50 40N 2 30w
22 North Downs, England 51 18N 0 20E
13 North Dvina R., U.S.S.R. 62 30N 43 0E
65 North East Frontier Agency, India 28 0N 95 0E
*82 North East New Guinea, Terr. of New Guinea 5 0s 145 0E
33 North Esk R., Scotland 56 54N 2 45w
13 North European Plain 57 0N 26 0E
23 North Foreland, England 51 23N 1 28E
49 North Frisian Is., Ger. 55 0N 8 20E
84 North I., New Zealand 38 0s 176 0E
67 North Korea, st., Asia 40 0N 127 0E
65 North Moscos Is., *see* Heinze Is.
51 North Ossetian, A.S.S.R., U.S.S.R. 43 0N 44 10E
68 North Pageh, I., Indon. 3 0s 100 10E
24 North Petherton, Eng. 51 6N 3 0w
90 North Platte R., U.S.A. 42 30N 105 0w
31 North Queensferry, Scot. 56 1N 3 22w
46 North Rhine-Westphalia, Land, Germany 51 0N 7 0E
**27 North Riding, England 54 20N 1 30w
32 North Roe, dist., Scot. 60 35N 1 20w
33 North Ronaldsay, I., & Firth, Scotland 59 25N 2 25w
88 North Saskatchewan R. Canada 54 0N 112 30w
13 North Sea, Europe 56 0N 3 0E
27 North Somercotes, Eng. 53 26N 0 9E
34 North Sd., Ireland 53 10N 9 48w
33 North Sd., Scotland 59 17N 2 45w
84 North Taranaki Bight, New Zealand 38 50s 174 0E
92 North Tonawanda, U.S.A. 43 0N 78 50w
32 North Tolsta, Scotland 58 21N 6 14w
48 North Tröndelag, Co., Norway 64 15N 12 0E
32 North Uist, I., Scotland 57 37N 7 20w
68 North Vietnam, st., Asia 22 0N 105 0E
95 North Village, Bermuda 32 19N 64 47w
23 North Walsham, England 52 49N 1 24E
80 North-West C., Austral. 21 42s 114 10E
32 North-West Highlands, Scotland 57 30N 5 2w
89 North-West River, Can. 53 45N 60 10w
88 Northwest Terr., Canada 65 0N 97 0w
27 North York Moors, Eng. 54 25N 0 50w
27 Northallerton, England 54 21N 1 27w
80 Northam, Australia 31 40s 116 40E
24 Northam, England 51 2N 4 13w
80 Northampton, Australia 28 24s 114 37E
28 Northampton, & Co., England 52 14N 0 54w
65 Northern Circars, India 17 30N 82 30E
36 Northern Ireland, U.K. 54 40N 6 50w
80 Northern Terr., Australia 19 30s 134 0E
23 Northfleet, England 51 27N 0 20E
22 Northleach, England 51 50N 1 51w
83 Northumberland, C., Australia 38 0s 140 30E
28 Northumberland, Co., England 55 13N 2 0w
82 Northumberland Is., Australia 21 45s 150 20E
93 Northumberland Str., Canada 46 20N 64 15w
26 Northwich, England 53 16N 2 32w
27 Norton, England 54 8N 0 47w
92 Norwalk, U.S.A. 41 6N 82 46w
48 Norway, Europe 65 30N 12 0E
16 Norwegian Sea 70 0N 0 2E
23 Norwich, England 52 38N 1 19E
67 Noshiro, & R., Japan 40 12N 140 0E
60 Nosok, U.S.S.R. 69 20N 82 20E
75 Nossi Bé, I., Madag. 13 25s 48 15E
75 Nossi Mitsio, Madag. 12 55s 48 20E
76 Nossob, R., Botswana 25 0s 20 20E
47 Notec, R., Europe 53 5N 17 10E
40 Noto, Sicily, Italy 36 59N 15 10E
28 Nottingham, & Co., Eng. 52 58N 1 8w
72 Nouadhibou (Port Etienne), Mauritania 21 0N 17 0w
76 Noupoort, South Africa 31 10s 24 57E
44 Nouzonville, France 49 49N 4 45E
†74 Nova Chaves, Angola 10 20s 21 26E
75 Nova Lisboa, Angola 12 35s 15 48E
68 Nova Sagres, Port. Timor 8 20s 127 30E
93 Nova Scotia, Prov., Can. 45 0N 64 0w
60 Novaya Lyalya, U.S.S.R. 59 0N 60 50E
60 Novaya Zemlya, Is., U.S.S.R. 75 0N 55 0E
47 Nové Zámky, Cz-slov. 48 2N 18 8E
50 Novgorod, U.S.S.R. 58 30N 31 10E
41 Novi Pazar, Yugoslavia 43 8N 20 30E
41 Novi Sad, Yugoslavia 45 17N 19 44E
60 Novo Kuznetsk, U.S.S.R. 53 30N 87 10E
74 Novo Redondo, Angola 11 3s 13 46E
51 Novocherkassk, U.S.S.R. 47 22N 40 8E
47 Novograd Volynsk, U.S.S.R. 50 6N 27 33E
60 Novokazalinsk, U.S.S.R. 45 50N 62 5E
50 Novokuybyshevsk, U.S.S.R. 53 10N 49 52E
60 Novokuznetsk, U.S.S.R. 54 0N 87 10E
100 Novolazarevskaya, Antarctica 70 45s 2 0E
52 Novomoskovsk, U.S.S.R. 54 5N 38 15E
51 Novorossiysk, U.S.S.R. 44 40N 37 50E
52 Novoshakhtinsk, U.S.S.R. 47 45N 39 55E
60 Novosibirsk, U.S.S.R. 55 10N 83 5E
51 Novouzensk, U.S.S.R. 50 30N 48 10E
40 Novska, Yugoslavia 45 22N 16 59E
60 Novy Port, U.S.S.R. 67 40N 73 20E
65 Nowgong, India 26 22N 92 40E
83 Nowra, Australia 34 51s 150 38E
47 Nowy Sacz, Poland 49 39N 20 42E
46 Nowy Tomysl, Poland 52 20N 16 5E
43 Noyon, France 49 35N 3 0E
75 Nsanje, Malawi 16 55s 35 15E
73 Nubian Des., Sudan 21 0N 33 0E
98 Nudo Coropuna, mt., Peru 16 0s 72 30w
88 Nueltin, L., Canada 59 40N 99 30w
90 Nuesces, R., U.S.A. 28 40N 99 0w
94 Nueva Rosita, Mexico 28 0N 101 20w
94 Nuevo Laredo, Mexico 27 25N 99 35w
84 Nuhaka, New Zealand 39 0s 177 47E
62 Nukha, U.S.S.R. 41 28N 47 5E
73 Nukheila, Oasis, Sudan 19 7N 26 15E
84 Nuku'alofa, Tonga Is. 21 9s 175 14w
60 Nukus, U.S.S.R. 42 30N 60 0E
80 Nullarbor Plain, Austral. 30 40s 129 30E
73 Numan, Nigeria 9 29N 12 3E
67 Numata, Japan 36 45N 139 4E
67 Numazu, Japan 35 10N 138 50E
83 Numurkah, Australia 36 3s 145 30E
22 Nuneaton, England 52 31N 1 28w
74 Nunivak Is., Alaska 60 0N 166 0w
44 Nunspeet, Netherlands 52 22N 5 46E
40 Nuoro, Sardinia, Italy 40 20N 9 20E
83 Nuriootpa, Australia 34 27s 139 0E
45 Nürnberg (Nuremberg), Germany 49 28N 11 7E
68 Nusa Tenggara, Prov., Indonesia 7 40s 118 0E
62 Nusaybin, Turkey 37 3N 41 10E
64 Nushki, Pakistan 29 35N 65 57E
76 Nuweveldberge, mts., S. Africa 32 10s 21 45E
80 Nuyts, Pt., Australia 35 1s 116 40E
80 Nyabing, Australia 33 30s 118 10E
74 Nyahanga, Tanzania 2 10s 33 32E
83 Nyah, Australia 35 8s 143 26E
73 Nyala, Sudan 12 2N 24 58E
65 Nyalam Dz., Tibet, China 28 10N 85 50E
73 Nyamlell, Sudan 9 0N 27 3E
75 Nyasa, L., E. Africa 12 0s 34 30E
74 Nyasaland, E. Africa, *see* Malawi
49 Nybro, Sweden 56 43N 15 55E

* *Incorporated within Papua New Guinea*

** *Incorporated within the county of North Yorkshire*

† *Renamed Huambo*

60 Nyda, U.S.S.R. 66 40N 73 28E
66 Nyenchen Tanghla, Ra., Asia 30 30N 90 0E
74 Nyeri, Kenya 0 34S 37 0E
47 Nyiregyhaza, Hungary 47 47N 21 43E
49 Nyköbing, Denmark 54 51N 11 50E
49 Nylöping, Sweden 58 46N 17 0E
75 Nylstroom, S. Africa 24 40S 28 0E
83 Nymagee, Australia 32 7S 146 20E
49 Nynashamn, Sweden 58 55N 17 57E
83 Nyngan, Australia 31 39S 147 13E
45 Nyon, Switzerland 46 24N 6 15E
39 Nyons, France 44 20N 5 5E
47 Nysa, Poland 50 40N 17 22E
67 Nyudo, C., Japan 40 0N 139 30E
74 Nzega, Tanzania 4 12S 33 11E
72 Nzérekoré, Guinea 7 46N 8 58W

O

31 Oa, Mull of, Scotland 55 35N 6 20W
22 Oadby, England 52 37N 1 7W
90 Oahu, Hawaii 21 30N 158 0W
83 Oakbank, Australia 32 58S 140 50E
22 Oakengates, England 52 42N 2 29W
83 Oakey, Australia 27 28S 151 33E
23 Oakham, England 52 40N 0 47W
90 Oakland, U.S.A. 37 55N 122 5W
84 Oamaru, New Zealand 45 1S 171 0E
100 Oasis, Antartica 77 0S 101 0E
100 Oates Coast, Antarctica 70 0S 165 0E
94 Oaxaca, Mexico 17 15N 96 38W
60 Ob, G. of, U.S.S.R. 70 0N 73 0E
60 Ob, R., U.S.S.R. 62 40N 66 0E
92 Oba, Canada 48 50N 84 10W
84 Oban, New Zealand 46 55S 168 10E
30 Oban, Scotland 56 25N 5 27W
44 Oberhausen, Germany 51 28N 6 50E
83 Oberon, Australia 33 40S 149 50E
68 Obi Is., Indonesia 1 40S 128 0E
98 Obidos, Brazil 1 48S 55 37W
62 Obock, Fr. T.A. & I. 12 0N 43 15E
34 O'Briensbridge, Ireland 52 46N 8 30W
72 Obuasi, Ghana 6 17N 1 40W
98 Ocaña, Colombia 8 0N 73 35W
37 Ocaña, Spain 39 55N 3 30W
31 Ochil Hills, Scotland 56 15N 3 40W
61 October Revolution I., U.S.S.R. 79 30N 97 0E
62 Oda, Gebel, Sudan 20 15N 36 50E
48 Odadahraun, Iceland 65 10N 17 0W
49 Odda, Norway 60 3N 6 35E
48 Oddeyri, Iceland 65 40N 18 5W
76 Odendaalsrus, S. Africa 27 53S 26 45E
49 Odense, Denmark 55 22N 10 23E
49 Oder, R., Poland 53 3N 14 20E
90 Odessa, U.S.A. 31 50N 102 25W
61 Odessa, U.S.S.R. 46 37N 30 16E
72 Odienné, Ivory Coast 9 30N 7 15W
23 Odiham, England 51 16N 0 57W
47 Odorhei, Rumania 46 20N 25 20E
41 Odzak, Yugoslavia 45 3N 18 18E
75 Odzi, Rhodesia 19 0S 32 20E
40 Ofanto, R., Italy 41 10N 16 50E
45 Ofenpass, Switzerland 46 40N 10 20E
35 Offaly, Co., Ireland 53 10N 7 30W
45 Offenbach, Germany 50 7N 8 51E
45 Offenburg, Germany 48 28N 7 57E
45 Oftringen, Switzerland 47 20N 7 56E
67 Ogaki, Japan 35 25N 136 30E
72 Ogbomosho, Nigeria 8 5N 4 10E
90 Ogden, U.S.A. 41 22N 111 50W
91 Ogdensburg, U.S.A. 44 42N 75 20W
67 Oginohama, Japan 38 27N 141 30E
40 Oglio, R., Italy 46 0N 10 20E
83 Ogmore, Australia 22 37S 149 35E
25 Ogmore Vale, Wales 51 35N 3 32W
84 Ohakune, New Zealand 39 26S 175 25E
44 Ohey, Belgium 50 26N 5 8E
91 Ohio, R., U.S.A. 39 45N 81 30W
91 Ohio, st., U.S.A. 40 40N 82 30W
46 Ohre, R., Czechoslovakia 50 10N 12 30E
41 Ohrid, Yugoslavia 41 10N 20 50E
76 Ohrigstad, S. Africa 24 35S 30 32E
35 Oilgate, Ireland 52 25N 6 30W
61 Oimyakon, U.S.S.R. 63 20N 143 5E
60 Oirot-Tura, U.S.S.R. 52 0N 86 3E
42 Oise, Dépt., France 49 35N 2 12E
43 Oise R., France 49 20N 3 0E
44 Oisterwijk, Netherlands 51 35N 5 12E
67 Oita, & Pref., Japan 33 10N 131 30E
99 Ojos del Salado, mt., Arg. 27 0S 68 0W
75 Okahandja, S.W. Africa 22 0S 16 52E
84 Okarito, New Zealand 43 15S 170 10E
75 Okavango Swamp, Botswana 19 30S 23 0E
67 Okayama, & Pref., Japan 34 40N 133 6E
67 Okazaki, Japan 34 55N 137 10E
91 Okeechobee, L., U.S.A. 27 0N 80 50W
24 Okehampton, England 50 45N 4 0W
72 Okene, Nigeria 7 32N 6 11E
64 Okha, India 22 25N 69 0E
61 Okha, U.S.S.R. 53 40N 142 50E
61 Okhotsk, U.S.S.R. 59 25N 143 10E
61 Okhotsk, Sea of, U.S.S.R. 57 0N 149 0E
67 Oki Is., Japan 36 17N 133 10E
75 Okiep, S. Africa 29 41S 17 59E
67 Okinawa, I., Japan 26 30N 128 0E
90 Oklahoma City, U.S.A. 35 40N 97 20W
90 Oklahoma, st., U.S.A. 35 40N 97 0W
72 Okrika, Nigeria 4 47N 7 4E
84 Okuru, New Zealand 43 55S 168 58E
48 Olafsvik, Iceland 64 52N 23 45W
49 Oland I., Sweden 56 50N 16 40E
83 Olary, Australia 32 8S 140 7E
99 Olavarria, Argentina 37 0S 60 20W
40 Olbia, Sardinia, Italy 40 55N 9 30E
37 Old Castile, Prov. Spain 42 0N 4 0W
36 Old Castle, Ireland 53 46N 7 10W
33 Old Deer, Scotland 57 30N 2 3W
35 Old Head of Kinsale, Ire., *see* Kinsale
30 Old Kilpatrick, Scotland 55 56N 4 34W
62 Old Sennar, Sudan 13 52N 33 32E
22 Oldbury, England 52 30N 1 59W
44 Oldenburg, Germany 53 10N 8 15E
26 Oldham, England 53 34N 2 7W
44 Oldenzaal, Netherlands 52 19N 6 55E
92 Olean, U.S.A. 42 7N 78 27W
61 Olekma, R., U.S.S.R. 57 30N 121 30E
33 Oldmeldrum, Scotland 57 20N 2 19W
61 Olekminsk, U.S.S.R. 60 40N 120 30E
61 Olenek, R., U.S.S.R. 72 30N 122 30E
42 Oleron, I.d', France 46 0N 1 20W
47 Olésnica, Poland 51 13N 17 22E
61 Olga, U.S.S.R. 43 50N 135 20E
76 Olifants R., S. Africa 24 0S 31 25E
76 Olifantshoek, S. Africa 27 50S 22 55E
45 Olives, Mt. of Israel 31 47N 35 14E
27 Ollerton, England 53 12N 1 1W
23 Olney, England 52 0N 0 42W
46 Olomouc, Cz-slov. 49 35N 17 8E
42 Oloron, France 43 10N 0 40W
61 Olovyannaya, U.S.S.R. 50 55N 115 30E
49 Olsztyn, Poland 53 45N 20 30E
45 Olten, Switzerland 47 22N 7 54E
90 Olympia, U.S.A. 47 2N 122 50W
41 Olympia, Ruins of, Gr. 37 40N 21 39E
41 Olympus, Mt., Greece 40 2N 22 25E
86 Olympus, Mt., U.S.A. 48 7N 124 0W
36 Omagh, N. Ireland 54 35N 7 18W
91 Omaha, U.S.A. 41 28N 96 12W
63 Oman, Arabia 22 0N 52 0E
63 Oman, G. of, S.W. Asia 24 30N 59 0E
68 Ombai Str., East Indies 8 15S 124 45E
22 Ombersley, England 52 17N 2 12W
74 Omboue, Gabon 1 35S 9 15E
40 Ombrone, R., Italy 42 40N 11 3E
73 Omdurman, Sudan 15 50N 32 45E
67 Ominato, Japan 41 25N 141 8E
44 Ommen, Netherlands 52 32N 6 26E
61 Omolon, R., U.S.S.R 64 30N 161 0E
67 Omoto, Japan 39 57N 142 0E
66 Ompor, U.S.S.R. 49 50N 117 0E
60 Omsk, U.S.S.R. 55 0N 73 30E
47 Omul, Mt., Rumania 45 20N 25 20E
75 Omuramba Omatako, R., South-West Africa 20 0S 17 50E
67 Omuta, Japan 33 0N 130 26E
75 Ondangua, S.W. Africa 18 0S 16 0E
66 Ondörhaan, Mongolia 47 30N 110 15E
48 Ondverdarnes, Iceland 64 52N 24 0W
50 Onega, & G. of, & R., U.S.S.R. 60 40N 37 30E
84 Onehunga, New Zealand 36 58S 174 50E
61 Onekotan, I., U.S.S.R. 49 30N 154 30E
61 Onguren, U.S.S.R. 54 0N 108 0E
72 Onitsha, Nigeria 6 8N 6 55E
67 Onomichi, Japan 34 30N 133 5E
80 Onslow, Australia 21 44S 115 1E
91 Onslow Bay, U.S.A. 34 30N 77 0W
67 Ontake, Mt., Japan 35 57N 137 30E
90 Ontario, U.S.A. 43 50N 117 0W
92 Ontario, L., N. America 43 40N 78 0W
89 Ontario, Prov., Canada 50 0N 86 0W
92 Ontonagon, U.S.A. 46 58N 89 12W
80 Oodnadatta, Australia 27 30S 135 30E
80 Ooldea, Australia 30 30S 131 55E
44 Oosterhout, Netherlands 51 38N 4 51E
64 Ootacamund, India 11 30N 76 40E
76 Ootse, Botswana 25 0S 25 40E
74 Opala, Zaïre 1 13S 24 45E
64 Opanake, Sri Lanka 6 30N 80 35E
47 Opava, Czechoslovakia 49 57N 17 50E
80 Ophthalmia Ra., Austral. 23 14S 119 30E
37 Oporto, Portugal 41 10N 8 38W
49 Oppland, Dist., Norway 61 10N 10 0E
84 Opua, New Zealand 35 13S 174 0E
84 Opunake, New Zealand 39 27S 173 52E
62 Oqair, Saudi Arabia 25 45N 50 10E
63 Or Yehuda, Israel 32 1N 34 53E
48 Oraefa Jokull, mt., Ice. 64 10N 16 20W
47 Oradea, Rumania 47 3N 21 57E
64 Orai, India 26 3N 79 30E
72 Oran, Algeria 35 45N 0 38W
99 Oran, Argentina 23 5S 64 15W
83 Orange, Australia 33 13S 149 0E
43 Orange, France 44 10N 4 50E
91 Orange, U.S.A. 30 5N 93 47W
76 Orange, R., S.W. Africa 28 40S 16 30E
76 Orange Free State, Prov., South Africa 28 20S 27 0E
91 Orangeburg, U.S.A. 33 30N 80 51W
75 Orangemouth, S.W. Afr. 23 38S 16 24E
92 Orangeville, Canada 43 58N 80 2W
46 Oranienburg, Germany 52 43N 13 14E
76 Oranjefontein, S. Africa 23 30S 27 30E
34 Oranmore, Ireland 53 16N 8 57W
45 Orbe, Switzerland 46 44N 6 30E
40 Orbetello, Italy 42 25N 11 5E
80 Orbost, Australia 37 40S 148 28E
44 Orchies, France 50 28N 3 14E
66 Ordos, Desert, China 39 30N 108 0E
51 Ordzhonikidze, U.S.S.R. 43 20N 44 30E
46 Ore Mts., Germany, *see* Erz Gebirge
48 Orebro, & Co., Sweden 59 20N 15 18E
90 Oregon, St., U.S.A. 43 45N 120 30W
52 Orekhovo-Zuyevo, U.S.S.R. 55 0N 39 2E
52 Orel, U.S.S.R. 53 3N 36 8E
50 Orenburg, U.S.S.R. 51 42N 55 7E
37 Orense, Spain 42 19N 7 53W
23 Orford, England 52 6N 1 33E
44 Origny Ste. Benoite, Fr. 49 50N 3 30E
37 Orihuela, Spain 38 8N 0 58W
92 Orillia, Canada 44 42N 79 30W
98 Orinoco, Delta of, Ven. 9 0N 61 0W
98 Orinoco R., Venezuela 8 0N 64 50W
65 Orissa, Prov., India 21 0N 85 0E
40 Oristano, Italy 39 57N 8 39E
48 Orkanger, Norway 63 16N 9 57E
48 Orkla, R., Norway 63 0N 9 40E
76 Orkney, S. Africa 27 0S 26 35E
33 Orkneys Is., & Co., Scotland 59 5N 3 0W
100 Orkneys, South, Islands, Southern Ocean 61 0S 46 0W
91 Orlando, U.S.A. 28 30N 81 0W
43 Orléanais, Prov., France 47 50N 2 0E
43 Orléans, France 47 57N 1 53E
72 Orléansville, *see* El Asnam
64 Ormara, Pakistan 25 13N 64 37E
68 Ormoc, Philippines 11 5N 124 30E
84 Ormond, N.Z. 38 30S 177 55E
26 Ormskirk, England 53 34N 2 53W
45 Ornans, France 47 7N 6 8E
42 Orne, Dépt., France 48 40N 0 15W
48 Örnsköldsvik, Sweden 63 18N 18 44E
40 Orosei, Italy 40 20N 9 40E
83 Orroroo, Australia 32 45S 137 30E
45 Orsieres, Switzerland 46 2N 7 10E
50 Orsk, U.S.S.R. 51 8N 58 30E
47 Orsova, Rumania 44 42N 22 22E
45 Orta, L., Italy 45 48N 8 28E
37 Ortigueira, Spain 43 40N 7 50W
45 Ortles, Mt., Italy 46 19N 10 38E
26 Orton, England 54 28N 2 35W
40 Ortona, Italy 42 20N 14 22E
98 Oruro, Bolivia 17 50S 67 25W
40 Orvieto, Italy 42 45N 12 5E
23 Orwell, R., England 52 10N 1 0E
41 Oryakhovo, Bulgaria 43 43N 23 55E
91 Osage, R., U.S.A. 38 0N 94 0W
67 Osaka, & Pref., Japan 34 40N 135 39E
92 Oshawa, Canada 44 0N 78 59W
75 Oshikango, S.W. Africa 17 9S 16 10E
72 Oshogbo, Nigeria 7 55N 4 50E
74 Oshwe, Zaïre 3 10S 19 35E
41 Osijek, Yugoslavia 45 32N 18 42E
61 Osinino, U.S.S.R. 71 0N 148 57E
91 Oskaloosa, U.S.A. 41 17N 92 44W
49 Oskarshamn, Sweden 57 18N 16 23E
49 Oslo, Norway 59 54N 10 50E
49 Oslo Fjord, Norway 59 0N 10 30E
64 Osmanabad, India 18 6N 76 4E
51 Osmaniye, Turkey 37 7N 36 15E
44 Osnabrück, Germany 52 19N 8 2E
45 Osogna, Switzerland 46 18N 8 58E
99 Osorno, Chile 40 30S 73 0W
44 Oss, Netherlands 51 47N 5 32E
83 Ossa, Mt., Australia 41 47S 146 0E
27 Ossett, England 53 40N 1 35W
44 Ostend, Belgium 51 14N 2 56E
49 Öster Dal, R., Seden 61 30N 13 50E
49 Östergötland, Sweden 58 20N 15 30E
48 Östersund, Sweden 63 14N 14 40E
49 Östfold, Co., Norway 59 30N 11 0E
40 Ostia, Italy 41 40N 12 20E
47 Ostrava, Cz.slov. 49 55N 18 19E
49 Ostróda, Poland 53 40N 20 1E
47 Ostróg, U.S.S.R. 50 20N 26 30E
47 Ostroleka, Poland 53 1N 21 34E
47 Ostrów, Poland 51 40N 17 50E
47 Ostrów Mazowiecka, Pol. 52 48N 21 55E
47 Ostrowiec, Poland 51 0N 21 25E
67 Osumi Chan. (Van Diemen Str.), Japan 30 55N 131 0E
26 Oswaldtwistle, England 53 44N 2 27W
91 Oswego, U.S.A. 43 25N 76 33W
22 Oswestry, England 52 15N 3 5W
67 Ota, Japan 36 42N 140 30E
84 Otago, Dist., N.Z. 45 20S 169 0E
84 Otaki, New Zealand 40 38S 175 10E
67 Otaru, Japan 43 10N 141 0E
75 Otavi, S.W. Africa 19 35S 17 25E
75 Otjiwarongo, S.W. Afr. 20 22S 16 37E
27 Otley, England 53 56N 1 31W
84 Otorohanga, N.Z. 38 10S 175 12E
41 Otranto, & Str., Italy 40 11N 18 28E
67 Otsu, Japan 35 0N 136 0E
93 Ottawa, & R., Canada 45 20N 75 41W
91 Ottawa, U.S.A. 38 40N 95 20W
89 Ottawa Is., Canada 59 30N 81 0W
22 Otter, R., England 50 48N 3 15W
24 Ottery St. Mary, Eng. 50 45N 3 16W
91 Ottumwa, U.S.A. 41 5N 92 20W
72 Oturkpo, Nigeria 7 10N 8 15E
47 Otwock, Poland 52 10N 21 20E
91 Ouachita, Mts., U.S.A. 34 58N 94 20E
91 Ouachita, R., U.S.A. 32 30N 92 5W
73 Ouadda, Central Africa 8 15N 22 20E
72 Ouagadougou, Volta 12 25N 1 30W
72 Ouallene, Algeria 24 30N 1 20E
74 Ouanda Djalé, Central Africa 8 55N 22 53E
74 Ouango, Central Africa 4 19N 22 30E
72 Ouargla, Algeria 31 50N 5 20E
72 Ouarzazate, Morocco 31 0N 6 40W
74 Oubangi, R., Congo (Fr.) 1 0N 17 30E
44 Oudenaarde, Belgium 50 51N 3 37E
44 Oudensbock, Neth. 51 35N 4 30E
75 Oudtshoorn, S. Africa 33 32S 22 8E
74 Ouesso, Congo (Fr.) 1 40N 16 10E
72 Ouezzane, Morocco 34 51N 5 42W
44 Ougrée, Belgium 50 35N 5 30E
72 Ouidah, Dahomey 6 25N 2 0E
72 Oujeft, Mauritania 20 0N 13 0W
72 Ouled Djellal, Algeria 34 20N 6 30E
23 Oulton Broad, England 52 28N 1 44E
48 Oulu, Co., Finland 64 53N 25 23E
48 Oulu, L. & R., Finland 64 20N 27 15E
48 Ounas, R., Finland 67 45N 24 55E
23 Oundle, England 52 29N 0 27W
44 Our, R., Germany 50 3N 6 8E
99 Ouro Preto, Brazil 20 17S 43 48W
44 Ourthe, R., Belgium 50 13N 5 33W
33 Ousdale, Scotland 58 10N 3 34W
23 Ouse, Great, R., Cambs., England 52 21N 0 6E
23 Ouse, R., Sussex, Eng. 50 50N 0 5E
27 Ouse, R., Yorks., Eng. 54 0N 1 10W
32 Out Skerries, Scotland 60 25N 0 44W
*32 Outer Hebrides, Scot. 57 40N 7 0W
83 Ouyen, Australia 35 0S 142 30E
99 Ovalle, Chile 30 35S 71 17W
75 Ovamboland, reg., S.W. Africa 17 40S 16 0E
37 Ovar, Portugal 40 50N 8 40W
33 Overbister, Scotland 59 16N 2 33W
44 Overijssel, Prov., Neth. 52 24N 6 33E
48 Overtornea, Sweden 66 25N 23 32E
37 Oviedo, Spain 43 25N 5 53W
84 Owaka, New Zealand 46 30S 169 48E
91 Owatonna, U.S.A. 44 8N 93 34W
92 Owen Sound, Canada 44 40N 81 0W
82 Owen Stanley Ra., Papua 9 0S 148 0E
91 Owensboro, U.S.A. 37 47N 87 7W
92 Owosso, U.S.A. 43 2N 84 12W
36 Ox Mts., *see* Slieve Gamph
49 Oxelösund, Sweden 58 43N 17 15E
22 Oxford, & Co., England 51 45N 1 15W
84 Oxford, New Zealand 43 20S 172 10E
83 Oxleys Pk., Australia 31 50S 150 20E
33 Oykel R., Scotland 57 58N 4 40W
72 Oyo, Nigeria 7 58N 3 59E
43 Oyonnax, France 46 15N 5 40E
83 Oyster B., Australia 42 10S 148 0E
68 Ozamiz, Philippines 8 10N 123 40E
91 Ozark Plateau, U.S.A. 37 0N 92 30W
91 Ozarks, L. of the, U.S.A. 38 0N 93 0W

P

65 Paan, China 29 55N 99 5E
76 Paarl, Cape Prov. 33 45S 18 59E
48 Paatsi, R., U.S.S.R. 68 55N 29 0E
64 Pab Hills, Pakistan 26 20N 66 45E
32 Pabbay I., & Sd., Scot. 57 47N 7 14W
65 Pabna, Bangladesh 24 0N 89 10E
95 Pacaraima, Sa, mts., Venezuela 4 0N 63 0W
98 Pacasmayo, Peru 7 28S 79 30W
64 Pachpadra, India 25 57N 72 0E
94 Pachuca, Mexico 20 13N 98 45W
4 Pacific Ocean 45 0S to 60 0N, 120 0E to 75 0W
68 Padang, Indonesia 1 5S 100 25E
46 Paderborn, Germany 51 47N 8 52E
26 Padiham, England 53 48N 2 20W
88 Padlei, Canada 62 10N 97 5W
24 Padstow, & B., England 50 32N 4 57W
46 Padua (Padova), Italy 45 23N 11 51E
91 Paducah, U.S.A. 37 1N 88 29W
84 Paeroa, New Zealand 37 18S 175 39E
46 Pag I., Yugoslavia 44 20N 15 0E
68 Pagadian, Philippines 7 55N 123 30E
90 Page, U.S.A. 37 0N 111 25W
84 Pago Pago, Samoa 14 5S 171 48W
68 Pahandut, Indonesia, *see* Palangka Raya
84 Pahiatua, New Zealand 40 27S 175 48E
62 Pahlevi, Iran 37 37N 49 8E
67 Paicheng, China 45 40N 122 30E
24 Paignton, England 50 26N 3 33W
49 Päijänne, L., Finland 61 40N 25 30E
42 Paimboeuf, France 47 20N 2 0W
42 Paimpol, France 48 42N 3 2W
30 Paisley, Scotland 55 51N 4 25W
22 Painswick, England 51 47N 2 11W
90 Painted Desert, U.S.A. 36 0N 111 10W
65 Paiyu, China 31 10N 98 45E
68 Pajakumbuh, Indonesia 0 20S 100 40E
68 Pakanbaru, Indonesia 0 30N 101 35E
66 Pakhoi, China 21 30N 109 12E
64 Pakistan, Asia 30 0N 70 0E
64 Pakistan, West *see* Pakistan
65 Pakistan, East *see* Bangladesh
65 Pakokku, Burma 21 15N 95 6E
68 Pakse, Laos 15 5N 105 47E
64 Paktya, prov., Afghan. 33 0N 69 0E
64 Palam, India 19 0N 77 0E
37 Palamos, Spain 41 52N 3 13E
68 Palangka Raya (Pahandut), Indonesia 2 25S 114 0E
64 Palanpur, India 24 15N 72 30E
75 Palapye, Botswana 22 30S 27 28E
91 Palatka, U.S.A. 29 37N 81 42W
5 Palau Is., Pacific Ocean 7 20N 135 0E
68 Palawan, I., Philippines 9 30N 119 0E
49 Paldiski, U.S.S.R. 59 23N 24 9E
68 Paleleh, Indonesia 1 0N 122 0E
68 Palembang, Indonesia 3 0S 104 47E
37 Palencia, Spain 42 1N 4 35W
40 Palermo, Italy 38 8N 13 18E
62 Palestine, *see* Israel and Jordan
91 Palestine, U.S.A. 31 46N 95 40W
64 Palghat, India 11 1N 76 59E
23 Palgrave, England 52 22N 1 6E
64 Pali, India 25 45N 73 10E
64 Palitana, India 21 48N 71 49E
64 Palk Bay, Sri Lanka 9 20N 80 0E
64 Palk Str., India 10 0N 80 0E
45 Pallanza, Italy 45 58N 8 35E
34 Pallaskenry, Ireland 52 38N 8 52W

* *Incorporated within the region of Western Isles*

82 Palm Is., Australia 18 45S 146 35E
37 Palma, Balearic Is., Spain 39 37N 2 40E
72 Palma, I., Canary Is. 28 50N 17 50W
40 Palmas, G. of, Italy 38 50N 8 25E
84 Palmerston, N.Z. 45 30S 170 45E
84 Palmerston North, N.Z. 40 18S 175 36E
40 Palmi, Italy 38 20N 15 55E
98 Palmira, Colombia 3 40N 76 20W
62 Palmyra, Syria 34 20N 37 55E
64 Palni Hs., India 10 30N 77 30E
94 Palo Seco, Trinidad 10 5N 61 32W
51 Palu, Turkey 38 37N 40 0E
43 Pamiers, France 43 5N 1 40E
55 Pamir, mts., Cent. Asia 37 0N 73 0E
90 Pampa, U.S.A. 35 32N 101 0W
98 Pampas, The, Argentina 36 20S 62 0W
37 Pampiona, Spain 42 48N 1 37W
95 Panama, & G., Panama 9 3N 79 30W
95 Panama Canal Zone, Pan. 9 3N 79 45W
95 Panama, Cent. Amer. 9 0N 80 0W
91 Panama City, U.S.A. 30 13N 85 14W
41 Pancevo, Yugoslavia 44 55N 20 42E
64 Pandharpur, India 17 36N 75 24E
22 Pangbourne, England 51 29N 1 6W
68 Pangkal Pinang, Indon. 2 0S 106 8E
64 Pangon Tso, L., Tibet 33 50N 78 50E
65 Pangyang, Burma 22 10N 98 45E
64 Panjim, Goa, India 15 30N 73 45E
64 Panna, India 24 45N 80 15E
64 Pannani, India 10 40N 75 55E
40 Pantelleria, I., Italy 36 50N 12 0E
94 Panuco, R., Mexico 21 30N 98 30W
72 Panyam, Nigeria 9 27N 9 8E
66 Paoki, China 34 30N 106 50E
66 Paoshan, China 25 16N 99 35E
66 Pao-ting, China 39 0N 115 47E
66 Paotow, China 40 45N 110 1E
73 Paoua, Central Africa 7 25N 16 30E
47 Pápa, Hungary 47 20N 17 30E
32 Papa Stour I., Scotland 60 19N 1 40W
33 Papa Stronsay, Scotland 59 9N 2 34W
33 Papa Westray I., Scot. 59 21N 2 54W
94 Papantla, Mexico 20 27N 97 15W
30 Paps of Jura, Scotland 55 55N 6 0W
82 Papua New Guinea 7 0S 145 0E
82 Papua, G. of, New Guinea 8 30S 145 0E
98 Para, st., Brazil 4 0S 52 30W
98 Pará, *see* Belém
98 Para, R., Brazil 1 0S 48 15W
68 Paracel Is., S. China Sea 16 30N 111 30E
91 Paragould, U.S.A. 36 4N 90 29W
98 Paraguana Pen., Ven. 12 0N 70 0W
99 Paraguari, Paraguay 25 30S 57 15W
99 Paraguay R., S. Amer. 23 0S 58 0W
97 Paraguay, S. Amer. 21 0S 60 0W
98 Paraiba, st., Brazil 7 12S 38 0W
49 Parainen, Finland 60 21N 22 17E
72 Parakou, Dahomey 9 30N 2 35E
98 Paramaribo, Surinam 5 45N 55 15W
61 Paramushir I., U.S.S.R. 50 10N 156 0E
99 Paraná, Argentina 32 0S 60 30W
99 Paraná R., Argentina 29 0S 59 30W
99 Parana, St., Brazil 24 0S 52 0W
99 Paranagua, Brazil 25 45S 48 30W
98 Paranaiba, R., Brazil 18 40S 48 30W
99 Paranapanema, R., Brazil 22 30S 52 0W
99 Paranpiacaba, Sa., mts., Brazil 24 30S 49 0W
83 Paratoo, Australia 32 45S 139 15E
43 Paray le Monial, France 46 25N 4 5E
64 Parbhani, India 19 30N 77 0E
46 Parchim, Germany 53 30N 11 50E
46 Pardubice, Cz-slov. 50 0N 15 45E
98 Parecis, Sa. dos, mts., Brazil 13 50S 59 0W
61 Paren, U.S.S.R. 62 30N 163 0E
93 Parent, Canada 47 50N 74 40W
95 Paria, G. of, S. America 10 15N 62 0W
99 Parintins, Brazil 2 30S 56 20W
43 Paris, France 48 52N 2 18E
91 Paris, U.S.A. 33 42N 95 34W
90 Park, Ra., U.S.A. 40 0N 106 30W
76 Park Rynie, S. Africa 30 20S 30 25E
92 Parkersburg, U.S.A. 39 18N 81 35W
83 Parkes, Australia 33 0S 148 6E
40 Parma, Italy 44 48N 10 19E
98 Parnaiba, Brazil 3 10S 41 40W
98 Parnaiba, R., Brazil 6 45S 44 0W
41 Parnassos, Mt., Greece 38 30N 22 40E
49 Pärnu, U.S.S.R. 58 24N 24 37E
83 Paroo R., Australia 30 0S 144 40E
64 Paropamisús Ra., Afghan. 34 40N 63 0E
41 Paros, I., Greece 37 3N 25 10E
24 Parracombe, England 51 20N 3 50W
83 Parramatta, Australia 33 48S 151 0E
100 Parry Is. Arctic Ocean 78 30N 112 0W
91 Parsons, U.S.A. 37 18N 95 18W
42 Parthenay, France 46 40N 0 18W
35 Partry, Mts., Ireland 53 40N 9 24W
98 Paru, R., Brazil 1 0N 54 40W
65 Parvatipuram, India 18 56N 83 30E
64 Parwan, Prov., Afghan. 35 0N 69 0E
90 Pasadena, Calif., U.S.A. 34 0N 118 0W
91 Pasadena, Texas, U.S.A. 29 42N 95 23W
42 Pas-de-Calais, Dépt., Fr. 50 27N 2 15E
91 Pascagoula, U.S.A. 30 30N 88 30W
90 Pasco, U.S.A. 46 16N 119 3W
68 Pasir Mas, Malaya 6 0N 102 20E
64 Pasni, Pakistan 25 15N 63 25E
30 Pass of Brander, Scot. 56 24N 5 8W
47 Pass of the Tartars, U.S.S.R. 48 20N 24 50E
35 Passage E., Ireland 52 13N 6 59W

34 Passage W., Ireland 51 55N 8 26w
46 Passau, Germany 48 33N 13 21E
40 Passero, C., Sicily, Italy 36 41N 15 10E
99 Passo Fundo, Brazil 28 10s 52 25w
98 Pastaza, R., Ecuador 3 30s 76 40w
98 Pasto, Colombia 1 12N 77 25w
48 Pasvik R., U.S.S.R. 69 15N 29 30E
99 Patagonia, S. Argentina 45 0s 69 0w
64 Patan, India 23 56N 72 5E
23 Patcham, England 50 52N 0 9w
83 Patchewollock, Austral. 36 27s 142 0E
84 Patea, New Zealand 39 45s 174 28E
72 Pategi, Nigeria 8 50N 5 45E
40 Paterno, Italy 37 35N 14 50E
93 Paterson, U.S.A. 40 59N 74 10w
90 Pathfinder Res., U.S.A. 42 10N 105 50w
64 Patiala, India 30 22N 76 28E
65 Patkai Bum, mts., India 26 39N 95 0E
41 Patmos, I., Greece 37 18N 26 35E
65 Patna, Bihar, India 25 40N 85 10E
41 Pátrai, Greece 38 15N 21 47E
27 Patrington, England 53 42N 0 1w
40 Patti, Italy 38 10N 14 55E
65 Patuakhali, Bangladesh 22 20N 90 15E
42 Pau, France 43 21N 0 23w
65 Pauk, Burma 21 25N 94 30E
74 Paulis, see Isiro
96 Paulistana, Brazil 8 0s 41 15w
98 Paulo Afonso Rapids, Brazil
9 20s 37 40w
76 Paulpietersburg, S. Africa 27 25s 30 50E
40 Pavia, Italy 45 11N 9 11E
60 Pavlodar, U.S.S.R. 52 25N 77 10E
52 Pavlograd, U.S.S.R. 48 40N 36 0E
52 Pavlovo, U.S.S.R. 56 0N 43 10E
52 Pavlovsk, U.S.S.R. 50 32N 40 7E
52 Pavlovskiy-Posad, U.S.S.R.
55 47N 38 40E
93 Pawtucket, U.S.A. 41 55N 71 25w
45 Payerne, Switzerland 46 50N 6 56E
90 Payette, U.S.A. 44 6N 116 55w
89 Payne, L., Canada 59 30N 74 30w
99 Paysandu, Uruguay 32 19s 58 0w
90 Payson, U.S.A. 40 4N 111 45w
41 Pazardzhik, Bulgaria 42 12N 24 19E
88 Peace, R., Canada 58 47N 114 0w
88 Peace River, Canada 56 0N 117 18w
83 Peak Hill, N.S.W., Australia
32 36s 148 9E
80 Peak Hill, W.A., Australia
25 42s 118 47E
27 Peak, The, England 53 25N 1 52w
90 Pearl City, Hawaii 21 15N 157 55w
41 Pec, Yugoslavia 42 41N 20 14E
50 Pechenga, U.S.S.R. 69 30N 31 25E
50 Pechora, G. of, U.S.S.R. 68 40N 54 0E
90 Pecos, & R., U.S.A. 31 25N 103 35w
47 Pécs, Hungary 46 4N 18 13E
*31 Peebles, & Co., Scotland 55 39N 3 11w
93 Peekskill, U.S.A. 41 15N 73 57w
26 Peel, Isle of Man 54 13N 4 43w
23 Peel Fell, mt., England 55 19N 2 34w
83 Peel R., Australia 30 58s 150 30E
49 Peene, R., Germany 53 52N 13 40E
84 Pegasus B., New Zealand 43 13s 173 0E
65 Pegu, Burma 17 33N 96 25E
65 Pegu Yoma, mts., Burma 19 0N 96 0E
67 Pehan, China 49 10N 126 20E
66 Pei Kiang, China 24 10N 113 10E
68 Pekalongan, Indonesia 6 50s 109 45E
92 Pekin, U.S.A. 40 30N 89 43w
66 Peking, China 39 49N 116 30E
47 Peleaga, mt., Rumania 45 17N 22 58E
88 Pelly, R., Canada 62 20N 133 0w
41 Peloponnese, Pen., Greece 37 50N 22 0E
99 Pelotas, Brazil 31 45s 52 20w
42 Pelvoux, Mt., France 44 52N 6 10E
68 Pematang Siantar, Indon. 3 0N 99 15E
70 Pemba I., Tanzania 0 5s 39 40E
80 Pemberton, Australia 34 28s 115 59E
22 Pembridge, England 52 13N 2 54w
92 Pembroke, Canada 45 40N 77 10w
**28 Pembroke, & Co., Wales 51 41N 4 55w
23 Pembrey, Wales 51 42N 4 16w
37 Penalara, Mt., Spain 40 55N 3 50w
25 Penarth, Wales 51 27N 3 12w
99 Peñas, G. de, Chile 47 30s 75 0w
24 Pencoed, Wales 51 31N 3 30w
90 Pend Oreille L., U.S.A. 47 20N 116 30w
72 Pendembu, Sierra Leone 8 6N 10 45w
26 Pendle Hill, Hs., Eng. 53 52N 2 20w
90 Pendleton, U.S.A. 45 42N 118 47w
63 Pendzhikent, U.S.S.R. 39 20N 67 30E
66 Pengpu, China 32 50N 117 50E
83 Penguin, Australia 41 4s 146 7E
37 Peniche, Portugal 39 20N 9 22w
31 Penicuik, Scotland 55 50N 3 11w
27 Penistone, England 53 32N 1 38w
67 Penki, China 41 15N 122 40E
25 Penmaenmawr, Wales 53 16N 3 56w
42 Penmarch, Pte. de, Fr. 47 50N 4 30w
92 Penn Yan, U.S.A. 42 40N 77 0w
64 Penner R., India 14 40N 80 10E
26 Pennines, mts., England 54 20N 2 10w
92 Pennsylvania, st., U.S.A. 41 10N 77 30w
83 Penola, Australia 37 12s 140 51E
80 Penong, Australia 32 0s 133 0E
83 Penrith, Australia 33 48s 150 40E
26 Penrith, England 54 40N 2 47w
24 Penryn, England 50 10N 5 7w
91 Pensacola, U.S.A. 30 30N 87 15w
100 Pensacola Mts., Antarctica
84 0s 45 0w
83 Penshurst, Australia 37 55s 142 25E
88 Penticton, Canada 49 30N 119 30w

* *County incorporated within the region of Borders*

82 Pentland, Australia 20 37s 145 27E
33 Pentland Firth, Scot. 58 41N 3 0w
31 Pentland Hills, Scotland 55 47N 3 35w
22 Penybont, Wales 52 16N 3 15w
26 Pen-y-ghent, mt., Eng. 54 8N 2 10w
25 Pen-y-groes, Wales 51 48N 4 3w
52 Penza, U.S.S.R. 53 8N 45 0E
24 Penzance, England 50 8N 5 33w
61 Penzhina G., U.S.S.R. 61 0N 163 0E
61 Penzhino, U.S.S.R. 63 50N 168 3E
92 Peoria, U.S.A. 40 40N 89 35w
37 Perdido, mt., Spain 42 45N 0 15w
51 Perekop, U.S.S.R. 46 0N 33 0E
51 Pereyaslav Khmelnitski, U.S.S.R.
50 5N 31 27E
99 Pergamino, Argentina 33 45s 60 40w
43 Perigueux, France 45 16N 0 42E
98 Perija, Sa. de. mts., Colombia
9 30N 73 3w
62 Perim I., Red Sea 12 40N 43 17E
50 Perm, U.S.S.R. 58 0N 55 15E
98 Pernambuco (Recife), Brazil
8 20s 35 0w
98 Pernambuco, st., Brazil 8 0s 39 0w
41 Pernik, Bulgaria 42 37N 23 4E
43 Peronne, France 49 55N 2 55E
52 Perovo, U.S.S.R. 55 40N 37 45E
43 Perpignan, France 42 43N 2 55E
24 Perranporth, England 50 20N 5 9w
24 Perranzabuloe, England 50 18N 5 7w
90 Perryton, U.S.A. 36 25N 100 55w
22 Pershore, England 52 7N 2 4w
62 Persia, see Iran
62 Persian G., S.W. Asia 27 0N 51 0E
80 Perth, Australia 32 0s 115 50E
92 Perth, Canada 44 52N 76 28w
†31 Perth, & Co., Scotland 56 24N 3 27w
93 Perth Amboy, U.S.A. 40 30N 74 25w
96 Peru, S. America 88 0s 75 0w
40 Perugia, Italy 43 8N 12 25E
50 Pervomaisk, U.S.S.R. 47 58N 31 0E
40 Pesaro, Italy 43 57N 12 55E
40 Pescara, Italy 42 30N 14 18E
64 Peshawar, Pakistan 34 3N 71 30E
63 Petah Tiqva, Israel 32 5N 34 52E
44 Petange, Luxembourg 49 33N 5 55E
100 Peter 1st, I., S. Ocean 69 0s 91 0w
92 Peterborough, Canada 44 21N 78 27w
83 Peterborough, Australia 32 58s 138 49E
23 Peterborough, England 52 35N 0 14w
28 Peterborough, Soke of, England
52 35N 0 14w
22 Peterchurch, England 52 3N 2 58w
33 Peterculter, Scotland 57 7N 2 20w
33 Peterhead, Scotland 57 32N 1 47w
27 Peterlee, England 54 45N 1 18w
92 Petersburg, U.S.A. 37 13N 77 25w
23 Petersfield, England 51 0N 0 56w
89 Petitsikapau, L., Canada 54 40N 66 30w
64 Petlad, India 22 30N 72 40E
94 Peto, Mexico 20 3N 89 0w
84 Petone, New Zealand 41 5s 174 50E
92 Petoskey, U.S.A. 45 20N 84 58w
41 Petrich, Bulgaria 41 25N 23 12E
92 Petrolia, Canada 42 54N 82 5w
61 Petropavlovsk-Kamchatsky, U.S.S.R.
53 10N 158 30E
99 Petropolis, Brazil 22 30s 43 10w
41 Petrograd, see Zrenjanin
47 Petroseni, Rumania 45 30N 23 28E
41 Petrovaradin, Yugoslavia 45 15N 19 58E
52 Petrovsk, U.S.S.R. 52 23N 45 18E
61 Petrovsk, U.S.S.R. 51 20N 108 50E
50 Petrozavodsk, U.S.S.R. 61 50N 34 25E
76 Petrusburg, S. Africa 29 0s 25 20E
36 Pettigo, Ireland 54 38N 7 50w
23 Petworth, England 50 59N 0 37w
61 Pevek, U.S.S.R. 69 35N 170 50E
22 Pewsey, Vale of, Eng. 51 20N 1 48w
43 Pézenas, France 43 28N 3 50E
45 Pfafers-Dorf, Switzerland 46 58N 9 28E
45 Pfaffikon, Switzerland 47 21N 8 48E
45 Pforzheim, Germany 48 50N 8 25E
64 Phagwara, India 31 10N 75 40E
64 Phalodi, India 27 5N 72 25E
68 Phan Rang, Vietnam 11 38N 109 4E
68 Phan Thiet, Vietnam 11 0N 108 9E
68 Phanom Dang Raek, mts., Thailand
14 30N 104 0E
66 Phari, Tibet, China 27 53N 89 10E
93 Philadelphia, U.S.A. 39 55N 75 18w
72 Philippeville, see Skikda
44 Philippeville, Belgium 50 12N 4 33E
82 Philippi, L., Australia 24 20s 138 55E
68 Philippines, Asia 13 0N 123 0E
76 Philippolis, S. Africa 30 15s 25 16E
35 Philipstown, see Daingean
76 Philipstown, S. Africa 30 28s 24 28E
83 Phillip I., Australia 38 22s 145 18E
68 Phnom Penh, Khmer Rep. 11 40N 105 0E
90 Phœnix, U.S.A. 33 45N 111 50w
4 Phœnix Is., Pacific Ocean 4 0s 171 0w
68 Phu Quoc, I., Vietnam 10 20N 104 0E
40 Piacenza, Italy 45 0N 9 40E
83 Pialba, Australia 25 18s 152 50E
47 Piatra Neamt, Rum. 46 59N 26 20E
99 Piaui, R., Brazil 7 55s 42 30w
99 Piaui, st., Brazil 6 30s 42 30w
98 Piaui, Sa. do, mts., Brazil 10 0s 43 0w
40 Piazza, Italy 37 20N 14 20E
37 Pic de Aneto, mt., Spain 42 35N 0 45E
43 Picardy, Prov., France 49 50N 3 0E
91 Picayune, U.S.A. 30 43N 89 43w
99 Pichilemu, Chile 34 20s 72 5w
27 Pickering, England 54 15N 0 45w

** *County incorporated within the county of Dyfed*

27 Pickering, Vale of, Eng. 54 12N 0 45w
37 Pico Guina, mt., Spain 42 50N 6 45w
37 Picos de Europa, mts. Sp. 43 15N 5 0w
83 Picton, Australia 34 5s 150 38E
92 Picton, Canada 43 59N 77 0w
84 Picton, New Zealand 41 20s 174 1E
93 Pictou, Canada 45 45N 63 5w
23 Pidley, England 52 23N 0 4w
64 Pidurutalagala, mt., Sri Lanka
7 0N 80 50E
91 Piedmont Plat., U.S.A. 34 0N 82 0w
40 Piedmont, Prov., Italy 45 0N 7 40E
94 Piedras Negras, Mex. 28 50N 100 35w
90 Pierre, U.S.A. 44 30N 100 15w
45 Pierrefontaine, France 47 14N 6 32E
76 Piet Retief, S. Africa 27 2s 30 52E
75 Pietermaritzburg, S. Africa
29 38s 30 28E
75 Pietersburg, S. Africa 23 45s 29 30E
47 Pietrosul, mt., Rumania 47 36N 24 56E
47 Pietrosul, mt., Rumania 47 7N 25 13E
90 Pike's Pk., mt., U.S.A. 38 50N 105 0w
76 Piketberg, South Africa 32 54N 18 42E
49 Pila, Poland 53 10N 16 48E
99 Pilar, C., Chile 52 40s 75 0w
80 Pilbara, Australia 21 13s 118 21E
99 Pilcomayo, R., S. Amer. 22 30s 62 20w
64 Pilibhit, India 28 20N 79 58E
47 Pilica, R., Poland 51 25N 20 45E
41 Pilion, mt. Greece 39 23N 23 0E
41 Pilos, Greece 36 55N 21 45E
68 Pinang, I., Malaya 5 20N 100 12E
95 Pinar del Rio, Cuba 22 0N 84 30w
47 Pinczów, Poland 50 30N 20 35E
72 Pindiga, Nigeria 9 58N 10 53E
41 Pindus Mts., Greece 39 30N 21 30E
91 Pine Bluff, U.S.A. 34 5N 91 58w
80 Pine Creek, Australia 13 40s 131 37E
82 Pine Hill, Australia 23 42s 147 0E
50 Pinega, R., U.S.S.R. 63 48N 45 0E
40 Pinerolo, Italy 44 53N 7 23E
75 Pinetown, South Africa 29 48s 30 54E
68 Ping, R., Thailand 16 30N 99 40E
66 Pingliang, China 35 30N 106 50E
37 Pinhel, Portugal 41 46N 6 57w
24 Pinhoe, England 50 44N 3 28w
41 Pinios R., Greece 39 37N 22 23E
67 Pinkiang, China see Harbin
83 Pinnaroo, Australia 35 5s 141 0E
99 Pino Hachado P., Chile 38 45s 71 0w
100 Pionerskaya, Antarctica 69 30s 97 0E
47 Piotrków, Poland 51 25N 19 40E
93 Pipmuacan, L., Can. 49 40N 70 20w
92 Piqua, U.S.A. 40 10N 84 15w
41 Piraievs, Greece 37 57N 23 30E
98 Pirapora, Brazil 17 25s 44 50w
41 Pirgos, Greece 37 38N 21 32E
41 Pirin Pl., Bulgaria 41 40N 23 20E
45 Pirmasens, Germany 49 12N 7 36E
41 Pirot, Yugoslavia 43 10N 22 39E
42 Pirou, France 49 12N 1 31w
40 Pisa, Italy 43 42N 10 25E
40 Pisciotta, Italy 40 7N 15 12E
98 Pisco, Peru 13 55s 76 10w
46 Pisek, Czechoslovakia 49 20N 14 8E
37 Pisuerga, R., Spain 42 45N 4 20w
90 Pit, R., U.S.A. 41 30N 120 45w
72 Pita, Guinea 11 0N 12 15w
4 Pitcairn I., Pacific Ocean 24 55s 131 0w
48 Pitea & R., Sweden 65 24N 21 30E
47 Pitesti, Rumania 44 52N 24 55E
65 Pithapuram, India 17 0N 82 20E
31 Pittenweem, Scotland 56 12N 2 44w
91 Pittsburg, Kan., U.S.A. 37 8N 94 40w
92 Pittsburgh, Pa., U.S.A. 40 30N 79 52w
93 Pittsfield, U.S.A. 42 28N 73 20w
83 Pittsworth, Australia 27 41s 151 37E
98 Piura, Peru 5 20s 80 35w
45 Piz Bernina, Pk., Switz. 46 22N 9 55E
40 Pizzo, Italy 38 42N 16 10E
89 Placentia, & B., Newf. 47 14N 54 2w
30 Pladda I., Scotland 55 25N 5 7w
90 Plainview, U.S.A. 34 15N 101 44w
91 Plant City, U.S.A. 28 3N 82 15w
37 Plasencia, Spain 40 3N 6 6w
43 Plateau de Langres, Fr. 47 45N 5 30E
90 Plateau du Coteau du Missouri, U.S.A.
47 0N 100 0w
90 Platte R., U.S.A. 41 0N 99 0w
46 Plauen, Germany 50 30N 12 7E
99 Plaza Huincal, Argentina 39 0s 69 0w
68 Pleiku, Vietnam 14 0N 108 15E
84 Plenty, Bay of, N.Z. 37 45s 177 0E
50 Plesetsk, U.S.S.R. 62 40N 40 10E
93 Plessisville, Canada 46 15N 71 48w
41 Pleven, Bulgaria 43 22N 24 41E
47 Plock, Poland 52 37N 19 40E
32 Plockton, Scotland 57 20N 5 39w
47 Ploësti, Rumania 44 58N 26 0E
41 Plovdiv, Bulgaria 42 7N 24 48E
75 Plumtree, Rhodesia 20 27s 27 55E
24 Plymouth, England 50 22N 4 10w
95 Plymouth, Montserrat. W.I.
16 38N 62 5w
24 Plympton, England 50 23N 4 2w
24 Plymstock, England 50 22N 4 4w
25 Plynlimon, mt., Wales 52 29N 3 47w
46 Plzeň, Czechoslovakia 49 48N 13 20E
40 Po, R., Italy 45 2N 9 20E
60 Pobedy Pk., Mt., U.S.S.R. 42 10N 79 57E
90 Pocatello, U.S.A. 43 10N 111 0w
27 Pocklington, England 53 56N 0 46w
61 Podkamennaya Tunguska, U.S.S.R.
61 40N 90 5E
52 Podolsk, U.S.S.R. 55 20N 37 40E

† *County incorporated within the region of Tayside*

72 Podor, Sénégal 16 30N 14 50w
76 Pofadder, South Africa 29 10s 19 22E
76 Point, C., S. Africa 34 22s 18 30E
94 Point Fortin, Trinidad 11 0N 61 50w
26 Point of Ayre, I. of Man
54 25N 4 22w
74 Pointe Noire, Congo (Fr.) 4 48s 12 0E
94 Point Saline, Grenada, W.I.
12 12N 61 40w
43 Poitiers, France 46 38N 0 20E
43 Poitou, Prov., France 46 40N 0 10w
44 Poix Terron, France 49 40N 4 38E
64 Pokaran, India 27 0N 71 50E
83 Pokataroo, Australia 29 34s 148 50E
40 Pola, Yugoslavia, see Pula
47 Poland, Europe 52 20N 20 0E
24 Polden Hills, England 51 5N 2 50w
74 Poli, Cameroon 8 34N 12 54E
43 Poligny, France 46 50N 5 40E
68 Polillo I., Philippines 14 50N 121 50E
41 Poliyiros, Greece 40 15N 23 10E
64 Pollachi, India 10 40N 77 0E
60 Polnovat, U.S.S.R. 63 50N 66 10E
50 Polotsk, U.S.S.R. 55 30N 28 42E
24 Polruan, England 50 17N 4 36w
52 Poltava, U.S.S.R. 49 37N 34 30E
50 Polyarny, U.S.S.R. 69 0N 33 10E
37 Pombal, Portugal 39 55N 8 40w
91 Ponca City, U.S.A. 36 43N 97 13w
95 Ponce, Puerto Rico 18 7N 66 48w
65 Pondicherry, India 12 0N 79 50E
76 Pondoland, dist., S. Africa 31 10s 29 40E
37 Ponferrada, Spain 42 34N 6 35w
76 Pongola, R., S. Africa 27 28s 32 7E
65 Ponnyadaung, mts., Burma 22 0N 94 0E
50 Ponoi, & R., U.S.S.R. 67 0N 41 15E
42 Pons, France 45 35N 0 35w
43 Pont-à-Mousson, France 48 58N 6 0E
42 Pont-l'Abbé, France 47 50N 4 16w
43 Pont St. Esprit, France 44 18N 4 40E
99 Ponta Grossa, Brazil 25 0s 50 10w
25 Pontardawe, Wales 51 43N 3 51w
43 Pontarlier, France 46 52N 6 20E
91 Pontchartrain, L., U.S.A. 30 10N 90 10w
40 Pontedera, Italy 43 40N 10 40E
27 Pontefract, England 53 41N 1 20w
37 Pontevedra, Spain 42 29s 8 37w
74 Ponthierville (Ubundu), Zaïre
0 22s 25 30E
92 Pontiac, U.S.A. 42 40N 83 20w
68 Pontianak, Indonesia 0 12s 109 29E
40 Pontine Is., Italy 40 58N 13 0E
51 Pontine Mts., Turkey 40 40N 39 0E
42 Pontivy, France 48 5N 3 0w
43 Pontoise, France 49 5N 2 5E
43 Pontremoli, Italy 44 22N 9 50E
45 Pontresina, Switzerland 46 30N 9 53E
25 Pontypool, England 51 43N 3 1w
25 Pontypridd, Wales 51 36N 3 19w
22 Poole, England 50 43N 1 59w
32 Poolewe, Scotland 57 46N 5 36w
64 Poona, India 18 25N 73 57E
83 Poopelloe, L., Australia 31 30s 144 0E
98 Poopo L., Bolivia 19 0s 67 0w
98 Popayan, Colombia 2 10N 76 45w
44 Poperinge, Belgium 50 51N 2 44E
61 Popigai, U.S.S.R. 72 55N 106 5E
91 Poplar Bluff, U.S.A. 36 45N 90 27w
83 Poplita, L., Australia 33 0s 141 50E
94 Popocatepetl, Mt., Mex. 18 45N 99 40w
74 Popokabaka, Zaïre 5 40s 16 33E
64 Porbandar, India 21 37N 69 46E
88 Porcupine R., Alaska 67 0N 143 0w
49 Pori, Finland 61 30N 21 35E
48 Porjus, Sweden 67 0N 19 50E
49 Porkkala, Finland 60 15N 24 30E
24 Porlock Hill, England 51 12N 3 40w
42 Pornic, France 47 10N 2 10w
61 Poronaisk, U.S.S.R. 49 25N 142 57E
45 Porrentruy, Switzerland 47 25N 7 4E
40 Porreta P., Italy 44 0N 11 10E
48 Porsangen Fjord, Norway 70 45N 26 0E
83 Port Adelaide, Australia
34 50s 138 42E
88 Port Alberni, Canada 49 20N 124 50w
75 Port Alfred, S. Africa 33 37s 26 58E
82 Port Alma, Australia 23 38s 150 53E
95 Port Antonio, Jamaica 18 12N 76 28w
83 Port Arthur, Australia 43 10s 147 40E
92 Port Arthur, see Thunder Bay
91 Port Arthur, U.S.A. 29 56N 94 5w
30 Port Askaig, Scotland 55 51N 6 6w
95 Port-au-Prince, Haiti 18 40N 72 20w
83 Port Augusta, Australia
32 22s 137 49E
89 Port aux Basques, Can. 47 43N 59 20w
30 Port Bannatyne, Scotland 55 52N 5 5w
75 Port-Berge, Madagascar 15 38s 47 40E
37 Port Bou, Spain 42 25N 3 5E
65 Port Canning, Bangladesh
22 25N 88 40E
89 Port Cartier, Canada 50 10N 66 50w
84 Port Chalmers, N.Z. 45 45s 170 40E
30 Port Charlotte, Scotland 55 44N 6 24w
43 Port de Bouc, France 43 23N 5 0E
95 Port de Paix, Haiti 19 50N 72 50w
68 Port Dickson, Malaya 2 43N 101 45E
82 Port Douglas, Australia 16 30s 145 30E
94 Port Elizabeth, Bequia I. 13 0N 61 15w
76 Port Elizabeth, S. Africa 33 58s 25 42E
30 Port Ellen, Scotland 55 37N 6 12w
26 Port Erin, Isle of Man 54 6N 4 47w
33 Port Erroll, Scotland 57 24N 1 51w
72 Port Étiènne, see Nouadhibou
83 Port Fairy, Australia 38 18s 142 15E
74 Port Francqui, see Ilebo
74 Port Gentil, Gabon 0 47s 8 40E
30 Port Glasgow, Scotland 55 56N 4 41w
72 Port Harcourt, Nigeria 4 45N 7 5E
89 Port Hawkesbury, Can. 45 35N 64 40w
80 Port Hedland, Australia
20 16s 118 36E
93 Port Hood, Canada 46 2N 61 30w
92 Port Huron, U.S.A. 42 59N 82 30w
83 Port Jackson, Australia 33 55s 151 12E
68 Port Kelang, Malaya 3 0N 101 20E
83 Port Kembla, Australia 34 29s 150 56E
35 Port Laoise, Ireland 53 3N 7 15w
91 Port Lavoca, U.S.A. 28 35N 96 50w
80 Port Lincoln, Austral. 34 40s 135 47E
30 Port Logan, Scotland 54 42N 4 57w
42 Port Louis, France 47 40N 3 0w
83 Port Macdonnell, Austral. 38 0s 140 39E
83 Port Macquarie, Australia 31 29s 153 0E
82 Port Moresby, Terr. of New Guinea
9 15s 147 12E
88 Port Nelson, Canada 57 2N 93 0w
75 Port Nolloth, S. Africa 29 12s 16 55E
94 Port of Spain, Trinidad 10 47N 61 23w
31 Portpatrick, Scotland 54 50N 5 8w
83 Port Phillip, B., Australia 38 17s 144 40E
83 Port Pirie, Australia 33 10s 138 0E
88 Port Radium, Canada 66 10N 117 40w
73 Port Safaga, Egypt 26 48N 34 0E
73 Port Said, Egypt 31 28N 32 6E
43 Port St. Louis, France 43 20N 4 50E
75 Port Shepstone, S. Africa 30 45s 30 30E
88 Port Simpson, Canada 54 20N 130 28w
92 Port Stanley, Canada 42 40N 81 12w
73 Port Sudan, Sudan 19 40N 37 20E
25 Port Talbot, Wales 51 36N 3 48w
43 Port Vendres, France 42 30N 3 5E
68 Port Weld, Malaya 4 45N 100 40E
36 Portaferry, N. Ireland 54 23N 5 31w
92 Portage, U.S.A. 43 36N 89 28w
88 Portage la Prairie, Can. 50 0N 98 25w
37 Portalegre, Portugal 39 18N 7 27w
35 Portarlington, Ireland 53 10N 7 11w
42 Portbail, France 49 20N 1 42w
36 Portglenone, N. Ireland 54 52N 6 29w
25 Porthcawl, Wales 51 29N 3 42w
25 Porthmadog, Wales 52 54N 4 7w
22 Portishead, England 51 29N 2 47w
33 Portknockie, Scotland 57 42N 2 48w
83 Portland, N.S.W., Australia
33 25s 150 0E
83 Portland, Vic., Austral. 38 13s 141 35E
93 Portland, Me., U.S.A. 43 42N 70 18w
90 Portland, Ore., U.S.A. 45 35N 122 37w
83 Portland B., Australia 38 [illegible]s 142 0E
24 Portland, Bill of, Eng. 5[illegible] 30N 2 27w
24 Portland, I. of, England 50 33N 2 27w
94 Portland Pt., Jamaica 17 40N 77 0w
89 Portland Promontory, Canada
58 40N 79 30w
25 Portmadoc, see Porthmadog
34 Portmagee, Ireland 51 53N 10 24w
35 Portmarnock, Ireland 53 26N 6 8w
99 Porto Alegre, Brazil 30 7s 50 55w
75 Porto Alexandre, Angola 16 0s 11 40E
75 Porto Amelia, Mozam. 13 0s 40 42E
40 Porto Empedocle, Italy 37 20N 13 25E
72 Porto Novo, Dahomey 6 27N 2 40E
72 Porto Santo I., Madeira 33 0N 16 40w
40 Porto Torres, Italy 40 51N 8 22E
98 Porto Velho, Brazil 8 50s 63 56w
40 Portoferraio, Italy 42 48N 10 20E
40 Portoscuso, Italy 39 10N 8 25E
98 Portoviejo, Ecuador 0 55s 80 30w
32 Portree, Scotland 57 25N 6 11w
34 Portroe, Ireland 52 53N 8 22w
36 Portsalon, Ireland 55 13N 7 37w
33 Portskerra, Scotland 58 35N 3 55w
23 Portslade, England 50 51N 0 13w
22 Portsmouth, England 50 47N 1 7w
93 Portsmouth, N.H., U.S.A.
43 15N 71 0w
92 Portsmouth, Ohio, U.S.A. 38 46N 83 5w
91 Portsmouth, Va., U.S.A. 36 48N 76 25w
33 Portsoy, Scotland 57 41N 2 40w
48 Porttipahta Res., Finland 68 10N 26 30E
37 Portugal, Europe 39 40N 8 0w
75 Portuguese E. Africa, see Mozambique
††72 Portuguese Guinea, W. Afr. 12 0N 15 0w
34 Portumna, Ireland 53 7N 8 12w
49 Porvoo, Finland 60 30N 25 40E
99 Posados, Argentina 27 30s 56 0w
72 Poste Maurice Cortier (Bidon 5),
Algeria 22 20N 1 5E
76 Postmasburg, S. Africa 28 25s 23 1E
61 Potapovskoye, U.S.S.R. 68 40N 86 55E
40 Potenza, Italy 40 41N 15 50E
84 Poteriteri L., N.Z. 46 0s 166 0E
75 Potgietersrus, South Africa 24 10s 29 3E
51 Poti, U.S.S.R. 42 20N 41 30E
72 Potiskum, Nigeria 11 39N 11 2E
92 Potomac, R., U.S.A. 39 10N 77 20w
98 Potosi, Bolivia 19 45s 65 45w
66 Potow, China 38 20N 117 0E
46 Potsdam, Germany 52 19N 13 15E
23 Potters Bar, England 51 42N 0 11w
64 Pottuvil, Sri Lanka 6 55N 81 50E
35 Poulaphouca Falls, & Res., Ireland
53 7N 6 35w
26 Poulton-le-Fylde, Eng. 53 51N 2 59w
50 Povenets, U.S.S.R. 62 48N 35 0E
84 Poverty B., N.Z. 38 42s 178 0E
37 Povóa de Varzim, Port. 41 28N 8 45w
90 Powder R., U.S.A. 45 20N 105 40w
90 Powell, L., U.S.A. 37 20N 110 35w

†† *Now independent and renamed Guinea-Bissau*

80 Powell Creek, Australia 18 0s 133 50E
66 Poyang, L., China 29 0N 116 25E
67 Poyarkova, U.S.S.R. 49 35N 128 45E
41 Pozarevac, Yugoslavia 44 39N 21 10E
46 Poznan, Poland 52 23N 16 57E
37 Pozoblanco, Spain 38 35N 5 1w
43 Prades, France 42 40N 2 28E
46 Prague, Czechoslovakia 50 8N 14 25E
46 Praha, see Prague
41 Prahova, R., Rumania 45 0N 25 40E
85 Prairies, N. America 43 0N 97 0w
40 Prato, Italy 43 53N 11 7E
90 Pratt, U.S.A. 37 42N 98 46w
37 Pravia, Spain 43 30N 6 10w
99 Pre-Cordilleras, mts., Arg. 29 0s 68 0w
80 Premier Downs, Austral. 30 30s 126 30E
49 Prenzlau, Germany 53 18N 13 52E
65 Preparis I., & Chans., India
15 0N 93 40E
47 Prerov, Czechoslovakia 49 27N 17 4E
26 Prescot, England 53 26N 2 49w
93 Prescott, Canada 44 46N 75 32w
90 Prescott, U.S.A. 34 24N 112 30w
90 Presidio, U.S.A. 29 35N 104 20w
47 Presov, Czechoslovakia 49 1N 21 33E
93 Presque Isle, U.S.A. 46 35N 68 3w
25 Prestatyn, Wales 53 20N 3 24w
25 Presteigne, Wales 52 16N 3 1w
26 Preston, England 53 47N 2 43w
31 Preston, Scotland 55 48N 2 18w
90 Preston, U.S.A. 42 6N 111 50w
31 Prestonpans, Scotland 55 57N 2 59w
26 Prestwich, England 53 32N 2 17w
30 Prestwick, Scotland 55 30N 4 36w
76 Pretoria, S. Africa 25 36s 28 12E
41 Preveza, Greece 38 58N 20 46E
46 Pribram, Czechoslovakia 49 42N 14 0E
90 Price, U.S.A. 39 33N 110 46w
76 Prieska, S. Africa 29 40s 22 38E
41 Prilep, Yugoslavia 41 19N 21 34E
88 Prince Albert, Canada 53 15N 105 47w
88 Prince Albert Pen., Can. 71 0N 115 0w
89 Prince Charles I., Can. 67 0N 76 0w
93 Prince Edward I., Prov., Canada
46 30N 63 30w
71 Prince Edward Is., Ind. Oc. 45 30s 38 0E
88 Prince George, Canada 54 0N 123 0w
88 Prince of Wales I., Alaska
55 30N 132 30w
88 Prince of Wales I., Can. 73 0N 99 0w
88 Prince Rupert, Canada 54 20N 130 25w
23 Princes Risborough, England
51 43N 0 51w
94 Princes Town, Trinidad 10 15N 61 28w
82 Princess Charlotte B., Australia
14 0s 144 0E
92 Princeton, U.S.A. 37 14N 87 54w
24 Princetown, England 50 33N 4 0w
71 Principé I., West Africa 1 45N 7 20E
50 Pripyat R., U.S.S.R. 52 10N 27 10E
50 Pripyat Marshes, Poland 51 53N 27 5E
41 Pristina, Yugoslavia 42 39N 21 9E
43 Privas, France 44 46N 4 40E
41 Prizren, Yugoslavia 42 12N 20 46E
94 Prógreso, Mexico 21 31N 89 37w
60 Prokopyevsk, U.S.S.R. 53 58N 86 30E
65 Prome, Burma 18 52N 95 25E
43 Propriano, Corsica, Fr. 41 44N 8 55E
82 Proserpine, Australia 20 27s 148 40E
46 Prostejov, Cz-slov. 49 5N 17 0E
83 Proston, Australia 26 2s 151 32E
43 Provence, Prov., France 43 55N 6 10E
93 Providence, U.S.A. 41 42N 71 23w
91 Providence Channels, Bahama
26 0N 78 0w
88 Provideniya, U.S.S.R. 64 25N 173 15w
43 Provins, France 48 37N 3 15E
90 Provo, U.S.A. 40 18N 111 36w
26 Prudhoe, England 54 57N 1 51w
88 Prudhoe Bay, Alaska 70 20N 149 40w
47 Pruszków, Poland 52 9N 20 49E
47 Prut, R., Rum.-U.S.S.R. 46 20N 28 32E
47 Przemysl, Poland 49 44N 22 49E
47 Przeworsk, Poland 50 5N 22 45E
60 Przhevalsk, U.S.S.R. 42 30N 78 30E
50 Pskov, U.S.S.R. 57 30N 28 30E
27 Pudsey, England 53 47N 1 41w
94 Puebla, Mexico 19 11N 98 15w
90 Pueblo, U.S.A. 38 18N 104 48w
37 Pueblonuevo, Spain 38 16N 5 16w
37 Puente Genil, Spain 37 24N 4 17w
66 Puerh, China 23 0N 100 50E
94 Puerto Barrios, Guat. 15 50N 88 35w
95 Puerto Berrio Colombia 6 30N 74 30w
95 Puerto Cabello, Ven. 10 22N 67 58w
95 Puerto Cabezas, Nicar. 14 5N 83 20w
95 Puerto Colombia, Col. 11 0N 75 0w
94 Puerto Corte's, Honduras 15 50N 88 0w
72 Puerto de Cabras, Canary Is.
28 40N 13 30w
98 Puerto Esperanca, Brazil 19 25s 57 25w
99 Puerto Madryn, Arg. 43 0s 65 0w
98 Puerto Maldonado, Peru 12 25s 69 0w
99 Puerto Montt, Chile 41 22s 72 40w
94 Puerto Morelos, Mexico 21 0N 86 0w
95 Puerto Rico, I., W.I. 18 15N 66 30w
4 Puerto Rico Trough, Atlantic Ocean
20 0N 65 0w
98 Puerto Suarez, Bolivia 19 0s 57 45w
98 Puerto Wilches, Col. 7 25N 73 45w
50 Pugachev, U.S.S.R. 52 0N 48 50E
90 Puget Sd., U.S.A. 48 0N 122 30w
43 Puge-Théniers, France 44 0N 7 0E
37 Puigcerda, Spain 42 23N 1 53E
84 Pukekohe, New Zealand 37 12s 174 55E
40 Pula, Yugoslavia 44 53N 13 53E
98 Pulacayo, Bolivia 20 25s 66 40w
92 Pulaski, Va., U.S.A. 37 0N 80 54w
47 Pulawy, Poland 51 28N 22 0E
23 Pulham Market, England
52 25N 1 13E
64 Pulicat, L. of, India 13 45N 80 12E
90 Pullman, U.S.A. 46 45N 117 0w
47 Pultusk, Poland 52 45N 21 9E
98 Puna I., Ecuador 3 0s 80 20w
99 Puna d'Atacama, Plat., Argentina
25 0s 67 0w
66 Punakha, Bhutan 28 0N 89 15E
64 Punch, India 33 40N 74 12E
64 Punjab, Prov., India 31 45N 74 30E
98 Puno, Peru 15 50s 70 12w
99 Punta Arenas, Chile 53 6s 71 5w
94 Puntarenas, Costa Rica 9 58N 84 40w
60 Pur R., U.S.S.R. 65 30N 78 0E
22 Purbeck I., England 50 38N 2 0w
65 Puri, India 19 50N 85 57E
22 Purley, England 51 29N 1 4w
44 Purmerend, Netherlands 52 30N 4 56E
65 Purnea, India 26 0N 87 38E
65 Purulia, India 23 20N 86 15E
98 Purus, R., Brazil 7 40s 66 0w
67 Pusan, Korea 35 12N 129 0E
61 Pushchino, U.S.S.R. 54 25N 158 10E
50 Pushkino, U.S.S.R. 51 16N 47 9E
65 Putao (Fort Hertz), Burma 27 24N 97 28E
84 Putaruru, N.Z. 38 3s 175 46E
40 Putignano, Italy 40 52N 17 10E
64 Puttalam, Sri Lanka 8 1N 79 55E
44 Putten, Netherlands 52 17N 5 37E
98 Putumayo, R., Col. 2 15s 72 0w
42 Puy-de-Dôme, Dépt., Fr. 45 40N 2 52E
90 Puyallup, U.S.A. 47 15N 122 22w
25 Pwllheli, Wales 52 54N 4 26w
67 Pyongyang, N. Korea 39 0N 126 0E
90 Pyramid L., U.S.A. 38 47N 120 0w
37 Pyrenees, mts., Europe 42 30N 1 0E
42 Pyrénées Orientales, dépt., France
42 30N 2 30E

Q

63 Qabatiya, Jordan 32 25N 35 16E
62 Qadhima, Saudi Arabia 22 15N 39 15E
62 Qal' at el Mudauwara, Saudi Arabia
29 28N 36 3E
64 Qal'eh Shaharak, Afghan. 34 10N 64 20E
63 Qalqilyah, Jordan 32 10N 34 58E
76 Qamata, S. Africa 32 1s 27 30E
62 Qamr B., South Yemen 16 0N 52 30E
73 Qara, Egypt 29 38N 26 30E
63 Qasr Dabà, Jordan 31 36N 36 2E
73 Qasr Farafra, Egypt 27 2N 28 0E
62 Qasr Umm Ramad, Saudi Arabia
23 10N 49 0E
63 Qatana, Syria 33 27N 36 5E
62 Qatar Sheikhdom, Arabia 25 30N 51 0E
62 Qatif, Saudi Arabia 26 30N 50 0E
63 Qatrana Sta., Jordan 31 12N 36 2E
62 Qattara Depression, Egypt 30 0N 28 0E
51 Qazvin, Iran 36 15N 50 0E
73 Qena, Egypt 26 16N 32 37E
64 Qila Safed, Pakistan 29 3N 61 27E
64 Qila Saifullah, Pakistan 30 45N 68 20E
63 Qiryat Gat, Israel 31 36N 34 46E
63 Qishm, & I., Iran 26 45N 56 0E
62 Qishn, South Yemen 15 30N 51 30E
62 Qizan, Saudi Arabia 16 58N 42 35E
51 Qizil Uzun, R., Iran 37 0N 48 40E
83 Quambatook, Australia 35 55s 143 45E
83 Quambone, Australia 30 56s 148 0E
68 Quan Long, Vietnam 7 10N 105 15E
83 Quandialla, Australia 34 2s 147 50E
68 Quang Ngai, Vietnam 15 2N 109 20E
68 Quang Tri, Vietnam 16 45N 107 7E
88 Quatsino, Canada 50 30N 127 40w
75 Que Que, Rhodesia 18 54s 29 45E
83 Queanbeyan, Australia 35 23s 149 17E
89 Quebec, & Prov., Can. 46 50N 71 30w
88 Queen Charlotte Is., Can. 53 0N 132 0w
88 Queen Charlotte Sd., Canada
51 0N 128 0w
88 Queen Maud G., Can. 68 25N 101 30w
100 Queen Maud Land, Antarc.
74 0s 15 0E
26 Queensbury, England 53 46N 1 50w
83 Queenscliff, Australia 38 12s 144 35E
82 Queensland, st., Australia 24 0s 145 0E
83 Queenstown, Australia 41 1s 145 38E
76 Queenstown, S. Africa 31 55s 27 1E
74 Quela, Angola 9 10 16 56E
75 Quelimane, Mozambique 17 55s 36 58E
67 Quelpart, see Cheju Do. I.
94 Queretaro, Mexico 20 47N 100 12w
88 Quesnel, Canada 52 25N 122 30w
64 Quetta, Pakistan 30 7N 66 55E
68 Quezon City, Philippines 14 50N 120 35E
68 Qui Nhon, Vietnam 13 37N 109 10E
74 Quibaxi, Angola 8 24s 14 27E
98 Quibdo, Colombia 6 0N 76 50w
42 Quiberon, France 47 31N 3 7w
75 Quilengues, Angola 14 12s 14 12E
64 Quilon, India 9 0N 76 40E
83 Quilpie, Australia 26 33s 144 17E
34 Quilty, Ireland 52 50N 9 27w
42 Quimper, France 48 0N 4 7w
42 Quimperlé, France 47 52N 3 37w
34 Quin, Ireland 52 50N 8 52w
91 Quincy, Ill., U.S.A. 39 55N 91 23w
93 Quincy, Mass., U.S.A. 42 15N 71 0w
37 Quintanar, Spain 39 35N 3 5w
83 Quirindi, Australia 31 27s 150 38E
98 Quito, Ecuador 0 20s 78 45w
62 Qum, Iran 34 30N 50 50E
62 Qumisheh, see Shahriza, Iran
32 Quoich, L., Scotland 57 4N 5 20w
83 Quondong, Australia 33 0s 140 15E
83 Quorn, Australia 32 30s 137 55E
92 Quorn, Canada 49 30N 91 0w
66 Qurug Tagh, mts., China 41 30N 90 0E
73 Quseir, Egypt 26 8N 34 20E

R

49 Raahe, Finland 64 40N 24 30E
63 Ra'anana, Israel 32 10N 34 53E
32 Raasay I. & Sd., Scot. 57 25N 6 3w
40 Rabat, Malta 35 53N 14 22E
72 Rabat, Morocco 34 0N 6 42w
82 Rabaul, New Britain 4 15s 152 12E
62 Rabigh Qasr, Si. Arabia 22 54N 39 1E
89 Race, C., Canada 46 40N 53 15w
63 Rachaya, Syria 33 30N 35 50E
72 Rachid, Mauritania 18 45N 11 45w
91 Racine, U.S.A. 42 41N 87 49w
47 Radauti, Rumania 47 53N 25 48E
26 Radcliffe, Lancs., Eng. 53 35N 2 19w
27 Radcliffe, Notts., Eng. 52 57N 1 3w
47 Radekhov, U.S.S.R. 50 15N 24 40E
91 Radford, U.S.A. 37 8N 80 33w
83 Radium Hill, Australia 32 30s 140 35E
68 Radja Ampat Arch., Indon. 1 0s 129 30E
22 Radley, England 51 42N 1 14w
*25 Radnor, Co. & Forest, Wales
52 19N 3 20w
47 Radom, Poland 51 24N 21 24E
41 Radomir, Bulgaria 42 37N 23 4E
47 Radomsko, Poland 51 5N 19 28E
24 Radstock, England 51 17N 2 25w
24 Radyr, Wales 51 32N 3 16w
88 Rae, Canada 62 45N 115 50w
65 Rae Bareli, India 26 20N 81 5E
89 Rae Isthmus, Canada 66 40N 87 30w
84 Raetihi, New Zealand 39 27s 175 20E
99 Rafaela, Argentina 31 10s 61 25w
73 Raga, Sudan 8 30N 25 45E
64 Ragama, Sri Lanka 7 0N 79 50E
83 Raglan, Australia 23 48s 150 45E
84 Raglan, New Zealand 37 55s 174 55E
40 Ragusa, Sicily 37 0N 14 48E
73 Rahad el Berdi, Sudan 11 20N 23 40E
64 Raichur, India 16 15N 77 24E
63 Raifoun, Syria 33 58N 35 33E
65 Raigarh, India 21 56N 83 25E
83 Railton, Australia 41 25s 146 25E
90 Rainier, Mt., U.S.A. 46 42N 121 40w
88 Rainy L., Canada 48 40N 93 0w
64 Raipipla, India 21 45N 73 30E
65 Raipur, India 21 16N 81 42E
65 Raj Nandgaon, India 21 0N 81 0E
65 Rajahmundry, I., India 16 0N 81 46E
64 Rajapalaiyim, India 9 20N 77 30E
64 Rajasthan, Prov., India 27 15N 73 0E
64 Rajgarh, India 24 3N 76 35E
64 Rajkot, India 22 15N 70 34E
65 Rajshahi, Bangladesh 24 30N 88 35E
84 Rakaia, & R., N.Z. 43 45s 172 1E
64 Rakaposhi, Kashmir 36 10N 74 0E
49 Rakvere, U.S.S.R. 59 20N 26 30E
91 Raleigh, U.S.A. 35 46N 78 43w
91 Raleigh Bay, U.S.A. 34 50N 76 0w
63 Ram Allah, Jordan 31 55N 35 11E
62 Ramadi, Iraq 33 26N 43 15E
64 Ramanathapuram (Ramnad), India
9 10N 78 57E
63 Ramat David, Israel 32 41N 35 11E
63 Ramat Gan, Israel 32 5N 34 48E
63 Ramat Hakovesh, Israel 32 12N 34 56E
63 Ramat Hashofet, Israel 32 39N 34 59E
43 Rambouillet, France 48 40N 1 50E
65 Ramechhap, Nepal 27 20N 86 5E
65 Ramgarh, Bihar, India 23 23N 85 30E
64 Ramgarh, Rajasthan, India
27 25N 70 20E
63 Ramishk, Iran 26 55N 58 47E
63 Ramla, Israel 31 55N 34 52E
64 Ramnad, see Ramanathapuram
47 Râmnicu Sărat, Rum. 45 26N 27 3E
47 Ramnicu Valcea, Rum. 45 6N 24 20E
76 Ramotswa, Botswana 24 50s 25 50E
64 Rampur, India 28 50N 79 10E
65 Rampur Hat, India 24 15N 87 45E
65 Ramree, I., Burma 19 10N 93 50E
26 Ramsbottom, England 53 38N 2 20w
23 Ramsey, England 51 55N 1 12E
26 Ramsey, & B., I. of Man 54 19N 4 24w
25 Ramsey I., Wales 51 51N 5 20w
23 Ramsgate, England 51 20N 1 26E
64 Ramtek, India 21 20N 79 15E
65 Ranaghat, India 23 5N 88 35E
99 Rancagua, Chile 34 18s 70 45w
65 Ranchi, India 23 29N 85 18E
90 Randall Res., U.S.A. 43 25N 99 30w
36 Randalstown, N. Ireland 54 45N 6 20w
49 Randers, Denmark 56 30N 10 0E
48 Ranea, & R., Sweden 65 52N 22 20E
84 Rangaunu B., N.Z. 34 51s 173 15E
65 Rangia, India 26 30N 91 20E
84 Rangiora, New Zealand 43 26s 172 37E
65 Rangoon, & R., Burma 16 55N 96 25E
65 Rangpur, Bangladesh 25 42N 89 22E
64 Ranibennur, India 14 40N 75 35E
65 Raniganj, India 23 35N 87 4E
64 Raniwara, India 24 50N 72 10E
83 Rankins Springs, Austral.
33 45s 146 12E

* *County incorporated within the county of Powys*

41 Rankovicévo (Kraljevo), Yugoslavia
43 43N 20 40E
64 Rann of Kutch, India 24 0N 70 0E
82 Rannes, Australia 24 6s 150 11E
30 Rannoch, L. & Dist., Scotland
56 41N 4 15w
30 Rannoch Moor, Scotland
56 37N 4 43w
75 Ranohiro, Madagascar 22 30s 45 25E
43 Rapallo, Italy 44 20N 9 18E
36 Raphoe, Ireland 54 52N 7 32w
90 Rapid City, U.S.A. 44 0N 103 20w
33 Rapness, Scotland 59 15N 2 51w
45 Rapperswil, Switzerland 47 15N 8 49E
51 Raqqa, Syria 36 2N 39 0E
73 Ras Abu Shagara, Egypt 21 0N 37 30E
63 Ras al Hadd. C., Oman 22 30N 59 48E
63 Ras al Madraka, C., Oman 19 0N 57 47E
71 Ras Asir, C., Somali Rep. 11 50N 51 12E
73 Ras Banas, C., Egypt 24 0N 35 45E
74 Ras Dashen, mt., Ethiopia 13 8N 37 45E
73 Ras el Milh, C., Egypt 31 55N 25 10E
73 Ras Hadarba, C., Sudan 22 0N 36 50E
73 Ras Lanuf, Libya 30 30N 18 30E
62 Ras Rakan, C., Tr. States 26 7N 51 20E
99 Rasa, Pt., Argentina 40 30s 62 0w
73 Rashad, Sudan 11 55N 31 0E
62 Rasht, Iran 37 18N 49 40E
74 Rat Is., Alaska 50 10N 177 30E
64 Ratangarh, India 28 4N 74 56E
34 Ráth Luirc (Charleville), Ireland
52 21N 8 40w
35 Rathangan, Ireland 53 13N 7 0w
35 Rathcoole, Ireland 53 17N 6 29w
34 Rathcormac, Ireland 52 5N 8 19w
35 Rathdowney, Ireland 52 52N 7 36w
35 Rathdrum, Ireland 52 55N 6 13w
46 Rathenow, Germany 52 36N 12 22E
34 Rathkeale, Ireland 52 31N 8 57w
36 Rathlin I., N. Ireland 55 17N 6 12w
34 Rathmore, Kerry, Ireland 52 5N 9 12w
36 Rathmullen, Ireland 55 7N 7 32w
35 Rathnew, Ireland 53 0N 6 5w
35 Rathvilly, Ireland 52 53N 6 42w
45 Ratische Alpen, Switz. 46 50N 10 10E
64 Ratlam, India 23 21N 75 2E
64 Ratnagiri, India 17 1N 73 22E
35 Ratoath, Ireland 53 30N 6 27w
90 Raton, U.S.A. 36 57N 104 30w
31 Rattray, Scotland 56 36N 3 20w
33 Rattray Hd., Scotland 57 40N 1 53w
48 Raufarhofn, Iceland 66 30N 15 53w
84 Raukumara Ra., N.Z. 38 0s 178 0E
49 Rauma, Finland 61 10N 21 20E
49 Raumo, see Rauma.
23 Raunds, England 52 22N 0 32w
63 Ravar, Iran 31 10N 56 50E
40 Ravenna, Italy 44 26N 12 14E
45 Ravensburg, Germany 47 48N 9 33E
82 Ravenshoe, Australia 17 45s 145 30E
80 Ravensthorpe, Australia 33 31s 120 7E
64 Ravi, R., Pakistan 31 0N 73 20E
64 Rawalpindi, Pakistan 33 40N 73 2E
80 Rawlinna, Australia 31 0s 125 25E
80 Rawlinson Ra., Australia 25 0s 129 0E
27 Rawmarsh, England 53 27N 1 20w
26 Rawtenstall, England 53 42N 2 18w
89 Ray, C., Canada 47 42N 59 25w
65 Rayagada, India 19 5N 83 15E
63 Rayâk, Lebanon 33 52N 36 0E
23 Rayleigh, England 51 36N 0 38E
88 Raymond, Canada 49 28N 112 42w
42 Raz, Pte. du, France 48 2N 4 47w
41 Razgrad, Bulgaria 43 33N 26 33E
42 Ré, I. de, France 46 16N 1 25w
23 Reading, England 51 27N 0 57w
90 Reading, U.S.A. 40 25N 75 46w
33 Reay, Scotland 58 33N 3 48w
73 Rebiana, Libya 24 12N 22 10E
98 Recife (Pernambuco), Brazil
8 5s 35 0w
90 Red Bluff, U.S.A. 40 15N 122 25w
88 Red Deer, Canada 52 14N 113 55w
88 Red Lake, Canada 51 10N 93 45w
91 Red Lake, U.S.A. 48 0N 95 0w
91 Red R., U.S.A. 31 30N 92 30w
66 Red R., Vietnam & China 22 10N 104 0E
70 Red Sea, Arabia-Africa 20 0N 39 0E
94 Red Tank, Panama Canal Zone (Inset).
47 Red Tower Pass, Rumania 45 38N 24 20E
25 Red Wharf B., Wales 53 18N 4 10w
23 Redbridge, Greater London, England
51 35N 0 7E
27 Redcar, England 54 38N 1 4w
83 Redcliffe, Australia 27 12s 153 0E
83 Redcliffs, Australia 34 12s 142 4E
90 Redding, U.S.A. 40 35N 122 25w
22 Redditch, England 52 18N 1 58w
27 Rede R., England 55 18N 2 20w
23 Redhill, England 51 14N 0 10w
90 Redlands, U.S.A. 34 2N 117 12w
27 Redmile, England 52 54N 0 48w
42 Redon, France 47 40N 2 5w
37 Redondela, Spain 42 15N 8 35w
37 Redondo, Portugal 38 40N 7 35w
24 Redruth, England 50 14N 5 14w
91 Redwing, U.S.A. 44 35N 92 40w
34 Ree, L., Ireland 53 30N 7 57w
84 Reefton, New Zealand 42 1s 171 50E
46 Regensburg, Germany 49 0N 12 5E
40 Reggio, Calabria, Italy 38 7N 15 41E
40 Reggio, Emilia Romagna, Italy
44 41N 10 39E
88 Regina, Canada 50 30N 104 37w
75 Rehoboth, S.W. Africa 23 18s 17 1E
63 Rehovot, Israel 31 55N 34 48E
46 Reichenbach, Germany 50 37N 12 18E
23 Reigate, England 51 13N 0 11w
43 Reims, France 49 18N 4 0E
88 Reindeer L., Canada 57 30N 102 28w
84 Reinga C., New Zealand 34 28s 172 36E
37 Reinosa, Spain 43 3N 4 11w
76 Reitz, S. Africa 27 50s 28 35E
61 Rekiniki, U.S.S.R. 60 50N 163 20E
68 Rembang, Indonesia 6 38s 111 15E
43 Remiremont, France 48 0N 6 35E
44 Remscheid, Germany 51 11N 7 12E
49 Rendsburg, Germany 54 19N 9 41E
**29 Renfrew, & Co., Scot. 55 53N 4 23w
68 Rengat, Indonesia 0 30s 102 40E
47 Reni, U.S.S.R. 45 30N 28 19E
32 Renish Pt., Scotland 57 44N 6 59w
62 Renk, Sudan 11 50N 32 50E
44 Renkum, Netherlands 51 58N 5 43E
83 Renmark, Australia 34 9s 140 48E
42 Rennes, France 48 10N 1 41w
90 Reno, U.S.A. 39 35N 119 45w
40 Reno, R., Italy 44 34N 11 30E
22 Repton, England 52 50N 1 32w
90 Republican R., U.S.A. 40 10N 99 0w
37 Requena, Spain 39 34N 1 14w
99 Resistencia, Argentina 27 30s 59 0w
47 Resita, Rumania 45 18N 21 53E
84 Resolution I., N.Z. 45 35s 166 40E
25 Resolven, Wales 51 43N 3 42w
43 Rethel, France 49 30N 4 20E
41 Rethimnon, Crete, Greece 34 45N 24 30E
76 Retreat, S. Africa 34 55s 18 20E
71 Réunion I., Indian Ocean 21 15s 56 0E
37 Réus, Spain 41 9N 1 5E
45 Reutlingen, Germany 48 30N 9 15E
43 Revel, France 43 26N 2 0E
88 Revelstoke, Canada 50 59N 118 5w
86 Revilla Gigedo Is., Pacific Ocean
18 50N 111 0w
44 Revin, France 49 57N 4 39E
65 Rewa, India 24 35N 81 25E
64 Rewari, India 28 18N 76 43E
48 Reykafjord, Iceland 66 0N 21 20w
48 Reykjahlid, Iceland 65 40N 16 55w
48 Reykjanæs, Iceland 63 50N 22 40w
48 Reykjavik, Iceland 64 10N 21 53w
80 Reynolds Ra., Australia 22 30s 133 0E
94 Reynosa, Mexico 26 0N 98 0w
51 Reza'iyeh, Iran 37 40N 45 5E
45 Rhätikon, mts., The Alps 46 50N 10 0E
25 Rhayader, Wales 52 18N 3 31w
44 Rheine, West Germany 52 17N 7 25E
44 Rheydt, Germany 51 12N 6 27E
44–45 Rhine (Rhein), R., Ger. 50 45N 7 10E
46 Rhineland Palatinate, Land, Germany
50 55N 6 50E
91 Rhinelander, U.S.A. 45 48N 89 27w
30 Rhins, The, Scotland 54 50N 5 3w
25 Rhiw, Wales 52 49N 4 37w
91 Rhode I., st., U.S.A. 41 20N 71 20w
41 Rhodes, see Ródhos.
75 Rhodesia, Africa 19 0s 30 0E
41 Rhodope Mts., Bulgaria 41 40N 24 10E
25 Rhondda, Wales 51 40N 3 29w
42 Rhône, Dept. & R., Fr. 45 58N 4 35E
25 Rhos-on-Sea, Wales 53 18N 3 49w
25 Rhosllanerchrugog, Wales 53 3N 3 4w
32 Rhu Coigach, Scotland 58 6N 5 27w
25 Rhuddlan, Wales 53 17N 3 28w
32 Rhum I., Scotland 57 0N 6 20w
25 Rhyl, Wales 53 20N 3 28w
25 Rhymney, Wales 51 45N 3 17w
33 Rhynie, Scotland 57 20N 2 50w
64 Riasi, Kashmir 33 10N 74 45E
37 Ribadéo, Spain 43 35N 7 0w
64 Ribat, Pakistan 29 50N 60 55E
37 Ribatejo, Prov., Portugal 39 10N 8 30w
26 Ribble, R., England 53 56N 2 20w
49 Ribe, Denmark 55 20N 8 43E
99 Ribeirao Preto, Brazil 21 15s 47 40w
44 Ribemont, France 49 48N 2 55E
43 Riberac, France 45 15N 0 15E
98 Riberalta, Bolivia 11 0s 66 0w
84 Riccarton, New Zealand 43 31s 172 28E
31 Riccarton Junc., Scot. 55 16N 2 43w
93 Richibucto, Canada 46 39N 65 5w
90 Richland, U.S.A. 46 25N 119 30w
82 Richmond, Australia 20 45s 142 13E
23 Richmond, Greater London, England
51 27N 0 17w
27 Richmond, Yorks., Eng. 54 24N 1 45w
84 Richmond, New Zealand 41 20s 173 14E
91 Richmond, Ind., U.S.A. 39 47N 85 0w
91 Richmond, Ky., U.S.A. 37 45N 84 18w
91 Richmond, Va., U.S.A. 37 30N 77 28w
83 Richmond Ra., Australia 29 0s 152 45E
23 Rickmansworth, England 51 40N 0 27w
46 Ried, Austria 48 15N 13 30E
46 Riesen Geb., mts., Poland 50 50N 16 0E
76 Rietfontein, S. Africa 26 45s 20 0E
40 Rieti, Italy 42 25N 12 50E
48 Rifstangi, Iceland 66 32N 16 0w
73 Rig Rig, Chad 14 15N 14 26E
49 Riga, & G., U.S.S.R. 56 58N 24 12E
49 Riihimaki, Finland 60 44N 24 45E
40 Rijeka, Yugoslavia 45 1N 14 22E
44 Rijn, R., Netherlands 52 5N 4 30E
44 Rijssen, Netherlands 52 18N 6 31E
44 Rijswijk, Netherlands 52 3N 4 20E
65 Rima, China 28 25N 97 5E
40 Rimini, Italy 44 2N 12 38E
89 Rimouski, Canada 48 25N 68 30w
34 Rineanna (Shannon Airport), Ireland
52 42N 8 57w

** *County incorporated within the region of Strathclyde*

Ringford, Scotland 54 55N 4 3W
Ringköbing, Denmark 56 15N 8 15E
Ringvassöy I., Norway 69 53N 19 25E
Ringville, Ireland 52 3N 7 37W
Ringwood, England 50 50N 1 48W
Rinia I., Greece 37 15N 25 20E
Rio Claro, Brazil 22 20S 47 35W
Rio Claro, Trinidad 10 12N 61 15W
Rio Cuarto, Argentina 33 0S 64 0W
Rio de Janeiro, & st., Brazil 22 5S 43 12W
Rio de la Plata, S. Amer. 35 0S 57 0W
Rio Gallegos, Arg. 51 40S 69 10W
Rio Grande, New Mexico, U.S.A. 34 20N 106 48W
Rio Grande, R., Mexico 29 0N 107 0W
Rio Grande de Santiago, Mexico 22 0N 103 35W
Rio Grande del Norte, Mexico 25 55N 97 12W
Rio Grande do Norte, st., Brazil 5 30S 36 0W
Rio Grande do Sul, & st., Brazil 32 0S 52 0W
Rio Preto, Brazil 21 0S 49 20W
Riobamba, Ecuador 1 40S 78 48W
Riohacha, Colombia 11 33N 72 45W
Riom, France 45 52N 3 5E
Riouw Arch., Indonesia 0 50N 104 50E
Ripley, England 53 3N 1 24W
Ripon, England 54 9N 1 32W
Riq'ai, Saudi Arabia 29 0N 46 33E
Risca, England 51 36N 3 6W
Rishon le Zion, Israel 31 58N 34 47E
Rishton, England 53 46N 2 26W
Risör, Norway 58 43N 9 10E
Riva, Italy 45 54N 10 52E
Rivarolo, Italy 45 20N 7 45E
River Cess, Liberia 5 30N 9 25W
Rivera, Uruguay 31 0S 55 40W
Riversdale, S. Africa 34 10S 21 35E
Riverside, U.S.A. 33 55N 117 25W
Riverton, Australia 34 0S 138 50E
Riverton, Canada 51 5N 97 0W
Riverton, New Zealand 46 20S 168 5E
Riviere au Renard, Can. 49 5N 64 25W
Riviera di Levante, Italy 44 23N 9 15E
Riviera di Ponente, Italy 43 58N 8 0E
Rivière du Loup, Can. 47 50N 69 27W
Rivière Pilote, Martinique, W.I. 14 30N 60 50W
Riyadh, Saudi Arabia 24 40N 46 50E
Rize, Turkey 40 59N 40 30E
Rizzuto, C., Italy 38 54N 17 5E
Rjukan Fos., Norway 59 54N 8 40E
Road Weedon, England 52 14N 1 6W
Roanne, France 46 4N 4 2E
Roanoke, & R., U.S.A. 37 18N 80 1W
Roaringwater B., Ireland 51 30N 9 30W
Robert, Martinique, W.I. 14 40N 60 57W
Robert Williams, Angola 12 40S 15 45E
Robertson Ra., Australia 23 20S 121 0E
Robertsport, Liberia 6 45N 11 26W
Robertstown, Ireland 53 16N 6 50W
Roberval, Canada 48 24N 72 20W
Robin Hood's B., Eng. 54 25N 0 31W
Robinson Ranges, Austral. 25 40S 119 0E
Robson, Mt., Canada 53 15N 118 0W
Roca, Cabo de, Portugal 38 46N 9 30W
Rocamadour, France 44 46N 1 40E
Rochdale, England 53 38N 2 11W
Rochechouart, France 45 50N 0 45E
Rochefort, Belgium 50 12N 5 15E
Rochefort, France 45 57N 0 57W
Rochester, England 51 22N 0 29E
Rochester, Minn., U.S.A 44 2N 92 29W
Rochester, N.H., U.S.A. 43 18N 71 0W
Rochester, N.Y., U.S.A. 43 12N 77 40W
Rochford, England 51 36N 0 42E
Rochfortbridge, Ireland 53 25N 7 19W
Rock Island, U.S.A. 41 30N 90 32W
Rock Springs, U.S.A. 41 38N 109 13W
Rockall I., Atlantic Oc. 57 37N 13 42W
Rockall Deep, Atlantic Ocean 56 45N 11 0W
Rockcliffe, England 54 58N 3 0W
Rockcorry, Ireland 54 7N 7 0W
Rockford, U.S.A. 42 19N 89 8W
Rockhampton, Australia 23 28S 150 31E
Rockingham, & For., Eng. 52 30N 0 40W
Rockland, U.S.A. 44 10N 69 10W
Rocky Mount, U.S.A. 35 57N 75 52W
Rocky Mts., N. America 40 0N 110 0W
Roden, Netherlands 53 7N 6 20E
Rodez, France 44 22N 2 39E
Ródhos I., Greece 36 21N 28 17E
Roding R., England 51 43N 0 16E
Roebourne, Australia 20 43S 117 10E
Roebuck B., Australia 18 10S 122 0E
Roermonde, Netherlands 51 12N 6 0E
Roes Welcome, Sd., Can. 65 0N 87 0W
Roeselare, Belgium 50 57N 3 7E
Rogaland, Co., Norway 59 0N 6 30E
Rogliano, Corsica, France 42 55N 9 25E
Rohri, Pakistan 27 47N 68 50E
Rohtak, India 28 57N 76 30E
Roisel, France 49 58N 3 6E
Rojo, C., Mexico 21 30N 97 20W
Rolla, U.S.A. 37 59N 91 46W
Rollingstone, Australia 19 0S 146 15E
Roma, Australia 26 32S 148 49E
Roma, Sweden 57 35N 18 27E
Romaine, R., Canada 51 40N 63 40W
Roman, Rumania 46 59N 26 55E
Roman, U.S.S.R. 60 25N 112 10E
43 Romans, France 45 2N 5 0E
43 Romanshorn, Switz. 47 35N 9 22E
40 Rome, Italy 41 53N 12 33E
91 Rome, Ga., U.S.A. 34 15N 85 8W
91 Rome, N.Y., U.S.A. 43 15N 75 30W
43 Romilly, France 48 30N 3 46E
23 Romney Marsh, England 51 0N 0 54E
45 Romont, Switzerland 46 42N 6 54E
43 Romorantin, France 47 20N 1 45E
48 Romsdal, val., Norway 62 30N 7 50E
22 Romsey, England 50 59N 1 29W
32 Rona, I., Scotland 57 33N 6 0W
32 Ronay, I., Scotland 57 30N 7 10W
37 Roncesvalles & P., Spain 43 1N 1 20W
37 Ronda, Spain 36 48N 5 9W
49 Rondane, Plat., Norway 61 66N 95 7E
49 Rönne, Denmark 55 5N 14 41E
44 Ronse, Belgium 50 44N 3 36E
64 Roorkee, India 29 45N 78 20E
100 Roosevelt I., Antarctica 80 0S 161 0E
36 Roosky, Ireland 53 50N 7 47W
80 Roper R., Australia 14 58S 134 0E
43 Roquefort, France 43 58N 3 0E
98 Roraima, mt., Venezuela 5 45N 62 0W
98 Roraima, state, Brazil 2 30N 62 0W
48 Röros, Norway 62 35N 11 22E
45 Rorschach, Switzerland 47 29N 9 29E
99 Rosario, Argentina 33 3S 60 40W
94 Rosario, Mexico 23 0N 105 40W
99 Rosario de la Frontera, Argentina 25 45S 65 0W
37 Rosas, Spain 42 18N 3 10E
42 Roscoff, France 48 40N 4 0W
36 Roscommon, & Co., Ire. 53 38N 8 8W
34 Roscrea, Ireland 52 58N 7 48W
95 Roseau, Dominica, W.I. 15 15N 61 15W
83 Rosebery, Australia 41 52S 145 38E
90 Roseburg, U.S.A. 43 13N 123 20W
82 Rosedale, Australia 24 38S 151 53E
33 Rosehearty, Scotland 57 42N 2 8W
62 Roseires, Sudan 11 50N 34 30E
33 Rosemarkie, Scotland 57 35N 4 8W
46 Rosenheim, Germany 47 55N 12 5E
88 Rosetown, Canada 51 30N 108 10W
73 Rosetta, Egypt 31 20N 30 21E
83 Rosewood, Australia 27 38S 152 20E
49 Röskilde, Denmark 55 39N 12 3E
52 Roslavl, U.S.S.R. 53 57N 32 40E
22 Ross on Wye, England 51 54N 2 34W
84 Ross, New Zealand 42 55S 170 52E
100 Ross Dependency, Antarctica 70 0S 170 0E
100 Ross Ice Shelf, Antarc. 82 0S 175 0W
100 Ross Sea, Antarctica 75 0S 178 0E
*29 Ross & Cromarty, Co., Scotland 57 45N 4 50W
36 Rossan Pt., Ireland 54 42N 8 49W
34 Rosscarbery & B., Ireland 51 34N 9 1W
36 Rosses Bay, Ireland 55 2N 8 30W
36 Rosses Point, Ireland 54 17N 8 34W
88 Rossland, Canada 49 5N 117 35W
35 Rosslare & Hr., Ireland 52 15N 6 20W
72 Rosso, Mauritania 16 40N 15 45W
52 Rossosh, U.S.S.R. 50 17N 39 30E
88 Rosthern, Canada 52 58N 106 10W
46 Rostock, Germany 54 3N 12 7E
52 Rostov, U.S.S.R. 47 12N 39 40E
48 Rosvatn L., Norway 65 40N 14 0E
90 Roswell, U.S.A. 33 28N 104 36W
31 Rosyth, Scotland 56 2N 3 25W
27 Rothbury & For., Eng. 55 19N 1 52W
23 Rother, R., Kent, England 51 1N 0 37E
27 Rotherham, England 53 26N 1 20W
33 Rothes, Scotland 57 33N 3 13W
30 Rothesay, Scotland 55 50N 5 3W
46 Rothhaar, G., mt., Ger. 51 6N 8 10E
23 Rothwell, Northants, England 52 25N 0 48W
27 Rothwell, Yorks., Eng. 53 46N 1 29W
84 Rotoroa, L., N.Z. 41 50S 172 39E
84 Rotorua, & L., N.Z. 38 13S 176 20E
44 Rotterdam, Netherlands 51 55N 4 30E
23 Rottingdean, England 50 48N 0 3W
45 Rottweil, Germany 48 12N 8 20E
87 Rotuma I., Pacific Oc. 12 0S 177 0E
43 Roubaix, France 50 43N 3 4E
43 Rouen, France 49 28N 1 7E
34 Rough Pt., Ireland 52 19N 10 0W
34 Roundstone, Ireland 53 24N 9 55W
35 Roundwood, Ireland 53 4N 6 14W
33 Rousay, I., Scotland 59 9N 3 4W
43 Roussillon, Dist., France 42 40N 2 40E
89 Rouyn, Canada 48 6N 79 0W
48 Rovaniemi, Finland 66 35N 25 40E
40 Rovereto, Italy 45 53N 11 2E
40 Rovigo, Italy 45 2N 11 41E
40 Rovinj, Yugoslavia 45 18N 13 40E
47 Rovno, U.S.S.R. 50 30N 26 22E
31 Rowanburn, Scotland 55 5N 2 54W
68 Roxas, Philippines 11 40N 122 45E
84 Roxburgh, New Zealand 45 30S 169 27E
**29 Roxburgh, & Co., Scot. 55 34N 2 30W
23 Royston, Herts., England 52 3N 0 1W
26 Royton, Lancs., England 53 34N 2 7W
44 Rozoy-sur-Serre, France 49 40N 4 8E
52 Rtishchevo, U.S.S.R. 52 27N 43 50E
25 Ruabon, Wales 52 59N 3 3W
84 Ruahine Ra., N.Z. 39 45S 176 0E
22 Rubery, England 52 24N 1 59W
30 Rubha a' Mhail, C., Scot. 55 57N 6 7W
40 Rubicone, R., Italy 44 9N 12 29E
63 Rud-i-Khoran R., Iran 29 0N 56 30E
52 Rudnichny, U.S.S.R. 59 40N 52 20E
64 Rudok, Tibet, China 33 30N 79 40E
††74 Rudolf, L., Kenya 3 30N 36 0E
43 Rudolstadt, Germany 50 45N 11 55E
42 Ruffec, France 46 0N 0 18E
74 Rufiji, R., Tanzania 8 0S 38 0E
72 Rufisque, Sénégal 14 42N 17 8W
22 Rugby, England 52 21N 1 17W
22 Rugeley, England 52 45N 1 54W
46 Rügen I., Germany 54 32N 13 30E
46 Rühr, R., Germany 51 25N 8 0E
74 Ruki R., Zaïre 0 10S 18 30E
74 Rukwa, L., Tanzania 8 5S 33 0E
32 Rum I., *see* Rhum
80 Rum Jungle, Australia 13 20S 131 12E
47 Rumania, Europe 45 40N 25 20E
73 Rumbek, Sudan 6 50N 29 30E
84 Runanga, New Zealand 42 25S 171 15E
26 Runcorn, England 53 21N 2 44W
74 Rungwa & R., Tanzania 6 40S 33 50E
65 Rupa, India 27 15N 92 25E
89 Rupert, R., Canada 51 30N 78 40W
75 Rusape, Rhodesia 18 32S 32 5E
41 Rusé (Ruschuk), Bulgaria 43 53N 25 57E
35 Rush, Ireland 53 31N 6 7W
23 Rushden, England 52 17N 0 37W
60 Russian S.F.S.R., Europe and Asia 58 0N 80 0E
60 Russkaya Polyana, U.S.S.R. 54 5N 74 0E
76 Rustenburg, S. Africa 25 34S 27 10E
62 Rutba, Iraq 33 4N 40 15E
47 Ruthenia, reg., U.S.S.R. 48 30N 23 40E
30 Rutherglen, Scotland 55 48N 4 13W
25 Ruthin, Wales 53 8N 3 18W
33 Ruthven, Scotland 57 4N 4 2W
91 Rutland, U.S.A. 43 47N 72 55W
†28 Rutland, Co., England 52 38N 0 40W
74 Rutshuru, Zaïre 1 0S 29 28E
44 Ruurlo, Netherlands 52 5N 6 27E
74 Ruwenzori, Mt., Uganda 0 40N 29 50E
52 Ruzayevka, U.S.S.R. 54 10N 44 55E
47 Ruzomberok, Cz. 49 12N 19 15E
74 Rwanda, Africa 2 0S 30 0E
30 Ryan, L., Scotland 55 0N 5 4W
52 Ryazan, U.S.S.R. 54 35N 39 45E
52 Ryazhsk, U.S.S.R. 53 43N 40 0E
60 Rybache, U.S.S.R. 46 40N 81 20E
50 Rybachi Pen., U.S.S.R. 69 40N 32 0E
50 Rybinsk (Shcherbakov), U.S.S.R. 58 0N 38 51E
50 Rybinsk Res., U.S.S.R. 58 30N 37 50E
22 Ryde, England 50 44N 1 11W
23 Rye, & B., England 50 58N 0 44E
27 Ryhope, England 54 53N 1 21W
83 Rylstone, Australia 32 40S 149 58E
47 Rypin, Poland 53 0N 19 30E
67 Ryukyu Is., Japan 26 30N 128 0E
52 Rzhev, U.S.S.R. 56 20N 34 25E

S

45 Saanen, Switzerland 46 29N 7 17E
45 Saar, Land, Germany 49 38N 6 33E
45 Saar (Sarre), R., Fr. & Germany 49 20N 6 45E
45 Saarbrücken, Germany 49 19N 7 0E
44 Saarburg, Germany 49 38N 6 33E
45 Saarlouis, Germany 49 18N 6 44E
45 Saas Fee, Switzerland 46 8N 7 56E
68 Sabah, state, Malaysia 6 0N 117 0E
63 Sabastiya, Jordan 32 16N 35 11E
62 Sabha, Wadi, Si. Arabia 23 50N 50 0E
94 Sabinas, Mexico 27 40N 101 10W
94 Sabinas Hidalgo, Mex. 26 25N 100 15W
40 Sabine Mts., Italy 42 20N 12 50E
91 Sabine R., U.S.A. 31 45N 93 45W
93 Sable, C., Canada 43 28N 65 50W
91 Sable, C., U.S.A. 25 15N 81 5W
89 Sable, I., Canada 43 57N 60 00W
63 Sabzawar, Iran 36 25N 57 55E
63 Sabzawar, Afghanistan 33 12N 62 0E
45 Säckingen, Germany 47 35N 7 55E
90 Sacramento, & R., U.S.A. 38 37N 121 25W
90 Sacramento Mts., U.S.A. 32 20N 105 0W
27 Sacriston, England 54 49N 1 38W
37 Sadaba, Spain 42 20N 1 15W
30 Saddell, Scotland 55 31N 5 30W
35 Saddle Hd., Ireland 54 0N 10 10W
67 Sado, I., Japan 38 0N 138 15E
65 Sadon, Burma 25 25N 97 50E
49 Säffle, Sweden 59 9N 12 55E
23 Saffron Walden, England 52 1N 0 15E
72 Safi, Morocco 32 15N 9 15W
67 Saga, & Pref., Japan 33 18N 130 6E
65 Sagaing, Burma 21 58N 95 56E
67 Sagami B., Japan 35 0N 139 30E
64 Sagar, India 23 50N 78 50E
25 Sageston, Wales 51 41N 4 48W
91 Saginaw, & B., U.S.A. 43 29N 84 0W
37 Sagres, Portugal 37 1N 8 57W
95 Sagua la Grande, Cuba, 22 58N 80 2W
93 Saguenay, R., Canada 48 18N 70 0W
37 Sagunto, Spain 39 42N 0 18W
37 Sahagúna, Spain 42 20N 5 0W
63 Sahah, Jordan 31 51N 36 0E
72 Sahara Atlas, mts., Algeria 34 0N 3 0E
72 Sahara, Des., N. Africa 20 0N 12 0E
64 Saharanpur, India 29 57N 77 38E
64 Sahiwal, Pakistan 30 48N 73 5E
63 Saidabad, Iran 29 27N 55 48E
64 Saidapet, India 13 0N 80 15E
74 Sa'id Bundas, Sudan 8 24N 24 48E
64 Saidu, Pakistan 34 50N 72 15E
68 Saigon, Vietnam 10 40N 106 37E
62 Saihut, South Yemen 15 25N 51 20E
66 Saikhoa Ghat, India 28 5N 95 0E
50 Saimaa, L., Finland 61 20N 28 0E
31 St. Abb's, Scotland 55 54N 2 7W
31 St. Abb's Hd., Scotland 55 55N 2 8W
43 St. Affrique, France 43 58N 2 55E
24 St. Agnes, & Hd., Eng. 50 19N 5 15W
23 St. Albans, England 51 46N 0 20W
91 St. Albans, U.S.A. 44 50N 73 0W
22 St. Albans Hd., England 50 35N 2 4W
44 St. Amand, France 50 26N 3 27E
43 St. Amand-Montrond, France 46 40N 2 30E
44 St. Amandsberg, Belgium 51 5N 3 42E
43 St. André, France 44 0N 6 30E
75 St. André, C., Madagascar 16 0S 44 25E
31 St. Andrews, Scotland 56 20N 2 48W
42 St. Anne, Channel Is. 49 44N 2 10W
26 St. Annes, England 53 46N 3 4W
95 St. Ann's, & B., Jamaica 18 10N 77 15W
83 St. Arnaud, Australia 36 33S 143 15E
25 St. Asaph, Wales 53 17N 3 26W
89 St. Augustin, Canada 51 30N 58 30W
91 St. Augustine, U.S.A. 29 58N 81 21W
24 St. Austell, England 50 20N 4 48W
45 St. Avold, France 49 8N 6 41E
94 St. Barthélemy I., W.I. 17 56N 62 45W
26 St. Bees & Hd., England 54 31N 3 39W
88 St. Boniface, Canada 49 50N 97 0W
31 St. Boswells, Scotland 55 34N 2 39W
42 St. Brelade's, Jersey, Channel Is. 49 12N 2 13W
25 St. Bride's B., Wales 51 48N 5 11W
42 St. Brieuc, France 48 34N 2 45W
43 St. Calais, France 47 55N 0 40E
94 St. Catherine, Mt., Grenada, W.I. 12 13N 61 40W
22 St. Catherine's Point, England 50 35N 1 19W
43 St. Céré, France 44 50N 1 50E
92 St. Clair L., Canada-U.S.A. 42 38N 82 30W
43 St. Claude, France 46 22N 5 50E
91 St. Cloud, U.S.A. 45 28N 94 10W
24 St. Columb Major, Eng. 50 26N 4 56W
95 St. Croix, I., W. Indies 17 45N 64 45W
33 St. Cyrus, Scotland 56 47N 2 25W
25 St. Davids, & Hd., Wales 51 53N 5 16W
95 St. David's I., Bermudas 32 23N 64 38W
43 St. Dié, France 48 20N 7 0E
43 St. Dizier, France 48 40N 5 8E
88 St. Elias, Mt., Canada 60 40N 140 0W
43 St. Étienne, France 45 27N 4 22E
94 St. Eustatius I., W.I. 17 30N 63 30W
93 St. Félicien, Canada 48 38N 72 30W
43 St. Florent, France 42 40N 9 15E
43 St. Flour, France 45 0N 3 10E
45 St. Gallen, & Canton, Switzerland 47 26N 9 21E
43 St. Gaudens, France 43 5N 0 45E
95 St. George, Bermudas 32 25N 64 43W
90 St. George, U.S.A. 37 10N 113 35W
95 St. George's, Grenada, W.I. 12 5N 61 40W
44 St. Georges, Belgium 50 36N 5 22E
43 St. Germain, Yvelines, France 48 52N 2 5E
24 St. Germans, England 50 24N 4 19W
42 St. Gilles, France 46 41N 2 0W
43 St. Girons, France 43 0N 1 8E
25 St. Govan's Hd., Wales 51 35N 4 56W
75 St. Helena B., S. Africa 32 40S 18 0E
5 St. Helena I., S. Atlan. Oc. 10 20S 7 50W
26 St. Helens, Eng. 53 28N 2 43W
90 St. Helens, U.S.A. 45 50N 122 52W
42 St. Helier, Jersey 49 15N 2 8W
43 St. Hippolyte, France 47 20N 6 50E
44 St. Hubert, Belgium 50 2N 5 22E
89 St. Hyacinthe, Canada 45 40N 73 0W
45 St. Ingbert, Germany 49 16N 7 6E
24 St. Ives, & B., Corn., Eng. 50 14N 5 30W
23 St. Ives, Hunts., England 52 19N 0 4W
43 St. Jean, France 45 20N 6 20E
93 St. Jean, L., Canada 48 39N 72 10W
42 St. Jean de Luz, France 43 25N 1 40W
93 St. Jerôme, Canada 45 57N 74 0W
93 St. John, N.B., Canada 45 18N 65 55W
93 St. John, R., U.S.A. 46 42N 69 35W
95 St. John's, Antigua, W.I. 17 0N 61 50W
89 St. John's Newf'd., Can. 47 37N 52 40W
36 St. Johnston, Ireland 54 56N 7 29W
91 St. Joseph, U.S.A. 39 49N 94 50W
89 St. Joseph, L., Canada 51 10N 90 50W
92 St. Joseph R., U.S.A. 42 8N 85 30W
43 St. Junien, France 45 50N 0 55E
24 St. Just, England 50 7N 5 41W
18 St. Kilda, I., Atlantic Oc. 57 50N 8 40W
84 St. Kilda, N.Z. 45 53S 170 31E
94 St. Kitts I., West Indies 17 20N 62 49W
93 St. Lawrence, G. of, Can. 48 0N 62 0W
93 St. Lawrence, R., Canada 49 0N 68 30W
23 St. Leonards, England 50 51N 0 33E
42 St. Lô, France 49 12N 1 5W
72 St. Louis, Senegal 16 0N 16 27W
91 St. Louis, U.S.A. 38 40N 90 20W
94 St. Lucia, I. & Chan., Wind. Is., W. Indies 14 0N 61 0W
76 St. Lucia, L., S. Africa 27 45S 32 30E
94 St. Maarten I., Neth. W.I. 18 5N 63 0W
32 St. Magnus B., Scotland 60 23N 1 35W
42 St. Malo, France 48 42N 2 2W
95 St. Marc, Haiti, W.I. 19 0N 72 50W
42 St. Martin, Jersey, Channel Is. 49 15N 2 5W
43 St. Martin, France 44 2N 7 15E
95 St. Martin I., W.I. 18 15N 63 0W
83 St. Mary Pk., Australia 31 30S 138 40E
83 St. Mary's, Australia 41 30S 148 15E
24 St. Mary's I., England 49 55N 6 18W
42 St. Mathieu, Pte. de, Fr. 48 20N 4 50W
43 St. Maur, France 48 44N 2 30E
45 St. Maurice, Switzerland 46 14N 7 1E
25 St. Mellons, England 51 31N 3 8W
24 St. Michael's Mt., Eng. 50 7N 5 29W
31 St. Monance, Scotland 56 12N 2 45W
45 St. Moritz, Switzerland 46 30N 9 51E
42 St. Nazaire, France 47 20N 2 13W
23 St. Neots, England 52 13N 0 16W
44 St. Niklaas, Belgium 51 10N 4 8E
43 St. Omer, France 50 42N 2 12E
43 St. Paul, France 42 50N 2 30E
91 St. Paul, U.S.A. 44 58N 93 6W
40 St. Paul's Bay, Malta 36 57N 14 24E
42 St. Peter Port, Channel Is. 49 30N 2 35W
91 St. Petersburg, U.S.A. 27 49N 82 44W
89 St. Pierre and Miquelon, Fr. Overseas Terr., N. Amer. 46 49N 56 15W
46 St. Polten, Austria 48 10N 15 38E
43 St. Quentin, France 49 54N 3 13E
43 St. Raphael, France 43 26N 6 50E
43 St. Rémy, France 43 43N 4 50E
42 St. Servan, France 48 40N 2 0W
42 St. Sever, France 43 47N 0 40W
93 St. Stephen, Canada 45 12N 67 18W
92 St. Thomas, Canada 42 45N 81 20W
95 St. Thomas, I., W. Indies 18 20N 65 0W
44 St. Trond, Belgium 50 49N 5 11E
43 St. Tropez, France 43 18N 6 35E
43 St. Valéry-en-Caux, Fr. 49 52N 0 45E
43 St. Valéry sur Somme, Fr. 50 10N 1 40E
43 St. Vallier, France 45 12N 4 50E
37 St. Vincent, C., Portugal 37 0N 9 0W
83 St. Vincent, G. Australia 35 0S 138 0E
94 St. Vincent I., W. Indies 13 17N 61 15W
44 St. Vith, Belgium 50 17N 6 5E
43 St. Yrieix, France 45 32N 1 15E
94 Sainte Anne, Guadeloupe, Fr. W.I. 16 13N 61 23W
94 Sainte Anne, Martinique, Fr. W.I. 14 25N 60 52W
75 Ste. Marie, I., Madag. 16 55S 50 0E
94 Sainte Marie, Martinique, Fr. W.I. 14 46N 61 0W
44 Sainte Ménéhould, France 49 10N 4 52E
94 Sainte Rose, Guadeloupe, W.I. 16 18N 61 40W
42 Saintes, France 45 47N 0 40W
36 Saintfield, N. Ireland 54 28N 5 50W
42 Saintonge, Dist., France 45 30N 0 40W
65 Sairang, India 23 50N 92 40E
67 Saitama, Pref., Japan 36 20N 139 45E
62 Saiun, South Yemen 15 52N 48 55E
98 Sajama, Mt., Bolivia 17 30S 68 30W
67 Sakai, Japan 34 30N 135 30E
67 Sakashima Gunto, Is., Jap. 25 0N 124 0E
67 Sakata, Japan 38 58N 139 56E
61 Sakhalin, U.S.S.R. 52 0N 143 0E
76 Sakrivier, S. Africa 31 10S 20 28E
49 Sala, Sweden 59 56N 16 30E
99 Salado, R., Argentina 29 0S 63 0W
72 Salaga, Ghana 8 35N 0 45W
68 Salajar, I., Indonesia 6 12S 120 25E
37 Salamanca, Spain 40 59N 5 40W
82 Salamaua, Terr. of New Guinea 7 10S 147 0E
41 Salamis, Greece 37 58N 23 30E
98 Salaverry, Peru 8 12S 79 0W
43 Salbris, France 47 22N 2 8E
37 Saldaña, Spain 42 30N 4 48W
83 Sale, Australia 38 7S 147 0E
26 Sale, England 53 26N 2 19W
72 Salé, Morocco 33 29N 6 47W
60 Salekhard, U.S.S.R. 66 30N 66 50E
64 Salem, India 11 35N 78 0E
93 Salem, Mass., U.S.A. 42 30N 71 0W
90 Salem, Ore., U.S.A. 44 48N 123 0W
40 Salerno, Italy 40 42N 14 50E
26 Salford, England 53 29N 2 18W
90 Salida, U.S.A. 38 25N 106 0W
75 Salima, Malawi 13 50S 34 30E
90 Salina, U.S.A. 38 57N 97 58W
94 Salina Cruz, Mexico 16 23N 95 25W
90 Salinas & R., U.S.A. 36 40N 121 42W
99 Salinas Grandes, Arg. 29 15S 63 30W
43 Salins, France 46 59N 5 50E
83 Salisbury, Australia 34 45S 138 35E
22 Salisbury, England 51 5N 1 47W
75 Salisbury, Rhodesia 17 50S 31 2E
91 Salisbury, Md., U.S.A. 38 25N 75 33W
91 Salisbury, N.C., U.S.A. 35 42N 80 30W
22 Salisbury Plain, England 51 14N 1 57W
62 Sallom, Sudan 19 22N 37 6E
90 Salmon, & R., U.S.A. 45 10N 113 50W
90 Salmon River Mts., U.S.A. 44 45N 120 0W
49 Salo, Finland 60 22N 23 3E
43 Salo, Italy 45 40N 10 30E
43 Salon, France 43 40N 5 5E
64 Salsette, I., India 18 30N 72 10E
52 Salsk, U.S.S.R. 46 10N 41 30E
43 Salsomaggiore, Italy 44 50N 10 0E
48 Salt Fd., Norway 67 10N 14 10E
90 Salt Fork R., Texas, U.S.A. 33 15N 101 0W
90 Salt Lake City, U.S.A. 40 45N 111 50W
99 Salta, Argentina 24 47S 65 20W
24 Saltash, England 50 25N 4 12W
27 Saltburn, England 54 35N 0 58W
30 Saltcoats, Scotland 55 38N 4 47W
35 Saltee Is., Ireland 52 7N 6 35W

Incorporated within the regions of Highland and Western Isles

** *County incorporated within the region of Borders*

† *Incorporated within the county of Leicester*

†† *Renamed Turkana, L.*

27 Saltergate, England 54 20N 0 40w
94 Saltillo, Mexico 25 28N 101 0w
99 Salto, Uruguay 31 25s 58 0w
98 Salto Augusto, Falls, Fs., Brazil
8 30s 58 0w
90 Salton Sea, U.S.A. 33 20N 115 45w
72 Saltpond, Ghana 5 15N 1 3w
23 Saltwood, England 51 4N 1 5E
73 Salum, G. of, Egypt 31 30N 25 10E
65 Salur, India 18 36N 83 12E
40 Saluzzo, Italy 44 40N 7 30E
99 Salvador (Bahia), Brazil 12 50s 38 25w
94 Salvadore, C. Amer. 13 45N 88 50w
65 Salween, R., China-Burma
19 30N 97 40E
46 Salzburg, & prov., Austria 47 46N 13 1E
46 Salzgitter, Germany 52 7N 10 19E
60 Sama, U.S.S.R. 60 25N 60 27E
61 Samagaltai, U.S.S.R. 51 40N 95 0E
63 Samar, Jordan 32 40N 35 47E
68 Samar, I., Philippines 11 30N 125 0E
82 Samarai, Papua 10 30s 151 0E
63 Samaria, Dist., Jordan 32 21N 35 15E
63 Samaria, Mts. of, Jordan 32 15N 35 15E
68 Samarinda, Indonesia 0 48s 117 18E
60 Samarkand, U.S.S.R. 39 45N 66 55E
62 Samarra, Iraq 34 30N 43 55E
62 Samawa, Iraq 31 15N 45 15E
65 Sambalpur, India 21 32N 83 59E
68 Sambas, Indonesia 1 35N 109 20E
75 Sambava, Madagascar 14 10s 50 3E
64 Sambhal, India 28 40N 78 35E
64 Sambhar, India 26 55N 74 45E
40 Sambiase, Italy 38 57N 16 16E
47 Sambor, U.S.S.R. 49 30N 23 15E
44 Sambre, R., Fr.-Belg. 50 20N 4 15E
74 Same, Tanzania 4 1s 37 45E
51 Samnan, Iran 35 31N 53 20E
41 Samos, I., Greece 37 41N 26 50E
41 Samothraki, I., Greece 40 28N 25 38E
68 Sampit, Indonesia 2 23s 113 0E
66 Samshui, China 23 15N 112 55E
51 Samsun, Turkey 41 20N 36 12E
68 Samut Songkhram, Thailand
13 20N 100 0E
72 San Mali 13 15N 4 45w
95 San Andres, I., Colombia
12 30N 81 35w
90 San Andres, Mts., U.S.A.
33 0N 106 40w
94 San Andres Tuxtla, Mex. 18 25N 95 15w
90 San Angelo, U.S.A. 31 25N 100 28w
99 San Antonio Oeste, Arg. 40 40s 65 5w
99 San Antonio, Chile 33 30s 71 40w
90 San Antonio, U.S.A. 29 27N 98 32w
94 San Antonio, C., Cuba 21 58N 85 0w
91 San Antonio, R., U.S.A. 28 45N 97 30w
91 San Benito, U.S.A. 26 5N 97 45w
90 San Bernardino, U.S.A. 34 11N 117 25w
68 San Bernardino Str., Philippines
12 30N 124 17E
91 San Blas, C., U.S.A. 29 40N 85 20w
68 San Carlos, Philippines 11 0N 124 20E
99 San Carlos de Bariloche, Argentina
41 20N 71 0w
90 San Clemente I., U.S.A. 32 50N 118 30w
99 San Cristobal, Argentina 30 25s 61 10w
94 San Cristobal, Mexico 17 14N 92 32w
95 San Cristobal, Venezuela 7 30N 72 15w
78 San Cristobal, I., Solomon Is.
11 0s 162 0E
90 San Diego, U.S.A. 32 45N 117 12w
99 San Felipe, Chile 32 40s 70 45w
95 San Felipe, Venezuela 10 10N 68 50w
37 San Feliu, Spain 41 45N 3 0E
94 San Fernando, Mexico 24 50N 98 2w
37 San Fernando, Spain 36 36N 6 14w
95 San Fernando, Trinidad 10 10N 61 28w
98 San Fernando, Venezuela 7 50N 67 30w
90 San Francisco, U.S.A. 37 40N 122 25w
95 San Francisco de Macoris, Dominican
Republic 19 15N 70 5w
99 San Ignacio, Bolivia 16 10s 61 0w
90 San Joaquin, R., U.S.A. 37 0N 120 0w
94 San Jorge B., Mexico 31 0N 113 30w
99 San Jorge, G. de, Arg. 46 0s 66 30w
99 San José, Bolivia 18 0s 60 30w
95 San José, Costa Rica 9 50N 84 2w
68 San Jose, Philippines 10 45N 122 0E
90 San Jose, Cal., U.S.A. 37 20N 122 50w
99 San José, Uruguay 34 7s 57 0w
99 San Juan, Argentina 31 38s 68 38w
95 San Juan, Puerto Rico 18 27N 66 10w
90 San Juan Mts., U.S.A. 37 30N 107 0w
99 San Julian, Argentina 49 20s 67 35w
99 San Lorenzo, Mt., Arg. 47 30s 72 0w
94 San Lucas, C., Mexico 23 0N 110 0w
99 San Luis, Argentina 33 24s 66 15w
90 San Luis Obispo, U.S.A.
35 18N 120 38w
94 San Luis Potosi, Mex. 22 10N 100 37w
40 San Marino, Italy 43 58N 12 30E
90 San Mateo, U.S.A. 37 30N 122 15w
99 San Matias, G. de, Arg. 41 30s 64 0w
94 San Miguel, Salvador 13 25N 88 10w
99 San Nicolas, Argentina 33 20s 60 10w
94 San Pedro, Mexico 26 0N 102 58w
99 San Pedro, Paraguay 24 0s 57 10w
95 San Pedro de Macoris,
Dominican Republic 18 30N 69 20w
94 San Pedro Sula, Honduras
15 35N 88 0w
99 San Rafael, Argentina 34 30s 68 20w
40 San Remo, Italy 43 50N 7 50E
94 San Salvador, Salvador 13 59N 89 18w
95 San Salvador I., Bahama
24 0N 74 30w
37 San Sebastian, Spain 43 20N 1 58w
40 San Severo, Italy 41 40N 15 20E
94 San Vicente, Salvador 13 45N 88 50w
37 San Vicente de la Barquera, Spain
43 28N 4 30w
62 San'a, Yemen 15 25N 44 15E
63 Sanamein, Syria 33 5N 36 10E
68 Sanana, I., Indonesia 2 20s 126 0E
95 Sanchez, Dominican Republic
19 10N 69 35w
43 Sancoins, France 46 50N 2 58E
95 Sancti Spiritus, Cuba 22 0N 78 0w
68 Sandakan, Malaysia 6 0N 118 12E
68 Sandalwood I., Indonesia 10 0s 120 0E
33 Sanday, I. & Sd., Orkneys, Scotland
59 12N 2 30w
26 Sandbach, England 53 8N 2 23w
83 Sandgate, Australia 27 26s 152 57E
23 Sandgate, England 51 4N 1 7E
23 Sandhurst, England 51 21N 0 48w
49 Sandnes, Norway 58 50N 5 45E
74 Sandoa, Zaïre 9 48s 22 4E
47 Sandomierz, Poland 50 40N 21 42E
65 Sandoway, Burma 18 14N 94 30E
90 Sandpoint, U.S.A. 48 27N 116 35w
32 Sandray, Hebrides, Scot. 56 53N 7 30w
23 Sandringham, England 52 49N 0 30E
80 Sandstone, Australia 27 55s 119 25E
91 Sandusky, U.S.A. 41 25N 82 45w
49 Sandviken, Sweden 60 38N 16 58E
23 Sandwich, England 51 16N 1 22E
23 Sandy, England 52 8N 0 18w
82 Sandy, C., Australia 24 45s 152 30E
64 Sandy Desert, Pakistan 28 0N 65 0E
91 Sanford, U.S.A. 28 48N 81 27w
88 Sanford, Mt., Alaska 62 5N 143 30w
64 Sangamner, India 19 35N 74 10E
61 Sangatolon, U.S.S.R. 61 50N 149 30E
68 Sangihe Is., Indonesia 3 57N 125 14E
64 Sangli, India 16 55N 74 25E
74 Sangmelina, Cameroon 2 57N 12 1E
37 Sangonera, R., Spain 37 40N 2 0w
90 Sangre de Cristo Ra., U.S.A.
37 30N 105 20w
94 Sangre Grande, Trinidad 10 36N 61 8w
74 Sangwa, Zaïre 5 30s 26 5E
74 Sankuru, R., Zaïre 4 0s 21 0E
37 Sanlúcar la Mayor, Spain 36 46N 6 21w
37 Sanlúcar de Barrameda, Spain
36 40N 6 28w
47 Sanok, Poland 49 35N 22 14E
31 Sanquhar, Scotland 55 22N 3 55w
72 Sansanné-Mango, Togo 10 28N 0 25E
94 Santa Ana, Salvador 14 0N 89 35w
90 Santa Ana, U.S.A. 33 40N 117 48w
90 Santa Barbara, U.S.A. 34 30N 119 40w
90 Santa Barbara Is., U.S.A.
33 15N 118 30w
90 Santa Blanca Pk., U.S.A.
33 20N 105 45w
90 Santa Catalina I., U.S.A.
33 10N 119 0w
99 Santa Catarina I., Brazil 27 45s 48 20w
95 Santa Clara, Cuba 22 30N 79 40w
90 Santa Clara, U.S.A. 37 22N 122 3w
98 Santa Cruz, Bolivia 17 50s 63 26w
72 Santa Cruz, Canary Is. 28 25N 16 19w
90 Santa Cruz, U.S.A. 36 57N 122 0w
90 Santa Cruz I., U.S.A. 34 5N 119 50w
81 Santa Cruz Is., Pac. Oc. 10 20s 168 0E
94 Santa Eugenia, Pt., Mex. 27 50N 115 5w
99 Santa Fé, Argentina 31 40s 60 45w
90 Santa Fe, U.S.A. 35 40N 105 50w
99 Santa Inés I., Chile 54 0s 73 0w
74 Santa Isabel, Equatorial Guinea
3 45N 8 50E
99 Santa Maria, Brazil 29 30s 53 40w
90 Santa Maria, U.S.A. 34 50N 120 28w
41 Santa Maria di Leuca, C., Italy
39 50N 18 23E
95 Santa Marta, Colombia 11 13N 74 12w
95 Santa Marta, Sa. Nevada de, mts.,
Colombia 11 0N 73 0w
90 Santa Monica, U.S.A. 34 5N 118 31w
99 Santa Rosa, Argentina 36 35s 64 0w
94 Santa Rosa, Honduras 14 50N 88 45w
90 Santa Rosa, U.S.A. 38 25N 122 45w
94 Santa Rosalia, Mexico 27 10N 112 32w
66 Santai, China 31 20N 104 30E
37 Santander, Spain 43 28N 3 52w
98 Santarém, Brazil 3 12s 54 30w
37 Santarém, Portugal 39 17N 8 43w
91 Santee, R., U.S.A. 33 30N 80 15w
99 Santiago, Chile 33 35s 70 40w
95 Santiago, Dominican Republic
19 25N 70 40w
37 Santiago, Spain 42 54N 8 31w
95 Santiago de Cuba, Cuba 20 5N 75 48w
99 Santiago del Estero, Arg. 27 45s 64 27w
74 Santo Antonio do Zaire, Angola
5 50s 12 10E
98 Santo Antonio Falls, Brazil 9 0s 64 0w
95 Santo Domingo, Dominican Republic
18 32N 69 50w
37 Santona, Spain 43 28N 3 29w
99 Santos, Brazil 24 0s 46 10w
67 Santuaho, China 26 50N 119 50E
74 Sanza Pombo, Angola 7 16s 15 5E
99 São Borja, Brazil 28 30s 56 0w
98 São Francisco R., Brazil 8 45s 40 0w
98 São Luiz (Maranhao), Brazil
2 45s 44 10w
98 Sao Manuel R., Brazil 11 0s 55 35w
99 São Paulo, & st., Brazil 23 35s 46 30w
98 São Roque, C., Brazil 5 0s 35 0w
74 São Salvador do Congo, Angola
6 30s 14 25E
99 São Sebastião I., Brazil 24 0s 45 30w
99 São Tomé, C., de, Brazil 22 0s 41 10w
43 Saône, R., France 46 10N 3 50E
42 Saône-et-Loire, Dept., Fr. 46 42N 4 25E
72 Sapele, Nigeria 5 50N 5 40E
67 Sapporo, Japan 43 1N 141 15E
73 Saqota, Ethiopia 12 30N 38 45E
41 Sar Planina, Mts., Y-slav. 42 0N 20 45E
41 Sarajevo, Yugoslavia 43 56N 18 46E
63 Sarakhs, U.S.S.R. 36 35N 61 2E
65 Sarangarh, India 21 30N 82 57E
52 Saransk, U.S.S.R. 54 13N 45 5E
50 Sarapul, U.S.S.R. 56 35N 53 47E
91 Sarasota, U.S.A. 27 15N 82 29w
91 Saratoga Springs, U.S.A. 43 6N 73 50w
52 Saratov, U.S.S.R. 51 35N 45 59E
68 Saravane, Laos 15 35N 106 25E
68 Sarawak, St., Malaysia 2 40N 113 15E
65 Sarda, R., India 28 55N 80 30E
72 Sardalas, Libya 25 48N 10 40E
40 Sardinia, I., Italy 40 20N 9 5E
63 Sardarshahr, India 28 30N 74 30E
48 Sarektjakko, Mt., Nor. 67 30N 17 30E
50 Sarema, I., U.S.S.R. 58 20N 22 45E
45 Sargans, Switzerland 47 4N 9 30E
64 Sargodha, Pakistan 32 10N 72 35E
60 Sargumei, U.S.S.R. 45 20N 74 53E
82 Sarina, Australia 21 22s 149 13E
43 Sarlat, France 44 52N 1 10E
99 Sarmiento, Argentina 45 30s 69 0w
45 Sarnen, Switzerland 46 54N 8 14E
92 Sarnia, Canada 43 0N 82 30w
47 Sarny, U.S.S.R. 51 18N 26 40E
41 Saros, G. of, Turkey 41 37N 26 35E
49 Sarpsborg, Norway 59 16N 11 12E
45 Sarrebourg, France 48 44N 7 2E
43 Sartène, Corsica, France 41 38N 8 55E
42 Sarthe, Dépt., France 48 5N 0 3E
60 Sartynya, U.S.S.R. 63 25N 63 7E
63 Sarur, Oman 23 20N 58 7E
42 Sarzeau, France 47 30N 2 50w
65 Sasaram, India 24 56N 84 0E
67 Sasebo, Japan 33 6N 129 50E
64 Saser, Mt., Kashmir 35 0N 77 45E
88 Saskatchewan, Prov., Can. 54 0N 106 0w
88 Saskatchewan R., Can. 53 20N 104 30w
88 Saskatoon, Canada 52 10N 106 38w
61 Saskylakh, U.S.S.R. 72 0N 114 40E
61 Sasnovka, U.S.S.R. 54 20N 109 50E
52 Sasovo, U.S.S.R. 54 25N 41 55E
72 Sassandra, & R., Ivory Coast
5 0N 6 0w
40 Sassari, Italy 40 45N 8 35E
46 Sassnitz, Germany 54 33N 13 35E
47 Sasyk, L., U.S.S.R. 45 32N 29 12E
72 Satadougou, Mali 12 40N 11 25w
64 Satara, India 17 50N 74 0E
64 Satmala Hills, Andhra Pradesh, India
19 30N 78 30E
64 Satmala Hills, Maharashtra, India
20 20N 74 30E
65 Satna, India 24 40N 80 50E
47 Sátoraljaújhely, Hungary 48 25N 21 40E
64 Satpura Hills, India 22 0N 77 0E
47 Satu Mare, Hungary 47 50N 23 0E
48 Saudharkrókur, Iceland 65 45N 19 37w
62 Saudi Arabia, S.W. Asia 25 0N 45 0E
44 Sauer, R., Luxembourg 49 51N 6 17E
43 Saulieu, France 47 20N 4 15E
92 Sault Ste. Marie, Canada 46 35N 84 22w
91 Sault Ste. Marie, U.S.A. 46 30N 84 24w
42 Saumur, France 47 18N 0 10w
48 Saurbœr, Iceland 64 21N 21 35w
40 Sava, R., Yugoslavia 46 14N 14 20E
84 Savaii I., Samoa (Inset)
72 Savalou, Dahomey 8 0N 2 9E
95 Savanna la Mar., Jamaica 18 14N 78 6w
91 Savannah, & R., U.S.A. 32 0N 81 5w
68 Savannakhet, Laos 16 35N 105 0E
75 Save, R., Mozambique 21 16s 34 0E
51 Saveh, Iran 35 0N 50 10E
72 Savelugu, Ghana 9 38N 0 4w
43 Saverne, France 48 40N 7 15E
43 Savigliano, Italy 44 40N 7 40E
42 Savoie, Dépt., France 45 33N 6 20E
40 Savona, Italy 44 21N 8 32E
68 Sawah Lunto, Indon. 0 30s 100 48E
64 Sawai Madhopur, India 26 5N 76 22E
67 Sawara, Japan 35 58N 140 36E
90 Sawatch Ra., U.S.A. 38 30N 106 30w
23 Sawbridgeworth, Eng. 51 49N 0 10E
33 Sawel, Mt., N. Ireland 54 47N 7 2w
73 Sawknah, Libya 29 10N 16 0E
75 Sawmills, Rhodesia 19 30s 28 2E
68 Sawu I., Indonesia 10 30s 122 0E
23 Saxmundham, England 52 13N 1 29E
72 Say, Niger 12 57N 2 25E
61 Sayan Mts., U.S.S.R. 54 0N 98 0E
63 Sayda (Sidon), Lebanon 33 33N 35 21E
66 Saynshand, Mongolia 45 0N 110 8E
92 Sayre, Pa., U.S.A. 41 57N 76 35w
41 Sazan, Albania 40 30N 19 20E
46 Sazava, R., Cz-slov. 49 42N 15 10E
64 Sazin, Kashmir 35 35N 73 25E
26 Scafell Pikes, England 54 28N 3 13w
27 Scalby & Ness, C., Eng. 54 18N 0 24w
32 Scalloway, Scotland 60 7N 1 22w
32 Scalpay I., Inner Hebrides 57 18N 6 0w
32 Scalpay I., Outer Hebrides, Scotland
57 51N 6 40w
48 & 49 Scandinavia, Europe 65 0N 15 0E
33 Scapa Flow, Scotland 58 53N 3 2w
30 Scarba I., Scotland 56 10N 5 42w
27 Scarborough, England 54 13N 0 25w
34 Scariff, Ireland 52 55N 8 30w
32 Scarp, I., Scotland 58 1N 7 8w
34 Scattery I., Ireland 52 38N 9 30w
45 Schaffhausen & Canton, Switzerland
47 43N 8 38E
89 Schefferville, Canada 54 50N 66 55w
44 Schelde, R., Belgium 51 10N 4 15E
93 Schenectady, U.S.A. 42 47N 73 55w
44 Scheveningen, Neth. 52 7N 4 20E
44 Schiedam, Netherlands 51 55N 4 24E
31 Schiehallion, Scotland 56 39N 4 9w
44 Schiermonnikoog, Neth. 53 30N 6 15E
40 Schio, Italy 45 40N 11 20E
44 Schleiden, Germany 50 32N 6 26E
46 Schleswig, Germany 54 50N 9 30E
46 Schleswig Holstein, Länd, Germany
54 30N 9 36E
61 Schmidt I., U.S.S.R. 81 0N 91 0E
45 Schorndorf, Germany 48 47N 9 32E
44 Schoten, Belgium 51 15N 4 30E
44 Schouwen I., Neth. 51 41N 3 53E
45 Schramberg, Germany 48 13N 8 23E
92 Schreiber, Canada 48 50N 87 20w
45 Schwabischer Alb (Swabian Jura), mts.,
Germany 48 30N 9 30E
45 Schwäbisch Gmünd, Germany
48 48N 9 47E
68 Schwaner Ra., Indonesia 0 35s 112 30E
67 Schwangcheng, China 45 30N 126 20E
45 Schwarzwald (Black Forest), Germany
48 15N 8 10E
45 Schweinfurt, Germany 50 3N 10 12E
76 Schweizer Reneke, S. Africa
27 10s 25 20E
45 Schwenningen, Germany 48 4N 8 30E
45 Schwyz, & Cn., Switz. 47 2N 8 39E
40 Sciacca, Italy 37 30N 13 0E
40 Scilla, Italy 38 18N 15 44E
24 Scilly, Isles of, England 49 55N 6 20w
83 Scone, Australia 31 58s 150 57E
31 Scone, Scotland 56 25N 3 24w
29 Scotland, U.K. 56 0N 4 0w
100 Scott, Antarctica 78 15s 167 0E
90 Scottsbluff, U.S.A. 41 55N 103 37w
83 Scottsdale, Australia 41 9s 147 30E
36 Scrabby, Ireland 53 53N 7 32w
91 Scranton, U.S.A. 41 25N 75 30w
31 Scremerston, England 55 44N 1 59w
30 Scridain L., Scotland 56 22N 6 10w
27 Scunthorpe, England 53 33N 0 35w
23 Seaford, England 50 46N 0 7E
32 Seaforth L., Scotland 57 53N 6 38w
27 Seaham, England 54 50N 1 20w
26 Seaton, Cumb., England 54 41N 3 32w
24 Seaton, Devon, England 50 42N 3 3w
90 Seattle, U.S.A. 47 45N 122 20w
94 Sebastien Vizcaino B., Mexico
28 30N 115 0w
51 Sebin Karahisar, Turkey 40 20N 38 21E
44 Seclin, France 50 33N 3 2E
73 Second Cataract of Nile, Sudan
21 45N 31 12E
84 Secretary I., N.Z. 45 13s 166 58E
64 Secunderabad, India 17 40N 78 35E
91 Sedalia, U.S.A. 38 40N 93 20w
83 Sedan, Australia 34 33s 139 20E
43 Sedan, France 49 40N 5 0E
26 Sedbergh, England 54 18N 2 35w
84 Seddon, N.Z. 41 42s 174 5E
84 Seddonville, N.Z. 41 30s 172 0E
27 Sedgefield, England 54 40N 1 27w
72 Sedihou, Sénégal 12 50N 15 30w
63 Sedom, Israel 31 4N 35 24E
60 Sedov Pk., U.S.S.R. 73 30N 54 10E
75 Seeheim, S.W. Africa 26 48s 17 50E
50 Seg L., U.S.S.R. 63 20N 33 20E
72 Ségou, Mali 13 28N 6 16w
37 Segovia, Spain 40 58N 4 7w
37 Segre, R., Spain 42 10N 1 25E
72 Séguéla, Ivory Coast 8 5N 6 30w
37 Segura, R., Spain 38 8N 0 38w
64 Sehore, India 22 39N 77 4E
30 Seil I., Scotland 56 18N 5 37w
48 Seiland, Norway 70 30N 23 15E
61 Seimchan, U.S.S.R. 62 50N 152 30E
48 Seinäjoki, Finland 62 47N 22 58E
42 Seine, R., France 48 57N 2 25E
42 Seine-et-Marne, Dépt., Fr. 48 53N 3 0E
42 Seine-Maritime, Dépt., Fr. 49 40N 1 5E
42 Seine-St Denis, Dépt., Fr. 49 0N 2 30E
76 Sekoma, Botswana 24 35s 23 55E
72 Sekondi-Takoradi, Ghana 4 56N 1 43w
27 Selby, England 53 48N 1 5w
40 Sele, R., Italy 40 31N 15 0E
66 Selenge Mörön, R., China 49 0N 102 0E
43 Sélestat, France 48 18N 7 30E
72 Sélibaby, Mauritania 15 20N 12 15w
73 Selima Oasis, Sudan 21 20N 29 35E
88 Selkirk, Canada 50 8N 96 40w
*31 Selkirk, & Co., Scotland 55 34N 2 51w
88 Selkirk Ra., Canada 51 0N 117 0w
91 Selma, U.S.A. 32 30N 86 59w
23 Selsey, England 50 44N 0 47w
23 Selsey Bill, England 50 43N 0 48w
75 Selukwe, Rhodesia 19 37s 30 0E
82 Selwyn, Australia 21 37s 140 32E
41 Seman, R., Albania 40 50N 19 50E
68 Semarang, Indonesia 6 55s 110 40E
91 Seminole, U.S.A. 35 10N 96 45w
60 Semipalatinsk, U.S.S.R. 50 30N 80 20E
60 Semiyarsk, U.S.S.R. 51 25N 78 30E
46 Semmering P., Austria 47 39N 15 50E

* *County incorporated within the region of Borders*

62 Semna, Sudan 20 28N 31 7E
44 Semois, R., Belgium 49 48N 5 12E
45 Sempach, Switzerland 47 9N 8 12E
43 Semur, France 47 30N 4 20E
75 Senanga, Zambia 15 59s 23 15E
67 Sendai, Japan 38 15N 141 0E
92 Seneca, L., U.S.A. 42 30N 77 0w
72 Sénégal, Africa 14 45N 15 0w
72 Senegal, R., Mali 13 55N 11 0w
70 Senegambia, Dist., West Africa
15 0N 14 0w
76 Senekal, O.F.S. 28 20s 27 40E
65 Senge Khambab (Indus), R., Tibet
32 30N 81 0E
40 Senigallia, Italy 43 43N 13 12E
48 Senja I., Norway 69 25N 17 30E
43 Senlis, France 49 10N 2 35E
98 Sena Madureira, Brazil 9 0s 68 45w
73 Sennar, Sudan 13 42N 33 57E
89 Senneterre, Canada 48 25N 77 15w
43 Sens, France 48 12N 3 18E
41 Senta, Yugoslavia 45 59N 20 1E
37 Séo de Urgel, Spain 42 18N 1 28E
67 Seoul, Korea 37 49N 127 15E
82 Sepik, R., Terr. of New Guinea
4 0s 143 0E
89 Sept Iles, Canada 50 10N 63 30w
90 Sequoia National Park, U.S.A.
36 20N 118 30w
44 Seraing, Belgium 50 36N 5 33E
65 Serampore, India 22 44N 88 30E
68 Serang, Indonesia 5 55s 106 15E
41 Serbia Fed. Unit, Yugoslavia
43 20N 21 20E
52 Serdobsk, U.S.S.R. 52 33N 44 8E
68 Seremban, Malaya 2 35N 102 10E
75 Serenje, Zambia 13 2s 30 50E
41 Sereth, R., *see* Siret, R.
99 Sergipe, st., Brazil 10 40s 37 30w
68 Seria, Malaysia 4 30N 114 25E
41 Serifos, I., Greece 37 11N 24 30E
60 Serny Zavod, U.S.S.R. 40 5N 59 10E
60 Serov, U.S.S.R. 59 45N 60 20E
75 Serowe, Botswana 22 19s 27 1E
75 Serpa Pinto, Angola 14 45s 17 59E
98 Serpents Mouth, Ven. 10 0N 61 30w
52 Serpukhov, U.S.S.R. 54 52N 37 40E
75 Serra da Bandeira, Angola 15 0s 13 3
41 Serrai, Greece 41 0N 23 30E
43 Serres, France 44 22N 5 42E
75 Serule, Botswana 21 52s 27 32E
75 Sesfontein, S.W. Africa 19 7s 13 39E
37 Sestao, Spain 43 23N 3 5w
43 Sète, France 43 21N 3 40E
72 Sétif, Algeria 36 10N 5 23E
72 Settat, Morocco 33 0N 7 35w
74 Setté Cama, Gabon 2 32s 9 57E
26 Settle, England 54 4N 2 18w
37 Setubal, & B. of, Port. 38 33N 8 53w
88 Seul, L., Canada 50 25N 92 30w
62 Sevan L., U.S.S.R. 40 15N 45 20E
51 Sevastopol, U.S.S.R. 44 37N 33 30E
34 Seven Heads, C., Ireland 51 32N 8 40
23 Sevenoaks, England 51 16N 0 12E
43 Sévérac, France 44 20N 3 5E
24 Severn Beach, England 51 34N 2 39w
22 Severn R., England 51 40N 2 35w
22 Severn Stoke, England 52 5N 2 13w
61 Severnaya Zemlya, U.S.S.R.
79 30N 97 0E
61 Severo-Yeniseisky, U.S.S.R.
60 25N 93 25E
50 Severodvinsk, U.S.S.R. 64 45N 40 0E
50 Severouralsk, U.S.S.R. 60 10N 59 30E
90 Sevier, R. & L., U.S.A. 39 0N 113 20
37 Seville, Spain 37 27N 5 58w
88 Seward, Alaska 60 0N 149 30w
5 Seychelle Is., Indian Oc. 4 30s 55 30E
48 Seydisfjordur, Iceland 65 15N 13 52w
83 Seymour, Australia 36 58s 145 10E
43 Sézanne, France 48 40N 3 45E
47 Sfântu Gheorghe, Rum. 45 50N 25 50
73 Sfax, Tunisia 34 49N 10 42E
44 's Gravenhage, Netherland, *see* The
Hague
32 Sgurr Mor, Mt., Scotland 57 42N 5 0
32 Sgurr na Ciche, Scotland 57 0N 5 29
32 Sgurr na Lapaich Mt., Scotland
57 21N 5 14w
65 Shaba Gomba, China 32 10N 89 0E
75 Shabani, Rhodesia 20 15s 30 14E
62 Shabicha, Iraq 30 52N 43 45E
100 Shackleton, Antarctica 79 0s 39 0w
60 Shadrinsk, U.S.S.R. 56 15N 64 0E
22 Shaftesbury, England 51 1N 2 12w
64 Shahgarh, India 27 15N 69 50E
73 Shahhat (Cyrene), Libya 32 40N 21 3
63 Shahr-i-Zabul, Afghanistan 31 0N 61 2
64 Shahrig, Pakistan 30 12N 67 35E
62 Shahriza, Iran 32 0N 51 57E
64 Shajapur, India 23 20N 76 15E
52 Shakhty, U.S.S.R. 47 40N 40 10E
72 Shaki, Nigeria 8 41N 3 21E
74 Shala, L., Ethiopia 7 30N 38 30E
73 Shallal, El, Egypt 24 0N 33 0E
66 Shamo, Desert, *see* Gobi Desert
74 Shamo, L., Ethiopia 5 50N 37 40E
75 Shamva, Rhodesia 17 15s 31 40E
65 Shan State, Burma 21 5N 100 0E
34 Shanagolden, Ireland 52 35N 9 6w
72 Shanga, Nigeria 11 1N 4 40E
75 Shangani, R., Rhodesia 18 37s 28 0E
67 Shanghai, China 31 15N 121 35E
66 Shangiao, China 28 20N 116 15E
66 Shangkiu, China 34 35N 116 0E

37 Spain, Europe 39 50N 3 40W
83 Spalding, Australia 33 27S 138 30E
23 Spalding, England 52 47N 0 9W
46 Spandau, Germany 52 35N 13 7E
90 Spanish Fork, U.S.A. 40 6N 111 40W
††72 Spanish Sahara, Africa 25 0N 13 0W
95 Spanish Town, Jamaica, W.I. 18 0N 76 59W
90 Sparks, U.S.A. 39 30N 119 37W
91 Spartanburg, U.S.A. 34 58N 81 57W
41 Sparti, Greece 37 7N 22 18E
40 Spartivento, C., Italy 38 56N 8 57E
40 Spartivento, C., Italy 37 58N 16 7E
67 Spassk-Dalni, U.S.S.R. 44 45N 132 55E
41 Spatha, C., Greece 35 40N 23 50E
33 Spean Bridge, Scotland 56 53N 4 55W
94 Speightstown, Barbados, W.I. 13 15N 59 8W
83 Spencer, C., Australia 35 20S 136 50E
83 Spencer G., Australia 34 0S 137 0E
27 Spennymoor, England 54 43N 1 35W
84 Spenser Mts., N.Z. 42 0S 172 30E
36 Sperrin Mts., N. Ireland 54 50N 7 5W
46 Spessart Mts., Germany 50 10N 9 25E
33 Spey, R., Scotland 57 40N 3 5W
45 Speyer, Germany 49 22N 8 28E
34 Spiddal, Ireland 53 14N 9 19W
40 Spinazzola, Italy 41 0N 16 5E
23 Spithead, England 50 43N 0 56W
100 Spitsbergen (Svalbard), Arctic Ocean 80 0N 20 0E
40 Split, Yugoslavia 43 32N 16 30E
45 Splugen Pass, Switzerland 46 30N 9 20E
90 Spokane, U.S.A. 47 48N 118 25W
40 Spoleto, Italy 42 46N 12 47E
41 Sporades Is., N., Greece 39 20N 24 0E
68 Spratly I., S. China Sea 8 45N 111 30E
46 Spree, R., Germany 51 30N 14 30E
45 Spremberg, Germany 51 33N 14 21E
75 Springbok, S. Africa 29 48S 17 57E
91 Springfield, Ill., U.S.A. 39 23N 89 42W
93 Springfield, Mass., U.S.A. 42 0N 73 0W
91 Springfield, Ohio, U.S.A. 39 42N 84 15W
90 Springfield, Ore., U.S.A. 44 0N 123 0W
93 Springhill, Canada 45 45N 64 0W
76 Springs, Trans., S. Afr. 26 14S 28 21E
82 Springsure, Australia 24 2S 148 0E
90 Springville, Utah, U.S.A. 40 13N 111 35W
27 Sproatley, England 53 46N 0 9W
75 Spungabera, Mozam. 20 28S 32 47E
27 Spurn Hd., England 53 37N 0 8E
88 Squamish, Canada 49 45N 123 10W
40 Squillace, Italy 38 50N 16 26E
61 Sredinny Ra., U.S.S.R. 57 0N 159 0E
61 Sredne Kolymsk, U.S.S.R. 67 20N 153 25E
61 Sredne Tambovskoye, U.S.S.R. 50 50N 137 50E
61 Sredne Vilyuisk, U.S.S.R. 63 50N 123 10E
41 Sremska Mitrovica, Yugoslavia 44 59N 19 35E
68 Srepok, R., Khmer Rep. & Vietnam 13 30N 107 0E
61 Sretensk, U.S.S.R. 52 10N 117 50E
64 Sri Lanka, Asia 8 0N 80 45E
64 Srinagar, Kashmir 34 5N 74 55E
40 Srnetica, Yugoslavia 44 25N 16 35E
49 Stade, Germany 53 38N 9 31E
30 Staffa, I., Scotland 56 26N 6 22W
22 Stafford & Co., England 52 40N 2 4W
27 Staindrop, England 54 35N 1 49W
23 Staines, England 51 25N 0 30W
27 Stainforth, England 53 37N 0 59W
26 Stainmore Forest, Eng. 54 29N 2 5W
52 Stalingrad, see Volgograd
52 Stalino, U.S.S.R., see Donetsk
26 Stalybridge, England 53 29N 2 3W
82 Stamford, Australia 21 15S 143 46E
93 Stamford, U.S.A. 41 5N 73 30W
27 Stamford Bridge, Eng. 54 0N 0 54W
75 Standerton, S. Africa 27 0S 29 30E
26 Standish, England 53 35N 2 39W
76 Stanger, S. Africa 29 22S 31 15E
26 Stanhope, England 54 45N 2 0W
41 Stanke Dimitrov, Bulgaria 42 27N 23 9E
83 Stanley, Australia 40 45S 145 20E
27 Stanley, England 54 53N 1 42W
74 Stanleyville, see Kisangani
26 Stanlow, England 53 16N 2 45W
27 Stannington, England 55 7N 1 41W
61 Stanovoy Ra., U.S.S.R. 55 0N 130 0E
83 Stanthorpe, Australia 28 40S 152 0E
88 Stanton, Canada 69 40N 128 40W
27 Stapleford, England 52 56N 1 16W
41 Stara-Zagora, Bulgaria 42 22N 25 41E
46 Stargard, Poland 53 19N 15 1E
52 Staritsa, U.S.S.R. 56 33N 34 59E
47 Starogard, Poland 53 59N 18 30E
47 Staroskonstantinov, U.S.S.R. 49 45N 27 8E
24 Start Bay, England 50 14N 3 35W
24 Start Pt., England 50 14N 3 38W
61 Stary Kheidzhan, U.S.S.R. 60 0N 144 50E
99 Staten I., (I. de los Estados), Argentina 54 50S 64 30W
91 Staunton, U.S.A. 38 11N 79 0W
49 Stavanger, Norway 58 58N 5 32E
27 Staveley, England 53 16N 1 20W
44 Stavelot, Belgium 50 25N 5 56E
44 Staveren, Netherlands 52 53N 5 25E
49 Stavern, Norway 59 0N 10 3E
50 Stavropol, U.S.S.R. 45 5N 42 0E
†† *Renamed Western Sahara*

83 Stawell, Australia 37 0S 142 48E
74 Stefanie, L., see Chew Bahir
45 Steffisburg, Switzerland 46 48N 7 40E
48 Steinkjer, Norway 63 59N 11 40E
76 Stella, South Africa 26 35S 24 45E
93 Stellarton, Canada 45 32N 62 45W
75 Stellenbosch, S. Africa 34 0S 18 55E
40 Stelvio Pass, Italy 46 32N 10 20E
43 Stenay, France 49 30N 5 15E
46 Stendal, Germany 52 38N 11 50E
31 Stenhousemuir, Scotland 56 2N 3 46W
51 Stepnoi, U.S.S.R., see Elista
51 Stepnoi Divnoe, U.S.S.R. 46 0N 43 20E
60 Stepnyak, U.S.S.R. 53 5N 70 55E
76 Sterkstroom, S. Africa 31 32S 26 32E
90 Sterling, U.S.A. 40 38N 103 15W
60 Sterlitamak, U.S.S.R. 53 34N 55 47E
46 Stettin, see Szczecin
88 Stettler, Canada 52 20N 112 45W
91 Steubenville, U.S.A. 40 24N 80 37W
23 Stevenage, England 51 54N 0 11W
91 Stevens Point, U.S.A. 44 40N 89 35W
30 Stevenston, Scotland 55 38N 4 45W
84 Stewart I., N.Z. 47 0S 168 0E
88 Stewart River, Canada 63 0N 139 30W
30 Stewarton, Scotland 55 40N 4 30W
36 Stewartstown, N. Ireland 54 35N 6 40W
46 Steyr, Austria 48 1N 14 21E
76 Steytlerville, S. Africa 33 20S 24 16E
88 Stikine, R., Canada 57 40N 132 0W
91 Stillwater, Minn., U.S.A. 45 2N 92 54W
91 Stillwater, Okla., U.S.A. 36 5N 97 7W
41 Stip, Yugoslavia 41 41N 22 10E
*31 Stirling & Co., Scotland 56 7N 3 55W
80 Stirling Ra., Australia 34 27S 118 0E
31 Stobo, Scotland 55 38N 3 18W
46 Stockerau, Austria 48 25N 16 15E
49 Stockholm, & Co., Sweden 59 21N 18 3E
26 Stockport, England 53 25N 2 10W
27 Stocksbridge, England 53 30N 1 36W
27 Stockton on Tees, Eng. 54 34N 1 20W
90 Stockton, U.S.A. 37 58N 121 18W
32 Stoer, Pt. of, Scotland 58 15N 5 22W
23 Stoke Mandeville, Eng. 51 46N 0 47W
26 Stoke-on-Trent, Eng. 53 2N 2 12W
27 Stokesley, England 54 27N 1 12W
48 Stokkseyri, Iceland 63 47N 20 52W
41 Stolac, Yugoslavia 43 5N 18 0E
45 Stolberg, Germany 50 47N 6 12E
61 Stolbovoi, I., U.S.S.R. 74 10N 135 30E
61 Stolbovoye, U.S.S.R. 64 50N 153 50E
26 Stone, England 52 54N 2 9W
33 Stonehaven, Scotland 56 58N 2 12W
22 Stonehouse, England 51 45N 2 18W
31 Stonehouse, Scotland 55 42N 4 0W
88 Stonewall, Canada 50 10N 97 20W
61 Stony Tunguska, R., U.S.S.R. 62 0N 97 0E
48 Storuman L., Sweden 65 10N 16 30E
48 Stora Lulevatten, Sweden 67 10N 19 30E
48 Stora Sjöfallet, Sweden 67 30N 18 30E
48 Storavan, L., Sweden 66 0N 18 30E
49 Store Bælt, Denmark 55 30N 11 0E
48 Storen, Norway 63 0N 10 20E
48 Storisandur, Dist., Ice. 65 10N 20 0W
83 Storm B., Australia 42 10S 147 22E
32 Stornoway, Scotland 58 12N 6 21W
48 Storolfshvoll, Iceland 63 48N 20 15W
47 Storozhinets, U.S.S.R. 48 14N 24 45E
48 Storsjön L., Sweden 63 15N 14 22E
23 Stort, R., England 51 56N 0 11E
48 Storuman, L., Sweden 65 15N 17 0E
22 Stour, R. (Dorset), Eng. 50 52N 2 10W
22 Stour, R. (Essex), Eng. 51 57N 1 0E
23 Stour R. (Suffolk), Eng. 52 5N 0 40E
22 Stourbridge, England 52 25N 2 9W
22 Stourport, England 52 21N 2 17W
22 Stow-on-the-Wold, Eng. 51 55N 1 42W
23 Stowmarket, England 52 11N 0 59E
36 Strabane, N. Ireland 54 49N 7 25W
33 Strachan, Scotland 57 1N 2 31W
30 Strachur, Scotland 56 9N 5 3W
35 Stradbally, Laois, Ire. 53 2N 7 10W
35 Stradbally, Waterford, Ire. 52 7N 7 28W
83 Strahan, Australia 42 5S 145 15E
48 Stralsund, Germany 54 18N 12 58E
76 Strand, South Africa 34 5S 18 45E
36 Strangford, & L., N. Ire. 54 21N 5 43W
36 Stranorlar, Ireland 54 48N 7 47W
30 Stranraer, Scotland 54 54N 5 1W
43 Strasbourg, France 48 35N 7 46E
92 Stratford, Canada 43 20N 81 12W
84 Stratford, New Zealand 39 22S 174 20E
22 Stratford-on-Avon, Eng. 52 11N 1 42W
33 Strath Dearn, Scotland 57 26N 4 10W
31 Strath Earn, Scotland 56 20N 3 50W
32 Strath Halladale, Scot. 58 30N 3 51W
33 Strath Spey, Scotland 57 18N 3 32W
31 Strath Tay, Scotland 56 40N 3 40W
83 Strathalbyn, Australia 35 18S 138 59E
31 Strathaven, Scotland 55 40N 4 3W
33 Strathbogie, Dist., Scot. 57 25N 2 45W
33 Strathdon, Scotland 57 12N 3 4W
31 Strathmiglo, Scotland 56 16N 3 15W
33 Strathmore, Dist., Scot. 56 40N 3 10W
33 Strathmore R., Scotland 58 25N 4 40W
33 Strathpeffer, Scotland 57 37N 4 30W
24 Stratton, England 50 49N 4 31W
22 Stratton St. Margaret, England 51 35N 1 45W
48 Straumnes, Iceland 66 27N 23 7W
80 Streaky B., Australia 32 37S 134 10E
24 Street, England 51 7N 2 43W
61 Strelka, U.S.S.R. 58 5N 93 5E
* *County incorporated within the region of Central*

43 Stresa, Italy 45 55N 8 30E
27 Stretford, England 53 27N 2 19W
33 Strichen, Scotland 57 35N 2 5W
36 Strokestown, Ireland 53 47N 8 9W
40 Stromboli, I. Italy 38 50N 15 17E
32 Stromeferry, Scotland 57 20N 5 37W
33 Stromness, Scotland 58 59N 3 20W
48 Ströms Vattudal L., Swed. 64 0N 15 30E
49 Strömstad, Sweden 58 59N 11 10E
48 Strömsund, Sweden 63 52N 15 39E
33 Stronsay F. & I., Scot. 59 3N 2 35W
23 Strood, England 51 23N 0 30E
22 Stroud, England 51 45N 2 11W
49 Struer, Denmark 56 30N 8 35E
41 Struma, R., Bulgaria 41 50N 23 14E
25 Strumble Hd., Wales 52 2N 5 4W
41 Strumica, Yugoslavia 41 30N 22 41E
47 Stry, U.S.S.R. 49 18N 23 50E
80 Stuart Ra., Australia 29 30S 135 30E
68 Stung-Treng, Khmer Rep. 13 42N 105 55E
80 Sturt, R., Australia 19 30S 127 40E
76 Stutterheim, S. Africa 32 33S 27 28E
45 Stuttgart, Germany 48 49N 9 15E
91 Stuttgart, U.S.A. 34 32N 91 32W
48 Stykkisholmur, Iceland 65 5N 22 45W
47 Styr, R., U.S.S.R. 51 5N 25 40E
46 Styria, Prov., Austria 47 18N 15 0E
62 Suakin, Sudan 19 30N 37 25E
66 Süanhwa, China 40 40N 115 5E
65 Subarnarekha R., India 22 30N 86 45E
41 Subotica, Yugoslavia 46 2N 19 33E
47 Suceava, Rumania 47 32N 26 20E
67 Suchan, U.S.S.R. 43 5N 133 0E
66 Süchow, Kiangsu, China 34 17N 117 15E
34 Suck, R., Ireland 53 25N 8 12W
98 Sucre, Bolivia 19 0S 65 20W
73 Sudan, Africa 15 30N 31 0E
70 Sudan Reg, Africa 11 0N 8 0E
92 Sudbury, Canada 46 35N 81 10W
22 Sudbury, Suffolk, Eng. 52 3N 0 45E
73 Sudd, Reg., Sudan 8 0N 30 0E
46 Sudeten Highlands, Ger. 50 0N 17 20E
37 Sueca, Spain 39 13N 0 20W
73 Suez, Egypt 30 0N 32 30E
73 Suez Canal, Egypt 30 30N 32 15E
73 Suez, G. of, Egypt 29 30N 33 0E
**23 Suffolk East, Co., Eng. 52 15N 1 10E
**23 Suffolk West, Co., Eng. 52 15N 0 45E
35 Sugar Loaf, Gt., mt., Ire. 53 7N 6 10W
83 Sugarloaf Pt., Australia 32 30S 152 30E
35 Suir, R., Ireland 52 18N 7 20W
52 Sukhinichi, U.S.S.R. 54 15N 35 17E
50 Sukhona, R., U.S.S.R. 59 30N 42 0E
62 Sukhumi, U.S.S.R. 43 10N 41 5E
89 Sukkertoppen, Greenland 65 40N 53 0W
64 Sukkur, Pakistan 27 45N 68 56E
62 Sulaiyil, Saudi Arabia 20 30N 45 25E
64 Sulaiman Range, Asia 31 0N 70 10E
51 Sulaimaniya, Iran 35 32N 45 25E
68 Sulawesi, I., Indonesia 2 0S 120 0E
47 Sulina Mouth, Danube, Rumania 45 0N 29 40E
48 Sulitjelma, mt., Norway 67 2N 16 30E
98 Sullana, Peru 5 0S 80 30W
65 Sultanpur, India 26 8N 82 5E
68 Sulu Arch., Philippines 6 0N 121 0E
68 Sulu Sea, Philippines 8 0N 120 0E
73 Suluq (Soluk), Libya 31 44N 20 14E
45 Sulzbach, Germany 49 17N 7 2E
68 Sumatra, I., Indonesia 0 30N 101 0E
68 Sumba I., see Sandalwood I.
68 Sumbawa I., Indonesia 8 30S 118 0E
74 Sumbawanga, Tanzania 8 0S 31 38E
32 Sumburgh Hd., Scotland 59 53N 1 16W
41 Sumen, Bulgaria 43 17N 26 55E
35 Summerhill, Ireland 53 30N 6 44W
93 Summerside, Canada 46 25N 63 50W
46 Sumperk, Czechoslovakia 49 59N 17 0E
91 Sumter, U.S.A. 33 55N 80 17W
52 Sumy, U.S.S.R. 50 58N 34 45E
32 Sunart, Dist., Scotland 56 42N 5 30W
30 Sunart, L., Scotland 56 40N 5 50W
83 Sunbury, Australia 37 48S 144 50E
93 Sunbury, U.S.A. 40 50N 76 50W
57 Sunda Sea, Indonesia 6 30S 118 0E
68 Sunda Str., Indonesia 6 0S 105 43E
65 Sundarbans, E. Pak. 22 10N 89 30E
65 Sundargarh, India 22 10N 84 7E
27 Sunderland, England 54 55N 1 23W
23 Sundridge, England 51 15N 0 11E
48 Sundsvall, Sweden 62 21N 17 18E
23 Sunninghill, England 51 24N 0 39W
67 Suo B., Japan 33 56N 131 35E
65 Supaul, India 26 10N 86 35E
91 Superior, Wis., U.S.A. 46 40N 92 1W
92 Superior, L., N. America 47 30N 88 0W
50 Sura, R., U.S.S.R. 55 0N 46 30E
68 Surabaja, Indonesia 7 12S 112 48E
68 Surakarta, Indonesia 7 45S 110 50E
64 Suratgarh, India 29 15N 74 0W
83 Surat, Australia 27 13S 149 1E
64 Surat, India 21 12N 73 5E
68 Surat Thani, Malaya 9 5N 99 25E
44 Sure R., Luxembourg 49 50N 6 0E
60 Surgut, U.S.S.R. 61 27N 73 7E
65 Suri, India 23 55N 87 30E
64 Suriapet, India 17 5N 79 30E
96 Surinam (Netherlands Guiana), S. America 4 0N 56 0W
98 Suriname, R., Surinam 6 0N 55 0W
23 Surrey, Co., England 51 5N 0 20W
45 Sursee, Switzerland 47 12N 8 6E
73 Surt, Libya 31 10N 16 50E
92 Susquehanna, R., U.S.A. 42 0N 76 0W
** *United to form the county of Suffolk*

93 Sussex, Canada 45 42N 65 33W
23 Sussex E., Co., England 50 55N 0 16E
23 Sussex W., Co., England 50 54N 0 32W
76 Sutherland, S. Africa 32 21S 20 44E
†33 Sutherland, Co., Scotland 58 10N 4 30W
64 Sutlej, R., India 30 7N 73 10E
23 Sutton, England 51 21N 0 11W
23 Sutton Bridge, England 52 46N 0 12E
22 Sutton Coldfield, England 52 32N 1 47W
27 Sutton-in-Ashfield, Eng. 53 8N 1 15W
67 Suttsu, Japan 42 47N 140 5E
76 Suurberge, C. Prov. 33 8S 25 30E
84 Suva, Fiji Is. 18 5S 178 20E
47 Suwalki, Poland 54 6N 22 53E
63 Suweilih, Jordan 32 2N 35 50E
52 Suzdal, U.S.S.R. 56 27N 40 20E
100 Svalbard (Spitsbergen), Arctic Ocean 78 0N 15 0E
48 Svartisen, mt., Norway 66 55N 13 30E
49 Svealand, Dist., Sweden 59 55N 15 0E
49 Sveg, Sweden 62 2N 14 27E
49 Svendborg, Denmark 55 7N 10 38E
60 Sverdlovsk, U.S.S.R. 56 52N 60 32E
100 Sverdrup I., Arctic Oc. 80 0N 100 0W
50 Svir, R., U.S.S.R. 61 0N 34 0E
41 Svishtov, Bulgaria 43 36N 25 23E
61 Svobodny, U.S.S.R. 51 30N 128 5E
48 Svolvær, Norway 68 20N 14 30E
46 Swabian Jura, mts., Germany, see Schwabishe Alb.
22 Swadlincote, England 52 47N 1 34W
23 Swaffham, England 52 38N 0 40E
75 Swakopmund, S.W. Afr. 22 33S 14 35E
27 Swale, R., England 54 13N 1 28W
83 Swan Hill, Australia 35 15S 143 31E
22 Swanage, England 50 36N 1 57W
36 Swanlinbar, Ireland 54 11N 7 42W
83 Swansea, Australia 33 3S 151 35E
25 Swansea, & B., Wales 51 38N 3 57W
76 Swartberge, S. Africa 33 15S 22 0E
66 Swatow, China 23 30N 116 50E
75 Swaziland, S.E. Afr. 26 30S 31 30E
16 Sweden, Europe 63 0N 16 0E
88 Swift Current, Canada 50 20N 107 49W
36 Swilly, L. & R., Ireland 55 14N 7 33W
22 Swindon, England 51 33N 1 47W
36 Swinford, Ireland 53 55N 8 58W
46 Swinoujscie, Poland 53 54N 14 16E
26 Swinton, Lancs., Eng. 53 31N 2 21W
27 Swinton, Yorks., Eng. 53 28N 1 20W
45 Switzerland, Europe 46 50N 8 10E
35 Swords, Ireland 53 28N 6 14W
83 Sydney, Australia 33 55S 151 12E
89 Sydpröven, Greenland 60 30N 45 20W
50 Syktyvkar, U.S.S.R. 61 45N 50 40E
48 Sylarna Mt., Sweden 63 2N 12 20E
65 Sylhet, Bangladesh 24 50N 91 52E
48 Sylt, I., Denmark 55 0N 8 19E
60 Sym, U.S.S.R. 60 20N 87 55E
31 Symington, Scotland 55 35N 3 36W
22 Symonds Yat, England 51 50N 2 38W
60 Syr Darya, R., U.S.S.R. 44 40N 65 0E
40 Syracuse, see Siracusa
91 Syracuse, U.S.A. 43 0N 76 10W
62 Syria, S.W. Asia 35 0N 38 0E
62 Syrian Des., Si. Arabia 32 0N 40 0E
52 Syzran, U.S.S.R. 53 12N 48 30E
46 Szczecin, Poland 53 25N 14 31E
46 Szczecnek, Poland 53 43N 16 41E
66 Szechwan, Prov., China 30 0N 104 0E
47 Szeged, Hungary 46 17N 20 9E
47 Székesfehérvár, Hungary 47 17N 18 24E
47 Szentes, Hungary 46 39N 20 19E
67 Szeping, China 43 15N 124 15E
47 Szolnok, Hungary 47 15N 20 10E
46 Szombathely, Hungary 47 17N 16 27E

T

66 Ta Liang Shan, mts., China 28 0N 102 20E
76 Table, Mt., S. Africa 34 1S 18 27E
46 Tabor, Czechoslovakia 49 23N 14 29E
74 Tabora, Tanzania 5 0S 33 0E
72 Tabou, Ivory Coast 4 30N 7 20W
62 Tabriz, Iran 38 3N 46 24E
67 Tachima, Japan 37 9N 139 48E
68 Tacloban, Philippines 10 15N 124 55E
98 Tacna, Peru 18 5S 70 20W
90 Tacoma, U.S.A. 47 15N 122 12W
99 Tacuarembo, Uruguay 31 30S 56 0W
98 Tacutu, R., S. America 3 0N 59 40W
27 Tadcaster, England 53 54N 1 18W
72 Tademait, Plat. du, Alg. 28 28N 2 0E
60 Tadzhikistan, Rep., U.S.S.R. 39 0N 72 6E
67 Taegu, Korea 35 48N 129 30E
63 Tafa, Syria 32 44N 36 4E
37 Tafalla, Spain 42 30N 1 42W
52 Taganrog, U.S.S.R. 47 16N 38 55E
52 Taganrog Gulf, U.S.S.R. 46 50N 37 57E
35 Taghmon, Ireland 52 21N 6 43W
88 Tagish, Canada 60 20N 134 0W
37 Tagus (Tajo) R., Spain 40 40N 2 12W
68 Tahan, Mt., Malaya 4 15N 102 50E
66 Tahcheng, China 46 45N 83 10E
4 Tahiti, Pacific Ocean 17 50S 149 40W
90 Tahoe, L., U.S.A. 39 0N 120 0W
62 Tahiri, Iran 27 35N 52 20E
73 Tahta, Egypt 26 44N 31 32E
67 Tai Shan, mts., China 36 0N 118 30E
67 Taichung, Taiwan 24 10N 120 35E
62 Taif, Saudi Arabia 21 0N 41 2E
84 Taihape, New Zealand 39 42S 175 49E
60 Tailakovy, U.S.S.R. 59 20N 74 5E
† *Incorporated within the region of Highland*

83 Tailem Bend, Australia 35 12S 139 29E
62 Taima, Saudi Arabia 27 23N 39 20E
61 Taimyr Pen., U.S.S.R. 75 0N 100 0E
33 Tain, Scotland 57 48N 4 3W
67 Tainan, Taiwan 23 0N 120 22E
41 Tainaron (Matapan), C., Greece 36 20N 22 30E
67 Taipei, Taiwan 25 0N 121 38E
68 Taiping, Malaya 4 55N 100 45E
67 Taira, Japan 37 4N 140 58E
61 Taishet, U.S.S.R. 56 0N 98 5E
99 Taitao Pen., Chile 46 0S 75 0W
66 Taitung, China 30 45N 117 40F
67 Taitung, Taiwan 22 55N 121 5E
67 Taiwan (Formosa), China 24N 121 0E
66 Tai-yüan, China 38 2N 112 20E
62 Ta'izz, Yemen 13 43N 44 7E
37 Tajo, R., Spain 40 40N 2 12W
73 Tajura, Libya 32 51N 13 27E
55 Ta-Khingan Shan, China 50 0N 120 0E
55 Ta-Liang Shan, China 28 20N 103 0E
67 Takamatsu, Japan 34 15N 134 0E
67 Takana, Japan 34 0N 135 6E
67 Takaoka, Japan 36 40N 137 4E
84 Takapuna, New Zealand 36 47S 174 47E
67 Takasaki, Japan 36 10N 139 0E
67 Takata, Japan 37 12N 138 12E
74 Takaungu, Kenya 3 35S 39 45E
67 Takefu, Japan 35 57N 136 5E
67 Taketoyo, Japan 34 56N 137 0E
66 Takla-Makan, China 39 45N 85 0E
61 Tala, U.S.S.R. 72 50N 113 57E
98 Talara, Peru 4 20S 81 10W
60 Talas, U.S.S.R. 42 45N 72 0E
68 Talaud, Is., Indonesia 4 10N 126 50E
37 Talavera, Spain 39 59N 4 46W
68 Talayan, Philippines 6 55N 124 25E
99 Talca, Chile 35 18S 71 45W
99 Talcahuano, Chile 36 35S 73 12W
65 Talcher, India 20 55N 85 3E
60 Taldy Kurgan, U.S.S.R. 45 5N 78 50E
64 Talguppa, India 14 10N 74 45E
66 Tali, China 25 57N 100 7E
74 Tali Post, Sudan 5 55N 30 44E
68 Taliabu, Indonesia 1 45S 125 0E
32 Talladale, Scotland 57 41N 5 20W
91 Tallahassee, U.S.A. 30 30N 84 10W
83 Tallangatta, Australia 36 8S 147 5E
49 Tallinn, U.S.S.R. 59 29N 24 58E
34 Tallow, Ireland 52 6N 7 59W
62 Talodi, Sudan 10 42N 30 22E
99 Taltal, Chile 25 40S 70 35W
83 Talwood, Australia 28 25S 149 25E
25 Tal-y-Lyn, Wales 52 40N 3 53W
72 Tamale, Ghana 9 30N 0 38W
24 Tamar, R., England 50 45N 4 22W
75 Tamatave, Madagascar 17 50S 49 40E
72 Tambacounda, Sénégal 13 10N 13 40W
82 Tambo, Australia 24 54S 146 14E
52 Tambov, U.S.S.R. 52 43N 41 30E
37 Tamega, R., Portugal 41 15N 8 0W
72 Tamgak Mts., Niger 19 10N 8 35E
65 Tamil Nadu, st., India 11 0N 78 0E
45 Tamins, Switzerland 46 50N 9 22E
91 Tampa, & B., U.S.A. 28 10N 82 20W
49 Tampere, Finland 61 34N 23 38E
94 Tampico, Mexico 22 20N 98 12W
72 Tamsagout, Mali 24 5N 6 35W
83 Tamworth, Australia 31 8S 151 0E
22 Tamworth, England 52 38N 1 42W
48 Tana Fjord, Norway 70 45N 28 20E
73 Tana L., Ethiopia 12 0N 37 20E
74 Tana R., Kenya 1 0S 40 0E
80 Tanami Desert, Australia 20 0S 136 0E
75 Tananarive, Madagascar 19 0S 47 20E
40 Tanaro, R., Italy 44 47N 8 10E
83 Tanbar, Australia 25 30S 141 58E
74 Tandah, Ethiopia 10 0N 40 45E
99 Tandil, Argentina 37 8S 59 10W
68 Tandjong Selor, Indon. 2 50N 116 40E
68 Tandjungpandan, Indon. 2 45S 107 40E
64 Tando Adam, Pak. 25 40N 68 34E
67 Tanega Shima, I., Japan 30 40N 131 0E
72 Tanezrouft, Dist., Algeria 22 30N 2 0E
71 Tanganyika, see Tanzania
74 Tanghanyika, L., Cent. Afr. 6 30S 29 40E
66 Tanghla Ra., Mts., China 33 0N 92 0E
72 Tangier, N. Africa 35 46N 5 47W
68 Tangshan, China 39 45N 118 0E
64 Tanjore, see Thanjavur
73 Tanta, Egypt 30 50N 30 48E
83 Tanunda, Australia 34 30S 139 0E
22 Tanworth, England 52 20N 1 50W
71 Tanzania, Africa 6 0S 34 30E
67 Taonan, China 45 29N 122 57E
72 Taourirt, Morocco 34 20N 3 2W
66 Tapa, Mts., China 31 50N 109 0E
98 Tapajos, R., Brazil 6 30S 57 30W
51 Tarabulus, Lebanon, see Tripoli
73 Tarabulus, Libya, see Tripoli
68 Tarakan, Indonesia 3 15N 117 30E
84 Taranaki, Dist., N.Z. 39 0S 174 50E
32 Taransay, I. & Sd., Scot. 57 54N 7 1W
40 Taranto, & G., Italy 40 30N 17 14E
43 Tarare, France 45 52N 4 30E
84 Tararua Ra., N.Z. 40 47S 175 30E
43 Tarascon, France 43 50N 4 40E
72 Tarat, Algeria 26 4N 9 7E
84 Tarawera, N.Z. 39 2S 176 35E
34 Tarbert, Ireland 52 35N 9 22W
30 Tarbert & L.W., Argyll, Scotland 55 58N 5 25W
32 Tarbert, & L., W & E, Harris, Scotland 57 55N 6 50W
42 Tarbes, France 43 13N 0 1E

30 Tarbet, Scotland 56 13N 4 44W
80 Tarcoola, Australia 30 48S 134 52E
83 Taree, Australia 31 48S 152 17E
72 Tarfaya, Morocco 27 55N 12 55W
37 Tarifa, Spain 36 2N 5 37W
62 Tarim, South Yemen 16 15N 49 22E
66 Tarim Basin, China 40 30N 85 0E
66 Tarim R., China 41 0N 85 0E
51 Tarkhankut C., U.S.S.R. 45 25N 32 30E
72 Tarkwa, Ghana 5 23N 2 0W
68 Tarlac, Philippines 15 25N 120 35E
26 Tarleton, England 53 41N 2 51W
42 Tarn, Dépt., France 43 50N 2 10E
42 Tarn-et-Garonne, Dépt., France 44 10N 1 10E
47 Tarnow, Poland 50 1N 21 2E
47 Tarnowskie Góry, Poland 50 30N 19 0E
72 Taroudant, Morocco 30 30N 9 0W
37 Tarragona, Spain 41 7N 1 13E
37 Tarrasa, Spain 41 30N 2 0E
51 Tarsus, Turkey 37 0N 34 50E
47 Tartars, P. of the, U.S.S.R. 48 20N 24 30E
61 Tartary Str., U.S.S.R. 53 10N 141 30E
50 Tartu, U.S.S.R. 58 22N 26 40E
73 Tasawah, Libya 26 0N 13 30E
89 Taschereau, Canada 48 45N 78 45W
60 Tashauz, U.S.S.R. 42 7N 59 30E
60 Tashkent, U.S.S.R. 41 7N 69 15E
60 Tashkumyr, U.S.S.R. 41 40N 72 20E
70 Tasili Plateau, N. Africa 25 30N 8 0E
48 Tasjön, L., Sweden 64 15N 16 0E
84 Tasman B., N.Z. 41 0S 173 30E
84 Tasman Mts., N.Z. 41 0S 172 30E
83 Tasman Pen., Australia 43 0S 147 40E
84 Tasman Sea, Australasia 38 0S 163 0E
83 Tasmania, I., Australia 42 0S 146 30E
47 Tatabanya, Hungary 47 35N 18 30E
50 Tatar, A.S.S.R., U.S.S.R. 55 30N 51 30E
60 Tatarsk, U.S.S.R. 55 30N 76 3E
67 Tateyama, Japan 35 0N 139 58E
66 Ta-tung, China 40 0N 113 20E
51 Tatvan, Turkey 38 33N 42 12E
46 Tauern Mts., Austria 47 15N 12 40E
84 Taumarunui, N.Z. 38 55S 175 15E
76 Taung, South Africa 27 32S 24 45E
65 Taunggyi, Burma 20 55N 97 3E
65 Taungun & P., Burma 18 50N 94 20E
24 Taunton, England 51 1N 3 5W
46 Taunus Mts., Germany 50 18N 8 20E
84 Taupo & L., N.Z. 38 47S 175 50E
49 Taurage, U.S.S.R. 55 15N 22 18E
84 Tauranga, New Zealand 37 40S 176 12E
40 Taurianova, Italy 38 22N 16 1E
51 Taurus Mts., Turkey 37 30N 34 30E
60 Tavda, U.S.S.R. 58 7N 65 8E
37 Tavira, Portugal 37 5N 7 40W
24 Tavistock, England 50 34N 4 10W
64 Tavoy, Burma 13 49N 98 22E
24 Taw, R., England 50 57N 3 55W
73 Taweisha, Sudan 12 25N 26 55E
68 Tawitawi, I., Phil. 5 15N 120 0E
36 Tawnyinah, Ireland 53 55N 8 45W
31 Tay, Firth of, Scotland 56 27N 2 45W
31 Tayport, Scotland 56 26N 2 53W
68 Taytay, Philippines 10 40N 119 25E
60 Taz R., U.S.S.R. 65 40N 82 40E
51 Tbilisi, U.S.S.R. 41 45N 44 48E
74 Tchibanga, Gabon 2 45S 11 12E
84 Te Anau, L., N.Z. 45 12S 167 48E
84 Te Awamutu, N.Z. 38 1S 175 20E
84 Te Kuiti, New Zealand 38 20S 175 11E
72 Tébessa, Algeria 35 38N 8 5E
68 Tebingtinggi, Indonesia 3 30S 103 0E
47 Tecuci, Rumania 45 20N 27 25E
26 Tees, R., England 54 39N 1 9W
*27 Teesside, England 54 34N 1 16W
68 Tegal, Indonesia 7 0S 108 35E
25 Tegid, L., Wales 52 55N 3 37W
72 Tegina, Nigeria 10 5N 6 11E
94 Tegucigalpa, Honduras 14 20N 87 12W
92 Tehachapi P., U.S.A. 35 5N 119 30W
66 Tehchow, China 37 35N 116 15E
62 Tehran, Iran 35 37N 51 22E
66 Tehtsin, China 28 45N 98 10E
94 Tehuantepec, & G., Mex. 16 40N 95 35W
25 Teifi, R., Wales 52 2N 4 20W
24 Teign, R., England 50 40N 3 40W
24 Teignmouth, England 50 33N 3 31W
74 Teixeira de Sousa, Angola 10 39S 22 14E
37 Tejo (Tagus), R., Port. 39 15N 8 30W
84 Tekapo, L., N.Z. 43 55S 170 30E
41 Tekirdag, Turkey 41 0N 27 25E
63 Tel Aviv-Jaffa, Israel 32 4N 34 45E
94 Tela, Honduras 15 45N 87 25W
68 Telanaipura, Indonesia 1 40S 103 35E
51 Telavi, U.S.S.R. 42 0N 43 30E
49 Telemark, Co., Norway 59 32N 8 20E
22 Telford, England 52 42N 2 29W
64 Tellicherry, India 11 45N 75 43E
68 Telok Anson, Malaya 3 50N 101 0E
50 Telpos Iz, Mt., U.S.S.R. 64 12N 59 30E
49 Telsiai, U.S.S.R. 56 2N 22 30E
68 Teluk Betung, Indon. 5 30S 105 20E
84 Temuka, N.Z. 44 14S 171 17E
72 Tema, Ghana 5 41N 0 0
94 Temax, Mexico 21 15N 88 50W
76 Tembuland, dist., S. Afr. 31 40S 28 0E
22 Teme, R., England 52 23N 3 7W
60 Temir, U.S.S.R. 49 3N 57 3E
60 Temir Tau, U.S.S.R. 53 15N 87 40E
92 Temiskaming, Canada 46 50N 79 0W
83 Temora, Australia 34 29S 147 33E
91 Temple, U.S.A. 31 3N 97 27W
82 Temple B., Australia 12 15S 143 3E
34 Templemore, Ireland 52 47N 7 49W
36 Tempo, N. Ireland 54 23N 7 27W
99 Temuco, Chile 39 0S 72 0W
65 Tenali, India 16 15N 80 40E
22 Tenbury, England 52 18N 2 36W
43 Tenda, France 44 6N 7 39E
72 Tenerife, I., Canary Is. 28 30N 18 0W
37 Tenes, Algeria 36 36N 0 32W
66 T'eng Ch'ung, China 25 5N 98 25E
66 Tengkow, China 40 0N 106 20E
64 Tenkasi, India 8 45N 77 10E
80 Tennant Creek, Austral. 19 30S 134 15E
43 Tenneins, France 44 22N 0 20E
91 Tennessee, R., U.S.A. 34 45N 87 30W
91 Tennessee, st., U.S.A. 35 40N 86 30W
67 Tenryu, R., Japan 35 30N 137 56E
23 Tenterden, England 51 5N 0 41E
83 Tenterfield, Australia 29 0S 152 0E
98 Teofilo Otoni, Brazil 17 50S 41 30W
94 Tepic, Mexico 21 20N 104 50W
46 Teplice, Czechoslovakia 50 39N 13 50E
72 Téra, Niger 14 0N 0 57E
40 Teramo, Italy 42 39N 13 46E
83 Terang, Australia 38 7S 142 59E
98 Teresina, Brazil 5 2S 42 45W
83 Terewah or Narran, L., Australia 29 52S 147 35E
44 Tergnier, France 49 49N 3 17E
63 Termez, U.S.S.R. 37 25N 67 12E
40 Termini, Italy 37 57N 13 45E
40 Termoli, Italy 42 0N 15 3E
68 Ternate, I., Indonesia 0 45N 127 20E
40 Terni, Italy 42 35N 12 40E
47 Ternopol, U.S.S.R. 49 30N 25 40E
91 Terre Haute, U.S.A. 39 29N 87 20W
34 Terryglass, Ireland 8 14N 53 3W
45 Terschelling, I., Neth. 53 23N 5 20E
37 Teruel, Spain 40 22N 1 6W
41 Tesanj, Yugoslavia 44 40N 18 0E
88 Teslin, Canada 60 20N 132 45W
72 Tessalit, Mali 20 5N 0 57E
72 Tessaoua, Niger 13 55N 8 18E
22 Test, R., England 51 3N 1 32W
22 Tetbury, England 51 38N 2 9W
75 Tete, Mozambique 16 10S 33 37E
41 Teteven, Bulgaria 42 58N 24 15E
90 Teton, Mts., U.S.A. 43 45N 110 45W
41 Tetovo, Yugoslavia 42 1N 21 2E
22 Tettenhall, England 52 35N 2 7W
72 Tetuan, Morocco 35 32N 5 22W
61 Tetyukhe, U.S.S.R. 44 30N 135 57E
99 Teuco R., Argentina 24 0S 62 0W
31 Teviot, R., Scotland 55 20N 2 57W
83 Tewantin, Australia 26 27S 153 3E
22 Tewkesbury, England 51 59N 2 8W
91 Texarkana, U.S.A. 33 28N 94 11W
83 Texas, Australia 28 43S 151 3E
90 Texas, st., U.S.A. 31 15N 98 30W
44 Texel, I., Netherlands 53 5N 4 48E
65 Tezpur, India 26 50N 92 40E
76 Thaba Nchu, S. Africa 29 10S 26 57E
76 Thabana Ntlenyana, mt., Lesotho 29 12S 29 22E
63 Thaih, U.A.E. 23 57N 54 0E
57 Thailand (Siam), Asia 15 0N 101 0E
64 Thal, Pakistan 33 30N 70 30E
65 Thala Pass, Burma 28 15N 98 10E
68 Thale Luang, Thailand 7 30N 100 15E
83 Thallon, Australia 28 36S 149 0E
23 Thame, England 51 45N 0 59W
23 Thame R., England 51 52N 0 47W
84 Thames, N.Z. 37 3S 175 32E
22 Thames, R., England 51 29N 0 40E
64 Thana, India 19 30N 72 58E
23 Thanet, I., England 51 21N 1 20E
64 Thanjavur, India 10 45N 79 17E
43 Thann, France 47 46N 7 5E
64 Thar Des., India 27 30N 72 20E
64 Tharad, India 24 30N 71 30E
65 Tharrawaddy, Burma 17 42N 95 57E
41 Thasos, I., Greece 40 40N 24 40E
22 Thatcham, England 51 24N 1 16W
45 Thawil, Switzerland 47 18N 8 32E
65 Thazi, Burma 21 0N 96 5E
90 The Dalles, U.S.A. 45 35N 121 15W
44 The Hague ('s Gravenhage), Netherlands 52 5N 4 18E
80 The Johnston Lakes, Australia 32 30S 120 40E
88 The Pas, Canada 53 40N 101 20W
24 The Quantocks, England 51 8N 3 10W
49 The Skaw, see Skagen
36 The Skerries Is., N. Ire. 55 14N 6 40W
49 The Sound, Denmark 56 7N 12 30E
24 The Sound, England 50 17N 4 10W
83 The Warburton, R., Austral. 27 50S 138 0E
83 Theodore, Australia 25 0S 150 1E
41 Thermopylae, P., Greece 38 48N 22 45E
41 Thessaloniki, Greece 40 38N 23 0E
41 Thessaly, Dist., Greece 39 30N 22 20E
23 Thetford, England 52 24N 0 45E
93 Thetford Mines, Canada 46 15N 71 5W
76 Theunissen, S. Africa 28 30S 26 40E
43 Thiers, France 45 50N 3 32E
65 Thimphu, Bhutan 27 31N 89 45E
48 Thingvallavatn, Iceland 64 10N 21 5W
43 Thionville, France 49 20N 6 10E
41 Thira, I., Greece 36 24N 25 26E
27 Thirsk, England 54 14N 1 22W
48 Thjorsá R., Iceland 64 20N 19 15W
88 Thompson, R., Canada 51 0N 119 0W
82 Thomson, R., Australia 23 50S 144 0E
**74 Thomson's Falls, Kenya 0 2N 36 27E
45 Thonon, France 46 20N 6 30E
52 Thorez, U.S.S.R. 48 0N 38 38E
65 Thori, India 27 23N 84 30E
48 Thórisvatn L., Iceland 64 10N 18 7W
48 Thorlákshöfn, Iceland 63 50N 21 20W
27 Thornaby-on-Tees, Eng. 54 33N 1 18W
23 Thorndon, England 52 16N 1 8E
27 Thorne, England 53 37N 0 58W
27 Thornham, England 52 59N 0 35E
31 Thornthwaite, England 54 36N 3 13W
26 Thornton-Cleveleys, Eng. 53 50N 3 4W
23 Thorpe, England 52 38N 1 20E
48 Thorshöfn, Iceland 66 12N 15 15W
42 Thouars, France 47 0N 0 18W
41 Thrace, Prov., Greece 41 27N 26 30E
23 Thrapston, England 52 24N 0 32W
84 Three Kings I., N.Z. 34 0S 172 0E
26 Threshfield, England 54 5N 2 2W
80 Throssell Ra., Australia 22 0S 122 0E
44 Thuin, Belgium 50 20N 4 17E
100 Thule, Greenland 76 22N 69 0W
45 Thun, Switzerland 46 46N 7 39E
92 Thunder Bay, Canada 48 20N 89 23W
45 Thunersee, Switzerland 46 42N 7 40E
45 Thur, R., Switzerland 47 37N 8 40E
45 Thurgau, Canton, Switz. 47 38N 9 4E
46 Thuringian Forest, Ger. 50 35N 11 0E
23 Thurlby, England 52 45N 0 21W
34 Thurles, Ireland 52 40N 7 53W
23 Thurrock, England 51 28N 0 20E
81 Thursday, I., Australia 10 35S 142 10E
45 Thusis, Switzerland 46 43N 9 26E
74 Thysville (Mbanza Ngungu), Zaïre 5 12S 14 53E
73 Tibati, Cameroon 6 30N 12 52E
40 Tiber, R., Italy 43 33N 12 10E
63 Tiberias, Israel 32 47N 35 32E
73 Tibesti, Dist., Sahara 20 30N 17 0E
65 Tibert, A.R., China 32 30N 88 0E
63 Tibnin, Lebanon 33 11N 35 24E
94 Tiburon, I., Mexico 29 0N 112 30W
72 Tichit, Mauritania 19 20N 8 55W
45 Ticino, Canton, Switz. 46 20N 8 45E
40 Ticino, R., Italy 45 20N 8 53E
72 Tidjikja, Mauritania 18 25N 11 55W
44 Tiel, Netherlands 51 54N 5 26E
44 Tielt, Belgium 51 0N 3 20E
44 Tienen, Belgium 50 49N 4 57E
55 Tien Shan, mts., Asia 43 40N 86 0E
66 Tienshui, China 34 45N 105 15E
66 Tientsin, China 39 0N 117 5E
66 Tientu, China 18 30N 109 30E
100 Tierra del Fuego Terr., South America 54 0S 68 0W
37 Tietar, R., Spain 40 0N 5 45W
93 Tignish, Canada 46 55N 64 15W
62 Tigris, R., Iraq 32 30N 46 0E
65 Tigu, Tibet 28 45N 91 40E
65 Tigyaing, Burma 23 45N 96 10E
94 Tijuana, Mexico 32 30N 117 30W
51 Tikhoretsk, U.S.S.R. 45 55N 40 10E
61 Tiksi, U.S.S.R. 71 50N 129 0E
44 Tilburg, Netherlands 51 34N 5 6E
23 Tilbury, England 51 27N 0 23E
61 Tilichiki, U.S.S.R. 60 50N 166 0E
31 Till, R., England 55 35N 2 0W
72 Tillabéri Niger 14 15N 1 40E
31 Tillicoultry, Scotland 56 9N 3 44W
41 Tilos I., Greece 36 22N 27 21E
83 Tilpa, Australia 30 58S 144 30E
33 Tilt, R., Scotland 56 50N 3 48W
50 Timan Ridge, U.S.S.R. 64 30N 51 30E
84 Timaru, New Zealand 44 20S 171 21E
83 Timboon, Australia 38 32S 143 0E
72 Timbuktu, see Tombouctou
72 Timerein, Sudan 15 57N 36 30E
72 Timimoun, Algeria 29 10N 0 10E
47 Timisoara, Rumania 45 43N 21 8E
89 Timmins, Canada 48 30N 81 30W
41 Timok, R., Yugoslavia 43 30N 22 18E
34 Timoleague, Ireland 51 39N 8 46W
68 Timor, I., Indonesia 9 30S 125 0E
80 Timor Sea, Indian Ocean 14 0S 120 0E
35 Tinahely, Ireland 52 48N 6 28W
72 Tindouf, Algeria 27 30N 8 15W
65 Tindzhe Dzong, China 28 25N 88 10E
67 Ting-hai, China 30 10N 122 12E
72 Tinjoub, Algeria 29 20N 5 40W
49 Tinnoset, Norway 59 42N 9 3E
99 Tinogasta, Argentina 28 0S 67 30W
41 Tinos I., Greece 37 38N 25 10E
24 Tintagel, England 50 40N 4 45W
25 Tintern, England 51 42N 2 41W
83 Tintinara, Australia 35 58S 140 1E
65 Tipongpani, India 27 15N 95 50E
34 Tipperary, & Co., Ire. 52 29N 8 8W
22 Tipton, England 52 32N 2 3W
41 Tirane, Albania 41 20N 19 50E
41 Tirano, Italy 46 15N 10 15E
47 Tiraspol, U.S.S.R. 46 50N 29 30E
63 Tirat Karmel, Israel 32 46N 34 58E
51 Tirebolu, Turkey 40 59N 38 50E
30 Tiree I., Scotland 56 30N 6 55W
47 Tîrgoviste, Rumania 44 58N 25 30E
47 Tîrgu-Jiu, Rumania 45 0N 23 20E
47 Tîrgu Mures, Rumania 46 31N 24 38E
64 Tirodi, India 21 35N 79 35E
40 Tirso, R., Italy 40 0N 8 45E
64 Tiruchchirappalli, India 10 52N 78 40E
64 Tirunelveli, India 8 45N 77 45E
64 Tiruvannamalai, India 12 15N 79 10E
88 Tisdale, Canada 52 50N 104 10W
49 Tisted, Denmark 56 58N 8 40E
47 Tisza, R., Hungary 47 50N 21 0E
98 Titicaca, L., Bolivia-Peru 16 0S 69 30W
41 Titograd, Yugoslavia 42 30N 19 19E
41 Titov Veles, Yugoslavia 41 40N 21 49E
41 Titovo Uzice, Y-slav. 43 55N 19 50E
74 Titule, Zaïre 3 5N 25 25E
92 Titusville, U.S.A. 41 38N 79 40W
24 Tiverton, England 50 55N 3 31W
40 Tivoli, Italy 41 58N 12 25E
48 Tjeggelvas, L., Sweden 66 30N 18 0E
68 Tjirebon, Indonesia 6 5S 108 30E
94 Tlacotalpan, Mexico 18 50N 95 40W
94 Tlaxcala, Mexico 19 23N 98 10W
94 Tlaxiaco, Mexico 17 15N 97 40W
72 Tlemcen, Algeria 34 55N 1 20W
68 Toba, L., Indonesia 2 30N 98 57E
64 Toba Kakar, Hills, Pak. 31 20N 68 40E
94 Tobago, I., W. Indies 11 17N 60 40W
36 Tobercurry, Ireland 54 3N 8 44W
30 Tobermory, Scotland 56 38N 6 4W
60 Tobol R., U.S.S.R. 54 0N 63 30E
60 Tobolsk, U.S.S.R. 58 10N 68 30E
82 Tobriand or Kiriwina Is., Papua 8 35S 151 0E
73 Tobruk, Libya, see Tubruq
98 Tocantins, R., Brazil 3 30S 49 30W
45 Toce, R., Italy 46 13N 8 19E
67 Tochigi, Pref., Japan 36 40N 139 45E
99 Tocopilla, Chile 22 12S 70 20W
83 Tocumwal, Australia 35 54S 145 56E
26 Todmorden, England 53 42N 2 5W
72 Togba, Mauretania 7 40N 10 20W
50 Togliatti, U.S.S.R. 53 37N 49 18E
72 Togo, W. Africa 7 45N 1 0E
73 Toinya, Sudan 6 17N 29 46E
47 Tokaj, Hungary 48 7N 21 22E
84 Tokanui, New Zealand 46 51S 169 0E
84 Tokarahi, New Zealand 44 56S 170 39E
51 Tokat, Turkey 40 27N 36 35E
4 Tokelau Is., Pac. Oc. 9 0S 172 0W
60 Tokmak, U.S.S.R. 42 55N 75 45E
67 Tokushima, & Pref., Jap. 34 0N 134 30E
67 Tokuyama, Japan 34 0N 131 50E
67 Tokyo, & Pref. Japan 35 48N 139 45E
37 Toledo, Spain 39 55N 4 0W
92 Toledo, U.S.A. 41 47N 83 30W
72 Tolga, Algeria 34 49N 5 26E
98 Tolima, Mt., Colombia 4 0N 75 0W
37 Tolosa, Spain 43 9N 2 5W
68 Tolo, G. of, Indonesia 2 0S 121 30E
94 Toluca, Mexico 19 25N 99 37W
66 Tolun, China 42 30N 116 30E
37 Tomar, Portugal 39 35N 8 28W
47 Tomaszów, Mazowiecki, Poland 51 30N 20 0E
98 Tombador, Sa. do, mts., Brazil 12 0S 57 10W
72 Tombouctou, Mali 16 50N 3 0W
32 Tomdoun, Scotland 57 3N 5 3W
37 Tomelloso, Spain 39 13N 2 1W
68 Tomini G., Indonesia 0 0 120 30E
33 Tomintoul, Scotland 57 16N 3 24W
61 Tommot, U.S.S.R. 59 0N 126 30E
41 Tomorrit, Mt., Albania 40 40N 20 30E
60 Tomsk, U.S.S.R. 56 30N 85 5E
94 Tonala, Mexico 16 10N 94 0W
45 Tonale P., Italy 46 18N 10 36E
23 Tonbridge, England 51 11N 0 16E
24 Tone, R., England 51 0N 3 22W
22 Tong, England 52 40N 2 17W
84 Tonga (Friendly) Is., Pacific Ocean 19 50S 175 0W
76 Tongaat, South Africa 29 35S 31 5E
84 Tongatapu I., Pac. Oc. 21 0S 175 20W
44 Tongeren, Belgium 50 37N 5 20E
68 Tongian Is., Indonesia 0 20S 122 30E
83 Tongio, Australia 37 10S 147 35E
99 Tongoy, Chile 30 10S 71 45W
90 Tongue, R., U.S.A. 45 20N 106 3W
64 Tonk, India 26 10N 76 0E
66 Tonkin, G. of, China 20 0N 109 0E
68 Tonlé Sap, Khmer Rep. 12 30N 105 30E
43 Tonnerre, France 47 52N 3 58E
49 Tönning, Germany 54 19N 8 58E
90 Tonopah, U.S.A. 38 4N 117 13W
49 Tonsberg, Norway 59 15N 10 25E
25 Tonyrefail, Wales 51 35N 3 26W
90 Tooele, U.S.A. 40 32N 113 22W
34 Toomevara, Ireland 52 50N 8 3W
83 Toora, Australia 38 40S 146 20E
83 Toowoomba, Australia 27 30S 152 0E
64 Top, Afghanistan 34 15N 68 35E
50 Top, L., U.S.S.R. 65 30N 32 0E
91 Topeka, U.S.A. 39 0N 95 40W
60 Topki, U.S.S.R. 55 40N 85 40E
94 Topolobampo, Mexico 25 45N 108 48W
24 Tor B., England 50 25N 3 33W
24 Torbay, England 50 28N 3 32W
37 Tordesillas, Spain 41 30N 5 0W
61 Torei, U.S.S.R. 50 45N 104 45E
46 Torgau, Germany 51 35N 12 58E
44 Torhout, Belgium 51 4N 3 7E
40 Torino, see Turin
73 Torit, Sudan 4 29N 32 35E
37 Tormes, R., Spain 41 10N 6 0W
48 Torne, R., Sweden 67 30N 22 0E
48 Torneträsk, L., Sweden 68 20N 19 25E
48 Tornio, & R., Finland 65 57N 24 12E
99 Toro, Cor del, Chile 29 10S 69 0W
41 Toronaios, G., Greece 40 0N 23 35E
83 Toronto, Australia 32 58S 151 30E
92 Toronto, Canada 43 42N 79 30W
74 Tororo, Uganda 0 43N 34 13E
24 Torquay, England 50 28N 3 32W
37 Tôrre de Moncorvo, Port. 41 12N 7 10W
37 Torrelavega, Spain 43 20N 4 5W
83 Torrens, L., Australia 31 0S 137 40E
82 Torrens Creek, Austral. 20 48S 145 3E
94 Torreon, Mexico 25 30N 103 12W
94 Torres, Mexico 28 40N 110 55W
82 Torres Strait, Australia 10 0S 142 30E
37 Torres Vedras, Portugal 39 3N 9 19W
37 Torrevieja, Spain 37 59N 0 40W
32 Torridon, & L., Scot. 57 33N 5 30W
93 Torrington, U.S.A. 41 50N 73 5W
42 Torteval, Guernsey, Channel Is. 49 26N 2 38W
43 Tortona, Italy 44 55N 8 55E
83 Torrowangee, Australia 31 25S 141 30E
37 Tortosa, Spain 40 48N 0 47E
98 Tortuga I., Venezuela 11 0N 65 30W
47 Torun, Poland 53 2N 18 37E
52 Torzhok, U.S.S.R. 57 10N 34 55E
67 Tosa B., Japan 33 15N 133 30E
24 Totnes, England 50 25N 3 51W
83 Tottenham, Australia 32 10S 147 20E
67 Tottori, & Pref., Japan 35 30N 134 10E
72 Toubkal, Djebel, Morocco 31 15N 7 20W
72 Touggourt, Algeria 33 5N 6 0E
43 Toul, France 48 42N 5 53E
43 Toulon, France 43 9N 5 55E
43 Toulouse, France 43 37N 1 18E
43 Touraine, Dist., France 47 20N 0 40E
43 Tourcoing, France 50 46N 3 3E
44 Tournai, Belgium 50 37N 3 23E
43 Tournus, France 46 35N 4 50E
43 Tours, France 47 24N 0 41E
76 Touws, South Africa 33 32S 20 32E
76 Touwsrivier, S. Africa 33 20S 20 2E
23 Towcester, England 52 8N 1 0W
82 Townshend I., Australia 22 15S 150 38E
82 Townsville, Australia 19 15S 146 47E
25 Towy, R., Wales, see Tywi
25 Towyn, see Tywyn
67 Toyama, B. & Pref., Jap. 36 40N 137 10E
67 Toyohashi, Japan 34 40N 137 28E
51 Trabzon, Turkey 40 58N 39 50E
93 Tracadie, Canada 47 30N 65 0W
37 Trafalgar, C., Spain 36 13N 6 7W
88 Trail, Canada 49 6N 117 58W
41 Trajan's Gate, Bulgaria 42 21N 23 46E
47 Trajan's Wall, Rumania 44 18N 28 20E
34 Tralee, & B., Ireland 52 16N 9 43W
35 Tramore & B., Ireland 52 9N 7 10W
49 Tranås, Sweden 58 5N 14 58E
68 Trang, Malaya 7 30N 99 40E
83 Trangie, Australia 31 58S 148 2E
40 Trani, Italy 41 17N 16 27E
76 Transkei, Bantu Area, S. Africa 32 0S 28 0E
75 Transvaal, Prov., S. Afr. 25 20S 28 30E
47 Transylvania, reg., Rum. 46 18N 24 30E
47 Transylvanian Alps, Rum. 45 35N 24 30E
40 Trapani, Italy 38 1N 12 35E
83 Traralgon, Australia 38 17S 146 35E
37 Tras os Montes E Alto-Douro, Prov., Portugal 41 25N 7 20W
40 Trasimeno, L., Italy 43 8N 12 5E
68 Trat, Cambodia 12 20N 102 30E
83 Traveller's L., Australia 33 14S 142 0E
84 Travers, Mt., N.Z. 42 1S 172 45E
92 Traverse City, U.S.A. 44 50N 85 40W
41 Travnik, Yugoslavia 44 12N 17 38E
40 Trebbia, R., Italy 44 50N 9 30E
46 Trebic, Czechoslovakia 49 15N 15 50E
41 Trebinje, Yugoslavia 42 43N 18 17E
46 Trebon, Czechoslovakia 49 0N 14 50E
25 Tredegar, England 51 46N 3 16W
25 Treharris, Wales 51 38N 3 17W
99 Treinta y Tres, Uruguay 33 30S 54 0W
44 Trélon, France 50 5N 4 6E
49 Trelleborg, Sweden 55 21N 13 2E
25 Tremadoc, & B., Wales 52 55N 4 8W
37 Tremp, Spain 42 10N 0 50E
27 Trent, R., England 53 33N 0 44W
40 Trentino-Alto-Adige, Reg., Italy 46 5N 11 0E
40 Trento, Italy 46 3N 11 5E
92 Trenton, Canada 44 6N 77 37W
92 Trenton, U.S.A. 40 17N 74 39W
89 Trepassey, Canada 46 34N 53 25W
99 Tres Arroyos, Argentina 38 30S 60 30W
99 Tres Puntas, C., Arg. 47 30S 65 0W
43 Treviglio, Italy 45 35N 9 40E
40 Treviso, Italy 45 41N 12 18E
24 Trevose Hd., England 50 33N 5 3W
43 Trévoux, France 46 0N 4 50E
64 Trichur, India 10 30N 76 15E
83 Trida, Australia 32 58S 144 59E
45 Trier, Germany 49 45N 6 40E
40 Trieste, Italy 45 39N 13 50E
41 Trikkala, Greece 39 35N 21 42E
35 Trim, Ireland 53 35N 6 47W
64 Trincomalee, Sri Lanka 8 40N 81 12E
98 Trinidad, Bolivia 14 30S 65 12W
95 Trinidad, Cuba 21 55N 80 7W
90 Trinidad, U.S.A. 37 5N 104 30W
94 Trinidad, I., W. Indies 10 5N 61 0W
94 Trinidad & Tobago, see Inset
99 Trinidad I., Argentina 39 0S 62 0W
94 Trinité, Martinque, Fr., W.I. 14 42N 60 58W
94 Trinity R., U.S.A. 31 30N 95 3W
73 Trinkitat, Sudan 17 30N 37 50E
51 Tripoli, Lebanon 34 40N 36 0E
73 Tripoli, Libya 32 58N 13 12E
41 Tripolis, Greece 37 29N 22 37E
73 Tripolitania, Libya 30 0N 14 0E
65 Tripura, Prov., India 24 0N 91 40E
5 Tristan da Cuñha, Atlantic Ocean 38 0S 12 20W
64 Trivandrum, India 8 40N 76 50E
47 Trnava, Czechoslovakia 48 20N 17 30E

* *Incorporated within the county of Cleveland*

** *Renamed Nyahururu*

* Tyne and Wear, Co., England
  54 55n 1 35w
** In April 1973 districts replaced
  counties in N. Ireland

30

52 Vichuga, U.S.S.R. 57 20N 41 50E
43 Vichy, France 46 10N 3 28E
91 Vicksburg, U.S.A. 32 12N 90 47W
83 Victor Hr., Australia 35 50S 138 40E
83 Victoria, st., Australia 37 0S 145 0E
72 Victoria, Cameroon 4 0N 9 12E
90 Victoria, Canada 48 28N 123 20W
72 Victoria, Guinea 10 57N 14 50W
40 Victoria, Malta 36 1N 14 18E
68 Victoria, Sabah, Malaysia 5 15N 115 40E
91 Victoria, U.S.A. 28 46N 97 0W
75 Victoria Falls, Rhodesia 17 59S 25 57E
88 Victoria I., Canada 70 30N 109 0W
74 Victoria, L., Africa 1 0S 33 0E
100 Victoria Ld., Antarctica 80 0S 160 0E
66 Victoria, Mt., Burma 21 15N 94 5E
68 Victoria Point, Burma 10 0N 98 30E
80 Victoria, R., Australia 15 40S 131 0E
80 Victoria River Downs, Australia 16 22S 131 8E
76 Victoria W., S. Africa 31 37S 23 5E
93 Victoriaville, Canada 46 0N 72 5W
41 Vidin, Yugoslavia 43 59N 22 52E
99 Viedma, L., Argentina 49 30S 72 30W
43 Viella, Spain 42 43N 0 47E
46 Vienna (Wien), Austria 48 12N 16 20E
43 Vienne, France 45 32N 4 57E
43 Vienne R., France 47 10N 0 20E
42 Vienne, Dépt., France 46 23N 0 20E
66 Vientiane, Laos 18 6N 102 30E
95 Vieques, I., Puerto Rico 18 10N 65 30W
45 Vierwaldstattersee (L. of Lucerne), Switzerland 47 2N 8 10E
44 Viersen, Germany 51 16N 6 24E
68 Vietnam North, Asia 22 0N 105 0E
68 Vietnam South, Asia 14 0N 108 0E
94 Vieux Fort, St. Lucia, W.I. 13 45N 60 58W
68 Vigan, Philippines 17 32N 120 20E
37 Vigo, Spain 42 12N 8 42W
65 Vijayawada, India 16 30N 80 39E
41 Vijose, R., Albania 40 40N 20 21E
48 Vikna I., Norway 65 0N 11 0E
60 Vikulovo, U.S.S.R. 56 50N 70 40E
75 Vila Arriaga, Angola 14 35S 13 30E
75 Vila Cabral, Mozam. 13 8S 35 30E
75 Vila Coutinho, Mozam. 14 34S 34 21E
75 Vila de Joao Belo, Moz. 25 2S 33 34E
37 Vila Franca, Portugal 39 0N 8 58W
75 Vila General Machado, Angola 11 58S 17 22E
74 Vila Henrique de Carvalho, Angola 9 45S 20 30E
76 Vila Luiza, Mozambique 25 40S 32 35E
75 Vila Luso, Angola 11 45S 19 58E
75 Vila Nova de Seles, Angola 11 35S 14 22E
75 Vila Pereira d'Eça, Angola 16 48S 15 50E
37 Vila Real, Portugal 41 15N 7 42W
74 Vila Salazar, Angola 9 12S 14 48E
75 Vila de Sena, Mozam. 17 23S 34 40E
74 Vila Verissimo Sarmento, Angola 8 15S 20 50E
42 Vilaine, R., France 47 50N 1 50W
48 Vilhelmina, Sweden 64 38N 16 50E
61 Viliga, U.S.S.R. 61 20N 156 20E
49 Viljandi, U.S.S.R. 58 23N 25 38E
94 Villa Ahumada, Mex. 30 35N 106 30W
*72 Villa Cisneros, Spanish Sahara 23 55N 15 50W
99 Villa Encarnación, Para. 27 20S 56 0W
99 Villa Maria, Argentina 32 20S 63 15W
46 Villach, Austria 46 37N 13 45E
37 Villagarcia, Spain 42 34N 8 46W
94 Villahermosa, Mexico 18 0N 92 55W
37 Villalba, Spain 43 19N 7 43W
37 Villanueva de la Serena, Spain 39 0N 5 48W
37 Villarreal, Spain 39 50N 0 1W
99 Villarrica, Paraguay 25 45S 56 30W
37 Villarrobledo, Spain 39 20N 2 30W
45 Villars, Switzerland 46 18N 7 6E
37 Villaviciosa, Spain 43 30N 5 30W
42 Ville de Paris, Dépt., France 49 0N 2 15E
43 Villefranche, Alpes-Maritimes, France 43 43N 7 20E
43 Villefranche, Aveyron, Fr. 44 20N 2 0E
43 Villefranche, Rhône, Fr. 46 0N 4 40E
37 Villena, Spain 38 42N 0 52W
43 Villeneuve, France 44 22N 0 40E
44 Villerupt, France 49 28N 5 55E
43 Villeurbanne, France 45 42N 4 55E
50 Vilnius, U.S.S.R. 54 42N 25 15E
44 Vilvoorde, Belgium 50 56N 4 28E
61 Vilyui, R., U.S.S.R. 63 58N 125 0E
61 Vilyuisk, U.S.S.R. 63 20N 121 20E
99 Vina del Mar, Chile 33 0S 71 30W
37 Vinaroz, Spain 40 25N 0 30E
91 Vincennes, U.S.A. 38 49N 87 30W
66 Vinh, Vietnam 18 55N 105 49E
68 Vinh Loi, Vietnam 9 29N 105 50E
41 Vinkovci, Yugoslavia 45 20N 18 45E
47 Vinnitsa, U.S.S.R. 49 10N 28 30E
64 Viramgam, India 23 12N 72 3E
42 Virandeville, France 49 35N 1 44W
88 Virden, Canada 49 50N 100 55W
99 Vírgenes, C., Argentina 52 15S 68 10W
95 Virgin Is., W. Indies 18 20N 65 0W
36 Virginia, Ireland 53 50N 7 5E
76 Virginia, S. Africa 27 53S 26 45E
91 Virginia, st., U.S.A. 37 15N 79 0W
44 Virton, Belgium 49 35N 5 33E
64 Virudhungar, India 9 30N 77 55E
40 Vis I., Yugoslavia 43 0N 16 10E
90 Visalia, U.S.A. 36 23N 119 16W

** Renamed Dakhla*

68 Visayan Sea, Philippines 11 30N 123 30E
49 Visby, Sweden 57 41N 18 20E
88 Viscount Melville Sd., Canada 75 0N 110 0W
44 Visé, Belgium 50 44N 5 42E
41 Visegrad, Yugoslavia 43 47N 19 15E
37 Viseu, Portugal 40 40N 7 53W
65 Vishakhapatnam, India 17 44N 83 16E
76 Vishoek, South Africa (Inset) 34 8S 18 40E
40 Viso, Mt., Italy 44 45N 7 10E
45 Visp, Switzerland 46 19N 7 54E
47 Vistula, R., *see* Wisla
50 Vitebsk, U.S.S.R. 55 15N 30 20E
40 Viterbo, Italy 42 26N 12 10E
84 Viti Levu, I., Pac. Oc. 18 0S 178 0E
61 Vitim, & R., U.S.S.R. 59 45N 112 25E
98 Vitoria, Brazil 20 15S 40 15W
37 Vitoria, Spain 42 52N 2 35W
42 Vitré, France 48 10N 1 18W
43 Vitry le Francois, France 48 42N 4 30E
43 Vittoria, Italy 37 0N 14 30E
40 Vittorio Veneto, Italy 45 58N 12 19E
37 Vivero, Spain 43 40N 7 34W
43 Viviers, France 44 26N 4 40E
65 Vizianagaram, India 18 8N 83 24E
44 Vlaardingen, Neth. 51 55N 4 21E
52 Vladimir, U.S.S.R. 56 2N 40 35E
47 Vladimir Volynski, U.S.S.R. 50 50N 24 18E
61 Vladivostok, U.S.S.R. 42 58N 131 50E
44 Vlieland, I., Netherlands 53 15N 4 57E
44 Vlissingen, *see* Flushing
41 Vlöre (Vlöne), Albania 40 30N 19 31E
46 Vltava, R., Cz-slov. 49 20N 14 10E
57 Vogelkop Pen., Indon. 1 25S 133 0E
46 Vogels Berg, mt., Ger. 50 37N 9 30E
43 Voghera, Italy 45 0N 9 0E
75 Vohémar, Madagascar 13 25S 50 0E
75 Vohipeno, Madagascar 22 21S 47 51E
74 Voi, Kenya 3 20S 38 35E
43 Voiron, France 45 21N 5 38E
48 Vojmsjön, L., Sweden 65 0N 16 30E
48 Volda, Norway 62 12N 6 5E
44 Volendam, Netherlands 52 30N 5 4E
50 Volga, R., U.S.S.R. 57 30N 42 0E
52 Volgograd (Stalingrad), U.S.S.R. 48 42N 44 28E
50 Volkhov, R., U.S.S.R. 59 30N 32 0E
45 Volklingen, Germany 49 15N 6 51E
47 Volkovysk, U.S.S.R. 53 10N 24 30E
76 Volksrust, S. Africa 27 20S 29 58E
61 Volochanka, U.S.S.R. 70 55N 94 10E
61 Volochayevka, U.S.S.R. 48 27N 134 40E
50 Vologda, U.S.S.R. 59 10N 39 57E
41 Vólos, & G., Greece 39 26N 22 57E
52 Volsk, U.S.S.R. 52 5N 47 30E
72 Volta, R., W. Africa 5 40N 0 23E
40 Volterra, Italy 43 23N 10 54E
43 Voltri, Italy 44 26N 8 45E
40 Volturno, R., Italy 41 3N 14 0E
52 Volzhskiy, U.S.S.R. 48 53N 44 55E
44 Voorburg, Netherlands 52 4N 4 18E
48 Vopnafjördur, Iceland 65 45N 14 50W
46 Vorarlberg, Prov., Austria 47 15N 10 0E
50 Vorkuta, U.S.S.R. 67 30N 64 10E
52 Voronezh, U.S.S.R. 51 37N 39 10E
52 Voroshilovgrad, U.S.S.R. 48 35N 39 29E
52 Voroshilovsk, U.S.S.R., *see* Kommunarsk
42 Vosges, Dépt., France 48 5N 6 25E
42 Vosges, Mts., France 48 20N 7 0E
49 Voss, Norway 60 38N 6 28E
100 Vostok, Antarctica 78 30S 107 0E
100 Vostok I., Antarctica 72 0S 97 0E
50 Votkinsk, U.S.S.R. 57 5N 53 50E
37 Vouga, R., Portugal 40 45N 8 0W
43 Vouziers, France 49 20N 4 44E
43 Voves, France 48 18N 1 35E
51 Voznesensk, U.S.S.R. 47 30N 32 0E
61 Voznesenskaya, U.S.S.R. 55 15N 95 50E
50 Voznesenye, U.S.S.R. 61 6N 35 20E
47 Vranje, Yugoslavia 42 33N 21 55E
41 Vratsa, Bulgaria 43 13N 23 30E
40 Vrbas, R., Yugoslavia 45 0N 17 22E
76 Vrede, S. Africa 27 30S 29 15E
76 Vredendal, South Africa 31 35S 18 25E
75 Vredenburg, S. Africa 32 55S 18 0E
45 Vrin, Switzerland 46 40N 9 6E
41 Vrsac, Yugoslavia 45 10N 21 15E
76 Vryburg, S. Africa 26 48S 24 44E
76 Vryheid, S. Africa 27 50S 30 40E
44 Vught, Netherlands 51 39N 5 17E
40 Vulcano, I., Italy 38 29N 15 0E
50 Vyatka, R., U.S.S.R. 57 30N 49 30E
50 Vyatskiye Polyany, U.S.S.R. 56 15N 51 30E
52 Vyazma, U.S.S.R. 55 15N 34 20E
50 Vyborg, U.S.S.R. 60 45N 28 40E
50 Vychegda, R., U.S.S.R. 61 30N 48 0E
25 Vyrnwy, L. & R., Wales 52 46N 3 30W
52 Vyshniy Volochek, U.S.S.R. 57 30N 34 30E
50 Vytegra, U.S.S.R. 61 15N 36 40E

W

72 Wa, Ghana 10 5N 2 27W
44 Waal, R., Netherlands 51 33N 5 40E
44 Waalwijk, Netherlands 51 42N 5 2E
92 Wabash, & R., U.S.A. 40 54N 85 48W
88 Wabiskaw, R., Canada 57 40N 115 30W
47 Wabrzezno, Poland 53 15N 19 0E
90 Waco, U.S.A. 31 50N 97 0W
73 Wad Banda, Sudan 13 3N 27 58E

*** Incorporated within the region of Lothian*

73 Wad Medani, Sudan 14 23N 33 58E
44 Wadden Zee, Neth. 53 15N 5 0E
23 Waddesdon, England 51 51N 0 51W
88 Waddington, Mt., Can. 51 20N 125 25W
24 Wadebridge, England 50 31N 4 49W
45 Wadenswil, Switzerland 47 13N 8 40E
23 Wadhurst, England 51 4N 0 21E
63 Wadi es Sir, Jordan 31 57N 35 50E
73 Wadi Halfa, Sudan 21 52N 31 22E
25 Waenfawr, Wales 53 7N 4 10W
44 Wageningen, Neth. 51 58N 5 40E
89 Wager Bay, Canada 65 45N 91 0W
89 Wager, B., Canada 65 45N 90 0W
83 Wagga Wagga, Australia 35 10S 147 23E
80 Wagin, Australia 33 19S 117 20E
72 Wagin, Nigeria 12 42N 7 10E
68 Wahai, Indonesia 2 50S 129 35E
84 Waiau, New Zealand 42 54S 173 0E
84 Waihi, New Zealand 37 19S 175 58E
84 Waikaremoana L., N.Z. 38 45S 177 5E
84 Waikato, R., N.Z. 37 18S 174 43E
83 Waikerie, Australia 34 1S 140 0E
84 Waikokopu, N.Z. 39 0S 177 58E
84 Waikouaiti, N.Z. 45 38S 170 41E
84 Waimarino, New Zealand 39 7S 175 26E
84 Waimate, New Zealand 44 45S 171 7E
64 Wainganga, R., India 21 30N 80 0E
88 Wainwright, Canada 52 57N 111 0W
84 Waiouru, New Zealand 39 28S 175 36E
84 Waipara, New Zealand 43 3S 172 46E
84 Waipawa, New Zealand 39 54S 176 36E
84 Waipiro, New Zealand 38 2S 178 25E
84 Waipukurau, N.Z. 40 0S 176 31E
84 Wairoa, N.Z. 39 3S 177 25E
84 Waitaki, R., N.Z. 44 52S 171 14E
84 Waitara, New Zealand 38 57S 174 12E
84 Waiuku, New Zealand 37 6S 174 38E
66 Waiyeng, China 23 10N 114 30E
67 Wajima, Japan 37 28N 137 0E
74 Wajir, Kenya 1 57N 40 10E
67 Wakamatsu, Honshu, Japan 37 30N 139 58E
67 Wakamatsu, Kyushu, Japan 33 58N 130 50E
67 Wakasa B., Japan 35 50N 135 30E
84 Wakatipu, L., N.Z. 45 0S 168 30E
67 Wakayama, & Pref., Jap. 34 10N 135 12E
11 Wake I., Pacific Ocean 19 0N 167 0E
27 Wakefield, England 53 41N 1 30W
84 Wakefield, N.Z. 41 25S 173 7E
67 Wakkanai, Japan 45 20N 141 49E
76 Wakkerstroom, S. Africa 27 30S 30 12E
83 Wakool, & R., Australia 35 30S 144 20E
23 Walberswick, England 52 18N 1 39E
46 Walbrzych, Poland 50 45N 16 18E
83 Walcha, Australia 31 0S 151 38E
44 Walcheren, I., Neth. 51 39N 3 35E
49 Walcz, Poland 53 17N 16 27E
45 Wald, Switzerland 47 19N 8 54E
25 Wales, Gt. Britain 52 0N 3 30W
83 Walgett, Australia 30 15S 147 32E
83 Walhalla, Australia 37 48S 146 30E
90 Walker, L., U.S.A. 38 45N 118 42W
82 Walkerston, Australia 21 11S 149 8E
90 Walla Walla, U.S.A. 46 6N 118 25W
90 Wallace, U.S.A. 47 35N 115 58W
92 Wallaceburg, Canada 42 33N 82 26W
47 Wallachia, reg., Rum. 44 42N 25 20E
83 Wallaroo, Australia 33 56S 138 0E
26 Wallasey, England 53 26N 3 5W
83 Wallerawang, Australia 33 25S 150 0E
22 Wallingford, England 51 36N 1 8W
32 Walls, Scotland 60 13N 1 34W
27 Wallsend, England 54 59N 1 32W
83 Wallsend, Australia 33 0S 151 10E
83 Wallumbilla, Australia 26 30S 149 5E
23 Walmer, England 51 11N 1 24E
76 Walmer, South Africa 34 0S 25 25E
22 Walsall, England 52 35N 1 59W
90 Walsenburg, U.S.A. 37 42N 104 47W
23 Walsoken, England 52 40N 0 11E
27 Waltham, England 53 32N 0 6W
23 Waltham Abbey, England 51 39N 0 0
23 Waltham Forest, Greater London, England 51 37N 0 2E
26 Walton-le-Dale, England 53 45N 2 41W
23 Walton-on-the-Naze, Eng. 51 50N 1 18E
75 Walvis Bay, S.W. Africa 22 40S 14 30E
66 Wampo, Tibet, China 31 25N 86 35E
64 Wana, Pakistan 32 25N 69 30E
83 Wanbi, Australia 34 48S 140 30E
83 Wandoan, Australia 25 58S 149 59E
23 Wandsworth, Greater London, England 51 27N 0 12W
84 Wanganui, New Zealand 39 53S 175 7E
83 Wangaratta, Australia 36 25S 146 23E
66 Wanhsien, China 31 3N 108 30E
75 Wankie, Rhodesia 18 23S 26 25E
95 Wanks, R., Cent. America 15 0N 83 5W
22 Wantage, England 51 35N 1 22W
64 Warangal, India 17 57N 79 36E
83 Waratah, Australia 41 32S 145 48E
83 Warburton, Australia 37 58S 145 57E
84 Ward, New Zealand 41 58S 174 2E
33 Ward Hill, Scotland 58 54N 3 23W
76 Warden, S. Africa 27 50S 29 1E
64 Wardha, India 20 53N 78 36E
22 Wardington, England 52 8N 1 17W
26 Wardle, England 53 39N 2 38W
23 Ware, England 51 49N 0 2W
22 Wareham, England 50 40N 2 8W
83 Warialda, Australia 29 32S 150 30E
27 Warkworth, England 55 22N 1 38W
84 Warkworth, N.Z. 36 28S 174 35E
22 Warley, England 52 29N 2 2W

**** West Midlands, Co., England 52 30N 1 55W*

76 Warmbad, South Africa 24 50S 28 10E
75 Warmbad, S.W. Africa 28 23S 18 40E
22 Warminster, England 51 12N 2 12W
49 Warnemünde, Germany 54 10N 12 0E
83 Warragul, Australia 38 7S 146 0E
83 Warrego, R., Australia 29 20S 145 50E
83 Warren, Australia 31 33S 147 58E
92 Warren, Ohio, U.S.A. 41 8N 80 57W
91 Warren, Pa., U.S.A. 41 54N 79 12W
83 Warrenville, Australia 25 40S 147 20E
72 Warri, Nigeria 5 35N 5 57E
80 Warrina, Australia 28 7S 136 0E
26 Warrington, England 53 24N 2 36W
83 Warrnambool, Australia 38 18S 142 29E
47 Warsaw (Warszawa), Pol. 52 16N 21 0E
27 Warsop, England 53 13N 1 9W
47 Warszawa, *see* Warsaw
47 Warta (Warthe), R., Poland 51 20N 19 0E
83 Warwick, Australia 28 15S 152 10E
22 Warwick, & Co., Eng. 52 18N 1 35W
90 Wasatch Ra., U.S.A. 39 30N 111 30W
27 Washington, England 54 54N 1 31W
92 Washington, D.C., U.S.A. 38 58N 77 0W
91 Washington, N.C., U.S.A. 35 32N 76 54W
90 Washington, st., U.S.A. 47 45N 121 0W
64 Washir, Afghanistan 32 15N 63 50E
44 Wassenaar, Netherlands 52 8N 4 24E
43 Wassy, France 48 30N 5 0E
26 Wast Water, L., Eng. 54 26N 3 19W
92 Waswanipi, L., & R., Canada 49 30N 76 25W
24 Watchet, England 51 1N 3 18W
75 Waterberg, S.W. Africa 20 23S 17 9E
76 Waterberge, mts., South Africa 24 30S 28 0E
93 Waterbury, U.S.A. 41 32N 73 0W
35 Waterford, & Co., Ire. 52 15N 7 7W
34 Watergrasshill, Ireland 52 1N 8 21W
44 Waterloo, Belgium 50 43N 4 24E
26 Waterloo, England 53 29N 2 59W
72 Waterloo, Sierra Leone 8 26N 13 8W
91 Waterloo, U.S.A. 42 30N 92 16W
32 Waternish, Scotland 57 32N 6 35W
93 Watertown, N.Y., U.S.A. 43 57N 75 50W
91 Watertown, S.D., U.S.A. 44 58N 97 4W
76 Waterval-Boven, S. Africa 25 40S 30 20E
34 Waterville, Ireland 51 49N 10 11W
93 Waterville, U.S.A. 44 30N 69 0W
93 Watervliet, U.S.A. 42 40N 73 40W
23 Watford, England 51 39N 0 23W
95 Watling's I., Bahamas 24 0N 74 35W
23 Watlington, Norfolk, England 52 40N 0 24E
23 Watlington, Oxford, England 51 39N 1 1W
88 Watrous, Canada 51 40N 105 30W
74 Watsa, Zaïre 3 0N 29 30E
33 Watten, Scotland 58 29N 3 18W
45 Wattwil, Switzerland 47 20N 9 6E
73 Wau, & R., Sudan 7 50N 28 2E
83 Wauchope, Australia 31 27S 152 44E
91 Waukegan, U.S.A. 42 23N 87 51W
92 Wausau, U.S.A. 45 0N 89 35W
80 Wave Hill, Australia 17 32S 130 58E
23 Waveney, R., England 52 21N 1 13E
84 Waverley, N.Z. 39 46S 174 35E
44 Wavre, Belgium 50 43N 4 37E
91 Waxahachie, U.S.A. 32 23N 96 52W
44 Waxweiler, Germany 50 6N 6 22E
91 Waycross, U.S.A. 31 10N 82 25W
64 Wazi Khwa, Afghanistan 32 5N 68 15E
64 Wazirabad, Pakistan 32 30N 74 5E
23 Weald, The, England 51 9N 0 20E
26 Wear, R., England 54 48N 1 33W
26 Weaver, R., England 53 0N 2 31W
90 Weatherford, U.S.A. 32 45N 97 47W
91 Webster City, U.S.A. 42 30N 93 48W
68 Weda, Indonesia 1 15N 127 50E
100 Weddell Sea, Antarctica 68 0S 40 0W
83 Wedderburn, Australia 36 28S 143 37E
22 Wednesbury, England 52 33N 2 2W
22 Wednesfield, England 52 36N 2 3W
83 Wee Waa, Australia 30 3S 149 30E
44 Weert, Netherlands 51 16N 5 44E
67 Weifang, China 36 45N 119 0E
67 Weihai, China 37 30N 122 0E
46 Weimar, Germany 50 59N 11 15E
45 Weinheim, Germany 49 37N 8 45E
66 Weining, China 27 0N 103 50E
90 Weiser, U.S.A. 44 15N 117 3W
65 Weisi, China 27 10N 99 15E
62 Wejh, Saudi Arabia 26 15N 36 30E
47 Wejherowo, Poland 54 36N 18 15E
76 Welkom, South Africa 28 0S 26 45E
92 Welland, & Can., Canada 43 0N 79 6W
23 Welland, R., England 52 40N 0 20W
82 Wellesley Is., Australia 16 45S 139 30E
44 Wellin, Belgium 50 5N 5 6E
23 Wellingborough, Eng. 52 19N 0 42W
83 Wellington, Australia 32 30S 148 58E
22 Wellington, Salop., Eng. 52 42N 2 30W
24 Wellington, Som., Eng. 50 58N 3 14W
76 Wellington, South Africa 33 35S 19 0E
91 Wellington, U.S.A. 37 14N 97 26W
84 Wellington, & Dist., N.Z. 41 15S 176 46E
99 Wellington I., Chile 49 30S 75 0W
35 Wellington Bridge, Ire. 52 15N 6 45W
24 Wells, England 51 13N 2 38W
80 Wells, L., Australia 27 0S 123 35E
46 Wels, Austria 48 10N 14 0E
25 Welshpool, Wales 52 39N 3 9W
23 Welwyn, England 51 48N 0 13W
22 Wem, England 52 52N 2 44E

† Incorporated within the counties of North, West & South Yorkshire

90 Wenatchee, U.S.A. 47 25N 120 25W
67 Wenchow, China 27 59N 120 30E
23 Wendover, England 51 47N 0 45W
45 Wengen, Switzerland 46 28N 7 56E
82 Wenlock, R., Australia 12 15S 142 0E
22 Wenlock Edge, England 52 30N 2 46W
27 Wensleydale, England 54 18N 2 10W
23 Wensum, R., England 52 47N 0 55E
83 Wentworth, Australia 34 10S 141 50E
22 Weobley, England 52 9N 2 53W
76 Wepener, South Africa 29 46S 27 1E
46 Werra, R., Germany 51 10N 10 0E
83 Werribee, Australia 38 0S 144 40E
83 Werris Creek, Austral. 31 8S 150 36E
44 Wesel, Germany 51 41N 6 39E
46 Weser, R., Germany 52 30N 9 0E
65 West Bengal, St., India 23 0N 87 0E
47 West Beskids, Mts., Czechoslovakia 49 30N 19 20E
27 West Bridgford, England 52 56N 1 8W
22 West Bromwich, England 52 31N 1 59W
32 West Burra I., Scotland 60 7N 1 5W
31 West Calder, Scotland 55 52N 3 34W
13 West Dvina R., Europe 55 40N 28 0E
44 West Flanders, Belgium 50 58N 3 0E
91 West Frankfort, U.S.A. 37 49N 88 46W
46 West Germany, Europe 51 0N 9 0E
23 West Grinstead, Eng. 50 58N 0 18W
30 West Kilbride, Scotland 55 42N 4 51W
26 West Kirby, England 53 23N 3 11W
31 West Linton, Scotland 55 45N 3 24W
24 West Looe, England 50 20N 4 27W
**31 West Lothian, Co., Scot. 55 55N 3 37W
***75 West Nicholson, Rhodesia 21 1S 29 20E
64 West Pakistan, Asia 27 0N 67 0W
91 West Palm Beach, U.S.A. 26 40N 80 12W
93 West Pt., C., Canada 49 50N 64 40W
27 West Rasen, England 53 23N 0 23W
†27 West Riding, Yorks., Eng. 53 50N 1 30W
44 West Schelde, R., Neth. 51 23N 3 50E
60 West Siberian Plain, U.S.S.R. 62 0N 76 0E
23 West Suffolk, England 52 9N 0 45E
23 West Sussex, England 50 53N 0 30W
92 West Virginia, st., U.S.A. 39 0N 81 0W
83 West Wyalong, Australia 33 56S 147 10E
23 Westbourne, England 50 22N 0 56W
83 Westbury, Australia 41 32S 147 0E
22 Westbury, Salop., Eng. 52 41N 2 57W
22 Westbury, Wilts., England 51 15N 2 11W
46 Wester Wald, mts., Ger. 50 40N 8 0E
23 Westerham, England 51 16N 0 5W
80 Western Australia, st., Australia 25 0S 121 30E
64 Western Ghats, mts., India 15 0N 74 0E
84 Western Samoa, Pacific Ocean (Inset)
61 Western Sayan, U.S.S.R. 52 30N 94 0E
44 Westfriesche Eilanden, Netherlands 53 30N 5 15E
26 Westhoughton, England 53 34N 2 30W
84 Westland Dist., N.Z. 43 0S 170 0E
35 Westmeath, Co., Ireland 53 30N 7 30W
††26 Westmorland, Co., Eng. 54 27N 2 40W
22 Weston, England 52 51N 2 2W
24 Weston-super-Mare, Eng. 51 21N 2 58W
35 Westport, & B., Ireland 53 48N 9 32W
84 Westport, New Zealand 41 50S 171 52E
33 Westray, I. & Firth, Scot. 59 17N 2 58W
31 Westruther, Scotland 55 45N 2 34W
68 Wetar I., Indonesia 7 50S 126 20E
88 Wetaskiwin, Canada 52 58N 113 20W
27 Wetherby, England 53 57N 1 24W
44 Wetteren, Belgium 51 0N 3 53E
46 Wetzlar, Germany 50 34N 8 27E
82 Wewak, Terr. of New Guinea 3 40S 143 30E
35 Wexford, & Co., Ireland 52 19N 6 28W
35 Wexford Hr., Ireland 52 20N 6 23W
23 Wey, R., England 51 18N 0 30W
27 Weybourne, England 52 58N 1 8E
23 Weybridge, England 51 22N 0 28W
88 Weyburn, Canada 49 40N 104 56W
89 Weymont, Canada 47 50N 73 50W
22 Weymouth, England 50 36N 2 28W
84 Whakatane, New Zealand 37 59S 177 0E
89 Whale R., Canada 55 25N 76 0W
100 Whales, B. of, Antarc. 78 30S 165 0W
26 Whaley Bridge, England 53 20N 1 59W
32 Whalsay I., Scotland 60 21N 0 58W
84 Whangamomona, N.Z. 39 8S 174 44E
84 Whangarei, N.Z. 35 41S 174 20E
26 Wharfedale, England 54 8N 2 0W
90 Wheeler Pk., U.S.A. 39 20N 114 30W
92 Wheeling, U.S.A. 40 0N 80 38W
26 Whernside, mt., England 54 15N 2 24W
23 Whiston, England 53 25N 2 45W
31 Whitburn, Scot., U.K. 55 52N 3 41W
27 Whitby, England 54 29N 0 38W
24 Whitchurch, Devon, Eng. 50 31N 4 7W
22 Whitchurch, Hants., Eng. 51 15N 1 21W
22 Whitchurch, Salop., Eng. 52 58N 2 41W
25 Whitchurch, Wales 51 32N 3 15W
82 Whitecliffs, N.Z. 43 26S 171 55E
47 White Crisul, R., Rum. 46 18N 22 20E
41 White Drin, R., Y.-slav. 42 30N 20 34E
31 White Esk, R., Scotland 55 15N 3 10W
22 White Horse Vale, Eng. 51 39N 1 35W
84 White I., New Zealand 37 29S 177 14E
47 White Mts., Cz-slov. 49 0N 17 40E
90 White Mts., U.S.A. 37 15N 118 15W
73 White Nile, *see* Bahr el Abiad
50 White Russia (Byelorussia), S.S.R., U.S.S.R. 53 30N 30 0E
50 White Sea, U.S.S.R. 65 30N 37 30E

†† Incorporated within the county of Cumbria

31 Whiteadder, R., Scotland 55 50N 2 25w
91 Whitefish B., U.S.A. 47 0N 85 0w
34 Whitegate, Ireland 51 49N 8 14w
26 Whitehaven, England 54 33N 3 36w
88 Whitehorse, Canada 60 40N 135 5w
31 Whitekirk, Scotland 56 2N 2 36w
83 Whitemark, Australia 40 4s 148 0E
83 Whitfield, Australia 36 50s 146 23E
30 Whithorn, Scotland 54 44N 4 24w
84 Whitianga, N.Z. 36 50s 175 40E
25 Whitland, Wales 51 49N 4 37w
27 Whitley B., England 55 3N 1 26w
90 Whitney, Mt., U.S.A. 36 45N 118 30w
23 Whitstable, England 51 21N 1 2E
82 Whitsunday I., Australia 20 15s 149 4E
88 Whittier, Alaska 60 5N 140 50w
27 Whittington, Derby, Eng. 53 17N 1 24w
27 Whittington, Salop., Eng. 52 53N 2 59w
23 Whittlesey, England 52 33N 0 7w
27 Whitwell, England 53 16N 1 11w
27 Whitworth, England 53 39N 2 11w
88 Wholdaia L., Canada 60 40N 104 20w
83 Whyalla, Australia 33 0s 137 28E
83 Whyjonta, Australia 29 40s 142 25E
91 Wichita, U.S.A. 37 48N 97 12w
90 Wichita Falls, U.S.A. 33 58N 98 36w
33 Wick, Scotland 58 27N 3 8w
23 Wickford, England 51 37N 0 31E
35 Wicklow, & Co., Ireland 52 58N 6 2w
35 Wicklow Mts., Ireland 53 5N 6 25w
31 Widdrington, England 55 15N 1 35w
24 Widemouth, England 50 45N 4 34w
26 Widnes, England 53 21N 2 46w
47 Wieliczka, Poland 49 59N 20 5E
47 Wielun, Poland 51 12N 18 45E
46 Wien, *see* Vienna
46 Wiener Neustadt, Austria 47 48N 16 13E
45 Wiesbaden, Germany 50 5N 8 14E
26 Wigan, England 53 33N 2 38w
*22 Wight, Isle of, England 50 40N 1 20w
22 Wigmore, England 52 19N 2 52w
22 Wigston, England 52 35N 1 6w
26 Wigton, England 54 50N 3 9w
**30 Wigtown, & Co., Scot. 54 52N 4 27w
30 Wigtown B., Scotland 54 48N 4 17w
45 Wil, Switzerland 47 28N 9 3E
83 Wilcannia, Australia 31 36s 143 20E
47 Wilhelmshaven, Germany 43 34N 8 8E
100 Wilkes, Antarctica 66 0s 111 0E
93 Wilkes Barre, U.S.A. 41 18N 75 48w
100 Wilkes Basin, Antarctica 77 0s 138 0E
88 Wilkie, Canada 52 20N 108 40w
44 Willebroek, Belgium 51 5N 4 20E
95 Willemstadt, Neth., Antilles
12 0N 69 0w
22 Willenhall, England 52 36N 2 3w
23 Willesborough, England 51 8N 0 55E
88 Williams L., Canada 52 20N 122 10w
92 Williamson, U.S.A. 37 38N 82 10w
92 Williamsport, U.S.A. 41 19N 77 7w
83 Williamstown, Australia 37 45s 144 49E
23 Willingdon, England 50 47N 0 16E
27 Willington, England 54 43N 1 41w
45 Willisau, Switzerland 47 7N 8 0E
76 Williston, South Africa 31 20s 20 59E
90 Williston, U.S.A. 48 2N 104 3w
24 Williton, England 51 10N 3 18w
76 Willowmore, S. Africa 33 10s 23 37E
83 Willunga, Australia 35 27s 138 32E
83 Wilmington, Australia 32 30s 138 0E
24 Wilmington, England 50 46N 3 8w
93 Wilmington, Del., U.S.A. 39 47N 75 35w
91 Wilmington, N.C., U.S.A.
34 12N 77 50w
26 Wilmslow, England 53 19N 2 14w
22 Wilnecote, England 52 37N 1 39w
91 Wilson, U.S.A. 35 44N 77 55w
83 Wilson's Promontory, Australia
39 1s 146 29E
22 Wilton, England 51 5N 1 51w
22 Wiltshire, Co., England 51 18N 1 55w
44 Wiltz, Luxembourg 49 58N 5 57E
80 Wiluna, Australia 26 30s 120 4E
22 Wimborne Minster, Eng. 50 48N 1 58w
76 Winburg, S. Africa 28 25s 27 22E
24 Wincanton, England 51 3N 2 25w
23 Winchelsea, England 50 56N 0 42E
22 Winchester, England 51 4N 1 19w
92 Winchester, U.S.A. 39 18N 78 10w
90 Wind River Ra., U.S.A.
43 45N 109 40w
83 Windera, Australia 25 59s 151 37E
26 Windermere & L., Eng. 54 20N 2 57w
75 Windhoek, S.W. Africa 22 37s 17 8E
83 Windsor, Australia 33 40s 150 45E
93 Windsor, Nova Scotia, Canada
45 0N 64 08w
93 Windsor, Ontario, Can. 42 17N 83 0w
23 Windsor, England 51 28N 0 36w
76 Windsorton, S. Africa 28 20s 24 50E
95 Windward Is., W. Indies 13 30N 61 0w
95 Windward Passage, W. Indies
20 0N 73 30w
31 Windygates, Scotland 56 12N 3 1w
91 Winfield, U.S.A. 37 20N 97 15w
83 Wingen, Australia 31 55s 150 55E
83 Wingham, Australia 31 42s 152 3E
23 Wingham, England 51 16N 1 12E
* *Created a county, separate from Hampshire*
** *County incorporated within the region of Dumfries and Galloway*

89 Winisk, R., Canada 54 40N 87 0w
72 Winneba, Ghana 5 25N 0 36w
90 Winnemucca, U.S.A. 40 59N 117 45w
88 Winnipeg, Canada 49 55N 97 15w
88 Winnipeg, L., Canada 52 0N 98 0w
88 Winnipegosis, L., Can. 52 30N 99 50w
92 Winona, U.S.A. 44 0N 91 44w
26 Winsford, England 53 12N 2 31w
44 Winschoten, Netherlands 53 10N 7 3E
23 Winslow, England 51 56N 0 53w
90 Winslow, U.S.A. 35 5N 100 45w
91 Winston Salem, U.S.A. 35 8N 80 24w
44 Winterswyk, Neth. 51 58N 6 44E
45 Winterthur, Switzerland 47 30N 8 42E
82 Winton, Australia 22 23s 143 2E
84 Winton, New Zealand 46 10s 168 21E
27 Wirksworth, England 53 6N 1 35w
26 Wirral Pen., England 53 20N 3 5w
23 Wisbech, England 52 39N 0 9E
91 Wisconsin Rapids, U.S.A.
44 26N 89 43w
92 Wisconsin, st., U.S.A. 45 0N 90 0w
47 Wisla (Vistula) R., Pol. 53 0N 18 55E
49 Wismar, Germany 53 54N 11 23E
43 Wissembourg, France 49 0N 7 58E
75 Witbank, South Africa 25 52s 29 8E
23 Witham, England 51 48N 0 38E
27 Witham R., England 53 7N 0 13w
27 Withern, England 53 20N 0 8E
27 Withernsea, England 53 45N 0 1E
23 Witley, England 51 9N 0 39w
22 Witney, England 51 48N 1 29w
46 Wittenberge, Germany 53 0N 11 41E
46 Wittenburg, Germany 51 52N 12 45E
80 Wittenoom, Australia 22 15s 118 20E
44 Wittlich, Germany 49 59N 6 52E
47 Wlocklawek, Poland 52 36N 19 5E
47 Wlodawa, Poland 51 30N 23 30E
23 Woburn, England 51 59N 0 36w
23 Woburn Sands, England 52 1N 0 38w
83 Wodonga, Australia 36 3s 146 57E
23 Woking, England 51 18N 0 34w
23 Wokingham, England 51 24N 0 50w
45 Wolhusen, Switzerland 47 4N 8 5E
46 Wolin, I., Poland 53 40N 14 37E
88 Wollaston, L., Canada 58 20N 103 20w
88 Wollaston Pen., Canada 69 30N 113 0w
83 Wollongong, Australia 34 25s 151 0E
76 Wolmaransstad, S. Africa 27 20s 26 0E
83 Wolseley, Australia 36 20s 141 0E
26 Wolsingham, England 54 44N 1 52w
44 Wolvega, Netherlands 52 53N 6 0E
22 Wolverhampton 52 36N 2 8w
23 Wolverton, England 52 3N 0 47w
27 Wombwell, England 53 32N 1 24w
83 Wondai, Australia 26 12s 151 48E
67 Wonsan, Korea 39 20N 127 25E
83 Wonthaggi, Australia 38 28s 145 38E
23 Woodbridge, England 52 7N 1 20E
83 Woodend, Australia 37 20N 144 33E
34 Woodford, Ireland 53 3N 8 24w
82 Woodlark I., Pac. Oc. 9 0s 152 45E
23 Woodley, England 51 26N 0 54w
80 Woodroffe, Mt., Austral. 26 16s 131 30E
80 Woods, L., Australia 18 0s 133 0E
88 Woods, L., of the, Canada-U.S.A.
49 30N 94 30w
83 Woodside, Australia 38 45s 147 0E
93 Woodstock, N.B., Can. 46 12N 67 45w
92 Woodstock, Ont., Can. 43 7N 80 46w
84 Woodville, New Zealand 40 19s 175 59E
24 Wookey Hole, England 51 14N 2 40w
22 Wool, England 50 41N 2 14w
24 Woolacombe, England 51 11N 4 12w
83 Woolgoolga, Australia 30 7s 153 12E
83 Woombye, Australia 26 40s 152 58E
81 Woomera, Australia 31 5s 136 50E
93 Woonsocket, U.S.A. 42 1N 71 30w
83 Wooroorooka, Australia 27 59s 145 58E
67 Woosung, China 31 20N 121 25E
22 Wootton Bassett, Eng. 51 32N 1 55w
76 Worcester, South Africa 33 40s 19 28E
†22 Worcester, & Co., Eng. 52 11N 2 13w
91 Worcester, U.S.A. 42 18N 71 45w
22 Worfield, England 52 34N 2 22w
26 Workington, England 54 38N 3 34w
27 Worksop, England 53 19N 1 8w
44 Workum, Netherlands 52 59N 5 27E
44 Wormerveer, Netherlands 52 30N 4 45E
45 Worms, Germany 49 40N 8 20E
23 Wortham, England 52 22N 1 3E
23 Worthing, England 50 48N 0 22w
74 Wota, Ethiopia 7 4N 35 51E
22 Wotton-under-Edge, Eng. 51 38N 2 21w
73 Wour, Chad. 21 20N 15 48E
61 Wrangel I., U.S.S.R. 71 30N 180 0E
88 Wrangell, Alaska 56 30N 132 52w
88 Wrangell Mts., Alaska 61 40N 143 30w
32 Wrath, C., Scotland 58 38N 5 0w
22 Wrekin, Mt., England 52 40N 2 33w
25 Wrexham, Wales 53 4N 3 0w
68 Wright, Philippines 11 45N 125 0E
88 Wrigley, Canada 63 0N 123 30w
24 Writhlington, England 51 18N 2 16w
46 Wroclaw (Breslau), Poland 51 6N 17 0E
23 Wrotham, England 51 18N 0 20E
22 Wroughton, England 51 32N 1 48w
66 Wu Kiang, R., China 27 30N 107 30E
† *County incorporated within Hereford and Worcester*

55 Wu Yis Shan, mts., China 28 0N 118 0E
66 Wuchang, China 30 45N 114 25E
66 Wu-chow, China 23 35N 110 49E
66 Wuhan, China 30 45N 114 15E
66 Wu-hu, China 31 12N 118 20E
64 Wun, India 20 0N 79 0E
65 Wuntho, Burma 24 0N 95 30E
44 Wuppertal, Germany 51 15N 7 15E
45 Würzburg, Germany 49 45N 9 59E
67 Wusih, China 31 30N 120 5E
66 Wuwei, China 38 0N 102 25E
83 Wyandra, Australia 27 15s 145 58E
83 Wycheproof, Australia 36 0s 143 17E
25 Wye, R., Wales 52 15N 3 27w
23 Wymondham, England 52 45N 0 42w
23 Wymondham, England 52 33N 1 8E
76 Wynberg, South Africa 34 0s 18 27E
84 Wyndham, New Zealand 46 20s 168 51E
80 Wyndham, Australia 15 18s 127 58E
25 Wynnstay, Wales 52 36N 3 33w
83 Wynnum, Australia 28 0s 152 58E
83 Wynyard, Australia 41 0s 145 45E
90 Wyoming, St., U.S.A. 43 30N 107 30w
83 Wyong, Australia 33 5s 151 25E
26 Wyre, R., England 53 54N 2 48w
22 Wyre Forest, England 52 23N 2 25w

X

41 Xánthi, Greece 41 5N 24 55E
75 Xinavane, Mozambique 25 2s 32 47E
98 Xingu, R., Brazil 6 0s 53 0w

Y

66 Yaan, China 30 10N 101 50E
83 Yaapeet, Australia 35 48s 142 0E
63 Ya'bad, Israel 32 27N 35 10E
74 Yaballo, Ethiopia 4 57N 38 8E
63 Yabis, Wadi, Jordan 32 25N 35 40E
61 Yablonovy Ra., U.S.S.R. 52 0N 114 0E
64 Yadgir, India 16 50N 77 0E
65 Yakiang, China 30 2N 101 10E
90 Yakima, U.S.A. 46 40N 120 35w
72 Yako, Volta 12 58N 2 11w
73 Yakoma, Zaïre 4 0N 22 17E
67 Yakoshih, China 49 30N 120 45E
61 Yakutsk, U.S.S.R. 62 0N 129 0E
61 Yakut, A.S.S.R., U.S.S.R. 66 0N 130 0E
88 Yakutat, Alaska 59 38N 139 40w
82 Yalleroi, Australia 24 3s 145 42E
83 Yallourn, Australia 38 10s 146 18E
51 Yalta, U.S.S.R. 44 28N 34 10E
67 Yalu R., Korea 40 40N 126 20E
66 Yalung, R., China 27 30N 101 45E
67 Yamagata, & Pref., Jap. 38 10N 140 6E
67 Yamaguchi, & Pref., Jap. 34 8N 131 30E
60 Yamal Pen., U.S.S.R. 70 0N 70 0E
67 Yamanashi, Pref., Japan 35 30N 138 30E
50 Yaman Tau, Mt., U.S.S.R. 54 0N 59 0E
83 Yamba, N.S.W., Austral. 29 25s 152 15E
73 Yambio, Sudan 4 38N 28 24E
41 Yambol, Bulgaria 42 30N 26 33E
65 Yamdrok Tso L., China 29 0N 90 30E
65 Yamethin, Burma 20 29N 96 18E
83 Yamma Yamma, L., Australia
26 20s 141 25E
64 Yamuna, R. (Jumna), India
27 10N 79 0E
61 Yana R., U.S.S.R. 69 0N 135 0E
83 Yanac, Australia 36 4s 141 12E
65 Yandoon, Burma 17 0N 95 40E
66 Yangchuan, China 38 5N 113 0E
66 Yangtze (Kinsha) R., China
32 30N 98 0E
66 Yang-tze-kiang, R., China
31 45N 121 15E
91 Yankton, U.S.A. 42 58N 97 26w
83 Yanna, Australia 26 55s 146 5E
73 Yao, Chad 12 58N 17 32E
72 Yaoundé, Cameroon 4 0N 11 20E
94 Yaqui, R., Mexico 27 30N 110 0w
82 Yaraka, Australia 24 53s 144 3E
23 Yare, R., England 52 35N 1 28E
62 Yarim, Yemen 14 14N 43 23E
57 Yarkand, China 38 15N 77 0E
64 Yarkhun, R., Pak. 36 30N 72 30E
31 Yarm, England 54 31N 1 20w
93 Yarmouth, Canada 43 50N 66 20w
52 Yaroslavl, U.S.S.R. 57 40N 40 0E
83 Yarram, Australia 38 29s 146 40E
83 Yarraman, Australia 26 50s 151 59E
31 Yarrow, Scotland 55 32N 3 0w
61 Yartsevo, U.S.S.R. 60 20N 90 0E
83 Yass, Australia 34 50s 148 58E
88 Yathkyed L., Canada 62 45N 98 0w
63 Yatta, Jordan 31 28N 35 5E
67 Yawata, Japan 33 54N 130 56E
23 Yaxley, England 52 31N 0 14w
64 Yazdan, Iran 33 30N 60 45E
91 Yazoo City, U.S.A. 32 51N 90 26w
91 Yazoo, R., U.S.A. 32 48N 90 45w
65 Ye-Byu, Burma 14 10N 98 15E
47 Yedintsy, U.S.S.R. 48 5N 27 20E
52 Yegoryevsk, U.S.S.R. 55 23N 39 2E
67 Yehsien, China 37 10N 119 55E
51 Yeysk, U.S.S.R. 46 38N 38 10E
72 Yeji, Ghana 8 11N 0 41w

52 Yelets, U.S.S.R. 52 42N 38 33E
72 Yelimane, Mali 15 4N 10 30w
32 Yell I. & Sd., Scotland 60 35N 1 5w
67 Yellow Sea, China 35 30N 123 0E
88 Yellowhead P., Canada
52 40N 117 45w
88 Yellowknife, & R., Can. 62 14N 114 2w
90 Yellowstone National Park, U.S.A.
44 15N 110 0w
90 Yellowstone R., U.S.A. 46 20N 107 0w
62 Yemen, Arabia 16 0N 44 30E
52 Yenakiyevo, U.S.S.R. 48 20N 38 10E
66 Yenan, China 37 5N 108 55E
62 Yenbo, Saudi Arabia 24 0N 38 20E
60 Yenisey, G. & R., U.S.S.R.
72 20N 80 0E
61 Yeniseysk, U.S.S.R. 58 25N 91 30E
67 Yenki, China 43 10N 129 25E
66 Yenki, China 42 30N 86 0E
67 Yentai, China, *see* Chefoo
24 Yeo, R., England 51 0N 2 48w
64 Yeola, India 20 0N 74 25E
64 Yeotmal, India 20 26N 78 4E
24 Yeovil, England 50 57N 2 38w
82 Yeppoon, Australia 23 0s 150 45E
60 Yerbent, U.S.S.R. 39 30N 58 50E
51 Yerevan, U.S.S.R. 40 10N 44 20E
61 Yermakovo, U.S.S.R. 52 35N 126 20E
61 Yerofei Paulovich, U.S.S.R.
54 0N 122 0E
98 Yerupaja, Mt., Peru 10 20s 77 0w
24 Yes Tor, England 50 43N 3 57w
61 Yessei, U.S.S.R. 68 25N 102 10E
42 Yeu, I. d', France 46 43N 2 20w
51 Yevpatoriya, U.S.S.R. 45 15N 33 20E
52 Yevstratovskiy, U.S.S.R. 50 7N 39 44E
62 Yezd, Iran 31 55N 54 22E
41 Yiannitsa, Greece 40 45N 22 22E
66 Yinchwan (Ningsia), China
38 45N 106 5E
66 Yingtan, China 28 20N 116 25E
65 Yinmabin, Burma 22 10N 94 55E
74 Yirol, Sudan 6 30N 30 30E
41 Yithion, Greece 36 40N 22 40E
66 Yiyang, China 28 45N 112 30E
48 Ylitornio, Finland 66 25N 23 45E
48 Ylivieska, Finland 64 2N 24 30E
72 Yobe, R., Nigeria 13 0N 12 0E
74 Yokadouma, Cameroon 3 35N 14 50E
73 Yoko, Cameroon 5 35N 12 28E
67 Yokohama, Japan 35 25N 139 35E
67 Yokosuka, Japan 35 18N 139 36E
67 Yokote, Japan 39 20N 140 30E
73 Yola, Nigeria 9 10N 12 37E
67 Yonago, Japan 35 30N 133 20E
67 Yonezawa, Japan 37 57N 140 4E
91 Yonkers, U.S.A. 41 0N 73 57w
42 Yonne, Dépt., France 47 50N 3 45E
43 Yonne, R., France 48 0N 3 20E
82 York, Australia 31 50s 116 48E
27 York, England 53 58N 1 5w
82 York, C., Australia 10 50s 142 30E
89 York Factory, Canada 56 4N 92 35w
80 York Sd., Australia 14 57s 125 5E
27 York Wolds, England 54 0N 0 40w
83 Yorke Pen., Australia 34 45s 137 38E
28 Yorkshire, Co., England 54 4N 1 15w
88 Yorkton, Canada 51 17N 102 35w
90 Yosemite National Park, U.S.A.
37 30N 119 30w
50 Yoshkar Ola, U.S.S.R. 56 40N 47 50E
34 Youghal & Bay, Ireland 51 57N 7 51w
83 Young, Australia 34 18s 148 18E
91 Youngstown, U.S.A. 41 2N 80 43w
51 Yozgat, Turkey 39 53N 34 48E
44 Ypres, Belgium 50 50N 2 52E
48 Ystad, Sweden 55 25N 13 48E
25 Ystwyth, R., Wales 52 20N 3 48w
33 Ythan, R., Scotland 57 26N 2 15w
94 Yucatan, Dist., Mexico 19 30N 89 30w
94 Yucatan Str., Mexico 22 0N 86 20w
60 Yudino, U.S.S.R. 55 10N 67 55E
46-47 Yugoslavia, Europe 44 30N 18 0E
66 Yukiang, China 22 50N 109 0E
86 Yukon R., Alaska 65 0N 154 0w
88 Yukon, Terr. Canada 61 45N 133 30w
66 Yungan, China 26 0N 117 0E
67 Yunkia, China, *see* Wenchow
66 Yulin, China 18 25N 109 20E
90 Yuma, U.S.A. 32 40N 114 35w
66 Yunnan, Prov., China 25 30N 102 0E
66 Yushan, China 28 46N 119 3E
67 Yushan, Mt., Taiwan 23 30N 121 5E
66 Yushu, China 33 10N 96 10E
66 Yutze, China 37 45N 112 25E
67 Yuzhno Sakhalinsk, U.S.S.R.
46 50N 143 30E
42 Yvelines, Dépt., France 49 0N 1 50E
45 Yverdon, Switzerland 46 47N 6 39E
43 Yvetot, France 49 38N 0 45E

Z

44 Zaandam, Netherlands 52 27N 4 48E
63 Zabdani, Syria 33 44N 36 7E
62 Zabid, Yemen 14 8N 43 15E
94 Zacapa, Guatemala 15 0N 89 35w
94 Zacatecas, Mexico 22 52N 102 15w

94 Zacoalco, Mexico 20 5N 103 33w
40 Zadar, Yugoslavia 44 9N 15 15E
37 Zafra, Spain 38 28N 6 28w
62 Zagazig, Egypt 30 33N 31 12E
52 Zagorsk, U.S.S.R. 56 23N 28 10E
40 Zagreb, Yugoslavia 45 47N 15 58E
51 Zagros Mts., Iran 33 45N 47 0E
64 Zahidan, Iran 29 35N 60 50E
63 Zahlah, Lebanon 33 50N 35 55E
74 Zaïre, Rep. of, Africa 3 0s 23 0E
74 Zaïre, R., Africa 2 0N 22 0E
60 Zaisan, L., U.S.S.R. 48 10N 83 35E
41 Zákinthos, & I., Greece
37 48N 20 57E
47 Zaleshchiki, U.S.S.R. 48 48N 25 45E
75 Zambezi, Zambia 13 38s 23 7E
75 Zambezi, R., Africa 18 50s 36 20E
74-75 Zambia, Africa 15 0s 28 0E
68 Zamboanga, Philippines 6 55N 122 0E
52 Zametchino, U.S.S.R. 53 30N 42 38E
94 Zamora, Mexico 20 0N 102 10w
37 Zamora, Spain 41 30N 5 49w
47 Zamosc, Poland 50 43N 23 18E
44 Zandvoort, Netherlands 52 21N 4 33E
74 Zanzibar I., E. Africa 6 0s 39 17E
72 Zaouiet el-Kahla, Algeria 27 10N 6 40E
99 Zapala, Argentina 39 0s 70 0w
52 Zaporozhye, U.S.S.R. 47 45N 35 10E
37 Zaragoza, Spain 41 38N 0 50w
99 Zárate, Argentina 34 0s 59 0w
72 Zaria, Nigeria 11 0N 7 25E
46 Zary, Poland 51 37N 15 10E
73 Zarzis, Libya 33 30N 11 0E
61 Zashiversk, U.S.S.R. 67 25N 142 40E
64 Zaskar Mts., Kashmir & India
33 0N 77 20E
76 Zastron, South Africa 30 10s 27 3E
61 Zavitinsk, U.S.S.R. 50 10N 129 20E
47 Zawiercie, Poland 50 20N 19 30E
47 Zdunska Wola, Poland 51 38N 19 0E
44 Zeebrugge, Belgium 51 19N 3 12E
44 Zeeland, Prov., Neth. 51 30N 3 50E
76 Zeerust, South Africa 25 33s 26 1E
62 Zeila, Somali Rep. 11 0N 43 30E
44 Zeist, Netherlands 52 5N 5 15E
47 Zelenogradsk, U.S.S.R. 54 53N 20 29E
44 Zelzate, Belgium 51 12N 3 49E
73 Zemio, Central Africa 5 3N 25 11E
41 Zemun, Yugoslavia 44 51N 20 25E
51 Zenjan, Iran 36 39N 48 30E
46 Zerbst, Germany 51 59N 12 8E
45 Zermatt, Switzerland 46 1N 7 44E
45 Zerriez, Switzerland 46 43N 10 6E
††29 Zetland Co., Scotland 60 20N 1 20w
61 Zeya, & R., U.S.S.R. 54 10N 127 20E
51 Zeytin, Turkey 37 53N 36 53E
37 Zezere, R., Portugal 40 10N 7 40w
47 Zhabinka, U.S.S.R. 52 17N 24 3E
52 Zhdanov, U.S.S.R. 47 2N 37 36E
52 Zhitomir, U.S.S.R. 50 20N 28 42E
50 Zhlobin, U.S.S.R. 53 0N 30 0E
47 Zhmerinka, U.S.S.R. 49 1N 28 2E
61 Zhupanovo, U.S.S.R. 53 50N 159 35E
46 Zielona Gora, Poland 51 57N 15 31E
44 Zierikzee, Netherlands 51 40N 3 55E
73 Ziguei, Chad 14 45N 15 48E
72 Ziguinchor, Sénégal 12 25N 16 20w
63 Zikhron Yaagov, Israel 32 35N 34 57E
62 Zilfi, Saudi Arabia 26 30N 45 22E
47 Zilina, Czechoslovakia 49 15N 18 50E
73 Zillah, Libya 28 29N 17 50E
66 Zilling Tso, L., China 31 45N 89 0E
61 Zima, U.S.S.R. 54 0N 102 5E
72 Zinder, Niger 13 45N 9 3E
62 Zira, Iran 28 12N 51 29E
41 Zlatograd, Bulgaria 41 20N 25 0E
50 Zlatoust, U.S.S.R. 55 5N 59 25E
73 Zillah, Libya 28 29N 17 50E
46 Znojmo, Czechoslovakia 48 50N 16 2E
45 Zofingen, Switzerland 47 18N 7 57E
75 Zomba, Malawi 15 23s 35 19E
73 Zongo, Zaïre 4 10N 18 50E
51 Zonguldak, Turkey 41 30N 32 0E
73 Zouar, Chad 20 28N 16 32E
72 Zouérabe, Mauritania 22 35N 12 30w
41 Zrenjanin, Yugoslavia 45 23N 20 26E
45 Zug, & Cn., Switzerland 47 11N 8 31E
45 Zugersee, L., Switzerland 47 10N 8 30E
44 Zuid Holland, Neth. 51 50N 4 30E
75 Zumbo, Mozambique 15 30s 30 24E
72 Zungeru, Nigeria 9 57N 6 45E
45 Zürich, & Canton, Switz. 47 22N 8 32E
45 Zürichsee, (L. of Zürich), Switzerland
47 15N 8 38E
40 Zurrieq, Malta 35 52N 14 26E
44 Zutphen, Netherlands 52 18N 6 12E
73 Zuwarah, Libya 32 50N 12 5E
60 Zverinogolovskoye, U.S.S.R.
54 30N 62 30E
60 Zverovo, U.S.S.R. 71 40N 83 20E
47 Zvolen, Czechoslovakia 48 33N 19 10E
46 Zwettl, Austria 48 40N 15 10E
46 Zwickau, Germany 50 42N 12 25E
45 Zweibrücken, Germany 49 14N 7 22E
45 Zweisimmen, Switzerland 46 32N 7 24E
44 Zwolle, Netherlands 52 22N 6 7E
47 Zyrardow, Poland 52 0N 20 30E
60 Zyryanovsk, U.S.S.R. 49 20N 85 12E
†† *Renamed Shetland*

PRINTED IN GREAT BRITAIN BY GEORGE PHILIP PRINTERS LIMITED, LONDON